Foch in Command

CH00968524

Ferdinand Foch ended the First World War as Marshal of France and supreme commander of the Allied armies on the Western Front. *Foch in Command* is a pioneering study of his contribution to the Allied victory. Elizabeth Greenhalgh uses contemporary notebooks, letters and documents from previously under-studied archives to chart how the artillery officer, who had never commanded troops in battle when the war began, learned to fight the enemy, to cope with difficult colleagues and allies, and to manoeuvre through the political minefield of civil–military relations. She offers valuable insights into neglected questions: the contribution of unified command to the Allied victory; the role of a commander's general staff; and the mechanisms of command at corps and army level. She demonstrates how an energetic Foch developed war-winning strategies for a modern industrial war, and how political realities contributed to his losing the peace.

ELIZABETH GREENHALGH is a QEII Research Fellow at the University of New South Wales, based at the Australian Defence Force Academy, Canberra. Her previous publications include *Victory through Coalition: Britain and France during the First World War* (Cambridge, 2005).

Cambridge Military Histories

Edited by

HEW STRACHAN Chichele Professor of the History of War, University of Oxford and Fellow of All Souls College, Oxford

GEOFFREY WAWRO Major General Olinto Mark Barsanti Professor of Military History, and Director, Center for the Study of Military History, University of North Texas

The aim of this new series is to publish outstanding works of research on warfare throughout the ages and throughout the world. Books in the series will take a broad approach to military history, examining war in all its military, strategic, political and economic aspects. The series is intended to complement Studies in the Social and Cultural History of Modern Warfare by focusing on the 'hard' military history of armies, tactics, strategy and warfare. Books in the series will consist mainly of single-author works – academically vigorous and groundbreaking – which will be accessible to both academics and the interested general reader.

A full list of titles in the series can be found at:
www.cambridge.org/militaryhistories

Illustration 1 Foch in marshal's dress uniform
revealing the 'quaint, kindly glance' that Aston describes (in his *Foch*,
facing p. 280).

Foch in Command

The forging of a First World War general

Elizabeth Greenhalgh

CAMBRIDGE
UNIVERSITY PRESS

The Edinburgh Building, Cambridge CB2 8RU, UK

Published in the United States of America by Cambridge University Press, New York

Cambridge University Press is part of the University of Cambridge.

It furthers the University's mission by disseminating knowledge in the pursuit of education, learning and research at the highest international levels of excellence.

www.cambridge.org
Information on this title: www.cambridge.org/9781107633858

© Elizabeth Greenhalgh 2011

First published 2011
First paperback edition 2013

A catalogue record for this publication is available from the British Library

Library of Congress Cataloguing in Publication data
Greenhalgh, Elizabeth.
Foch in command : the forging of a First World War general / Elizabeth Greenhalgh.
    p.   cm. – (Cambridge military histories)
Includes bibliographical references.
ISBN 978-0-521-19561-4 (hardback)
1. Foch, Ferdinand, 1851–1929 – Military leadership.   2. Marshals – France –
Biography.   3. Generals – France – Biography.   4. France. Armies –
Biography.   5. World War, 1914–1918 – Campaigns – Western
Front.   6. Command of troops – Case studies.   I. Title.   II. Series.
DC342.8.F6G74   2011
940.4´1244092–dc22
[B]

2010050055

ISBN 978-0-521-19561-4 Hardback
ISBN 978-1-107-63385-8 Paperback

For Michael

Contents

Illustrations

Maps

Preface

This study of the command of the French First World War general, Ferdinand Foch, who became supreme Allied commander in 1918 and was raised to the dignity of Marshal of France, has been long in the writing. Hence the list of debts incurred is correspondingly lengthy. First, however, some housekeeping.

For clarity I have italicised enemy units such as armies and divisions, and have used Allied (capitalised) to indicate the Entente Allies: principally, Britain, France, Italy and Russia. Although the USA became an associated, not an Allied, power when they joined the war in 1917, I have included the USA among the 'Allies' so as to avoid tedious repetition of 'Allied and associated countries'. I have preferred 'British' to 'English' when translating from French documents (and all translations are my own unless otherwise stated). Where the colloquial expression in diaries and other personal documents required a move from literal translation so as to make better sense in English, I have given the original French as well. I have preferred to use Sir Douglas Haig's manuscript diary, but usually there is little difference between manuscript and the typescript in the National Archives. Hence readers wishing to pursue a reference need not feel obliged to go to Edinburgh. In identifying documents in the footnotes, I have used names (for brevity) rather than titles: hence I have substituted 'Foch to Pétain' for 'Le Maréchal commandant les armées alliées au général commandant en chef les armées françaises du nord et du nord-est'. Maps are a perennial problem. I have used a variety of contemporary maps, sketches and diagrams, amended as far as possible to reflect the text. When citing casualty figures (which are notoriously unreliable), I use the term 'casualties' to include the missing, the wounded and the killed. The references show the sources used, but the reader must make allowances for figures which may include or exclude the lightly wounded, may include or exclude prisoners, may be based on incomplete data, and may have been massaged for propaganda purposes.

The extensive research for this study could not have been undertaken without financial support. I am very grateful to the University of New

South Wales for the award of a three-year research fellowship, which allowed me the time to be thorough. In addition, King's College London awarded me a Libraries and Archives fellowship in 2004 which enabled me to spend time in the marvellous Liddell Hart Centre for Military Archives; and the Australian Academy of the Humanities awarded me a travelling fellowship in 2006 which enabled me to visit archives in the USA and in Brussels.

Friends and colleagues have provided invaluable support. I thank especially and alphabetically: General André Bach, who kindly answered my questions about the French army and pointed me towards several useful archival collections; Dr Jim Beach, who sent me chapters of his doctoral thesis; General Robert A. Doughty, who read and commented on several draft chapters; Professor Keith Jeffery, who answered my questions about Henry Wilson; Dr Edwin Jurriëns and Dr Eleanor Hancock, who helped with translations from the Dutch and German respectively; Baron Christian de Posch, who sent me copies of his grandfather's papers; and Dr Mitchell Yockelson, who proved a helpful guide to the American archival collections. Most of all, I thank Professor John Horne; without his wise and thoughtful counsel on previous drafts, this would be a much worse book. All at Cambridge University Press have supported my endeavours efficiently and patiently.

The staff of the Academy Library of UNSW@ADFA and all the libraries and archives that I used were unfailingly helpful. Especial thanks go to the Service historique de la Défense, whose staff in the army archives remained friendly and welcoming despite having to work under very difficult conditions as the reading room was shifted from one building in the Château de Vincennes to another. For permission to quote from material they hold I am grateful to: the Virginia Historical Society (Mott papers); the Library of Congress (department of manuscripts); the Royal Archives and the Army Archives in Brussels; les Archives nationales, Paris; les Archives diplomatiques, Paris; la Bibliothèque de l'Institut, Paris; the National Archives (Public Record Office), Kew; the Bodleian Library, Oxford; Churchill Archives Centre, Cambridge; the Trustees of the Imperial War Museum, London; the Trustees of the National Library of Scotland, Edinburgh; the Trustees of the Liddell Hart Centre for Military Archives, King's College London; and the manuscripts department of the British Library, London. I am grateful to Earl Haig for permission to use the Haig papers, and to the Warden and Fellows of New College Oxford (Milner papers). I thank also the DITEEX in Vincennes for permission to consult the papers of Generals Brugère, Cointet and Weygand. Finally, M. André Prunet-Foch received me most kindly in Paris and gave me permission to consult and quote from the Marshal's illuminating letters in the Bibliothèque nationale de France.

Abbreviations

ADC	aide-de-camp (military assistant)
AEF	American Expeditionary Forces
AFGG + vol. no.	*Les Armées françaises dans la Grande Guerre* (see Bibliography)
AS	Artillerie spéciale (i.e. tanks)
AS + vol. no.	Poincaré, *Au service de la France* (see Bibliography)
BEF	British Expeditionary Force
CA	Corps d'Armée
CCC	Churchill Archives Centre, Cambridge
CIGS	Chief of the Imperial General Staff
CinC	commander-in-chief
COS	chief of staff
CS	Fayolle, *Cahiers secrets* (see Bibliography)
CWF	Prior and Wilson, *Command on the Western Front* (see Bibliography)
[d]	dossier
DA	Direction de l'Arrière (dealt with transport and supply matters in rear areas)
DAB	Détachement d'Armée de Belgique
DAN	Détachement d'Armee du Nord
DC	Division de Cavalerie
DGCRA	Direction Générale des Communications et des Ravitaillements aux Armées (organisation to control all the army's transport and supply services)
DI	Division d'Infanterie
DIC	Division d'Infanterie Coloniale
DMO	Director of Military Operations (at the War Office in London)
DR	Division de Réserve
E-M	Etat-Major (general staff)

EWB	Executive War Board
FF	Ferdinand Foch
FRUS	*Foreign Relations of the United States* (see Bibliography)
GAN	Groupe des Armées du Nord
GB	groupe de bombardement (bomber force)
GHQ	General Headquarters (British)
GQG	Grand Quartier Général (French HQ)
GQGA	Grand Quartier Général Allié (Allied headquarters)
IV	Weygand, *Idéal vécu* (see Bibliography)
JM	Journal de Marche (war diary)
JMO	Journal des Marches et des Opérations
Joffre, JM	Pedroncini (ed.), *Journal de Marche de Joffre* (see Bibliography)
LHCMA	Liddell Hart Centre for Military Archives, King's College London
MAE	Ministère des Affaires Etrangères
MC + vol. no.	Mordacq, *Le Ministère Clemenceau* (see Bibliography)
NCO	non-commissioned officer
OH + year	Edmonds *et al.*, *Military Operations: France and Belgium* (see Bibliography)
OH Italy	Edmonds and Davies, *Military Operations: Italy* (see Bibliography)
OHL	Oberste Heeresleitung (German high command)
PMR	Permanent Military Representative (to the SWC)
POW	prisoner of war
PPC	*Paris Peace Conference* (volume in *FRUS*; see Bibliography)
PV	Doughty, *Pyrrhic Victory* (see Bibliography)
PWW + vol. no.	Link (ed.), *The Papers of Woodrow Wilson* (see Bibliography)
QMG	Quartermaster General (head of logistics in the British army)
RAW + vol. no.	Reichsarchiv, *Der Weltkrieg 1914 bis 1918* (see Bibliography)
RFC	Royal Flying Corps
SHD/T	Service Historique de la Défense/Département de l'Armée de Terre, Château de Vincennes
SWC	Supreme War Council

USAWW + vol. no.	*United States Army in the World War* (see Bibliography)
VTC	Greenhalgh, *Victory through Coalition* (see Bibliography)
WO	War Office (British)

Introduction

On 7 August 1918 the President of the French Republic raised General Ferdinand Foch to the dignity of Marshal of France. Foch had reached the pinnacle of his military career. Less than five months earlier, on 26 March 1918, he had been chosen by unanimous consent of the British and French military and political leaders to be Generalissimo of the Allied armies on the Western Front. To undertake the terrible responsibility thrust on him Foch would be required to draw on all he had learned as a soldier in the prewar period and to reflect on his performance as a commander since August 1914. This book is a study of Foch's command in the positions that he occupied during the war; its aim is to examine how Foch's ideas evolved as he moved along the path that led to the supreme command. As Foch himself wrote: one does what one can to apply what one knows.

Foch was an artillery officer who had never commanded troops in battle before the war. Neither did he become commander-in-chief of the French army. However, he commanded a corps, an army and an army group between 1914 and 1916. He fought defensive battles – most famously before Ypres at the end of 1914 – and offensive battles – two in Artois in 1915 and the following year on the Somme. He commanded a desk from May 1917 until March 1918 as chief of the army general staff, before becoming supreme Allied commander for the final months leading to victory. He presented the terms that the Germans had to sign on 11 November 1918, and his fight to obtain the Rhine frontier was a dominant element during the peace treaty talks. Even the desk-job was important, for 1917 was a critical year as Russia left the war and the United States joined. Foch's experience in the War Ministry gives us an insight both into logistic problems and the difficulties of coordinating strategy and logistics with allies. His 1918 experience is unique in that the role of supreme Allied commander was new and had to be defined and refined as events unfolded.

A detailed analysis of Foch's wartime career as he moved toward the supreme command illuminates some of the important yet neglected questions that remain about the First World War. He began the war as a corps commander and commanded an army during the Battle of the Marne in September 1914. These intermediate ranks of command have been neglected as subjects of study in favour of, on the one hand, high command and strategy or, on the other, the experience of the individual soldier on the battlefield. This gap in the historiography is being corrected to some extent for the intermediate levels of command in the British army, but not for French generals. Apart from Pedroncini's study of General Pétain, and Gras' study of General de Castelnau, little has been published in French that utilises the immense resources of the archives of the Service historique de la défense in the Château de Vincennes to illuminate the careers of the hundreds of French generals who exercised command at army or corps level. Foch's early progress through these levels to army group command sheds light on this neglected area, and reveals how great or how circumscribed a role a corps or army commander might play in planning battles. An examination of his two years at the operational level of army group commander should answer the question of how much credit an army group commander deserves for what subordinate units achieve or, more frequently, how much blame he deserves for failure.

The nature of command in a coalition war and the significance of national sensibilities are important elements in Foch's diplomatic role as army group commander, coordinating French, British and Belgian armies; these aspects of the First World War are also frequently neglected. The eventual victory was, after all, a victory for coalition rather than for the British army alone, as Haig occasionally implies. The Franco-British facet of the coalition victory was perhaps at its most significant for the Western Front, but in addition Foch had to work with King Albert and the Belgian army; by 1918 he also had to deal with General Pershing and the American Expeditionary Forces, and with Generals Cadorna and Diaz, and the Italian army. His interactions with those national commanders reveal much about the operation of a coalition in a modern, industrial war. How well did Foch, who had studied German along with his contemporaries at the Ecole Supérieure de Guerre, cope with the demands of collaborating with foreigners? Did his performance improve with time? Did he discover the most effective methods for coordinating action with allies, given that he spoke no English? Of all the First World War generals, Foch was the only one who negotiated regularly with Allied colleagues, and so his early experience with the British and Belgians and his 1918 experience with the Americans and the Italians provide an excellent perspective on coalition warfare.

The next stage in Foch's career, after being removed from command of his army group in December 1916, provides a very different insight into a modern war. As chief of the army general staff in 1917, Foch had to advise and persuade French war ministers, and Allied politicians. He was involved in the arrangements for the introduction of the American Expeditionary Forces to the Western Front, and in the enormous industrial effort that France made in order to arm and equip itself and those new armies for the combined-arms battles of the year of victory. Then, as supreme commander in 1918, his tasks involved much political infighting alongside dealing with the enemy. Indeed, the relationship between Foch and France's last wartime Premier and War Minister, Georges Clemenceau, is a fascinating story of how difficult it is to manage civil–military relations both in wartime and in making the subsequent peace. If Foch deserved any credit for the victory, did this entitle him any role in the peace negotiations? J. C. King's two books have long been the standard reference work on the politicians and generals in France, but both were written before the archives were opened.[1] This book therefore takes the marvellous opportunity to use the archival record to revise conclusions reached decades ago. Foch's involvement with politics right from 1914 is one of the surprises in the pages that follow.

Finally, Foch's actions in the months between March and November 1918 illustrate what a supreme Allied commander actually does. The conditions of his appointment and the constraints under which he worked were very different from those that governed General Dwight D. Eisenhower a generation later. Most historians dismiss the First World War version of supreme command as of little value and Foch's role in the victory as minimal. This book will counter that view. Indeed, more generally, the question of the manner of the Entente's victory on the Western Front has been a strangely neglected topic. Many histories of the war in 1918 concentrate on the stunning German gains made during the five spring offensives, thereby surprising the reader with the final Allied military victory. Admiration for German technical efficiency and innovation is also often joined to the judgement that Allied military leaders were incompetent, with the occasional corollary that the wisdom of the New World was required to bring the conflict to an end. Yet it was the German plenipotentiaries who asked for terms, and it was Foch who drew up the military clauses of the armistice presented in the railway wagon at Rethondes in the forest near Compiègne. How far did his earlier command positions prepare him for the final victory? His command is an important element in the victory, but his role in the peace treaty negotiations was highly contested.

---

[1] King, *Generals and Politicians* (1951), and *Foch versus Clemenceau* (1960).

Running through all the stages of Foch's wartime career is a further question: how important are staff and liaison work for victory in an industrialised war? Great captains cannot be great all alone. With politicians and allies always at their heels, they require the administrative services of a general staff, and they need smooth liaison with the allies. Foch had the same chief of staff, General Maxime Weygand, right from the early weeks of the war until its end, except for a brief period when Weygand was France's permanent military representative in the Supreme War Council – and even there, he continued to act as his chief's mouthpiece. Weygand's devotion to Foch has bequeathed a mass of documentary evidence and an important memoir.[2] Moreover, in a coalition consisting of armies speaking different languages (as in the multi-lingual *kaiserlich und königlich* enemy army), the need to provide a trusted method of communication through translation, not of words but of the meaning behind the words, was acute. Since Foch acted in an international context for most of the war, the evidence of liaison officers provides further insights into the exercise of command. We are particularly fortunate in that the archives contain well-informed, articulate and perceptive accounts by his liaison officers of their dealings with Foch. They give particularly valuable insights into Foch's 'learning experience'.

So an examination of the evolution of Foch's thinking and actions between 1914, when he commanded only a corps, and 1919, when the peace treaty was signed and he became commander of the Allied occupation forces, illuminates many neglected questions: the contribution of unified command to the Allied victory; the resolution of national conflicts within an international coalition; the intricacies of civil–military relations and the importance to be accorded to the administrative post of chief of the army general staff; the role of a commander's general staff; and the mechanism of command at corps and army level. As he learned how to play effectively all his various roles, Foch's war experience gives us an insight into the lessons that enabled him to undertake successfully the task of supreme commander.

These questions have been neglected because most of the writing in English about Foch is based on biographies and on Foch's own postwar memoirs, hence limited by its sources. This book is not a biography, except insofar as the war became Foch's life, and so there is no discussion of his prewar career or of his postwar battles about France's future defence policy. Several good general biographies have already been published, the most recent in French, and the standard English-language one by

[2] Weygand, *Idéal vécu* (1953).

B. H. Liddell Hart.[3] Neither do I attempt to link Foch's prewar writings, the two volumes of his lectures at the Ecole Supérieure de Guerre, published in 1903 and 1904, to events between 1914 and 1918. If the prewar writings are opaque, the posthumous memoirs are uninformative. The two volumes of his *Mémoires pour servir à l'histoire de la guerre de 1914–1918* were published in 1931, two years after Foch's death, and he did not complete them (they deal only with 1914 and 1918). Although Foch's hand is discernible on every page because each may be compared to the drafts that have been conserved, yet the tone of a general staff account remains. The drafts were prepared by his staff officer Commandant de Mierry in the same format as the French official history, namely a text with hundreds of documents as annexes. French historian and veteran Pierre Renouvin pointed out in his review of the volumes how disappointingly little of the man appeared in the pages. He lamented their report format, and claimed that the memoirs would not inspire the general public; nor would they please historians who 'seek above all the quality of the witness'.[4] The reader will find, therefore, very few references to them in these pages. Writing so soon after Foch's death, Liddell Hart was forced to use Foch's postwar utterances collected by his staff and journalists. These are frequently bombastic or self-serving; they are not to be preferred to contemporary documents, which reveal not only his attractive personality, but also the devotion he inspired in his staff.

Instead of relying on Foch's postwar account or on biographies in order to examine Foch's various commands and what he learned from the experience, this book relies heavily on archival research, using collections that in some cases have only recently become available (Madame la maréchale's informative diary, for example). I have used contemporary documents (letters, the notebooks, official documents) and contemporary comments from informed observers. There is much Foch material in the French army archives in Vincennes, the Archives nationales in Paris, and the Bibliothèque nationale de France. I have also used the valuable records of Foch's various liaison officers. Probably the same qualities that make for a good liaison officer mean that the records they leave are particularly useful. In sum, the sources for an in-depth study of this important First World War military commander are not lacking.

As a corps commander, Foch led France's national day military parade on 14 July 1914 in Nancy, the capital of what remained to France of

---

[3] Notin, *Foch* (2008); Autin, *Foch ou le triomphe de la volonté* (1987); Liddell Hart, *Foch: The Man of Orleans* (1931). Less well known but better are Falls, *Foch* (1939), and Hunter's study for the Canadian army. Full publication details are in the Bibliography.
[4] Renouvin, Review, 303.

Lorraine. As Marshal Foch, and supreme Allied commander, he led the 14 July victory parade in 1919 in Paris. The variety of positions that he held in between those two parades permits an insight into the workings of command. The following analysis of his achievements in those roles – the lessons learned, the mistakes made in the fire of war – all build a picture of the forging of a general. This hard-won education helps us to understand how the difficult task of mastering the First World War battlefield was completed, and how victory was won in 1918 – and also to appreciate the tangled relations of civilian and military powers, not only in France but also among Allied generals and politicians. Foch was central in all these matters.

So this book analyses the stages of that journey from Nancy to Paris in order to answer some of the questions outlined above, and, along the way, to put the achievements of Marshal Ferdinand Foch into better perspective by studying what he did rather than accepting what others say that he preached. Foch is better known in the English-speaking world as one of the prewar authorities accused of educating a generation of generals who threw away more than a million French lives in senseless offensives. The following pages correct that perspective by examining what the teacher learned.

Part I

From theory to practice

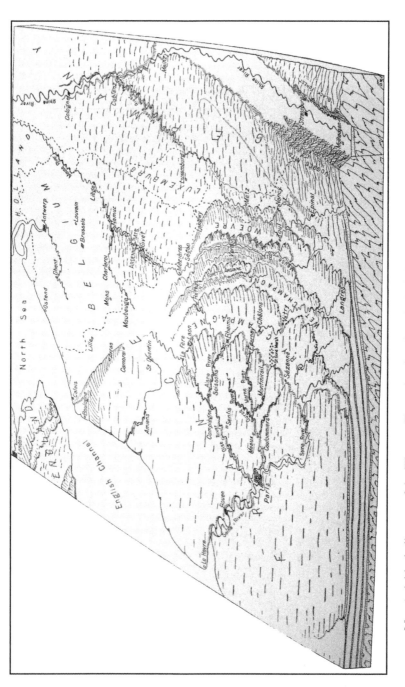

Map 1 A block diagram of the Western Front showing the principal plateaux and plains, mountains and lowlands, cliff scarps and river trenches which influenced military operations

Note especially how the valley of the river Meuse, running between Sedan and Mézières with the Ardennes to the north, became the vital corridor for the Germans in supplying their armies in northern France and Belgium.

1   From the Ecole de Guerre to August 1914 in Lorraine

In 1914 the French national day, 14 July, was celebrated as usual with military parades, and in Nancy, the capital of the province of Lorraine, the élite XX Corps performed that duty. Nancy was the former capital of the Duchy of Lorraine and, following the amputation of a large portion of the province in 1871, the elegant town lay close to the new German border. In case of war XX Corps had the task of covering that sector of the frontier with Germany as the French army mobilised to meet the threat from across the Rhine. Since August 1913, the corps commander was General Ferdinand Foch. He had reached the highest rank in the army, divisional general, in 1911, and when he reached his sixty-third birthday on 2 October 1914 he would be just two years short of the retirement age for generals. He had no experience at all of commanding troops in battle. Indeed, he had little experience of command, since most of his prewar career had been spent in staff appointments or, most famously, as an instructor.

Between 1895 and 1901 he taught in the Ecole Supérieure de Guerre in Paris, later publishing the lectures that he gave there. Between 1908 and 1911 he was the school's commandant. There followed a succession of brief appointments which took him through several of France's military regions (Nice, Chaumont, Bourges) before he reached Nancy in 1913. Foch owed this succession of posts, rather than a comfortable pre-retirement billet, to General Joseph Joffre. Joffre had become chief of the army staff in 1911, a post which made him automatically the commander-in-chief of the French armies in time of war. Joffre had known Foch for a long time and appreciated his qualities.[1]

Joffre even had Foch's name on his short-list for the post of his deputy, but the War Minister, Adolphe Messimy, vetoed Foch's selection and General Noël de Curières de Castelnau was given the job instead. Joffre gave the head of his military cabinet and confidant, Colonel Maurice Gamelin (better known as the Second World War general), the task of

---

[1] Autin, *Foch*, 105.

explaining to Foch why he had not been chosen. Gamelin described how Foch waved away his explanations and went straight to what he saw as the heart of the question of how to foil the Schlieffen plan, which aimed to envelop the French army's left wing by an invasion of Belgium. Foch advised Gamelin to remember: thirty-five German corps on the coast.[2] As early as 1911 Foch was thinking about the uncertain future.

The intrusion of politics into military appointments would have come as no surprise to Foch. Leaving aside the Dreyfus affair (about which he was careful to express no opinions openly), Foch had suffered from political discrimination when he was removed from his teaching post at the Ecole de Guerre as a result of the purges of officers with overt religious affiliation (hence supposedly anti-republican sentiments), and he expected to suffer from it again in 1908 when it was a question of appointing its new commandant. However, Premier Georges Clemenceau showed, not for the last time, that he cared little for religious affiliation or presumed political opinions when it came to important and influential positions. To Foch's surprise, Clemenceau appointed him commandant of the Ecole Supérieure de Guerre.

As a result of that selection, Foch had the chance to make international contacts, especially with Britain, that proved highly useful when war came. He was keen to create closer ties with the British because he saw Russia's lack of readiness for war. Despite the long-standing military agreement with Russia and despite French loans for railway construction, that lack of readiness meant that French military planners could not count on Russian help if war came. Therefore Joffre sought to increase the effectiveness of the Russian alliance in his revision of the French war plan.[3] Foch was fortunate in his wish for closer relations with the British because his British counterpart, Henry Wilson, was very keen to visit France and its war college. Wilson first went to see Foch in December 1909, and he returned in January 1910; October 1910 (when he was invited to the wedding of Foch's daughter, Marie); in February 1911; in February, August and October 1912 (when he was invited to but did not attend the wedding of Foch's younger daughter Anne); three more visits in 1913 and again in May 1914. Foch went to Britain less frequently: in June 1910 and December 1912. He also went to Russia for the Russian army manoeuvres in 1910 and 1912.

There is no need to posit a deep, personal friendship between Wilson and Foch simply because of wedding invitations. They were congenial colleagues who found it easy to work together and, more importantly, had a common interest in strengthening the military ties between their two

[2] Reynaud, *Au cœur de la mêlée*, 912.   [3] Williamson, *Politics of Grand Strategy*, 120, 208.

countries. The fact that the weddings gave the two men the opportunity to talk at length and in private is sufficient reason for the invitations. Nonetheless, there was an easy comradeship that is revealed in the following letter, written to Wilson in July 1914 just after the last French manoeuvres before war broke out.[4]

we missed you, we miss you a lot. Not a day goes by without someone saying this or speaking of you. Last night, in his toast to your generals, General Castelnau proposed your health, regretting your absence and saying how much we were thinking of you.

If Foch did not have any experience of leading troops in battle – Joffre and other generals had experience of at least colonial fighting – he did know something of the armies of France's Allies.

When he took command of XX Corps Nancy itself was not fortified, although just across the frontier, only fifty-seven kilometres distant, the Germans had done considerable work around Metz and Thionville [Diedenhofen] to create a massive fortified region, the *Moselstellung*. France's main defensive line of forts ran behind Nancy, with Toul directly west of the town and the next fort (Epinal) to the south. Nancy itself was protected, however, to the northeast by an arc of hills, the Grand Couronné de Nancy, that formed the edge of the river valley of the river Moselle, enlarged by the Meurthe, which runs into the Moselle north of the town. (See the diagrammatic representation of the Western Front shown in Map 1.) When Foch took over XX Corps in 1913, his army commander, General Castelnau, asked that defensive positions be built along these hills. It was essential to hold the line as protection against a German sortie from Metz. Foch appears to have done little towards completing the defensive works, if Castelnau's letter of January 1914 complaining of 'hesitation and apathy' is a guide.[5] The work was still not complete on the outbreak of war.

When the French mobilised on 2 August 1914, the units of XX Corps were two infantry divisions, 11 (the 'iron division') and 39 Division d'Infanterie (DI), and a regiment of cavalry, 5th Hussars. France's recent Three-Year Law, passed as Foch took command of his corps, had increased the length of military service from two years to three, but the war started before any conscripts with three years of training were produced and the immediate effects of the measure merely increased expenditures on extra barracks, hospitals and equipment. Like the Nancy defences, the extra building and supplies were not ready by August

[4] Letter, Foch to Henry Wilson, 3 July 1914, Wilson mss, HHW 2/73/21.
[5] Gras, *Castelnau*, 140; Weygand, *IV*, 137.

1914. There had not been enough cloth, for example, for the uniforms of all XX Corps' soldiers in that year's 14 July military parade.[6] Joffre's new field service regulations had not had time to percolate through all the ranks. Financial considerations had meant that training facilities to keep the reserves up to scratch were also lacking.[7] Although as one of the corps who 'covered' the French mobilisation XX Corps was better off than much of the rest of the French army, nonetheless Foch did not begin the war as commander of a well-equipped, well-trained, homogeneous military force.

It took time to assemble reservists, equip them and transport all units to the allotted sectors. (The Three-Year Law of 1913 decreed that men were liable for service as reservists for eleven years after they completed the three years of active duty.) It was only on the twelfth day of mobilisation that action could start. Joffre had agreed with the Russians that both countries would take the offensive on 14 August. The task of XX Corps during this period was *couverture*, that is, to 'cover' or protect Second Army during this process of assembly and preparation. After being recalled to Nancy from leave, Foch began on 27 July to deploy his divisions to the incomplete defensive positions on the Couronné, both to continue entrenching and to prevent an enemy capture of the area, since the Germans could easily make a dangerous sortie from the nearby heavily fortified Metz–Thionville area. When the government ordered French troops to remain ten kilometres from the border so as to prevent any provocation and to ensure that the first act of war would not be committed by the French, Foch ignored the instruction. The defence of Nancy was too precarious to permit the risk of losing the Grand Couronné to enemy action, despite the fact that parts of the heights lay within the ten-kilometre zone. By 31 July his 11 DI occupied a line including the two high points of Mont Amance and Montenoy.[8]

This disobedience showed that Foch had no fear that his lack of experience might cause him to do something rash, despite his chapter on discipline in *Des principes*. He was very impatient to start doing something, and found the two weeks of the *couverture* trying. The morale of his corps was 'excellent', and he was keen to see some action. He would feel 'humiliated', he wrote to his wife, if the important battles took place further north, where the main German thrust seemed to be aimed, while troops in Lorraine stood still 'hypnotised' by the Château-Salins gap.[9]

[6] *Eclair de l'Est*, 15 July 1914, 2.   [7] Goya, *La Chair et l'acier*, ch. 3.
[8] Colin, *Division de fer*, 16.
[9] Foch, *Des principes*, ch. 4; letters, Foch to Mme Foch, 2 and 3 August 1914, vol. 32.

The town of Château-Salins itself lay just across the frontier in German Lorraine.

Whether Foch was permitted or not to contravene the ten-kilometre order (and Joffre would not have minded, for he chafed at the restriction), there were certainly cavalry infractions. This resulted in a sharp reminder from War Minister Messimy, sent late on 1 August to all corps commanders involved in the *couverture*. The ban on crossing the demarcation line applied to all arms, including cavalry, Messimy reminded them, and there should be no patrols, no reconnaissances, no element whatsoever east of the line. The final paragraph was addressed specifically to Foch: 'This applies above all to XX Corps because of its proximity to the enemy, and a reliable source has seen [German cavalry units] "nose to nose" with a squadron of hussars.'[10] So Foch did not keep his cavalry in check, and the first Frenchman killed was probably one of the 5th Hussars.[11] Moreover there were further incidents: on 5 August a reconnaissance patrol dislodged two Bavarian cavalry units but then were chased back across the frontier; and on the 11th units of 2 Cavalry Division were pushed out of a village that they had captured from the Bavarians the previous day.[12]

Joffre planned an advance by two armies (First and Second) into German-held Alsace and Lorraine. Any success in recapturing parts of the lost provinces for France would boost morale and, more importantly, pin down large numbers of German troops so that they could not be moved to add weight to the right wing swinging through Belgium. The objective for XX Corps was Juvelize, and its place in the attacking formation was on the left of both armies. Foch would have to keep an eye on the possibility of an enemy attack from the heavily fortified Metz region because the Nancy defences were now in the hands of reserve divisions.[13] Castelnau advised his corps commanders that the German tactics 'imposed' a methodical approach on the French: all the artillery should be in place before putting in an infantry attack; all captured positions should be 'organised' before setting off again; advantage should be taken of the superiority of French artillery to dominate the enemy's artillery before giving battle.[14] While one cannot fault the first two recommendations, the third was irrelevant. The Germans had heavier guns with a

[10] War Minister to commanders of II, VI, XX, XXI and VII Corps, 1 August 1914, 22h30, *AFGG* 1/1, annex 26.
[11] Weygand, *IV*, 75.   [12] Gazin, *Cavalerie française*, 62.
[13] Second Army, Instruction générale et secrète no 1, 12 August 1914, *AFGG* 1/1, annex 207.
[14] Second Army, Communication secrète aux commandants de C.A. et de D.C., 12 August 1914, ibid., annex 208.

greater range, and this fact was to cause many casualties in the coming days.

The terrain through which Second Army was to pass did not favour the attacker. It was hilly, heavily forested and full of waterways: rivers, canals and lakes. The river Seille ran more or less east–west across their front, and had been made into an even bigger obstacle by the German opening of flood gates, which inundated the river valley. As the French advanced slowly and prudently as ordered, the two German armies under Crown Prince Rupprecht of Bavaria withdrew. Rupprecht's orders were to draw the French into a noose, pulling back as far as the river Saar, before launching attacks on the flanks from Metz on the one side and from Strassburg and the Vosges on the other. The French had poor intelligence about the numbers of enemy troops that faced them and did not realise that the German chief of staff, Helmuth von Moltke (the Younger), anticipating a French attack in Lorraine, had allocated eight army corps to his left wing. Facing Second Army were *I*, *II* and *III Bavarian Corps*; *I Bavarian Reserve Corps*; and *XXI Corps*, further reinforced on 17 August by six *Ersatz* divisions.[15] Most of these corps each had twenty-eight batteries (160 guns), and in addition the army commander had heavy guns and mortars. The French were out-gunned.

XX Corps had a relatively easy first day, reaching its assigned objective early, but the two neighbouring corps had a much more difficult time of it. This was repeated over the next three days (15–17 August), as the roads became rivers of mud in torrential rain after the great heat of the war's first days. Foch had time to write confident and reassuring letters to his wife. He even seemed to be enjoying the activity, claiming that he felt extremely well despite the very long days. It was a vast improvement over being caged up in Nancy.[16] By midday on the 17th he had entered Château-Salins in Lothringen (German Lorraine) and held some of the Seille river crossings.

Because of the easy captures of Château-Salins and of Sarrebourg by First Army, Castelnau changed the slow prudent advance. Joffre wanted as many troops as possible held down in Lorraine so as to relieve his other armies, who were taking the brunt of the German advance. Consequently Castelnau's orders for 19 August were to employ as much 'vigour and speed as possible', thus marking a complete change from the earlier prudence and method. Second Army was to cross the Seille and XX Corps' objective was Faulquemont (Falkenberg). Because there were no enemy forces in front of it, Castelnau wanted XX Corps to free the way for the two other corps.[17] This change of tempo was made more difficult

---

[15] *RAW*, 1: 678–80.   [16] Letters, Foch to Mme Foch, 15, 16, 17 August 1914, vol. 32.
[17] Jacquand memoirs, 19 August 1914, fo. 19, 1K/795/37.

because Joffre had withdrawn two corps from Second Army, thus leaving only a group of reserve divisions instead of a regular corps as protection between Foch's corps and the fortifications of Metz. (See Map 2.)

Once again there was little enemy activity in front of XX Corps, but the two neighbouring corps came under artillery fire from the ridges in front of them. Hence, by the evening of the 19th XX Corps was in advance of the other units of Second Army, and facing the small town of Morhange and a line of ridges between it and the corps objective, Faulquemont. Castelnau knew that the hills around Morhange were strongly held, because his aviation observers had reported large numbers of guns in prepared positions, with trench lines and hidden troop reserves. One pilot described the enemy army as setting a 'trap' before them like a 'compressed spring ready to let go forwards instead of retreating backwards'.[18] He had tried to report this intelligence to XX Corps when they first began to advance, but Foch's chief of staff (Colonel Duchêne) had rejected, most forcefully, the value of aerial observation. Since the pilot noted that his request to see Foch personally to explain his findings had been denied, it is impossible to judge how far (if at all) Foch shared his staff's prejudice.[19]

Castelnau's orders for the next day, 20 August, were issued at 5pm. The two corps who had been held up were to advance, while XX Corps was to remain where it was. Foch's instructions for 20 August, however, were sent just after midnight on the 20th and ordered a continuance of the offensive along the whole front of the corps, to begin at 6am. So Foch's order contradicted Castelnau's.

Rupprecht was just as impatient as Foch to see some action. His orders were to keep withdrawing as far back as behind the Saar river, so as to bring the French far enough forward to be able to close the neck of the trap and attack on both flanks. Moltke wanted the French held down in Lorraine because he intended to begin operations with his right wing in Belgium on the 18th. Rupprecht thought, however, that he could just as well hold down the French by attacking as by continuing to withdraw, and sought permission for an offensive. He knew the French order of battle because it had been found on a prisoner captured in an early skirmish. Despite the preference of the German high command (Oberste Heeresleitung, OHL) that Rupprecht continue to retreat, the Bavarian commander was persistent and on 18 August extracted permission to act as he saw fit from OHL, who abdicated responsibility.[20] He planned a joint attack on the French: his own *Sixth Army* against Castelnau's Second, and von Heeringen's *Seventh Army*

[18] Gras, *Castelnau*, 153.   [19] Ibid., 150–1.
[20] Duffour, *Joffre et la guerre de mouvement*, 143; Bayerische Kriegsarchiv, *Die Schlacht in Lothringen*, 1: 134–6.

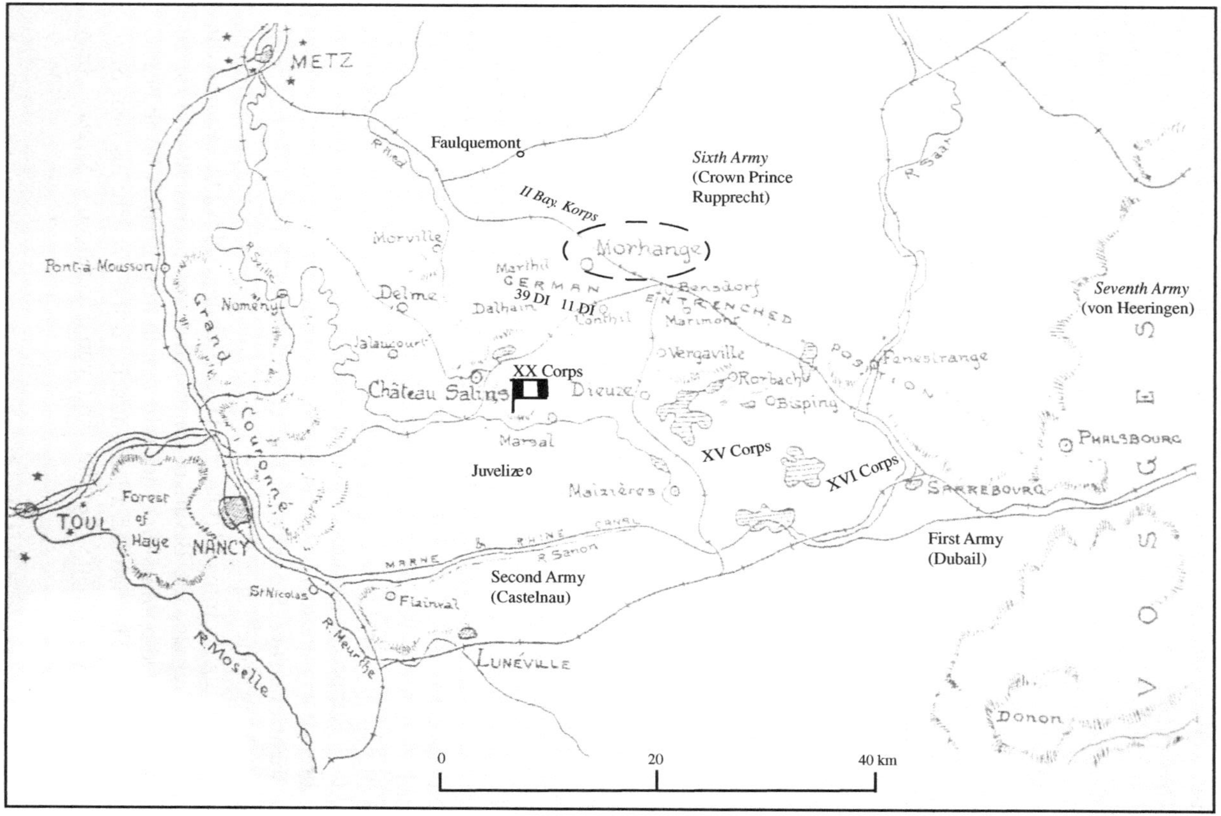

Map 2 XX Corps at Morhange, 19–20 August 1914

against French First Army. His own units were mainly Bavarian, and his wish for an offensive may have been a way of ensuring some territorial advantage for Bavaria in the peace settlement.

Heeringen was not quite ready and so his attack was delayed until 20 August, the same date that Castelnau had decreed for two of his corps to advance, whilst Foch's XX Corps held on to the positions they already occupied. The events of 20 August caused considerable postwar dispute.[21] Foch claimed that he never received Castelnau's operational order no. 27, instructing him to remain where he was, timed at 5pm on the 19th, a claim he repeated in his memoirs. Castelnau called this claim 'puerile'. The previous instruction had covered only action on the 19th, and so XX Corps should have awaited further orders for the next day and queried the reason for their non-arrival, had that been the case. When Castelnau found out early in the morning of 20 August what Foch intended, he sent a liaison officer to insist that Foch follow the intentions of his army commander. That officer made no reference to any loss of an operational order. The liaison officer was followed by a telephone message at 6.20am, ordering XX Corps to conform to army orders. No enquiry was made at that point as to what those army orders might have been. Further, Castelnau hinted that a cover-up might have taken place, since XX Corps records for August 1914 were 'clearly incomplete'.[22] In fact, today, they are not extant.[23] The war diary and records of XX Corps operational orders begin when General Balfourier took over from Foch on 28 August.

Short of the discovery of a document clearing the matter up one way or the other, it is now impossible to adjudicate between Castelnau's insistence that such an order could not have gone astray and Foch's insistence that the order was not received. The balance of probability would seem to favour the army rather than the corps commander. Whether Duchêne pocketed the order and did not show it to Foch (his refusal to pass on intelligence from the aviation service was noted above; and Castelnau's biographer writes that after the engagement Duchêne altered the war diary of one of the corps' divisions),[24] whether Foch was ill and simply did not see the order (as suggested by Castelnau's biographer), or whether Foch believed that as the commander on the ground he had the right to do as he

---

[21] See the correspondence relating to the *Revue des deux mondes* article by Victor Giraud of 1 August 1921 reproduced in *Le Matin*, 30 August 1921.

[22] Letter, Castelnau to War Minister, 22 November 1922, 1K/795/11, [d] 'Lorraine polémiques'.

[23] The XX Corps records are in 22N 1350 and the war diary in 26N 193. The 'ordres généraux' begin 1 September 1914, although several of them for 20 August are reproduced in *AFGG* 1/1.

[24] Gras, *Castelnau*, 157.

saw fit (his order to attack stated that there were no enemy troops west of the Château-Salins forest, and that there were few troops on the crests before the corps),[25] the outcome was a bloody nose. The question of the (non-)arrival of the order would not have mattered if the day had been a French success. It was not.

The day began misty. Consequently, at 6am, Castelnau ordered the two attacking corps to delay until the aerial observation reports came in. At the same time, in accordance with Foch's orders, XX Corps began assembling ready to attack. His 39 DI drew up all their units on the flat ground below the ridges and in front of Château-Salins. The units of his 11 DI on their right were slightly later getting into attack formation since their divisional commander sent out his orders only at 5.45. This probably saved the division from much higher casualties.

As the French were preparing to attack, two corps in accordance with Castelnau's wishes and XX Corps in direct contradiction, Rupprecht launched his own attack at 5.15am, thus pre-empting the French operations. The Bavarians overran Foch's left flank guard, and pushed 11 DI out of the village where it had spent the night. The two Bavarian divisions that attacked 39 DI as they assembled in the open caused so many casualties that the division was placed in reserve on 23 August.[26] Nonetheless, although XX Corps had been pushed back all along the line, they were not fleeing in confusion, and Foch still had all his reserves in his hand.

The enemy had started even earlier in the morning against the other two corps of Second Army. From 4am the enemy pushed these two corps back, so that Castelnau called on Foch to assist XV Corps, his immediate neighbour, but he was unable to help because the retreat was becoming too pronounced. At 10.10am Castelnau sent out directions for the line of retreat of the whole army, which took effect at 13.15. Foch was given the task of covering the army's retreat by holding on to the Château-Salins bridgehead as long as possible. Conditions were so difficult on the roads jammed with artillery trains, and XV Corps on Foch's right was so badly mauled, that Castelnau advised Foch to have his troops slip away in the night rather than wait for morning. Eventually Castelnau ordered Second Army to collect itself behind the river Meurthe, with its left on the Nancy defences and in touch with First Army on its right. The retreat was completed the following day, with the enemy following up only slowly. Thus, on 22 August, the French were back where they had started in

---

[25] Ordre général d'opérations no 31 pour le 20 août, 20 August 1914, *AFGG* 1/1, annex 673.
[26] XX Corps order for 23 August 1914, *AFGG* 1/1, annex 1209.

French Lorraine, after an advance into German Lothringen of about twenty kilometres.

The Germans had had the advantage of surprise, and of greater numbers of both men and heavy guns. They might have drawn the French deeper into Lorraine, so deep that they could not have escaped a pincer attack from the heavily fortified fortresses of Metz (on the French left) and Strassburg (on their right). Rupprecht's impatience prevented that. It is doubtful whether Foch's failure to obey orders (if such it was) made any difference, given Rupprecht's actions. On the other hand, Foch had already argued against the order keeping the French army ten kilometres away from the frontier and had had his argument accepted. His offensive spirit met with Joffre's approval. He handled his corps competently and carried out the difficult mission of acting as rearguard during the retreat. The Battle of Morhange, as the engagement was named, left Foch in an equivocal position. Was he a commander always ready to take the initiative, or was he hot-headed and careless of authority?

At any rate, he was not down-hearted. On 23 August he wrote to his wife that all was well: 'the troops always superb; command excellent; my staff of the first order; – but obviously it's not us who are going to settle the important matters – Those are going to be resolved in Belgium.'[27] Nevertheless, XX Corps had suffered 4–5000 casualties, and Rupprecht reported to OHL on the evening of 21 August that his *Sixth Army* had captured 8000 prisoners and more than thirty guns from Second Army. *Seventh Army* had taken a further seventy guns and several thousand prisoners.[28]

Immediately, Castelnau set about not only getting defences dug but also preparing for a counter-attack if the opportunity presented itself. Fortunately the German pursuit was slow, thus giving Second Army time to get back on its feet. German losses had not been insignificant, and Rupprecht had not intended a pursuit at first. Now Rupprecht was to suffer for his initial boldness; the Kaiser, Rupprecht noted, was 'nearly ecstatic' at the success. Moltke too was delighted with the Lorraine success, and imagined a vast pincer movement encircling the French army with his left wing in Lorraine in the east and with his right wing in Belgium and northern France. This represented a change of plan, much criticised later, from the original intention to strengthen the right wing with some of the corps originally used in Lorraine. Moltke ordered Rupprecht to continue the pursuit southwards towards Epinal. Rupprecht was now less enthusiastic, but having insisted on attacking,

---

[27] Letter, Foch to Mme Foch, 23 August 1914, vol. 32.
[28] XX Corps report, 25 August 1914, *AFGG* 1/1, annex 566; *RAW*, 1: 292.

despite Moltke's suggestion that such an attack was premature, he was obliged to finish the job.[29]

The reason for giving Epinal as the direction of march was to reach the Charmes gap. This gap in France's eastern chain of fortresses between Toul (behind Nancy) and Epinal to the south had been designed to act as a funnel for any German invasion force. Moltke could not have given the French anything better. In order to reach Lunéville then Epinal, Rupprecht would have to march his troops southwards, presenting his right flank to the Second Army as he went. Moltke's belief that the Second Army was a spent force was greatly mistaken.

On the morning of 24 August Second Army aviators reported a German manoeuvre of 'great temerity'. Two army corps at least were moving from the Nancy area towards the junction of Second and First Armies 'carrying out a flank movement under the nose of Second Army along the western slopes of the valley of the Meurthe, covered by a single division deployed on a wide front'.[30] Castelnau decided to take the offensive, and ordered XX Corps to attack out of the Nancy defences whilst First Army met the advancing Germans head on.

In a series of violent attacks Foch's two divisions of XX Corps crashed into the enemy's left on 25 August. Although they did not gain much territory they tied down a significant number of enemy troops, and contributed to the success along the rest of the front. By evening the Battle of the Mortagne had been won and Morhange avenged. The Germans were pushed back eastwards across the eponymous river. The French continued the pursuit the next day in torrential rain, but did not manage to get across the Meurthe. Both armies were worn out, and Castelnau ordered a day's rest on 27 August so that units could re-form and re-organise.

Foch, however, believed that the enemy should be given no respite and Castelnau's liaison officer was obliged once again to reinforce the order to XX Corps not to attack.[31] Castelnau ordered the advance to be continued on 28 August, but both sides remained too exhausted to achieve very much and the fighting died down. Second Army had achieved Joffre's aim of tying down troops in the east, and the left of Moltke's pincer was broken.

Command of XX Corps now passed to General Balfourier, until then commander of 11 DI, because Foch was called away for another task. General Emile Fayolle, commanding 70 DI (a reserve division) protecting XX Corps' left, and a friend of Foch, was nonetheless pleased by the

---

[29] Mombauer, *Moltke*, 239–43, 248.
[30] Report of Captain Armengaud, 24 August 1914, cited in Gras, *Castelnau*, 162.
[31] Ibid., 165.

change of command. Balfourier was much less boisterous than Foch, he noted in his diary.[32] In a telegram sent early in the morning of 28 August, the commander-in-chief asked Castelnau to remove Foch from command of XX Corps and to send him to headquarters as quickly as possible. He was to bring with him Colonels Weygand (then serving in XX Corps' cavalry) and Devaux (head of operations on Castelnau's general staff), because he was needed 'for an important command'.[33] Foch left that afternoon. The Foch–Weygand duo, which was to last the whole war and to prove one of the most fruitful combinations of commander and chief of staff, was thereby constituted through sheer chance. It was Joffre who had selected Weygand as he had Foch; and because Weygand had three months' seniority over Devaux the former got the top job, despite not having attended the Ecole Supérieure de Guerre. Foch told Joffre that if Weygand proved to be not up to the job, he would get another chief of staff. The question did not arise.

Foch had distinguished himself in Lorraine by his competent handling of his corps. He had been lucky not to meet much opposition from the enemy as he advanced, and lucky that his failure (deliberate or not) to follow orders at Morhange had been overtaken by events. Second Army would have been forced to retreat when the Bavarians attacked with superior numbers, whatever Foch did, and Joffre was unlikely to criticise a commander for too much offensive spirit. Foch had then carried out the difficult task of rearguard and had participated in the counter-attacks at the Mortagne river. His few weeks of command experience in Lorraine looked even better when compared with the commanders of Foch's two neighbouring corps. Generals Espinasse and Taverna, in command of XV and XVI Corps respectively, were both relieved a few weeks later after their failure to make much headway in the advance into Lorraine. These two corps were recruited in the south of France, and the Parisian press publicised their retreat, which appears to have turned into a rout among some units.[34] Foch's energy and determination stood out among his peers, even if this led to taking matters into his own hands rather than following orders. The relationship with Castelnau never recovered from the events of August.

---

[32] Fayolle, *CS*, 27 (entry for 29 August 1914). Fayolle wrote that Balfourier was much less 'capitaine Fracasse' than Foch. Capitaine Fracasse is a character in a Gautier novel, based on the *commedia dell'arte* figure of the boisterous soldier.

[33] Telegram, CinC to II Army commander, 28 August 1914, 7am, *AFGG* 1/2, annex 981.

[34] Rocolle, *Hécatombe*, 98–9.

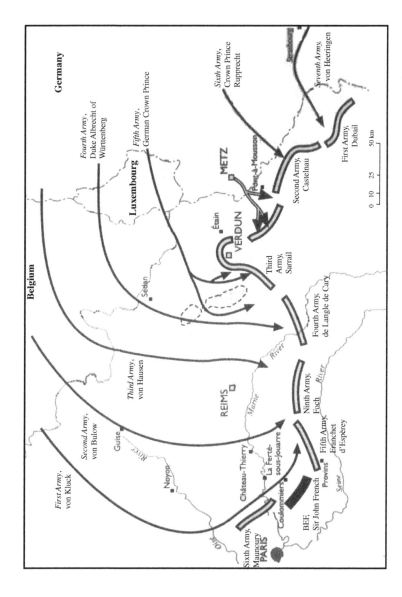

Map 3 Arrival of the armies on the Marne, September 1914

2   'He held to the last quarter hour': with Ninth Army on the Marne

While Foch had been carrying out his role as commander of XX Corps within Second Army by holding down as many German forces as possible on the eastern frontier, the main battles of August 1914, known collectively as the Battles of the Frontiers, had taken place. By using First and Second Armies in Alsace and Lorraine, Joffre had retained the flexibility to deploy France's Third and Fourth Armies in the centre and Fifth Army on the left of the line. Joffre knew that German troops were marching through Luxembourg and Belgium, but he did not know their strength or their exact route. As it became clear that the German right wing was stronger than had first been estimated, Joffre drew the conclusion that therefore the centre must have been weakened. First and Second Armies had fulfilled their roles of holding enemy forces admirably, and so, if the German right was indeed stronger, then the forces deployed in front of Third and Fourth Armies in the centre must be weaker. As a consequence, Joffre sent these two armies into Belgium on 21 August (the day after Rupprecht's attack at Morhange) with orders to attack the enemy wherever he was found. Although Fourth Army was six-corps strong, the opposing German forces were stronger still. Joffre had miscalculated disastrously and the costly Battles of the Frontiers were the result.[1]

The Great Retreat then began and the French army, now extended on its left by the British Expeditionary Force, marched further and further back, southwards. Casualties had been enormous. By the end of August 128,000 French soldiers had been killed or had 'disappeared' (some of whom were in fact wounded but had been left on the battlefield) out of a total of 206,000 casualties.[2] It was the worst period for casualties of the whole war. Among them were Paul Bécourt, the husband of Foch's daughter Marie, and Foch's only son, officer cadet Germain Foch. However it was only a month later that Foch and his wife learned that

---

[1] On the thinking that led to these errors of appreciation, see Doughty, 'French Strategy in 1914'.
[2] *AFGG* 1/2, 825.

Bécourt had been killed and that Germain was missing; his death was not confirmed until much later, in February 1915.

Following the retreat from the frontier Joffre had to recast his operational plan, but his calm temperament and experience of logistics stood him in good stead. He collected troops from the east and moved them by train across to France to constitute a new force to bolster the retreating troops. This newly constituted French army (named Sixth) made its stand eventually northeast of Paris. Next in line were the British, then Fifth, Fourth, Third Armies with Foch's old Second Army in Lorraine, and finally First Army in Alsace. The line ran like an 'S' on its back, dipping south from Paris to below the Marne, then rising northwards towards and around Verdun, finally dipping south again as far as the Swiss frontier. (See Map 3.) Joffre called for Foch to help fill a gap in this line that the retreat had opened up between Fourth Army and Fifth Army on its left. Fourth Army commanded by General de Langle de Cary was now very large, and Joffre intended to lighten Fourth Army's task by detaching some of its units and placing them under Foch's command so as to fill the dangerous gap. Hence Foch moved from the eastern periphery to the centre of the Allied army disposition.

Foch arrived at French headquarters (Grand Quartier Général, GQG) on the evening of 28 August and left the next morning with his 'lettre de service'. He collected two more officers for his staff, one of whom he already knew and who would become a useful contact, André Tardieu. Tardieu claims that it was he who had suggested to Clemenceau in 1908 that Foch might be a suitable commandant for the Ecole de Guerre, and Tardieu and Foch had worked together on the matter of the three-year conscription law passed in 1913.[3] A parliamentary *député* of mobilisable age, Tardieu – who spoke English – had been employed at GQG as an interpreter in 2e Bureau but he wanted a more exciting job. He was also an influential journalist. An officer at GQG called him a 'political power'.[4] He provided a link to Georges Clemenceau (with whom he would work closely during the peace negotiations in 1919) and himself became Premier in 1929.

After leaving GQG, Foch drove straightaway to Fourth Army headquarters in Machault (Champagne), where General de Langle de Cary greeted him as a gift from 'Providence', although he was not too sure where his army units were that were to constitute Foch's army detachment.[5] Those units were somewhat miscellaneous: General Dubois'

---

[3] Tardieu, *Avec Foch*, 12–14; Weygand, *Foch*, 89–90.

[4] Dupont memoirs, fo. 71, 1KT/526, SHD/T: 'c'est une puissance politique'.

[5] Journées, 29 August 1914, 414/AP/10.

IX and General Eydoux' XI Corps, plus General Grossetti's 42 DI (which joined later by train), plus two reserve divisions and some cavalry. The first mentioned, IX Corps, had started the war in Second Army and so Foch had some idea of its value, but XI Corps was exhausted because it had been in the fierce fighting on the frontiers and had suffered large casualties, especially among its officers. The cavalry division had lances and cuirasses but few bullets; Grossetti's division lacked some of its elements that had stayed with the division's original corps. The two reserve divisions had been so badly shaken by the fighting that their exact location was unknown. Right from the start they had lacked cohesion and experienced leadership, and were now so ill disciplined as to be guilty of panic and looting.[6] Joffre was not giving Foch a well-trained and cohesive set of units for his army detachment. The detachment's task was to fill the gap between Fifth Army on its left and Fourth Army on its right, as the whole line continued to withdraw. Fourth Army's left flank had been uncovered by the actions of Fifth Army. Both it and the British had been retreating, and blaming each other for that fact, ever since the actions at Mons and Le Cateau when the British Expeditionary Force (BEF) first arrived in France.

Foch took command of his army detachment at 3pm on 29 August. His first order was both characteristic and unrealistic: an attack to begin at 6am the next morning with the aim of protecting Fourth Army's flank by offensive action.[7] This was to ask too much of units that had been fighting hard as well as retreating. Rear areas were full of confusion, and enemy units were pushing forward in strength. It is not certain that the order reached all units before it was overtaken by events. New orders had to be given to continue the retreat and all Foch's men had retired across the Aisne by the end of the day. It was vital to get those units, especially the reserve divisions, re-organised. Foch put two measures in place to deal with the confusion. First, military police were given precise orders to round up stragglers and collect the reserve divisions in rear of active forces, with a strict geographic limit beyond which no combatant could go. Second, because the roads were crowded with civilian refugees, Foch enforced a rigid separation: refugees were not permitted to use the roads between midnight and 3pm, but were so permitted during the remaining time.[8]

---

[6] Villate, *Foch à la Marne*, ch. I, section 1.
[7] Ordre général no 1, *AFGG* 1/2, annex 1272.
[8] Instruction générale aux Commandants de C.A. et D.R., 30 August 1914, *AFGG* 1/2, annex 1490; Weygand, *IV*, 97.

As the armies retreated, Joffre contemplated an operation by Fourth Army's right, and asked Foch on 31 August whether he judged that he would be able to protect Fourth Army's left flank while such an operation was under way. Foch's reply was a measured statement. He would find it difficult to hold on for the two or three days that Joffre wanted in the face of the two German corps already identified on his front because the terrain favoured the Germans (it was flat and there were no river obstacles); because his IX Corps lacked artillery; and because his troops were very tired. The only way he would be able to keep fighting was by manoeuvring in retreat, and this was likely to compromise Fourth Army's security, which was his primary task.[9] Joffre accepted Foch's judgement and told Fourth Army to continue the fighting retreat. Also on 31 August new arrivals brought Foch's staff up to establishment. Commandant Desticker became head of 3e Bureau (operations), and allocations of typewriters, secretaries and cars, together with mess personnel, meant that the army detachment could begin to operate properly.[10]

Between 1 and 4 September Fourth Army and Foch's detachment alongside continued its move southwards. They crossed river after river; they passed through Reims on 3 September and they crossed the Marne. They marched in the great heat amid crowds of refugees with their belongings piled onto carts. Joffre had commanded the retreat to continue until he was sure that the enemy could no longer threaten his open left wing with envelopment. Finally, late on 4 September, the order arrived to stop marching southwards and to turn around to face the enemy. On that day Foch's army detachment became Ninth Army, and General Humbert's Moroccan Division joined it. Foch did not let the promotion from corps to army command go to his head, writing to his wife: 'It makes no difference [Cela ne me fait pas une plus belle jambe] – May God grant me inspiration.'[11]

The enemy units that faced the new Ninth Army were General von Bülow's *Second Army*, and on its left *Third Army* made up of Saxon units under Generaloberst Max Freiherr von Hausen. The two and a half corps of *Third Army* (the weakest of the German armies on the right wing) spent the day of 5 September at rest in and around Châlons-sur-Marne. *Second Army* had continued to advance that day, and so was well ahead of its neighbour, but did not know of the existence of Ninth Army.[12] Foch, however, knew from aerial reconnaissances that large columns of enemy

[9] Réponse du général Foch, 31 August 1914, *AFGG* 1/2, annex 1698.
[10] Weygand, *IV*, 97–8.
[11] Letter, Foch to Mme Foch, 5 September 1914, vol. 32.
[12] Bülow, *Mein Bericht zur Marne-Schlacht*, 54.

troops were crossing the Marne and from prisoner interrogations that *Third Army* consisted of *XII Corps* and *XII Reserve Corps.*[13]

By the time that the Germans reached the Marne, having marched all the way from Belgium in very hot weather, their railheads were between 120 and 160 kilometres behind them. They were running short of ammunition, food rations and fodder for the horses who had to pull most of the German supplies to the front line. *First Army* alone required almost a million kilos of fodder for its horses every day. The invading armies could not live off the land because the fields of northern France could not supply such quantities.[14]

Both British and French aerial reconnaissance had identified *First Army*'s turn southeastwards, passing to the east of Paris. Joffre intended to seize the opportunity to take the offensive along the entire front with all his armies, including the BEF, and also including the new Sixth Army under the command of General Michel Maunoury. Sixth Army was to march eastwards out of Paris and attack the flank of von Kluck's *First Army*, which presented a tempting target as it marched southeastwards. The Allies now had numerical superiority for the battle: fifty-six British and French infantry divisions and nine and a half cavalry divisions, facing forty-four infantry and seven cavalry divisions.[15] Joffre intended that Sixth Army, the BEF and Fifth Army attack the Germans' right flank as they marched into the salient between Paris and Verdun. In the middle of the salient stood Foch's Ninth Army with orders to hold the line, while at the same time supporting Fifth Army's attack and maintaining contact with Fourth Army. The remaining French armies (Fourth, Third, Second and First) were to maintain the pressure on the enemy forces facing them to prevent any detachment of units to help the German right flank.

The terrain on which Ninth Army was to operate consisted of three different sectors (see Map 4).[16] On the western left flank lay the last limestone escarpment of the Paris basin with the landmarks of the church and château of Mondement. Then the wooded escarpment dropped away sharply to the east to the muddy valley of the Petit Morin, with the marshes of Saint-Gond, three kilometres across at the widest point and nineteen kilometres from east to west. The marshes could be crossed from north to south only by five roads and three tracks, thus making them easy to defend with artillery fire. South of the marshes the ground rose again to the Allemant–Mont Août ridge, giving good observation to and protection for the artillery covering the marshes. As will be seen, later the ridge also

---

[13] Compte-rendu de renseignements du 5 septembre 1914, *AFGG* 1/2, annex 2552.
[14] Herwig, *First World War*, 100–1.   [15] *AFGG* 1/2, 818, note 3.
[16] There is a good description of the terrain in Villate, *Foch à la Marne*, ch. II.

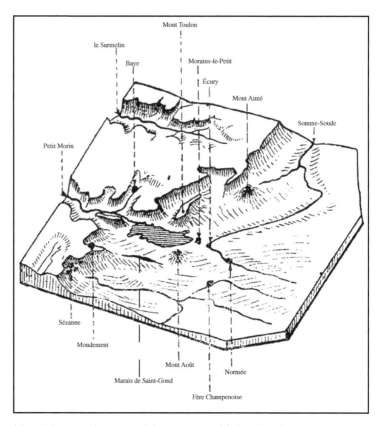

Map 4 Perspective map of the marshes of Saint-Gond area

protected French infantry movements from enemy observation. Finally, on the right, eastern flank of Foch's front, began the chalky, flat, dry Champagne plain. This was good attacking ground for infantry because it lacked any obstacles for the defenders to use. After the war Foch described the three sectors as rampart, ditch and gap.[17]

On Ninth Army's left flank Grossetti's 42 DI had the task of supporting the attack of Fifth Army alongside. They were operating in the hilly, wooded country of the escarpment. Next to 42 DI and down in the valley was IX Corps (General Dubois). Its task was to prevent the enemy from getting across the valley by holding the marshes of Saint-Gond, and the

---

[17] Bugnet, *En écoutant Foch*, 130.

troops were mostly in line along the southern edge, with outposts held on the higher ground to the north. On the right of the deployment was General Eydoux' XI Corps, which held the line of the Somme river, but they were in open, flat country and here the Somme was not the large river that Foch would know in 1916 further west and north, but another insignificant watercourse of the same name, little more than a ditch in places, that presented only a minor obstacle to an enemy attacking in such flat country. In fact the town of Fère-Champenoise was the only notable feature round about. To the right of XI Corps and between it and Fourth Army lay a gap of thirty-six kilometres that was patrolled by Ninth Army's cavalry division. This was a very wide gap, hence represented the main weakness in Foch's line of battle, but it was rendered less dangerous by the fact that a similar gap existed between Hausen's *Third Army* and the Duke of Württemberg's *Fourth Army*. Foch's corps reserve was 18 DI, but it had not yet completed its move from Lorraine.

Joffre's instructions to Ninth Army were very general and a combination of offensive and defensive action: to cover the right of Fifth Army's attack by holding on to the marshes of Saint-Gond and by getting a portion of its forces onto the high ground north of Sézanne.[18] Ninth Army along with Fifth, the BEF, and Sixth Army were to begin the offensive early on the morning of 6 September. So Foch had freedom to decide how best to support an offensive by the neighbouring army on his left while remaining in contact with the non-attacking army (the Fourth) on his right. He ordered IX Corps, the forces in the centre of his disposition, to take up advance positions on the two high points north of the marshes as well as holding a line to the south. Foch has been criticised for this, with the argument that he should have kept his IX Corps together and used its artillery to dominate the marshes from the higher ground to the south.[19] However, IX Corps was missing three of its artillery groups, left behind in Lorraine, and Foch judged that it would be more secure if they could prevent the Germans from occupying the high ground north of the marshes. Further, holding northern outposts would protect IX Corps when (if) they advanced.[20]

The results of the first day's fighting on 6 September were mixed (see Map 5). On the left 42 DI managed to advance as Fifth Army progressed, but only after some heavy fighting and a considerable number of casualties. In the centre IX Corps was unable to withstand the attacks of von Bülow's *Second Army* and had to abandon the outposts north of the marshes, so that the entire corps was south of the marshes by the end of the

---

[18] Ordre général no 6, 4 September 1914, 22h, *AFGG* 1/2, annex 2332.
[19] Anon., 'General Foch'.   [20] Dubois, *Deux ans*, 1: 169–73.

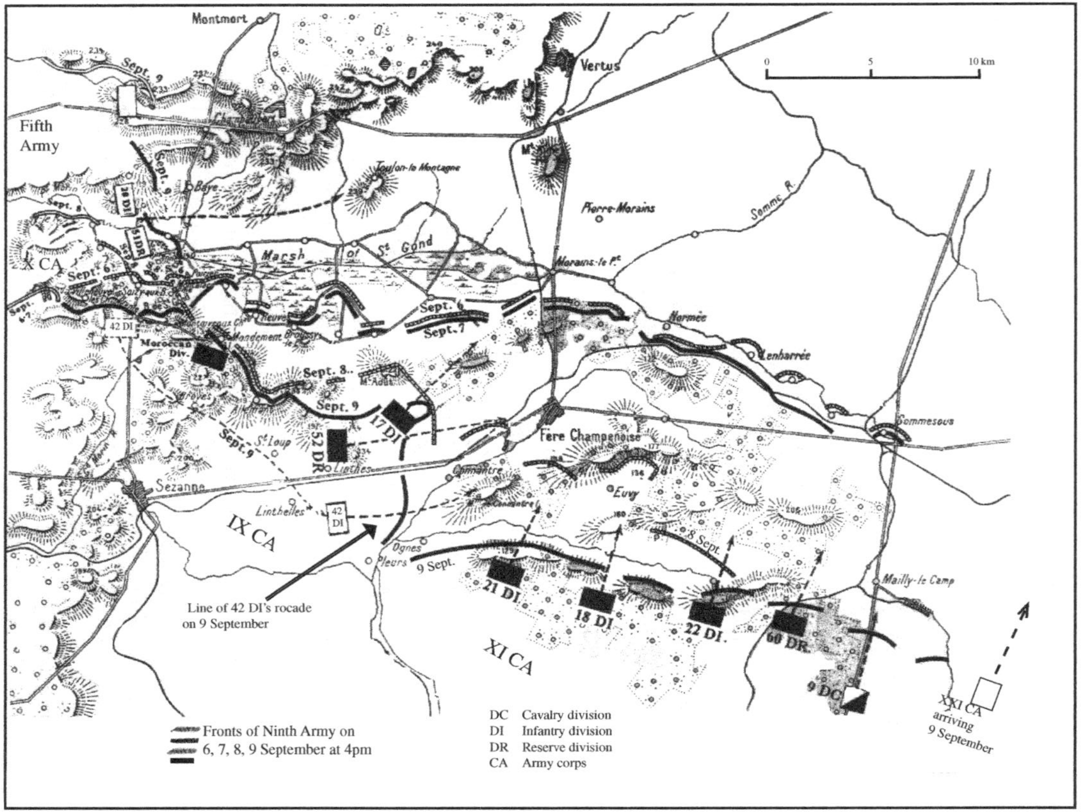

Map 5 Ninth Army on the Marne, 6–9 September 1914

day. The Prussian *Corps of Guards* began crossing the marshes on the few available roads, but were easy targets for the French artillery on the south side and the Germans were obliged henceforth to pass them either to the east or to the west. On the right, XI Corps was unable to resist the oncoming Saxons (who had had a day's rest on 5 September, although they were still very tired with the heat and the marching and had not expected to find much in the way of opposition until they reached the river Seine). The divisions of XI Corps were forced to abandon the line of the river Somme, and were clearly considerably disorganised despite Foch's two notes of encouragement about how vital it was to hang on.[21] The confusion meant that the position on the right had become very dangerous.

The next day, 7 September, Foch's intentions remained unaltered: an attack towards the northeast in liaison with Fifth Army, whilst holding on to the marshes of Saint-Gond and the roads leading northeastwards towards Châlons and Vertus.[22] The gap on the right between the weakening XI Corps and Fourth Army was a worry. GQG informed Foch at 10am on 7 September that the units of XXI Corps that were being sent to help fill the gap were delayed. It was likely that only the artillery and perhaps one brigade of infantry would arrive by evening.[23] Nonetheless Foch's orders issued at 4am began and ended on an optimistic note. He began by explaining how well Sixth Army had progressed eastwards from Meaux and how the BEF was ready for action in liaison with Fifth Army. He ended by calling on all Ninth Army troops to act with the 'greatest activity and energy' so as to consolidate the results already achieved against a 'heavily tried enemy'. The infantry should be engaged with economy, but the artillery 'without counting', whilst any ground captured was to be organised defensively without delay. How far the tired troops could carry out these tactics was doubtful; yet they knew what their commanding officer expected of them. It is noteworthy that Foch was keeping the whole battlefront in view, and keeping his subordinate commanders informed.

Ninth Army had little chance to make any headway against the enemy, who dominated the action on 7 September. In the centre IX Corps took a considerable beating; but so long as they maintained the liaison with the heights on their left, where 42 DI was making good progress alongside Fifth Army, they were in no immediate danger. Foch kept IX Corps informed of the progress being made on its left via messages at 8.10 and

---

[21] Villate, *Foch à la Marne*, ch. IV/6.
[22] IX Armée, Compte-rendu de situation, 5 September 1914, *AFGG* 1/2, annex 2563.
[23] QGQ (Berthelot) to Plancy [Ninth Army], 7 September 1914, *AFGG* 1/3, annex 775.

9.30 in the morning and then at 1.30 and 2.15 in the afternoon. It was otherwise on the right where XI Corps was struggling. Foch allocated them a brigade of his reserve 18 DI at 3.45pm so that they could mount an offensive to recapture some of the ground they had lost. Whether Foch really believed that XI Corps was in any state to attack, or whether he judged that an offensive attitude would keep the corps together more effectively than another retirement, is difficult to know. Weygand explained how his chief believed that an advance unified and that an order to retreat 'dissociated' an army; orders for an attack obliged officers and men to look forward instead of backwards. Hence, if the will of the chief is expressed firmly and clearly, then even the most timid take heart. Some attacking troops at least will succeed, even if it is impossible for all to carry out the attack. At the end of a battle, energetic action lasting an hour or a retreat lasting an hour might mean final success or defeat.[24]

Although the pressure was unrelieved on Foch's Ninth Army front, elsewhere the French and British troops were achieving some success. Sixth Army's offensive had forced von Kluck to pull back two of his corps from south of the Marne in order to help with his defence against Sixth Army further north. This decision opened up a gap between the two German armies, *First* and *Second*, into which the BEF was marching. Furthermore the impossibility of getting across the marshes forced von Bülow to separate the corps of his *Second Army* so that they could get around the obstacle to the east and to the west.

Clearly the German high command would have to try a new tactic. This was a move by von Hausen's *Third Army*. If Foch is to be criticised for issuing orders to attack to a weakened XI Corps, what is to be made of von Hausen's plan for 8 September? Hausen had been forced to split his forces, just like *Second Army*, because of his support role. He had to respond to calls for assistance from von Bülow on his right and from Duke Albrecht of Württemberg's *Fourth Army* on his left. He decided now, at 6pm on the evening of 7 September (5pm French time), that a frontal attack was the right tactic. The whole of his *Third Army*, together with units from the wings of both neighbouring armies, would make a bayonet attack at dawn the next day before the French artillery could see well enough to fire on them. (The French army has been criticised severely for such tactics as frontal attacks made with the bayonet.) The aim was simply to probe the French defences so as to find the weak spots that would enable a breakthrough as far as the French artillery positions in the rear. As the historian of the Saxons on the Marne has pointed out,

---

[24] Weygand, *Foch*, 68.

Moltke's hands-off approach meant that any idea of Hausen's for breaking through Ninth Army and rolling it up would have to be organised not by OHL but by agreement with the neighbouring army commanders. Communications were too poor for that, even if the commanders had had time to spare from protecting their own fronts. Further, the concept of exploiting the breach between Ninth and Fourth Armies so as to roll up Ninth Army was 'not even discussed. Hausen's writings are completely silent on the point.'[25]

Foch's orders for the XI Corps action on 8 September had been that all units, including his reserve division which was committed to the corps, should carry out the attack that the enemy had prevented them from making on the 7th. All men should be under arms by 5am and ready to begin attacking.[26] The Germans moved first, however. In complete silence they removed bullets from their rifles, fixed bayonets and set off in close ranks in the dark, at 3.45 (2.45 French time). The result was panic. By the beginning of the afternoon, XI Corps had retreated twelve to thirteen kilometres along a twenty-kilometre-wide front, taking with them the army's only reserves, 18 DI who had been destined to join in the French *attack*. German casualties were high (about 4500 for the western attack group alone), but XI Corps casualties were higher, about 6500. The French also lost between twenty and thirty artillery pieces, some machine-guns and thousands of prisoners.[27] Hausen was pleased. He sent a radio message to OHL that evening stating that he intended to continue the next day to 'push back the enemy'.

Foch knew that his right was the weaker flank and that the gap between IX Corps and Fourth Army was too wide for comfort, and so he made sure that liaison officers kept him informed. He had a better appreciation of the danger than Hausen had of the opportunity. He dispatched a staff officer to XI Corps early in the morning, and, on hearing his report, sent Tardieu to General Eydoux, the XI Corps commander. Eydoux was with his artillery batteries and Tardieu gave him Foch's message: 'It is not a question of victory. Victory is for tomorrow. But to be victorious tomorrow you must hold on today. The safety of the whole army is in the balance and the honour of your corps. Counter-attack as soon as possible.' Tardieu then returned to Foch's command post, but Foch sent him straight back again to ensure that the order was carried out. Despite universal scepticism, the counter-attack was carried out, and so the positions held by the corps were consolidated for the night.

[25] Kleinhenz, 'La Percée saxonne', 148, 150.
[26] IX Armée, Ordre préparatoire, 7 September 1914, *AFGG* 1/3, annex 934.
[27] Kleinhenz, 'La Percée saxonne', 162–3.

Matters were less desperate on the left and in the centre where, despite heavy fighting, the units were able to remain in touch with each other. Having used up his army reserves, Foch was obliged to ask his neighbours for help for his right wing. He telephoned the Fourth Army commander at 7am to ask whether the newly arriving XXI Corps might be able to support his right flank. Foch knew from GQG that the corps had been delayed, but de Langle de Cary claimed that the gap was too wide for him to be able reach out to Foch's flank with Fourth Army troops. Next Foch telephoned Fifth Army to ask Franchet d'Espèrey to attack so as to ease the pressure on Foch's IX Corps who could then, in their turn, help to ease the pressure on the right. In a series of written and verbal instructions Foch directed General Eydoux to use some of his IX Corps troops to support the beleaguered XI Corps by joining with them in an attack to recapture Fère-Champenoise. The last of these orders was timed as late as 15.30.[28] Despite the weariness of troops who had been attacked at bayonet-point twelve hours earlier and had been pushed back many kilometres, both corps managed to make some progress towards their objective before nightfall. Foch backed up these orders by visiting the commanders personally to insist on the urgency of keeping the line intact.[29]

The intelligence bulletin that evening is probably the source of the rather silly phrase that has been attributed to Foch ever since: 'My right is driven in; my left is giving way; the situation is excellent, I am attacking!' Weygand is definite that Foch said no such thing, and it may have been a telephoned message from Tardieu to GQG that used those or similar words. Nonetheless the intelligence bulletin sent to GQG that evening after a day of violent fighting and retreats gave no sign of weariness or pessimism. Ninth Army had borne the brunt of the attacks on 7 September on its left, the bulletin stated, and now on 8 September on its right. The violent enemy attacks were obviously designed to cover the retreat back to the Marne of von Kluck's *First Army* and part of the *Second Army*. The general situation was therefore 'excellent'.[30] Foch's confidence derived from his consideration of the whole picture, not simply his battered Ninth Army's part within it.

The 'excellent' situation may have been true for the French army as a whole, but the Ninth still faced a dangerous threat. Foch's orders for the next day, 9 September, were that positions held were to be organised as strongly as possible and that XI Corps should occupy and defend Fère-Champenoise, with the aid of IX Corps. He had no reserves left, and so he resorted to a highly irregular stratagem (for which he was mocked because

---

[28] *AFGG* 1/3, annex 1533.   [29] Villate, *Foch à la Marne*, ch. VI.
[30] *AFGG* 1/3, annex 1521.

it would never have been approved by the professors in the Ecole Supérieure de Guerre). He would withdraw the units of 42 DI, who had been engaged in some very hard fighting in support of Fifth Army on the left, order them to march sixteen kilometres across the south of the battle-field behind the hills marking the edge of the valley containing the marshes, and then launch them in an offensive in support of XI Corps. It was a desperate measure to meet desperate circumstances. As he told his liaison officer with 42 DI, there was nothing else he could do.[31]

Foch rang Franchet d'Espèrey that evening at 9.40 to ask if he could liberate General Grossetti's 42 DI, given that Fifth Army was making some progress. Franchet d'Espèrey not only agreed to relieve 42 DI, but he also put the whole of his X Corps under Foch's orders so that Foch would be able to concentrate on the dangerous right flank and have no worries about his left. Immediately Foch drew up the orders for both 42 DI and X Corps and sent his staff officer, Captain Edouard Réquin, to deliver them in person. There was no time to waste, especially if the Saxons intended to repeat their early morning surprise tactic of a bayonet attack.

Réquin reached General Grossetti's headquarters at 10.30pm. Naturally Grossetti asked if he were mad. How could a division that had been fighting for three days and two nights be relieved under the nose of the enemy? Foch's orders were clear, however. At 5am on 9 September X Corps was to relieve 42 DI, whose men would form up to the south of the battlefield.[32]

On the right of Ninth Army's front things went badly for XI Corps on 9 September. Foch sent Tardieu to see if the Germans had made any progress. They had captured Euvy and the XI Corps commander was holding a ridge two kilometres to the south of the village while infantry columns streamed past to the rear. Tardieu reported the situation to Foch, who sent him straight back again with an order that XI Corps must hold on. By the time Tardieu reached them, however, they had retreated still further as the Prussian *Guards* came on. Once more Tardieu reported back to Foch who wrote out a brief order: 'General attack, whatever happens.' Before Tardieu left to deliver the order, Foch took back the page torn out of his notebook and underlined twice the phrase 'whatever happens'. It was vital to hold on until 4pm, when 42 DI would be arriving to make their assault on Fère-Champenoise. The commander and rem-nants of XI Corps greeted Tardieu and his order with stupefaction. Nonetheless an attempt was made to carry it out.

---

[31] Général Réquin, 'Extraits de mon carnet de route', 9 September 1914, Lecomte mss, 1K/108/3.
[32] *AFGG* 1/3, annex 2147.

On both right and left, then, Foch's orders were met with incredulity. Were those orders as mad as their recipients believed? Foch had no resources other than those under his hand, and they had all been hard pressed since the fighting began on 6 September. It was imperative that the thin French line should hold. Foch knew that his best general and best troops were in 42 DI on the left, where Fifth Army was progressing (and where the BEF would soon cross the Marne) and that the danger was on the right. He could not order a retreat; XI Corps clearly could not stand. Tardieu's reports left Foch in no doubt as to the state of the disorder. The only action left was to press XI Corps to attack, with the assurance that 42 DI were coming to help. Yet moving a division on foot while German aircraft were out spotting was desperately dangerous. In Foch's view, something had to be done, and moving 42 DI was all that could be done. It requires a special sort of character to be able to issue such orders, but Foch had the necessary energy and conviction, and he knew what his subordinate commanders were capable of. Weygand described such behaviour as 'audace réfléchie', or audacity consciously decided.[33]

On other fronts, the events of 9 September were more promising. The BEF between the French Sixth and Fifth Armies had already reached the Marne and they would begin to cross early on the 9th, the Germans having failed to destroy all the bridges. Sixth Army had been reinforced by a division's worth of men who had joined the battle thanks to the 'taxis of the Marne'. The gap on Fourth Army's left was filled by another cavalry division and the delayed XXI Corps. In Lorraine Castelnau's troops had withstood the critical German attacks against the defences of Nancy. Although fighting in Lorraine continued, Moltke had decided on 8 September that the position of his right-hand armies did not permit him to continue with the attempt to take Nancy, where the Kaiser was expecting to make a triumphal entry.[34] Thus, on the flanks, the French situation as a whole was looking better. Furthermore, Moltke had despatched Colonel Hentsch on the morning of 8 September to all the army headquarters to judge whether the BEF advance (which Moltke had discovered through radio intercepts) necessitated a retreat in order to close the gap between his *First* and *Second Armies* into which the BEF was moving (albeit slowly).

On 9 September on Foch's front, however, the Germans were still attacking. The plan to disengage 42 DI and re-deploy the troops on the right flank of Ninth Army did not go smoothly. The relief was due to begin at 5am but there was confusion about whether X Corps had the right to

[33] Weygand, *IV*, 110.   [34] Gras, *Castelnau*, 169–70.

order its right-hand units to relieve 42 DI, and the process was not completed until 11am. In addition the Prussian *Guards* got past the marshes and, in a violent attack, captured the landmark of the château of Mondement. The Moroccan Division of IX Corps, who had suffered huge losses in men and officers in fighting in the same area since 6 September, bore the brunt of the attack. Its commanding officer, General Humbert, asked 42 DI for help. The château overlooked the centre of the battlefield, and if the Germans had managed to install heavy artillery in its grounds they would have gained a priceless advantage. General Grossetti judged, therefore, that the loss of Mondement would be so dangerous as to make his action further east redundant; hence he delayed collecting all his division for the march east and lent to the Moroccan Division two battalions of infantry and two groups of artillery (about twenty-four guns). Finally 42 DI started its march in the early afternoon. The morale effect was enormous on those who saw the infantry moving in deployed columns with their remaining artillery groups, led by the cavalry and General Grossetti on horseback. Weygand (sent by Foch to check on progress) thought the spectacle very fine. Réquin also saw the 'admirable' sight, and spotted that the division did not have its full complement of artillery. He sped back to ask Humbert if he could return the two groups that he had borrowed. Humbert assented, although the château would not be re-captured until 7pm.[35]

Réquin had been keeping Foch informed of 42 DI's progress. He told him at 1pm that the orders were being carried out, but with about a three-hour delay. Foch sent him back to Grossetti with the instruction that, even if he could not attack before 6pm, he should still attack. In September it is getting dark by that time at that latitude in France. Foch also kept IX and XI Corps informed about Grossetti's progress. He told IX Corps in the morning that 42 DI were on their way and would be ready to go into action at midday. At midday he told them that the division was delayed and it was vital that they hold on until it arrived. In a message to all Ninth Army troops Foch said that intelligence showed that the 'German Army, after having marched without letup since the start of the campaign, had arrived at the extreme limit of fatigue ... The vigorous offensive of our troops has surprised the enemy, who had thought that we would not offer any further resistance.'[36] It takes little imagination to guess what Ninth Army thought. They too were at 'the extreme limit of fatigue'. Nevertheless, there was little more Foch could do than offer encouragement.

---

[35] Weygand, *IV*, 116; Réquin, Carnet, 9 September 1914.
[36] Communication du général commandant la IXe armée aux troupes, 9 September 1914, midday, *AFGG* 1/3, annex 2148.

Foch gave Réquin the instructions for 42 DI's action. They were to attack northwards out of Pleurs (which had been Foch's command post until the German advance), and IX and XI Corps would join the attack, which was to start about 4pm. Foch also ordered his left flank to attack northwards from the marshes. It was as though he had to get his whole army on the move for one last effort. He even sent Weygand to the totally disorganised XI Corps on the right with an order to support 42 DI with an attack along its whole front – wherever that was.

In the end, it was almost dark when 42 DI arrived at the point where they were to begin their attack. The artillery opened fire at 6.10pm and a few infantry set off to the north. Grossetti wanted to see where they had gone and told Réquin to set fire to a haystack after thirty minutes so that he would be able to find his way back.[37] Thus ended a heroic manoeuvre. The orders went out for the next day, 10 September, at 11pm.[38]

At 6.10pm, when Grossetti set off in the gathering dark after his infantry, it was already forty minutes after the German *Third Army* had issued orders to its corps commanders to retreat between fifteen and thirty kilometres.[39] Although the headway made against the Ninth Army had been great, and despite feeling nearly certain that another's day offensive would break right through Ninth Army, Hausen was obliged to obey the order to pull back and shorten the line because *Second Army* had already begun to retreat (at 1pm) and Hentsch ordered *First Army* to conform. There was much argument about the correctness of the decision to retreat from the Marne, both at the time and after the war.[40] Yet *First Army* was outnumbered; the BEF's crossing of the Marne on the morning of 9 September threatened the flanks of both *First* and *Second Armies*; and the Germans were running out of supplies (ammunition; fodder for the horses; rations for the men). Nonetheless the Germans greeted the order to retreat with incredulity. Chief of Staff of *First Army*, General Hermann von Kuhl, believed that 'complete victory beckoned'; Hausen stated that his army left the 'field of victory south of the Marne neither compelled by the enemy nor by its own decision'.[41] His army's great

---

[37] Réquin, 'La Journée du 9 septembre 1914 à la gauche de la IXème Armée (Foch)', ts of article that appeared in the *Revue de l'infanterie*, November 1930, 24, Lecomte mss, 1K/108/3.

[38] Ordre général d'opérations (pour la journée du 10 septembre), 9 September 1914, *AFGG* 1/3, annex 2162.

[39] Kleinhenz, 'La Percée saxonne', 178.

[40] See Mombauer, *Moltke*, 257–60; and Jäschke, 'Zum Problem der Marne-Schlacht'.

[41] Von Kuhl, cited in Zabecki, *Chief of Staff*, 1: 155; Hausen, *Bewegungskrieg*, 125, cited in Kleinhenz, 'La Percée saxonne', 181–2.

inroads into the cellars of Champagne were probably intended to be a form of recompense.

Foch's Ninth Army entered Fère-Champenoise next morning without opposition. Broken bottles filled the streets to a depth of twenty-five centimetres and German corpses swelled as the champagne in their stomachs fermented.[42] Foch installed his command post there, and slept that night in the town hall. His daring rocade (chess move) 'castling' 42 DI had certainly not caused the German retreat, but now at least the weakened and weakening right-hand corps had someone to follow and now pointed in the right direction, in pursuit of the enemy. Joffre sent his congratulations for the 'valour, vigour and tenacity' of the men, and Foch passed them on to his Ninth Army.[43] They were well deserved, for since 29 August Ninth Army had retreated, then turned around, and held on despite repeated battering.

Foch attempted to press the pursuit by attacking the German rearguards, but although constantly he urged speed and energy, the men were simply too tired. In September 1914 Ninth Army suffered 27,919 casualties, of whom 13,229 had been killed or were missing, and 14,690 had been wounded.[44] Since the army existed only from 5 September to 5 October, that represented an average daily casualty rate of about 900 men. There was still no news of Germain Foch, and his father was becoming worried.

Despite the demands in Foch's orders for the days after 10 September for speed and energy in pursuing the retiring enemy forces, the pursuit was slowed by the aggressive German rearguard actions. Furthermore, shells for the 75s were becoming scarce, and Foch felt particularly the lack of heavy artillery. The 75s had done sterling work on the flat Champagne plain and in defending the exits from the marshes of Saint-Gond, but heavy artillery was required to dislodge the enemy from entrenched and elevated positions. Neither the shrapnel nor the high-explosive shell of the 75mm gun was capable of destroying fortified positions, and he told his wife that he was waiting to receive some heavy artillery before re-starting attacks in earnest.[45] Eventually, also, Foch was asked to help Fifth Army by extending his front to defend Reims, and then to give up one of his corps to GQG because Joffre was now moving troops to envelop the German right wing. Consequently, offensive action on the part of Ninth Army became increasingly difficult. On 21 September Foch even

[42] Tardieu, *Avec Foch*, 59, 77.
[43] Ninth Army order, 10 September 1914, *AFGG* 1/3, annex 2791.
[44] 'Etat numérique des Pertes des Armées pendant les mois de septembre, octobre et novembre 1914', *AFGG* 1/4, 554.
[45] Compte rendu, IX Corps artillery, 18 September 1914, *AFGG* 1/4, annex 477; letter, Foch to Mme Foch, 20 September 1914, vol. 32.

suggested to Joffre that his attack proposed for the next day be delayed because without the means to exploit any success it would be premature.[46] So much for the unthinking offensive at all costs. Foch could see that the main battle lines were moving away from his front, now that the Germans had reached the strong defensive position on the high ground of the river Aisne. He told Tardieu: 'We had to win the Battle of Marne so as not to lose the war. Soon it will be necessary to win the Battle of the North Sea.'[47]

On 12 September Foch moved his headquarters further north to Châlons on the river Marne. The next day, finally, there was news of his family. General Sarrail, commanding Third Army, sent one of his officers to tell Foch that his son-in-law Paul Bécourt had been killed on 22 August. Why, Foch asked his wife, did a veil of grief have to cover the glory of recapturing Fère-Champenoise? Nevertheless, he accepted Providence's decrees and would continue to do his duty. He counted on his wife to comfort their daughter and her children. A few days later (19 September) Sarrail's chief of staff informed Foch that his son had disappeared on the same day that Bécourt had been killed. There was a chance that he had been wounded and taken prisoner, although Foch did not put much faith in the possibility. He resolved that none of the French deaths should be in vain: 'I'm working to that end with all the strength of my spirit and my character', he told his wife.[48] His energetic pursuit of the retreating German troops reveals the strength of his resolution.

The events across the whole French front that were given the name of the Battle of the Marne represented a significant moment, despite the fact that neither the Germans nor the Allies could be said to have won a tactical victory. The few days' fighting might be described as a draw, in some respects like events at sea in 1916 at the Battle of Jutland. In strategic terms, however, the Marne marked the end of Germany's hope of defeating France in short order. Consequently (and very quickly) the battle entered the realms of legend. What the Germans called the 'Marne drama', not acknowledging defeat, became for France the 'miracle of the Marne' with Joffre becoming known as the 'saviour of the Marne' or (more familiarly) 'Papa Joffre'.

Foch's role in the battle also partook of legend. The chess move, 'castling' 42 DI across the rear of the battlefield, the mythical communiqué and throwing the Prussian *Guard* into the marshes (the last untrue) all fed into the desire for some good news at last. The château at Mondement with its

[46] Letter, Foch to Joffre, 21 September 1914, *AFGG* 1/4, annex 758.
[47] Tardieu, *Avec Foch*, 75.
[48] Letters, Foch to Mme Foch, 13, 14, 19, 20 September 1914, vol. 32.

view over the marshes became a tourist destination after the war. If the legends do not reflect the whole truth, yet it is undeniable that Foch's Ninth Army played an important role in the battle. He admitted after the war (in the *Echo de Paris*, January 1920) – when, of course, he could afford to do so – that he had been defeated at the Marne. Nor did his actions impel the German retreat. As British historians frequently point out, French accounts omit the factor of the BEF's crossing of the Marne in the German decision to withdraw; Sixth Army's offensive against Kluck's *First Army* disrupted Germans plans, such as they were; Sarrail's Third Army hung on to Verdun; and Castelnau's Second Army retained Nancy. Nonetheless, if the middle of the line had not held, then the Germans would have been able to break through and split the Allied deployment, rolling up the British and French against the coast, or continuing east to crush the French against the Vosges as originally planned. This would have rendered useless the BEF's slow penetration of the original breach between German *First* and *Second Armies*.

Foch's achievement in inspiring Ninth Army to hold on to the vulnerable centre of the French line is all the more remarkable when the speed of the operation is taken into account. Foch created the army from a disparate collection of units, created a staff *ab nihilo*, conducted a fighting retreat, and finally turned and faced the enemy – all in just under two weeks. He repaid amply Joffre's confidence in his abilities. He knew what he wanted from the units in his army, and insisted on getting it. He 'knew' that against a resolute enemy there must be no voluntary retreat. He 'knew' that a successful defence against such an enemy required offensive action. This was not always possible – and Foch never railed against commanders whom force majeure prevented from attacking – but an offensive attitude kept the enemy under constant threat and kept a small degree of initiative in French hands. Weygand claims that Foch never expected the arrival of 42 DI on the right of his front to get the whole line forward; rather, he expected the infusion of new blood to give heart to the weary XI Corps. Weygand claims also that the rocade of 42 DI was less risky a manoeuvre than it seemed at first glance because Foch knew Grossetti, and both men knew the terrain and the situation on the whole battlefield.[49] Foch had complete confidence in his own judgement.

The outstanding characteristics of his exercise of command are clear from the foregoing account. Foch's mental and physical stamina was enormous; and he put great emphasis on his communications with the higher command (so as to be able to keep a sense of the whole battle, not

[49] Weygand, *IV*, 120–3.

simply his own army's part in it) and with lower commands (so as to ensure that his commands were carried out as far as possible). He did not consider that his job was over when orders had been issued, but urged and exhorted and encouraged constantly. If the troops held, it was partly in response to this urging and encouragement. Many of his instructions were pious hopes rather than practical orders, yet, as any teacher knows, to expect little is to receive little. One must ask for a lot in order to obtain at least something. Foch used boundless energy, as tight a control over the battlefield as enemy action permitted, and a desperate transfer of troops across the rear of a battlefield to achieve his aims.

What is more, he wrote many of his own orders (they still exist in the Ninth Army records), and sent them to the units on his flank via Tardieu and Réquin, his liaison officers. Although he could not leave his command post because he had to be findable at all times, he sent his officers out, including Weygand on occasion. This feature of his command style contrasts greatly with German methods. Moltke did not know what was going on because he was too far away in Luxembourg and he had no direct line of communication with his right wing. The two army commanders there had no telephone line connecting them until 9 September. Kluck's decision to pull back two corps to meet the threat from Sixth Army, thus exposing Bülow's right, was taken without reference to the *Second Army* commander. The latter's decision to retreat forced both neighbouring armies to follow suit, but most unwillingly.

In sum, Foch proved himself a very hands-on commander during the Battle of the Marne. He had indeed held to the vital 'last quarter hour'.[50] One historian reckoned that Foch's attitude during the battle was worth an army corps to Ninth Army.[51] The government showed its appreciation of his efforts with a promotion in the Légion d'honneur; and Joffre showed his by entrusting Foch with another vital mission.

---

[50] Berthelot diary, fo. 110 (entry for 9 September 1914).   [51] Tyng, *Marne*, 266.

3   Commander-in-chief's deputy in the north, October–November 1914

The French may have conducted a successful defence on the Marne, but the Germans were not beaten. Although Foch had tried to make Ninth Army pursue the retreating enemy forces with all speed, little progress had been made and once the Germans reached the high ground north of the river Aisne progress ended. Moltke intended the retreat to be merely a temporary measure, and so the Germans dug defensive positions as soon as they reached the tactically favourable high ground. There Moltke filled the gap between *First* and *Second Armies*, and turned his attention to Belgium. Then War Minister Erich von Falkenhayn replaced Moltke as chief of the general staff on 14 September and set about re-starting the offensive so as to defeat the French as speedily as possible.

With the end of active operations on his front Foch turned to thinking about infantry tactics. The doctrine had been formation in depth ['l'ordre en profondeur'], but this meant that when the heads of columns reached an obstacle such as a heavily defended trench and were held up, then all the rearward elements (reinforcements, second line and so on) stopped as well. As a tactic it was useless for getting troops forward without significant losses, and putting more troops into the first line only increased the casualties. A much more 'rational' method of proceeding when approaching a significant obstacle was to widen the attack, taking advantage of the terrain to seek out the weak points of the enemy's defences. In other words, more activity, more manoeuvre, and less of the immobilisation caused by the 'ordre en profondeur'. Foch issued this advice in a note to his troops on 30 September, advising company and section commanders to adopt its recommendations 'without hesitation'.[1] This document was not drawn up by the staff but by Foch himself, as the various drafts in his notebooks reveal.

The next day Foch sent out instructions for the defensive as well, now that Ninth Army was stretched more thinly following the withdrawal of

---

[1] Note relative à l'emploi de l'infanterie, 30 September 1914, *AFGG* 1/4, annex 1713.

one of its corps. A linear defence was too dangerous, he advised, because it placed too many troops in the front line. A defensive position in depth was both stronger and more economical in men. In order to achieve such a position he proposed centres of resistance with a wide field of fire in front and at the sides; wide gaps between those centres that could be covered by artillery fire from them; artillery placed to cover likely avenues of approach by the enemy; careful study of the lines of access between centres; and finally the reduction of front-line troops to a minimum so as to create reserves for use in counter-attacks or offensive actions.[2]

Amid all the re-thinking of tactics, Foch did not neglect GQG. He sent Tardieu there five times between the end of the Marne battle and 30 September because he knew that Tardieu would be able to speak freely with Joffre. Foch wanted to keep in touch with the big picture, pressing Tardieu to try to 'see clearly' what was happening. He also sent Tardieu to obtain more shells, but Joffre replied that Foch should leave him in peace; he did not have any to spare. Foch accepted Joffre's decision, saying that a long siege war was beginning that would last for years.[3] Foch was looking to the future.

Joffre too was looking to the future. He was very pleased with Foch's actions on the Marne, but annoyed by the campaign that had started up to give the glory for the victory of the Marne to the military governor of Paris, General Gallieni. So Joffre decided to kill two birds with one stone. On 24 September he sent a strictly personal telegram to the War Minister in Bordeaux, where the government was now based, requesting that Foch should be designated his eventual successor instead of, as currently, General Gallieni. Joffre described Foch in highly flattering terms: 'among the army commanders, General Foch has shown an unquestioned superiority, from the point of view of character and of military thought'. If the government accepted his proposal, Joffre would take Foch as his *ad latus* in order to lighten the heavy task of commander-in-chief. As a sign of their confidence in Joffre War Minister Millerand accepted on behalf of the government, but suggested that the decision not be made formal and definite until after the current military operations had ended.[4] Millerand probably had no wish to upset the Gallieni applecart at this juncture. Indeed, the government seems never to have made this 'formal and definite resolution', because Joffre had to repeat the request to replace

---

[2] Instruction sur l'organisation défensive des fronts étendus, 1 October 1914, ibid., annex 1791.
[3] Tardieu, *Avec Foch*, 76–85.
[4] Cypher telegrams, Joffre to War Minister, #7026, 24 September 1914, and War Minister to Joffre, #1481/G, 25 September 1914, in Fonds Joffre, 1K/268, 'Dossier strictement personnel'.

Gallieni with Foch some months later. Poincaré knew of Joffre's proposal, and knew also that Foch was one of the army's brightest hopes. He agreed that Joffre needed an assistant and that it would be impossible to find a better man than Foch for the role. Gallieni's status as Joffre's successor had not been made public, but Poincaré feared that he would be dissatisfied if he were superseded.[5]

It seems that Joffre's thinking was to bring the Ninth Army commander to GQG, an idea that did not please Foch, who preferred the command of troops to a headquarters job. He composed a note with his objections and gave it to Tardieu to present, the next time he went to GQG. This note gives an insight into how Foch saw his current role. He began by explaining why he enjoyed his army command: it gave him a measure of independence and also responsibility; it allowed him to use what he called his 'activity and his impulsion' whilst keeping in close touch with his subordinate commanders. Command of an army conferred authority and prestige and so, in order to prevent a move to GQG being seen as a disgrace, he would require similar attributes in any new role. Becoming Joffre's deputy would mean an office job, lacking any influence on the execution of orders. Foch ended with an important statement: certainly, the execution of orders needed to be studied in an office, but the execution must be 'followed and directed closely on the ground'.[6] Foch was convinced that his hands-on approach was correct.

By the time Tardieu next went to GQG, the thinking there had changed. Colonel Maurice Gamelin, Joffre's confidant and head of his military cabinet, told Tardieu that it was the government who wanted to give Joffre a deputy (so as to be able to 'divide and rule'), but they did not want Gallieni, whom they accused of making himself 'king of Paris' (the move to Bordeaux left ministers feeling powerless). Gamelin suggested that the new strategic situation meant that GQG could accept a deputy for Joffre by putting such a deputy in charge of the northern armies, which could not be easily controlled from GQG in central France.[7] The front line was being stretched ever further, from Alsace and the Swiss border to reach eventually Belgium and the North Sea, which was too much for one man to control effectively. Gamelin told Poincaré's liaison officer that the battle in the north could be decisive if the armies there were 'coordinated by the impulsion of an active and energetic will . . . Foch is ideal to fill this role.'[8]

---

[5] Poincaré, *AS*, 5: 323 (entry for 24 September 1914).
[6] Tardieu, *Avec Foch*, 80–1. Tardieu cites the full document verbatim (presumably he had kept the paper).
[7] Ibid., 83–5.
[8] Herbillon, *Du général*, 1: 52 (entry for 4 October 1914).

The stretching of the front line to the north had changed the strategic situation. After the Germans halted their retreat from the Marne and dug into ideal defensive positions on the heights above the river Aisne, they also moved troops northwards to envelop the open French left flank, with the result that in turn Joffre had to make a similar manoeuvre so as to envelop the German right. Consequently the front extended further and further north as each side tried to envelop the other. Eventually, this fluid situation was complicated by two further factors. First, Joffre had to answer Sir John French, who wanted to move the BEF from the Aisne front and return to positions closer to the coast and to his army bases. In addition, on 28 September the Germans began investing Antwerp, which tied up the Belgian Army, who were trying to defend the city, encouraged enthusiastically by Winston Churchill. Joffre wanted the Belgian Army to retire from Antwerp in order to fight another day, rather than remain shut up in a besieged fortress. So the strategic situation in the north presented three challenges: the French troops and the open left flank; the British and their CinC; and the Belgians.

On 4 October Joffre called Foch into GQG and told him that he was to be named as the commander-in-chief's 'adjoint' or deputy. If Joffre could not get formal permission to make Foch his successor, he could at least co-opt him as his deputy. As one of the few French generals with knowledge of the British army, Foch was an obvious choice. His friendship with Henry Wilson, dating from the days when both were heads of their respective war colleges, might produce better results than had been experienced when Sir John French and General Lanrezac, commanding Fifth Army alongside, had clashed during the Great Retreat. The head of the British mission at GQG, General G. S. Clive, considered Foch to be 'the most able' of France's generals.[9] Foch's first task would be to coordinate as an army group the action of the French troops in the north, where Joffre wanted a more energetic general with 'guts'.[10] These troops were General Castelnau's Second Army, which Joffre had moved from Lorraine to begin the enveloping operation (Foch had been under Castelnau's command at the start of the war); then, a detachment on Castelnau's left flank, commanded by General de Maud'huy, that grew very large as more units were added, and so became on 5 October Tenth Army; and finally a group of territorial divisions commanded by the seventy-three-year-old General Brugère who, despite being on the retired list, had requested a return to service. Brugère was one of Joffre's predecessors as vice-president of the

---

[9] Clive diary, 4 October 1914, Clive mss 2/1, LHCMA.
[10] Berthelot diary, fo. 157 (entry for 28 September 1914): 'un chef qui ait du cran'.

Conseil supérieur de guerre and had drawn up Plan XV. Brugère's territorials occupied the sector in between Sixth and Tenth Armies.

If the French were reorganising their forces, then so too were the Germans. Their new commander, Erich von Falkenhayn, regrouped the German forces and brought from Lorraine Crown Prince Rupprecht's *Sixth Army*. Hence Castelnau and Rupprecht faced each other once again as they had done in Lorraine in August. The task of *Sixth Army* was to carry out as rapidly as possibly the decision battle [*Entscheidungsschlacht*].[11] Unfortunately for the French and despite their greater railway facilities, the Germans always seemed to be one move ahead, with the result that each French attempt to envelop the German right wing found heavy enemy troop concentrations instead of open country. The Germans, however, had a similar problem because damage to the French and Belgian rail networks hampered their rail movements.

By 4 October, when Joffre called Foch to his headquarters to explain his new role, the situation was this: Second Army and Maud'huy's army detachment (under Second Army's command) were spread over a 100-kilometre front, running northwards from the river Aisne, with the river Somme bisecting their front. The Germans had been attacking Second Army south of the Somme around Roye during the last ten days of September; now they were attacking Maud'huy's troops north of the Somme towards the important communications hubs of Douai and Arras. Foch's first task, therefore, was to evaluate the position on the French left flank and then to coordinate action to contain the German attacks, so that Joffre's aim of enveloping the German flank could be achieved. He lost no time, handing Ninth Army over to General Humbert for the few days until it was dissolved, its units allocated to the neighbouring armies. Foch left that night by car with a few of his staff officers, and he arrived at Castelnau's headquarters at 4.30 next morning, 5 October.

Castelnau had spent the previous two weeks attempting Joffre's enveloping manoeuvre with troops exhausted by continuous fighting. Instead of enveloping, the French were being enveloped, and the older French troops, General Brugère's territorials, were facing the élite Prussian *Corps of Guards*. During the evening of 4 October Maud'huy sent a message to Castelnau stating that unless he was permitted to retire immediately, the French faced another Sedan,[12] for the Germans had launched on his front a pincer attack against Arras from both the southeast and the north via Vimy Ridge. So matters were serious, although GQG did not appear to

---

[11] Mombauer, *Moltke*, 269–71; Foley, *German Strategy*, 98–102.

[12] Maud'huy's message to Captain Tournès, 4 October 1914, cited in Gras, *Castelnau*, 188.

have a true appreciation of the situation, believing that all that was required to defeat the Germans was sufficient boldness.

The meeting between Foch and Castelnau could not have been other than difficult. It was barely two months since the action at Morhange, when Foch had failed to follow the orders of Castelnau, his army commander. Now Foch was that army commander's superior. General Fayolle, for one, could not believe how Foch could have reached such a position.[13] The interview between the two men went badly and led to shouting. Although held in private with only Castelnau's chief of staff, General Anthoine, in attendance, the meeting was overheard easily by one of Castelnau's staff officers, who was on duty in the next room. Castelnau pointed out that unless he received reinforcements he would be obliged either to give ground or to watch the enemy break through.[14] Although Anthoine was permitted to give his view that a retreat was essential, Foch refused to listen. 'You are speaking to a deaf man', Foch wrote later (or 'to a wall' as Weygand recorded Foch's words on leaving). The instruction that Foch left for Castelnau stated that he must hold on, whatever the cost, and that Joffre would send reinforcements as soon as he could.

There is little doubt that Foch spoke harshly to his former superior. Weygand takes pains in his memoirs to show how afterwards Foch attempted, unsuccessfully, to mend fences.[15] A letter Foch sent a few days later, for instance, is addressed to 'Mon cher ami'.[16] It appears to have been an unfortunate characteristic of Foch's to jump in feet first, especially when the situation seemed critical. It will happen again with the Italians in 1917, and with General Gough of Fifth Army in March 1918. Usually relations were repaired or repairable with time, but the relationship with Castelnau never mended and the events at Morhange were not forgotten. The purely human dimension should not be underestimated: both men were very tired, Foch having been driven from his Ninth Army headquarters overnight and Castelnau having been roused early to see him; both men had lost children (Castelnau had lost two sons already in the fighting, one of them in Foch's XX Corps, and a third was missing; and Foch and his wife were still hoping that their own son had not been killed, in fact, but merely taken prisoner).[17] In Foch's defence, it must be said that Joffre's instructions to him were to buck up the two northern armies, and 'to get them forward'. Foch was in no position, therefore, to

---

[13] Fayolle, *CS*, 41 (entry for 9 October 1914).
[14] Armengaud's account cited in Gras, *Castelnau*, 191. See also accounts in Foch, Journées, 414/AP/10, [d] 3; Weygand, *IV*, 135; and Tardieu, *Avec Foch*, 87–9.
[15] Weygand, *IV*, 135–7.
[16] Letter, Foch to Castelnau, 11 October 1914, *AFGG* 1/4, annex 2644.
[17] See, for example, letter, Foch to Mme Foch, 8 October 1914, vol. 32.

permit Second Army to retire, and Joffre had already sent a telegram to Castelnau forbidding any withdrawal that could be interpreted as a retreat.[18] On the other hand, Castelnau's orders for 5 October were clear: Maud'huy was to use all his reinforcements to hold the line whilst waiting for Foch to give his instructions. Furthermore, Foch had to take into account the bigger picture, not simply the position of the French troops in northern France, and the junction with the British troops, who were moving back to the left of the line from their trenches on the Aisne, but also the Belgians, who began retreating southwards as Antwerp fell (its fate was sealed on 7 October, with the Germans completing possession by the 10th).

After his acrimonious meeting with Castelnau, Foch left for Maud'huy's headquarters west of Arras (about three hours' drive away). Before Foch's arrival, Maud'huy had ordered the construction of a line of retreat for the two divisions that were arriving as reinforcements. After talking to Foch, the orders were changed: a cavalry advance was to combine with an infantry attack from the north, whilst X Corps before Arras was to resist where they were.[19] Fayolle's 70 DI was forced back four or five kilometres onto Vimy Ridge, and the offensive gained little ground. Yet at least the French managed to compel the German cavalry to break off their attack, its commanding officer General von der Marwitz informing the Kaiser that he had given up the idea of breaking through the French front.[20] The Kaiser had arrived before Arras and commanded his cavalry to pursue the French, and his presence explains the especial violence of the German attacks on 4 October that had disturbed General Anthoine. Foch was content, however, with what had been achieved on the first day of his new command. His sunny message to GQG that evening concluded that the morrow seemed to promise even better results.[21]

Unfortunately, the hopes were disappointed. Southeast of Arras the territorials gave way completely, and the Germans made another violent assault on Second Army, forcing the French to concede some more ground. At 5pm Second Army even rang Foch and asked him to come back. Joffre asked Foch to act energetically to restore the Second Army's morale, which appeared to be seriously weakened, and sent more infantry reinforcements.[22] Joffre also asked General Gough's 2 Cavalry Division to help. (Gough's men were on their way from the Aisne to the north and, on hearing Castelnau's personal appeal, delayed for a day to support Second

---

[18] *AFGG* 1/4, 220; telegram, Joffre to Castelnau, 4 October 1914, ibid., annex 2004.
[19] Ibid., annexes 2168, 2169; Fayolle, *CS*, 37 (entry for 5 October 1914).
[20] *AFGG* 1/4, 223, from a captured German message.
[21] Ibid., annex 2131.   [22] Ibid., 523.

Army around Roye.)[23] The crisis was over, and Second Army only had to dig in on the following days. Falkenhayn decided to break off this attack in favour of action towards Lille.[24]

Yves Gras combats the 'legend', supported by Joffre's memoir account, of a pessimistic Castelnau intending to abandon Arras and to retreat behind a defensive line formed by the Somme river. However, Second Army's liaison officer's report in the early hours of 3 October, that Castelnau was envisaging a retirement south of the Somme, confirmed GQG's decision to appoint Foch as coordinator.[25] Furthermore, Joffre's dismissal a few days later of Castelnau's chief of staff, General Anthoine, for 'lack of sang-froid and lucidity', bears a great resemblance to events in 1918, when Anthoine was similarly sacked as Pétain's chief of staff for pessimism. The liaison officer between Castelnau and Maud'huy confirms the latter's expectation of a new Sedan and intention to retire to the west of Arras, which probably fed the pessimism in Second Army. The same officer also confirms how easily Maud'huy could veer between despair and 'robust' optimism, which explains in part how Foch's arrival could change an intention to retire into an order to take the offensive.[26] *Contra* Gras, British generals witnessed the atmosphere at Castelnau's headquarters as they passed through the town on their way northwards. Henry Wilson noted that Castelnau was 'a tired old man', but that Foch, whom they saw later that afternoon, was full of fight. (Castelnau was two months younger than Foch.) Sir John French thought Castelnau 'seemed anxious and depressed', but Foch to be 'the exact opposite'.[27] This independent evidence casts doubt on Gras' defence of Castelnau, which is based on the doubtless partisan accounts of his staff. Moreover, General Brugère found Second Army's orders confused and was grateful to have a single commander in Foch.[28]

How much influence on the action around Arras on 5 and 6 October did Foch's actions have? The son of General Humbert (Moroccan Division) was an officer in one of the divisions fighting north of Arras, and his account indicates that Arras might have been lost without Foch's authoritative action. Certainly orders were changed on the mornings of 5 and 6 October following Foch's arrival at Maud'huy's headquarters.[29] One of Second Army's liaison officers is equally clear that, although he did

[23] Gough, *Fifth Army*, 55.   [24] Gras, *Castelnau*, 194.
[25] Ibid., 195–6; Berthelot diary, fos. 168–9 (entry for 3 October 1914).
[26] Letter, General R. Tournès to Weygand, 2 April 1931, Fonds Castelnau, 1K/795/11, [d] Lorraine polémiques.
[27] Wilson diary, 8 October 1914; French diary, 5–8 October 1914, cited in French, *Life of Field-Marshal Sir John French*, 247.
[28] Brugère diary, 7 October 1914, 1K/160.   [29] Humbert, 'Foch'.

not know precisely what Foch contributed, yet Foch's arrival at the critical moment helped them to win a lost battle.[30] On the other hand, the staff of Second Army maintained that Foch did not have much effect since they had already restored the situation by the time that Foch arrived.[31] This was certainly the case on the Somme, but further north, around Arras, the effect of his bustle and optimism was tangible. A member of Maud'huy's staff, General Molinié, wrote to Weygand after the Second World War, recalling how Foch had reversed the position almost instantly, as though by a magic spell, so that there were no further retreats.[32] Indeed, Arras remained in Allied hands. On 6 October Falkenhayn decided to give up on Arras and turned his attention further north to the larger prize of Lille and the coast.[33] Thus ended the first Artois battle for possession of the former capital of the province and the crucial ridge to its north that would cost so many lives.

What is undeniable is the energy that Foch displayed once again during these days. He arrived in the middle of a crisis, with no knowledge of the terrain or the events that had led to that point, yet he encouraged and insisted on a single idea: no voluntary retreat. To achieve this aim, he travelled many kilometres back and forth between the various headquarters whilst Tardieu managed Foch's own headquarters in Doullens, constantly on the telephone or the cypher machines. However, Foch's orders did not always inspire his subordinates. His friend and critic, Colonel Emile Mayer, was on General Brugère's staff during this period. Brugère's group of territorial divisions lost a village on 8 October, and Foch ordered its recapture the next day. When no effort was made to do this, Foch repeated the order. This went on for several days, to the amusement of the various generals who never attempted to obey because they judged the task impossible.[34]

Now that the situation in Picardy and Artois was restored, Foch could turn his attention to the second element of the northern problem – the British. On 29 September Sir John French had requested that the three British corps move from their trenches on the Aisne (where their pursuit of the Germans after the Marne had come to a halt), and that they return to their original position on the French left, where they would have the advantage of shorter lines of communication with their bases. Although Joffre had no objection in principle to such a request, it created a double difficulty for the French, both in arranging for French units to fill the gap left by the British, and in supplying the rail transport or freeing up the roads for the transfer. The last British corps to leave the Aisne required,

[30] Jauneaud, 'Souvenirs', 836.   [31] Gras, *Castelnau*, 195, citing Commandant Jacquand.
[32] Weygand, *IV*, 139–40.   [33] *RAW*, 5: 198.   [34] Mayer, *Trois maréchaux*, 144.

for example, fifty-one trains for the men and thirteen for their supplies, each train being made up of fifty wagons.[35]

The gradual arrival of units of the BEF from the Aisne meant that Joffre could extend his line northwards once more, and by the evening of 11 October III Corps were in line next to the French around Béthune, with the Cavalry Corps covering the gap between III and II Corps, the latter still detraining around St Omer. Foch had been given authority over the port of Dunkirk and its garrison on 6 October, and he arranged to use those troops to cover the disembarkation of the BEF around St Pol. Joffre gave Foch permission to negotiate directly with Sir John French over the details of the disembarkation and concentration.

So, after coping with Second and Tenth Armies, Foch now had to deal with the prickly British commander-in-chief. That task would require a different set of skills and greater tact. He could not speak to a British field marshal in the same tones as he had used with Castelnau. As he wrote to his wife: 'I am now in contact with the British Army. We get on with our neighbours French and Wilson as best we can. They are the same as ever, but the more or less delicate diplomatic relations are an additional charge on me.'[36] The task was made even more difficult by the aggravation that the BEF's move had created. Sir John had been slow to make up his mind; but, encouraged by Wilson and Churchill, he made an official request to shift the BEF. Joffre refused initially because he did not believe that sending the BEF to the open left wing would be profitable, judging that Sir John would not act decisively or even quickly once he arrived there. He only agreed, in a conference on 5 October, that the move could take place after receiving assurances that Sir John would engage each corps as it arrived. This was a concession because Joffre had wanted each *division* to be engaged as it arrived, but Sir John insisted on waiting for a complete corps to have arrived before moving it into line. The tension between the two commanders was increased when Joffre asked Poincaré to intervene with Kitchener to ensure that the British did not lose any time. However, since Sir John had also asked Poincaré to intervene with Kitchener over another matter – the command of Sir Henry Rawlinson's troops sent to defend Antwerp – Joffre was able to make up some ground by asking Kitchener to place Rawlinson under Sir John's command. All in all, an unseemly quadrille of the governments and the military chiefs of two nations, jockeying for advantage, that augured very badly for the future conduct of the coalition war.[37]

[35] Beckett, *Ypres*, 17.   [36] Letter, Foch to Mme Foch, 10 October 1914, vol. 32.
[37] Prete, War of Movement, 339–90.

The tension that resulted became manifest immediately. Between Sir John and Kitchener, the tension had begun when Kitchener came over to Paris and ordered Sir John not to withdraw and re-group before the Marne battle. Sir John in his turn found Joffre overbearing, and he was so furious when Kitchener's letter arrived about employing the BEF's divisions immediately upon arrival that he lost his temper with Huguet, head of the French mission.[38] Hence the energetic Foch would have come at least as a change, if not as a pleasant surprise. Sir John had met Foch several times in England before the war, and commented in 1912 to the then Secretary of State for War that Foch was a man with whom he could 'get on'.[39] Although this opinion would fluctuate over the next few weeks, as was to be expected of someone of his mercurial temperament – the fact that Foch had both lower rank and lower status than himself was galling at times, as will be seen – the final verdict on the relationship during the coming weeks around Ypres was positive.

Sir John and Wilson had called in to see Foch on 8 October on their way from the Aisne to their new headquarters. The latter found Foch 'absolutely full of fight', and so delighted to see him that he kissed him 'twice! in front of the whole crowd!' Indeed, Foch made a particular effort to be welcoming, putting on a guard of honour and a 'kind of tea and champagne party'. As it was an afternoon party, the French knew that they had to provide tea, but were unsure what to offer to eat. After a fruitless search for some Huntley & Palmer biscuits, the mess was reduced to providing cream cakes, of which they felt somewhat ashamed. Weygand remembered how amazed they were at the speed with which the cream cakes disappeared and how the replacement 'petit beurre' biscuits were ignored, disproving yet another 'preconceived notion' about their ally.[40]

Foch went to see Sir John two days later, and they agreed a plan which aimed to safeguard the important industrial centre of Lille.[41] Lille was France's fifth largest city and its textile industry (cotton and linen yarn and fabric) provided for four-fifths of the country's needs. Its capture would constitute a grievous loss to the French economy as well as a disaster for its citizens. Foch proposed a British advance eastwards to the north of the city, and a French advance eastwards to its south. Then, with Lille behind them and the British move from the Aisne complete, the British and the

---

[38] Wilson diary, 6 October 1914; Huguet, *Britain and the War*, 124; Clive diary, 6 October 1914, Clive mss 2/1, LHCMA.
[39] Seely, *Adventure*, 180.   [40] Wilson diary, 8 October 1914; Weygand, *IV*, 146.
[41] *AFGG* 1/4, annex 2567.

French could join up with the Belgian Army so as to re-assemble all their scattered forces. If the British could reach Courtrai on the Lys and the French Tournai on the Scheldt, then the assembly area would be well protected, with the rivers on the flanks and Lille at their back (see Map 6).

Foch had tried to be tactful, by bringing a copy of this proposal in person to Sir John's headquarters and asking for his agreement. Wilson put the matter rather more bluntly, writing that 'Foch simply said what he wanted done & <u>when</u>.' Notwithstanding, Sir John accepted the plan 'cordially' the next day, 11 October, and promised 'every possible' assistance. Joffre also approved the plan the same day. Indeed, the existence of a definite plan of action probably induced Joffre to cooperate in the matter of relieving I Corps, which was still on the Aisne. Sir John had been demanding its early relief in the face of Joffre's insistence that he was

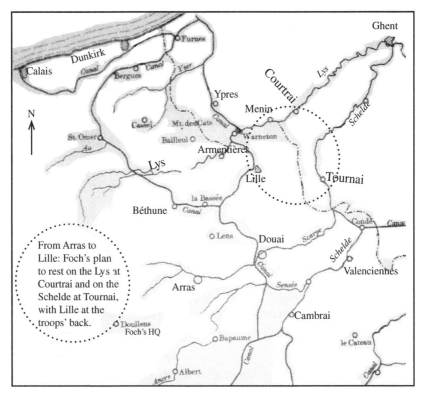

Map 6 From Arras to Lille, and the race to the sea, October 1914

unable to comply. Joffre told Foch to inform Sir John that he was studying how to relieve one of the corps' divisions as soon as possible.[42]

While the British were getting organised the Germans were still pressing Maud'huy's Tenth Army very hard, although the French cavalry managed to hold them off. Foch offered motor transport to speed the move of the II Corps infantry from the disembarkation to the concentration zone, because speed was of the essence if the German enveloping manoeuvre was to be foiled and the safety of Lille assured. Although, by the evening of 11 October, the British cavalry and troops of II Corps had extended Maud'huy's left ready to carry out Foch's plan, the enemy forestalled them once again. That night, after a forced march over a mere seven days from the *Third Army*'s front around Reims, men of the German *XIX Corps* entered Lille and took prisoner its defending garrison, a detachment of French territorials. The city remained in enemy hands for four years, until October 1918, its citizens used as a source of deportations for forced labour.

Joffre was so displeased with Sir John's failure to save the important manufacturing centre of Lille by not moving quickly enough that he told Poincaré's liaison officer that the British could have taken the town without a shot being fired.[43] Yet the loss of Lille did not affect the optimistic tenor of Foch's telephoned report to GQG on the evening of 12 October. He made four points: the BEF was now in position; XX Corps had made progress and captured a gun; Lille was captured by the enemy; and the general situation was 'considered to be good'.[44] Thus he downplayed the loss of Lille by not placing it first in his list, and he was already considering another operation. He took account of the fact that, although the British were moving at last, they were moving very slowly; furthermore the French were tired and, despite, their numerical superiority, were not strong enough to make an effective enveloping manoeuvre of the enemy's flank. The alternative was, therefore, to make an attack on the centre of the enemy's line, rather than on the open flank (which was closing rapidly as Belgian and British troops left Antwerp), relying on heavy artillery rather than on infantry to make the breakthrough.[45] Such an operation in combination with a similar attack in the Champagne region could not be carried out, however, because the enemy launched a different assault: an offensive towards Calais to gain control of the straits. This time the

---

[42] Wilson diary, 10 October 1914; *AFGG* 1/4, annexes 2631, 2628.
[43] Poincaré, *AS*, 5: 392 (entry for 23 October 1914).
[44] Telephoned message from General Foch, 12 October 1914, 21h25, *AFGG* 1/4, annex 2705.
[45] Letter, Foch to Joffre, 13 October 1914, secret correspondence, 16N 2034.

action also involved the Belgians, the third element of Joffre's strategic problem.

So Foch had succeeded in avoiding the feared desk job at GQG, and remained in contact with the action. He had seen that the focus of the fighting would move away from central France and towards the North Sea, and he had issued new directives on infantry tactics and on the construction of defensive positions. He had acted promptly and with great energy to reverse the situation before Arras, where he had a greater influence on Maud'huy than he did on Castelnau. Indeed, the relationship with Castelnau deteriorated further. Since Foch clearly put greater effort and tact into the relationship with the BEF and its commander than he did with Second Army, perhaps some of the blame for the deterioration lies at Foch's door. As well as the Second Army commander, he also rubbed its staff up the wrong way. They complained that Foch's staff did not organise troop movements efficiently.[46] Maud'huy's chief of staff, Colonel Pierre des Vallières, was also critical. He judged that Foch's reassurances that the British were arriving rallied Tenth Army, and that Foch's optimism was 'contagious', yet to some extent dangerous. For, in Vallières' opinion, Foch went too far in denying the danger and in looking solely at the big picture.[47]

Foch's actions on the northern flank consisted of oversight rather than issuing orders directly, although he countermanded orders when necessary, as with Maud'huy on 5 October at Arras. He devoted much bustle and energy to this oversight role – on 5 and 6 October, during his first forty-eight hours as Joffre's adjoint, for example, he travelled 800 kilometres between the various headquarters. It took two hours by car to travel between Foch's headquarters in Doullens and St Omer, where British headquarters (GHQ) was installed.[48] Picardy and Artois had been short engagements, involving mainly the French, but had given Foch a good insight into the problems of the task that Joffre had given him. The next battle, the final outflanking action in Flanders, lasted much longer and involved troops of three nationalities, French, British and Belgian, thus proving a greater test of Foch's abilities.

The fighting in Flanders, along the river Yser and before Ypres in October and November 1914 (see Map 7), was significant strategically and for Foch personally. It marked the last German attempt to gain a victory in the west and to take some profit from the 1914 military campaign. It marked also a personal triumph for Foch in that his actions in the

---

[46] Jacquand memoirs, 15 and 17 October 1914, Fonds Castelnau, 1K/795/36.
[47] Vallières, *Au soleil*, 100.
[48] Weygand, *IV*, 141; letter, Foch to Mme Foch, 15 October 1914, vol. 32.

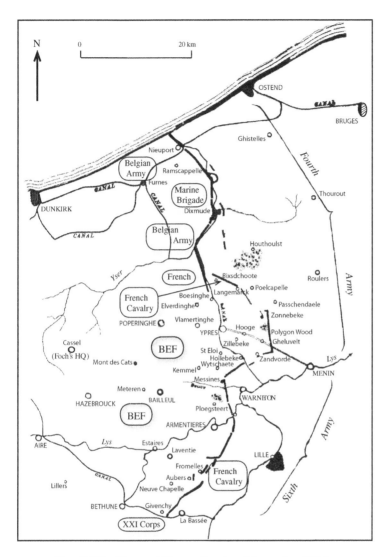

Map 7 The Yser and Ypres, October–November 1914

desperate fighting gained him considerable credit with the Allies, credit that would be cashed in under even more desperate circumstances in 1918. The first phase of the fighting began on the Yser (18–30 October) and overlapped the second phase before Ypres (21 October–12 November).

After recognising Rupprecht's failure to win in Picardy the decisive battle that he wanted, Falkenhayn decided to make his next effort on the extreme right of the line. The capture of Calais would constitute a sort of consolation prize for the failure of the Schlieffen plan. He took the remnants of the Duke of Württemberg's *Fourth Army* and reconstituted it in Flanders, bolstering it with four new reserve corps made up of some trained reservists (twenty-five per cent) and under-age and over-age volunteers. In addition, the fall of Antwerp freed up General Beseler's *III Reserve Corps* and large quantities of heavy artillery. This new large force was to act in conjunction with *Sixth Army* to split the Allied armies. The specific aim of this new *Fourth Army* was to advance down to Dunkirk and Calais with its flank on the coast and thence, at St Omer, southwards. *Sixth Army* was to strike westwards out of Lille towards the coast. Together the two armies were to deal 'an annihilating blow' to the enemy.[49]

The immediate threat posed by the new German offensive was to the Belgian Army and to what remained of Belgian territory – the third element of the coordination task in the north that Joffre had given to Foch. The Belgian government and King (who was also commander-in-chief of the national army) had left Brussels for Antwerp on 17 August and were trapped there when the Germans laid siege to the forts, beginning seriously to invest the place with heavy artillery on 28 September. Foch had not been involved in the failed attempt (instigated by Churchill) to relieve Antwerp. The King left the city on 7 October, reaching the coast at Ostend on the 10th. Following a meeting of his council of ministers attended also by General Pau, the head of the French mission that Joffre had sent to Antwerp, the government requested permission for Belgian troops to enter France so as to get some relief after their weeks of fighting and retreating. They also requested permission for the Belgian government to establish itself at Le Havre, but Joffre had no wish to see the Belgians retire along the coast into France. Instead General Pau presented an alternative scheme for the Belgian Army to remain in Belgium, ready to join the French and British offensive. He explained Foch's scheme for the junction of the Belgians with the Franco-British forces on the Lille–Courtrai line by 13 October. Although certainly King Albert wished to remain on Belgian territory, he had no wish to engage his army in an offensive. In any case, the approaching German *Fourth Army* was likely to impede the BEF's arrival on the Lille–Courtrai line, as indeed happened, and so Albert ordered his army to stand on the line of the river Yser.

[49] Foley, *German Strategy*, 102; *RAW*, 5: 279; Beckett, *Ypres*, 37.

This short river runs northwards, more or less parallel to the coast, and then after Dixmude wobbles its way to the sea. Just before the river turns seawards a canal cuts off to the east towards Ypres. Hence the Yser, prolonged by the Ypres canal, presented a muddy obstacle to the advancing Germans as well as a definite line behind which to mount a defence. Foch sent a message insisting that there should be no retreat unless forced by the enemy, and that the Belgian divisions should remain in contact with Ypres, where a centre of resistance was being created. Nonetheless, there was some defiance from the Belgian troops, and some voluntary withdrawals. On 15 October, Foch asked whether the line would hold and the reply was sent that strict orders had been given to that effect but that it would be impossible without help. Albert visited his divisions the next morning encouraging resistance and raising morale, and threatening that commanders would be sacked if their men retreated.[50]

Foch was not convinced, and so decided to see for himself. He visited Albert in his headquarters at Furnes that afternoon. He had already driven in the morning to see the British commander-in-chief at St Omer, thence to Dunkirk to check on the defences. There he spoke to Baron Charles de Broqueville, the Belgian President of the Council of Ministers, then the chiefs of the Belgian army and his liaison officer in Furnes before speaking to the King at 2pm. He was displaying considerable energy in seeing to his defences.

The interview with the King on 16 October clearly impressed both men, but it led to a postwar dispute about who was responsible for making the Belgians stand on the Yser. Foch's memoirs state that Albert visited his troops the day after Foch's visit instead of earlier that morning, thereby implying cause and effect. However, Albert's own account, and the account drawn up in 1924 as a result of various press articles, are categorical. Albert's visit to the troops, when commanders were threatened with discharge if they retreated, lasted from 9 to 12 in the morning, and Foch arrived at 2pm. The King told Foch that the Belgian army would do what it could, but what it could do was limited. It required support. Foch is said to have replied: 'hold on for forty-eight hours, and you will be supported'. The King's later recollection was that the interview had the 'happy result' of convincing Foch that a division had to be sent to help maintain the Belgian front.[51] Colonel Brécard, the head of the French mission to the

[50] This account is based on King Albert's own 'Récit par le roi Albert des événements militaires du 7 au 16 octobre 1914', in Thielemans (ed.), *Albert Ier*, 173–9.
[51] Ibid.; 'Note pour la section historique de l'Etat-Major', 15 December 1924, in file, 'Bataille de l'Yser 16 Octobre 1914', box 1320, Russian returned archives, Army Archives, Brussels.

Belgian army, was the only witness to the meeting. He confirms that
Foch spent part of the morning with the Belgian general staff and saw
the King after lunch. According to Brécard, Foch told the King that
nations that wished to survive must be prepared to defend themselves.
The Belgian army had to be alongside the French, who were fighting
the invader. As a soldier of the Republic, Foch went on, 'I can affirm
to Your Majesty that our cause is just and holy, and that Providence
will give us victory.' After Foch left, the King told Brécard how happy
he was to hear a French general speaking thus.[52] Hence Foch spoke
very firmly, but the King's decision to stand had already been made
and action already taken. (The story became embroidered in Foch's
mind. Two years later, in December 1916, he told the writer Henry
Bordeaux, who may have done some of his own embroidery, that when
the King demurred, saying that he had no army left, Foch insisted. In
response to the King's statement that he had to consult his ministers
because of the country's constitution, Foch claimed that he replied: 'Je
me f ... de la Constitution, Sire. We must save your country and your
honour.')[53]

Foch reported that evening to Joffre that both the King and the
Belgian Premier seemed prepared to enforce the order that the
enemy must be resisted with all energy. In a postscript to the letter,
Foch added that notwithstanding his confidence in the Belgians, some
good French troops would have a very beneficial effect on the Belgians'
left, from all points of view, once Joffre could spare any.[54] In fact,
whilst Foch was in Furnes speaking with King Albert, Joffre had
informed his headquarters that he proposed sending 42 DI (from
Fifth Army) and IX Corps (from the former Ninth Army on the
Aisne), plus as a general reserve another infantry and another cavalry
division. On the Marne 42 DI and IX Corps had carried out Foch's
orders in exemplary fashion, and so he knew that he would be able to
rely on them. The very next day (17th) Weygand sent an early message
to Belgian HQ announcing that a French division would be disembark-
ing in Dunkirk beginning on the evening of 19 October. Admiral
Ronarc'h's brigade of marines had already arrived in Dixmude on
the 15th at midday.[55] As a final support measure, Foch encouraged
Sir John to maintain his advance eastwards to the river Lys and the
Lille–Courtrai line so as to take pressure off the Belgian front.

The forces to be coordinated by Foch comprised, from south to north,
the French Second and Tenth Armies, then a mixture of French and

[52] Brécard, *En Belgique*, 48–9. [53] Bordeaux, *Histoire d'une vie*, 5: 275.
[54] Secret letter, Foch to Joffre, 16 October 1914, 16N 2034. [55] Ronarc'h, *Souvenirs*, 59.

British cavalry and infantry units receiving reinforcements as General Rawlinson's IV Corps came south from Antwerp and Douglas Haig's I Corps began arriving from the Aisne. They formed an arc around Ypres. Finally the Belgians occupied the line from Dixmude to the sea at Nieuport, thus making the Allied line continuous, albeit tenuous. In fact the line extended into the North Sea, because on 15 October the Belgian government had asked for the Admiralty's help in safeguarding their flank, and Joffre sent a further request the next day (the same day that Foch met Albert) for the Royal Navy to use its long-range guns if the Germans reached the coast. The Admiralty had already seen the risk to the Dover area after the fall of Antwerp and Zeebrugge, and had created a new command, the Dover Patrol under Admiral Hood. On 17 October three shallow-draught monitors and twenty-four scouts and destroyers took up position off the Belgian coast, despite the unfavourable weather. Joffre asked that the naval commander concert operations with General Foch through Dunkirk.[56]

Joffre and Foch were not the only ones to be thinking about the sea. Before the war, in the context of the debate over a Channel Tunnel, Sir John had studied the question of turning Boulogne into an entrenched camp for the British army.[57] On the evening of 13 October, Sir John and his chief of staff, General Archibald Murray, discussed the possibility that the need for such a camp had indeed risen. Wilson found this prospect 'simply terrifying' and asked Foch to write with a proposal that defensive positions be prepared behind St Omer and behind the Somme, so that 'the idea of going to Boulogne should be nipped at once'. Foch agreed to supply such a letter for Wilson to pass on to Sir John. After Wilson and Huguet had read it beforehand as Foch wanted, the letter was duly delivered on 16 October, with a suggestion for a defensive position to be dug along the Béthune–St Omer canal. The plan backfired, however, as Sir John was furious. Wilson recorded the reaction in his diary: 'he [Sir John] would be d – if he would be dictated to by Foch who had better mind his own business etc. etc.[,] bursting out like the d – fool he is, & ending by saying he was going to base himself on Boulogne'.[58] Nevertheless, the Béthune–St Omer position was prepared gradually by British engineers, helped by some French territorial battalions.[59]

This angry reaction is the probable explanation for the unsatisfactory meeting between Foch and Sir John the next day, 17 October, held to discuss future plans. Wilson thought that his commander-in-chief 'talked

[56] Corbett, *Naval Operations*, 1: 213–15.
[57] Wilson, *Channel Tunnel Visions*, 86, and appendix 3.
[58] Wilson diary, 14 and 16 October 1914.   [59] Edmonds *et al.*, *OH 1914*, 2: 83–4.

arrant nonsense' – so much so that Foch told the head of the French Mission to GHQ that Sir John should be sent home.[60] Nevertheless, agreement was reached that the push eastwards towards Lille would continue despite the earlier failure of the more southerly Anglo-French attacks on the Lys. The French cavalry (under de Mitry) should press on to Roulers, whilst Rawlinson's IV Corps newly arrived from Antwerp should attack towards Menin. British III and II Corps should continue their movement against La Bassée and along the banks of the Lys respectively. The gap between these two corps was covered by French cavalry, and the British attack on La Bassée was supported by French artillery further south.[61] Sir Douglas Haig was ordered to support Rawlinson, despite the fact that his I Corps divisions had only just started moving from the Aisne (they were the last troops to leave, and only completed detraining on the 19th); and Foch formed the Détachement d'Armée de Belgique (DAB) under General d'Urbal, and received reinforcements from Joffre. Thus, in effect, Sir John accepted Foch's general plan that the Belgians should hold along the Yser whilst British and French pushed eastwards as far as the Lille–Courtrai line.

That evening Foch went to see Castelnau and Second Army. He had asked them to prepare a supporting offensive, but was not pleased by the length of time before it would be launched. There was another stormy scene with Castelnau, who seems to have told Foch either to sack him or to let him get on with his job. He refused to be rushed and told Foch that he would not be ready before 24 October. Foch told his wife that Castelnau was 'demoralised' by the loss of his sons, and was finding it difficult to accept that Foch was now his superior. Whilst Foch and Castelnau were talking, Tardieu was telling Second Army staff what a marvellous job Foch had done in restoring Belgian morale.[62] The listeners were probably even less inclined to listen to such praise because Joffre had imposed General Duchêne on Second Army as Anthoine's replacement chief of staff. Duchêne had been Foch's chief of staff at Morhange, where he may have played a role in the XX Corps failure to follow orders (see chapter 1). Duchêne's brutal ways were proving most unpopular.[63]

So Foch's plan was in place: the Belgian Army was to hold along the line of the river Yser while the British and French attacked eastwards towards the Lille–Courtrai line. His methods, however, were beginning to rub

[60] Wilson diary, 17 October 1914. Prete discusses the question of replacing Sir John in War of Movement, 425–32.
[61] Maréchal French, général Foch réunis à Anvin, 17 October 914, *AFGG* 1/4, annex 2968.
[62] Jacquand memoirs, Fonds Castelnau, 1K/795/36, 17 October 1914; letter, Foch to Mme Foch, 18 October 1914, vol. 33.
[63] Gras, *Castelnau*, 199–200, 202.

Second Army up the wrong way, and relations with Castelnau had not improved. His attempts with Wilson to deal with Sir John's Boulogne plan had backfired, and merely brought out the fact that Foch stood lower in the military hierarchy than the British commander-in-chief.

The time for planning offensives was now over, because the German armies had advanced to meet the thin lines of Allied troops. They launched attacks on 17 October against the Belgians along the Yser, which intensified over the following two days. By 21 October the whole line from the sea, around the Ypres salient, and down southwards towards Lille and La Bassée was under violent attack. The British and French attempts to progress eastwards to the Lille–Courtrai line had all been repulsed. Yet reinforcements were arriving: on the 20th Haig's I Corps moved into the front line from their billets after detraining, and, as promised, Joffre allocated IX Corps to d'Urbal's new DAB. In order to support the coastal end of the Belgian line at Nieuport, Foch hastened the disembarkation of Grossetti's 42 DI, which was completed on 21st in time for Joffre and King Albert to review it at Furnes. What is more, the Belgians were managing to hold on to their positions on the Yser. In addition the Royal Navy together with four French destroyers began bombarding enemy positions on the coast, although the ships' shells were not suited to such a purpose and the ships did not carry large numbers of them. Consequently, the naval action did not last very long.[64]

The strength of the German attacks now made taking defensive measures even more urgent. If the enemy broke through the Belgian line and moved along the coast to take Dunkirk, Boulogne and Calais, then the British would be looking constantly over their shoulder at their bases and communications and, for the Belgians, their country would be wiped off the map of Europe. Foch concentrated his energies, therefore, on getting all the troops in Flanders to hold on. When the Germans got a bridgehead across the Yser, 42 DI was ready to intervene,[65] and Foch promised King Albert, after a 'stormy interview', that he would send what reinforcements he could, although Joffre had control of the reserves.[66] It proved impossible to dislodge the Germans from their bridgehead; the Belgians were beginning to run out of munitions and even guns; the naval support ceased because of the weather, and on 25 October Admiral Ronarc'h reported that he could maintain his position at Dixmude for only one more day. Consequently the Belgians decided to

[64] Thomazi, *Marine française*, 53–4; Corbett, *Naval Operations*, 1: 225.
[65] Telegram, Brécard [head of French mission to Belgian army] to Foch, 22 October 1914, *AFGG* 1/4, annex 3192.
[66] File, 'Bataille de l'Yser', box 1320, Army Archives, Brussels.

retire behind the next defensible line, namely the straight line of the railway that ran to Nieuport along a built-up embankment, and to flood the land between the river and the railway, despite the damage that the flooding would do. (Foch claimed later that the idea of retiring behind the railway was his, and discussed the previous day in his meeting with the King. However, the King's brief account of the interview makes no mention of this, and his military adviser's account states unequivocally that the idea was suggested by a Belgian liaison officer and approved by the King.)[67]

The flooding began in earnest on 27 October, when the Belgian Army orders were to defend to the last the positions it occupied. The inundations between Dixmude and the coast at Nieuport closed down the battle on the Yser, which ended officially on 30 October. Although the Germans managed to wade through the rising flood waters and get across the railway line to capture the village of Ramscapelle on that day, Grossetti counter-attacked immediately and the Germans were thrown back. Thus the Yser battle ended with an Allied success and the left flank was secured.

Foch had attempted to ease the pressure on the Belgians by getting the British and the French to take the offensive according to the agreed plan, namely joint attacks towards the east on 22/23 October: on Roulers by the French and towards Courtrai by the British.[68] This proved too optimistic, as both Haig's I Corps and Rawlinson's IV Corps were under severe attack and the French reinforcements (IX Corps) were arriving as separate units with their heavy artillery following. As the flooding began its work, Foch repeated the orders on 27 and 28 October for attacks by I Corps and IX Corps, but for little gain. Nonetheless Foch was not down-hearted. He sent a brief note to IX Corps repeating his instruction about infantry tactics that he had issued whilst on the Aisne in September. Formations in depth are pointless in the flat terrain close to the enemy where they were now engaged. If the heads of the columns are held up during an advance, the rear échelons should manoeuvre to get around the obstacle.[69] He wrote to his wife: 'we are advancing everywhere, slowly but continuously'.[70]

However, the battle for Ypres itself had already begun before the Yser front closed down under water. Falkenhayn had been compelled to make another plan. His *Fourth Army* had neither broken through the Yser front

---

[67] Galet, *S. M. Le Roi Albert*, 349–50.
[68] Telegram, Huguet to Foch and Brécard, and Foch, Note, both 22 October 1914, *AFGG* 1/4, annexes 3191 and 3197.
[69] Instruction, Foch to IX Corps commander, 28 October 1914, *AFGG* 1/4, annex 3473.
[70] Letter, Foch to Mme Foch, 28 and 27 October 1914, vol. 33.

to move down the coast to capture the Channel ports nor made any progress in the northern half of the Ypres salient; similarly, Rupprecht's *Sixth Army* had failed to break through the British and Tenth Army lines at the southern end of the salient. Accordingly, more troops were brought from points further east and a new army group, *Group Fabeck*, created. It consisted of six infantry divisions (not the inexperienced volunteers that Albrecht had had to use, but troops who had already seen action), and a cavalry corps, thus giving the Germans a more than two-to-one numerical superiority. Their superiority in heavy guns was even more significant. They had over 250, including mortars and howitzers, which supplied the plunging fire that was so devastating against defenders.[71] General Fabeck's task was to slip between *Fourth* and *Sixth Armies* and to attack between Zandvoorde and Messines so as to break through and take Mt Kemmel, the high ground that dominated the southern approaches to Ypres. Thus, on 29 October, began the battle for Gheluvelt that fell mainly on Haig's I Corps, although the two flanking German armies also attacked in order to draw off what they considered to be the few reserves that the Allies had left.

On 29 and 30 October the Allies suffered violent attacks and towards evening on the 30th Foch learned that I Corps had lost Hollebeke and Zandvoorde. He went to GHQ to see Wilson, who had been prevented from making his usual 9pm visit to Foch's headquarters in Cassel. Foch was afraid that a gap had opened up in the line, through which the Germans could approach Ypres from the south, and, lacking up-to-the-minute information from Wilson, decided that something had to be done. He spent about an hour at GHQ with Wilson and a hastily roused Sir John. Reinforcements were expected, namely 32 DI (of XVI Corps), and Foch promised that the three battalions already disembarked plus another five and six batteries of guns would be moved immediately to the Saint-Eloi region to plug the gap.[72]

The next day, 31 October, the battle for Ypres reached crisis point. Despite the French reinforcements, the British were driven back still further, losing part of Messines in the morning and in the afternoon Gheluvelt on the Ypres–Menin road. It seemed to both Sir John and Haig that they would have to withdraw to a shorter line. The British line held by 1 Division had broken and men and guns were retiring towards Ypres, although this was not a rout, more an orderly move to an already marked out defensive line. It was only a temporary setback, however, as

---

[71] Edmonds, *et al.*, *OH 1914*, 2: 259.

[72] Wilson diary, 30 and 31 October 1914; Note sur les relations entre les E.-M. anglais et français, 30 October 1914, *AFGG* 1/4, annex 3552.

the Worcesters re-took Gheluvelt in the early afternoon. Foch and Sir John met by chance on the road, and Foch argued that to retreat would be to cause a rout. Dismissing Sir John's histrionic outburst that there was nothing for it but to join his men and get killed alongside them, Foch persuaded the British commander-in-chief to order Haig to remain where he was. Foch would relieve the pressure by attacking on both flanks of the hard-pressed British.[73]

Surely Foch was right to argue that to hold on at all costs was the correct action. There was very little room for manoeuvre between the front line and the sea, and any giving way without a properly organised position to fall back onto would have been bound to turn into panic and even rout. Equally, Sir John was temperamentally unsuited to maintain the calm exterior and overall control that the dangerous situation required. When Foch noted on a piece of paper at 15.00 on 31 October that the only possible course of action was to hold on, and when Sir John endorsed that paper with the comment that Haig should conform to that course of action, Foch was not simply 'ingratiating' himself and extracting the maximum from the British, as Professor Prete argues.[74] He was also acting promptly and efficaciously to prevent a precursor to Dunkirk in 1940 that could have left the Germans in control of Calais and wiped Belgium off the map of Europe. Moreover, the reserves were being fed in to the British lines, as they arrived and in fractions – battalions and regiments were what was available, not divisions with their HQ staffs.

The ad hoc arrangements – feeding in reserves piecemeal as they arrived, without reference to nationality, and permitting commanders of reinforcements to communicate directly with the British they were supporting – were working. Foch sent his liaison officer to Haig to discuss the outline of his plan: the British should hold in the middle whilst the French attacked on the flanks. However, renewed German attacks on 1 November achieved the capture of Messines and part of Wytschaete. Sir John French would recall in his memoirs the 'thin and straggling line' that stood between the Empire and ruin.[75]

That same day, 1 November, Kitchener arrived in France and so Foch had to dash to Dunkirk to meet him, with Joffre and President Poincaré. Kitchener was visibly shaken by the crisis. Poincaré noted Kitchener's

---

[73] Journées; Note sur les relations entre les E.-M. anglais et français, 31 October 1914, *AFGG* 1/4, annex 3640. Sir John's own comment in his *1914* was that he spent the 'worst' half hour of his life in the early afternoon of 31 October (p. 252).

[74] Note remise au maréchal French, 31 October 1914, with endorsement, *AFGG* 1/4, annex 3636; Edmonds *et al.*, *OH 1914*, 2: 342. Sir John does not even mention this note in his *1914*. Haig's diary is equally silent about its receipt. Prete, War of Movement, 445.

[75] French of Ypres, *1914*, 237.

'considerable anxiety' about the BEF, and Wilson, who spoke on the telephone with Kitchener, recorded that Kitchener was 'upset'.[76] According to Weygand, Kitchener's first words were 'So we are beaten.'[77] The gathering of bigwigs in Dunkirk, an unusual event for the midst of a desperate battle, was the result of Joffre's actions after he learned from Sir John on 21 October of the scheme for an entrenched camp at Boulogne, described earlier. Joffre knew that relations between Kitchener and Sir John were difficult, and he knew from Foch what opinion Wilson had of his commander-in-chief. By the time Kitchener arrived, however, they were all in the midst of heavy fighting, when it would be highly dangerous to change commanders. Besides, Sir John had shown much more aggression and energy during the Flanders fighting than had been the case on the Marne or in the march on Lille. In any case, Kitchener's offer of the services of Sir Ian Hamilton as the new CinC foiled the French scheming. The French had hoped to get Wilson in the job but, failing that, the devil they knew was clearly a better bet. The liaison between Foch's headquarters and those of Sir John was working very well through Wilson. Thus the offer of Hamilton was rejected 'energetically' (Weygand's word), and the only 'benefit' that Foch and Joffre extracted from the proceeding was that they were able hypocritically to present their rejection of Kitchener's offer of Hamilton as support for and a 'defence' of Sir John's position. Just as the proposal to get Rawlinson's Antwerp forces put under Sir John's command had been used to bind Sir John more closely to the French command, so too this failed attempt to obtain a more 'useful' CinC for the BEF was put to the same purpose.[78]

What was Foch's role in this intrigue? After all, it was he who had suggested in exasperation that Sir John should be sent home (see page 62). Swapping Sir John for Wilson would certainly have made Foch's life easier, but it was an impossible proposal from the British point of view. Prete, who has studied this episode, states that there is nothing in the archives to indicate whether Foch was involved in Joffre's action in summoning Kitchener or, indeed, whether he even knew what Joffre had done. It seems more likely than not, however, that Joffre informed the man he had sent to the north as coordinator of Allied action about his attempt to seek Sir John's replacement. On the other hand, Poincaré believed that it was Foch's influence that had changed Joffre's mind about removing Sir John when the meeting took place.[79] So Foch's part

---

[76] Poincaré, *AS*, 5: 408, 411 (entry for 1 November 1914); Wilson diary, 1 November 1914.
[77] Weygand, *IV*, 175.
[78] This account is based on the meticulous research in Prete, 'Command Crisis'.
[79] Poincaré, Notes journalières, 2 November 1914, NAF 16028.

in the affair remains unclear. Joffre's memoirs imply that it was at Poincaré's request that he himself was in Dunkirk on 1 November, and he states that his rejection of Kitchener's offer of Ian Hamilton was a 'service' to Sir John, revealing the strength of the 'bonds of affection and esteem' between the two commanders-in-chief.[80] There is no mention of his role in inviting Kitchener to France – further proof, if any were needed, of the unreliability of many postwar memoirs.

By 2 November, the day after the Dunkirk conference, the German onslaughts were abating. More French reinforcements arrived to support Haig's I Corps as the rising flood waters freed the French from the need to support the Belgians. Also Joffre sent Foch's old corps, XX Corps, as further relief. Now, French and British units were so intermingled that close liaison between the two headquarters became vital. Indeed, it was these events at Ypres in 1914 that revealed the need for unity of command, and it was the memory of these days that enabled Haig to accept Foch as Generalissimo in 1918, when another crisis beckoned. Henry Wilson described the liaison to his wife on 2 November:

I am spending a good deal of time these days with Foch on this curious hill on the way between Ypres and St. Omer [that is, Foch's headquarters at Cassel]. We have got our troops so much mixed up with his that no order can be issued without the other's approval etc. I think we are going to beat this attack with the aid the French have given us. It has been a stiff business.[81]

It was fortunate that the relationship between Wilson and Foch was so cordial, because Sir John was less appreciative of the help being given to the hard-pressed British who, after all, were only where they were because he had insisted on the move from the Aisne a month earlier.

Since the battle seemed to have ended Foch began to think of attacking again, despite low stocks of ammunition and Haig's calls for more support for his exhausted units. However, Joffre refused to permit an offensive until munitions supply improved, and the enemy had not finished with the battle. So Foch's desire to straighten out the dents in the salient in order to shorten the front thus releasing more troops proved impossible. Repeated German attacks on 5 and 6 November pushed in the Allied line still further, and strident demands for relief and assistance (both British and French) became more insistent. Although Joffre sent what were absolutely the last available reserves, considerable resentment built up as the British were too exhausted to do anything more than hold on and the French had to bear the brunt of the attacks. Nevertheless the Allies managed to parry the final German attack by the Prussian *Guards* on 11 November, so the

---

[80] Joffre, *Mémoires*, 1: 479.   [81] Callwell, *Wilson*, 1: 186.

line remained intact. The French held the line of the canal from Ypres to Dixmude. Although they had lost Dixmude itself, Ronarc'h's marines had prevented the Germans from getting beyond the town; the Belgians were safe behind the railway embankment, and the flooded areas between the river and railway line were now impassable; finally, on the coast, the troops under the governor of Dunkirk were installed solidly in Nieuport. The enemy was stalled, Foch reported. In a long letter to Joffre on 19 November he claimed that the enemy could not repeat the violent attacks on Ypres, and that the German offensive in the west had been *halted definitively*.[82]

The cost had been substantial. The French suffered 125,000 killed in October and November (this figure excludes the wounded and officers, but includes those killed in the First Battle of Artois). British casualties totalled 55,000 for the same two months, of whom approximately half had been killed or were missing. Accurate German figures are not available, but an estimated 700,000 became casualties (killed and wounded) between the start of the war and the end of November.[83] At the time, the Kaiser's adjutant, Colonel General Plessen, noted that attacking units around Ypres suffered 160,000 casualties in the ten days up to 16 November.[84] During the month from 15 October the DAB's 75mm guns fired almost 350,000 shells, and Foch's two other armies (Second, Tenth) almost 400,000 more.[85] Units still in line were worn out, and were intermingled because of the way small units had been fed hurriedly into line as reinforcements. There had not been time to dig proper defensive lines. Capitaine Réquin, Foch's liaison officer with d'Urbal's army, pointed out that it was vital to complete the construction of defences, to relieve those units who were incapable of continuing in line, and to gather artillery and everything necessary for a siege. It would require considerable preparations to break the fortified front that the enemy now presented.[86] Finally the intermingled troops were restored to their correct units. On 14 November Foch and Sir John agreed separate British and French zones of action: I Corps was relieved from the front between IX and XVI Corps and joined the rest of the BEF further south around Messines; the French front then ran to join up with the Belgians, and

---

[82] Secret letter, Foch to Joffre, 19 November 1914, fo. 8, 16N 2034.
[83] French figures from the 1920 parliamentary report, British figures from *Statistics of the British Military Effort*, and German estimates supplied by the Reichsarchiv, all tabulated in Churchill, *World Crisis*, 289–92.
[84] Plessen, 'Tagebuch', 16 November 1914, cited in Foley, *German Strategy*, 104, note 90.
[85] Consommation des munitions de 75, 15 October–14 November 1914, *AFGG* 1/4, 556.
[86] Réquin report to Foch, 11 November 1914, ibid., annex 4191.

from the 16th the units became Eighth Army. There was a further fraction of French troops at Nieuport, thus enclosing the Belgian Army.

In an earlier report on the battle sent to his commander-in-chief on 14 November, Foch summed up his thoughts on the events of the previous weeks. The Allied position was strengthening daily and the Germans appeared to have given up the idea of taking Ypres, although the effort the enemy had made to take the town was witness to the importance that they attributed to it. Neither French nor British were ready yet to take the offensive again, but Foch thought that minor actions might straighten out the line, if they were jointly organised. Combined Allied action had resulted in a victory of sorts: securing the maritime bases and joining together all the Allied armies. However, it was a 'purely negative' tactical result, he concluded; the enemy had simply been prevented from carrying out his plan. However, with his usual optimism, Foch suggested that the Allies might be able to derive some advantage from the enemy's inability to progress.[87]

Yet something more than a purely negative result had been achieved. In a letter to his wife's uncle, Foch wrote of his satisfaction: 'I am very pleased with what I have obtained – I have united all the Allied armies in a battle which stopped the Germans dead, with considerable losses, I have rendered their offensive powerless, and prepared a future full of promise.'[88] Combining three Allied armies in one defensive battle was no mean achievement. Foch had encouraged the demoralised Belgian army by his personal intervention with the King, and he had managed to win over the irascible and erratic British commander-in-chief, his superior in rank. Sir John was difficult to deal with and a repeat of the ill effects of the failures in cooperation between him and General Lanrezac during the Great Retreat in the opening weeks of the war could have been fatal. It was vital for Foch to secure amicable relations, and this required tact. Foch told Generals Dubois (who was complaining about the British) and d'Urbal (who was complaining about everybody): 'They take you as you are. Take them as they are'[89] – which is sound advice about any sort of relationship. Yet he did not find it easy to take his own advice, as he complained in a letter to his aunt at the end of the year. As the British and Belgians did what Foch wanted only when it suited them, he was 'reduced to [using] as much diplomacy as command'.[90] Nonetheless, this was an important skill to learn, and one that would be required even more in 1918.

[87] 'Rapport', 14 November 1914 [written in the form of a letter to Joffre], 1K/129/1, [d] '1914 et ensuite'; also in *AFGG* 1/4, annex 4252.
[88] Foch to Eugène Rochard, 14 November 1914, 1K/129/2.
[89] Tardieu, *Avec Foch*, 127.
[90] Foch to Mme Louis Bienvenüe, 26 December 1914, 1K/129/2.

Foch also gained practice in one further skill that would be vital in 1918: the handling of reserves and reinforcements. Prete criticises Foch for withstanding the German attacks 'only by reinforcing the British in crisis rather than by relieving their hard-pressed forces'.[91] This is too harsh, because French reserves were few, and were battalion-sized or smaller. Joffre certainly felt that he had no more to feed into the battle, and eventually sent a message that if Foch and Sir John could not hold the present line then they would simply have to retire to a shorter one. He could not send one single soldier more.[92] If Joffre was resigned to giving up territory, albeit Belgian territory, then surely he spoke the truth when he stated that he had no reserves left. No commander would willingly cause the muddle that had ensued before Ypres, when units were separated from their HQ staffs, if it could be avoided, and Joffre urged Foch not to 'dislocate' the reserves that he was sending.[93]

More importantly, relief of, say, a whole British corps was simply not possible in the conditions on the ground. Troops were holding a thin line of shallow, waterlogged ditches, not a properly prepared defensive position with plentiful munitions, in whose shelter reliefs could be carried out safely. (During a relief neither the troops being relieved nor those doing the relieving are able to respond to an enemy attack.) Surely it is unrealistic to imply that Foch could have done more in this regard. He reinforced, and he supported by taking the offensive with French troops. Whatever (large) suspicions remained in the minds of both British and French commands, Foch's method was vindicated at First Ypres. The 'mêlée des Flandres' had exhausted French resources. The battle took so many men, guns and shells that Tenth and Second Armies were incapable of anything more than small offensive actions as their contribution to the main battle. They could only strengthen their defences and hold on. It would have been very difficult for Foch to coordinate any more troops than he controlled already.

The Yser and Ypres battles had a greater significance than their inconclusive fighting might indicate. First of all, the German failure to break through the Allied lines marked the failure of the only strategic plan they had. The Marne could be (and was) passed off as a temporary breathing space – merely a strategic withdrawal, not a defeat, and no bulletin was issued for fear of alarming the home front. Germany did not accept it as a

---

[91] Prete, War of Movement, 467.
[92] Telephone message from Clive [head of the British Mission at GQG], 17 November 1914, 17N 338, Coopération franco–britannique et interalliée, [d] 1.
[93] Prete, War of Movement, 442; Berthelot diary, fo. 210 (entry for 27 October 1914). See also telegrams, Joffre to Foch, 25 and 27 October 1914, *AFGG* 1/4, annexes 3335, 3423.

defeat, either at the time or postwar. Moltke's replacement by Falkenhayn was kept secret; and the Austrians were not informed.[94] The Flanders defeat, by contrast, was patent; it could not be passed off or disguised. The Kaiser had come to Flanders to enter Ypres in triumph, but returned disappointed to his headquarters. The defeat prompted Falkenhayn to tell the German Chancellor that victory was now impossible. His armies were exhausted, and the only way to break the Entente alliance was to negotiate a separate peace with Russia.[95] Bethmann Hollweg refused the suggestion, but the fact that it was even uttered is eloquent testimony to the bankruptcy of German strategic planning.

The Entente, on the other hand, had overcome the initial setbacks. Although the enemy still occupied most of Belgium and a large segment of France's industrial areas and their mineral resources, yet the Allies had managed to pull together in a common purpose. A tri-national line of tired troops held a continuous front, extended into the North Sea by the Royal and French navies. Symbolically, the first occasion when a British admiral flew his flag in a French ship as a wartime ally occurred during the Flanders fighting, when Admiral Hood went aboard the French destroyer *Intrépide*.[96] More importantly, during the Dunkirk conference that otherwise represented a failure for French plotting, the French had won an acknowledgement from Kitchener that he would commit his New Armies to the Western Front, even if not as rapidly as the French would have liked. When Kitchener promised a million men by the middle of 1915, Foch retorted that he would prefer fewer sooner.[97]

Finally, mention must be made of the personal significance of Ypres for Foch. Clearly the experience affected him deeply, and he dedicated five chapters of his memoirs to those October/November days. His diary record, called 'Journées' (its date is unknown, but is postwar), is likewise much fuller than earlier entries. He had come a long way since August: from corps command to the commander-in-chief's 'adjoint'. His handwritten reports to Joffre reveal a commander who was thinking seriously about what the war entailed. Although the battle was conducted by lower-level commanders (the recapture of Gheluvelt by 2nd Worcesters on 31 October is a good example; they did not wait for orders to be issued), Foch kept himself fully informed, reassured Sir John (to whom he brought a 'lively bustling optimism'), and created 'a warm spirit of comradeship' among the intermingled troops.[98] Above all, he was still optimistic.

---

[94] Mombauer, 'Marne', 759–60.   [95] Sweet, 'Leaders and Policies', 230–3.
[96] Thomazi, *Marine française*, 54.   [97] Weygand, *IV*, 176.
[98] Farrar-Hockley, *Death of an Army*, 70–1; Falls, *Foch*, 84.

Despite the loss of his son and son-in-law – Bécourt's death was only confirmed around 20 November, and Foch and his wife were still hopeful that Germain was not killed, but interned somewhere as late as 5 December[99] – he displayed prodigious energy travelling miles between various headquarters, constantly urging and encouraging. His method for commanding a group of armies was set in those weeks around Ypres. In Hew Strachan's judgement, Foch displayed during those weeks 'an inner certainty, a belief in ultimate success, a bloody-minded obstinacy'[100] – qualities which he shared with Douglas Haig and which would be sorely needed in the years to come.

[99] Letters, Foch to Mme Foch, 20, 23 November, 5 December 1914, vol. 33.
[100] Strachan, *To Arms*, 280.

4   The end of the war of movement and reflections on 1914

The end of the Ypres fighting did not mean an end to activity for Foch. Joffre wanted an offensive in Flanders to take advantage of the relative quiet of the German artillery, which he believed was due to lack of munitions and to their heavy casualties in the recent fighting. Also, train movements indicated that enemy troops were being transported either to another part of the front or to Russia. In August the French and Russians had launched their attack on the same date as agreed, and now the Russians needed support. Their armies were under heavy pressure from the new German *Ninth Army* that the recently promoted Field Marshal Hindenburg had launched on 11 November against the important industrial town of Lodz. By the time that the weather forced an end to operations there ten days later, *Ninth Army* had taken 136,000 prisoners.[1] The Russians sent an appeal for the Allies to take the offensive in the west in order to relieve the pressure. The British ambassador in St Petersburg, Sir George Buchanan, sent a wire to GHQ stating that the country would 'come to a standstill if we did not prevent more Germans from going over'.[2] The telegrams from Russia made Millerand more depressed than Poincaré had ever seen him.[3]

Foch spent three days at Romilly with Joffre at GQG to discuss what offensive action he could take while the Germans were still disorganised. He arrived there on 24 November in time for the presentation by President Poincaré and War Minister Millerand of the *médaille militaire* to Joffre. Just as Foch had kept in touch with GQG via Tardieu after the Marne fighting, so he made sure not to miss such an important occasion.

The operations bureau at GQG believed that an attack in the north was the best option, since the army as a whole had neither the men nor the munitions for attacks along the whole front. Success in the north would free the rich industrial areas of France, and perhaps make the British less

---

[1] Herwig, *First World War*, 108–9.   [2] Wilson diary, 4 December 1914.
[3] Poincaré, *AS*, 5: 486 (entry for 5 December 1914).

concerned about invasion.[4] After his discussions with Joffre, Foch immediately conferred with his Tenth Army commander about an attack 'to
break through [*percer*]' the enemy's lines between Bailleul and Givenchy,
north of Arras, beginning around 18–20 December.[5] This was the area
where Foch had first seen action in October as Joffre's deputy, and it was
of great strategic importance. The infamous Vimy Ridge lay to the west of
Bailleul and Givenchy, and possession of the ridge would give observation
over the plain of Douai, with its communications hub. Its capture would
constitute an important prize.

However, Joffre wanted something bigger than a single operation on
Foch's front in the north; he was now preparing an attack in Champagne
as well. In addition, he wanted supporting attacks by the British in the
north, and by French troops in the Vosges. Despite the poor winter
weather, Joffre wished to take advantage of the enemy's disorganisation.
His instructions to his generals proposed, therefore, an ambitious two-
pronged main attack on the enemy's communications, in Flanders and in
Champagne, together with four secondary actions.[6]

Meanwhile Foch tried to create some reserves by making greater use of
Belgian troops. On 17 November he suggested to Joffre placing a Belgian
brigade with each of Eighth Army's four corps, thereby freeing up a strong
French division.[7] Two days later, Foch proposed moving four Belgian
divisions into the Ypres sector; alternatively, the Belgian army might be
spread amongst the French with one Belgian brigade per French division.
The King's answer to these ideas left no room for doubt: the Belgian army
must remain united and independent; it would take the offensive when the
French did; its past service to France was a guarantee of that.[8] The British
supporting attack proved equally difficult to arrange. Sir John was proposing yet another move for the BEF, this time to the coast. The First Lord of
the Admiralty also had in mind a scheme to attack up the Belgian coast in
order to re-take Ostend and Zeebrugge, and the Cabinet had been discussing the double proposal. The British ambassador, Sir Francis Bertie, made
a formal request for cooperation to the French government on 9 December.
Churchill had already visited Sir John two days earlier in order to explain

---

[4] Note sur les conditions d'un mouvement d'offensive générale, 29 November 1914, *AFGG*
2, annex 227.
[5] Tenth Army, Instruction personnelle et secrète, 6 December 1914, ibid., annex 265.
[6] Instruction générale no 8 pour les généraux commandant les armées, 8 December 1914,
ibid., annex 280.
[7] Foch's letter cited in 'Note sur les conditions d'un mouvement d'offensive générale',
29 November 1914, ibid., annex 227.
[8] Letter, Foch to Joffre, 19 November 1914, ibid., annex 156; Thielemans and Vandewoude
(eds.), *Le Roi Albert*, 544.

the scheme. So, if the British were to start moving their divisions once again, they would be unable to support the flank of the planned French offensive in the north.

For many reasons, the Zeebrugge scheme was unrealistic. Not all British politicians were convinced of the danger of invasion (Asquith wished that the 'very fussy & jumpy' Foreign Secretary had 'more sense of proportion and perspective').[9] Churchill had lost much credibility as a result of the Antwerp fiasco, and his 'Dunkirk circus' received a great deal of criticism. Admiral Hood had wanted to destroy the two Belgian ports when he was helping the Belgians, as described earlier, but the War Office had objected. Now it appeared to have changed its mind. The Belgians would be most unlikely to swap places with the BEF to facilitate the scheme, because this would mean abandoning the defence of the remnants of their national territory. King Albert received with little enthusiasm the suggestion that the Belgian and British armies should amalgamate. The terrain was unsuitable for such an operation because the coastal dunes between the two ports and Nieuport, where the Allied line reached the sea, were open (so lacking any defensive features) and criss-crossed with streams and drainage ditches (so making progress difficult). Moreover, the weather at that time of year was awful and would have prevented the shallow-draught vessels in the North Sea from operating; and the Admiralty would not risk battleships on such an operation. Finally, of course, the French could not agree to a scheme that would throw into confusion all they had planned. Before Churchill's visit Sir John had already agreed to support the northerly French attack, and so would be guilty of bad faith if he pulled out. Foch was much amused by the whole idea of a Zeebrugge scheme, Wilson recorded, because he guessed that it was Churchill rather than Kitchener or Sir John who had dreamed it up. Wilson himself called it 'idiotic' and Foch treated it 'with the greatest contempt'.[10]

Thus the planning for Foch's northern army group offensive for an attack to capture Vimy Ridge was complicated by the need to hurry in order to help the Russians, and by the need to deal with a British proposal for an operation that had no connection with it. Moreover, Foch needed British cooperation to take over the front held by units of his XXI Corps, so that he could use the whole corps in the main attack. On 8 December Wilson and Sir John went to see Foch in Cassel and Sir John stated that he could either relieve XXI Corps or he could put in the supporting attack (against Messines) – he could not do both. Foch agreed to manage

[9] Asquith to Venetia Stanley, 23 October 1914, in Brock and Brock (eds.), *Asquith Letters*, 283.
[10] Wilson diary, 11 December 1914.

without the relief, commenting privately to Wilson, 'How he loves to cry, that Baby.'[11]

Foch's northern offensive began on 14 December for the BEF and Eighth Army (the DAB had become Eighth Army a month earlier), followed two days later by Tenth Army's preliminary attacks. The northern Ypres attacks made little headway, and the BEF made even less against Messines. Sir John did not have his heart in the operation and impressed on his corps and divisional commanders that everybody was to 'wait for the man on his left'. Since the last man on the left was next to XVI Corps in Eighth Army, which made no progress, it is not surprising that the British did not get very far either. Operations continued in a half-hearted way for two more days. Foch blamed the British for the poor results obtained by the Eighth Army units, and the British (according to a report by the French Mission) refused to move until XVI Corps moved.[12] Even the requested help from the Admiralty was not forthcoming. Churchill was still pressing his Ostend/Zeebrugge scheme, despite political opposition to what was seen as his meddling in army affairs, and he bad-temperedly refused any naval support on the Belgian coast. 'We are receiving requests almost daily from French', he telegraphed to Sir John (who, presumably, was expected to forward the message to GQG). 'We regret inability to comply. The small vessels alone cannot face the shore batteries, and to expose the battleships to submarine risks, unless in support of a land attack of the first importance, is unjustifiable.'[13] Thus, with a disparaging comment, did Churchill refuse British cooperation in the larger French undertaking. All northern attacks were suspended on 20 December.

Each ally blamed the other. Foch wrote to Joffre that French gains would be small so long as the British did not attack whole-heartedly. In fact, the actions of the two British corps revealed 'desperate reservations'. Sir John informed Kitchener, on the other hand, that the attack 'was brought to a standstill ... because the French on our left failed to carry out the role which they accepted ... I am sure we cannot succeed unless the French put in greater strength.'[14]

However, despite the lack of success on the part of the BEF and Eighth Army in the north, there was no question of halting Foch's main operation because Tenth Army's offensive was being supported on its right flank by

[11] Ibid., 8 December 1914.
[12] Telegram, Huguet to Joffre, 16 December 1914, *AFGG* 2, annex 367.
[13] Quotations from *OH, 1915*, 1: 17, 19; telegram, Huguet to Foch, 20 December 1914, *AFGG* 2, annex 414.
[14] Secret letter, Foch to Joffre, 16 December 1914, *AFGG* 2, annex 368; Sir John French to Kitchener, 17 December 1914, PRO 30/57/49.

Second Army, and the operation in Champagne was even bigger. So Tenth Army began as planned with a preliminary action on 16 December, followed by the main action the next day.[15] There had already been several changes in the start date because of the tension between Joffre's desire to take advantage of the perceived German reductions and everyone's wish to have gathered, before launching the attack, all the necessary resources and to have sapped forward towards the enemy trenches so as to reduce the distance to be crossed in no-man's land. Foch had already put his own nominee in charge of the artillery because Tenth Army's commander, General Maud'huy, failed to demand results from his subordinates on the grounds that he was an infantry officer and did not understand artillery matters. Foch claimed that a general should be neither an infantry, nor a cavalry, nor an artillery officer, but all of them at the same time.[16]

Foch arrived at Tenth Army headquarters on the morning of 17 December and took over command of the battle from Maud'huy. Three corps attacks were planned: XXI Corps aimed for the Vimy Ridge from the north; in the centre General Pétain's XXXIII Corps aimed to break through south of Souchez and then work up the ridge to its highest point; further south X Corps was to protect Pétain's flank. Because there was insufficient artillery for this ambitious plan, Foch decided to concentrate all the heavy artillery to support a single corps, the northern XXI Corps attack towards Notre Dame de Lorette; he delayed General Pétain's attack, therefore, until the afternoon, when the heavy artillery would fire in support of the XXXIII Corps offensive towards Souchez. Neither attack made much headway, however, on either 17 or 18 December. So Foch suspended the action on 19th, in favour of trying a new tactic, concentrating solely on Pétain's corps. XXI Corps had sufficient munitions to hold on and contain enemy counter-attacks; Pétain's XXXIII Corps was to use armoured guns and armoured wire-cutters on the wire in front of the strong German defences after another bombardment using all the heavy artillery resources.[17] The attack was due to be renewed on 21 December, but the weather made all progress impossible. Instead of a war in the trenches, it was becoming a war in the water, Foch wrote to the commander-in-chief.[18] Also, although Pétain was willing to continue trying, the fog came down, making artillery observation impossible. Despite repeated orders for the attack over the days of Christmas, the weather won out and the orders for 29 December, approved by Foch, stated that the guns would be collected and made ready for whenever the

[15] See Doughty, *PV*, 127–30.   [16] Weygand, *IV*, 199.   [17] *AFGG* 2, 179.
[18] Secret letter, Foch to Joffre, 21 December 1914, 16N 2034.

ground firmed up. Tenth Army had captured a few metres of trench around Carency and Notre Dame de Lorette, together with some houses in the northern outskirts of Arras, for the loss of almost 3000 men killed or missing (a total of 7791 casualties in all).[19]

This was a depressing end to the 1914 campaign. After the successful defence of Ypres, offensive action had achieved almost nothing other than proving that the war of movement had come to an end. The British were being difficult about falling in with Joffre's plans (the Ostend/Zeebrugge scheme had not gone away), and the Belgians had refused to contribute to the fighting by amalgamating their troops. The German defences were becoming stronger, and the weather made them impregnable.

Between August and December 1914 Foch saw action in a variety of roles. As commander of XX Corps he had advanced into Lorraine, only to be given a bloody nose and forced to redeem matters by defensive action before Nancy. He had probably disobeyed orders and created tension and distrust with his then commander, General Castelnau, that would never be resolved. As commander of Ninth Army, he had fought a defensive action on the Marne on a vital sector of the front. As Joffre's deputy and then commander of forces in northern France, he coordinated more defensive action – first around Arras, where he arrived in the middle of events and so exerted limited, although important, influence; and then, to much greater effect, in Belgium, where he had to deal with the British and the Belgians as well as with French subordinate commanders. Finally he had his first experience of organising and coordinating an offensive oper-ation, which achieved very little. When compared to that of the approx-imately 180 French generals and acting generals relieved of their command by year's end, this was a rapid and impressive progression. Joffre told an aide that the reason for his confidence in Foch was this: 'His force of resolution is mistress of his imagination. And when it is a question not simply of wishing but also of improvising, when matters are desperate, he is incomparable.'[20]

From these experiences Foch took some important lessons. First, he had learned the power of the defence. Even in the waterlogged terrain on the Yser, the Germans rapidly installed barbed-wire defences after their capture of Dixmude. This was a hard lesson to absorb because he had taught that modern weapons and increased firepower helped the attacker. Yet all Foch's successes in 1914 were the results not of offensive action but were hastily organised defences, on the Marne and then at Ypres. Perhaps,

[19] *AFGG* 2, 175–84, 189.   [20] Fabry, *Joffre*, 223.

indeed, the defence at Ypres might have been achieved with greater German and fewer Allied casualties if he had not tried to ease the pressure on the Belgians by attacking out of the salient, but had simply stood firm and allowed the Germans to batter themselves to pieces.

A second lesson showed the vital necessity of husbanding reserves. On the Marne Foch had none left after the first days' fighting and had been forced to the desperate tactic of marching a division across the rear of the battlefield. At Ypres he had been forced to feed in bits and pieces of units as they arrived, with the result that French and British were completely intermingled by the end of the battle, with all the attendant confusion. Joffre had tried to be parsimonious, and the British had been demanding, but the manpower resources were simply not available. Joffre had to intervene to stop Foch from stripping both men and guns from Tenth Army to feed the battle.[21] By the time that the Allies fought once again over the same ground in 1918, Foch was able to demonstrate that the reserves lesson had been well learned.

The French were out-gunned from the start, and Foch, the artillery officer, also learned very early what guns were required to fight this modern war. In the advance into Lorraine the French 75s had been unable to respond adequately to the greater range and greater weight of shell of the German guns. In static warfare mortars were essential, and the French had nothing to reply to the plunging fire of German mortars. In August 1914 all German divisions were allocated heavy guns, and in total the German armies had about 2000 of them, in addition to their 5500 field guns, of which about one-quarter were howitzers. French divisions began the war with about 3840 field guns (the 75s), which were generally better than the German 77mm (although the 77s had greater range and there were many more of them); no howitzers; and about 680 heavy guns, only half of which were mobile.[22] Foch was so convinced of the primordial importance of artillery that he had used someone he could trust (General Besse, who had done excellent work on the Marne in charge of IX Corps artillery) to prepare Tenth Army's December offensive, and Foch had taken charge himself of the artillery work once the fighting began. In the confined conditions around Ypres the 75s had done sterling work, because the terrain was flat and because they were crowded so closely together that they covered the ground completely. Yet he realised that the French needed much more than their standard field gun. In a letter to Joffre after the Ypres operations ended, Foch listed what he believed was required: large numbers of siege guns with plenty of shells to deal with

[21] Telegram, GQG to Foch, 3 November 1914, *AFGG* 1/4, annex 3801.
[22] Herr, *Artillerie*, ch. 1.

fortified enemy positions; mortars and other weapons capable of lobbing bombs into enemy positions; and sappers for mining operations and digging equipment such as had been used for constructing the Paris métro. He wanted many more machineguns as well.[23] He was also thinking about artillery tactics. In addition to superior numbers of guns, Foch saw the need for counter-battery (silencing enemy guns during an infantry attack), for getting the 75s as close to enemy trenches as possible, and for 'an intimate union' between the infantry and the artillery, instead of treating the two arms separately.[24]

Just as important as these tactical lessons was the experience of dealing with allies. Foch was able to establish good relations with King Albert of the Belgians. Although there would be a postwar dispute over their first meeting on 16 October (and it is likely that Foch spoke rather more harshly than the King was accustomed to hear), Foch bolstered the King's resolve to hang on to the last portion of national territory despite the poor morale of the Belgian government and high command. Queen Elisabeth described Foch as their 'ray of sunshine'.[25] Although he was unable to make greater use of Belgian troops, Foch would pay particular attention to maintaining that relationship in the months and years ahead – a task that required some tact because Albert was sure that the Belgian sacrifices had not been appreciated.

Among the British, Sir John found Foch much more congenial than Joffre. He wrote to Churchill on 25 October that he was 'on the very best of terms with Foch who is doing splendid work and will be at Ostend and probably Bruges within a week'.[26] Foch has been blamed by many commentators (especially Liddell Hart) for 'infecting' Sir John with such excessive optimism. Yet it is clear from his letters and dealings with Wilson that Foch believed that he had to boost morale and act positively because contemplation of retreat or even of stalemate was counterproductive. Surely Foch was right to exude optimism – if high command cannot be optimistic, there is little chance of positive action lower down the chain of command. His friendship with Henry Wilson was a vital factor in his ability to act effectively in this regard because they were able to communicate honestly with each other, with Wilson reporting daily Sir John's changing state of mind. Thus Foch was helped to find the right words whenever Sir John was being difficult. After one such occasion,

---

[23] Secret letter, Foch to Joffre, 19 November 1914, 16N 2034; Foch, Carnets, [end of December], fo. 32, 1K/129/10.

[24] Secret letter, Foch to Joffre, 1 January 1915, 16N 2034.   [25] Weygand, *IV*, 193.

[26] Letter, Sir John French, to Churchill, 25 October 1914, in Gilbert, *Churchill*, 3, *Companion*, pt 1: 219.

Foch told the head of the French Military Mission: 'It is of no importance; you only have to tell him that he has just saved England; that will put him in all his good humour again!' Foch was correct, for on this occasion Sir John responded: 'I know it only too well. I knew it from the beginning!'[27] Bertie relayed to London the cordial relations that existed between the two armies and between Sir John and Joffre and Foch, reports of which he had heard from Poincaré's liaison officer with GQG and from Aristide Briand, France's next premier.[28]

Most importantly for the future of the coalition, Foch had built a relationship with Sir John's eventual successor. Despite some cross words spoken in the heat of the moment – on 8 November Haig wrote: 'Foch said he had issued "formal order" to retake old position near Klein Zillebeke & I said too many orders had already been issued, what was wanted was execution!'[29] – Haig was grateful for the help he had received. His generous letter to his neighbouring French corps is proof of that, and he wrote to his wife in praise of French officers.[30] In the dark days of March 1918 Haig would remember what Foch had done around Ypres as, finally, he accepted unity of command. Hence Foch's command method in October and November 1914 eased the resentments engendered during the Great Retreat, when Sir John complained that the French on his flank kept disappearing without warning. The Marne had not resulted in any intermingling; the BEF simply filled the gap in between two French armies. In Flanders, however, the non-canonical way that reserves and reinforcements had been fed piece-meal into portions of the line that threatened to give way allowed British and French the opportunity to discover the other's qualities, as all faced the same enemy, the same mud and the same exhaustion. As a British liaison officer pointed out, the battles on the frontier and the retreat 'were not actually caused but intensified by the want of pulling together of the whole show'. What was needed was a 'master hand pulling all the strings and taking a grip of the situation'.[31] It was Foch's hand that had taken grip of the Flanders situation: see Illustration 2.

Foch also impressed other important British figures during the course of the Flanders campaign. When Lord Kitchener met Foch at the Dunkirk

[27] Huguet, *Britain and the War*, 147.
[28] Draft letter to Sir Edward Grey, 21 November 1914, and draft telegram to same, 13 December 1914, Bertie mss, add. mss 63,035.
[29] Haig diary, 8 November 1914.
[30] Haig's letter of 20 November 1914, reproduced in facsimile and in translation in Dubois, *Deux ans*, 2: 100; letter, Haig to Lady Haig, 3 November 1914, acc. 3155, ms. 141.
[31] Letter, Lord Loch [liaison officer between II Corps and GQG] to his wife, 11 October 1914, cited in Jeffery, *Wilson*, 139–40.

Illustration 2 'Winter in 1914–1915 in Flanders'
Réquin's drawing shows Foch urging on his Allies, Henry Wilson and the
Belgians fishing in the Yser, from south of Amiens to the coast at
Nieuport.

conference on 1 November he thought him more impressive and less
'inelastic' than Joffre, calling him 'brilliant', and noting Foch's confidence
in victory.[32] Paul Cambon, France's ambassador in London, was also
present at the Dunkirk conference and recorded the 'ineradicable impression' that Foch had made on Kitchener.[33] Poincaré noted that Foch made
a special point of reassuring Kitchener during the meeting, repeating
constantly 'We will hold, we will hold.'[34] Foch had met future prime
minister David Lloyd George on 19 October and apparently convinced
him that there would be no more French retreats.[35] However, he does not
appear to have met the politician who would play such an important role in
1918, namely Viscount Milner, although there was an indirect link
through the former British commander-in-chief Lord Roberts. Foch had
met Roberts in England before the war, the pair becoming instant friends,
and they saw each other in Foch's headquarters just before Roberts died
on 14 November at St Omer. Foch represented the French Army at the
funeral service before the body was returned to England. When Wilson
returned to London for Lord Roberts' funeral in St Paul's, Milner had a
two-hour lunch with Wilson at his home,[36] and Foch's name must have
come into the conversation. Moreover Wilson had been keeping Milner
well informed about the progress of the war (as well as about the government's failings). Milner was also involved, along with Georges
Clemenceau, in the search for news of George Cecil (the only son of
Lady Cecil, the former Violet Maxse and his future wife). George Cecil
had been killed on 31 August whilst in action with the Grenadier Guards,
but his death was not confirmed until two weeks later.[37] Thus Milner was
in touch with events in France – another benefit of Foch's friendship with
Henry Wilson.

Of course, Foch had done rather more than simply impress British
politicians; he had intervened in the matter of the British CinC. If Foch
did not know beforehand that Joffre had convened the Dunkirk conference in an attempt to replace Sir John with (preferably) Henry Wilson
because of anger over the British failure to occupy Lille and over the
Boulogne question, nonetheless he played a schemer's role after the
conference. On 5 November Foch went to see Wilson (normally Wilson

[32] Letter, Asquith to Venetia Stanley, 2 November 1914, Brock and Brock (eds.), *Asquith Letters*, no. 198; David (ed.), *Inside Asquith's Cabinet*, 205; Stevenson, *Lloyd George Diary*, 5 November 1914, 10.
[33] Letter, Cambon to Foch, 13 November 1914, 414/AP/3.
[34] Poincaré, *AS*, 5: 412 (entry for 1 November 1914).
[35] Lloyd George, memorandum, 31 December 1914, in Gilbert, *Churchill*, 3, *Companion*, pt 1: 351.
[36] Wilson diary, 19 November 1914.   [37] Cecil, *Imperial Marriage*, 246–51.

went to Foch's headquarters each evening) to tell him what had transpired: namely, Kitchener's offer of Ian Hamilton to replace Sir John, and Joffre's refusal because he 'had worked cordially & well' with the British CinC. Foch told Wilson that 'he thought Sir J. ought to know of it'. This was mischief-making of considerable proportions: it was bound to worsen relations between Sir John and Kitchener, even if the intention was to improve Allied relations by making Sir John feel grateful for French support. This was achieved the next day, when Sir John went to thank Foch in person and indicated that he would also thank Joffre.[38] The episode does not reflect well on Foch, however.

As well as making an impression on British politicians, Foch had had an effect on his own political leaders. Poincaré had been present at the Dunkirk conference and visited Foch at Cassel the next day, where the President was impressed by the 'masterly' exposition of the action that Foch gave and by his knowledge of the history of the region, the cockpit of Europe. However, in the original manuscript notes on which Poincaré based his published memoirs, he was somewhat more equivocal, describing Foch as on edge. When General Brugère spoke to Poincaré at the end of the year, this judgement was confirmed as both men agreed that Foch was not calm enough.[39] Nonetheless, Joffre informed Foch that the latter had made a good impression on both Poincaré and War Minister Millerand. As a result they had 'ratified' Joffre's choice of Foch as his deputy.[40]

Foch was also in touch with other French politicians. Although he had lost Tardieu from his staff (Joffre had recalled him to GQG in order to write communiqués), another *député* had joined him on 17 November. This was Charles Meunier-Surcouf, who represented the Côtes du Nord and knew Madame Foch's family. Since the mobilised *députés* moved between their military and their parliamentary duties, Foch had a source of information about what was happening in Paris, especially regarding the growing criticism of Joffre and GQG as parliamentarians returned to the capital from Bordeaux.

In early December Foch had a visit from Senator Paul Doumer, who had acted as the head of General Gallieni's civil cabinet during the government's absence in Bordeaux. Gallieni's friends were criticising Joffre's so-called incompetence; they believed that Gallieni should have received greater recognition for the 'miracle' of the Marne. Weygand recounts

---

[38] Wilson diary, 5, 6 November 1914.
[39] Poincaré, *AS*, 5: 417–18 (entry for 2 November 1914); Notes journalières, 2 November 1914, NAF 16028; Brugère diary, 23 December 1914, 1K/160.
[40] Letter, Joffre to Foch, 3 October [sic, sc. November] 1914, Foch mss, 414/AP/2.

Doumer's visit (without naming him) and claims that Foch did not let him develop the criticisms and showed him the door.[41] Foch himself told his wife that he had tried to argue against any change in command whilst operations were continuing. Politicians seemed to believe that they had several command 'teams' to hand, he continued, just as they had teams to fill ministries. It would be 'disastrous' to make a change in the high command at the moment. Nevertheless, and he warned his wife to keep his words confidential, Doumer had included him in his scheming.[42] Foch duly reported the visit to Joffre, who then told Poincaré.[43]

Much more importantly, Foch had contact with another senator, namely Georges Clemenceau. He had met Clemenceau in 1908 when the latter appointed him, to his surprise, as commandant of the Ecole Supérieure de Guerre, but they do not seem to have had much to do with each other after that. Using his daughter Anne (wife of his aide, Alex Fournier) as an intermediary, Foch arranged to speak to Clemenceau in Beauvais on 13 December.[44] The reason for Foch's initiative is unclear, and the only account of the meeting is Clemenceau's, and that much after the event. In his final work, which is a response to Foch's criticisms and was written after Foch's death – it must be viewed therefore in the light of the postwar disagreements over the terms of the peace treaty – Clemenceau describes their unsatisfactory meeting ('a string of commonplaces') as a fishing expedition on Foch's part as to the attitude of politicians towards any change in the high command.[45]

Whether or not Foch was seeking answers to the question of his own future (he was, after all, Joffre's man and Joffre was being criticised), it is easy to see why Foch would wish to speak to Clemenceau. The senator-journalist had shown as much drive and energy as Foch himself. Premier René Viviani was overwhelmed, and the approach of the Germans to Paris was said to have caused a near panic in the capital. Hence Clemenceau's pungent articles in his newspaper *L'Homme Libre* (re-named *L'Homme Enchaîné* after censorship was introduced) attacking the government, especially over the inadequate medical arrangements and the inadequate supplies of munitions, gave a much stronger impression of decisiveness than any government action. The paper's circulation went up as a result. Foch called him 'un fort type'.[46] Clemenceau would be elected to the Senate's influential Army Commission in January 1915. Furthermore,

---

[41] Weygand, *IV*, 180.   [42] Letter, Foch to Mme Foch, 10 December 1914, vol. 33.

[43] Poincaré, *AS*, 5: 500 (entry of 11 December 1914). Doumer's visit is there described as 'recent'.

[44] Letters, Foch to Mme Foch, 14 and 15 December 1914, vol. 33.

[45] Clemenceau, *Grandeur and Misery of Victory*, 15.

[46] Letter, Foch to Mme Foch, 15 December 1914, vol. 33.

Foch had a channel of communication to him because Albert Clemenceau, the Tiger's favourite and much younger brother, was attached to Foch's lines of communication staff.[47] Foch came away from the meeting in Beauvais with the impression that Clemenceau would support his ideas about both 'internal and external' matters.[48] Foch did not expound on what these ideas were, but this early hint of the cooperation that would come to fruition in 1918 is very interesting. Thus there is early proof that Foch was paying attention to matters political even before the end of 1914.

As far as relations within his own French Army were concerned, Foch had developed a good working relationship with the CinC. This is demonstrated by Joffre's considerable confidence in Foch in promoting him so rapidly and Foch's response in keeping him fully abreast of developments and of his thinking. The confidential letters that Foch sent most evenings were kept in the 'secret cupboard no. 2', and did not enter the regular GQG correspondence registers, although some were stamped as having been seen by the chief of staff and his assistant. Relations with other generals were less good. The quarrel with Castelnau has been mentioned already; General Brugère also bore Foch a grudge, blaming him for his removal from command. He had commanded the group of territorial divisions in September and October which Joffre later disbanded. (Despite his age Brugère was so annoyed about being removed from command that he even threatened to offer his services to the BEF!) He accused Foch of never visiting his divisions and of praising him to his face but acting differently behind his back.[49] In Third Army General Sarrail was stirring trouble, and Foch informed Joffre that Sarrail had told a *député* and reserve officer that the country was heading to a military dictatorship. When the Germans were defeated, Joffre would be made a marshal, Foch would succeed him, and that would mean 'the return of caesarism and the end of the Republic'. Sarrail is alleged to have told the *député* to return to the Parliament and 'prevent the coup d'état'. This unlikely scenario is more a product of Sarrail's ambition than a reflection of Foch's political views, but accords well with what is known of Sarrail.[50] The fact that it was Foch who informed Joffre of this, in addition to Brugère's complaints about Foch's two-faced behaviour, accords with the scheming to replace Sir John French related above.

---

[47] He was appointed on 12 September 1914: Ninth Army records, 19N 1539, [d]2 Ordres de bataille.
[48] Letter, Foch to Mme Foch, 14 December 1914, vol. 33.
[49] Brugère diary, 8 December 1914, 1K/160.
[50] Letter, Foch to Joffre, 3 December 1916, Fonds Joffre, 1K/268. See Tanenbaum, *Sarrail*, 53.

Indeed, it seems on the whole that Foch got on better with Allied generals than with French ones (with the exception of his CinC), perhaps because in part there could be no threat from, or rivalry for promotion with, the former. The British ambassador in Paris informed Sir Edward Grey after the end of the Ypres fighting that he had heard that the 'understanding between General Foch and Sir John French is complete & that there is confraternity between the French and British Troops'.[51] This derived probably from Foch's lack of authority to issue orders to his Allies as he could to his army commanders. Moreover, both Belgians and British were commanded by hierarchical superiors: King Albert and a field marshal. Hence Foch was reduced to using more tact and diplomacy than command in his dealings with them. This was another good lesson to have learned early in the war, which seems to have spilled over into his relationship with his staff, if not with other French generals. He still had Weygand and Desticker and Naulin; and had requested and been granted the appointment to his staff of Capitaine Alex Fournier, his second, surviving, son-in-law.[52]

Foch's style of command style was well established by the end of the year. It forms a complete contrast to Moltke's distance from, hence ignorance of, events during the Battle of the Marne. Foch was not aloof, quite the opposite. In fact he might be said to have been too 'hands-on' in some instances. For example, he had taken it upon himself to issue an order to attack on 20 August at Morhange, contrary to his army commander's wishes, and he took over Maud'huy's Tenth Army in December. Maud'huy's chief of staff, Colonel des Vallières, found Foch bombastic and unwilling to discuss matters.[53] Yet Jean de Pierrefeu, who wrote communiqués for GQG, thought that Foch identified himself with the conduct of operations, and that this simple identification was the reason for his command style. Pierrefeu describes Foch rushing into various headquarters during the Flanders fighting, waving his arms about, responding 'attack' to every request for reinforcements, and then rushing out again 'charged like an electric battery with wild energy and unconscious aggression'.[54]

Not surprisingly, therefore, Foch's technique came in for criticism. The staff of Second Army were told mockingly that their former XX Corps commander had covered himself with glory on the Marne and that Foch was to become the Duke of Saint-Gond.[55] The failure of the December

[51] Draft letter, Bertie to Grey, 21 November 1914, Bertie mss, add. mss 63,035, fos. 46–8.
[52] Letters, Foch to Mme Foch, 19, 20 October 1914, vol. 33.
[53] Vallières, *Au soleil*, 103, 107.   [54] Pierrefeu, 'Foch au pouvoir', p. 10, 1K/120.
[55] Bary memoirs, p. 12, 1K/795/39.

fighting in Artois gave rise to some amusement, with generals comparing Foch's teaching in the Ecole de Guerre with his actions in issuing counter-orders: ordering all the artillery to support first one corps and then the next day to support the other.[56] Such criticism and mockery may be the result of Foch's lack of experience. It must be remembered that he had no prior experience of command in battle, hence little knowledge of troops. During the forty years between graduating from the artillery Ecole d'Application in Fontainebleau and the outbreak of war he had spent one year as a lieuten-ant, six years commanding an artillery battery or group of batteries, and two years in command of a regiment, with breaks between these postings – less than a quarter of his military career spent in command of troops.[57]

The other facet of Foch's hands-on style is the personal contact that he insisted upon. He achieved this by using liaison officers on the Marne, and in Flanders spent many hours driving between King Albert, Sir John French and his own army commanders. The need for such personal and continual contact was unique on the Western Front, not only because the army group command was new but because Belgian and French Flanders was the only theatre of operations where the Allies had to cooperate so closely. The physical and mental stamina that Foch displayed in develop-ing the job description as well as doing the job of coordinator is undeni-able, especially given his age. Clearly action gave him an adrenalin rush. When, after the war, President Poincaré gave the speech admitting Foch to the Académie Française, he referred to the apocryphal saying from the Marne battle – everything giving way, but the situation is excellent, 'I am attacking.' Poincaré stated that even if Foch had never said those words, he acted as though he had.

Constant optimism was another prominent feature of his command style. It is important for high command to retain faith in ultimate victory, yet Liddell Hart is disparaging – he refers to 'gusts of optimism', infusing Sir John 'with his own assurance', and injecting Sir John with 'Fochian serum'. Although Liddell Hart perhaps did not mean to imply by these medical similes that Sir John was sick, or that Foch was malign, there can be little doubt that in the extreme circumstances of the beleaguered forces in Flanders energy and optimism were vital. Foch managed to maintain these qualities despite still having no definite news of the fate of his son. On 8 November he wrote to his wife that a colleague's brother posted missing on 20 August had just been found as a labourer in Germany, and so hope remained. Even when his son-in-law's death was confirmed on 19 November, Foch continued to hope for Germain.[58]

---

[56] Brugère diary, 22 December 1914, 1K/160.   [57] See Mayer, *Nos chefs de 1914*, 68–9.
[58] Letters, Foch to Mme Foch, 8, 20 November 1914, vol. 33.

Foch summed up his views on what the 1914 fighting had achieved in a letter to Joffre. The German plan of destroying their adversary in the west before turning against their adversary in the east had fallen through; they were now in a painful and powerless position in the west and had everything to do in the east, but could not withdraw troops for the purpose. Foch was mistaken, however, in thinking that the next German offensive would come via Strassburg, Metz and the Meuse.[59] He was equally upbeat in talking to Tardieu. Although Joffre had recalled Tardieu to GQG to write battle accounts for the press (Joffre thought that France's exploits needed greater publicity), Tardieu liked to return to Cassel and talk with Foch. After the Flanders fighting had died down, Foch summed up for him the situation as he saw it. The longer the war continued the greater the supply problems Germany would have; the French armies were 'magnificent' and all the poor commanders had been removed; the British were arriving and the Belgians had reconstituted their divisions and their morale. Most importantly, Germany having sought war had started out with a tradition of victory, whereas France began with a tradition of defeat, but it was not France who had been beaten. He did not know when France would take the offensive, but it was being prepared in the munitions factories and training schools; the armies were constituting reserves and transport resources; the offensive was being prepared in the soul. Foch claimed to see no disadvantage for France in all this.[60] As he wrote to his wife, 'We don't have a *victory* in the full sense of the word, but we have inflicted a *great defeat* on the enemy.'[61]

[59] Letter, Foch to Joffre, 19 November 1914, 16N 2034.   [60] Tardieu, *Avec Foch*, 155.
[61] Letter, Foch to Mme Foch, 23 November 1914, vol. 33 (original emphasis).

5   Second Artois, January–June 1915

At lunch in his headquarters to celebrate New Year's Day 1915, Foch summed up the past four months and was confident of victory. He could think of no better position after the war was over than that of Governor of Metz, where he had been when the Franco-Prussian war began. For the moment, what was needed, once the weather improved, was more artillery and more munitions – munitions in sufficient quantities so as to be able to economise on men.[1] Foch was equally upbeat in his New Year greetings to the commander-in-chief. French artillery, he wrote, had proved its ability to silence that of the enemy. The French infantry were stopped not by the enemy's artillery but by his defensive works, so the answer was to exploit their own artillery superiority in order to destroy those defences, by bringing the 75s nearer to the front lines and protecting them with dugouts or shields. There should be intimate coordination between infantry and artillery, shelters and communication trenches to get support troops up close, and lots of observers for the artillery. Tenth Army was undertaking all these preparations. Whilst the rain continued, that was all they could do, but, when the weather improved, the results of their preparation would be seen.[2]

If Foch had seen what the answer was to the problem of the First World War battlefield – artillery, and lots of it – the events of 1915 were to show how difficult it was to achieve that artillery superiority. Not only had industrial mobilisation barely started, so that it would be months before the shells crisis was over, but other problems intervened as well, especially those created by the Allies. Politicians in Paris and London began to consider other fronts, not simply the trench lines that ran across northern France into Belgium. Furthermore, the enemy had an annoying habit of intervening with improved methods of his own. Foch's lot in 1915 was repeated battering at the Vimy Ridge as he attempted to carry out Joffre's offensive strategy and break the German lines, repeated demands

---

[1] Weygand, *IV*, 208–10.   [2] Letter, Foch to Joffre, 1 January 1915, *AFGG* 2, annex 526.

for greater artillery resources, and repeated negotiations with (mainly) Sir John French over coordinating operations. Following on from First Artois, the uninspired nomenclature of the 1915 battles, Second and Third Artois, underlines the repetitive nature of what Foch was asked to do that year.

On 20 December Foch had described himself as a spider, sending out his representatives whilst waiting for his web to be strong enough to catch not a fly, but 'a sparrow-hawk'.[3] In order to catch that larger prey, Foch's de facto position as army group commander was regularised on 5 January. Hence, in addition to being Joffre's 'adjoint', he and the former First Army commander, General Yvon Dubail, now became his 'délégués' as well, with the same powers as the CinC as regarded the conduct of operations 'according to the directives that will be given them'. The length of the front was now so extended that Joffre could not oversee the whole, hence Foch was appointed to coordinate the two northern armies (Eighth and Tenth – Castelnau's Second Army remained under Joffre's hand), and General Dubail was to carry out a similar function in the east. The mission of the two 'delegated generals' was to oversee the execution of orders without hampering the initiative of the individual army commanders.[4]

However, Joffre retained strategic and administrative control of the armies, and did not hand over much freedom to his two delegates, maintaining the tight control over his generals that he had exercised in 1914. A very large majority of the divisional, corps and army commanders in January 1915, including of course Foch himself, now owed their position to the commander-in-chief. It was Joffre who issued notes on offensive and on defensive operations to all the armies and, as far as the north went, he informed Foch that the Zeebrugge–Ostend project should not be pursued. In one further respect, Foch's influence was limited. The question of who was to succeed Joffre should anything happen to him was sharpened by continuing criticism and by the feud between Joffre and Gallieni over whose was the glory for the victory on the Marne. Joffre had already tried to replace Gallieni as his official successor when he appointed Foch his 'adjoint' in October. The government had agreed to Joffre's request but refused to make a formal decision that Foch should be that successor. In March Joffre tried again, seeking permission from the Minister to make his own appointment. Millerand put the matter to the Conseil des ministres, but Poincaré, ever the constitutionalist, objected that Gallieni's formal 'lettre de service' could not be taken from him.

[3] Letter, Foch to Mme Foch, 20 December 1914, vol. 33.
[4] Instruction pour Messieurs les généraux Foch et Dubail, 5 January 1915, *AFGG* 2, annex 555.

However, the Cabinet accepted that Joffre would never agree to Gallieni standing in for him, even temporarily, and so the ministers decided on 10 March that General Dubail, commanding the Eastern Army Group, might be so designated.[5]

Why was Foch, already appointed the commander-in-chief's 'adjoint', overlooked? The decision could be interpreted as a snub. Liddell Hart relates how Foch enquired about the succession following a minor car crash (so minor that the only trace of it is to be found in Foch's own postwar memoirs) in which both Foch and Joffre were involved on 17 January, and how 'the Ministry had replied, rather caustically, that he need not concern himself'. Yet, the selection of Dubail is entirely in line with army practice to follow seniority. Dubail had reached the rank of divisional general in 1908 (three years before Foch), and he had been chief of the army general staff and a member of the Conseil supérieur de la guerre. Castelnau, too, was senior to Foch, although Castelnau was not an army group commander. Liddell Hart's account of a 'jesuitical' attempt by Foch to gain greater power for himself is, therefore, ungenerous.[6]

If Foch was disappointed by this decision, nevertheless he was gaining more public attention. At the end of January the bi-monthly review, *Le Correspondant*, featured him in its anonymous series of articles on various commanders.[7] Across the Channel, Colonel Charles à Court Repington wrote a eulogistic piece in *The Times*. Foremost amongst the French generals who were making a name for themselves beyond the army, wrote Repington, was General Foch, to whom Sir John had expressed his gratitude in his recent dispatch. His article brought Foch to the attention of those British who read *The Times*, namely the decision-makers. The article was taken up later by the *New York Times* in its *Current History Magazine*, which expatiated for American readers on the French general's rising star, in even more glowing terms.[8]

Foch was also making a name for himself in Paris salons. Whilst posted in Paris before his marriage, Foch had frequented the circle that met in Gustave Doré's home, and he had been one of the executors of the artist's will, which contained several charitable benefactions. Furthermore, Foch maintained his connections with artistic circles through Philippe Berthelot even after the war began. Berthelot was influential in the French Foreign Ministry, and would become more so after October

---

[5] Poincaré, *AS*, 6: 102.   [6] Liddell Hart, *Foch*, 160–1.
[7] 'Miles', 'Le Général Foch', *Le Correspondant*, 25 January 1915.
[8] 'General Foch, The Man of Ypres, Philosopher and Strategist', *The Times*, 18 February 1915, 9; 'General Foch, the Man of Ypres: An Account of France's New Master of War', *New York Times Current History Magazine*, April 1915.

1915, when Aristide Briand replaced Viviani as Premier.[9] The writer
Marthe Bibesco recorded hearing Foch pronounce in February: 'Si on
m'enveloppe, je perce; et si l'on me perce, j'enveloppe' [If I am surrounded, I break out; and if they break through, I surround them] – a
sentiment that works better as a *bon mot* than as a military maxim.[10]

Furthermore, there is some evidence of a campaign to put Foch into the
top job. The British ambassador, Sir Francis Bertie, heard of 'intrigues' to
remove Joffre to the War Ministry and to replace him with Foch 'who, it is
thought, would be more enterprising'. Bertie gave little credence to these
rumours because he believed that the public had confidence in Joffre.[11]
Foch had already spoken to Millerand about these so-called intrigues
when the Minister visited Tenth Army in December, claiming that he
could do nothing about the campaign since he was so far from Paris, and
hinting that some politicians were attempting to split the political union by
such methods. He also warned his wife to stop his brother getting mixed
up in the business.[12] With no evidence to hand, it is impossible to say
whether Foch was using the press to further his own career, or whether he
was simply being used to attack Joffre. The press publicity and the campaign to replace Joffre may have been factors in the government's decision
to designate Dubail instead of Foch as the commander-in-chief's eventual
successor.

Whilst waiting for the weather to improve so that operations could
begin again, Foch could deal with two matters: improving the relationship
with the Belgians and the British, which had to be done tactfully since
Foch lacked any hierarchical authority; and improving his own army's
tactics. King Albert had been angered by what he perceived as French lack
of appreciation of the Belgian stand on the Yser, and had written a
memorandum on 23 October 'protesting strongly' about 'false accusations', although he never sent it.[13] On 3 January Foch went to see him to
offer New Year wishes and to explain that he appreciated fully the sacrifices the Belgian army had made. His praise of the Belgian army was
somewhat hypocritical – Wilson recorded that Foch thought it 'almost
useless', and when he arrived in the north Foch had found the Belgian
chief of staff, General Hanoteau, completely demoralised[14] – but required
by diplomacy. Foch recorded the King's high opinion of his (Foch's)

[9] Tardieu, *Avec Foch*, 131.   [10] Diesbach, *Princesse Bibesco*, 214.
[11] Bertie, *Diary*, 1: 111 (entry for 13 February 1915).
[12] Letters, Foch to Mme Foch, 8 and 3 March 1915, vol. 34.
[13] 'Au commandement français', 23 October 1914, in Thielemans and Vandewoude (eds.),
     Le Roi Albert, 531–2.
[14] Wilson diary, 29 December 1914; Autin (*Foch*, 146) cites the much harsher comments of
     the draft, toned down in Foch, *Mémoires* 1: 186.

integrity, energy and frankness, and Albert told Weygand that Foch would have made dead men fight.[15] Good relations were re-established, and Joffre commended Foch's action in mending fences with the Belgians.[16]

As for the British, Foch had distributed photographs of himself as Christmas presents to Sir John, Wilson and Huguet with an appropriate ('sensationnelle') dedication, and Sir John had reciprocated with cigarettes and cigars and had been 'very kind'.[17] Foch still had a low opinion of Sir John as commander-in-chief of the BEF, and both he and Henry Wilson blamed the lack of support during First Artois on Sir John's chief of staff, Sir Archibald Murray. Foch admitted that Sir John was difficult – he refuses 'to accept what I propose', Foch wrote to his wife, but 'knows even less what he wants himself' – and that without Wilson's cheerful cooperation the British and the French would never be able to settle matters.[18] Accordingly Joffre began to agitate to replace the obstructive Murray with the cooperative Wilson.[19] Foch knew what was afoot, telling Joffre that Sir John was incapable of carrying anything through because he did not know his own mind. Foch claimed that, in trying to carry out Sir John's wishes, he had found that not only would he change his mind about what he wanted but he would refuse to 'advance' further. Hence, the French 'manoeuvres' to remove Murray had caused Sir John to dig in his heels. Since both Kitchener and Asquith opposed any appointment of that 'serpent' Wilson as chief of staff, Foch recommended leaving Sir John to muddle along by himself for the time being.[20]

In the event, at the end of January Sir William Robertson, who in 1914 had been the BEF's highly efficient quartermaster general (QMG), replaced Murray. Conveniently, Murray had fallen ill and so could be removed without the British seeming to give in to French pressure. Wilson became, however, 'Principal Liaison Officer' with the French, an entirely new position, instead of chief of staff (see Illustration 3). Although Foch did not realise it, for several reasons Wilson's new position was not particularly beneficial to Foch in his relations with the BEF. First, the role of such a liaison officer did not exist in army establishment and so the job had no place in the headquarters hierarchy; next, the job clashed with

---

[15] Letter, Foch to Mme Foch, 4 January 1915, vol. 34; Foch, Journées, 3 January 1915 (two similar accounts); Weygand, *IV*, 185.

[16] Letter, Joffre to Foch, 6 January 1915, *AFGG* 2, annex 560.

[17] Letters, Foch to Mme Foch, 14, 24, 25 December 1914, vol. 33.

[18] Letter, Foch to Mme Foch, 29 December 1914, ibid.

[19] Prete, War of Movement, discusses this topic fully, 477–92; less fully in his *Strategy and Command*, 189–96.

[20] Secret letter, Foch to Joffre, 5 January 1915, 16N 2034; Asquith to Venetia Stanley, 28 December 1914, in Brock and Brock (eds.), *Asquith Letters*, 342.

Illustration 3 The long and the short of it: Foch and Wilson in a dark
office
Despite the formal pose, both men seem to be trying not to laugh.

the official liaison mission, run by General Clive at GQG; finally, Wilson had been sub-chief of staff and also Sir John's first choice to replace Murray, thus making the relationship with Robertson difficult. In consequence, Foch would not have the same insights into GHQ thinking in 1915 as he had enjoyed through Wilson during 1914. His and Joffre's plotting had not only failed, but had resulted in a worse situation from the point of view of getting the British to fall in with French planning.

In addition to managing the Allies, Foch had also been thinking hard about the problem of getting onto the high ground of Vimy Ridge, and (more importantly) staying there (see Map 8). The reason for repeating an offensive at this point, despite the failure to make any headway earlier, is patent, for, in order to break through northwards from Arras between Bailleul and Givenchy, the French would have to capture the ridge. It was long and narrow, running NW–SE, with high points at 140, 132 and 119 metres. On its eastern side it dropped away sharply towards German-held territory, with the villages of Givenchy, Bailleul, and Vimy itself at its foot. Its importance lay in the observation that it gave over that German-occupied country, which became a flat plain extending eastwards towards the communications hub around Douai. At the northwestern tip, it was separated from another ridge dominated by the chapel of Notre Dame de Lorette. The little river Souchez had created the gap between the two ridges, and the eponymous village nestled in the low ground between them. The Germans held Souchez and the two villages, Ablain and Carency, that protected it. They had also constructed strong defensive works at the southern end of Vimy Ridge, nearer to Arras, around La Targette and Neuville Saint Waast, with an especially strong position called the 'Labyrinth'. The capture of Vimy Ridge, not completed until 1917, would cost many thousands of lives.

Foch identified the German strongpoints that would require destruction before the high ground could be captured. He thought about counter-battery work, about getting accurate photographs from aerial reconnaissances, and about flank attacks that would support the principal action.[21] He arranged for the construction of armoured carts ['brouettes blindées'] for getting guns and other materiel forward under fire.[22] His notebooks are full of ideas about how to proceed, which resulted in a 'Note' for all units of his army group.[23] He proposed a methodical artillery preparation to destroy the enemy wire, artillery barrages to protect the flanks of his attacking force, and counter-battery fire to suppress enemy

---

[21] Foch, Carnets, fo. 45 [n.d., January 1915].

[22] Letters, Foch to Mme Foch, 3 November and 5 December 1914, vol. 33; Weygand, *IV*, 198–200.

[23] Foch, Note, n.d. [3 February 1915], *AFGG* 2, annex 792.

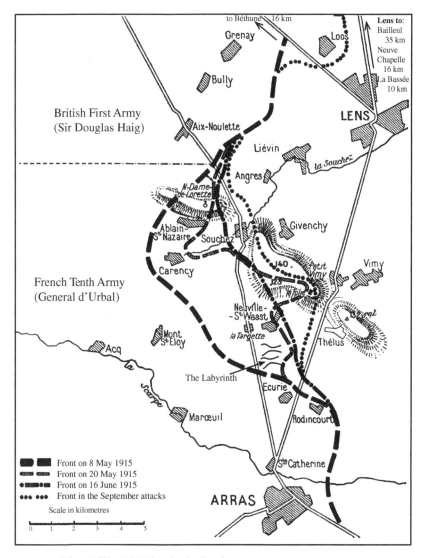

to Béthune 16 km

Grenay

Loos

Lens to:
Bailleul
35 km
Neuve
Chapelle
16 km
La Bassée
10 km

Bully

LENS

British First Army
(Sir Douglas Haig)

Aix-Noulette

Liévin

la Souchez

Angres

N-Dame-
de-Lorette

Givenchy

Ablain-
St-Nazaire   Souchez

Carency

140.

Petit
Vimy

Vimy

French Tenth Army
(General d'Urbal)

Neuville-
-St-Waast

la Targette

Mont
St-Eloy

Acq

la Scarpe

Thélus

The Labyrinth

Ecurie

Marœuil

Rodincourt

Ste Catherine

Front on 8 May 1915
Front on 20 May 1915
Front on 16 June 1915
Front in the September attacks
Scale in kilometres

0   1   2   3   4   5

ARRAS

Map 8 The 1915 battles in Artois

counter-attacks. Speedy capture of the second defensive line would create
a deeper lodgement better able to resist counter-attacks. Clearly Foch had
appreciated the importance of 'tempo', and the importance of artillery.
However, France still had not managed to match the production of armaments to these tactics. As Foch was writing, the French armies had not

even received replacements for all the 75s lost in the initial fighting. Although the shell shortage was being overcome, the speed of production had led to lower quality standards and a large number of gun barrels were bursting in consequence. Between 20 December 1914, when the shells made since the start of the war began to be used, and the end of January 1915, almost one hundred of the army's 75s were put out of action through premature explosion.[24] During the spring months, one gun barrel was bursting for every 3000 rounds fired, whereas prewar the rate of such losses had been one per half a million rounds.[25]

Despite occupying himself in mending fences with the Allies and thinking about the tactical problem of taking the ridge, Foch was beginning to feel the strain of enforced inaction. He even felt somewhat 'humiliated', he wrote to his wife, by the lack of movement, but was pushing preparations as much as possible in order to be as effective as possible when better weather arrived.[26] Meanwhile Foch kept a close watch on Tenth Army preparations. On 7 February he dictated a set of instructions to its chief of staff, Colonel des Vallières; the same day he asked General Pétain, who was to make the main attack with his XXXIII Corps, for his plan directly instead of going through Tenth Army channels; and he paid critical attention to the final army plan, demanding certain changes be made and progress on their implementation reported to him.[27] So Foch was intervening in areas that were within the province of the army commander. Certainly the role of an army group commander was new and had to be negotiated, but tactical details of attack plans were the responsibility of the army commander, General de Maud'huy. Foch's interference reflects his impatience with inactivity and accounts in part for the adverse opinion that several officers held of him.

Yet one activity required all Foch's attention and patience, namely the British relief so as to free up French units for the offensive. This relief was slowed by two factors. First of all, despite Joffre's refusal to entertain it, the Ostend–Zeebrugge operation was not yet dead, the Cabinet having discussed a possible British advance to the Dutch frontier (!) on 13 and 23 January. Second, the British in London were seeking more profitable theatres in which to act, which would deprive Sir John of the reinforcements that he needed in order to relieve the French. The Chancellor of the Exchequer, David Lloyd George, favoured an operation out of Salonika to rally the Balkan states, thus putting pressure on Austria-Hungary;

---

[24] Baquet, *Souvenirs*, 77, 109.   [25] Strachan, *To Arms*, 1056–8.

[26] Letter, Foch to Mme Foch, 3 February 1915, vol. 34.

[27] Instructions dictées par le général Foch le 7 février 1915, Tenth Army to General Foch, 7 February 1915, Foch, Note, 13 February 1915, *AFGG* 2, annexes 823, 824, 869.

Churchill proposed capturing the island of Borkum off the German coast as a stepping-stone to an operation against Germany itself; Maurice Hankey, secretary to the newly created War Council, suggested that an operation against Turkey might re-open communication with Russia through the Black Sea, and provide a platform for a further operation in alliance with various Balkan states against Austria-Hungary. The French politicians returning to Paris from Bordeaux were thinking similar thoughts about the high costs of fighting on French soil. Given the French commercial interests in the eastern Mediterranean, Aristide Briand, Minister of Justice in the Viviani government, had put forward a scheme in December for a joint Franco-British expedition to support Serbia and attack Austria-Hungary that way. There was support in the French military too (Generals Gallieni and Franchet d'Espèrey) for a Salonika expedition. Yet neither Joffre, nor Sir John, nor Foch would face with equanimity the prospect that resources be diverted from the Western Front, nor that the divisions of Britain's New Armies be sent anywhere other than to France.

On 14 February Foch took his ideas to GQG to explain how he intended to use Tenth Army to re-start offensive operations in Artois with an attack by XXXIII Corps on Vimy Ridge, supported by strong artillery action on the flanks. Possession of the ridge would allow the French guns to dominate the Douai plain, and also allow X Corps to attack out of Arras. At the same time as the Arras operation the British right should attack La Bassée so as to extend the French front of attack, and follow this with a second British attack on the Warneton–Messines front.[28] This was an ambitious scheme, especially given that he had no promise as yet of British cooperation. The Cabinet in London had now decided finally against the Zeebrugge plan, and as a consequence against sending to France the reinforcements that had been allocated for it, thereby reducing Sir John's ability to relieve Foch's two corps for the attack on Vimy Ridge.[29] The lack of proper coalition machinery for settling such questions made Foch's position very difficult. He was preparing for an offensive that required the relief of French troops by the British, but he had no authority to order such a relief; his commander-in-chief was in agreement with Sir John about the primacy of his front, but relations between the pair were bad otherwise; Robertson was now chief of staff rather than the hoped-for Wilson; and Sir John was coming under heavy criticism both at home and in France. Moreover, Kitchener was becoming critical of the failures of both Sir John's and French methods; as

[28] Note taken to GQG, 14 February 1915, ibid., annex 874.
[29] Secretary's Notes of War Council, 28 January 1915, CAB 42/1/28.

a result, he was having second, third and more thoughts about sending the last regular division (the 29th) to France.[30] Finally, as a result of these qualms, Kitchener informed Sir John on 27 February that 29 Division would not go to France after all; instead it was committed to the Dardanelles.

Furthermore, Kitchener's dislike of the failure to achieve any success in France led him to intervene by using the Belgian Premier, Baron Charles de Broqueville, as an intermediary.[31] During the course of a long conversation in the War Office on 16 February Kitchener told him that he was 'exasperated' by the fighting in France, and that the methods used there were leading to pointless massacres. He threatened not only to refuse to send any more troops to France unless the methods were changed, but also to withdraw troops that were already there. He delegated Broqueville to transmit his views to Joffre and Foch, but Wilson and Foch scorned Kitchener's idea for a night attack along the whole front, with the corps commanders only being informed of the day and time immediately before the operation began.[32] Broqueville showed Foch the reply to Kitchener that he had written for Joffre, and Foch told the premier that it represented 'perfectly' the feelings of the French army.[33] This laid squarely on Foch's shoulders the burden of maintaining harmony in order to dedicate the maximum resources to the forthcoming battle.

Increasingly stiff letters now flowed between GHQ and GQG. Joffre insisted that he could not undertake the action that Foch had been preparing unless the British relieved French units; Sir John insisted that the reinforcements he had received were not of a quality to enable him to extend his front and carry out the La Bassée operation. Indeed, the only people who seemed to be cooperating at this time were Foch and Wilson, who were united in their dislike of an operation at Salonika. For them, killing Germans in France was the correct strategy, and they agreed that Churchill and Lloyd George were mad.[34] Sir John remained adamant and his refusal to cooperate meant the end of Foch's operation. On 24 February Joffre postponed it.

Even though Joffre had refused to allow Foch to undertake the offensive in the north without the British relief, Sir John felt that he could not simply stand still. He had to show willing, both to Kitchener (to prove that a Western Front offensive could indeed achieve something) and to the

---

[30] On this question see Philpott, 'Kitchener and the 29th Division'.
[31] Note du Comte de Broqueville, n.d., Broqueville mss, mfm 1510/391.
[32] Wilson diary, 23 February 1915; letter, Foch to Mme Foch, 22 February 1915, vol. 34.
[33] Broqueville to Lord Kitchener, 23 February 1915, PRO 30/57/57/WH15.
[34] Wilson diary, 12, 15 February 1915.

French (to show that the BEF could obtain a victory with or without French support). The Battle of Neuve Chapelle was the result. Foch arranged for Tenth Army's heavy artillery to support the British (but without exceeding the munitions allocation laid down by Joffre), and he instructed Maud'huy to designate 43 DI to cover the British right should they succeed in advancing.[35] This was as much as he could offer because Joffre had been so angered by Sir John's refusal to relieve the French that he gave strict orders that Foch should not undertake any action around Arras.[36] However, Foch had already authorised Maud'huy to deal directly with Haig so as to ensure close cooperation, and Haig had been to see Maud'huy on 28 February. They had been neighbours earlier on the Aisne, although this was their first meeting. Haig found Maud'huy to be 'a small active man, about 58. Sandy coloured hair, probably dye! Quite the old type of Frenchman whom one has seen on the stage of the Louis 14th period.'[37] Maud'huy had already allocated four batteries to help Haig, and he informed Foch that he was able to support the British action.[38]

So, because Sir John had refused to agree to Foch's plan, Haig's First Army attacked alone on 10 March, well north of Vimy Ridge. Haig's aim had been to take the village of Neuve Chapelle, and then move onto the Aubers Ridge, to the north of La Bassée. Although this ridge was not captured, the advance on 10 March had been a complete success with capture of the village, and Foch was generous in praising this progress in his report to Joffre at 6pm that evening. The British had made greater and more rapid progress than anyone (including the British themselves) had expected. On the same day, in his letter to his wife, he wrote that he hoped that Sir John would display as much obstinacy in action as he had done in negotiation.[39] However, subsequent days saw little further progress and Haig stopped the battle on 13 March. Foch reported to Joffre that lack of munitions was an important factor in the British inability to continue, thereby underlining, consciously or not, his own requirements.[40]

At this point, then, Foch had nothing to show for the months of waiting and of preparation of his Northern Army Group. His efforts to move northwards from Arras to capture Vimy Ridge had been stopped first by the weather, and then by the British refusal to cooperate. He had been reduced to diplomacy rather than fighting, which he claimed did not suit

[35] Note, Foch to Maud'huy, 9 March 1914, *AFGG* 2, annex 1126.
[36] Wilson diary, 8 March 1915.   [37] Haig diary, 28 February 1915.
[38] Maud'huy to Foch, 9 March 1915, *AFGG* 2, annex 1134.
[39] Letter, Foch to Joffre, 10 March 1915, *AFGG* 2, annex 1143; letter, Foch to Mme Foch, 10 March 1915, vol. 34.
[40] Letter, Foch to Joffre, 13 March 1915, *AFGG* 2, annex 1177.

him.[41] Although Foch had managed to carry out the diplomacy with the Allies, despite Kitchener's heavy-handed intervention, and had paid particular attention to maintaining Belgian morale, he had found it harder to strike the right note with his subordinate commanders. Too few of them, he wrote to his wife, knew how to, or dared to, command. Instead of being the shepherds, three-quarters of them were simply sheep following the flock.[42] Relations with Castelnau in Second Army were still delicate. Foch visited Castelnau's headquarters on his way to GQG so as not to give the impression of avoiding him, even though it seemed that Castelnau behaved that way to him.[43] Relations with Tenth Army were even worse. Its chief of staff, Colonel Pierre des Vallières, found Foch too authoritarian, taking away 'all liberty of action and even of thought' from the army commander. After what Vallières described as three months of quarrels, eventually on 2 April Maud'huy was moved to a command in eastern France. By the end, Foch had been refusing to see him. (Weygand, however, claims that Foch had no part in the decision to move him.)[44] On the other hand, Foch considered that Vallières (a 'brilliant student and teacher' at the Ecole Supérieure de Guerre) was a failure as a chief of staff.[45]

At corps level also, Foch was found to be too demanding. Pétain's chief of staff blamed Foch for the fact that Maud'huy was harassing XXXIII Corps. Foch was pressing Maud'huy, who was simply passing on the pressure so as to avoid accusations of inertia. Pétain also mistrusted Foch's promise that the necessary resources would be provided for the operation.[46] At divisional level, one of Pétain's generals, artillery officer General Fayolle in command of 70 DI, was even more critical. Fayolle blamed the higher command (unfairly) for insufficient munitions and munitions of the wrong sort. Maud'huy had no ideas at all, Fayolle wrote on 8 March, simply repeating 'attack' with Foch, or else coming under the influence of Joffre and saying 'wait, economise munitions and men'.[47]

One possible explanation for Foch's overbearing command style may lie in his frustration. He had been preparing his attack since December, but first the weather then the British imposed delays. Foch did not have the temperament to accept such hitches calmly. Furthermore,

[41] Letter, Foch to Mme Foch, 16 March 1915, vol. 34.
[42] Letters, Foch to Mme Foch, 8 February 1915, vol. 34, 7 April 1915, vol. 35.
[43] Letter, Foch to Mme Foch, 13 February 1915, vol. 34.
[44] Vallières, *Au soleil*, 110; Weygand, *IV*, 217.
[45] Letter, Foch to Mme Foch, 24 February 1915, vol. 34.
[46] Serrigny, *Trente ans*, 11, 13 (entries for 28 and 30 November 1914).
[47] Fayolle, *CS*, 91 (entry for 8 March 1915).

confirmation of his son's death arrived around this time. His wife was in Orleans on 24 February, trying to find out where he was buried, and Foch wrote that he was consoled by the thought that Germain had been buried on French soil by French hands. All that he and his wife could do for their son was, after the war ended, to kneel by his grave.[48]

Hence it had been a frustrating few months since the action on the Yser and at Ypres. Nonetheless planning had continued, and at least the delay meant that the next Artois battle could take place in better weather. On 19 March Foch went to GQG to discuss matters and found Joffre still optimistic about winning a decisive victory on the principal front, that is in France. Despite 43,000 casualties in his Champagne offensive (for the liberation of three square kilometres of ground), Joffre had told Millerand on 17 March that the attack had succeeded in keeping German troops in France, thereby easing the Russian front; that the British success at Neuve Chapelle was due to the enemy's surprise at the contrast with previous British inertia; that British reinforcements were arriving; that the supply of munitions was improving; that German losses had been huge; and that French morale was high. Foch too wanted to carry out his Arras operation because the British and Champagne attacks had run out of steam.[49]

In a note for GQG Foch set out his ideas. Since manoeuvre was impossible, a general attack had to be undertaken along the whole front, with the decisive central attack aimed at a portion of the front where the terrain prevented the enemy from creating another fortified line. A wide front of attack solved the problem of vulnerable flanks, and fixed the enemy in place. A strong and careful artillery preparation would facilitate the exploitation of any success. The 'general' attack could be undertaken with a lesser density of troops, whereas the troops undertaking the 'decisive' attack must have trench mortars, bombs and so on. He argued that the 'decisive' action should take place north of Arras, aiming at the heights on Vimy Ridge, to be carried out by Tenth Army augmented by more infantry and more heavy guns. This should be supported by the 'general' action undertaken further north by the Belgian Army and two British armies, and on the right by the other French armies (Second, Sixth, Fifth, Fourth and Third), even though they would all have been stripped of some of their resources to strengthen Tenth Army. As for timing, that depended on the supply of munitions, the supply of the new 58mm trench mortars and bombs, and on reaching agreement with the Allies.[50] On 24 March Foch supplied his detailed proposal, with requirements in guns

---

[48] Letter, Foch to Mme Foch, 1 March 1915, vol. 34.
[49] Foch, Carnets, 19 and 14 March 1915, fos. 64, 62.
[50] Note du Général Foch, fin mars 1915, *AFGG* 3, annex 24.

and munitions.[51] The length and level of detail reveal that the plan to capture the ridge had been long in the making.

At a meeting with Joffre on 29 March attended by the British and French War Ministers, Sir John agreed to relieve Foch's IX and XX Corps in the Ypres salient for the operation. Kitchener promised two territorial divisions to enable Sir John to complete the relief by 20 April, in time for the offensive, which was set for 1 May.[52] These promises eased greatly the Foch–Sir John relationship, because the huge amount of bad will that had been generated between Joffre and Sir John over reinforcements now worked to Foch's advantage. Foch believed that he had gained Sir John's confidence, helped by the close working relationship with Wilson. After a meeting with him on 5 April, Foch wrote to his wife that Sir John had told him that in the dark days of last November he had always been pleased to see Foch. Now Foch was trying to make up for what he called Joffre's 'clumsy' and 'pointless' barbs in his dealings with the BEF's commander, by putting 'more oil in the works'.[53]

Now the enemy intervened. Falkenhayn had been forced to send troops to the east, where the Austrians especially were in considerable difficulties, and this gave the Allies numerical superiority in the west. However, the Germans had not remained inactive: new formations were created (*Eleventh Army* in March); new defensive measures (second defensive line on reverse slopes; stronger front line); and new weapons. Since only the *Fourth Army* commander was prepared to test one of those new weapons, the gas shells, this meant that it was around Ypres once again that the action would take place.

By 20 April the British relief of the two French corps was completed, as promised, and the units assembled behind Tenth Army. Meanwhile, on the northern face of the Ypres salient, the Germans of *XV Corps* had been waiting a long time for the wind to stop blowing in from the sea towards them. On 22 April, a beautiful spring day, the wind finally favoured the Germans, and at 5pm chlorine gas was released from cylinders which had been dug in as long ago as 11 March. The six weeks that the Germans had been obliged to wait proves the gas weapon's lack of utility from their point of view. Since the prevailing winds in northern Europe blow from the west, the British and French would always have a huge advantage if they chose to copy the Germans and develop such a weapon themselves.

[51] Projet d'attaque dans la région au nord d'Arras, 24 March 1915, ibid., annex 20.
[52] Extrait de procès-verbal . . ., 30 March 1915, sent to Foch for information, ibid., annex 23; Wilson diary, 29 March 1915.
[53] Letter, Foch to Mme Foch, 5 April 1915, vol. 35.

The long wait had given the Germans an enormous advantage, however, in that they faced Allied troops of three nationalities. Although the Belgians knew the area, the French troops had been reduced by the departure of two corps for the planned Artois offensive and were under the command of the newly arrived General Putz. The British segment of the front was held by the newly formed V Corps, and consisted of three recent divisions, the Canadian and 27 and 28 Divisions. Consequently the Germans faced a thin screen of recently arrived troops, under three national commands, whose headquarters were busy putting the final touches to a large offensive further south in Artois, due to begin just over a week later. What is more, the intelligence reports that something involving gas was being prepared had been discounted as lacking credibility.[54]

The gas drifted over the French troops of 45 DI, who fell back in disarray. A gap of 3.5 kilometres was created, due north of Ypres, opening the way into the city. Fortunately, the Germans did not press their advantage. There were no reserves at hand, and they had no desire to walk through their own gas. In any case, the gas had been tried as an experiment, to cover the removal of troops to the eastern front, and there was no plan to turn the temporary advantage into a large breakthrough. Nonetheless, despite the lack of an exploitation plan, a hole in the Allied line north of Ypres might give the Germans the opportunity to push on to the coast – which had been their aim in October.

At midnight Foch sent a message to General Putz that his troops should hang on to the points they occupied and prepare a counter-offensive, but the French counter-attacks on 23 April failed. Foch saw Putz that same afternoon, and fresh orders for counter-attacks were issued for the next day, for he was confident when he wrote to Joffre that evening that there were sufficient resources in the salient to re-take all the ground that had been lost. The agreement between the Allied armies was 'perfect and very active', he concluded.[55] Plans for the 24th were forestalled by yet another release of gas, and the Germans got across the Ypres canal. So Foch brought another division from Artois (using buses and trains, it was due to arrive on 25 April), and warned yet another to be ready to move. Once again, when he wrote to Joffre on the evening of 24 April, he was optimistic that the British had enough reserves of both infantry and cavalry to recapture the further ground lost that day. He had seen Sir John, who was 'in a good frame of mind'.[56]

[54] Belgian Army intelligence report 247, 16 April 1915, *AFGG* 2, annex 1392; Lepick, *Grande Guerre chimique*, 75–6; Edmonds *et al.*, *OH 1915*, 1: 163–4.
[55] Letter, Foch to Joffre, 23 April 1916, *AFGG* 2, annex 1422.
[56] Letter, Foch to Joffre, 24 April 1915, ibid., annex 1434.

Whatever his 'frame of mind', the next day Sir John was 'furious with Foch & Joffre & all Frenchmen'. He even threatened 'to clear out of France bag & baggage & go elsewhere'. Fortunately Wilson and Foch remained on good terms, for Sir John was so angry that he wanted to withdraw to a shorter line within the salient. Foch was not downcast by this setback. 'Whilst telephoning to Putz', Wilson wrote in his diary, 'Foch wore my cap & looked so funny & made me listen to Putz in the other Receiver.'[57]

Given the lack of progress in retaking the lost ground, Sir John went to Cassel on 28 April and stated that he wished to conserve his troops for the Artois operation, not use them up round Ypres. Foch pointed out that a withdrawal to a shorter line would not make the British line any safer, for German guns would then be installed on the hills to the northeast and east of Ypres, making the British position even more precarious. Certainly the Artois battle was the important affair, but it was not good tactics to resign oneself to losing one battle so as to be able to win the next one. Sir John agreed to wait twenty-four hours, until the evening of the 29th, and the arrival of some French heavy artillery, and Foch requested British support for the French attempt to re-capture the Langemarck region. Foch informed Joffre that he hoped to persuade Sir John to keep his troops in place, even if the Langemarck operation achieved little, until 6 or 8 May, when the postponed Artois campaign was due to start. Foch explained also that he had painted his assessment of the consequences of the proposed British withdrawal in darker terms than he felt to be the case because he believed that the enemy's only advantage was the gas weapon.[58] However, Sir John was not mollified. That same evening Wilson recorded 'one of the worst explosions ag[ains]t the French I ever heard. That he (Sir J.) had been infamously treated, that neither Joffre nor Foch knew a thing about soldiering, that he had given orders to Plumer to retire tomorrow night etc. Warned Foch by wire what would happen tomorrow.'[59] If Foch thought he had learned how to deal with Sir John, he had miscalculated this time.

On 29 April Putz put off the planned action until the following day, on the reasonable grounds that he had not been able to get his new guns registered because transporting them from Second Army had put the aiming mechanisms out of true. Sir John, however, had clearly changed

[57] Wilson diary, 25 April 1915.
[58] Résumé de la conversation du 28 avril 1915, à 11h., entre le général Foch et le maréchal French; letter, Foch to Joffre, 28 April 1915, Note pour le maréchal French, 28 April 1915: all in *AFGG* 2, annexes 1465–7.
[59] Wilson diary, 28 April 1915.

his mind yet again because he agreed to delay his retirement and support the French attack on the morrow. The danger of a possible enemy break-through to the coast was emphasised by German shelling of Dunkirk. Heavy shells had fallen on the town the previous day, and on the 29th a further twenty shells fired from a 380mm or 420mm gun killed thirty, wounded seventy and caused considerable damage.[60]

On 30 April fog delayed the action, but at last the French managed to make some progress. Foch saw Wilson in St Omer in the morning and Sir John twice at his advanced headquarters in Hazebrouck. Sir John claimed that the French troops had 'broken' because there were too few of them (something that he claimed to have warned Foch about 'constantly'). He repeated his threat that if no progress were made, he would begin the retirement that night. However, in light of the advances achieved, Sir John agreed that sufficient progress had been made to hang on for another day.[61]

After more delays, more threats from Sir John and more persuasion from Foch, finally Sir John ordered the retirement to the already con-structed line, thus reducing the salient by 4 May to a semi-circle with a three-mile radius around the town of Ypres. Finally, too, Foch accepted that further attempts to recapture the ground on the eastern side of the canal towards Langemarck would cost more resources than ought to be devoted to it, and so he would remain satisfied with having ejected the enemy from the western side of the canal. Foch and Sir John agreed that now they had to concentrate on the Artois attack. Weather permitting, Tenth Army would begin their artillery preparation on 3 May, with the infantry attack going in on the 7th, while the British continuation of the Neuve Chapelle operation would begin on the 8th.

German gas attacks continued in the Ypres salient against the French until 17 May and against the British until the 25th. The German interruption to the preparations for Second Artois had cost them almost 35,000 casualties; but the British (including the newly arrived Canadians) had lost nearly 60,000 and the French had well over 40,000 killed on all fronts in April. The number of those casualties attributable to the gas is, however, difficult to calculate. Recent research puts the British and French mortality rate at between 800 and 1400, for between 2000 and 3000 more or less seriously gassed.[62]

Foch has been much criticised by British historians for his handling of the events that became known as Second Ypres. This is because the task of

[60] Letters, Foch to Joffre, and Cdt Dufieux [liaison officer between GQG and Foch] to Joffre, 29 April 1915, ibid., annexes 1478, 1479; Ronarc'h, Souvenirs, 272.
[61] Wilson diary, 30 April 1915.
[62] Edmonds, et al., OH 1915 1: 355–9; Guinard, Devos and Nicot, Inventaire: Introduction, graph p. 212; Lepick, Grande Guerre chimique, 80–1; Cook, No Place to Run, 31–3.

restoring the line fell mainly on the BEF, in particular the Canadians. These criticisms focus on three factors: Foch's spirit of the offensive, which led him to expect too much from too few troops; his assumption that issuing orders meant that they were carried out ('his illusions' were 'of undiluted harm'); finally, his malign influence on Sir John, who was 'beguiled by Foch's optimism'.[63]

In his defence it may be said that the sector was considered British. The British official history devotes most of one volume to the Second Battle of Ypres; the President of the French Republic hardly mentions it. The sixteen British divisions in the salient after completing the relief of Tenth Army units faced eleven and a half German divisions. Since the whole BEF held some thirty miles or so of front, Foch might be forgiven for believing that Sir John had enough troops to cope with the emergency. In any case, Foch did return units to Ypres immediately, one division arriving on 23 April and two more two days later. Moreover, he had the wider picture to consider, namely the need to support the Russians and to encourage the newly joined Italians, as well as continuing preparations for Artois and dealing with a threat to Dunkirk from the German super-heavy gun.

As for his 'illusions', Foch was fully aware of what was happening. He received reports every evening and his liaison officers pointed out the poor artillery/infantry coordination. He made frequent visits to talk to Sir John and saw Wilson each evening. What was needed was more guns, not more troops to add to the intermingled confusion in the salient. Foch also reacted very quickly to the gas threat. Primitive gas masks were soon provided following advice from the Ministry of Public Works about the sort of protection miners used, and on 23 April Foch called to his head-quarters the head of the Paris municipal laboratory, a respected chemist, to prepare a report on what gases the Germans were using.[64]

Certainly Foch attempted to get Sir John to give up his plan to withdraw to a shorter front in the salient by painting the consequences of such a withdrawal blacker than he believed to be the case. Yet Sir John, as an independent commander-in-chief, out-ranked Foch and should have been capable of making up his own mind, however mercurial. Foch's insistence on re-taking Langemarck instead of pulling back was proved correct by subsequent events. A reduced salient made conditions even more crowded, and the enemy was encouraged to make yet more attacks against the new British lines. In the words of the British official history, 'some of the most desperate fighting that ever took place in the Salient'

---

[63] Liddell Hart, *Foch*, 182, 177.   [64] Lepick, *Grande Guerre chimique*, 105–6.

took place *after* the withdrawal to the shorter line. It was neither illusions nor malign influence on Foch's part that caused the British casualties, but the 'use of gas with a favourable wind proved the determining factor', despite the 'gallant behaviour of the infantry'.[65]

The planning for the Artois operation had taught Foch some hard lessons as he attempted to define his new role of army group commander. Despite the need to take advantage of Allied numerical superiority in France, to support the Russians and to encourage the Italians (who would declare war on Austria-Hungary on 24 May), he could not get his battle started. First of all the weather held up preparations, then the politicians delayed reinforcements because they were thinking about opening other fronts. Next Sir John refused to cooperate and achieved only a minor success when he went it alone at Neuve Chapelle. Finally the enemy intervened round Ypres and threw all the arrangements into disarray once more. It was not until 9 May that the delayed Second Battle of Artois got under way.

The biggest problem by far was the coordination of operations with the British. Foch did not have enough guns or men to achieve his aim solely with French resources. He needed the British to cover his northern flank and extend the operational front, but Sir John's outbursts and changes of mind made cooperation very difficult. Perhaps for that reason, Foch made a particular point of maintaining good relations with Haig who, as First Army commander, would be more closely involved. On 19 April he went with Weygand to Haig's headquarters and, according to Haig's account, Foch questioned him 'closely' about the Neuve Chapelle attack. Joffre had told all French corps commanders, he said, to study the British methods. Haig was clearly flattered by these complimentary words from the author of *Des principes de la guerre*, France's 'most capable general'. Foch, too, was pleased with the visit, telling his wife that he had had a 'very simple, very cordial, very comfortable' reception, and that they had been able to agree all they needed 'without difficulty, with enthusiasm and confidence'.[66] There was probably a degree of deliberate flattery in Foch's words; nevertheless at the time of Neuve Chapelle he had praised Haig's success generously to Joffre. Whether the visit would prove of benefit as Second Artois began on 9 May remained to be seen.

Because the 1915 class of recruits was now incorporated, Joffre was able to allocate six corps to the Artois operation (including IX Corps, which returned from Flanders), and to send a further two divisions once the battle had started. Artillery resources were still less than ideal, but

---

[65] Edmonds, *et al.*, *OH, 1915*, 1: 310, 306.
[66] Haig diary, 19 April 1915; letter, Foch to Mme Foch, 19 April 1915, vol. 35.

nevertheless Foch had considerably more than 700 field guns (most of them 75s), and 293 heavies plus some super-heavies. In addition Foch had requested mortars for the destructive force of their plunging fire, and he received ten (of which six were mounted on trucks). Guns were registered between 3 and 5 May, and Foch settled on 7 May for the infantry attack, but bad weather forced a further two days' delay. It was thus on 9 May that the British and French began their attacks. General Maistre's XXI Corps attacked the northern strongpoint of Notre Dame de Lorette, whilst General Balfourier's XX Corps attacked the southern one at Neuville St Waast.

Most progress was made in the centre by Pétain's XXXIII Corps. His Moroccan Division reached the crest of Vimy Ridge, an advance of four kilometres. Swiss novelist and Foreign Legion volunteer, Blaise Cendrars, was part of that Moroccan Division. One of his squad was an excellent cook and had been casseroling the cats in the villages that they had been attacking. The cook, who fired the only shot that Cendrars and his companions fired on their way to the crest of Vimy Ridge, killed a fine hare. As they cleared the Bavarian trenches on the crest, they discovered a stock of Munich beer, and rolled out three barrels to be collected later to drink with the jugged hare.[67] However, because the flanking strongpoints had not been captured, it proved impossible to remain in such a precarious position, enfiladed by enemy fire, and the division had to pull back. The legionnaires had been so far ahead that they had been fired on by the French as well as the enemy. The reserves that might have supported or even enlarged the deep but narrow breach in the enemy's front were seven kilometres away from the front; the troops in army reserve were even further back.

The British had made no headway at all, after an artillery barrage of only forty minutes, compared to Tenth Army's four-hour bombardment. The lesson of the first day of Second Artois appeared to be that a four-hour barrage was better than a forty-minute one, and that it was a mistake to hold the reserves too far back. (The latter ignored the fact that a narrow breach was unlikely to lead to a major breakthrough, however many reserves were pushed up behind.) Despite very heavy casualties, XXXIII Corps had managed to capture some enemy guns and to take 1000 prisoners. Joffre was delighted.

Subsequent days did not fulfil the promise of the first. All the attacks made on 10 May failed; the Germans had recovered very quickly and brought up reinforcements. Nevertheless, the French continued to attack and made some small gains around the chapel on Lorette hill and in

---

[67] Cendrars, *La Main Coupée*, 80–9.

Neuville. They also continued to take very heavy casualties, and they were running out of shells as the German reinforcements arrived. French guns were wearing out as well because poor quality control over the new supplies of shells had led to gun barrels bursting. Twenty-four of the 75s of XXXIII Corps, for example, had been put out of service in this way, compared to a mere four that the Germans had knocked out.[68] Consequently Foch told d'Urbal to reduce shell consumption in those corps that had made little progress, so as to concentrate the meagre supplies on the two successful corps.[69] Pétain, however, was beginning to look at a series of operations to deal with the enemy strongpoints that were holding them up. His defender, Professor Pedroncini, described this as realism, not the pessimism with which Pétain is usually charged, claiming that it would be a long time before d'Urbal and Foch would accept this method of proceeding.[70] Pétain's suggestion was to concentrate first of all on the left (Souchez, the left of the Vimy Ridge position), next on Neuville on the right, and only after these localities were taken would he return to the crest of the ridge that his troops had reached on the opening day of the battle.[71] Since d'Urbal accepted Pétain's proposal, and Foch approved d'Urbal's decision, Pedroncini is being less than fair in claiming that it would be a long time before Foch would accept such a proceeding.[72]

There was more arguing with Sir John over British reliefs to support the French who now faced German reinforcements. Haig's First Army had achieved little on the French left, and was suffering a shortage of munitions, compounded by the War Office decision to send shells to the Dardanelles. However, Wilson recorded that Foch took the bad news 'amazingly well' when he learned that one division was the total relief. Foch wrote to his wife that evening that he was finding the negotiations most interesting, and he compared himself to a cart horse that had to get firmly between the shafts and pull hard to get the cart moving.[73]

Joffre and Foch were determined to continue the battle, but it proved impossible to reduce the German strongpoints and to capture a jumping-off point for the assault on the ridge. So Foch declared that, since surprise was now no longer possible, Tenth Army must return to the careful preparation that had preceded the successful events of the first day of the offensive. Hence time was needed to bring up artillery, make reconnaissances and so

---

[68] Pedroncini, *Pétain, soldat*, 106, note 2.
[69] Note pour Monsieur le général commandant la Xe Armée, 11 May 1915, *AFGG* 3, annex 191.
[70] Pedroncini, *Pétain, soldat*, 104, note 1.
[71] Pétain to d'Urbal, 11 May 1915, *AFGG* 3, annex 200.
[72] D'Urbal to Foch, and Foch to d'Urbal, 12 May 1915, *AFGG* 3, annexes 211, 203.
[73] Wilson diary, 12 May 1915; letter, Foch to Mme Foch, 12 May 1915, vol. 35.

on. A 'base de départ' or jumping-off line, had to be created, and clearly such a line could not be created until the flanking strongpoints had been destroyed. He estimated that eight to ten days were required to complete these preparations. During that time the troops who would be doing most of the attacking should be rested and their morale restored by being informed that the successful method of 9 May was to be used once again.[74]

The new general attack was postponed repeatedly but, instead of the troops being rested in the interval, they had to face continual German counter-attacks while mopping up Neuville. This progressed house-to-house, was complete only on 9 June, and to take and to hold cost 3500 casualties in General Mangin's 5 DI alone. On the other hand, about 1000 German corpses littered the houses and communication trenches; a dozen machineguns, three 77mm guns and lots of ammunition had been captured.[75] The constant pressure from high command (Joffre on Foch, Foch on d'Urbal, d'Urbal on his corps commanders) was resented. Fayolle (commanding 70 DI in Pétain's corps) claimed that Foch did not listen and that he demanded attacks before the attackers were ready. Captain E. L. Spears (liaison officer between the British and Tenth Army) noted in his diary that Foch was 'awful' for always nagging. He was 'always yelling', but, since Spears added that in response d'Urbal only smiled, it was perhaps the case that Foch's bark was recognised to be worse than his bite.[76]

During this period of enforced delays, the arguments continued. Foch had to cope with the enemy, still making gas attacks in Flanders; with Haig, delayed by boggy ground, lack of munitions and new German defences; with Sir John, who demanded French artillery in return for relieving French units; and with Kitchener, threatening to refuse permission for his New Armies to be 'wasted' in futile operations. Finally Kitchener wired that he was not sending the remaining five divisions of the First Army because of the BEF's failure to break the line, the danger of invasion, and the lack of ammunition. Wilson called Kitchener both a fool and a knave, and Joffre and Foch claimed that Kitchener was 'mad'.[77] Foch commented sarcastically to Wilson, 'what a splendid Army which has everything except the means of attack'.[78]

---

[74] Colonel des Vallières, [untitled account of the conversation with Foch], 15 May 1915, *AFGG* 3, annex 247.

[75] *AFGG* 3, 69; Tenth Army report on events of 10 May and night 10/11 May 1915, *AFGG* 3, annex 564.

[76] Fayolle, *CS*, 106–7 (entry for 21 May 1915); Spears diary, 23 and 28 May 1915, 1/2, LHCMA.

[77] Wilson diary, 17 May 1915.

[78] Secret letter, Foch to Joffre, 29 May 1915, *AFGG* 3, annex 399; Wilson diary, 30 May 1915.

Yet the lack of munitions did not prevent Foch from asking Sir John to help in the forthcoming re-launch of operations. He wanted the British to attack along the Loos–La Bassée line. Sir John replied that he could not do that, even if he had the ammunition. In fact, he had already told Haig, who would have to carry out the operation, that he had no intention of embarking on an attack against the 'shell trap' of Loos unless the French captured Vimy Ridge first. Nonetheless he offered to attack 'in the Loos direction' on 6 or 7 June 'if Foch had made a hole'. Although Foch had indicated that he expected to begin his attack on 3 June (the date being postponed later), he thanked Sir John for his cooperation. Small wonder that the principal virtue that he had been cultivating since the war began, he wrote to his wife, was patience.[79] That patience, however, was beginning to wear a little thin, although he remained optimistic, believing that the Allies had caged up the enemy. All that was required to smash the cage was time, munitions and men.[80]

With all his corps commanders insisting that they could not complete preparations by the early date that Foch wanted (despite the constant postponements), Joffre advised that the general attack should not begin until all were ready. Haste should not compromise the chance of success.[81] Finally, after the completion of the capture of Neuville and the strongpoint of the 'Labyrinth' to its south, the date was fixed for 15 June, but delayed yet again by bad weather to the following day. The one advantage to be derived from the repeated postponements was that reinforcements had been brought in. On 16 June d'Urbal had twenty-three infantry divisions (three of which were territorials) and three cavalry divisions under his direct control. In addition, all the mortars that could be taken from the other armies had been sent to Tenth Army because it had been recognised that the only way to deal with lethal machineguns protected by casemates was to use the plunging fire of the new 58mm mortars. Although it had proved impossible to replace all the damaged 75s, Tenth Army had at its disposition on 15 June 799 field guns and 355 heavies. Six groups of mobile guns formed an army reserve; these had been taken from the individual corps and placed under a single command as an army reserve ready to intervene in support of any breakthrough. Munitions were so plentiful that Tenth Army could count on firing for several days at the intensity that had proved successful on 9 May, when the heavy artillery alone fired over 30,000 shells.[82]

---

[79] French diary, 28 May 1915, cited in French, *Life of Field-Marshal Sir John French*, 306; Wilson diary, 30 May 1915; letter, Foch to Mme Foch, 7 June 1915, vol. 35.

[80] Foch, Carnets, 2 June 1915, fos. 81–2.

[81] Telegram, Joffre to Foch, 30 May 1915, *AFGG* 3, annex 412.

[82] Ibid., 79, and annex 1125.

The artillery preparation had begun on 10 June and feint attacks were carried out with the aim of forcing the enemy to reveal the presence of his batteries. Surprise in the infantry attack was to be achieved by not making any alteration in the artillery fireplan immediately before it began. The intelligence report of 15 June showed that Tenth Army had a significant numerical superiority, since facing them were only a dozen German divisions in the front lines and in reserve.[83]

Once again, as on 9 May, the Moroccan Division made splendid progress when the infantry assault began after midday on 16 June, but then they found themselves in a pocket enfiladed by machineguns. The other corps made little or no progress. The British I Corps made no progress either. The bill for the capture of 600 German prisoners was 19,000 casualties. Nonetheless d'Urbal decided that the battle would continue all night and into the next day, which he was able to do because he had placed his reserves close at hand. The immediate lack of reserves had been judged to be the cause of the failure to follow up the first day's success on 9 May. These orders were overriden following a meeting between Joffre and Foch in the early morning of 17 June. Pressing the attack along the whole front would cost too many casualties, they decided. Consequently, follow-up pressure was to be applied only on the left of the front, where some progress had been made.[84] Despite all their efforts and a huge expenditure of shells, little progress was made that day, and again on the next day, when the same orders had been given once more. A further 10,000 men became casualties on those two days. During the evening of 18 June Foch and d'Urbal agreed that the operation would be suspended. Likewise Sir John ordered Haig to halt operations, but nevertheless he held out the prospect of re-grouping for a further offensive in which he would extend the French left so as to attack on as wide a front as possible.[85]

On 8 August Foch wrote a report for Joffre on Tenth Army's conduct of the Artois offensive.[86] The narrowness of the front was a factor in its failure. Foch had wished to extend the attack southwards to Arras, but had insufficient resources for this. The extension northwards was the responsibility of the British, but they had provided little help. Nevertheless the preparation had been very careful, surprise had been achieved, and the troops, full of *élan*, had gained success on the first day. The French had then required from 16 May until 9 June to carry out a series of small local actions in order to reach the jumping-off line for the

[83] Ibid., 91.   [84] GAN, JMO, 17 June 1915, ibid., annex 645.
[85] Letter (trans.), Sir John French to Joffre, [20] June 1915, ibid., annex 692.
[86] Foch to Joffre, 8 August 1915, ibid., annex 1125.

next 'general' attack. The June attack benefited from the lessons of the earlier venture, when the reserves had been held too far back. It was recognised that the *élan* of the first day of an attack could not be maintained, and the impossibility of achieving surprise once more was recognised by not firing the usual preparatory artillery barrage before the infantry attack went in. However, the enemy had brought up reinforcements very rapidly and, more importantly, had reinforced their heavy artillery. Consequently, the French no longer enjoyed in June the heavy artillery superiority that they had enjoyed in May. Despite the French having expended on 16 June more than double the volume of shells that they had fired on 9 May, the reinforced German artillery was now superior because its guns were all rapid-firing and because they had inexhaustible supplies of shells. It was enemy barrages of heavy artillery shells, kept up for hours at a time, that stopped the French advance. Despite the greatly increased resources allocated to Foch and his Tenth Army – resources which they had thought ample – they were still insufficient. Until the artillery situation improved, breakthrough was doubtful.

Foch remained optimistic, however. During Second Artois he had managed to keep up Sir John's spirits – the latter would call him a 'bottle of champagne' – and he had got to know Haig even better. After the battle he reiterated the 'cage' simile: the enemy could not get out of the cage, and now they had to finish off the beast by breaking that cage. Sooner or later the Allies would impose their will. In order to achieve this, they needed destructive power – yet more munitions.[87]

The picture was less rosy in other respects. As regards the British (still continuing their Dardanelles campaign), the renewed anti-Joffre agitation because of the repeated failures was unwelcome. Bertie informed the Foreign Office that Clemenceau and Doumer were pushing for Gallieni to succeed Millerand, and for Foch to succeed Joffre. The response was that this would be regarded 'with much dismay'.[88] Moreover, Asquith had been obliged to re-constitute his government as a coalition, and had gone over to France at the beginning of June on a tour of inspection. He had met Foch and Joffre in conference on 2 June. Although the optimism of the French generals had struck Asquith, the Prime Minister did not impress Foch – 'a drinker, it would appear'. Weygand called the conference a 'waste of time'.[89] Since the official British line stated that sending

---

[87] Letter, Foch to Mme Foch, 8 May 1915, vol. 35; Foch, Carnets, 21 June 1915, fo. 86.

[88] Bertie to Grey, 9 June 1915, and Lord Crewe [for Grey] to Bertie, 17 June 1915, FO 800/167/Fr/15/34 and 37.

[89] Letter, Asquith to Sylvia Henley, 2 June 1915, cited in Prete, 'Conflit stratégique', 30; Foch, Journées, 2 June 1915; Weygand, Carnets, 2 June 1915.

out more New Armies was pointless if they lacked munitions, Weygand's reaction is not surprising. Another cause for concern, had Foch known of it, was Asquith's recommendations on returning to London: there should be an immediate review of the BEF's defences and its line of retreat in case of disaster.[90] (A paper handed to Sir John on 6 July stated, however, that the BEF commander should not withdraw from joint operations with the French army, nor entertain the idea of a retreat to the Channel ports.)[91]

Hankey had accompanied Asquith on the trip to France, and found in Foch the 'gasconading blagueur' that Haig had described to him.[92] The bubbly optimism that worked with Sir John was apparently less attractive to the Scotsman. It is interesting that Haig's comment uses French terminology (a Gascon is reputed to be boastful, just as Scotsmen have the reputation for meanness). Perhaps he was simply repeating what French liaison officers had said to him, and the effect of Foch's earlier judicious flattery had worn off.

Relations with other French generals continued to prove difficult. Pétain was furious over Foch's insistence on attacking. Foch and d'Urbal were mad, he claimed, for not caring about the degree of preparation.[93] The soldier–*député* Abel Ferry reported that the latest Artois offensive had earned for d'Urbal the title of 'assassin'.[94] Castelnau called Foch the 'enragé du Nord' [the madman of the north], and answered Foch's tiger-in-a-cage simile by pointing out how solid the cage was. The bars were covered with barbed wire, making it very difficult to wield a stick with which to beat the tiger. Indeed, in Russia the tiger was well on the way to breaking out of the cage.[95] Vallières still judged that Foch harassed Tenth Army, was too demanding and did not always take enough account of contingencies. Jacquand thought that Foch was too much of a 'swashbuckler' to be let loose on strategy at GQG. He believed that Foch's tenacity and high morale had been marvellous on the Marne, and he had probably saved France in Flanders, but perhaps he was now failing to consider organisational matters and to make adequate allowance for coalition politics.[96]

Fayolle was even more critical. Neither Foch nor d'Urbal took enough account of the state of the ground, he wrote as the June battle got bogged down. On 26 June, after the end of the battle, he had lunch with Foch at the latter's headquarters. He noted that Foch still wanted to capture Hill

[90] Asquith note, n.d. [following the visit to France], cited in George H. Cassar, *Asquith as War Leader* (London: Hambledon Press, 1994), 114.
[91] Untitled paper, 5 July 1915, handed by Kitchener to Sir John French on 6 July 1915, WO 32/5591.
[92] Hankey diary, 2 June 1915, HNKY 1/1.   [93] Fayolle, *CS*, 111 (entry for 13 June 1915).
[94] Ferry, *Carnets secrets*, 125 (Conseil des ministres, 4 July 1915).
[95] Gras, *Castelnau*, 230, 225.   [96] Jacquand memoirs, 4 and 24 June 1915, 1K/795/36.

140, the highest point on the ridge, and that he believed that more shells were required. In Fayolle's view, however, it was an 'illusion' that enough shells could be poured onto a sector to create an empty space through which to advance. For Fayolle, good observation was the key. Nevertheless, by the end of the meal, he had to admit that Foch had 'the energy of a devil', and that what he had achieved on the Yser had been very fine. Foch had not hesitated to play for the big stakes: 'Either perish, or save the State.'[97]

Criticism of both Foch and Joffre reached Poincaré. Abel Ferry had already criticised to him at the end of April the generals ('selfish old men' who were sacrificing thousands of lives),[98] and the two Army Commissions of the Senate and the Chamber of Deputies were just beginning to flex their parliamentary muscle and demand greater accountability from the military. The President wondered whether it had been Joffre's obstinacy or Foch's urging that had resulted in the failed and costly offensives in Artois. Corps commanders were complaining of operations conducted by 'theoreticians' or 'professors' who were ignorant of the conditions of combat.[99]

Thus the second attempt to capture Vimy Ridge had failed. The preparations had been dislocated by the German gas attack at Ypres; the promise of the first day on 9 May had not been fulfilled; and the British ally had proved a disappointment once again. The political repercussions were mixed. Nevertheless, Foch was still hopeful. He told his wife that, although currently the Germans had more munitions, the position would be reversed in a couple of months. Since the Allies had numerical superiority, there was every reason to hope. The war had been a war of armies during the Marne and Ypres battles; now it was a war of munitions; next it would be an economic war.[100]

---

[97] Fayolle, *CS*, 113, 116–17 (entries for 18 and 26 June 1915).
[98] Ferry, *Carnets secrets*, 101–5 (23 and 27 April 1915).
[99] Poincaré, Notes journalières, 3 and 18 June 1915, NAF 16030.
[100] Mme Foch diary, 4 July 1915.

Planning began again immediately for the next campaign, in which Foch's part would be the dispiritingly named Third Battle of Artois. Both Foch and Joffre suffered from the effects of their previous failures. Joffre's freedom was curbed by Poincaré and his ministers, who insisted on properly constituted army groups and regular meetings. It was curbed further by the parliament, whose two Army Commissions began to demand and to win greater control over the commander-in-chief's actions through inspections on the ground. Clemenceau became famous in 1918 for his visits to the front, but, because of the calls for greater accountability, he had already begun making such visits from October 1915 as President of the Senate's Army Commission. Foch's own freedom of action in Artois was curtailed by the opposing arguments aired in the army group commanders' meetings, and also by increasing difficulties with Sir John French. These difficulties were exacerbated by the reduced role that Wilson played during the latter half of 1915. In addition, the supply of munitions was still less than Foch recognised as necessary, and the enemy's new defensive methods placed even greater demands on that supply.

The summer weeks between the end of the May–June operations and the start of the autumn battle in Artois were filled with Franco-British negotiations over men and munitions, both being consumed in the eastern Mediterranean.[1] Foch was not included in the high-level discussions in which Kitchener agreed to communicate the timetable for the arrival of new British divisions in France. Nor did he attend either the first Anglo-French wartime conference in Calais (6 July 1915), or the following day's military conference of all the Allies at French GQG, or the Anglo-French ministerial discussions between the two new munitions ministers, David Lloyd George and Albert Thomas. This highlights Foch's anomalous position as Joffre's representative in the north dealing with the British

---

[1] For the details see Doughty, *PV*, 165–90.

CinC but not invited, because of his lower position in the military hierarchy, to attend such conferences.

Of course, the enemy had not remained passive whilst the British and French were meeting and discussing manpower and munitions. The Germans had continued their victorious offensive through Poland, capturing Warsaw on 4 August, Brest-Litovsk on 25–26 August, and reaching Vilna in the north on 19 September. Even the Austrians (with a stiffening of German units) managed a victory. After recapturing the Przemysl fortress at the beginning of June, they pushed on to Lemberg, which fell on 22 June. They managed also to hold the Italian offensives, albeit at the cost of large casualties. By year's end the eastern front line of the Central Powers ran from Cernowitz in the south, near the Romanian border, to Riga in the north, within striking distance of St Petersburg. The Russians had suffered two million casualties,[2] and the enemy's huge successes in the east would play an important part in the planning for the autumn campaign in France.

Neither had the Germans in France been idle during the advances in the east, for their ad hoc defences of 1914 were replaced by a more systematic defensive system. OHL ordered each army on the Western Front to construct a second line, several kilometres behind the first, and situated wherever possible on a reverse slope while still holding the crest line in front.[3] The Allies had seen this second line through aerial observation, but the artillery procedures of the time meant that they could not fire accurately on targets that the gunners could not see. The enemy had learned from the French and British attacks that it was too dangerous to pack the front lines with troops and so they emphasised the creation of a fortified zone with strongpoints and garrisons behind the line in order to protect the infantry from the effects of French artillery fire. When the French and British made such meagre gains in Artois in May and June, the validity of the new defensive doctrine seemed confirmed. Falkenhayn inspected the Western Front armies in June and was so confident that the lines could not be broken that he sent yet more units to the east. He also sent two officers to update and unify the artillery and infantry doctrines of all the western armies. Artillery procedures were improved by new observation and ranging techniques; and emphasis was placed on destroying attacking troops as they left their trenches. The only positive note for the French in all this – and that a small one – was that the German defences had been improved so much that Falkenhayn did not even believe that the French would, or indeed could, mount another attack that year.[4]

[2] Herwig, *First World War*, 142–5.   [3] Samuels, *Command or Control*, 164–6.
[4] Foley, *German Strategy*, 163–8.

The demands for parliamentary control of Joffre's actions by means of missions reporting to the parliament's Army Commissions were now unanswerable in light of the enormous casualties that the French were suffering. Poincaré too became involved. He visited Tenth Army in July and learned from the corps commanders that their men were worn out, and unable to dig shelters in the new positions they occupied in the face of superior German artillery. Fayolle, now promoted to command XXXIII Corps, visited a neighbouring corps on 7 July and found its commander wearied by all the pointless deaths for which he felt responsible.[5] So increasing political pressure, a reaction to the enormous casualty bill, had an impact on the planning for the autumn campaign.

This pressure became manifest on 23 June, when Poincaré and the Premier (Viviani) and War Minister (Millerand) attended the first meeting of Joffre and his newly constituted army group commanders. By this means, Poincaré and the government hoped to establish better liaison with the military leaders. On 13 June Joffre had created formally three army groups to replace the two 'provisional' groups he had designated in January.[6] The centre group was to be commanded by Castelnau; Dubail already commanded the eastern group. Foch remained Joffre's 'adjoint' in command of the northern group, retaining his task of coordination with the British and Belgians.

Viviani began by recounting the 'emotion' in the parliament and in the country about the lack of any success since the Marne. Poincaré intervened to suggest that regular meetings to exchange views might dampen some of the criticisms. Although Castelnau agreed, Foch stated (somewhat tactlessly) that such meetings were 'useless', and Dubail did not seem to have an opinion one way or the other. Joffre was opposed, of course, but gave in so long as the meetings were not regular and so long as he could choose the date. As for operations, Joffre explained that the Tenth Army attacks would die down gradually and that a breakthrough was no longer possible. Foch, on the other hand, did not even want to predict that they would reach the crest of Vimy Ridge. He admitted that all the corps that had taken part in the attacks were badly in need of a rest, but claimed that two weeks would be enough for that purpose. All complained about the need for better coordination with the British, and Joffre condemned Kitchener's wish to remain on the defensive, stating that Kitchener did not have to deal with invaded provinces.[7]

---

[5] Poincaré, *AS*, 6: 335–7 (entry for 22 July 1915); Fayolle, *CS*, 114, 120 (entry for 7 July 1915).

[6] Ordre général no 39, 13 June 1915, *AFGG* 3, annex 581.

[7] Long account in Poincaré, *AS*, 278–83 (entry for 23 June 1915); see also Gras, *Castelnau*, 227–30. Oddly, Foch makes no mention.

Castelnau recounted how, during the meeting, Foch had repeated his favourite comparison, namely the tiger shut up in his cage. In response to Foch's claim that in Artois they would slash the tiger's claws on the bars of the cage and put an arm through the bars from time to time to attack him with a knife, Castelnau replied that the tiger had set up his cage in France, that the wire on the cage prevented the French from getting an arm through the bars, and that allegories are never exact. The 'stormy' meeting broke up without reaching a decision about future operations, according to Castelnau.[8] Foch's facile analogy and patent impatience with the meeting indicate that he was happier planning and conducting battles than he was sitting around a table.

GQG staff were still thinking through the results of Second Artois. Despite the original intention to make the main autumn offensive in the north, now General Pellé (head of operations) questioned whether the failure to capture the ridge did not compel a re-think. Pétain did not want a repeat performance because of the strength of the enemy defences. If operations around Arras could keep the enemy's attention fixed in the north, then making the principal attack in the centre (in Champagne) would have the added benefit of surprise.[9] Joffre asked Foch to let him know his views. Not surprisingly, Foch wished to retain the principal operation. In his view there was no obvious objective in Champagne, whereas the capture of Vimy Ridge would cause great problems for the enemy. Foch was arguing, therefore, for the capture of a specific objective whose loss would cause difficulties for the enemy, rather than a simple breakthrough for its own sake.[10] His colleagues were not convinced and following another army group commanders' meeting on 8 July Joffre decided on a double 'action d'ensemble' for the next offensive, allocating the greater resources to Champagne rather than to Foch's Artois operation (see Map 9).[11]

Next, after losing the argument over the focus of the principal attack, Foch had to gain Sir John French's assent to assist the Artois portion of the double offensive by extending its northern flank and taking over more of the front in order to release French troops. Joffre instructed Foch to attack two days before the main Champagne offensive so as to 'rupture' the enemy's front by conquering 'at least the ridge at points 119 and 140'.[12]

---

[8] Jacquand memoirs, 24 June 1915, fos. 587–8, 1K/795/36.
[9] Note sur la situation à la date du 24 juin et sur la préparation de l'offensive générale, 25 June 1915, *AFGG* 3, annex 751.
[10] Letter, Foch to Joffre, 1 July 1915, and Note, n.d. [1 July 1915], ibid., annexes 818, 819.
[11] Castelnau to Joffre, 7 July 1915, Instruction générale, personnelle et secrète, pour les généraux commandant les groupes d'armées, 12 July 1915, both in ibid., annexes 866, 894.
[12] Joffre, Instruction to Foch, 12 July 1915, *AFGG* 3, annex 896.

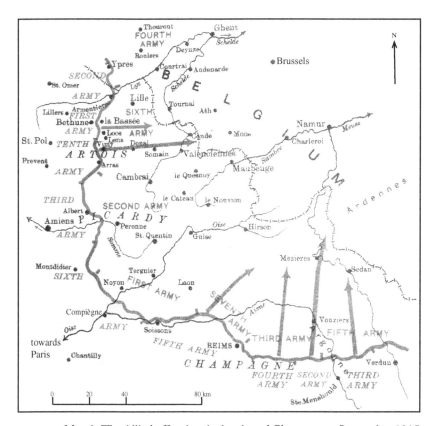

Map 9 The Allied offensives in Artois and Champagne, September 1915

Yet Joffre allocated fewer infantry and not many more heavy resources for this autumn repetition of what had failed in May. Moreover, Foch lost his Second Army, now commanded by Pétain, to Castelnau's Centre Army Group in Champagne. It was Pétain's troops who had gained the greatest success in May. So British help was vital.

Although the arrival of Kitchener's divisions enabled the constitution of a new Third Army which went into line on Tenth Army's right on 18 July, thereby encasing Tenth Army between Generals Haig and Monro, Third Army's commander, Sir John began to waver in his support. After learning that Foch's part of the autumn campaign was not to be the principal action, Sir John had inspected the terrain over which he had been asked to extend the front of attack northwards. From the Notre Dame de

Lorette heights he could see clearly the twenty or so kilometres north-wards towards Loos, Hulluch and La Bassée. On 11 July he had found the terrain promising, offering 'excellent "observation" of fire and ... many advantages to an attacker'. By 20 July, however, the terrain had become 'difficult', and he warned Joffre that he could do little more than a 'strong "holding" attack' because of his lack of munitions.[13] Foch's task of coordination became very difficult with these changes of mind, even more so because both Haig and Robertson were against an attack at Loos.[14] After judging on 14 June that an attack there was 'quite practical', Haig discovered a week later that the coal mines and miners' houses that filled the area would make such an attack 'very difficult'. Finally, on 23 July, he decided that a large-scale operation was impossible.[15] His IV Corps commander, Henry Rawlinson, who was next to the French and would have the largest role to play, was pessimistic. He knew that the German second and third lines had been strengthened, but accepted the need to extend the French front, although 'we shall have a hard time of it'.[16] In addition, General George Macdonogh (head of intelligence at GHQ) had identified eighteen new German corps, of which eleven or twelve were destined for the west.[17] The operation that Sir John had agreed to support was looking considerably more hazardous than it did when he gave that agreement. He could not afford another fiasco, nor use another 'shells scandal' to cover up failure, and he knew that moves were under way to have him removed. Haig, Robertson and Rawlinson were all in communication with King George V, and the King had concluded as early as 1 July 1915 that 'it would be better for all concerned if the CinC were changed'.[18] Clearly Sir John needed a success if he was to retain his job.

During the final days of July, in letters and in face-to-face meetings, Foch argued his case and Sir John vacillated, finally writing to Joffre that he would do as the French wished. Sir John thus moved the responsibility from his own to Joffre's shoulders. A similar letter went also to Foch.[19] Clive deduced from the two letters and from his discussions with Robertson that the British did not expect any great French success, and

[13] French diary, 12, 20 July 1915, in French, *Life of Field-Marshal Sir John French*, 312, 313.
[14] Clive diary, 28 July 1915, CAB 45/201.
[15] Prior and Wilson, *CWF*, 102–3.   [16] Rawlinson diary, 10 August 1915, RWLN 1/3.
[17] Wilson diary, 14 July 1915.
[18] King George V's diary, cited in Jeffery, *Wilson*, 150; see also Holmes, *Little Field-Marshal*, 298–9.
[19] Sir John French to Joffre, 29 July 1915, *AFGG* 3, annex 1040; Sir John French to Foch, 29 July 1915, WO 158/26. See the account of Sir John's havering in Holmes, *Little Field-Marshal*, 296–7.

so Sir John 'was not prepared to take the responsibility' for an attack decided upon 'for the general good'.[20]

The frustrating 'chopping and changing' (Robertson's words) continued into August. Foch complained that Sir John believed that other parts of the line offered better tactical advantages, yet the latter's suggestions – Aubers Ridge, Messines, Wytschaete – aimed simply to obtain for the BEF a better area in which to pass the winter. The only method, in Foch's view, was for the two armies to combine to attack together in the same or in converging directions so as to dominate the Douai plain. It would be a difficult task against enemy lines that had been strengthened, and would require powerful artillery and quantities of munitions. Nonetheless it was possible to achieve the precise objective, given the resources, but only if the British army joined in fully. Any other way of proceeding simply indicated that the intention was to undertake a 'restricted offensive'.[21]

After the disappointment of his offensive being reduced to second place behind that in Champagne, now it seemed to Foch that the British resolve was crumbling. He wrote in frustration in his notebook: 'The Tenth Army attack, reduced from twenty-two to twelve divisions before the same objective, doubtless reinforced, seems destined to be powerless, profitless. It has an objective; it lacks resources.' The Centre Army Group's attack, on the other hand, 'forty divisions strong, lacking a definite objective ("percer" is not one), does not appear to offer an appreciable tactical result, takes the greater part of our resources. It lacks an aim. It will be pure loss.'[22]

He developed this theme at another army group commanders' meeting on 11 August.[23] This meeting is interesting for it reveals Foch arguing for a greater supply of munitions than Joffre and Castelnau considered necessary for the Champagne offensive. They wanted a strong, wide-front attack, with the enemy's reserves pinned down by subsidiary action on the flanks. Castelnau stated that his aim was to break the enemy front (or, at least, to push it back [refouler] on a wide front) so as to be able to manoeuvre: 'we are seeking rupture, not with a methodical attack, but with an attaque brusquée'. In contrast, Foch was advocating the provision of munitions beyond the five days that Castelnau was suggesting because he likened the operation to 'siege warfare', to be carried out slowly and gradually. Foch's caution was at odds with his colleagues. As Castelnau's

---

[20] Clive diary, 29 July 1915, CAB 45/201.
[21] Letter, Foch to Joffre, 3 August 1915, *AFGG* 3, annex 1089.
[22] Foch, Carnets, fo. 107, n.d. [between 15 July and 19 August 1915].
[23] Réunion des commandants de groupe d'armées du 11 juillet [sic, sc. August], *AFGG* 3, annex 1150; Jacquand memoirs, 12 August 1915, fos. 690–3, 1K/795/36.

chief of staff put it, 'General Foch, former swashbuckler, seemed bruised [tapé] by his failure at Arras.'[24] Foch's own postwar account gives a different impression, of course, but his claim to have told War Minister Millerand that with limited munitions only limited pretensions were possible is confirmed in his contemporary notebook: 'limited aspirations, so long as limited means'. The French army had enough munitions to start a battle, but not to continue it. However successful Castelnau's initial 'attaque brusquée', a second and a third would have to follow, for which an assured supply of munitions was needed.[25]

On 15 August Foch summed up the strategic situation as he saw it:[26]

The French government does not want an attack.
    French command wants a powerful attack.
    Has neither the means nor a plan. The British government wants to do nothing for the moment. British command ditto.

Dealing with the changeable Sir John was made more difficult than in the past because Foch and Wilson were not seeing each other so frequently. This was not the result of any bad feeling, but rather the changed political situation in London. As a result of the 'shells scandal' and the resignation of Sir John Fisher over the Dardanelles operation, Asquith had reconstituted his Liberal Cabinet as a coalition on 26 May. This brought Wilson's Conservative political friends into prominence, and there was some agitation to get Wilson installed as Chief of the Imperial General Staff (CIGS) as a counterweight to Kitchener.[27] Worried about this possibility, Foch asked Clive about it.[28] Clive reassured him that Wilson was too valuable at GHQ, but Wilson made several trips to London during the latter half of 1915, an index of his growing interest in the political side of the war. In addition, Joffre began to run down the liaison services and to reduce the number of liaison officers, indicating a lack of appreciation of their value (as well as an index of the losses in junior officers that could not be replaced).[29] So not only was Foch expected to undertake the same mission as in May/June with reduced resources, he also had to deal with Sir John, Robertson and Haig (none of whom wanted to attack where Joffre wished) with reduced help from Wilson. Moreover neither GQG nor GHQ liked the cosy triangular relationship between

[24] Jacquand memoirs, 12 August 1915, fo. 693, 1K/795/36.
[25] Foch, Journées, 11 August 1915; Foch, Carnets, 11 August 1915, fo. 108.
[26] Foch, Carnets, 15 August 1915, fo. 108.
[27] Jeffery, *Wilson*, 149–51. Jeffery makes no mention of the September fighting, thus revealing its lack of importance as far as Wilson was concerned.
[28] Clive diary, 7 July 1915, CAB 45/201.   [29] See Greenhalgh, *VTC*, 84–7.

Huguet, Wilson and Foch; Robertson told Clive that he thought that Sir John should deal with Joffre direct, and less with Foch.[30]

If Wilson was of less help over the negotiations for the autumn campaign than he had been in the past, Foch received aid from another source in the task of making Sir John take (and keep to) a decision. Joffre had invited Kitchener to come to France and his visit on 16–19 August settled Sir John's vacillation. Kitchener told the Dardanelles Committee on his return that there was a risk that if the British did nothing in the forthcoming autumn offensive, either France or Russia (or both) might make a separate peace.[31] Asquith reported to the King that although Kitchener was 'not sanguine' about the prospects, he was 'strongly of the opinion that we cannot, without serious & perhaps fatal injury to the Alliance, refuse the co-operation which General Joffre invites & expects'.[32] Moreover, Kitchener accepted the command 'formula' that Joffre proposed, which gave the French CinC the 'initiative' so long as operations continued on French territory.[33] Hence Sir John's role was set: he was to extend the French left as Joffre wished.

Accordingly, a few days later on 22 August, the British and the French met at Joffre's headquarters when, if the procès-verbal is to be believed, all was sweetness and light. Sir John explained that his letters had merely set out his personal arguments against the proposed operation and did not represent a refusal to cooperate. He offered to take over a French division straight away, but demanded that their heavy guns remain in place; he stated that he would be ready for the start of operations, set provisionally for 8 September. Sir John announced that Haig had twelve divisions and more than 800 guns. For his part, Joffre stated that the French 75s had 1500 rounds, with virtually unlimited reserves in rear areas, while the heavy guns had more than 300 rounds per gun. Foch agreed to discuss with Sir John and the new Third Army the question of the French heavy guns to be left in sector. They ended by all agreeing to meet again soon.[34]

Four days later, at General Monro's Third Army headquarters, agreement was reached about the guns that Foch would leave when the British relief took place. Foch and Sir John each announced the resources that were to be devoted to the attack. The objectives of the British First Army were Loos (IV Corps), and the Hohenzollern redoubt and the mine west of Loos for I Corps alongside. Second Army would also make a

---

[30] Clive diary, 19 July 1915, CAB 45/201.
[31] Secretary's notes of a meeting of the Dardanelles Committee, 20 August 1915, CAB 42/3/16.
[32] Asquith to King, 20 August 1915, CAB 37/133.
[33] See Greenhalgh, *VTC*, 29–30.
[34] Procès-verbal d'une conférence tenue à Chantilly, le 22 août à 10h., *AFGG* 3, annex 1225.

diversionary attack around Ypres. There was a 'passive front' of 400 metres between British and French attacking troops, and Foch asked that the British extend their right to cover this gap. This matter was left to Haig and d'Urbal to settle between them. So, finally, the total length of front to be attacked from Loos to south of Arras was sixteen kilometres (nine French and seven British). Taking into account the longer Champagne front as well, the Germans were to face offensives along approximately forty-four kilometres. Foch announced that he intended to attack with twelve divisions in the northern sector and four divisions south of Arras. He had wanted to extend the front of attack further south still, because the experience of May/June had shown that a narrow front was dangerous, but this desire was a further casualty of Joffre's concentration on the Champagne attack. Joffre had no troops to spare.[35] Foch was very pleased with the meeting, writing to his wife after his return that everything had been agreed and arranged 'perfectly', and they had ended the meeting 'very comfortably, with tea'.[36]

If the high command was content, there was less harmony lower down the chain of command. Haig did not approve of the request to extend his right – 'yet another example of how the French try to work for their own hand in their dealings with the British' – and Sir Henry Rawlinson (IV Corps commander) had recognised Sir John's ambivalence. Rawlinson had 'gathered' that Sir John 'had given Joffre to understand' that he was going to make a wholehearted effort, 'whereas he is not going to do anything of the kind having limited [?] me to the capture of the front line trenches until we see how the French get on with their attack'. Among the French, Fayolle could not understand why they were attacking Vimy Ridge for the third time. 'Are we stronger than on 9 May and 16 June?', he asked his diary: 'No. Is the enemy stronger? Yes. So?' He believed that the offensive being prepared would make even less progress than the earlier attacks. In Fayolle's view, Foch's proposition that the French army would be better off at 140 metres (that is, occupying the ridge) was not necessarily the case. He added: 'we must lose another 60,000 men to be better off!', and left the sentence unfinished.[37]

Finally, the planning was completed, and the date settled, postponed from 8 to 25 September because Castelnau could not be ready by the earlier date. Foch wanted a wide-front attack on the whole front of Tenth

---

[35] Procès-verbal de la conférence tenue à Beauquesne le 26–8–15 (16h.), ibid., annex 1254, being a translation of Wilson's minutes in WO 158/26; Joffre to Foch, 19 August 1915, *AFGG* 3, annex 1204.

[36] Letter, Foch to Mme Foch, 26 August 1915, vol. 37.

[37] Haig diary, 6 August 1915; Rawlinson diary, 14 August 1915; Fayolle, *CS*, 126–7, 124 (entries for 21, 22, 9 August 1915).

Army, arguing against d'Urbal's original plan using only a portion of the available forces. Although the BEF would extend the attack northwards, Sir John refused to allow Third Army to extend it southwards, until there were 'signs of a general retreat of the Germans opposite Third Army'.[38] The final meeting of French army group commanders before the battle began took place on 14 September, and, as a sign of the British commander's new relationship to Joffre following the agreed command 'formula', Sir John attended too. Kitchener's acceptance of the formula left Sir John as the equivalent of an army group commander, which was justifiable when the number of armies is considered but difficult because it placed Foch and Sir John on the same footing. Joffre listed the numbers of divisions in each attack and the numbers of guns: a total of fifty-nine British and French divisions in both Artois and Champagne, supported by 1300 heavies and 2700 field guns. Wilson noted the main points as they struck him: 'terrific violence'; all the infantry were to move at the same time; arrangements for cavalry exploitation – all in all, a 'tremendous attack'.[39]

Foch does not appear to have been as convinced as Wilson by the scale of the forces to be used in the forthcoming operation, for as late as September he was still writing in his notebooks about a 'war of fortifications'. Fortified lines were being organised, defended and attacked. Great resources were needed for such a war, resources that the Germans possessed because they had been preparing for it. The French had to equal and then to surpass them, he wrote. Nothing was possible without these resources. The 'point of departure' for any commander to be able to command was the 'resources situation'.[40] With six army corps and an ample supply of shells for the forthcoming battle, Foch hoped that the 'resources situation' was good enough to ensure a success.

All the foregoing back-and-forth arguments and meetings beg a big question: why was Foch seeking to repeat the same exercise that had failed earlier? Certainly he was obeying Joffre's wish for a coordinated attack against both shoulders of the German salient in France, but the British were very unwilling. The answer is that Foch believed that he could now employ better methods against the same (still very valuable) objective. His troops were now nearer the crest of the ridge than they had been in May; and now the joint Franco-British front was much wider. If the British could capture the Lens heights and the French complete the capture of

---

[38] Tenth Army instructions for corps commanders, with Foch's marginalia, 1 September 1915; telegram, Joffre to Foch, 2 September 1915; Monro note, 22 September 1915: all in *AFGG* 3, annexes 1315, 1316, 1527.

[39] Wilson diary, 14 September 1915.

[40] Foch, Carnets, n.d. [after 3 September 1915], fo. 112.

Vimy Ridge, then together they would dominate the Douai plain and German communications.

However, despite Foch's insistence on the strategic importance of the terrain in Artois when compared to the Champagne sector, GQG preferred the latter precisely because the area lacked the heavily fortified villages such as Souchez and Neuville that had caused Tenth Army so many casualties. The German defences were stronger in Artois precisely because the terrain was more valuable to them. This conundrum illustrates the difficulty of dealing with the Western Front battlefield. In order to gain a local victory that might lead to a strategic advantage, the Allies had to attack the most heavily fortified fronts and suffer the consequent casualties. Foch knew that the answer lay with wide fronts, a speedy succession of blows, and ample guns and munitions. Unfortunately the French did not yet have the means to deliver such an offensive.

The planning for Third Artois had given Foch more practice in dealing firmly but tactfully with an ally; it allowed him to present (albeit unsuccessfully) his strategic views about the long siege war that lay before them to his CinC and army group commander colleagues; and it revealed that the politicians, both French and British, were beginning to play a bigger role than they had in 1914. Yet the man always credited with proposing an attack as the answer to all military situations was now advocating a very different form of attack from that which Joffre and Castelnau wanted. Foch still believed that the only way to evict the Germans from French soil was to attack them. Nevertheless, the method of attack had to be commensurate with the available means. He still favoured making the third attempt at capturing Vimy Ridge, and would have preferred that it be the major sector of the autumn campaign, but without significant cooperation from his Allies and sufficient artillery resources, he knew that he risked failure. His ideas were beginning to diverge from those of his commander-in-chief.

Given Sir John's frequent changes of mind, Foch was not sure that he could rely on the British to make an equal effort. He went to see Haig on 12 September to explain the French plan, which Haig already knew. 'I gathered', Haig wrote in his diary, 'that the real object of Foch's visit was to find out whether we British meant really to fight or not'. Haig reassured him on this score, and told him that the British troops had never been in better heart and were longing to have a fight.[41] In addition to making sure of Haig, Foch made further arrangements. For protection and flank support in the north, Admiral Bacon of the Dover Patrol had been in contact

[41] Haig diary, 12 September 1915.

with Foch since 7 September about menacing the German troops there with the possibility of a landing. When the battle opened on 25 September the Dover Patrol monitors with 12" guns fired nearly 200 rounds and, assisted by the Nieuport guns, 'appeared' to have done considerable damage to the German batteries. The ships were able to repeat the action the next day, but after that the weather forced an end to such operations for a week.[42]

In addition, Foch employed the air services. Starting on 23 September, two days before the infantry assault, Northern Army Group's aviation bombed German railway lines continuously.[43] The British and French had agreed to coordinate their bombing campaigns, and so Sir John was asked to begin attacking the large railway station at Valenciennes on the same date.[44] Foch was convinced of the value of aerial observation to the artillery, and he had already got the army group's aviation commander, Commandant Pujo, to work during the summer on two problems: how to destroy the enemy's means of observation (the balloons), and how to improve their own means of artillery observation. Pujo and his men experimented with mounting 37mm guns on aircraft to shoot down balloons, and with radio communications between gunners and aerial observers. In order to encourage their efforts, Foch made a point of reviewing the squadrons and congratulating them.[45]

The last pre-battle meeting between the French and British commanders took place at 5pm at Foch's headquarters on 24 September to agree the start time for their attacks the next day. The British had decided to supplement their artillery bombardment with gas and smoke shells to make up for their inadequate supplies of munitions.[46] The effect of this decision was to make the start of their infantry assault dependent on the wind, an element over which they had no control. If the weather permitted the use of gas, Haig stated that he would begin very early, at 4.50am, so as to take advantage of the slightly stronger winds that blew at daybreak. The timing of the French attack depended, as always, on conditions for artillery observation. As soon as it was light enough to observe the fall of shot, 'H' hour would be set to allow for at least two more hours of bombardment before the infantry assault began. It was agreed that if the weather did not permit the use of gas, Haig's reduced assault would conform to the French 'H' hour. If the weather was so awful as to forbid any attack at all, then the decision to postpone was Foch's.[47]

[42] Corbett, *Naval Operations*, 3: 148, 152–3.   [43] *AFGG* 3, 433.
[44] Weygand, Note pour Monsieur le Maréchal commandant les armées britanniques, 21 September 1915, 18N 167.   [45] Weygand, *IV*, 284.
[46] On the inadequate artillery plan for Loos using gas, see Prior and Wilson, *CWF*, 108–16.
[47] Wilson diary, 24 September 1915; Haig diary, 25 September 1915.

The great double battle began on the morning of 25 September, with the Champagne attacks beginning at 9.30 and making substantial gains. The British on Foch's left also made good progress, capturing Loos and Hill 70 (a kilometre or so directly east of Loos) after their early-morning release of gas. Most progress had been made near the junction with the French. Foch's Tenth Army troops made no progress on the right, little progress in the centre, but did better on the left next to the British. There XXI Corps completed the capture of Souchez village, and took both Givenchy wood and La Folie farm. It has been claimed that the potential for a great British breakthrough following the capture of Hill 70 was squandered because the British reserves had not been on hand to exploit the early success and because the French did not start their action as the same time as the British.[48] The potential has been shown to be illusory, but the widely differing start times caused trouble none-theless. The British had started so early because they believed that the wind blew more strongly immediately after daybreak. The morning dawned misty, however, as mornings do in northern climes in September, and so Foch decreed that 'H' hour should be set four hours after it became possible to observe the artillery preparation. Therefore d'Urbal set 12.25pm for the infantry assault. However, because of the early British success, Haig asked his French liaison officer as early as 9.45 to telephone Foch and ask him to launch his attack at once. By 11am Haig's 15 Division had captured Loos, and 1 Division Hulluch. As the enemy began counter-attacking Hill 70, Haig asked GHQ at 1.30 what d'Urbal was doing; but Tenth Army had advanced their attack a little because of the British calls, and had been in action for an hour by the time Haig contacted GHQ.[49]

Foch was very pleased with the British success, writing to his wife about the 'fine success' that they had achieved alongside the French.[50] He went to see Sir John that evening, and he ordered d'Urbal to support the British action the next day. He informed Joffre that he expected to reach the ridge by building on the successes on his left.[51] The window of opportunity was closing quickly, however, because Crown Prince Rupprecht called as early as 12.30 for 'further immediate reinforcement' for his *Sixth Army*.[52] The Germans had received an unpleasant surprise at being attacked on two fronts, in Artois and Champagne, and Falkenhayn ordered immediate troop movements. The *Guards Corps* was sent from its rest area south of

[48] Prior and Wilson, *CWF*, 126.   [49] Haig diary, 25 September 1915.
[50] Letter, Foch to Mme Foch, 26 September 1915, vol. 37.
[51] Foch to Joffre, 25 September 1915, *AFGG* 3, annex 1587.
[52] Cited in Foley, *German Strategy*, 173.

Brussels to support Rupprecht's men facing the British. The counter-attacks against the positions that Haig's troops had captured continued that night. Although the British had punched holes in the German front line, by next morning the German second line was held even more strongly than their front line before the battle began.

Action on the subsequent days was confused and mainly profitless. Foch wanted to support the British right and his successful left-hand French corps, but his intentions were hindered by the rain, which had started at 1pm on the 25th and continued for the rest of the battle. This made observation for the artillery, which Foch insisted must carry out a 'serious' preparation, very difficult, and caused the British to complain about the 'late' French starts. Sir John told his liaison officer with Tenth Army 'to kick the ass [sic]' of that army 'and get them on', and he told Clive that he could not get on unless the French came up on his right.[53] The perfectly valid reason for the late start times (namely, waiting for the mist to dissipate so as to get two hours' clear artillery observation before the infantry set off) seems to have escaped the British entirely. Robertson even wrote to King George V's secretary that the French waited until after lunch before attacking, as though the meal were more important than the battle.[54]

Then Joffre made Foch's life even more difficult. He had already asked Foch to identify which units might be withdrawn from Tenth Army and sent to Champagne if success looked unlikely in the north.[55] Now the commander-in-chief declared that the capture of the ridge line was impossible and he asked Foch as early as 10am on the second day of the battle to be circumspect ['agir sagement'] and set aside some 'intact' divisions.[56] Despite Joffre's prior assurances that he had enough munitions for everyone, expenditure had been so great that he decided to reinforce the greater success achieved in Champagne. The Artois operation was to be wound down. Joffre called Foch in to see him at 2.15pm and told him to stop the Artois attacks whilst avoiding giving either the British the impression that they were being left to attack alone or the enemy the impression that the attack was slowing.[57] Joffre did not explain quite how this was to be achieved. He ordered Foch further to 'economise' on munitions, and to reduce the density of troops in the

[53] Spears diary, 25 September 1915; Clive diary, 26 September 1915, CAB 45/201.
[54] Letter, Stamfordham to Robertson [in answer to the latter's report], 30 September 1915, Robertson mss, 7/1/17.
[55] Telegram, Joffre to Foch, 25 September 1915, *AFGG* 3, annex 1573.
[56] Telephone message, Joffre to Foch, 26 September 195, ibid., annex 1772.
[57] Résumé des directives données au général Foch par le général commandant en chef, 26 September 1915, ibid., annex 1797.

front line so as to free at least one and possibly two divisions to be placed at Joffre's disposal. All this was to be done 'carefully'.

Despite all these difficulties, the French managed to reach the top of the ridge and Foch offered to help Haig by relieving the British right in the Loos sector. The success made Foch eager to press on, but the unremitting rain, the weariness of troops who had endured a week's heavy fighting, the great casualties (almost 38,000 officers and men in the six attacking corps between 25 and 30 September)[58] combined to prevent this. Transport difficulties, then a German counter-attack, delayed the relief of the British and tempers began to fray. Foch described 'long and tortuous' negotiations with Sir John; Haig complained that that the French 'always try to make the British pull the chestnuts out of the fire for them'.[59] Fayolle, whose XXXIII Corps had been pushed off the very top of Hill 140 but was clinging to its western slopes, noted after a meeting between Foch and his corps commanders that the Northern Army Group commander had organised an offensive with the British. What did he hope to achieve, Fayolle wondered, noting that Foch had not said whether he expected to break through or not. Since the supply of heavy munitions was dangerously low, Foch presumably did *not* expect to break through; but the temptation to attack from the heights towards the plain was too great to resist.[60]

Although fighting continued until 13 October, the story was one of repeated delays as first the British and then the French were forced to postpone. In the end, the French attacked without the British on 11 October and made a few gains, which the enemy re-captured in the following days. They had attacked alone because the artillery preparation had begun the previous day and Tenth Army did not have enough munitions to extend it. Haig's own attack finally began on 13 October, without the French but with similar results: slight gains also lost again. Fayolle was appalled. The poor morale of worn-out troops who did not understand the purpose of the operation, poor artillery preparation because of the mist, and (although Fayolle does not mention it) insufficient munitions were all reasons for failure. Foch would never understand such things, Fayolle wrote, and d'Urbal was not the man to make Foch admit them.[61] The political decision to dispatch troops to Salonika brought the sorry campaign to an end.

---

[58] Ibid., 464.
[59] Letter, Foch to Mme Foch, 29 September 1915, vol. 37; Haig diary, 30 September, 1 October 1915.
[60] Fayolle, *CS*, 133 (entry for 30 September 1915); GAN JMO, 30 September 1915, *AFGG* 3, annex 2438.
[61] Fayolle, *CS*, 136 (entry for 12 and 14 October 1915).

Third Artois had been another frustrating experience for Foch. First, his preference for a 'methodical' attack had been overruled in favour of Castelnau's more rapid methods in Champagne. Then, coordinating the planning with the British had been even more difficult than back in May, and once the battle started coordination with Haig over such seemingly simple matters as start times was just as difficult. Most frustrating of all was being ordered to wind down operations for lack of munitions, despite having been allocated seemingly sufficient beforehand, yet at the same time having to keep the British in the dark about the order. Although the French had nearly reached the crest of the ridge and had cleared the important village of Souchez, expenditures of men and munitions had been huge. Tenth Amy casualties between 25 September and 15 October were 48,230, of whom 18,567 (about 38 per cent) were missing or killed.[62] Tenth Army captured 2135 prisoners, thirty-five machineguns, twenty-two *Minenwerfer* [trench mortars], and a considerable number of guns and other materiel.[63] The Germans too had suffered many casualties, but they had their successes in Russia as compensation, and had proved able to bring up rapidly considerable numbers of reinforcements for both their French fronts.

In his detailed report on the operations of his XXXIII Corps during the autumn campaign in Artois, Fayolle compared the success obtained on 25 September, the opening day, with the results of the last attack on 11 October. The first attack had an excellent jumping-off point; the men knew the ground and what the objectives were; they had good observation and good telephone communications; and finally the five-day preparation had been undertaken methodically, with close supervision. The latter attack had none of these advantages, despite their occupation of the ground won during the intervening twelve days. The artillery preparation lasted only two days and had not been supervised closely enough. Neither had the ground been prepared for the attack, and the enemy positions were not known. Against a well-entrenched enemy, Fayolle concluded, the attack is worth only as much as the preparation. He identified three causes of failure – uncut wire, machineguns, artillery barrages – of which the last was the most destructive. Some German batteries had not opened fire during the preparation period, but started up immediately the infantry attack began, firing on the positions where the second and third waves of infantry were waiting. Since it was impossible to hide all the infantry from aerial observation, the only answer to this German tactic was effective

[62] *AFGG* 3, 540.
[63] General d'Urbal, Report on Tenth Army operations, 25 September to 11 October 1915, 4 November 1915, ibid., annex 3050.

counter-battery. Every enemy gun must be suppressed beforehand, even if it took weeks to achieve, by making dummy attacks to force the batteries to reveal their position. It consumed huge amounts of shells, of course, but XXXIII Corps had managed to destroy all the enemy batteries before them on two occasions by having perfected the registration of their guns. He concluded that not only were more guns and more munitions needed, but also more aircraft per division, armed with explosive bullets to bring down enemy *Drachen* [observation balloons]. Faster fighter aircraft were needed as well. In short, Fayolle was recommending a technological solution to the problem of mastering the Western Front battlefield.[64]

In their respective reports on the operations both Foch and the Tenth Army commander pointed out that, although the amount of ground captured was not large, it was valuable ground. The determined German defence, despite their heavy losses, was proof of the great importance attached to keeping hold of the heights. Both men also pointed to the need to devolve command of the artillery to lower levels. The weather had impeded observation, and insufficient reserves of munitions meant that preparation could not be continued until observation was complete. The 'lesson' of the May attack – that reserves needed to be positioned close up behind the attacking troops – had been shown to be false, because where preliminary attacks failed the reserves took casualties through being bunched up too close. Foch recommended a methodical approach: groups of infantry exploiting zones that had been thoroughly prepared by the artillery, one after the other – hence a sort of infantry leapfrog. The most important consideration, added in his own hand at the end of his report, was speed ('tempo' in modern terms). He wrote that the successive zones should be dealt with in such a way that 'the enemy did not have time to recover'.[65]

These reports insisted on the artillery as the element essential for success. The army group and army and corps commanders identified differing problems and offered differing solutions, but were united in stressing the need for the artillery to do its job effectively before any success could be achieved. In his notebooks, Foch was writing that what was required for the next year's campaign was more field, trench and heavy artillery, more materiel, more munitions, more organisation. There was no room on the battlefield for manoeuvre. Rather they had to smash through the enemy's 'materiel organisations', using chemical weapons, aircraft, mechanical excavators. That was the 'price of victory'. The troops

---

[64] GOC XXXIII CA, 'Observations au sujet des récentes attaques', 30 November 1915, 16N 1976.
[65] Ibid; Foch to Joffre, 6 November 1915, *AFGG* 3, annex 3056.

were to be rested and instructed over the winter, but the high command needed to take stock as well. Otherwise, Foch wrote, 'the materiel necessary for an offensive will be insufficient. We shall be just as poor in spirit and in materiel and just as powerless as we are today.' Once again he emphasised the necessity for a rapid succession of attacks. Better and greater destructive means, adapted to the terrain, should enable a move on the German second line without any hold-up, where the artillery has *definitely* prepared the ground.[66]

The poor results of the autumn campaign placed considerable political pressure on Joffre and impelled him to send out a letter to all army group commanders on 23 October 1915, asking them to obtain from their officers information about the lessons to be learned from the 1915 campaign and about the main difficulties that they had faced.[67] Foch's response on behalf of the Northern Army Group was sent about six weeks later, on 6 December. His eight-point report was titled 'Lessons to be drawn from our last attacks'.[68] He began by stating that the war was no longer a matter of breaking through a couple of fortified lines, but of dealing with a wide and deep 'fortified area'. Consequently, in order to deal with the strong defences that the enemy had had time to develop, it was necessary to increase the attackers' ability both to destroy each line, and to repeat the procedure on successive lines with as little delay as possible. Since this would necessarily be a long process, bringing France to the limit of its manpower resources, success would depend on 'husbanding' the infantry by increasing the destructive power of the artillery. There was no point in learning the lessons from 1915 in order to deal solely with the immediate obstacle; the long view had to be taken.

Foch's first point dealt with the artillery's failure to suppress obstacles that held up the infantry, and he deduced the 'principle' that progress was impossible for the infantry 'without an effective artillery preparation'. The second point followed from the first. The artillery's ability to operate effectively depended on its ability to 'observe' the effects of its bombardment. Despite the limits to aerial or other observation, commanders must supervise the artillery closely, judging its effects by counting the number of rounds fired *that had been registered on the target*. Supervision of the artillery must be the commander's main task, because the infantry's progress depended on its actions. Simply counting the number of shells fired was inadequate.

---

[66] Foch, Carnets, 19, 20 October, 2 November 1915, fos. 122, 126–7.
[67] Note pour les généraux commandants de groupes d'armées, 23 October 1915, *AFGG* 3, annex 3005.
[68] Foch to Joffre, 6 December 1915, ibid., annex 3122.

Third, Foch emphasised the 'fragility' and 'rapid wearing-down' of the infantry. Instead of large numbers of infantry, commanders should employ an 'economical dose' of infantry to follow a large dose of artillery. Fourth, he recommended a change in the artillery organisation. Foch claimed that, in order to destroy one kilometre of trench at an average distance from the guns, it required 2000 rounds from a 155mm howitzer firing straight ahead, of which 140 might actually hit the trench and cause some destruction. On the other hand, it required only 300 rounds fired from the side in order to enfilade the trench for a similar effect. Thus an infantry attack must be supported by the artillery alongside, and it must not rely solely on its own divisional artillery firing directly ahead. Consequently, in addition to an infantry division's field artillery, adjoining corps and army should each have heavy artillery under its own command so as to 'concentrate' fire in support of the infantry attack. Moreover (the fifth point), counter-battery work was important. Any successful capture of a trench was threatened because the enemy batteries knew precisely where to fire to expel the opposing infantry. Successful counter-battery required aerial observers to spot for the gunners. Foch recommended that air superiority on the battlefield should be the aim, and the strategic bombing of distant areas abandoned.

The sixth and seventh points concerned the artillery support for attacking units. At the divisional level (the unit of attack), there should be the closest liaison between artillery and infantry, with supporting corps artillery under divisional control. Foch specified the minimum artillery and aviation (spotter planes) for each attacking division. Furthermore he insisted that an infantry commander should receive good intelligence about the state of artillery preparation before an action and that during it he should follow his infantry closely so as to be able judge progress accurately.

In conclusion Foch set out the requirements for a successful campaign. First, French industry should develop the 'material means' for success, especially in the production of spotter planes for the artillery, and, second, the high command should exercise closer control over the use of those means ['un emploi plus serré'] so as to support the infantry whenever the latter were held up.

It might appear that all the above is merely to state the obvious, and it is certainly an indictment of the methods employed in 1914 and 1915 that it needed to be said at all. Nevertheless, its good sense is obvious. In its statement of the precise types and numbers of guns required, it merits the appellation 'scientific method', which is used to distinguish the new, methodical offensive paradigm from the strategy of breakthrough that had prevailed in 1915. Foch would repeat this phrase throughout 1916's frustrating operations. He was not only writing about the methods he believed necessary for success, he was also making his gunners practise. Over the winter, when there were no operations under way, he had his armies practising artillery manoeuvres and making 'serious preparations' so as to be ready for action when the moment came.[69]

[69] Diary of Mme Foch, 15 and 25 January 1916.

7   The scientific method: planning the Somme, 1916

For the British the Somme carries a freight of meaning, whereas for the French it denotes merely a river or the département to which the river gives its name. For the French 1916 means Verdun and the more than 370,000 casualties in the epic ten-month struggle to repel the German assault.[1] Nevertheless, Joffre intended the 1916 campaign to take place on the Somme, maintained that intention through thick and thin, and finally devoted to it on 1 July approximately half the numbers of men that the British did. Hence, once again, Foch's role in 1916 was to attempt to achieve Joffre's strategic aims in cooperation with the British.

Although Foch's thinking about the failed methods of 1915 was incorporated into the revised army doctrine that Joffre disseminated, along with the after-action reports solicited from commanders on the other French fronts, 1916 became another disappointing and frustrating experience for the Northern Army Group commander. The new doctrine reflected ideas about the so-called 'scientific method', but Foch was unable to apply the method fully because once again the enemy forestalled the planning for the 1916 campaign by his attack on the French at Verdun that began on 21 February. Moreover, Foch had little to do with the strategic planning, led by his commander-in-chief, that settled those operational plans. He was not present at Chantilly in December 1915 when the Allies agreed unanimously that they would coordinate all their attacks in 1916, thus denying to the Central Powers the advantage of being able to move troops from one front to another along interior lines. No account was taken of Foch's dislike of the Northern Army Group sector chosen for the French and British portion of that Allied plan, namely where their lines joined, in Picardy around the valley of the river Somme. So, despite general acceptance of Foch's thinking about tactics, he was obliged to plan for a campaign in a sector of which he disapproved and with resources increasingly diminished by the German assault at Verdun.

---

[1] Table in *AFGG* 4/3, 551–2.

From the comments made by Foch and other army commanders, Joffre and GQG staff developed for 1916 new tactical doctrines. The lesson which Joffre and the French high command drew from these solicited reports on the expensive and fruitless attacks in Champagne and Artois was that a breakthrough capable of forcing the enemy to a decisive battle in open country could not be achieved in one single operation. Therefore, successive artillery preparations would have to precede a *series* of operations, linked by as short an interval of time as possible and by a common purpose, but separate, independent operations nonetheless. In the Champagne offensive the second German position had stopped the attackers, and the operations in Artois had soon run up against defensive works which the French artillery had been unable to subdue. Thus the concept of 'duration' replaced that of a single decisive breakthrough, with successive actions concentrating on carrying enemy positions to which sufficient artillery preparation had been devoted. Since the time scale implied in such a linked series of operations meant that the enemy would have time to create new defensive areas further back, it would be necessary to allow for the capture not of two front-line positions but of a number of such defensive lines.

Joffre's 'Instruction on the use of heavy artillery' of 20 November 1915 gave the main role in any future attack to the heavy artillery. It specified that each new phase of the infantry attack must be preceded by the re-positioning of the heavy artillery to enable it first to complete the destruction of strong points not destroyed in the original preparation and, second, to begin the destruction of all successive positions. A precise figure was set on the heavy artillery necessary for a successful action. Trench artillery and the 75 s should be used for wire-cutting; but destruction of defensive positions should be the task of the heavy artillery concentrating on precise points – flanking casemates, machinegun shelters, observation points and munition dumps. In sum, 'an attack can succeed only if it has been *prepared* and *supported continuously* by a powerful artillery' – otherwise the infantry would suffer 'excessive' losses.[2] In January 1916 Joffre issued a further instruction on small unit offensive tactics. It was acknowledged that infantry by themselves could not carry enemy defensive positions, and the principle of instructing troops to take a position 'at whatever cost' was recognised as erroneous. 'One does not fight with men against materiel.'[3] Battles conducted with strict and close liaison between artillery and infantry would have greater success, it was suggested, if conducted on as wide a front as possible so as to reduce flanking counter-attacks and to make it

---

[2] *AFGG* 4/1, 44–7. Quotation from p. 44, emphasis in the original.   [3] Ibid., 47.

difficult for the enemy to concentrate guns or men. The front should be continuous except for local actions, which might encircle a salient so as to take it from the flank or, by outflanking it completely, from the rear. Since surprise became impossible with these tactics, it was necessary to be able to act offensively all along the front line in order to keep the enemy on the alert to the possibility of attack over a wide area, thus pinning down as large a number of German troops as possible.[4]

So Foch's ideas coincided with the new tactical doctrine emanating from GQG. His strategic ideas differed, however. In preparing the 1916 campaign Joffre had asked his three army group commanders the previous October to study the possibility of action on each respective front that would be at least as large as 1915's operations in the Champagne region. Foch responded that the front of his southern Sixth Army, which ran between the rivers Aisne and Somme, was not propitious. Further north, however, the front of his Tenth Army offered greater possibilities. They already held a portion of Vimy Ridge, and an attack here to complete its capture would give good observation over the Douai plain and the enemy's communications. While the flat wheatfields in the southern sector might allow the capture of one or two enemy lines, the terrain beyond was the same. There was no height advantage to be gained, for example, to give better observation for the artillery; and the river Somme itself, which runs almost due north before turning (at Péronne) towards the sea, would be a barrier to further advance. Although an attack on Vimy Ridge meant hitting again at the same points that had been attacked in 1915, there was no other sector of the Northern Army Group's front that offered the same strategic advantages.

Whatever Joffre's decision, Foch concluded that it was vital to have much more heavy artillery than in 1915 to deal with the enemy's strengthened defences. Mobile field artillery had to be developed; incendiary and gas shells should be exploited; and machinery to dig galleries for placing mines under the enemy lines should be produced. Frontal attacks on the 1915 model were ineffective and costly. Foch underlined that 'the infantry attack fails or stops where the preparation was inadequate'. The infantry should be sent only against objectives that have been destroyed by registered and observed artillery fire.[5]

GQG did not much care for Foch's arguments. Although agreeing that the water obstacles of the Somme and the Oise, with their joining canal, created a cul-de-sac blocking any development towards the east, GQG

---

[4] On the new tactical doctrines see Lucas, *L'Evolution des idées tactiques*, ch. 4; and Goya, *La Chair et l'acier*, 261–6.

[5] Projet d'attaque, sent to Joffre on 2 February 1916, *AFGG* 4/1, annex 151.

argued that bottling up the Germans in that area might give a tactical victory with the capture of thousands of prisoners and 600 guns. Moreover, Joffre wanted a wide-front operation, which meant using both French and British armies; GQG's preferences lay therefore with the area south of the Somme, and Foch was asked to plan for the main front of attack there, instead of Vimy. GQG accepted his artillery calculations, but considered his infantry numbers too small. Instead GQG proposed three armies (forty divisions plus three territorials; 764 supplementary heavy guns in addition to the normal allocation, and fifty-seven super-heavies) for the forty-four kilometres between the Somme river and Lassigny. The aim should be to push the enemy back to both the Somme and the Oise rivers, and prevent them from debouching from around Péronne.[6] Foch's strictures on using the infantry parsimoniously were not accepted at GQG, despite the new 'powerful artillery' doctrine.

Once again, Foch was absent when the final decision was taken about the area of the 1916 offensive. Joffre and the new British CinC, Sir Douglas Haig, reached agreement on 14 February on the broad outlines of the proposed battle in the Somme area of northern France. Assuming that the Allies kept the initiative in the west, this would be a joint 'decisive' attack astride the river beginning on 1 July, on a front of sixty-five to seventy kilometres. North of the Somme Haig would contribute twenty-one divisions to the battle, or fourteen if he were obliged to take over the Tenth Army front. Foch's Northern Army Group would operate astride the river with thirty-nine infantry divisions, plus three territorials. Joffre promised that, whatever the date of the attack, Foch could have all the guns that he needed.

Seven days later the German onslaught began in eastern France against the fortified Verdun region. Falkenhayn aimed to take the heights to the east of the historic city, counting on the strength of his captured positions to inflict enormous casualties on the French who, he judged, would be bound to counter-attack. Recognising from the failed 1915 Western Front offensives (as had Foch) that massed infantry attacks could not succeed, Falkenhayn aimed to use heavy artillery instead to 'bleed' the French army white. He calculated that, whether the British mounted a relief operation by attacking elsewhere or whether they merely relieved French troops so that they could come to Verdun, the total casualty bill would force France to its knees, with the British following suit. The second part of Falkenhayn's strategy, a counter-offensive in northern France to finish off the weakened Allies, would follow the Verdun operation.[7] Joffre would

---

[6] Note du général Foch sur l'offensive entre la Somme et Lassigny, 6 February 1916, ibid., annex 159.

[7] This account of Falkenhayn's 1916 strategy is based on Foley, *German Strategy*.

have been prepared to call Falkenhayn's bluff by withdrawing from the Verdun salient because he had denuded France's fortresses of their heavy guns in order to palliate the great shortage of such guns at the front. All the heavy guns that were not fixed had left Verdun. However, French politicians from the President of the Republic down made it very plain that such a proceeding could not be contemplated. Ever since 843, when Charlemagne's heirs divided his lands and created the frontier between what became France and what became Germany, the fortified city had been a symbol of national pride.

The Germans made significant advances after the offensive began on 21 February, most notably capturing Fort Douaumont. On 27 February Haig offered to help by relieving the entire French Tenth Army, which previously he had intended to relieve only gradually, a division at a time. The relief was complete by 14 March. The Tenth Army's infantry corps were re-distributed onto other fronts or into reserve, and its headquarters transferred from Foch's Northern Army Group to GQG control. The British Third Army moved north to take over Tenth Army's former front, leaving the sector north of the Somme to a new army, Sir Henry Rawlinson's Fourth Army.

Notwithstanding Verdun, Foch continued his planning for the offensive astride the Somme that Joffre had approved, and he sent his detailed plan to GQG on 16 March (see Map 10).[8] It envisaged three armies attacking together. The centre army (of sixteen divisions) was to capture Roye and then push down the valleys leading to the Somme and cross the river upstream of Péronne. The right-hand or southern army (with eight divisions) would support the centre, by capturing the enemy bastion of Lassigny, an operation that would be made easier by extending the front of attack to the high ground south of the town. The northern or left-hand army (with nine divisions), astride the Somme and adjoining the British, would also support the centre. It would take up position north of the river on 1 May, and prevent enemy action against the centre from the heights above the river, whilst maintaining contact with the BEF. The latter task would probably involve waiting for the British to advance their lines a little, since the front curved back westwards at that point. South of the river, this left-flank army was to aim for the Somme between Cizancourt and Péronne. To this total of thirty-three divisions was added a six-division reserve, making thirty-nine in all. For this broad-front offensive, Foch calculated that 1069 heavy and super-heavy guns were required, together with 477 field batteries, 542 trench artillery pieces, twenty-five

---

[8] Projet d'attaque dans la région entre Somme et Oise, 16 March 1916, *AFGG* 4/1, annex 1282.

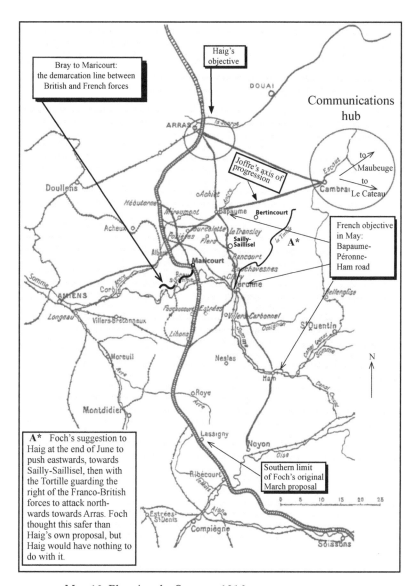

Map 10 Planning the Somme, 1916

anti-aircraft artillery posts, and twenty-four squadrons of aircraft with enough supplementary troops and aircraft to ensure continuous observation for the gunners and to man one observation balloon per division engaged. As for munitions, he calculated (for an initial seven-day period only) over four million field artillery shells, over a million shells for the heavy guns, and 238,800 trench artillery shells. In addition he listed such miscellaneous items as 55,000 spades, 2.2 million sandbags, 2.5 million grenades, 70,000 knives and 10,000 kilometres of telegraph wire. Thus, before the end of March, Foch had prepared a highly detailed plan for his offensive, with all the requirements precisely calculated, which his commander-in-chief approved a week after submission. Foch was confident that the peril of the enemy attacks at Verdun had been contained.[9]

On 20 April Foch sent out his 'general directives', entitled 'La Bataille offensive'.[10] This was a long document with three annexes, incorporating the various instructions from GQG and adapted to the particular conditions facing the Northern Army Group. It emphasised the depth of the enemy defensive positions, which imposed a sustained offensive, conducted methodically and supported by the artillery. Only the artillery could destroy the enemy positions and the infantry should attack only positions so destroyed. A longer artillery preparation was required for the first position, because this was the strongest, but once this was captured there should be a rapid shift to the next and any successive positions. Action should be on a wide front, and creating small local salients should be avoided.

So far, so obvious. The document then went on to describe the tasks involved in the preparation of the offensive (for example, counter-battery work was the province of the corps artillery), and to emphasise that the subsequent attacks must be prepared as far as possible, not simply the attack on the first position, as had been done in the past. The methodical nature of the preparation is seen clearly in the listing of the tasks for each calibre of the artillery and the insistence that firing must be controlled and the infantry action 'directed [conduite]', for simply committing troops pêle-mêle created disorder and made it impossible to coordinate their action. Speed was of the essence after a position had been taken and consolidated, and indeed the artillery should be moved up for the attack on the second and subsequent positions even before the capture of the previous one was complete.

Foch had set out detailed instructions for his subordinate commanders, but the document reveals a huge problem, one that would not be solved in

[9] Mme Foch diary, 29 February; 1 and 15 March 1916.
[10] *AFGG* 4/2, annex 2. It occupies fifty pages.

1916. Methodical artillery preparation was essential, however much time was required, but so too was speed in shifting the artillery into position to deal with second and subsequent enemy lines. Yet the more methodical and lengthy and successful the preparation on the first position, the more the ground was churned up, hence the slower the re-positioning of the guns. Greater success in the first phase ensured less success in the second and subsequent phases. More method in the first phase meant less speed in later phases.

The document contained three detailed annexes dealing with preparing the ground for the infantry, artillery fire and aviation. Against defensive works such as barbed wire, a battery of field artillery (that is, mainly the 75 s) needed to fire, in order to make a breach twenty to twenty-five metres wide and twenty-five metres deep, approximately 600 explosive shells at 2500m distance, the number of shells increasing as the distance increased. More shells were also needed if the ground rose in front of the guns, or if the depth of barbed wire to be destroyed was greater than 25m. If the defences were too far distant for the field artillery or too well concealed, the 155mm guns should be used. Fifty of one type of shell or eighty of the 'shell D' from these guns could make a 4–5m breach in a defensive position extending 15–20m at a distance of three kilometres. Machinegun shelters cannot be destroyed on the whole by field artillery. These guns can succeed only by firing a shell through one of the embrasures (probably scoring such a hit would owe more to luck than to accurate firing), and it would take 100 high-explosive shells to achieve a result. Instead the heavy guns should take on the machinegun shelters. Two direct hits from a 155 would be needed to destroy a shelter of the type consisting of three rows of logs; and, in order to achieve this, each gun would need to fire between seventy and 100 rounds. As for destroying trenches, the 155s had to fire 300–400 rounds (or 150 if enfilading the trench) to batter down distinct portions of a trench lying 50m away at points 25m distant from each other. Experience had shown that a 75 gun could keep up rapid fire, that is, six to eight shots per minute, for five minutes. Thus each battery of four guns could keep up a barrage 200m wide that would deliver one shell per 15m every thirty seconds. Such a weight of shell could neutralise temporarily an enemy battery which it had proved impossible to destroy. The heavy guns doing counter-battery work would need to have fired 100 rounds at 500m to score two hits. Finally air superiority was essential to provide intelligence to the commanders, to observe the fall of shot for the artillery and to supervise the battlefield. Thus Foch was leaving nothing to chance. Everything was calculated 'scientifically', down to the last detail.

None of Foch's precise calculations was plucked from the air. As noted earlier, Foch had his troops practising artillery manoeuvres after operations ceased at the end of 1915, and his own and Weygand's note-books contain earlier drafts, going back as far as January 1916, of what is contained in the 'Bataille offensive' document. Foch knew that artillery was the key to success on the Western Front – 'War is a race for muni-tions', he wrote on 21 January[11] – and his comments to his wife during the course of the year reveal his concern that France was not producing the necessary armaments quickly enough to make up for the forty-five-year lag that he calculated existed between France and Germany.

He was no less careful about aviation. Foch sent his director of aviation, Captain Pujo, to Verdun to study the lessons to be learned there. Pujo's view that air superiority was vital led to two decisions: each individual army was given its own fighter group, with another allotted to the Northern Army Group; and all the balloons and aircraft associated with observing for the artillery were placed under the same command. A system of signalling with lights was established so that the infantry and aircraft could communicate with each other; and each army aeronautical group had its own photographic section able to produce photographs within hours of their being taken. Foch sent out to all divisional and corps commanders an instruction on how to make use of the new arrange-ments, and Fayolle recorded in his diary at least one exercise in aviation–infantry liaison. In an atmosphere of friendly emulation, agreement was reached with the British over zones of attack when dealing with enemy observation balloons. The French won a bet with General Hugh Trenchard, commander of the Royal Flying Corps (RFC), by downing thirteen German balloons on 1 July as against the British total of nine.[12]

The meteorology service worked with the aviators. Foch got to know the chief meteorologist, naval Lieutenant Rouch, and tried to obtain accurate predictions. Rouch had a series of transmission stations across the Atlantic, and weather forecasts were issued to all army and corps commanders. Foch ordered Rouch to be available at all times during an attack and ensured that he (Rouch) had everything that he might need. Rouch was able to use published historical data sets for rainfall in the Somme department, and from this he drew up a table for Foch showing the days when it was least and most likely to rain (historically, at least).[13]

Foch needed all the help he could get from technical experts because the German defences on the Somme were some of the strongest on the Western Front. The advantage of open uncratered country had as its

[11] 'Note du Gal Foch', 21 January 1916, 1K/129/1, [d] 1914 et ensuite.
[12] Weygand, *IV*, 317–19; Fayolle, *CS*, 160 (entry for 4 May 1916).
[13] Weygand, *IV*, 318–19; J. Rouch, 'Souvenirs sur le Maréchal Foch', *Revue des Deux Mondes*, 15 May 1932, 337–58.

corollary that the German *Second Army* had had plenty of time to strengthen its defences and absorb the lessons of the 1915 defensive fighting. *Second Army* faced the Allies both north and south of the river. The southern sector opposite the French, however, where the river runs south–north, was less strong. Facing the British in the northern sector were two completed lines of trenches incorporating villages and fortified farms with cellars, and the beginnings of a third line a couple of kilometres further back. The two front trench systems were strongly wired, and the second was often sited on a reverse slope and so out of sight of the gunners. On the other hand, the trench lines south of the river were closer together, and the second line was often only a single trench, but there were several strong 'centres of resistance' sited in woods, between 1500 and 2500 metres in depth.[14]

Less than a week after putting out his 'offensive battle' directive, Foch learned that, after all, Joffre would not be able to give him the number of divisions originally envisaged and, more importantly, considerably fewer heavy guns. On 26 April Joffre wrote to Foch that he still intended to carry out the planned offensive, but that he did not intend to invoke the clause in the Chantilly agreement that provided for one ally to call for another's help in the event of being attacked. However, the men and guns that he could now devote to it must be reduced: thirty divisions instead of thirty-nine; and 660 guns, about half the original number. 'The front will be reduced', he wrote, 'but still joined to the front of the British attacks'.[15] The next day, Joffre authorised Foch to begin planning with Rawlinson the French artillery support around the juncture of the two armies, and informed him that he had asked Haig to have completed all the preparatory work for his twenty-five divisions by 1 June. Joffre expected to give Haig twenty days' notice of the date of the attack, once that date was decided, but he emphasised that liaison officers must be careful not to reveal any details of the forthcoming operation.[16]

By the end of April, then, planning was progressing. Joffre intended to carry out what he had decided, despite events at Verdun, which imposed a reduction in the numbers of men and guns that Foch could use. There was to be no invocation of the early action clause of the Chantilly agreement, however. Indeed, the French were holding on extremely well at Verdun, and Robert Foley's recent study of the German commander Erich von Falkenhayn concludes that the Germans were stalemated there by the end of April.[17] They had fought furiously on both sides of the river Meuse

---

[14] *AFGG* 4/2, 200–1.   [15] Joffre to Foch, 26 April 1916, ibid., annexes 2223 and 2224.
[16] Letter, Joffre to Foch, 27 April 1916, ibid., annex 2242.
[17] Foley, *German Strategy*, 236.

since 21 February, but had not achieved anything remotely approaching the spectacular capture of Fort Douaumont that they completed within four days of launching the offensive. They were also suffering enormous casualties, instead of imposing disproportionate casualties on the French as they had planned. In addition, the French defenders had regained air superiority, and so prospects for the enemy did not seem too favourable for any continuation of the battle.

In May, however, the French position worsened. First of all, at Verdun the Germans launched a series of offensives on the heights west of the Meuse. General Pétain commanding Second Army in the defence of Verdun had been making repeated calls for more resources, but Joffre demanded a more offensive-minded attitude. He 'promoted' Pétain to army group command, putting the offensive-minded Generals Nivelle and ('butcher') Mangin in charge of operations before Verdun. Second, as a consequence of the failure of French counter-offensives and further German gains, Foch's role on the Somme diminished even more, to the extent that it became dependent on the British action, which was elevated to the status of principal operation. Third and more importantly, at the end of May the politicians became involved. Finally, Foch had a car accident.

The last may be described briefly. The accident, which could easily have been fatal, occurred on 16 May as Foch was being driven to a meeting of army group commanders at Châlons. His driver swerved to avoid an animal on the road and the car hit a tree. It seems that Foch would have made a good advertisement for seat belts, as his injuries were considerable facial bruising and broken teeth. He was taken to a hospital in Meaux and the accident was kept a secret so as not to cause the public any despondency. It is not clear whether even the British were informed, because Haig did not mention the accident in his diary until he saw Foch on 31 May, when he wrote as though he already knew of it. On the other hand, Foch's resilience, despite his age (sixty-four), is very clear. As his wife recorded in a matter-of-fact entry in her diary, he insisted on continuing to work even though his doctor ordered rest and he received visits from Briand and Poincaré, and Joffre and Castelnau.[18] When his British liaison officer saw him a month after the accident, he commented that Foch had 'certainly made the most remarkable recovery', and that he was 'as quick as the devil'.[19] Nonetheless, the accident would prove useful later for Foch's critics as evidence of presumed physical incapacity to continue in command.

[18] Mme Foch diary, 23 and 27 May 1916.   [19] Dillon diary, 15 June 1916.

On 2 May Foch had already reduced the scope of his plan to take account of the fewer resources that Joffre could provide.[20] Two days later he informed Joffre that he still intended to use three armies to force a crossing of the Somme south of Péronne, but now the objective was to be the road that runs almost due north–south from Bapaume through Péronne to Ham, because his front of attack was now insufficiently wide to make a strategic breakthrough. Significantly, he ended with the comment that the operation might have to be halted in order to stop 'losses and sacrifices without any significant profit'.[21] The French were now 'far from a wide powerful offensive, capable of enduring, aiming at an achievable goal, these conditions being the only ones which would allow the attack to achieve a strategic result and avoid powerlessness'. Pétain at Verdun emphasised the struggle for resources when he wrote a personal letter to Foch, asking him not to press Joffre for the Somme offensive so as ensure that the more important battle (Verdun) should take priority.[22] Foch needed little persuasion; he was thinking of a limited operation which would be brought to an end after initial success rather than continued at enormous cost, as had happened during the 1915 battles.

Joffre's reply insisted that he aimed still to 'defeat the enemy, that is to say to expel him from the ground he occupies over as deep and as wide an area as possible', even if the return of troops from Verdun proved impossible. Foch should concentrate on the attacks on the Somme and on Roye 'more particularly the northern one', that is on the joint attack with the British.[23] So Joffre remained committed to his joint Allied strategy and to breakthrough, despite Foch's reservations. However, by 20 May, as the Germans captured and then lost again Hill 304 on the left bank above Verdun, and Mangin prepared his attack (which failed) to re-take Douaumont, Joffre could commit to the Somme only twenty-two infantry divisions (possibly increasing to twenty-six). As for heavy artillery, Foch could count on only 540 guns, of which only about one-fifth was the most useful calibre: the short 155 with its plunging fire. Even though Joffre foresaw being able to provide another 300 or so heavy guns, only 168 of them would be short 155s, and he could promise munitions for only twenty days' firing, not the thirty that Foch had specified a month earlier.[24]

Foch gave his Sixth Army commander, Fayolle, his instructions on 25 May (so the car accident had not slowed him down). Three army

[20] Instruction générale personnelle et secrète pour MM. les généraux commandant les VIe, IIIe et Xe Armées, 2 May 1916, *AFGG* 4/2, annex 19.
[21] Foch to Joffre, 4 May 1916, ibid., annex 42.
[22] Letter, Pétain to Foch, 8 May 1916, 414/AP/2.
[23] Commander-in-Chief to General Foch, 10 May 1916, *AFGG* 4/2, annex 217.
[24] Ibid., 193, and letter, Joffre to Foch, 20 May 1916, annex 396.

corps (eleven divisions) with a fourth corps (three divisions) in reserve were allocated to the operation, with everything to be ready for a start date of 1 July. Sixth Army south of the river was to capture only the Flaucourt plateau so as to prevent the enemy artillery firing across the river to disrupt the actions in the north. There Sixth Army's principal task was to support the British attack, and to enlarge its area of operations as the British progressed. The original intention to cross the Somme river was, therefore, abandoned.[25]

These repeated reductions had an unintended effect: the French contribution became a support operation, whilst the British attack was promoted to the principal role. Maintaining the ratio of eight guns per kilometre of front imposed a front of attack of only fifteen kilometres, instead of the original pre-Verdun forty kilometres from the river as far south as Lassigny. Anything wider, Foch insisted, would cause 'heavy and useless losses'. An attacking front of fifteen kilometres would extend as far south as Foucaucourt, but this village was in the middle of a defensive system. Foch argued that it would be foolish to leave the flank of an attack facing such a strongly defended position, and so either the attacking front might to be extended a further four kilometres to include Foucaucourt village itself or the front might be reduced. With the limited number of guns at his disposal, Foch reduced the front so that it ended at the straight Roman road that runs from Amiens almost to Péronne. Joffre approved this revision three days later, on 27 May.[26]

A further effect of Foch's revisions downward was to complicate the relationship with the BEF and its commanders, now the principal actors in the forthcoming operation. The 1915 autumn campaign in Artois had been a French campaign, with a little bit of British help around Loos, yet now, in May 1916, the BEF was a very different instrument. On 1 January 1916 there had been thirty-eight British infantry divisions in France, organised into three armies, with a further nine divisions in Egypt and ten more at Gallipoli or Salonika. By May a further twelve divisions had arrived in France, two of them territorial divisions, but many of the others hardened by their Gallipoli battle experience. (Another five divisions would arrive by 3 July.[27]) Moreover, the BEF had a new commander-in-chief and a new Fourth Army commander. Foch knew both Haig and Sir Henry Rawlinson, of course, and must have appreciated the departure

[25] Instruction personnelle et secréte pour M. le général commandant la VIe Armée, 25 May 1916, ibid., annex 581.
[26] Foch to Joffre, 24 May 1916, and Joffre to Foch, 27 May 1916, ibid., annexes 537 and 623.
[27] Edmonds *et al.*, *OH 1916*, 1: 18, 24.

of Sir John French in December 1915 after the success of the campaign to unseat him following the Loos battle, yet his position was still somewhat anomalous, as it had been vis-à-vis Sir John. In terms of numbers Haig was the equivalent of a French army group commander, which was Foch's position, and it was natural for Rawlinson eventually to deal directly with his French army commander counterpart, Fayolle, when Sixth Army came into line in June. Haig, however, was also commander-in-chief and had negotiated mainly with General Joffre (and without Foch) over planning the broad outlines of the forthcoming campaign. There was no British equivalent to Foch's position, which had been downgraded some-what since Castelnau's appointment at the end of 1915 to act as Joffre's chief of staff. Moreover, Foch had lost his ready access to and information about GHQ when Henry Wilson had been moved to command of IV Corps after Haig took over. Nonetheless, a direct line of liaison with the British was established when Colonel Eric Dillon was appointed as Foch's liaison officer and began work on 17 May. Dillon's diary record of his time at Northern Army Group headquarters reveals a growing admiration for Foch and his methods. Although Foch had lost his direct contact to GHQ through Wilson, he seems to have become fond of the man he called 'mon brave Dillon'.[28] He wrote to Wilson on 28 May: 'I am delighted with Colonel Dillon. I appreciate him a lot and my staff share completely my opinion of him'.[29]

Foch's anomalous position meant that he had to work slightly harder to maintain good and profitable relations with the British. As early as 10 January, soon after Haig took over as commander-in-chief, Foch invited him to dine, leaving a written invitation at British headquarters because Haig was out visiting his various units. The latter was not very enthusiastic: 'I shall have to go', he noted in his diary. Yet dinner the next day proved a great success, despite Haig being seated across the table from Foch and despite the fact that none of his staff spoke English. Haig recorded that 'Foch was greatly pleased at my dining with him and thanked me profusely for the honour which I paid him.'[30] It seems obvious that Foch had made a special effort to make friends. Yet there was an ulterior motive. If Weygand is to be believed, Joffre had sent Foch as an 'éclaireur' or scout to dissuade Haig from his preferred Belgian coast operation. Joffre did not wish to get involved in a debate over strategy so soon after Haig took over, and so Foch was to point out the difficulties posed by the Houthulst forest and by the flooding for any amphibious

[28] Lieutenant-Colonel R. I. Benson, letter to the editor, *The Times*, 8 May 1946.
[29] Letter, Foch to Wilson, 28 May 1916, HHW 2/83/16.
[30] Haig diary, 10, 11 January 1916.

operation against coastal batteries and submarine pens.[31] Haig makes no mention in his diary entry of any discussion about his Belgian operation, but Joffre certainly knew from his new head of the French Military Mission with the British army that such was Haig's preferred option.[32]

Foch's position was rendered even more anomalous by his opposition to the Somme offensive. He could see no strategic purpose in attacking there (as far back as October 1915, when Joffre wrote asking for army group commanders to put forward plans for an offensive, he had written 'with what aim?' on his copy of the letter).[33] He would have preferred action further north round Vimy Ridge, as we have seen, and once Verdun claimed ever greater resources he saw little point in the reduced action that he was compelled to take through lack of sufficient guns. He did not hide his views from the politicians; he had connections with some of the most influential. Both Albert and Georges Clemenceau (now President of the Senate's Army Commission) visited Foch on 3 May after Meunier-Surcouf (his former staff officer and *député*, who had decided to return to Paris and concentrate on politics) urged Clemenceau to go and talk to the only general 'who believed absolutely in a military victory'.[34]

Armed with knowledge of Foch's views, Clemenceau then went to see Haig the next day, 4 May. He impressed the latter during a conversation of more than an hour with his breadth of knowledge about 'what is going on in most of the theatres of war'. His aim, he told Haig, was to get him to 'exercise a restraining hand' on Joffre, and to prevent a large-scale offensive until all were at maximum strength. Clemenceau feared public reaction if failure followed a premature attack, since this would lead to the fall of the Ministry and the creation of a replacement under Joseph Caillaux that might ask for peace terms.[35] It is likely that Clemenceau's attempt to influence Joffre through Haig was the result of his talk with Foch the previous day, since Foch himself could make no headway in getting Joffre to reduce his aims to match his resources. This mixing of politics and military matters will recur.

Despite his dislike of what the campaign had become, Foch was obliged to become more involved, now that the detailed planning for supporting the principal British action was beginning. The demarcation line between

---

[31] Weygand, *IV*, 307.

[32] Vallières to Joffre, personal and secret report # 23, 10 January 1916, and # 35, 16 January 1916, in [d]Secret: Dossier personnel du Commandant en Chef # 3 (June 1915–June 1916), Fonds Joffre, 1K/268.

[33] Le général commandant en chef aux généraux commandant les G.A.N., G.A.C, G.A.E., 27 October 1915, *AFGG* 3, annex 3018, note 2 on p. 91.

[34] Charles Meunier-Surcouf, 'Mes cahiers, 1914–1919', cahier 6, p. 5, 1KT/83.

[35] Haig diary, 4 May 1916.

the British and French, which Joffre had insisted should be just north of the river (because it was not good military practice to have a river as a dividing line between different armies) proved very difficult to settle. The junction of the two army fronts was in the village of Maricourt, and the dividing line was eventually settled to run through the villages of Bray (on the river) up to Maricourt. French troops of XX Corps moved into position only on the nights of 1/2 and 2/3 June because Foch did not wish to cause too much congestion and wished Rawlinson's Fourth Army to have time and space to complete their preparations. Even so, it would be, as Rawlinson remarked, 'the hell of a squash'.[36] The constrained shape of the northern sector and the lack of roads gave the French a difficult problem (see Map 10). Because of the bend in the river, the French sector was cone-shaped, narrowing to meet the river in the west, and facing almost due east at its widest. The British, meanwhile, were facing in a much more northerly direction, which meant that any progress would serve only to widen the front and the gap between the armies. Small wonder that the demarcation of operational boundaries proved so difficult, with Fayolle in particular opposed to divergent attacks from the Maricourt salient.[37] A further result of the cone-shaped French sector was the need to share roads. There was only one road along the north bank, which the British were using. Since the bulk of the French forces was on the southern bank, more bridges would seem the obvious solution to the paucity of roads. Yet, having permitted one bridge to be built, Rawlinson refused to permit a second, on the grounds that it would give access to a road that his XIII Corps was already using. This particular problem was settled on 8 May, despite that corps commander's complaint that he was 'sadly shut in & deprived of roads'.[38]

At the end of May the French politicians intervened. It had been a political decision to defend Verdun; Joffre would have let the town go. Now the worsening situation and Pétain's lobbying for a greater share of the resources that Joffre was hoarding for the Somme combined to alarm Premier Briand and especially Poincaré. Poincaré had heard that Haig was concerned, following Clemenceau's visit, about the French commitment to the Somme offensive. Furthermore, Poincaré had received details of French casualties from Pétain and had spent the whole day of Sunday 28 May in Lorraine, his native province. Pétain had told the War Minister, General Roques, that he needed more artillery and that he did not believe that a French offensive was possible – the British should attack

[36] Rawlinson diary, 30 April 1916, RWLN 1/5.   [37] Ibid., 2 and 5 May 1916.
[38] 'Notes on Meeting with Generals Foch and Fayolles', Fourth Army Summary of Operations, WO 158/233; Congreve diary, 7 May 1916 (in private hands).

alone.[39] Joffre and GQG were coming under increasing press and parliamentary criticism for their handling of the Verdun defence, and were accused of having ordered the abandonment of the right bank of the Meuse. Tardieu had written two anonymous newspaper articles that appeared in *Le Petit Parisien* on 8 May and in *Le Matin* two days later. These criticised Joffre for his mistakes at Verdun and caused an uproar because, given the severe censorship, publication must have been authorised at a very high level indeed. Joffre was said to be furious that the censor had passed the articles. In addition to the press campaign, the Chamber of Deputies was agitating for a secret session to discuss what had gone wrong at Verdun. Among the leaders of those agitating, Poincaré noted, was a member of Foch's staff. The two Army Commissions added to the pressure: the Senate Army Commission, under the energetic Georges Clemenceau, criticised both Joffre and the government constantly; the Deputies' Commission under General Pédoya sent a series of questions about Verdun to the War Minister.[40] The pressure became so intense that a week later Bertie was recording in his diary the 'fresh movement against Joffre and the ministry', led by Clemenceau and Doumer.[41] Thus the criticisms of the French high command's conduct of operations at Verdun were reaching crisis proportions.

After a discussion in the Conseil des ministres on 27 May of the War Minister's report on the 'Verdun affair' and the casualty figures supplied by Pétain, Poincaré decided to call a meeting of himself and the War Minister with Haig, Foch and Pétain. Roques got Joffre to agree to attend, but without Pétain (Joffre declaring that he did not wish to 'disturb' Pétain).[42] It seems more likely that Joffre did not want to allow him to air his criticisms, especially given Joffre's aim of reassuring the politicians during the meeting that undue risks were not being taken. He composed a memorandum for the meeting that he transmitted to Haig via his liaison officer, who called the document 'eye wash'. Haig's French aide-de-camp (ADC) confirmed that the memorandum was 'badly put together and merely meant for the politicians'. Joffre had no intention of allowing political interference with his plans for the offensives programme agreed at Chantilly the previous December, despite what the enemy was doing at Verdun. Therefore he asked for Haig's support in reassuring the worried politicians that an offensive would indeed take place on the Somme that would 'extricate the French at Verdun'.[43] Nevertheless, Vallières

[39] Poincaré, *AS*, 8: 235, 216, 244–7 (entries for 24, 13, 28 May 1916).
[40] Ibid., 233, 243 (entries for 22 and 27 May 1916).
[41] Bertie, *Diary*, 1: 357 (entry for 5 June 1915).
[42] Poincaré, *AS*, 8: 245 (entry for 28 May 1916).
[43] Mémorandum pour la réunion du 31 mai, 30 May 1916, *AFGG* 4/2, annex 704; Haig diary, 30 May 1916.

(now head of the French Military Mission at GHQ) commented that the memorandum caused a 'bomb' at GHQ.[44]

The memorandum concluded that even if the forthcoming Russian part of the Allied multi-front offensive failed, it would still be necessary to attack in France in order to 'loosen the enemy's grip' at Verdun. The option of waiting for materiel superiority (that is, Foch's preference) should be rejected because that would allow the enemy to pursue his plan of driving a wedge between the coalition members. An offensive was the only way of forestalling this by preventing the enemy from concentrating his forces on each of the Allies in turn. After a long disquisition on numbers and resources and a full rehearsal of various possibilities consequent on various scenarios, the memorandum's final paragraph envisaged that the BEF might have to act alone if the pressure at Verdun intensified or the Germans attacked elsewhere (in Champagne, for example). Thus the politicians were to be reassured that Verdun, where 'France has poured out and is still pouring out [her strength] without counting the cost and for the benefit of the other Entente powers and in the general interests of the Coalition', would be relieved.

The meeting duly took place on 31 May in the presidential train in a railway siding in Saleux, near Amiens. Foch attended. Haig described him as looking 'untrustworthy and a schemer', but this might have been caused simply by his healing facial bruises (it was only a fortnight since the car accident). Haig adds that Foch 'came in for a reprimand' and that he had evidently been speaking 'very freely' to Clemenceau. According to Poincaré's account, Foch had to be pressed to give his opinion, although soldier–*députés* on his staff such as Tardieu were free with their views that there should be no offensive. Roques managed to get Foch to admit that an offensive might be useful, even necessary. Nevertheless it should not be an offensive aiming at breakthrough, but rather at simply easing the pressure on Verdun. A serious offensive, he admitted, should be undertaken only in 1917 when they had more resources. Thus did Foch stand by his 'scientific method' in the face of the war minister, his commander-in-chief, and the President of the Republic. Poincaré recognised that Foch was at odds with his commander-in-chief, who hankered after 'strategic results'.

Haig had assured Joffre beforehand that he would support him in any discussion of the possible need to attack earlier than planned. He carried out his promise, telling Poincaré that he would attack, whatever happened, on about 1 July, and that divisions should be brought back from

[44] Vallières, *Au soleil*, 159.

Salonika in order to push the advance to the Rhine (thereby displaying a breathtaking degree of optimism). He reported to the CIGS that the 'object of the meeting was to make sure that the soldiers were united in their views'. Clearly he was under no illusions as to the true purpose – to reassure the politicians by their unity. After the meeting, Joffre thanked Haig for his support.[45]

Foch told his wife that they had all conferred for two hours and said nothing. He himself did not know whether to be amused or distressed: amused at Briand's calling him 'pessimistic' for not believing that anything decisive could be achieved; or distressed by the politicians' clinging to 'illusions'.[46] Foch's own notes of the meeting state that after repeated questions, which he stalled by requesting to know what offensive they were talking about (presumably to emphasise that such matters ought to be secret), he drew a distinction between the needs of the moment – easing the Verdun situation – and the 'general' war situation, which required material means currently unavailable. Such an offensive must be organised as soon as possible: 'Therein lies the whole dimension of the war – Allies.'[47]

So the situation as June came in was as follows: the politicians were reassured that an offensive would indeed take place, such that it would relieve the pressure at Verdun; this offensive would not begin prematurely (in any case, the agreed twenty days' notice meant that the last week of June was the earliest possible date); Haig was reassured ('the meeting went off very well' and 'I believe the Army and the Govt [sic] are determined to go on for another year'); and Foch had made his disapproval evident, at the cost of some criticism if Haig is to be believed, but had stuck to his scientific method by reducing his front of attack in the face of the reduced resources. (This contrasts strongly with Haig, who would push Rawlinson to widen his objectives without any corresponding increase in resources.) Foch's chief of staff summed up the whole war council procedure in a short, pithy phrase: 'Linge sale [dirty washing]'.[48]

Following the Saleux conference the Somme offensive took on its own momentum. Despite Foch's fears that he did not have enough guns to do more than make a demonstration, the deterioration at Verdun meant that a demonstration was required nevertheless. Aware that something was being prepared further west as the élite French XX Corps arrived on the

[45] Haig diary, 31 May 1916; Poincaré, *AS*, 8: 250–2 (entry for 31 May 1916); secret letter, Haig to Robertson, 31 May 1916, Robertson mss, 7/6/43.
[46] Mme Foch diary, 9 June 1916; Weygand, *IV*, 325.
[47] Foch, Carnets, 31 May 1916, fo. 187.
[48] Haig to Lady Haig, 31 May and 2 June 1916, Haig mss, acc. 3155, ms. 144; Cahiers de notes personnelles, 31 May 1916, Weygand mss, 1K/130 partie déposée, carton 4, [d]15.

north bank of the Somme, the Germans pressed their assaults still further at Verdun. They captured Fort Vaux on 7 June, when its defenders were forced to surrender because of lack of water; Thiaumont fell on the 21st; finally they outflanked Fleury to overlook the city itself. This would be the closest that they would come to Verdun.

Political pressure mounted as German military pressure increased. Briand conceded a secret session of the Chamber of Deputies (16–22 June) and then another in the Senate (4–9 July). Despite much criticism of Joffre and of the state of Verdun's defences prior to the February attack, Briand won the two subsequent votes of confidence by a large margin. Clemenceau was one of only six Senators who voted against the government, after long discussion of Joffre's unwillingness to allow trained workers to return to the armaments factories to produce more guns – a theme dear also to Foch's heart. The Chamber's vote of confidence was significant. Although the motion declared that the Chamber would not interfere in the conception, direction or execution of military operations, yet it nevertheless reserved to itself the right to exercise 'effective supervision' over the conduct of the war.[49] Although the Premier had survived the vote of confidence, the motion made no mention of confidence in the commander-in-chief.

The Premier had saved his Ministry, but at the cost of much venting of criticism of the French high command (the proceedings of the secret sessions did not remain secret for long). If Briand still had any doubts after the Saleux conference as to the views of the Northern Army Group commander, he could not have entertained them as the secret sessions began. Tardieu wrote to him in his capacity a member of the Chamber Army Commission, reflecting (as Briand's biographer remarks) the views of both Foch and Pétain.[50] He predicted that, if the attack under preparation resembled the 1915 offensives, then it would suffer the same fate: failure through insufficient heavy artillery. By depriving Verdun of resources, it might also cause a defeat there as well. We do not have the evidence to know whether Foch was behind Tardieu's letter, although Tardieu had assured Poincaré as early as 19 May that Foch was opposed to any attack in 1916.[51]

On the Somme the detailed planning continued. At a 'dejeuner with Fosh [sic]' at Foch's headquarters on 16 June, Rawlinson and Fayolle and their respective chiefs of staff settled some of the remaining 'intricate

---

[49] On the two secret sessions, see King, *Generals and Politicians*, 115–23 (quotation p. 122); also Bonnefous, *Histoire politique*, 130–56; Allard, *Les Dessous de la guerre*, 11–55.
[50] Suarez, *Briand*, 3: 299, gives a long extract.
[51] Poincaré, *AS*, 8: 228 (entry for 19 May 1916).

points', including the boundaries 'in the advance as well as behind the lines'. Did Foch gather the army commanders together especially, because they could not settle matters otherwise? Certainly Dillon described their meeting as 'a pow-wow & lunch'. Whether Foch's influence and/or presence proved beneficial or not, agreement was reached quite easily. The 16 June seems very late, however, for reaching such critical decisions.[52]

Two further matters were less easy to solve: the date of the infantry attack; and its timing. Rawlinson wanted a 7am start, whilst Fayolle preferred to begin two hours later after having first observed the state of the enemy's defences. The British finally conceded thirty minutes and consented to 7.30, not wishing to make the infantry wait longer than this in the trenches. Rawlinson also stated that he could be ready to attack on the 25th, but would prefer two or three days more of preparation, were that possible. The French responded that they would check the position with Joffre, and communicate the decision later.

The question of the date was complicated both by the events at Verdun, and the action of the other Allies, whose offensives were to be concerted with that in France. At Verdun the German attacks continued to increase during June, both in numbers of units engaged and in artillery fire, and it seemed to Pétain that the enemy was trying to forestall the Allied attack by winning a decisive victory at Verdun. He wrote to his commander-in-chief on 11 June, saying that the right bank of the Meuse was threatened, especially as the French now had fewer guns than a month earlier because of wear. The fall of Verdun which might follow would raise German morale 'inestimably' and threaten the British offensive by freeing troops to move from Verdun to the Somme. He concluded by requesting that the date of 'the British offensive' (note the lack of reference to the French element) should be 'brought forward'. The lesser results of an operation launched prematurely were not to be weighed against the risk of seeing Verdun in German occupation.[53] Although Joffre's reply of the next day urged action worthy of Stonewall Jackson ('I am quite confident that you will continue to hold enemy'; 'reinforcements are coming'; 'I count on you'), he had already told his liaison officer to impress on the British the need to be ready to launch infantry attacks on 25 June.

The second complication concerned the other Allies, for it will be remembered that the Somme offensive was but part of a concerted effort on all fronts. The Italian and Russian portions of the Allied offensives

[52] Réunion tenue à Dury, 16 June 1916, *AFGG* 4/2, annex 1303; Dillon diary, 16 June 1916; Rawlinson diary, 16 June 1916, RWLN 1/5.
[53] Pétain to Joffre, 11 June 1916, *AFGG* 4/2, annex 1153.

were timed to precede the Somme by a fortnight, which was a further reason for Joffre to resist pressure for an earlier start to his offensive in the west. In northern Italy, however, the Austrians had forestalled the proposed Italian action on the Isonzo by attacking on 15 May. Despite the deep snow that still lay in the mountains, by the end of the month the Austrians had advanced to a point where they overlooked Italy's northern plains. Joffre responded to the subsequent Italian cries of alarm and requests for a Russian diversionary attack on the Austrians by insisting that it would be counter-productive for the Russians to attack before they were ready. Unconvinced, the Italians reiterated their demands, supporting them with a personal communication from the King to the Tsar, leading the French military attaché in Petrograd to report that the Russian staff thought that the Italians 'had lost their heads'. Fearing that the Italians might retreat, thus freeing enemy troops for the Russian front, the Russians had consented to begin their southern operation on 4 June, with the main operation further north to begin on 15 June.[54] General A. A. Brusilov's four Russian armies attacked around Lutsk in Bukovina on a 320-kilometre-wide front in a well-coordinated offensive that made spectacular gains, his Eighth Army breaking through three Austrian defensive lines. In three days Brusilov captured over 200,000 prisoners, and the Austro-Hungarians lost more than half their strength. Falkenhayn was obliged to send four German divisions to the east, thus depleting his strategic reserve for the coming battle in the west.[55] Further, in order to collect reserves for the Entente offensive that would obviously be not long in coming, Falkenhayn asked the German *Fifth Army* at Verdun on 24 June to study how the use of men, materiel and munitions might be limited.[56] It was the Russians who relieved the pressure on Verdun, not the British offensive, despite Haig's claim in December 1916.

This excellent news from the Russian front caused Joffre to rescind his request that the British begin their infantry attack on 25th, hence their artillery preparation on the 20th. He wanted to re-instate the original date of 1 July. On 16 June, in a series of telephone messages, he attempted to get Haig to agree, but Haig refused to delay beyond 29th because he had withdrawn troops from other parts of the line in readiness for the attack, and it would be too dangerous to wait longer. The next day in a private meeting at Haig's headquarters they agreed the date of 29 June for the infantry attack, to be communicated verbally to the army

[54] Telegram, Laguiche to Poincaré, Ministère de la Marine, Ministère des Affaires Etrangères, Etat-Major de l'Armée, 3 June 1916, 5N 139.
[55] Herwig, *First World War*, 204–14; Foley, *German Strategy*, 244–5, 253.
[56] Foley, *German Strategy*, 247.

commanders.[57] Northern Army Group headquarters continued to press for a postponement on the grounds that their XX Corps was not ready. As late as 23 June (that is, the day before the artillery preparation was due to start for the infantry attack on the 29th) Foch went personally to Rawlinson's headquarters and asked for a further two-day postponement. Rawlinson telephoned Haig, who refused. So Foch threatened humorously to leave the British to attack alone because he was not ready. ('Which, of course, was all nonsense', Dillon recorded. It is significant that Foch felt able to joke with Dillon and that Dillon could realise that he was joking after a mere five weeks' experience at Foch's headquarters.)[58] In the event, it was the weather that forced the further two-day postponement, and the infantry attack began, quite fortuitously, on 1 July, the very day that had been agreed back in February.

Difficult as operational boundaries, timings and dates were, there was a further question to be resolved. Despite its significance, it never received a satisfactory resolution. This was the matter of the direction of strategic exploitation following any breach of the German lines. Joffre still maintained his aim of 'driving the enemy as widely and as deeply as possible from the ground he occupies', even though Foch was preparing a limited offensive. Joffre expected to be able to move troops gradually from Verdun, and he told Rawlinson as late as 28 June that he wanted to send up a further twenty-eight to thirty divisions 'when we break through'.[59] On 21 June Joffre informed both Foch and Haig that the Bapaume–Cambrai road should constitute the 'axis of progression', with the British cavalry exploiting any breach north of that road and the French cavalry likewise to the south of the road. A long, hard battle would ensure the capture of the enemy's communications hub around Cambrai–Maubeuge–Valenciennes. That is to say, the direction of exploitation was eastwards.[60]

Haig, however, intended to go north. He would enlarge the breach he expected to create between Arras and Bapaume, and then the cavalry would be pushed, not eastwards along the Bapaume–Cambrai road, but northwards 'taking the enemy's lines in flank and reverse' and aiming for the village of Monchy, opposite Arras – it is approximately twenty-five kilometres from Bapaume to Arras, even further if the distance is

[57] Haig diary, 17 June 1916; des Vallières to GQG, 3e Bureau, 18 June 1916, *AFGG* 4/2, annex 1333.
[58] Rawlinson diary, 23 June 1916, RWLN 1/5; Dillon diary, 23 June 1916; Haig diary, 24 June 1916.
[59] Rawlinson, Short Note Diary, 28 June 1916, National Army Museum.
[60] Instruction personnelle et secrète pour M. le général Sir Douglas Haig et le général Foch, 21 June 1916, *AFGG* 4/2, annex 1385. In English in WO 158/14.

calculated from the southern boundary of the BEF's sector. If the enemy's resistance failed to break, the attack might be given up altogether, and the BEF's main efforts moved rapidly to another portion of the front.[61] This was cloud-cuckoo-land. The BEF had spent several months stock-piling supplies and building roads and railheads to support an attack on the Somme; hence the idea that a similar effort might be repeated so late in the campaigning season could not be entertained. In the event, such a change of plan was never contemplated.

Foch's staff examined Haig's proposal, praising the intention to widen any breach. It noted, however, that the move northwards would expose a flank to unsubdued German positions; therefore it was both dangerous and impossible.[62] Foch told Dillon that he disliked the plan. Haig would have to attack the German first position in flank, which Foch believed would be 'tough', or else Haig would be on too narrow a front. His southern flank would be weak and he would be operating alone, without French support. Foch suggested as an alternative that the British should push on eastwards as far as Sailly-Saillisel, supported by the French on their right. He would then take over more of the front north of the river, even as far as Ginchy, with the three or four corps that he anticipated then having available. This would give both the British and the French the protection on their right flank of the little tributary of the Somme, the Tortille. It was a narrow river, flowing in a southwesterly direction through a steep-sided valley.

Then the Anglo-French Army protected on the right by the Tortille could deploy on the line Sailly-Saillisel–Ancre and fight the enemy on the line Bettincourt–Bapaume. This would give them various advantages. They could use a larger force. They would be descending all the way. They would be in open country. They would have a large front. They would have good country to fight in & should be able to go straight on to the Arras–Cambrai road. Then they would really be able to take the front line near Arras right in reverse having cut the communications in that region.[63]

Thus Foch was prepared to make a thoughtful contribution to Haig's stated plan – one that accepted Haig's preferred direction of exploitation and seemed, on the face of it, to offer better prospects of success. Haig's plan to 'roll up' the German lines when a third system of defences was under preparation exposed the cavalry to flank attack. Foch's proposal

[61] Edmonds et al., OH 1916, vol. 1, appendix 13, pp. 86–7. On the British planning for the Somme, see Prior and Wilson, Somme, ch. 5.

[62] Undated, unsigned 'Note', [d] Bataille de la Somme: Armées Anglaises Sorties, Fonds Etat-Major Foch, 14N 48.

[63] Dillon diary, 28 June 1916. 'Bettincourt' should read Bertincourt (10 km due east of Bapaume).

was more ambitious, but offered greater chance of success by keeping British and French forces together. However, when Dillon took these suggestions to Haig, the latter refused to have anything to do with them, telling Dillon that Foch 'was a wily old devil'. Dillon reported back rather more tactfully that Haig was 'grateful for the paper but that he was going to stick to his original plan'.[64] As it happened, it did not matter. No breach in the enemy front occurred that permitted any rolling up of lines. It would be 12 November before Sailly-Saillisel fell to the French. Bapaume never fell at all.

This incident reveals that Foch was prepared to listen to the British plans and to make helpful comments, although Haig remained deeply suspicious of his motives. Despite Foch's aversion to the whole idea of the offensive, it is obvious that during June, when it was clear that an offensive would indeed take place, he became reconciled and even enthusiastic. Dillon noted Foch's 'roaring spirits' after a meeting at Rawlinson's headquarters, and Rawlinson himself noted '[v]ery good cheer', because Foch was on his 'best form' and 'most cordial'. He remarked that Foch was prepared to bring the whole Sixth Army north of the Somme, if the British cavalry got through, to help them capture Bapaume. But Haig stuck to his plan of making his main effort towards the north, whilst forming a defensive flank to the south of Bapaume until the French could get across the Somme.[65]

Joffre had placed the headquarters of Third Army at Foch's disposition after withdrawing it from alongside the Second Army at Verdun, and designating units from the Centre Army Group to move to the northern sector (21–22 June). This is an index of Joffre's determination to supply the Somme offensive as generously as he could. The arrival of the Third Army staff enabled Foch to withdraw Tenth Army from the defensive front so as to be held in readiness for joining the offensive. Tenth Army would be in a position either to support a British success north of the Somme, or to carry out a southern operation towards Roye.[66]

Clearly, then, Joffre had done his best to maintain his offensive strategy for 1916 and to support Foch's operation. Yet Foch made frequent complaints that the artillery provision was insufficient, and may have been working to destabilise Joffre politically through his contacts with parliamentarians. He told his wife on 8 June that Joffre neither organised

---

[64] Haig diary, 28 June 1916; Dillon diary, 28 June 1916. The British official history records that Foch's plan would expose the British left flank and that no reply was sent: Edmonds, *et al.*, *OH 1916*, 1: 50.

[65] Dillon diary, 25 June 1916; Rawlinson diary, 25 and 28 June 1916, RWLN 1/5.

[66] *AFGG* 4/2, 217.

nor ordered anything long term, and that the *députés* Meunier-Surcouf and Tardieu were leading the campaign to reorient policy so as to 'take in hand the important methodical means of arriving at definitive victory' – and Meunier-Surcouf had lunch with the Fochs on 12 June.[67] Certainly Dillon wondered, probably correctly, whether Foch was 'on the look out for his own glory'.[68]

In summary, Foch was obliged to mount an operation on the Somme, in an area which was not his preferred area of attack, and with resources which Verdun rendered too restricted, because his commander-in-chief insisted on maintaining the Somme plan. Nonetheless, Foch stuck to the principles of his 'scientific method', refusing to permit an attack on a wider front than he judged possible with the resources to hand. The last entry in Foch's notebooks before the infantry battle began is 'The [artillery] preparations on the villages still inadequate!'

[67] Mme Foch diary, 9 and 12 June 1916.   [68] Dillon diary, 28 June 1916.

8   Fighting on the Somme, July–November 1916

In order to carry out his 'scientific method' in the forthcoming Somme battle, Foch had to complete three tasks successfully. First he had to ensure that the artillery was employed effectively with good observation by his aviation services and efficient liaison between aviation, artillery and infantry. The different types of guns would have precisely delimited roles in order to destroy the enemy's front-line defences, before the infantry launched their assault. As for the heavy artillery, he himself kept control within the army group, with Fayolle's agreement. Second, he had to coordinate the successive operations against enemy lines, which entailed getting all units, French and British, to re-start operations in a concerted and synchronised manner against succeeding German lines. Finally, he had to divide his attention between the north and south banks of the Somme. To the north, one of Fayolle's Sixth Army corps (XX Corps) was in line, but the majority of troops were British to whom he could send only advice, not commands. To the south, the two remaining Sixth Army corps were in line, and another army (Tenth Army under General Alfred Micheler) was gradually formed as units were freed from Verdun. The geography of the two sectors on either side of the river was quite different. In the south lay a plateau, bounded by the river to the north and east, and by a line of villages to the south. Because the Somme upstream of Péronne flows south–north, any French penetration into the enemy front in this sector would soon reach the river, which could be crossed easily only if the Germans did not defend it – but this was unlikely. Downstream of Péronne the river flows from the east seawards and, except for communications with the southern bank, it did not affect the action of the BEF and the single French corps in the northern sector. Here the terrain rises to the watershed between the Somme and the Ancre rivers – the Thiepval Ridge, where so many British were to become casualties – with the heights crowned by fortified villages. The German lines on the far side of the ridge were situated on the reverse slope, hence invisible to British gunners whenever weather conditions prevented aerial observation.

The battle continued for four and a half months from the opening artillery barrages on 24 June, followed by the infantry assault on 1 July, ending mid-November. Except for a few set-piece attacks – 1 July itself, the tanks on 15 September – most of the action consisted of local operations on a restricted front, and most of these were postponed, often repeatedly. It would be tedious to relate all the constant negotiations, delays and frustrations, although there were lessons to be learned from the reasons for the repeated frustrations. Instead, in order to examine Foch's role, this chapter will concentrate on three main phases of the battle. These are, first, the fighting in the opening month of July, when a comparison between French successes and British casualties caused a re-think of the whole basis of the operation; second, the repeated and unsuccessful attempts during August and September to re-start wide-front operations such as had been successful on 1 July, a task complicated by Joffre's wish to synchronise such action with Romania's entry into the war on the side of the Entente; finally, the drift during October and November as the weather finally put a stop to further action.

Despite Verdun and all the difficulties of mounting an Allied operation, Foch's units were ready for the start on 1 July. (See Table 1.) The volume

Table 1: *Sixth Army infantry and artillery resources, 1 July 1916*

		Batteries of heavy artillery	Density of guns* (for whole army)
North of the Somme			
XX Corps	39 DI (next to BEF)	3 of 95s	528 heavy guns = 1 gun per 28m
		3 of 105s	61 extra heavy guns = 1 gun per
	11 DI	2 of long 120s	246m
		6 of long 155s	1 battery of short 155s per 500m
South of the Somme			1 battery of 220s per 600m
I Colonial	2 DIC	2 of quick-firing 100s	1 battery of long guns (46% were
Corps	3 DIC	5 of 95s	155s) per 250m
		7 of long 120s	1 battery of field guns per 144m
		14 of long 155s	1 heavy mortar per 267m
		4 groups extra-heavy mortars	
XXXV	6 DI	3 of 95s	
Corps		2 of 105s	
		10 long 155s	
		8 of neighbouring corps' heavies	

*Figures from Commandant Pagézy, 'L'Artillerie dans la préparation de l'attaque du 1er juillet à la VI Armée et pendant la Bataille de la Somme', Annexe, 16N 1982. In addition, the trench artillery provided one battery of 58s per 300m, and one battery of 240s per kilometre.

of artillery allocated to these units was a tribute to Joffre's determination to maintain his 1916 offensive plans despite the enemy's assault. Although some of the heavy artillery taken from the Centre and Eastern Army Groups was late arriving on the Somme or incomplete when it did arrive, 555 heavy guns were ready to fire on 24 June – an impressive total. The only drawback was a deficit in the munitions for the 155s, the most useful gun. The two other army groups were denied allocations of 155 shells, and even the Northern Army Group was ordered to be economical. French engineers had built over 272 kilometres of railway and had improved the Somme's lateral canal to help alleviate the lack of roads, especially for medical evacuations.[1] Foch had significant aviation resources to carry out spotting and reconnaissance for the troops on the ground and also to bomb targets such as railway stations, enemy troop concentrations and airfields. In fact, with 113 fighter aircraft and three groupes de bombarde-ment or bomber forces (GB 3 arrived in April in the Somme sector, and Escadrille 101 at the end of June, although GB 5 was not complete until mid-July), in addition to the 410 aircraft and 426 pilots of the RFC, the Allies had unrivalled air superiority at the start of the battle.[2] Foch had been careful to synchronise with Sir Hugh Trenchard (the RFC's commander) the start of air operations to destroy enemy balloons, arguing that it was vital to commence such operations before the artillery barrage began and not the day after, as Trenchard had ordered. Foch also sent a member of his staff to settle last-minute technical matters such as bad-weather contingency plans, timings, and synchronising watches.[3]

On 20 June Foch issued instructions for the forthcoming battle, which were distributed down to battalion level. They reflected the lessons that GQG had taken from the fighting at Verdun: infantry should not be used in dense formations. Rather, commanders should put in the first line of attackers the strict minimum of troops, with the remainder ready to reinforce and to manoeuvre as required.[4] Foch's directive repeated the need for economy in using the infantry, insisting over and over again on this single principle – the guns do the attacking:

the infantry's role is limited to capturing and occupying ground where the artillery has destroyed the defences effectively and completely, and to holding on to it. Furthermore, taking possession of the ground must be carried out *prudently* after reconnaissance, so as to avoid all surprise fire where the artillery destruction had not succeeded, and *under the constant protection of the guns.* [original emphasis]

[1] *AFGG* 4/2, 219, n. 1.
[2] Chagnon, '1916', 42; Martel, *French Bombardment Forces*, 116, 125.
[3] Foch to Haig and Trenchard, 23 June 1916, GAN Aviation Records, 18N 167.
[4] Joffre, Note pour les armées, 3 June 1916, *AFGG* 4/2, annex 868.

Hence the prewar doctrine, which had made the artillery's sole aim that of accompanying an infantry attack, had been replaced by methods that placed the artillery action *before* rather than simultaneous with the infantry's. From this desire for caution and protection Foch derived the attacking formation. The notion of an assault 'breaking all resistance by brute force' must be abandoned because successive waves of infantry lead to chaos, excessive losses and powerlessness. All units must be formed up in depth: 'So as to reduce the losses of succeeding combat échelons, they must be split up into small columns and largely linked together [articulés] from front to back and in depth.' The role of the commanding officer was to maintain an ordered and continuous line of attack, with no wild rushing about. Each commander in the field should be in the midst of his troops so as to be informed of events as quickly and as completely as possible, with divisional commanders placing themselves so as to be in contact with their brigade commanders. The directive ended with the statement that modern battle was of long duration, and so it was important to enable the infantry to last out: 'it is vitally important to be strictly economical with the infantry, only to ask it to carry out tasks of which it is capable, to exert close and methodical control'.[5]

In order to achieve his aim of sparing the infantry, Foch ensured that pilots photographed and mapped the terrain over which the infantry was to advance, and that lower-level commanders understood the necessity to observe artillery barrages to verify that each specific task had been completed. Joffre had supplied an unprecedented number of guns and munitions for the five-day artillery preparation that began on 24 June. It became a seven-day operation because bad weather in the middle prevented proper observation, and Foch and Rawlinson agreed a forty-eight hour postponement to compensate. The artillery barrage was overwhelming: Leutnant der Landwehr Richard Grün of *Reserve-Feldartillerie-Regiment 29* described it as a tempest such that no Dante could have imagined worse for his hell.[6]

Although Sixth Army had wanted to postpone the start date so as to complete construction of its 60cm gauge railways for bringing up supplies and munitions, Haig refused to delay any further and so Fayolle's Sixth Army began the assault north of the river on 1 July at 7.30am alongside the BEF's XIII Corps. They overran the entire German position that had been assigned to them in their narrow sector, for a casualty toll of about 800 in two days of fighting. South of the river, the two French corps did even better. The I Colonial Corps had gone beyond its first objective and

[5] Note à communiquer jusqu'aux bataillons, 20 June 1916, ibid., annex 1369.
[6] Cited in Lipp, 'Les Soldats allemands sur la Somme', 329.

by nightfall on 1 July was in position to attack the German second line. The XXXV Corps on the southern end of the attacking front also took all its objectives, although suffering more casualties because of its exposed position on the flank. The comparison with the poor results on the British front, where very little ground was taken except for the sector nearest the French, could not have been more stark.

The reasons for the disparity are easily understood. The two attacking divisions of XX Corps had left the hard fighting at Verdun at the end of April, arriving on the Somme at the beginning of June. Yet enemy artillery fire was just as deadly for well-trained or experienced infantry as it was for the inexperienced Kitchener divisions further north. Artillery was the key. On 1 July Sixth Army had 972 field guns and, more importantly, 528 heavy guns, or one gun per 28m of front. The large proportion of heavy guns devoted to counter-battery work in the French sector meant that there was one battery of such guns every 250m (see Table 1). Many attacking British battalions were wiped out by unsuppressed enemy artillery even before they reached their own front line because so few British guns were devoted to this important task. Foch's artillery liaison officer at Fourth Army headquarters reported as early as the end of May that artillery commanders in the British corps seemed not to believe in the usefulness of counter-battery, and that some even believed that the task was secondary. This attitude must be countered, the officer concluded.[7] South of the river the French attack was helped by the fact that the German lines were much closer together, so that over-shooting the first or second line might still result in a hit on an enemy position further back. (The reason usually attested for the French success in this sector – that the Germans did not know they were coming – is false, and there was no element of surprise.[8]) Success was due to the fact that the Germans were seriously out-gunned. At the start of the battle they had only 184 heavy guns (greater than 100mm calibre) against over 500 similar French guns and another 200 in Fourth Army alongside.[9]

So the attention that Foch gave to specific artillery tasks paid dividends for the French. However, the disparity in the achievements of the first two days of fighting caused problems in coordinating as speedily as possible another concerted push on the next objective. Coordination of the two battles north and south of the river became even more difficult when the

[7] Commandant Héring, 'Rapport au sujet de l'artillerie dans l'opération projetée à la IVe Armée', n.d. [received 27 May 1916], 16N 1916.
[8] Bülow, German 1st Army, 2.
[9] 'Deutsche und feindliche Artillerie bei Verdun und an der Somme 1916', RAW, 10: Anlage 1. The table is not very accurate for the numbers of British guns, and I have taken these from Prior and Wilson, CWF, 168.

results of the first two days' fighting were compared. North of the Somme the French were now obliged to wait for the British to catch up by completing the capture of the German first position before starting on a concerted attempt to capture the second. South of the Somme the easy capture of territory in the bend of the river gave rise to thoughts of taking back the initiative from the British and exploiting the greater success to the south.

This disparity between British and French results caused a row at Haig's headquarters. Joffre had been impressed by the 'atmosphere of methodical work and considered confidence' that he had seen in the various French corps headquarters.[10] On 3 July he collected Foch for a joint visit to Haig's headquarters in Beauquesne to discuss future arrangements. There he learned that Haig did not intend to continue to attack in the northern sectors, where operations had met with little success; rather he would exploit the greater success on his right and attack northwards towards Longueval. Thus Haig was proposing to substitute, for the wide front aiming generally eastwards, a narrow front to be pushed northwards. Joffre was furious. He thumped the table, ordered Haig to maintain the wide-front attack that had been agreed, and then left.

Haig was shocked by such ungentlemanly behaviour, and the story soon did the rounds. For Foch, Joffre's outburst had a double consequence. First, after having been informed by his liaison officer of Haig's displeasure, Joffre left it to Foch to sort things out with Haig. Besides, Joffre would be occupied for the next few weeks in negotiating the entry of Romania into the war and then, furthermore, Poincaré asked him to prepare an armistice in case the Germans asked for terms.[11] So Foch had the opportunity to forge a closer relationship with Haig who, as we have seen, did not trust his colleague. On 5 July the head of the British mission at Joffre's HQ noted that Haig looked on Foch as 'a theorist and an intriguer'.[12] The second effect of the row was to open up the possibility of exploiting the greater success south of the river, leaving the British, as Joffre put it, to 'muddle along' in their sector if they were refusing to stick to the principle of a wide front.[13] As Joffre was unable to insist on Haig acting according to the French plan, he resigned himself to letting the British do as they wished. His chief of staff, General Castelnau, pushed the idea of exploiting towards the south very energetically. He wished to aim for Noyon, the German-occupied town closest to Paris. Pushing the Sixth Army

---

[10] Joffre, JM, 2 July 1916, 14N 2.
[11] Pedroncini (ed.), *Joffre, JM*, 86 (entry for 12 August 1916).
[12] Clive diary, 5 July 1916, CAB 45/201.
[13] Pedroncini (ed.), *Joffre, JM*, 38 (entry for 4 July 1916).

southwards, he argued, would take the enemy lines along the river in flank and then Tenth Army might join in by attacking the German lines frontally. Since Georges Clemenceau's newspaper, *L'Homme Enchaîné*, declared as a banner headline in each issue that the Germans were at Noyon, any successful recapture of the town would have a huge morale effect.

The legend has grown up that a marvellous opportunity was lost at this moment, that Foch was slow to realise how well his southern corps had done. His refusal to allow the infantry to press on without halting angered the commanders on the spot, who would insist later that the chance to exploit an eight-kilometre breach in the German lines south of the river was thrown away. The I Colonial Corps cavalry had gone further than its assigned objective, and entered the village of Barleux that the Germans had abandoned. However, since the 'scientific method' required successive efforts to be prepared by the artillery, the Colonial Corps was withdrawn and Barleux remained in enemy hands. Castelnau was angry. In his view, Foch lacked vision and the 'crab' (Castelnau's private name for Joffre) lacked decision.[14]

Yet there are several problems with any decision to reverse the agreed priorities, changing from an operation with a north-easterly axis of attack in support of the British to an operation aiming towards the south. First of all, the French would lose all control over what the British were doing, and Haig had already indicated to Joffre on 3 July his unwillingness to fall in with the latter's plans. It would be a serious step to abandon the principle upon which the 1916 campaign had been built, namely a concerted wide-front operation in which the new British armies would play an important role (in the event, after Verdun, the more important role). Indeed Fayolle was resigned to losing the opportunity to exploit the eight-kilometre breach in the German lines in the south, because that would mean 'letting go of the British, and we won't do that because they would fall back into inaction'.[15] In any case, the French had insufficient troops to achieve very much on the south side of a marshy river, when the larger troop concentration (the British) was on the north bank. Moreover, even with Noyon as a prize, the area was a cul-de-sac bounded by another river, the Oise, and by canals linking it to the Somme. Foch had already indicated in the planning stage that all the strategic opportunities were in the north, and Weygand claimed that Foch always believed that the principal action was to take place north of the Somme, in accordance with the agreed plans.[16]

---

[14] Gras, *Castelnau*, 314.   [15] Fayolle, *CS*, 165 (entry for 3 July 1916).
[16] Weygand, *IV*, 334.

Nonetheless, despite Weygand's postwar defence, Foch *was* prepared to exploit the opportunity. What he was not prepared to do was to allow the infantry to press on without having fired another artillery barrage to open the way – hence the anger of the local commanders, who had wanted to press on without waiting. However, Fayolle was in complete agreement with Foch, who ordered him on 3 July to make for the old, straight Roman road which runs east–west from the Somme to Villers Bretonneux and to establish a front thereon facing south, so as to cover Tenth Army as it took up position to exploit the breach. Instead of the original intention to push I Colonial Corps eastwards towards the river and Péronne, Foch was now demanding a new direction – southwards. The time required to move and re-register guns meant that it was only on 5 July that the infantry could set off again, and by that time the Germans had reacted, had thrown in all their available reserves and had begun the construction of another defensive line along the river. The costly French infantry attacks were halted on 10 July, as the fleeting opportunity evaporated.

The possibility of exploitation south of the river remained, however, and that same day Fayolle ordered another three-day artillery preparation; Tenth Army was told to expect a substantial reinforcement of heavy artillery; and Foch requested another corps to replace the reserves that he had dedicated to the sector south of the river. Joffre agreed to send him VII Corps, since the position at Verdun had eased sufficiently to permit this.[17] GQG appeared to approve Foch's dispositions, and accepted that the French had enough resources to push hard both sets of attack, not only in the north supporting the British but also in the south.[18]

Meanwhile, on the north bank, the British Fourth Army completed the capture of the German second position by their night attack of 14 July, and so they and XX Corps alongside could move forward once again in a joint operation. Accordingly, a meeting with the British was arranged for 17 July at Foch's headquarters. Foch wanted another concerted push, as on 1 July, as speedily as possible, and he had already asked Fayolle to make for the line of the Tortille river but to maintain contact with the British.[19] If Fayolle could reach the line of the steep-sided river doubled by the unfinished Canal du Nord, his right flank would be protected and so he could keep step with the British as they advanced northwards. At the meeting on the 17th a new line of demarcation was settled that gave the

---

[17] *AFGG* 4/2, 252–4.
[18] Note sommaire sur les projets et les intentions de manœuvre des généraux Foch et Fayolle, 6 July 1916, ibid., annex 2070.
[19] Instruction personnelle et secrète pour M. général commandant la VIe armée, 6 July 1916, ibid., annex 2434.

French both a bit more room to manoeuvre, and a British-built railway line running into Maricourt. This enabled another French division to move into the northern sector. However, despite the increased numbers of French infantry, French and British operations remained interdependent. Haig realised that he had to extend his hold on the old German second position by taking Pozières on his left and Ginchy and Guillemont on his right. Until Ginchy and Guillemont were captured, the strongpoint of Falfemont Farm could not be taken; and the French objective of Maurepas could not be taken until the farm was captured. Consequently Fayolle's artillery was ordered to support the British right with counter-battery fire. All these arrangements were complicated and took time to finalise, and Foch became impatient. A concerted attack, he wrote in a note handed to Haig on 19 July, is the 'easiest and most profitable method ... the best way to obtain wide and lasting results, avoid losses and conserve the results gained by making it impossible for the enemy to concentrate his artillery fire'.[20] However, continued delays, caused by the weather preventing observation for the artillery and by necessary reliefs for troops who had been in line since 1 June, made Foch even more impatient. He returned to the seemingly better opportunities in the south, and, in order to bring in Tenth Army there, ordered XX Corps to take Hem, a village on high ground north of the Somme. Capture of the Hem plateau would give artillery observation over the Tenth Army's proposed sector of operation in the south.

The results of all this planning were disappointing, as a listing of the action in the second half of July shows. Between 15 and 22 July the British made six separate attacks on the Longueval–Delville Wood sector. Thus they could support the French XX Corps attack on Hem on 20 July with only a single British unit (35 Division). Next the joint attack planned for 23 July was postponed for twenty-four hours, and then Fayolle postponed it again. When the operation began finally on 30 July, there were some initial successes, but the enemy had recovered from his initial surprise and adopted a new tactic. German machinegunners established in shell holes stopped the French and British attacks, and so the order that the fighting be continued on 1 August was countermanded.

Despite Foch's urging that both armies needed to coordinate another wide-front attack like 1 July, neither Rawlinson nor Fayolle had been able to put a halt to small-scale local actions. This was not simply the result of British inexperience, because Fayolle's experienced Verdun veterans were doing the same thing. At least the French had the excuse that their

---

[20] Note handed to General Sir Douglas Haig, 19 July 1916, ibid., annex 2491.

restricted area on the north bank, a cone-shaped sector with the British on their left and the river on their right, made bringing up rations and munitions difficult. The bad weather did not help, neither on the ground nor in the skies, since aviators could not observe the enemy dispositions. Foch must bear a portion of the blame for the lack of coordination, because he was still distracted by the possibility of exploitation to the south. GQG were talking about cavalry exploitation and Weygand underlined a comment in his notebook about an attack towards the south being 'decided'. Indeed II Cavalry Corps was readied to reconnoitre a crossing of the Somme south of Péronne. It was no secret at Northern Army Group headquarters because Dillon (his liaison officer with Haig) noted that Foch was going 'to do a lot more in the South'.[21]

By the end of July, however, and given the meagre results of the joint French and British action on the 30th, Joffre decided to put a stop to the ideas of exploitation southwards from the Somme. He had spent a whole day in Verdun on 28 July and noted the easing of tension there as a result of the Somme offensive and also Second Army's confidence in Nivelle's command.[22] Consequently he called Foch to GQG on 31 July and informed him that the fundamental purpose of the Somme offensive, namely French support for British action northeastwards towards Cambrai, remained unchanged. In order to reaffirm this purpose, Fayolle's Sixth Army was restricted to north of the river, with Tenth Army taking over the units in line in the south; exploitation southwards was to be 'secondary or subordinate to results obtained in the north'; and Foch was to bring the British high command back to the original intention of concerted attacks on a wide front.[23] Foch passed on these instructions to Sixth and Tenth Army that evening on his return to his headquarters.

So July came to an end, the only rewards for the costly efforts made on the Somme being the relief of the tension at Verdun and the help afforded to the Russians by retaining German troops in the west. Foch had found the constant negotiations with the British very difficult, demanding a patience that he had not known he possessed, he told his wife. The British could throw aside agreements reached after much talking because they had 'forgotten' some detail, he complained, and then they all had to start again. Furthermore, he also had to act as a 'pot of glue' (one of Foch's favourite analogies), patiently dealing with the results of Joffre's lack of the

---

[21] Joffre, JM, 6 and 9 July 1916, 14N 2; Weygand, Cahier 2, entry for 9 July 1916, 1K/130/4, [d] 15; Dillon diary, 10 July 1916.

[22] Pedroncini (ed.), *Joffre, JM*, 69 (entry for 28 July 1916).

[23] Décision prise par le général en chef à la suite d'un entretien avec le général Foch et notifiée verbalement à ce dernier, 31 July 1916, *AFGG* 4/2, annex 2649.

necessary forms of politeness (as during the row on 3 July) and Haig's taking offence.[24]

Coordination with the British was not Foch's only difficulty, and more wide-ranging problems were beginning to surface. The first was man-power, the result of the huge losses at Verdun on top of those already suffered in 1914 and 1915. Joffre had been forced to write to the Minister of War on 19 July, requesting both that the class of 1917 begin their training and that the census of the class of 1918 be taken.[25] Newly formed divisions were now reduced from four to three regiments of infantry, a measure gradually extended to existing divisions. Second, reserves of artillery munitions were diminishing. The *daily* average of shells fired during July had been over 206,000 for the 75s and over 21,000 for the 155s (the principal heavy gun), in addition to the trench artillery, grenades, and smoke shells expended. Over 26,000 heavy artillery rounds had also been delivered to Sixth and Tenth armies during July.[26] Joffre turned down Foch's request of 22 July for increased allocation of shells for his 75s and a British request a few days later for 500 shells for their 220mm guns.[27] Yet it was important to keep up the pressure on the Somme to encourage the Romanians, with whom Joffre had been negotiating for some time. Finally, the Romanian Premier Ion Brătianu would sign the political and military conventions with the Entente on 17 August. As Sixth Army's liaison officer reported to London: 'French higher command is anxious to avoid even the appear-ance of a check just now ... there are probably some important foreign negotiations pending.'[28] Joffre's attempts to coordinate an offensive in France with Romanian action in the east would constitute another difficulty in the second phase of the Battle of the Somme.

The second phase (August and September) was characterised by Foch's attempts to stop small, local actions and return to a larger joint operation. (See Map 11.) Despite the professed intentions, and despite the symbolic splitting of Fayolle's command to reflect the commitment to support the British and principal action, the month of August saw more of the same methods with the same results. The British carried out limited (in scope, but not in frequency) and uncoordinated actions on the Somme front. Between 1 and 24 August, there were attacks of at least battalion strength made on fourteen days, mostly on positions on the left and centre of

---

[24] Letter, Foch to Mme Foch, 19 July 1916, vol. 41; Mme Foch diary, 31 July 1916.

[25] Pedroncini (ed.), *Joffre, JM*, 58 (entry for 19 July 1916).

[26] Figures calculated from *AFGG* 11, appendices 47 and 48.

[27] Pedroncini (ed.), *Joffre, JM*, 61 (entry for 23 July 1916), 64 (entry for 25 July 1916). Foch was told to make do with what he had until the end of September.

[28] Spears to CGS, 26 July 1916, SPRS 1/7, LHCMA.

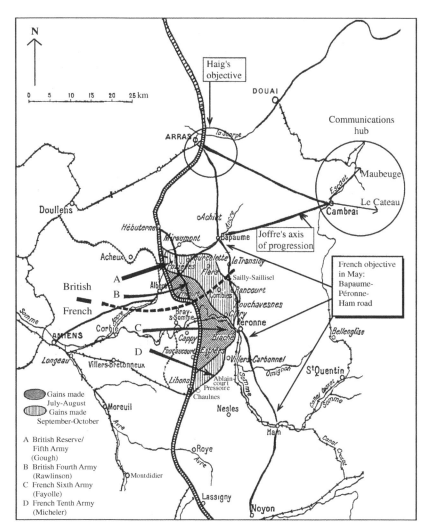

Map 11 Gains made during the Somme fighting, 1916

Fourth Army's front. On the right flank, in cooperation with the French, three battalions were involved in attacks on two occasions.[29] The French Sixth Army, too, was bogged down in local operations. The head of the French Military Mission to the British army, General des Vallières, reported to Joffre a list of delays in joint operations caused by that army,

[29] Prior and Wilson, *CWF*, 219, and table 20.2.

delays which had the effect of making the British slow down in their turn.[30]

In an attempt to halt such actions, Joffre composed a letter to Haig on 11 August, using the help of Foch and Vallières (whom Foch already knew, of course, from 1915 when Vallières was Tenth Army's chief of staff). Vallières had reported to Joffre that Foch was unable to exercise any control over the British high command, mainly it would appear because Haig preferred to receive directives from GQG rather than from Foch. This underlined further the difficulty of the army-group level of command that had dogged Foch from the start. Joffre took action, therefore, but did not risk another row with Haig as had happened on 3 July, and entrusted the letter to Vallières to deliver personally. In it Joffre urged a return to the 1 July wide-front method and an end to the small-scale actions of detail that seemed to be continuing. He proposed simultaneous attacks on 22 August to reach a position for the 1 September 'big push', when both armies would pass onto the offensive together: namely, on the Guillemont–Ginchy sector between the Bapaume road and the Somme and on the sector between the Bapaume road and the river Ancre.[31] At the same time Joffre reminded Foch in a telegram that the principal action was to support the British by having Sixth Army set a good example of energy.[32] Joffre had chosen skilfully the day on which to write to Haig, because the following day, 12 August, he and Foch attended GHQ and lunched with King George and Poincaré. Such an occasion might obviate the risk of a repeat of the 3 July row, although Joffre had to suffer the lemonade offered during the meal in observance of King George's pledge not to drink alcohol until the war had ended. Yet Joffre had a success with Haig, who said that he was in total agreement with the principle of wide-front attacks. He had already told Rawlinson on 2 August to concentrate on his right flank so as to facilitate operations with the French.

Joffre's insistence on hurrying the British and maintaining his original 1 September date owed its urgency to the Romanians. After much haggling the government in Bucharest signed an agreement with the Allies on 17 August, and Joffre wished to 'celebrate' their joining the Entente powers with another Allied 'big push' such as had occurred on 1 July. He maintained his multi-front strategy further by getting the Salonika army to make an attack at about the same time as well. He informed the Russians and the Italians, via the heads of the French missions at each headquarters, that the British and French were about to build on the success obtained on 1

---

[30] Mémorandum pour le chef du 3e bureau, 5 August 1916, *AFGG* 4/2, annex 2746.
[31] Letter, Joffre to Haig, 11 August 1916, ibid., annex 2864, and WO 158/15.
[32] Telegram, Joffre to Foch, 11 August 1916, *AFGG* 4/2, annex 2863.

July by mounting attacks astride the Somme on a front of some forty-six kilometres (twenty-four French divisions supported by 1200 heavy guns, and fifteen British divisions supported by 700 heavy guns). As this offensive was timed to coincide with Romania's entry into the war, he invited the Italians and the Russians to pursue their own offensives so as to take advantage of the concordance of Allied efforts.[33]

Haig was determined, however, despite his agreement in principle with Joffre, to wait for reinforcements of men and the arrival of tanks before starting the next 'big push'. He also needed to complete the capture of a number of local strongpoints so as to have a good jumping-off line. The repeated failures to secure Guillemont and Ginchy meant that he believed that the main portion of the September attack could not now take place until 10 September. Moreover Fayolle's army was feeling the strain, for XX Corps had been in line since April and was in urgent need of relief. This began on 21 August and caused further delays. The reliefs had to be effected, the new troops had to get to know the sector, and there were discipline problems with the colonial troops. Foch had to intervene to deal with these, for which Fayolle was grateful.[34]

Joffre disapproved of these delays and wrote again to Haig on 25 August, pressing the case for as early a date as possible. He was now prepared to delay until 5 September (not the 10th as Haig had agreed with Foch on 19 August), and tried some moral blackmail by pointing out the five months' defence at Verdun, the Russian and Romanian action, and the obligation for the British to intensify their efforts.[35] Two days later, in the presidential train at Saleux near Amiens, Joffre and Foch spent the day in conference with Haig as the sole British representative, and with Poincaré, Briand and General Roques, the War Minister. Joffre rehearsed the same arguments and Haig suggested that 15 September was now the likely date for the British offensive. The French also discussed the man-power question (Joffre wanted to incorporate the 1918 class into the armies in October 1916, whereas the Ministers decided that January 1917 was the earliest possible date), and the question of producing more powerful guns in order to make up for the falling numbers of infantrymen. It seems that, apart from outlining the forthcoming French contribution to the renewed Somme battle, Foch intervened only in the discussion of artillery. According to Poincaré, Foch insisted that production of artillery

---

[33] Cipher telegram, Joffre to head of French Military Mission to the Italian army, and same to head of French Military Mission to the Russian army, 23 August 1916, ibid., annexes 3042, 3043.

[34] Fayolle, *CS*, 172–3 (entry for 10 August 1916).

[35] Conventions en date du 19 août entre le général Foch et le général Haig, *AFGG* 4/2, annex 3004; letter, Joffre to Haig, 25 August 1916, ibid., annex 3073, and WO 158/15.

should be increased and perhaps he insisted too much, for Poincaré noted immediately afterwards that he (Foch) 'believes our production capacity to be unlimited'.[36]

So what had started (in his letter of 11 August) as an operation with everyone attacking together that Joffre wished to begin on 1 September was postponed to the 5th, then the 10th, and finally became staggered, not joint, attacks: Tenth Army south of the Somme on 4th and 5th, Sixth Army north of the river on 12th and 13th, and the BEF with their small fleet of tanks on the 15th. Joffre tried as late as 9 September to get Haig to advance his date, but in vain. Three days earlier the high hopes generated by Romania's accession had been dashed. The Romanian high command abandoned its war plan to invade Austria-Hungary and redeem their ethnic brothers after a German-led Bulgarian attack captured a southern Romanian fortress, followed by a series of military reverses that led (by December) to the enemy's occupation of Bucharest.

Joffre's refusal to delay and Haig's refusal to advance the date were mitigated by the dreadful weather, which caused the French to postpone a little. Tenth Army attacked south of the river on 4 and 5 September and made small, albeit significant, gains; but the success could not be exploited for lack of resources. Fayolle's army captured Bouchavesnes, north of the river, on 12 and 13 September, but was exhausted by the effort. Foch and Fayolle had a 'terrible meeting' the next day, when Foch insisted that Fayolle support the British attack on the 15th despite the weariness of his troops. The failure to coordinate the timing of British and French attacks reduced chances of success, and provides a lamentable example of Allied cooperation. After two and a half months, it should have been possible to come to an agreement over such a critical matter as a coordinated start date. Because of this failure Haig and Joffre must bear the responsibility for what Fayolle called his 'wasted day' on 15 September with 'useless casualties', and the first battlefield appearance of the British tanks was no compensation. Foch's responsibility for the casualties caused by failure to synchronise the date is less than that of the two commanders-in-chief who had argued about it. Finally Joffre seems to have appreciated the dangers caused by separate attacks. When he visited the Somme on 16 September he advised Fayolle to suspend operations for the time being until a new attack could be prepared on the German third position, this time in conjunction with the British.[37]

[36] Haig diary, 27 August 1916; Pedroncini (ed.), *Joffre, JM*, 100–1 (entry for 27 August 1916); Poincaré, *AS*, 8: 326 (entry for 27 August 1916).
[37] Pedroncini (ed.), *Joffre, JM*, 119 (entry for 16 September 1916).

September came to an end with some further progress. The Reserve Army managed to complete the capture of Thiepval Ridge, and Fourth Army took what had been the German third line, with honours going to weight of artillery rather than the new tanks. Another factor in the success was finally the proper cooperation of French and British, who encircled Combles, thereby cutting off its German defenders and pinching it out. This was the first chef-lieu of a canton to be liberated since October 1914.

Foch's role during August and September seems to have been limited. Joffre had taken over the task of dealing with Haig, not because he did not trust Foch but because he was receiving reports about British sensibilities and wished to deal as CinC to CinC. Moreover Joffre's strategy from the beginning of the war had been coordinated and simultaneous offensives on many fronts in order to deny the Central Powers' advantage of interior lines when shifting reserves from front to front. Now that the position around Verdun was greatly eased, and Romania's declaration of war on Austria-Hungary had come ten days after joining the Entente, Joffre was determined to bend Haig to his will (albeit, as we have seen, unsuccessfully). This left to Foch the task of coordinating Tenth Army's offensive with Sixth Army. Since Tenth Army had to play a secondary role because of limited munitions, both Foch and its commander Micheler felt dissatisfied. Micheler complained that he was in a 'delicate' situation and being criticised for expending too many shells, but that Foch had provided 'valuable moral support'.[38]

August and September had not been completely frustrating for Foch. He learned on 27 September that he was not to be retired when he reached the age limit for generals on his sixty-fifth birthday in October. Moreover, Joffre seemed to have been pleased with the (limited) British successes on 15 and 25 September, and Foch wrote to his wife that if the British could keep up the pressure there might be significant results. So there were grounds for optimism. Despite (or perhaps because of) being put aside by Joffre, Foch's relations with Haig appeared to have improved, and he took advantage of a visit by Lloyd George to the Somme front to further this improvement. Lloyd George was now Secretary of State for War following Kitchener's death by drowning earlier in June, when his ship was sunk by a German mine.

Lloyd George had visited Verdun on 7 September and gave an emotional speech in the citadel upon which the enemy's forces had broken 'as an angry sea breaks upon a granite rock'.[39] A few days later, on the 11th, and *before* going to see Haig and the BEF, he had lunch with Foch at his

---

[38] Micheler to Dubost, 15 September 1916, in Herbillon, *Micheler*, 90–1.
[39] Grigg, *Lloyd George* 4: 380–3, at p. 381.

headquarters and asked 'innumerable' questions about why the British took so little ground and suffered such heavy losses. The very next day Foch saw Wilson and relayed what had transpired, saying that he had explained that the British were 'green soldiers and his were veterans'. Wilson described Foch's account thus: 'Foch played up well as regards Haig and would not give him away.'[40] When Lloyd George went to Wilson's IV Corps headquarters on 13 September, he asked the same questions and received the same replies. Yet, during the day he spent at Haig's HQ, Lloyd George clearly hid any critical thoughts, because he impressed Haig with his desire 'to help in every way he can'.[41] However, Foch lost no time in letting Haig know what Lloyd George had said. This is Haig's diary account of what Foch told him on 17 September, privately in the garden at Haig's advanced headquarters:

He [Lloyd George] began by saying that he was a British Minister, and, as such, he considered that he had a right to be told the truth. He wished to know why the British who had gained no more ground than the French, if as much, had suffered such heavy casualties. Foch replied that the French Infantry had learnt their lesson in 1914, and were now careful in their advances. He often wished that they were not so well instructed. He would then have advanced much further and more quickly. In reply to questions about our Artillery, Foch said that, in his opinion, the British had done wonders. L.G. [sic] also asked his opinion as to the ability of the British Generals. Foch said 'L.G. was sufficiently patriotic not to criticise the Commander-in-Chief' but did not speak with confidence of the British Generals as a whole. Foch's reply was that he had no means of forming an opinion.

Unless I had been told of this conversation personally by Gen. Foch I would not have believed that a British Minister could have been so ungentlemanly as to go to a foreigner and put such questions regarding his subordinates.[42]

Apart from what it reveals about Lloyd George, this episode shows very clearly that Foch took the opportunity offered to him on a plate to bind himself more closely to Haig against their political masters. Foch had already complained to Wilson that he was 'dissatisfied' with his relations with Haig who 'is always civil and nice, but tells him nothing, and the relationship between them is not such that Foch can converse freely with Haig and tell him all his plans and hopes and experiences'.[43] So Lloyd George's intervention gave Foch the opportunity to profit from the situation. Foch's account to his wife of the Lloyd George visit led her to comment that Haig had thanked her husband

[40] Wilson diary, 12 September 1916. Note that Callwell, *Wilson*, has mis-dated this episode to 12 August (1: 292).
[41] Haig to Lady Haig, 13 September 1916, cited in Blake, *Haig Papers*, 166.
[42] Haig diary, 15 September 1916.   [43] Wilson diary, 12 September 1916.

for his 'praise'.[44] As a result of these actions, Foch was able to report at the end of the month that he was 'once again entirely in agreement' with Haig. Ever since Ypres, he continued, he and Haig had brought each other luck.[45] As had happened with Sir John French and Kitchener, Foch used the opportunities he was given to create ties to the British CinC by deepening any rift between the latter and his Minister, and involving Henry Wilson yet again in the combine.

He had a second opportunity to ingratiate himself with Haig a month later, when Lloyd George sent the former CinC, Sir John French, over to France to investigate French artillery methods in his capacity as director of training. In light of what Foch had told him about Lloyd George's questioning, Haig guessed correctly that the true purpose of Sir John's visit was to collect more 'evidence' against his conduct of the battle. Before meeting Sir John, Foch saw Haig on 10 October and again two days later, when Haig came to Foch's headquarters for lunch and a long, private talk. On 14 October Sir John spent the whole day at Foch's headquarters looking at the Northern Army Group artillery and aviation arrangements. Once again, Foch reported to Haig the very next day what Sir John had said (although Haig records no details in his diary), claiming to have been 'very non-committal' about Haig and unable to discuss British generals. Next Haig went to Foch's headquarters on 17 October with an offer to allocate roads and a railway in the British sector to the French in order to help with their Saillisel operations, because he had heard that GQG were criticising Foch for not devoting enough resources to them.[46] Obviously, Foch's tactic of drawing Haig closer in the face of possible criticism was working. Sir John returned to England on 15 October without visiting GHQ at all.

However, Foch's learning that he was not to be retired and his improving relationship with Haig were small compensations for the failure during August and September to re-create the relative success of 1 July, when British and French infantry had set off together across a wide front to attack the first German line of defences. The events on the British front on 15 September are treated in the British historiography as a major attack, mainly because of the first battlefield use of the tank, but the gains were modest and the cost heavy. When the events of that day are put into the Allied context and are related to the French attacks south of the river on 4 and 5 September and in the north on 12 September, the failure to give each other mutual support is manifest.

[44] Mme Foch diary, 24 September 1916.
[45] Letter, Foch to Mme Foch, 28 September 1916, vol. 41.
[46] French diary, 10–15 October 1916, cited in French, *Life of Field-Marshal Sir John French*, 244–5; Haig diary, 7, 10, 12, 15 October 1916; Wilson diary, 17 October 1916.

The third and final phase of the battle was even less productive. Despite the lateness of the season, Foch was determined to continue the offensive. He told his Belgian liaison officer, de Posch, that he intended to keep going through the winter, and Haig recorded on 15 October that Foch 'sees the necessity for doing as much as we possibly can to gain a big success before the wet weather comes in'.[47] Despite some days of relatively kind weather in the latter half of September, heavy autumn rains had to be expected, and so one has to wonder what the source was of Foch's determination. The most likely explanation is that Haig (and perhaps Rawlinson as well) were buoyed by their successes on 15 and 25 September and wished to continue operations. Rawlinson saw Haig on 6 October and concluded that the CinC intended to continue until they were stopped by the weather, and even to continue through the winter.[48] Since the main aim of the French was to support the BEF, obviously Foch had to show equal enthusiasm. This interpretation of Foch's intentions is supported by the entries in Madame Foch's diary during October. She had taken a lease on a villa near to Foch's headquarters and so was seeing him occasionally and thus able to record what he told her. When she asked him on 18 October whether the Somme campaign was to continue, Foch replied that, so long as the British wished it, the French would conform, although they could do nothing without the British and the weather had to be favourable as well. He had worked hard and consistently to get the British moving and now they were proud of what they had achieved. He was sure that they would not let go until Germany was destroyed.[49] However, the appalling weather began to create impossible conditions, with shells either losing their explosive power because they were falling into deep mud, or else failing to explode at all because the mud impeded the action of the fuse.[50]

Certainly Haig had not lost enthusiasm for the fight. In a letter to Robertson that was read out to the Cabinet on 9 October, Haig stated that there could be no question as to the right course to follow – 'our offensive must be continued without intermission as long as possible' – and that there were 'fair grounds for hope that very far-reaching success, affording full compensation for all that has been done to attain it, may be gained in the near future by a vigorous maintenance of our offensive'.[51] On 29 September he had communicated to Rawlinson a 'grandiose' plan to have Fourth Army pass to the east of Cambrai – a distance of well over

[47] De Posch diary, 1 October 1916; Haig diary, 15 October 1916.
[48] Rawlinson diary, 6 October 1916.   [49] Mme Foch diary, 18, 10 October 1916.
[50] Sheldon, *German Army*, 354, note 50.
[51] Haig to CIGS, OAD 173, 7 October 1916, CAB 42/21/3, appendix B.

thirty kilometres.[52] Consequently plans were made to progress in a north-easterly direction in order to capture Sailly-Saillisel (by the French) and the Le Transloy lines (by the British). The Germans had dug a new defence line, their fourth, running along the line of the Bapaume–Péronne road through the village of Le Transloy. Joint attacks – the capture of the French objective depended on the British capture of theirs, and vice versa – were carried out on 7, 12 and 18 October, for very few gains. Joffre intervened again with another letter to Haig on 18 October which claimed that 'public opinion' would not accept a slowing or a halt to the British operations when the BEF was supplied 'abundantly' with munitions and when the enemy was showing signs of 'indisputable disarray'. He insisted, therefore, that Haig reinstate wide-front operations no later than 25 or 26 October on Fourth Army's front. The GHQ staff were furious, and Haig sent a stiff response, stating that he alone was the judge of what he could undertake and when.[53] According to Dillon, Foch had a hand in either suggesting or drafting Joffre's letter, and so Joffre cannot be accused, as in the past, of causing difficulties and then expecting Foch to mend matters. The text may have been stronger than Foch had intended because he agreed with Dillon that the letter was 'rotten'.[54] Assuming that Foch's intention had been to keep the British in line and fighting, it must be said that the letter was counter-productive in that Haig asserted his independence even more.

Foch had problems with his two army commanders as well. Fayolle complained frequently to his diary about Foch's constant calls for an attack. What was the point of capturing Bapaume as Foch and Joffre wished, he asked rhetorically, if the capture cost 60,000 men? The only point of continuing operations was, as far as Fayolle could see, to 'carry the British along and force them to fight'.[55] As for Tenth Army, Micheler and Foch had a 'fairly active' exchange of views about the proposed action south of the Somme and disagreed further about the start dates. Nonetheless, an operation towards Chaulnes and then the two villages of Pressoire and Ablaincourt began on 10 October. Tenth Army captured several German trenches, along with 1377 prisoners, but was unable to progress on subsequent days and lost some of the gains to German counter-attacks. By 21 October, however, Tenth Army was within striking distance of completing the capture of Pressoire and Ablaincourt, but the weather prevented further action. Torrential rain on 30 October flooded

[52] Prior and Wilson, *CWF*, 250.
[53] Letters, Joffre to Haig, 18 October 1916, and Haig to Joffre, 19 October 1916, WO 158/15, also in *AFGG* 4/3, annexes 1094, 1137; Vallières, *Au soleil*, 167.
[54] Dillon diary, 19, 21 October 1916.   [55] Fayolle, *CS*, 182–3 (entry for 21 October 1916).

the trenches to a depth of between 40 and 80cm, drowning in mud the munitions stocked for the attack, and leaving duckboards floating about in the mess.[56] Finally the two villages were captured on 7 November and Tenth Army managed to resist fierce German counter-attacks and held on to them. Obviously, under such conditions, it proved impossible to synchronise Sixth and Tenth Army attacks. Each army had to do the best it could, when it could.

Hence there was no simultaneity with Sixth Army's final attack of the campaign supposedly in conjunction with another British attack on the Le Transloy lines. Haig ordered the attack, the seventh on the position, to begin on 5 November. However, the commander of the corps involved, Lord Cavan of XIV Corps, indicated that the task he had been given was impossible, although he was prepared 'to sacrifice the British right rather than jeopardise the French'.[57] Such unusually strong language from a subordinate commander convinced Rawlinson and Haig, and so when Foch met with them both in Rawlinson's headquarters on 4 November, the day before the infantry attack was due to start, Foch had to argue that the British should indeed support the three French corps that were about to attack towards Sailly-Saillisel. The Fourth Army commander explained what he was planning to do: the British would undertake some counter-battery work and bombard Le Transloy as if they 'were about to attack', as Haig put it. Not surprisingly Foch was (in Rawlinson's words) 'rather stuffy' about such a late abandonment of an agreed joint operation, and Rawlinson thought that Haig and Foch 'came to words' – 'Fosh [sic] was trying to make D.H. say that we were not going to continue the offensive so as to find an excuse for making us take over more line.'[58] The French attacked as planned on 5 November, but with mediocre results.[59] The French left, which the British should have covered by attacking Le Transloy woods, was exposed to the many German machinegun nests hidden among the trees, and so the final joint action on the Somme was a fiasco. Nonetheless Sixth Army managed to complete the capture of Sailly by the morning of 12 November. On both flanks, however, there were two small successes: Tenth Army's capture of Pressoire and Ablaincourt in the south, as recounted above, and British Fifth Army's capture of Beaumont Hamel in the relatively unscarred sector in the north of the battlefield. All that remained to close down the campaign was for some horse-trading about when and how far the British would extend their front and permit the relief of Sixth Army.

[56] *AFGG* 4/3, 277–8.   [57] Edmonds *et al.*, *OH 1916*, 2: 470.
[58] Haig diary, 4 November 1916; Rawlinson diary, 4 November 1916.
[59] Fayolle, *CS*, 185 (entry for 5 November 1916).

The Somme campaign was to have been a truly joint operation with the employment of two national armies to create a wide-front assault on the German lines in Picardy. As the above account has shown, joint operations were honoured more in the breach than in the observance, with small local attacks of detail by both the British and the French occurring on different days and at different times. The gains consisted of an advance of between fifteen and twenty kilometres at the widest point. The French reached almost to Péronne and the British almost to Bapaume. By the end of the battle Sixth Army was astride the Bapaume–Péronne–Ham road, which had been the original French aim. Yet they held only the portion of the road that ran between the villages of Sailly and Saillisel and Bouchavesnes; they did not hold its entire length, and they were threatened by German machinegun nests in the Saint-Pierre Vaast woods to the east of the road. The cost for these gains was some 202,000 French casualties, 432,000 British and 465,000 German.[60] By the end both nations had committed similar manpower resources (two armies each, although fewer French divisions than British), but the French suffered about half the number of casualties and took a much larger proportion of the recaptured territory than the British. German regimental histories and eye-witness accounts reflect the sense almost of outrage that they should have been attacked on the Somme.[61] Indeed, the German army had been profoundly shocked by the weight of the attack launched against them, but at the time neither the French nor the British had any accurate estimation of the extent of that shock.

Looking back to these events in 1928, Foch pointed to the slowness imposed by the need to reach agreements, so that it was impossible to maintain a 'suitable rhythm' in order to exploit the occasional real successes. Success was always possible, he claimed, when the Franco-British attacks were executed jointly on a wide front. Closer to the events, he commented on the Somme battle in September 1917, during the commission of enquiry into Nivelle's failed offensive earlier in the year. He described the Somme campaign as undertaken solely to bring in the British and to 'décongestionner' (to relieve) Verdun, not to achieve a breakthrough; it was carried out on a narrow front and with limited resources, using the tactic of capturing successive German defensive positions after a 'violent' artillery bombardment. The battering that the series of attacks imposed led finally to the German retirement to the

---

[60] British figures from Prior and Wilson, *Somme*, 301–2; French figures from *AFGG* 4/3, 552–3; German figures from Hirschfeld, 'Die Somme-Schlacht', 87.
[61] See Krumeich, 'Le Soldat allemand sur la Somme'.

Hindenburg Line. Foch claimed that if, instead of Nivelle's offensive on the Chemin des Dames, he had been able to repeat the Somme in 1917, but on a wider front of one hundred kilometres from Vimy to the Oise, the Germans might have been pushed back as far as the river Meuse. However, he concluded, that method of proceeding had been judged to be too slow.[62]

Such comments reflect more Foch's positive attitude in 1917 than they do his thoughts before and during the battle. Joffre had certainly been aiming at a breakthrough in 1916, and his instructions to Foch following the agreement with the Allies (once again in Foch's absence) on 15 November envisaged another joint but slightly separated offensive in 1917 with the aim of 'breaking through the enemy positions'. As to driving the enemy back to the Meuse, Foch's comments on Joffre's plan reveal a more realistic assessment of the possibilities. In his notebook on 21 November he wrote that the Germans could retire and then hold the Allies along the line of the Somme or the Canal du Nord with reduced forces and continue their offensives in the east.[63] However, the plans agreed by Joffre and the Allies did not come to fruition and a new commander-in-chief would lead the French armies in the 1917 campaign.

How faithful to his 'scientific method' had Foch been in 1916 on the Somme? Certainly he had shown that careful and observed artillery preparation was vital, as was allocating specific tasks such as counter-battery to specific guns, and the long opening barrage was very successful. However, it proved impossible to repeat such preparation in subsequent weeks because moving the heavy artillery forward became increasingly difficult as the weather deteriorated and the ground became cratered. Most of the French artillery pieces were older models and neither mobile enough nor sufficiently rapid firing for the sustained campaign that Foch wished to conduct. His comments to his wife lament the slowness that the campaign imposed.

Aviation had proved its usefulness, not only for reconnaissance and artillery observation, but also for harrying areas behind enemy lines such as railway stations and ammunition dumps. The station at Saint-Quentin, for example, was bombed on 1 July, disrupting the German response to the first day of the battle, again on the night of 7/8 August and again on 22/23 September.[64] By 18 July the Allies had destroyed so much of the enemy's observation capability that only one German balloon remained

---

[62] Joffre et al., Les deux batailles de la Marne, 98; Brugère commission hearings, 14 September 1917, 5N 255, fo. 67v.

[63] Joffre to Foch, 18 November 1916, AFGG 5/1, annex 129; Foch, Carnets, 21 November 1916, fo. 212.

[64] Martel, French Bombardment Forces, 126–8.

aloft, and that ten kilometres behind the lines.[65] Operations on the Somme had shown the 'absolute necessity' of possessing superiority in the air, Foch wrote on 23 November. Hence he wanted faster aircraft, better able to fly in windy conditions, and better armed to deal with enemy aircraft and barrage balloons.[66] Joffre was displeased by Foch's request for 400 such aircraft, because he believed that it was impossible to fulfil given France's current rate of production. In order to deal with the enemy's aircraft, Tenth Army had established for each corps three machinegun sections dedicated to anti-aircraft work, and the fact that the personnel of these sections was permanent proved superior to Sixth Army's use for the same work of territorial units that withdrew when their unit was rotated out of the line. Foch wrote to GQG on 16 December recommending that the Tenth Army system be adopted by all French armies.[67]

The most important and pressing concern for the next year's campaign, in Foch's view, was how to obtain the right tools. To his calls for mobile and rapid-firing artillery and for faster aircraft he added requests for armoured protection. The greater German use of machineguns had stopped the French infantry and so 'armoured infantry' were needed. Clearly Foch had been impressed by the British tanks, and he saw them as the answer to both the machinegun and enemy wire. (The caterpillar tracks would be used also for moving the heavy guns.) The offensive ran out of steam when the heavy artillery could not operate, and so different tools were needed: the tank.[68] These thoughts are the precursor to Foch's combined arms battle of 1918 that would defeat the enemy.

The reason for placing so much emphasis on artillery in the 'scientific method' was to spare the infantry. The French casualties – fewer than half the British casualties, although for greater gains – prove the method's relative efficacy. Several tactics protected the French infantry. The rolling barrage that was developed at Verdun and used extensively by the French and less so by the British on the Somme enabled the infantry to reach the enemy trenches before the defenders raised their heads (and weapons) from their trenches after the barrage passed. The use of gas shells neutralised enemy batteries that had escaped the initial artillery preparation. Counter-battery fire proved so effective that the British began to adopt the procedure and after the end of the battle instituted a corps-level dedicated Counter-Battery Staff Office.[69] The artillery intelligence service improved

[65] Lucas, L'Evolution des idées tactiques, 145.
[66] Letter, Foch to Joffre, 23 November 1916, SHD/SHAA A 277; Pedroncini (ed.), Joffre, JM, 167 (entry for 24 November 1916).
[67] Foch to Joffre (3e Bureau), 16 December 1916, 18N 167.
[68] Foch, Carnets, 24 November 1916, fo. 212.
[69] Palazzo, 'British Army's Counter-Battery Staff Office'.

markedly: when combined with the aerial photographs brought back by the aviators, the French gunners were able to fire with such accuracy that some German prisoners of war complained that their position must have been betrayed.[70] Finally, the use of motor transport meant that the infantry could be re-supplied more speedily. Pétain's organisation of the 'voie sacrée' feeding Verdun is well known, but it is less well known that motor transport in Picardy was just as tightly controlled as the railway traffic. On 22 July the main Amiens–Proyart road that ran east–west south of the Somme and bisected the two French army sectors carried 8000 horse and motor vehicles, a density of one vehicle every ten seconds.[71]

Just as there was a price to pay for a long and methodical artillery preparation, namely ground so churned up that it was difficult to move the guns forward, so there was a price for the secondary role that the infantry now believed it played. Fayolle noted as early as 16 July that his infantry was losing mobility, like an arthritic joint, because of the dominance of mechanical forces.[72] Troops would wait for the artillery to destroy everything before advancing to take possession, and this led in some cases to troops refusing to leave the trenches if they saw that the artillery had not, in fact, destroyed all the enemy defences.[73] Foch wrote in one of his 'instructions' that the methodical pursuit of defined objectives does not exclude prompt and deep exploitation of any opportunity that presents itself. This was one of the criticisms of the failure to exploit the breach in the enemy lines south of the Somme on 3 July.[74] If the troops had pushed on, the argument went, they might have widened the breach still further. The counter-argument states that losses among junior officers and non-commissioned officers (NCOs) are usually so high in the opening hours of an offensive that troops are left leaderless and incapable of pushing on without suffering further catastrophic casualties.

So Foch might be given credit for having stuck to his scientific method, although the twin problems of combining method with speed for the artillery and of restoring initiative to the infantry had not been solved.

There are two further points to make about Foch's command on the Somme. First, Foch's reluctance to embark on the Somme battle, expressed even before the head of state, contrasts vividly with his energy and drive once the battle began. The 'thinker' revealed in his notebooks before the battle began and as it wound down contrasts with the 'doer' as

[70] Lucas, *L'Evolution des idées tactiques*, 130.
[71] Ibid., 137–55; Porte, *Services automobiles*, 186–90.
[72] Fayolle, *CS*, 169 (entry for 20 July 1916).
[73] For an example of this see the operation to capture Falfemont Farm, completed by 5 September: Greenhalgh, 'Experience of Fighting with Allies'.
[74] Lucas, *L'Evolution des idées tactiques*, 146.

the battle unfolded. This tension may be explained by Foch's obedience to his superior officer, and by his realisation that he could not exhort Haig and the BEF to act if he was doing nothing himself. In any case, sitting on his hands was not one of Foch's fortes.

The second point concerns the contrast between the patience that Foch displayed when dealing with the British and the impatience in his dealings with Fayolle and Micheler. As noted in chapter 7, Foch had made a particular effort to begin on the right foot when Haig took over command in January. His informing Haig about Lloyd George's questioning of British methods obviously improved relations between the two generals. Dillon thought that Haig 'now really likes old Foch', a reflection written on 17 October, that is to say, immediately after Sir John French's visit recounted above. Foch also took pains to 'cultivate' Rawlinson – who found him 'very affable and agreeable'.[75] Rawlinson's diary reveals the frequency of Foch's appearances at his headquarters. During July, for example, he saw Foch nine times, every two or three days on average, and there were telephone conversations as well. Fayolle's diary, on the other hand, is full of complaints about Foch's demands, especially during the muddy final phase of the battle. After one row Fayolle's head still ached three days later.[76] Clearly Foch knew that he had to be more diplomatic with the British; indeed losing his temper would have been counter-productive.

For the 1917 campaign Foch believed that a wider, stronger and more varied offensive was required, extending from Vimy to Bapaume, with lots of tanks, lots of short 155mm guns and more railways. He feared that, if they did not succeed in 1917, it was doubtful whether the French would be able to make another big effort.[77] Yet the 1917 campaign did not take place between Vimy and Bapaume, and Foch was not involved because by then he had been removed from command. The year of the Somme and Verdun had ended with meagre gains, and both Foch and Joffre had to suffer the consequences. Haig, however, was rewarded with a field marshal's baton.

[75] Rawlinson diary, 2 March 1916, RWLN 1/5.
[76] Rawlinson, Short Note Diary, 1, 3, 5, 9, 14, 17, 19, 24, 27 July 1916, National Army Museum; Fayolle, CS, 174 (entries for 18 and 21 August 1916).
[77] Foch, Carnets, 21 November 1916, fo. 211.

9   In disgrace: reflections on two years
     of command

The story of Foch's sacking after the Battle of the Somme had ended is not only convoluted, as the following recital of events shows, but it is also somewhat mysterious. Late on 15 December 1916, after Foch had retired to bed, a telegram arrived at Northern Army Group headquarters that announced his removal from command and placed him at the disposition of General Joffre, still styling himself the commander-in-chief. This was followed by further telegrams. The *new* commander-in-chief, General Robert Nivelle, reiterated the sacking the next day, and informed Foch that he was to carry out a 'special mission' under his command. Then, on the 20th, another telegram announced that Foch was placed at the disposition of the War Minister. This was a euphemism for definitive sacking, with no further job in prospect. Finally, the following day, yet another telegram placed Foch once again at the disposition of the new commander-in-chief.[1]

The sacking is mysterious in that these decisions were all taken whilst there was no War Minister: Briand re-jigged his Ministry and on 13 December replaced General Roques by General Lyautey. At that date Lyautey was Resident General of Morocco and could not remove himself immediately to Paris, and so the functions of War Minister were carried out in the interim by Navy Minister Admiral Lacaze. It is odd that such important changes as appointing the commander-in-chief and army group commanders should be made by an acting minister in the midst of ministerial changes. A further complicating factor was Joffre's removal from effective command at the same time. What is abundantly clear, however, is that the roots of the matter went back a long way, and that Foch himself played a not inconsiderable role in his own downfall. It is necessary to go back to the beginning of the year, before the planning for the Somme and before Verdun, to understand what happened and why.

Relations between the Northern Army Group and GQG had already been strained by the September 1915 operations in Artois. Then Foch was

[1] *AFGG* 5/1, annexes 287, 298, 324, 328.

192

not present at the Allied conference in Chantilly in December that decided the strategic plan for 1916; nor was he present when Haig and Joffre agreed in February 1916 the Western Front portion of the strategic plan that became the Battle of the Somme. Foch's preferred option, it will be remembered, was for an operation further north. He resented the predominant role that Joffre played in the planning, dealing directly with the British and Belgians instead of leaving that task to Foch. Meunier-Surcouf described Joffre's actions as a great mistake.[2] After all, Foch had been sent to the north in 1914 precisely for that purpose.

An additional complication in the command structure had been the appointment of General Castelnau to act as Joffre's chief of staff in December 1915. That position had been created when Joffre's duties were increased to take responsibility for the Salonika front as well as the armies in France. The government felt that a deputy was required at GQG in order to help with the increased administration and with the task of Allied coordination, yet Foch had already been made 'adjoint' or deputy in 1914, responsible for affairs in the north. From the evidence of the comments made to his wife about Castelnau's appointment, Foch appears to have resented it, especially given the fact that he and Castelnau had clashed in 1914. He made several disparaging comments about the politicking in Paris involved in Castelnau's job, and claimed to be pleased that he had not been appointed to the responsibility. Yet the frequency of such comments indicates a degree of protesting too much.

The choice of the Somme battleground and the Castelnau appointment were not the only sources of discord. Foch had identified the need for greater quantities of heavy artillery as the key to success, as was demonstrated in chapter 5. Slow to recognise this, GQG had done little to remedy the position and it was not until 30 May 1916 that it produced a definitive programme for heavy artillery.[3] Since the manufacture of big guns requires specialist workers, great quantities of raw materials and a long lead-time, it is not surprising that the programme was not entirely completed even by the time of the Armistice. Foch had signalled many times during the planning for the Somme both the need for heavy artillery and also its lack. He even put in a request for 600 *Minenwerfer* (trench mortars) in February 1916 in order to supplement the offensive capabilities of his armies, but it was turned down apparently on the grounds that no provision had been made in the 1916 budget for the extra supply of such weapons.[4]

---

[2] De Posch diary, 23 and 24 April 1916.   [3] Bock, *Parlementarisme*, 161–8.
[4] De Posch diary, 21 February 1916.

Another source of dissatisfaction was the CinC himself. Foch complained on several occasions to his wife that Joffre was not sufficiently active, that he lacked energy and that he exerted no authority.[5] Although no friend of Foch's, Castelnau made the same criticisms, calling the commander-in-chief disrespectfully the 'crab', and describing him as a man of mediocre capacity who clung to power. Joffre had been caught off-balance by Verdun, Castelnau claimed, and had interfered with the well-prepared operation on the Somme. Instead of a decisive success, there was now a crisis of command, and his reputation that had lasted for two years was maintained simply by his political allies.[6] Joffre himself admitted that he was becoming tired. At Foch's headquarters in February he stated that he expected the war to be over by September, although the reason for this was his desire to see the end of the war, 'for I am beginning to have had enough' (see Illustration 4). Even the British ambassador noted that Joffre had had enough, and would retire with a field marshal's baton. King Albert also got the impression that Joffre would retire if the war was not settled by September.[7]

Criticisms of Joffre were not restricted to the military. Parliament was becoming restive, especially as there seemed to be no end to the slaughter at Verdun. Clemenceau had never had a high opinion of him: it is not enough to have a cap with braid ['un képi galonné'] to turn an idiot into an intelligent man, Clemenceau is reported to have said in the Army Commission as early as September 1915.[8] Furthermore, during his brief tenure of the War Ministry General Gallieni had produced a memorandum which advocated, in effect, reducing Joffre's powers and increasing those of the Ministry. The soldier–*député* André Maginot cited this document during the first secret session of the Chamber of Deputies in June, but, although Briand managed to survive the vote of confidence, he had to concede right of inspection. In July 1916 the Chamber's Army Commission won the assent of the Deputies for the Commission's delegates to inspect the zone of the armies (at their own risk). Thus parliamentary control was extended to the military as well as the political sphere of action.[9]

Indeed, the Army Commissions of both houses grew in importance and power throughout 1916. Both Commissions criticised the high command consistently for its failure over the provision of heavy artillery. The criticism had already begun in 1915, and it grew even fiercer during the

---

[5] See Mme Foch diary, entries for 16 February, 21 April, 6 May and 12 June 1916.
[6] Gras, *Castelnau*, 332.
[7] De Posch diary, 4 February, 5 May 1916; Bertie, *Diary*, 1: 314 (entry for 1 March 1916).
[8] Poincaré, *AS*, 7: 89.
[9] See King, *Generals and Politicians*, ch. 6; Bock, *Parlementarisme*, ch. 6.

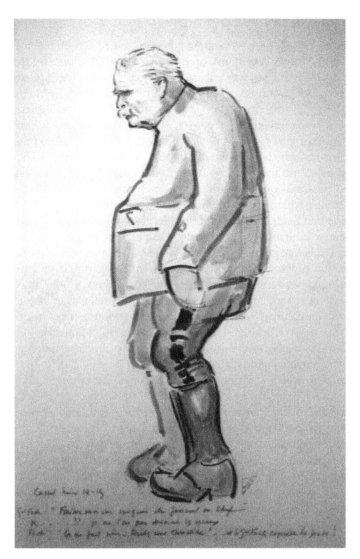

Illustration 4 Réquin's portrait of General Joffre, winter 1914–15
The caption reads:

Cassel, hiver 1914–15   Cassel, winter 1914–15
Gal Foch: Faites-moi une esquisse   Foch: Sketch the CinC for me
du Général en Chef
R: ! ! Je ne l'ai pas devant les yeux.   Réquin: But I don't have him in
    front of me.

Foch: Ça ne fait rien. Faites une   Foch: That doesn't matter. Do a
cariatide! – et il esquisse la pose!   caryatid! – and he indicates the pose!

course of 1916. There were some powerful critics of both the government and of the high command on the two Commissions. In the Senate Georges Clemenceau was a feared opponent, but he was not alone. Paul Doumer, for example, financial expert and future President of the Republic, played an important role; Charles Humbert published an influential newspaper and spoke with considerable authority. Among the *députés*, Abel Ferry, Albert Favre and André Tardieu created fear among the ministers who were obliged to appear before the commission to answer questions. With the country at war, the questioning of ministers during closed sessions by the parliamentary commissions provided the only means for parliament to influence the government.

Joffre had been furiously opposed to granting access to the zone of the armies to civilians, and he even threatened to resign over the matter. When the government had to give way over the question of parliamentary inspection of the military and a permanent delegation of twenty military *commissaires* was appointed to carry out inspections, Foch, however, was wise enough to welcome them. He assured the delegation 'it won't be me who will hide things from your sight'. His Northern Army Group generals were equally welcoming, unlike an unnamed GQG general.[10] One of the *commissaires* was André Tardieu, who had kept in close touch with Foch since leaving his headquarters.

Criticism was not confined to Joffre alone. The whole high command came under increasing scrutiny during 1916 as the Army Commissions flexed their muscles and the disasters – Verdun, Romania – piled up. Foch too was accused of being ill and dictatorial, and rumours about his poor health were circulating in Paris as early as January 1916.[11] As the battle for Verdun began, GQG was running the line that Foch was ill, in an effort to prevent his succeeding to Joffre's position should the latter be removed; but the rumours abated in March as fears about Verdun dominated public opinion.[12] His car crash in May provided additional fuel, despite the fact that his speedy recovery and energetic prosecution of the Somme offensive showed clearly that his strength was undiminished. On the other hand, as the campaign against Joffre started up even more strongly at the end of May and in June (when the first secret sitting of the Chamber of Deputies took place), Foch was named as a possible successor, as also was Pétain, who was now gaining his reputation as the saviour of Verdun.[13]

[10] Herbillon, *Du général*, 1: 323 (entry for 2 August 1916); Pédoya, *La Commission de l'armée*, 33.
[11] Letter, Foch to Mme Foch, 24 January 1916, vol. 39; de Posch diary, 21 February 1916.
[12] De Posch diary, 21 February 1916; letter, Foch to Mme Foch, 8 March 1916, vol. 39.
[13] Letter, Terrier [official in the French Foreign Ministry] to Lyautey [Morocco], 12 May 1916, ms 5903.

Although Foch *did* have a medical condition (probably either prostate or gall bladder problems), it did not affect his ability to do his job. He referred frequently to his excellent health in his letters to his wife. When Clemenceau visited him in May, perhaps to check on the rumours about his health, the Tiger found him full of energy. Since Clemenceau was a decade older than Foch, he would be unlikely to fault the latter on grounds of age. Joffre argued strongly for Foch to be exempted from the statutory retirement age, in the face of objections from the War Minister. Castelnau too argued that an army commander should not be changed whilst a battle is in progress, and requested that Foch be maintained.[14] The Conseil des ministres approved this on 26 September.

Indeed, neither too ill nor too old, Foch was active in keeping his finger on the political pulse. In April his ADC, Meunier-Surcouf, left for Paris, telling Foch that he had to do his duty as a *député*. He had written a forty-page account of his nearly two years with Foch, which repeated the arguments about the need for heavy artillery such as the Germans possessed, rapid-firing and mobile. After seeing this report, Foch agreed that he should go, but thereafter the *député* returned frequently to Foch's headquarters. Tardieu too had decided to devote all his energies to politics. After commanding the 7th Company of the 44 Bataillon de chasseurs at Verdun he decided that he could achieve more in Paris than in the army. Despite his three mentions in dispatches, after his unit was relieved on 3 April he decided to concentrate on the Chamber of Deputies, a decision that Pétain approved.[15] Tardieu was in total agreement with Foch, and he intended, so he told Meunier-Surcouf, to lead a serious campaign in the Chamber. Foch praised Tardieu's political skills and his knowledge of men and of the front. He believed that Tardieu was 'attached' to him, and could render him 'good service'.[16] If indeed Foch kept away from Paris, as he claimed, he was nonetheless very well aware of what was happening there.

Meunier-Surcouf sent his memorandum to the two Army Commissions, and organised with Abel Ferry the calling of the June secret session. He did more. He went to Clemenceau in person and showed him the memorandum, telling him that Foch was the only general who believed in victory and that GQG did not know what they were doing. He answered Clemenceau's criticisms of Foch: he was 'ill'– that was an infamous rumour; you could 'not understand a word he said'– that was because he was a *polytechnicien* and so spoke elliptically, unlike lawyers who always spoke 'en rond' and

[14] Pedroncini (ed.), *Joffre, JM*, 124–5; Gras, *Castelnau*, 350.
[15] Missoffe, *Tardieu*, 142–52.
[16] Letters, Foch to Mme Foch, 22 February, 1 March 1916, vol. 39.

padded things out; he had 'a lousy character'– he and Clemenceau would always be reconciled on the 'altar of the *patrie*'. Meunier-Surcouf recommended to Clemenceau that he go and see Foch. Although Meunier-Surcouf's testimony is postwar, hence may not be entirely credible, nonetheless Clemenceau *did* go to see Foch, and more than once. He had already spoken with him, it will be recalled, in December 1914 in Beauvais.

On 3 May 1916 Clemenceau had lunch at Foch's headquarters. His Belgian liaison officer, Major de Posch, concluded that he was checking on Foch's health, because his first comment was to congratulate Foch on how well he looked. They got on very well together, and Foch explained his polemics with GQG over the heavy artillery that the enemy possessed but the French did not. They agreed that the war would last another eighteen months because the French did not yet have all the materiel they needed for victory. In fact, neither the French nor the British were building enough guns: 'nobody was taking charge of the question'. Foch was pleased with the visit, describing Clemenceau as kind and sparkling with wit and energy. He told his wife that Clemenceau was a great patriot, 'the only man in the government; the others don't govern, they direct nothing; it's the same with Joffre'.[17] Foch explained to de Posch that the reason why he and Clemenceau had got on together so well, despite religious differences, was that Clemenceau was 'a great patriot'. De Posch concluded from Foch's 'deference' and amiability during Clemenceau's visit that he could be 'Clemenceau's man and become Generalissimo one day if [Clemenceau] managed to get rid of General Joffre, for whom he seemed to have very little esteem'[18] – a prophetic comment.

Clemenceau met Wilson in Rouen on 11 June. He spoke of getting rid of Joffre, who was now 'too old & too slow', and claimed that of the three possible replacements, Castelnau, Foch and Pétain, he favoured Foch. Clemenceau claimed also that Foch was still 'hostile' to attacking prematurely, and that 'it was all Joffre & the politicians' who were pushing the Somme operation. Wilson agreed with Clemenceau's preference, telling him that he knew 'all three and that Foch was the most brilliant by far, Castelnau the best staff officer, and Pétain a fine dogged fighter but without Foch's drive and wide outlook'.[19] Hence Clemenceau had learned that Foch would be an acceptable replacement for Joffre as far as the BEF (or at least a part of it) was concerned.

---

[17] De Posch diary, 3 May 1916; Mme Foch diary, 6 May 1916.
[18] De Posch diary, 4 May 1916.   [19] Wilson diary, 11 June 1916.

Clemenceau visited Foch's headquarters again on 1 July, the opening day of the Somme battle, and congratulated him warmly on the successes gained that morning. Weygand gives a vivid account of the visit, with Clemenceau disdaining the pills that had been set out for him and eating so heartily that the cook, who had thought that the fish prepared for lunch was big enough to do for dinner as well, had to find something else that evening. Foch had earlier told Weygand how much he admired the politician's powerful personality and above all his patriotism. 'He loves France jealously', Foch said, 'like a mistress'.[20] Again, on 8 October, Clemenceau visited and talked about the huge industrial effort that the French were starting to make, with much greater employment of women in factories and on the railways. He still anticipated that the war would continue for a long time yet. Foch described him as still full of energy, despite his seventy-five years. He told his wife that Clemenceau had paid him many compliments.[21] Clearly the relationship between the two men was becoming even warmer.

In fact it had been warm since May, when Clemenceau reportedly told Foch of his plan to attack the government so strongly as to overturn it and take power himself by making a few concessions to his main obstacle, the President of the Republic. Clemenceau would then defer the projected Somme offensive and replace Joffre. Foch told de Posch that he agreed entirely with Clemenceau. As de Posch summarised the situation in a report to King Albert of 6 May (that is, immediately following Clemenceau's first visit to Northern Army Group headquarters): 'in a word, Foch gave me clearly to understand that he was the candidate of Clemenceau, whose great praises he sang, painting him as a great patriot and comparing him even to Gambetta'. A week later Foch told de Posch that it was time to shake up both the British and the French governments.[22]

Foch was playing a risky game. He was pleased with the work that Meunier-Surcouf was doing in Paris, but it had not gone unnoticed. Poincaré told Foch at the Saleux conference on 31 May that he was well aware of the campaign to get Clemenceau into the government, that he knew that Foch had inspired Tardieu's articles criticising the artillery position, and that both Joffre and the government knew what Foch was up to. As de Posch commented, Foch was running 'the great risk of losing some of his feathers'.[23]

[20] Weygand, *IV*, 329–30.
[21] De Posch diary, 8 October 1916; letter, Foch to Mme Foch, 10 October 1916, vol. 42.
[22] De Posch diary, 6 and 14 May 1916.   [23] Ibid., 5 June, 1 June 1916.

The crunch came in November as the Somme wound down and attention returned to criticisms, both military and political. There had already been a crisis in June before the battle began as Joffre juggled the needs of Verdun and the Somme. The British ambassador noted the renewed agitation against Joffre, led by Clemenceau and Doumer in the Senate. (Foch was also keeping in touch with Doumer, whom he saw on 12 June.)[24] The Minister for Education, Paul Painlevé, told Foch that the Briand Ministry was certain to be overthrown and that someone who would follow Clemenceau's programme would replace him. Both Briand and Joffre were 'shaky', Bertie noted.[25] Many of Joffre's generals criticised him to their friends, who then passed on their comments to the députés. Nonetheless, both Briand and Joffre survived the agitation, and the start of operations on the Somme, together with the easing of pressure at Verdun, silenced the politicians and gossip-mongers, temporarily at least.

However, the end of operations on the Somme left France to face the prospect of yet another winter at war, and as the registration of the 1918 class provoked heated debate in the second secret session of parliament on 21 November, the pressure for change – whether in the high command, or in the Ministry, or both – became acute. The criticism of the high command and Joffre in particular crystallised around three matters: the Verdun defences, or rather, the lack thereof; the failure to set up artillery programmes that responded to the needs of the armies; and, third, resulting from these shortcomings, the lack of any great military success. Although Nivelle's final operations at Verdun had succeeded, they only restored the French to the line they had held before the German attack in February. The human cost of the successful defence (it could hardly be called a victory) was huge. The Romanian adventure was about to end in defeat with the capture of Bucharest. The only minor victories were in other theatres, such as Sarrail's capture of Monastir from the Bulgarians on 19 November. Even the inexperienced British managed to bring their portion of the Somme campaign to an end with a minor victory at Beaumont Hamel. Thus neither Joffre nor Foch gained any credit for the meagre gains of a few square kilometres of French territory on the Somme, and a new possible successor to Joffre had appeared in the person of General Nivelle.

Matters came to a head during the lengthy third secret session in the Chamber of Deputies (28 November to 7 December), followed by the second in the Senate (19–23 December). Whatever the truth of Foch's

[24] Letter, Foch to Mme Foch, 13 June 1916, vol. 40.
[25] De Posch diary, 12 June 1916; Bertie, Diary, 1: 359 (entry for 9 June 1916).

allegations about Joffre's lack of energy and drive, his criticism of artillery provision is valid. Abel Ferry declared in the Chamber on 21 November that the Army Commissioners had been able to obtain a global figure only for casualties for the whole war, rather than detailed figures for individual battles. He connected this failure 'directly' to the heavy artillery position: the necessity for heavy artillery 'was understood only on 30 May 1916 on the eve of the [first] secret sitting'.[26] Thus, when Foch complained about insufficient heavy artillery to the President of the Senate Army Commission in the person of Georges Clemenceau, and when he welcomed the parliamentary Commissioners to inspect where and what they wished, he was knocking nails into Joffre's coffin.

Next Joffre's position was called into even greater doubt because of events in Greece.[27] Briand was under considerable political pressure as a result of his pro-Greek policy. The ambush of a party of French marines in Athens on 1 December revealed King Constantine's duplicity, and French public opinion demanded a response in force. The British ambassador reported that Briand might have to 'jettison some of his cargo' in order to 'save his ship'.[28] In an astute political move, Briand persuaded Joffre over lunch on 3 December to move into an ill-defined role as the government's 'technical adviser', thus freeing Sarrail from his control and leaving open the position of command of the armies in France. Despite renewed attacks in the Chamber over this proposition, eventually Briand won a vote of confidence. The resolution took for granted, however, that the high command would be reorganised. The government's majority was reduced by a hundred votes from the result in June, but it was still a majority: 344 to 160 against.

However, by the time that the move to 'promote' Joffre to technical adviser was made, Foch's fate had been sealed by the decision on 1 December to remove him. On that day Joffre and Castelnau were called to the Elysée palace to meet with the President, with Briand and with War Minister General Roques in order to discuss what had been happening during the secret sessions in the Chamber. At that meeting it was decided that Castelnau would go to Russia for the proposed Allied conference in St Petersburg, to be given an army group command on his return so that Briand could satisfy the right wing in the Chamber (so Joffre reasoned, at least). As for Foch, Joffre stated that he did not want him to command the planned renewal of the offensive on the Somme; nor did he believe that

[26] *Journal Officiel. Débats. Chambre*, 10 November 1920, with minutes of secret session 21 November 1916, p. 111.
[27] On this episode see Dutton, 'Fall of Joffre'.
[28] Bertie, *Diary*, 2: 66 (entry for 28 November 1916).

Foch would be a suitable replacement for himself as commander-in-chief, even were that command to be lightened by excising the Salonika portion.[29]

The horse-trading then began. His British liaison officer thought that Foch had too many enemies to be given the job.[30] According to GQG's liaison officer with the government, Colonel Emile Herbillon, GQG's candidate to replace Joffre was Foch, but Castelnau's 'entourage' were working to install him rather than Foch; Joffre himself preferred Nivelle.[31] Chief of staff General Pellé thought that both Foch and Pétain were 'impossible' and Castelnau 'undesirable'. Pellé spoke about Foch to Joffre, who claimed that 'they' did not want Foch because of the 'unacceptable opinions' he had put forward at the Saleux conference (when he advised against the Somme operation).[32] Weygand was called to GQG and asked in confidence about Foch's health.[33] Amongst the ministers, Finance Minister Alexandre Ribot noted that there could be no question of beginning another Somme battle.[34] Albert Thomas and the acting War Minister both favoured Nivelle. Poincaré too preferred the short, sharp Nivelle method to Foch's 'methodical' battle. It was Nivelle who got the job.

Why then was Foch put on a different shelf, albeit temporarily, rather than set aside permanently on the shelf for 'ornamental china', not to be used, where Joffre was consigned? Who was responsible for the decision? It might be that Joffre had already sealed Foch's fate some time earlier. In September 1917 Nivelle informed the commission of enquiry charged with investigating his failed spring offensive that Joffre had told him as early as 10 November that he, Nivelle, had been chosen from among three candidates to succeed the CinC.[35] Certainly Briand's Education Minister, Paul Painlevé, confirms Joffre's significant role in Foch's dismissal, and there seems little reason to doubt the validity of his account. Even though the decree removing Foch was signed by the acting War Minister, Admiral Lacaze, writes Painlevé, it was only after a 'spirited resistance' and on General Joffre's 'formal, reiterated request to the war committee'.[36]

[29] Pedroncini (ed.), *Joffre, JM*, 171, 175 (30 November and 3 December 1916).
[30] Dillon diary, 21 November 1916.
[31] Herbillon, *Du général*, 1: 366 (entry for 5 December 1916).
[32] Letter, General Pellé to Albert Thomas, 3 December 1916, Albert Thomas mss, 94/AP/237.
[33] Weygand, *IV*, 359.   [34] Ribot, *Lettres à un ami*, 177.
[35] Brugère commission, procès-verbaux, 15 September 1917, 5N 225.
[36] Painlevé, *Foch et Pétain*, 12.

Joffre might request, but the decision was the government's and there was still some support for Foch amongst his colleagues.[37] Despite the strong criticisms of the government's policies and of the state of the army's heavy artillery made during the secret sessions by Foch's ally, Tardieu, the perceived failure of the Somme offensive weighed heavily, to be compared unfavourably a couple of weeks later with the recapture of ground in front of the shattered remains of Forts Vaux and Douaumont (Fort Douaumont itself recaptured on 24 October). Nivelle exulted that he had now found the method. The dash of the final phase at Verdun counted for more than the 'severe' Somme method.

Poincaré too was involved, at least in setting Joffre aside, although his role in Foch's removal is less clear-cut. A recent French biographer claims that the President played an active role in pushing forward Nivelle as commander-in-chief.[38] As for Foch, it was at Poincaré's official residence that the decision was taken on 1 December to remove him from command. Unfortunately Poincaré's 'notes journalières' are not extant for this period, and his memoirs (normally so very useful for knowledge of what went on at Cabinet meetings) are very coy for the beginning of December, although he has plenty to say on later meetings of the Comité de guerre (the French inner Cabinet) and Conseil des ministres on the 15th, 18th and 19th. Two pieces of evidence suggest Poincaré's involvement in Foch's removal. Foch's Belgian liaison officer heard that Poincaré was annoyed by the attacks made on the government by Meunier-Surcouf, especially after he had decorated him at Foch's request, and the President told Foch so. De Posch concluded that Foch had been removed by a 'political coup', organised by Briand and Poincaré in revenge for the attacks of Foch's patrons, Clemenceau and Tardieu.[39] The second piece of evidence is Poincaré's refusal to accept Briand's resignation on 9 December. Briand knew that, despite his gaining the vote of confidence after the secret sessions, he had to re-jig his Cabinet, and quickly. He favoured Nivelle to succeed Joffre, who would be a sort of super commander-in-chief presiding over the Allied councils; and he wired General Lyautey in Morocco to sound him out about taking over the War Ministry. Poincaré's refusal to allow Briand to resign rather than reconstitute his Ministry reveals the President's view that it was vital to hold on to the political unity ('l'union sacrée' or sacred union) that had been in place since 1914, replacing if only temporarily the ideological and political divisions of the Third Republic. Therefore, the departure of the

[37] Herbillon, *Du général*, 1: 366 (5 December 1916).
[38] Roth, *Poincaré*, 329.   [39] De Posch diary, 16 December 1916.

military leader could not be followed by that of a political leader. Poincaré's refusal reveals also the depth of the feud between himself and Clemenceau, who continued to attack the President and the government in a strong article in his newspaper, *L'Homme Enchaîné*, and in speeches during the secret session in the Senate.[40] Poincaré resisted calling on Clemenceau to form a government for as long as he could, and in turn this blocked Foch's candidacy for a higher command.

Lacaze has received some of the blame for the decision to remove Foch, but it would appear that his hand was forced. Certainly, it was his signature on the decree, but he was only acting War Minister. The fact that someone in his position should have been obliged to execute such an important decision, without waiting for the incoming General Lyautey (who would have chosen either Foch or Castelnau to succeed Joffre), is further evidence of a political plot. Lacaze never revealed what really went on, and according to someone who claimed to know him well was ashamed of his role. Weygand was equally mysterious about what happened, stating that in 1923 Lacaze told him the circumstances in confidence. Weygand, who had been asked to keep quiet about his interview at GQG on the subject of Foch's health, spoke to the French historian Guy Pedroncini in the 1960s, but he asked Pedroncini not to reveal his testimony.[41] Whatever the truth of the matter, whatever the relative responsibilities of the President of the Republic, the Premier or the acting War Minster, the events reveal a state of civil–military relations that could not be much worse. They rival those that would develop across the Channel a year later, at the end of 1917 after Passchendaele.

Briand's new Ministry took office on 13 December, but the decree making Nivelle commander-in-chief of the armies of the North and North-East is dated 12 December, with the decrees making Joffre the government's 'technical adviser' and defining the responsibilities of Nivelle and Sarrail (retained as commander in Salonika) dated the following day. On 15 December Joffre asked Nivelle to recommend those whom he wished to command the armies and army groups; but the very same day the Conseil des ministres confirmed the appointment of Castelnau to command the Northern Army Group, thus illustrating Joffre's lack of influence. Foch was placed at the disposition of Joffre, as we saw at the start of this chapter, in a telegram that was dispatched that evening. It is difficult to avoid the conclusion that Briand wanted Foch well out of the way before the arrival of Lyautey from Morocco.

---

[40] See Wormser, *Septennat*, 78–83; and Keiger, *Poincaré*, 226–8.
[41] Varillon, *Joffre*, 519–20; Pedroncini, 'Rapports', 123.

Thus the reasons for Foch's fall from grace, or his 'disgrace', as it is described in his papers, are complicated. In the first place, the failure on the Somme fed dissatisfaction, and Joffre repaid Foch's criticisms by feeding him in turn to the critics. Yet politics generally had as much to do with matters as the military situation. His so-called disgrace was fall-out from the fight between the parliament, the government and the high command for control of France's military effort, an effort which had seen huge casualties during more than two years but no real successes. Foch had tied his fate to Clemenceau, and Clemenceau had failed to unseat the government despite the secret sessions throughout 1916. We do not have enough evidence to elucidate all the political machinations, yet it is clear that Foch had his fingers burned. The usual reasons given for his sacking are clearly unsatisfactory. He was not ill, and Foch was furious that such a patently untrue excuse as his ill-health had been used, claiming at the end of 1916 that he had never felt better since the beginning of the war.[42] Hence when the letter that Admiral Lacaze sent to him about the award of the *médaille militaire* for his service gave poor health as the reason for his retirement from command, Foch wrote on it a formal denial in legal language.[43] As Herbillon noted when he spotted Foch leaving Lacaze's office, 'I declare that he looked pretty vigorous for a man supposed to be tired.'[44] Anyone, particularly anyone of his age, who could be back at work a few days after having been propelled through the windscreen of his car when it hit a tree and who could then prosecute a battle for four and a half months (a battle which he had not wanted to fight) could hardly be described as 'ill'. Another frequently proffered reason for Foch's removal from command is his religion; but this was not a factor, either. Foch never made a great show of his beliefs, and if Clemenceau himself was prepared to take no account of them then they weighed little in the balance. With France invaded, a general's beliefs or lack of them mattered very little.

Although Weygand and others among Foch's supporters have insisted that Foch accepted his dismissal quietly, it seems that there was an initial explosion of fury. Weygand gave Foch the telegram the morning after it arrived late on 15 December, having judged that it was not worth waking his chief for such news. Foch went immediately to see Joffre, who claimed that the decision was the government's, not his. The meeting was stormy, and Joffre was overheard shouting 'we shall all be sacked'. The next day, 17 December, Foch went to confront Lacaze, who said that the decision was Joffre's. Then there followed a 'violent meeting' between Lacaze and

---

[42] Letter, Foch to Mme Foch, 11 December 1916, vol. 42.
[43] Foch mss, 414/AP/2.   [44] Herbillon, *Du général*, 1: 371.

Joffre.[45] Joffre was beginning to realise that his position lacked power, and Nivelle was opposed to his nomination of Foch for 'special missions'. The 'violence' of the Lacaze–Joffre meeting probably derived from the fact that both realised they had been used. Furthermore, Nivelle was making it abundantly plain that he did not intend to leave any powers in Joffre's hands. He told Clive that Joffre had 'no right' to any sort of liaison with Haig, and he told Haig that Joffre would 'gradually disappear', and that he intended to appoint his own men as army commanders.[46]

The initial fury, however, gave way to resignation. Foch wrote to another victim of the purge, General Pellé, that he (Foch) had done his duty as a soldier, that he would continue to do so whatever happened, so long as there were Boches in France. He told journalist Raymond Recouly after the war that he had said to Lacaze that he would accept the command of a division, of even a brigade, it being no disgrace to lead French troops.[47]

Foch received some kind notes of sympathy, in particular from King Albert, Haig and Robertson. He hid his disappointment from his wife, and Dillon noted how happy Foch seemed, even describing him as in 'roaring spirits' as early as 18 December when Foch told him: 'It's not finished.'[48] He was consoled by receiving a kind letter from Lyautey when he arrived in Paris, and the new War Minister's first officially signed letter was to confer on him the *médaille militaire*. Lyautey wrote: 'I can't wait to see you and to take counsel of your advice in this task, whose crushing weight and responsibility are all I feel.'[49] Soon after his arrival in Paris Tardieu spent four hours with Lyautey, who stated that he could not understand why Foch had been set aside, as he had great esteem for him.[50] If Foch had made an enemy of Briand, he seemed to have at least one ally in the rejigged Briand Ministry.

Thus Foch had not given up on politics, even if he wrote on 15 December: 'It's war without action, parliamentary war.'[51] To his Belgian liaison officer Foch indicated that he still thought that the current Ministry would be overturned and that Clemenceau and Tardieu would come to power.[52] If further proof of the ambitions that he and Clemenceau had shared is

[45] Pedroncini (ed.), *Joffre*, *JM*, 189 (entry for 18 December 1916).
[46] Clive diary, 19 December 1916; Haig diary, 20 December 1916.
[47] Letter, Foch to Pellé, 26 December 1916, Pellé mss, 4435; Recouly, *Mémorial de Foch*, 158.
[48] Dillon diary, 18, 21, 29 December 1916.
[49] Letter, Lyautey to Foch, 29 December 1916, Foch mss, 414/AP/2.
[50] Ibid., [d] Lyautey.   [51] Foch, Carnets, 15 December 1916.
[52] De Posch diary, 14 and 21 December 1916.

required, the latter's short note sent on 18 December helps to confirm it. It is preserved in Foch's papers in the Archives nationales. Simply it states: 'Cher ami, // Dans l'épreuve on se serre. Avec vous je suis frappé. // A vous toujours // G. Clemenceau.'[53] Briand's vote of confidence in the Chamber had been secured over a week earlier, on 7 December.

It is interesting that Clemenceau makes no mention in his postwar *Guerres et misères d'une victoire* of his three visits during 1916 to Foch's headquarters. He merely makes fun of Foch for sending him a copy of the bust that the sculptor Léon Maillard made of Foch that year. And he recounts Foch's coming to his house in the rue Franklin to ask for advice after Joffre had apologised for consenting to Poincaré's order to sack him.[54] Since Clemenceau wrote these words after Foch's death and just before his own, as a response to the posthumous criticisms of the Versailles peace treaty, it is not surprising that he should have omitted or simply forgotten the ties that bound them in 1916.

On the last day of that year, Nivelle's chief of staff told Dillon that Foch was 'too old to command troops in battle! Anyhow, Nivelle is keeping him on and is at present using him Swisswards – what he will eventually do with him remains to be seen.'[55] In fact, in 1917 Foch would have much to do, in Switzerland and elsewhere, although he would have to wait until the end of the year before the Clemenceau half of the combo came to power and until March 1918 before the plans hatched in 1916 came to fruition.

Reflections on two years of command on the Western Front

At the end of the frustrating year of the Somme Foch set down his thoughts about the war's progress. The German offensive had been broken in November 1914 on the Yser, he wrote, and from that moment on the enemy had lost all chance of useful action on the Western Front – the proof of that being Verdun. In 1915, Foch continued, the Central Powers made progress on the Eastern Front in Russia and Serbia, but could not obtain a decisive victory there. In 1916 the attack on Romania had fizzled out, and the enemy now found himself in the same situation in the east as he had in 1914 in the west. Foch concluded that, in order to defeat the enemy, the Allies needed to mount powerful offensives together. These comments reflected those that Foch made even before the start of the

---

[53] Foch mss, 414/AP/3. 'Dear friend, // In adversity, we come closer together. Like you, I am affected. // Ever yours.'
[54] Clemenceau, *Grandeur and Misery of Victory*, 16, 19.
[55] Dillon, *Three Wars*, 78 (entry for 31 December 1916).

Somme fighting. In June 1916 he wrote that the Allies had managed to stop the German invasion in 1914 and inflicted a serious reverse, yet they had neither beaten nor expelled nor destroyed the enemy. That task remained to be completed. The Allies had had enough materiel to obtain 1914's negative result, but they did not have enough for what he called 'position' warfare. He argued that to attempt to achieve the defeat and destruction of the enemy with the same resources as in 1914 would lead to ruin, and that the failures of 1915 and 1916 were the result of attempting to do just that. He urged, therefore, that a special effort be undertaken to organise heavy and trench artillery.[56]

In Foch's opinion, then, France and its Allies had completed the first step in the necessary two-part effort: they had stopped the invasion. They had not completed the second element of the strategy, defeating the invader, because thus far they had tried to achieve it with inadequate means. The important task was to improve the means, but for Foch the method remained what it had always been: the offensive, leading to the decisive battle.

In this, Foch was in total agreement with French army doctrine. Joffre had established the new regulations in 1913, which returned the army to its traditional ways, accepting 'no law in the conduct of operations other than the offensive'.[57] Foch concurred. In his 1903 *Des principes de la guerre* he had written that in a modern war there was only one method of imposing one's will on the enemy: the destruction of the enemy's organised forces. Once he began the task of bringing about that destruction, he maintained that view. At the beginning of 1915 he wrote 'the offensive is the superior form of war', and at the end of that equally frustrating year, on 12 December, he wrote: 'to make war is to attack – without an attack, no decision, no victory, no results'. In January 1916, it was the same refrain: 'the war's aims can be achieved only by the attack'.[58]

So, over more than two years of war, Foch had not changed his opinion that the offensive was the only method for success, in spite of the loss of his son and son-in-law in two early offensives in August 1914. Indeed, since the Germans could not be expected to leave the richest areas of northern France without some humiliating and costly quid pro quo, France's *only* option was to attack, defeat and expel them After all, as Stalin remarked a generation later, you have to do more than force your enemy to the edge of the abyss; you have to push him in.

---

[56] Foch, Carnets, end November 1915 and 7 [?] June 1916, fos. 140–4, 189.
[57] See Doughty, *PV*, 26–7.   [58] Foch, Carnets, fos. 36, 144, 150.

However, Foch did not propose unthinking offensives under any and all circumstances, as some of his critics imply. Rather his appreciation that the offensive should be undertaken only when the material means necessary for success had been supplied led him, by 1916, to reject the idea of an offensive on the Somme. He saw that little could be achieved without greater numbers of guns and shells, and better types of gun, mobile and quick-firing. He displayed real courage in sticking to this view on 31 May when he confronted France's President, Premier, War Minister and commander-in-chief in the presidential train near Amiens. His removal in December 1916 was, to some extent, the result of that courage.

The rift between Joffre and Foch was partly the result of a divergence of opinion about mounting that Somme campaign. In opposition to Foch's view that such an offensive could achieve little without more heavy artillery, Joffre insisted that it go ahead, despite the German assault at Verdun. Yet it was only on 30 May 1916, after more than a year of sustained criticism from both Army Commissions about the types and quantities of artillery being ordered, that the Minister received Joffre's full heavy artillery programme setting up the structures and reinforcements to supply the army's needs. The programme had been presented so late in the day that it was not complete by war's end. Nevertheless, Joffre refused to allow the enemy at Verdun to dictate the abandonment of his multi-front strategy: he insisted that the Somme proceed, and he was still insisting that he was right a year later. On 19 December 1917 he told the Paris correspondent of the influential *Journal de Genève* that for six months he had fought the Allies, the government and his generals in order to wage the Battle of the Somme; and two days later he wrote that 1916 had been 'the greatest year of the war' because, it having been agreed the previous December that it would take place, the battle was indeed fought in the place and at the time decided upon, despite Verdun.[59]

Since early in the war, however, Foch had been arguing for more and better artillery resources, and he recognised very early that the war had become a war of siege. On 21 January 1916 he wrote a long document beginning with the statement that the war was 'a race for munitions', followed by precise calculations of how many guns were needed for each of the enemy lines on a single kilometre of front.[60] However, Foch gives no sign in his writing of any appreciation of the consequences of a race for armaments for the supply of military manpower. He demonstrated this

[59] Interview with Maréchal Joffre, 19 December 917, William Martin mss, Hoover Institution, Stanford, CA; 'Note no 2 du 21 décembre 1917', in Pedroncini (ed.), *Joffre, JM*, 247.
[60] 'Note du Gal Foch', 21 January 1916, 1K/129/1.

blind spot in 1918, with his constant pressure on the British to keep up their depleted divisions, thereby revealing that he never accepted those consequences – namely, that older men and women cannot dig all the coal, build all the tanks and railway locomotives, and man all the merchant ships that are needed for a modern, industrial war. Indeed, the French in general, and Foch in particular, never came to terms with the fact that, because their steel imports came from North America in British ships and were converted into shells in factories using British coal, the British armies in consequence could not be as large as the French ones.

It was not only lessons about artillery provision that Foch learned during the more than two years that he spent as a commander in the field prosecuting the strategy of the offensive. As we have seen, he disseminated to his troops notes about infantry tactics, and he reacted quickly to perceived changes. Thus, in the two Artois battles in 1915, the 'lesson' of the May attacks – that reserves must be pushed forward before the infantry assault begins, so as to follow up quickly any breach in the line – was abandoned in the September fighting because the tactic caused too many casualties. Similarly, in 1916, the success of the changed German defensive tactics – abandoning a linear front-line defence in trenches and placing machine-gunners in shell craters – demanded a response. Foch charged that trying to deal with such a tactic with artillery was like taking a sledge-hammer to attack a fly. After all, it was difficult enough to deliver shells on an established trench line accurately and consistently, without trying to hit shell craters. He judged that the correct response was 'armoured infantry', that is, infantry carried in tanks or armoured cars.[61] This response came, more or less, in the shape of the two-man Renault FT tank that played a significant role in the second Battle of the Marne in 1918.

Once the fighting died down on the Somme, Foch filled many pages of his notebooks with thoughts about the best way to proceed in 1917. For example,

13 November 1916:
Our basis of attack in 1916 was heavy artillery. The attack slows and dies down in front of the new position made up of scattered machineguns. We need something else. For 1917 we must prepare a manoeuvre that is not only wider but also more rapid and more deeply penetrating than in 1916 … It is not enough to do 1916 bigger in 1917, such an attack will be stopped.

14 November 1916:
The tank will allow us to gain results. A) In a battle based on artillery (divisional artillery or counter-battery), the tank should be used to extend the progress of the infantry who have captured the first position and beyond. B) In a battle based on

---

[61] Foch, Carnets, 24 November 1916, fo. 212.

surprise, against a weakly held position (Douaumont) or after a necessarily weak artillery preparation, the tank should be used to approach the first position [...] C) the enemy of the tank is the enemy artillery, against which powerful counter-battery techniques must be used. Thus counter-battery takes on particular importance.

16 November 1916:
The tactical offensive dies away in front of the tactical defensive because of the slowness of its progress. The offensive must be made more speedy with quick-firing heavy artillery and tanks.

19 November 1916:
It is not enough to break through a single line, we must conquer entire areas that have been organised for defence.

Foch's actions and thinking all reveal a general who is learning from experience. He meditated on the reasons for the failed offensives of 1915 and 1916, evaluated 1914's successful defences on the Marne and at Ypres, and never ceased agitating for the improvements that he knew were needed. Despite the frustrations of Artois and the Somme, he retained the inner confidence that his method was the right one, if only the necessary resources could be provided. It was not until 1918 that he was able to display how right he was, and there is no doubt that he profited greatly from the learning experience between August 1914 and December 1916.

The frustrations of 1915 and 1916 were caused by more than the lack of the right means to prosecute a decisive offensive battle; they also owed much to the constraints of coalition warfare. This was another important element in Foch's learning experience, and it too would be tested in 1918. In October 1914 Joffre had sent Foch to the north to act as coordinator of the French, British and Belgian troops in that theatre. He chose Foch because of his drive and energy, because of his contacts with the British, and (perhaps) because he felt he could trust Foch's loyalty when compared, for example, to a Sarrail or a Gallieni. Joffre's commission was not easy, for Foch had no formal authority for his relations with the British and Belgians in his new position. If Foch's situation vis-à-vis French army and corps commanders was regularised by the creation of the army group command (itself a completely new level of command), his situation vis-à-vis Sir John French, his successor Sir Douglas Haig, and King Albert of the Belgians could be only what Foch himself made of it. He could argue, cajole, persuade and even, at times, resort to underhand stratagems, but he could not issue orders. Instead he developed a procedure whereby he wrote a short summary of what he understood to have been agreed in discussion with British or Belgian commanders, and sent it to them for approval and for the record.

This procedure had served well enough when the BEF's contribution to the spring and autumn campaigns in Artois was little more than an extension of an essentially French battle, but the BEF and its new commander in 1916 created new challenges. It had been hard enough coping with the changeable Sir John French, but Scottish fixity of purpose was no less difficult. If Foch had succeeded with Haig as the I Corps commander at Ypres in 1914, the Haig of 1916 was a very different proposition. There was no conflict between the pair over the need to mount an offensive in order to gain victory, but Foch wanted to wait whereas Haig kept expanding his Somme objectives. The anomalies of Foch's position became more pronounced in 1916, as he was excluded from the strategic planning and as Haig grew in confidence and determination to be free of French control. The head of the French Military Mission at GHQ summed up the situation thus: 'Conscious of the experience gained and strengthened by its early successes, the British high command now refuses clearly to accept any intervention in the way it carries out operations.' Moreover, he concluded, the British were likely to stop operations on the Somme in order to 'perfect and to reinforce through the winter the instrument with which it thinks it can play in 1917 the main role in the Coalition'.[62]

Foch had been fortunate in his liaison officers (see Illustration 5) when explaining his strategic ideas to his Belgian and British allies. The evidence of his Belgian liaison officer's diary reveals a degree of sympathy and confidence; Wilson and Foch were similar in temperament and outlook, and it is doubtful if the fighting at Ypres in 1914 could have gained results without their friendly collaboration. Although Foch lost Wilson's services in 1916 with the changes in the British high command, Dillon proved a happy replacement. The efforts of liaison officers to explain the thinking of one national headquarters to the staff of another speaking a different language are generally ignored, yet it is difficult to see how Foch could have coordinated a battle such as that on the Somme in 1916 without Dillon carrying messages back and forth, massaging strong language, giving additional explanations, acting as a safety-valve, and generally smoothing the way.

Foch's role as coordinator in the north compelled him to consider the coalition aspect of the war, but he was thinking of more than simply the Western Front. In April 1916 he began putting onto paper his thoughts about Allied command.[63] The Russians had the manpower but lacked armaments; the Italians were fighting their own war; the British with their

[62] Vallières to commander-in-chief, Report # 1264, 22 October 1916, 17N 348.
[63] 'Le Commandement allié, avril–mai 1916', 1K/129/2, [d] Ecrits divers.

VILLERS -BRETONNEUX

(3 Septembre _ 26 Novembre 1916)

P.C. du G.A.N.

Dillon et de Posch

Officiers de liaison anglais
et belge

Illustration 5   Liaison officers Colonel Eric Dillon and Major de Posch

larger population held a much smaller front than the French and had only raised half the number of divisions that the French were fielding. Foch shared the common French perception that British policy was to wear out the French, rather than themselves (in other words, fighting to the last Frenchman). Because Foch believed that the enemy could be defeated only by an attack, that attack had to be delivered over as wide an area as possible and had to last for as long as possible in the new conditions of siege warfare. Since France could not deliver that attack alone, allies were needed, but the fighting on the Somme revealed how inexperienced the British still were, and Brusilov's offensive in Russia had petered out after an auspicious start.

Foch's thinking about coalition warfare led him to two conclusions: first, the Allies had to 'combine' their actions much more closely, forming a central directing 'organ' to eliminate individual initiatives; and second, the necessary wide-front and lengthy offensives depended entirely on the production of materiel. Hence 'the director of the war must be the director of production'. Since the greatest resources were in Britain, the 'tap' was in the hands of the government in London. If the French wanted the tap to be turned on for as long as the battle lasted, Foch implies (but does not say so explicitly), then the French had to control the tap. He ended thus: 'Before making a coalition of armies, we must make a coalition of governments.' Here we see Foch working towards the necessary structures – diplomatic, economic and industrial, as well as military – for a modern industrial war fought by a coalition. More than this, he was also coming to the conclusion that unity of command would be required.

In addition to the benefits of the experience of battle and of the experience of fighting with Allies in the development of his strategic thinking, Foch also learned from his sacking at the end of 1916. His removal from command taught him two valuable lessons. First, if he was to mix in politics or with politicians, then he had to be prepared to pay the price. Poincaré's memoirs reveal that Foch's connections to certain politicians were not only widely known, but also mistrusted. In the event, Foch was right to put his money on Georges Clemenceau, but once again the benefit would not appear for some time. Second, Foch was reminded most painfully that supreme command in a democracy lies in the hands of those politicians – and they had sacked both him and the commander-in-chief. Foch claimed to be a committed republican, but he wanted the Republic to be an intelligent republic.[64] He had little respect for Briand's new Ministry, and he told the War Minister General Lyautey in February 1917 that Briand had appointed him purely to save his Ministry; that Briand was all talk and nothing ever got done; that he (Lyautey) had the support of Poincaré and Albert Thomas, but as for all the rest: 'it's vaseline'.[65] Possibly this is why eventually he forgave Joffre, who realised that he had let his subordinate down and who apologised for so doing. Foch would have to bide his time patiently and wait (or so Clemenceau claimed to have advised him) to be recalled.

[64] De Posch diary, 11 November 1915.
[65] Foch, Journées, 19 February 1917, 414/AP/10.

Foch's approval of the arrival of Lloyd George in 10 Downing Street (on 11 December 1916) shows what he wanted from political leaders: energy and decision. He told his wife that the British were setting a 'fine example of awakening and energy', which he hoped would be followed in France. He approved the replacement of the 'endormeur' (soporific) Asquith, and believed that the new Premier was taking the lead and making some 'superb decisions'.[66] Obviously Foch wished for a similar lead from French politicians, preferably Georges Clemenceau. The (ditherer) Viviani and the (dilettante) Briand had proved inadequate war leaders, in Foch's eyes.

Foch had his critics. Although he himself spent little time as a corps or an army commander, he had to deal constantly with such commanders in his position as Northern Army Group commander. His command style led to some tensions and difficulties because the demarcation lines between Foch as army group commander and his army commanders had to be drawn as conditions developed. The relationship with Castelnau never recovered from the disastrous Morhange affair. Foch told his family after the war that he had been astounded to receive an order to halt.[67] There were other tensions revealed by Foch's tight control over his subordinates. Tenth Army's first commanding general, Maud'huy, felt harrassed and harried by Foch, according to that army's chief of staff. Maud'huy's successor, d'Urbal, had the same experience, although he seems to have weathered it with greater resilience. D'Urbal wrote in his postwar memoirs that at first he felt that Foch interfered too much in details that were the province of the army commander, causing mix-ups or merely repeating what had already been ordered. Nonetheless, he claimed that as they got to know each other better he grew to appreciate (at least with hindsight) Foch's 'constant and kindly goodwill'.[68] Of Foch's two army commanders on the Somme, Fayolle had been driven to write a letter of resignation, although it was later withdrawn, and his diary contains numerous entries about Foch's constant pressure.[69] Micheler had found Foch exacting, and rumours abounded about rows between them; but he disliked the way Foch had been used as the scapegoat for the Somme and believed that he would make a good commander-in-chief, being the army's 'only brain with wide views'.[70] Yet General

---

[66] Letters, Foch to Mme Foch, 5 and 10 December 1916, vol. 42.
[67] Denis Prunet, Notes de conversations, 20 October 1921, fo. 58, Mi 2907, BNF.
[68] D'Urbal, *Souvenirs*, 144–5.
[69] Fayolle, *CS*, entries for 17, 18, 19 (for the threat to resign), 21 August, 6, 7, 9, 23, 30 September, 21 October, 3 November 1916.
[70] Letters, Micheler to Antonin Dubost, President of the Senate, 19 November and 4 December 1916, cited in Herbillon, *Micheler*, 108–9. See also Ferry, *Carnets secrets*, 203 (entry for 7 September 1916).

Brugère continued to fulminate about the 'professor' soldiers. According to Brugère, Foch was both 'mad' and 'dangerous'. He disapproved of Foch's cautious waiting offensive strategy: 'he [Foch] wants to prepare everything himself and not to act until he has all the trumps in his hands. You never have them all, and it is necessary to act as quickly as possible and to gain the advantage of surprise.'[71] Brugère's lack of experience is revealed here. Foch had tried acting before obtaining all the trump cards, and had learned that the so-called 'advantage' of surprise was useless if lack of the right quantity and quality of munitions meant that it could not be exploited. Foch was right to demand the means of success before embarking on any offensive.

So Foch's career as a field commander on the Western Front ended in December 1916. His successes had all been defensive actions, and his offensives had all failed after the opening days, but his faith in his strategic vision was undimmed. The path to victory lay through offensive action, but only after the proper means had been provided. Meanwhile, Foch had learned useful lessons about how to deal (or attempt to deal) with the adversary, with allies and with politicians. He would not be long 'dans la coulisse', in the wings.[72]

[71] Brugère diary, 18 August, 6, 12 September 1916, 1K/160.
[72] Letter, Foch to Wilson, 9 January 1917, HHW 2/85/8.

End of Part I

10   Intermezzo 1917

Although Foch felt disgraced by his removal from command of the Northern Army Group, the new French commander-in-chief, General Robert Nivelle, put him to work immediately on various so-called 'special studies'. The first five months of 1917 have been portrayed as a period of 'make-work' for Foch, yet the three studies that he completed then were each of considerable potential importance. The stalemate of 1916 on the Western Front following the lack of German success at Verdun and the lack of Allied success on the Somme gave greater emphasis to sectors further to the southeast, namely Switzerland, the Alsace-Lorraine front where Foch had begun his wartime career, and Italy. The French feared that the Germans might transfer their attention to any of these three sectors, a fear greatly increased in March 1917 when the first Russian revolution made the Eastern Front less secure. Also in March the Germans on the Western Front completed their withdrawal (begun on 4 February) to the newly constructed and immensely strong defensive position, the *Hindenburgstellung*, thereby interfering with the French offensive that Nivelle was planning for the Aisne front.

Foch was instructed during these five months to study all three sectors: he drew up 'Plan H', a plan to coordinate action with the Swiss army in case the Germans violated Swiss neutrality and invaded either southern France or Italy; he took temporary command of the Eastern Army Group whilst its new commander, General Castelnau, was absent with an Allied mission to St Petersburg, and oversaw the preparation of offensive plans in case a relief operation was required in the east to support Nivelle's main action on the Aisne; then, finally, he visited Italy and drew up plans with General Luigi Cadorna to coordinate Allied help to that country in case of another attack such as the Austro-Hungarians had mounted in 1916. The third mission proved the most important because Italy was indeed attacked, and because the disaster at Caporetto in October 1917 led, finally, to the Allies taking concerted, political action to put the direction of the war effort onto a more efficient and effective footing. All three tasks gave Foch a much wider view of the war's complexity than his earlier concentration on the front in northern France had allowed.

Foch began work on Plan H immediately with his customary energy (his first report to Nivelle is dated 1 January 1917).[1] Landlocked neutral Switzerland was a significant importer of Entente foodstuffs and of German coal and iron ore; it was a centre for spying, black marketeering, and exploration of peace feelers; and it might provide an invasion route into southern France or northern Italy. Joffre had recognised France's vulnerability to a German violation of Swiss neutrality when he charged Foch in February 1916 with taking command of a Swiss frontier army group, should that become necessary.[2] So Nivelle's instruction to prepare 'Plan H' was not a completely new task for Foch, whose notebooks reveal considerable time spent thinking about the problems.

Foch envisaged a large army group (thirty to forty divisions), and requested permission to reconnoitre the Swiss railways. He submitted his final plan on 7 February and Nivelle approved it a few days later, expressing his great satisfaction with Foch's work.[3] By 3 March all the train and artillery moves were settled, and on 30 March Foch was designated the eventual commander of the Groupe des Armées d'Helvétie, or Army Group Switzerland.[4] Although the work remained a paper exercise against a possible invasion that did not occur, it had two benefits. It gave Foch experience in the logistical problems of transporting troops in mountainous country, and it gave Weygand the opportunity to play an independent role as he went to Switzerland and negotiated an agreement with the Swiss army's general staff about a possible French intervention at the request of the federal government.[5]

At the same time as preparing 'Plan H', Foch was deputed to take temporary command of the two armies in Eastern Army Group during the absence of its new commander, General Castelnau, who had gone to St Petersburg on 18 January with an Allied mission (returning to France on 4 March). Hence Foch went back to Lorraine, where he had begun the war and where General Lyautey, the new War Minister, decorated him with the *médaille militaire* on 20 February. The citation reads in part: 'outstanding tactician and accomplished leader ... inflexible tenacity, irrepressible energy and remarkable aptitude in the manoeuvre'.[6]

---

[1] Letter, Foch to Nivelle, 1 January 1917, *AFGG* 5/1, annex 376.
[2] GQG 3e Bureau, 22 April 1916, Instruction pour la Couverture de notre Aile Droite en cas de Violation du Territoire Suisse, 16N 1943 [d] Entrées.
[3] Letter, Nivelle to Foch, #10639, 12 February 1917, ibid.
[4] Note pour le G.A.E. – le Gal Foch, 30 March 1917, *AFGG* 5/1, annex 1079.
[5] Weygand, *IV*, 385–7; also *AFGG* 5/1, 341–2.
[6] Personnel dossier 9Y1d 528; Weygand, *IV*, 375–6.

Nivelle instructed Foch to prepare the two eastern armies to act as 'relief units' when his main attack was launched on the Aisne, and also to prepare an offensive plan in case the main attack failed to produce a decisive result. On 9 March Foch approved Seventh Army's plan for an attack on Mulhouse in Alsace, but he was recalled before the Eighth Army plan for an operation further north in Lorraine could be completed. Risk of German action around Nancy had held up the work, and the defences that Castelnau had complained were incomplete in 1914 were still incomplete in 1917.[7]

Once again, Foch had prepared for an operation that did not take place, yet once again the work was not wasted. It had shown Foch the need to reduce the Saint-Mihiel salient and had also reminded him of the considerable difficulties of an attack in Lorraine. In 1918 both these areas would become important.[8] The Lorraine episode deepened the antagonism between Foch and Castelnau. Foch departed on 30 March, the day before Castelnau arrived to take back command, leaving two staff officers to hand over. Castelnau's staff were not impressed by the scheme for Seventh Army that Foch had approved, seeing it as an example of Foch's 'je m'en fichisme' – his 'couldn't care less' attitude that they feared exposed Castelnau to the risks involved in carrying out a plan that he had not formulated.[9] Although Foch knew that the eastern sector was a backwater, with no definite role to play in Nivelle's forthcoming offensive, it is unlikely that the plan he had approved was careless. It is more likely that Castelnau's staff would have criticised any plan that Foch had approved, out of loyalty to their chief.

When Foch returned to his headquarters in Senlis, north of Paris, he had already heard rumours of his third task; it involved Italy, whose security was linked intimately with the Swiss question that he had been studying. The Italian question loomed very large during 1917, because of the significant changes in the diplomatic and political climate that had taken place by the time Foch returned from eastern France. Outside France, Russia underwent its first revolution and on 12 March the Tsar abdicated, leaving the Allies to wonder how much they might rely on any further military effort on the Eastern Front. This weakening of the eastern ally made the resilience of Italy even more critical. The Comando Supremo feared an Austrian attack in the Trentino, as had happened in spring 1916. Moreover, as the French

---

[7] Letter, Foch to commander-in-chief, 14 March 1917, *AFGG* 5/1, annex 857; Fayolle, *CS*, 202 (entry for 21 January 1917).

[8] See the draft chapter (ch. 2 of part 6) by de Mierry for Foch memoirs, Fonds Weygand, partie donnée, 1K/130/3.

[9] De Bary memoirs, 31 March 1917, fo. 11; *AFGG* 5/1, 315.

had already envisioned, the Germans might combine with the Austrians in a joint offensive against Italy, or might make an attack of their own following a violation of Swiss neutrality. The American declaration of war against Germany on 6 April, while welcome, was unlikely to make much difference to the European theatre in the immediate future. Meanwhile the German decision to restart unrestricted submarine warfare, which was a large factor in the American decision for war, was causing huge losses in Allied and neutral shipping: over 860,000 tons were lost in April 1917, which boded ill for any large transfers of American soldiers across the Atlantic.[10]

The domestic scene too had changed considerably by the time Foch gave up his temporary army group command. Haig had been put under Nivelle's command for the forthcoming offensive in France. That offensive was no longer the plan agreed when Joffre had been in command; rather a French Reserve Army Group was to destroy the German forces by attacking northwards from the river Aisne towards the Chemin des Dames, with the northern and British armies attacking in a convergent direction to cut off the large German salient. As in 1916, Russian and Italian offensives were to be launched as near simultaneously as possible. There were political as well as military changes. The Briand government was out, replaced on 20 March by a Ministry led by the experienced former Finance Minister, Alexandre Ribot, with Paul Painlevé as War Minister. Because of his scientific background, Painlevé had been Briand's Education Minister between October 1915 and December 1916 with responsibility for inventions, so worked with both French and British Munitions Ministers. In the discussions over Joffre's replacement back in December 1916 Painlevé had supported the more methodical Foch and Pétain methods over Nivelle's 'Verdun school', and had refused to serve in Briand's rejigged Ministry because Nivelle was chosen to succeed Joffre. Foch might expect, therefore, to be looked on with greater favour in the new Ribot Ministry than had been the case with the Briand government that had sacked him. He had already met Painlevé in June 1916, when they had a long talk at Foch's headquarters before the Battle of the Somme.[11] His former ADC, the *député* Charles Meunier-Surcouf, claims that he took the new War Minister Painlevé to meet Foch again. The two men had lunch and a two-hour conversation, after which Painlevé thanked Meunier-Surcouf for the meeting, calling Foch 'a remarkable man' for whom he would ensure that a 'special place' would be found.[12] There is no other trace of this meeting, and Foch seems to have left no record of his views, if any, on the new Cabinet, although he

[10] Halpern, *Naval History*, 341.   [11] Mme Foch diary, 12 June 1916.
[12] Charles Meunier [-Surcouf], 'Mes cahiers', cahier 6, fo. 17, 1KT/83.

had noted that Briand's departure would be no loss as he was doing nothing ['positivement trop inopérant'].[13]

What can be said with certainty about Foch's political views, however, is that he wanted a more energetic government, prepared to conduct the war 'vigorously', following Britain's example. 'What we need is a Lloyd George', he wrote to Henry Wilson, calling the change of government in London 'a magnificent model of parliamentary government in time of war'. As Briand's Ministry was coming to an end, Foch had nothing but scorn for the French politicians who sat around the table and merely talked, whereas Lloyd George was a man of action.[14] The Welshman was just as much of a 'squirrel' as Briand, but, in Foch's opinion, the former knew his way around his tree rather better.[15]

One of Lloyd George's first actions upon becoming Prime Minister had been to attempt to spring on the Allies a proposal for an Italian offensive against Austria-Hungary, supported by British and French artillery, as an alternative to yet another Western Front attack. He failed, however, to persuade the Allies in conference in Rome, and accepted instead Nivelle's proposal for a great attack in France which at least had the merit that it gave the French and not the British the main role. Yet the Italian front was clearly vulnerable, as the Austro-Hungarian attack, the *Strafexpedition* of May 1916, had shown. Neither France nor Britain could afford to see the enemy cut off Cadorna's troops in the eastern sector, where repeated battles near the Isonzo river were taking place, and Austro-Hungarian forces did not have to advance very far to reach the Adriatic and Venice. Such a disaster might force Italy to make a separate peace – the war had never been hugely popular in the country – thereby granting more liberty of action to the German and Austrian submarines operating in the Mediterranean from the Austrian base in Pola. The entire Mediterranean was declared one of the zones where all vessels were liable to attack without warning when the Germans re-started unrestricted submarine warfare on 1 February 1917. Anything that increased the submarine menace in the Mediterranean (hence endangering the sea routes to the Middle East and India) was to be avoided. For France, such a disaster would open its southern frontier to invasion.

Italian fears increased in March as operation ALBERICH was completed. The German withdrawal to the newly constructed *Hindenburgstellung* freed some of their divisions because their front was now shorter,

---

[13] Letter, Foch to Mme Foch, 11 March 1917, vol. 43.
[14] Letter, Foch to Wilson, 9 January 1917, HHW mss 2/85/8; Mme Foch diary, 24 February 1917.
[15] Comment probably dating from 1921, Rochard papers, 1K/129/2.

interfered with Nivelle's plans for his offensive, and made the Italians fear an Austrian offensive reinforced by some of those freed German divisions. By the time Foch left his temporary command of the Eastern Army Group, Lloyd George had already sent Robertson to Italy to see conditions. Robertson took Weygand as a French representative – another chance for Weygand to act independently. As a result of Robertson's mainly critical report, British and French staff officers were sent to establish closer relations with Cadorna and to oversee the transport and supply arrangements that might need to be put into effect.

On 1 April Nivelle asked the Comité de guerre to approve direct intervention in Italy, hoping that the British would agree to place their portion of any intervention force under Foch's orders because he did not want the British taking the credit.[16] War Minister Painlevé consulted with Pétain, now in command of the Centre Army Group. Pétain pointed to the chaotic situation in Russia (on 6 April the Petrograd Soviet would insist on opening peace negotiations), the real risk of failure in Nivelle's forthcoming offensive, and the likelihood of a German attack on Italy. He recommended sending four divisions, British and French, under Foch's command. Foch was the obvious candidate because he had been collaborating with the British since 1914.[17]

Foch expounded his own views to the Comité de guerre on 5 April in a typically brief but emphatic note.[18] The threat to Italy was real, he argued, and direct aid should be sent immediately. Consequently Painlevé dispatched Foch to Italy straight away, and Foch met Cadorna three days later in Vicenza after a long train ride via Milan, which would have given him a good idea of the transport difficulties across northern Italy. Then Foch inspected the Italian front and returned to Paris on 15 April. Cadorna was reassured by Foch's visit, and claimed to be in complete agreement with Foch, whom he found 'very open, decisive and *simpatico*'.[19] At a meeting in Paris on 21 April, Foch and Robertson reached agreement with Lloyd George and Painlevé that France would transport and supply four divisions with mountain artillery, and eight to ten squadrons of aircraft, the first units to begin moving within eight days of the order being given.[20]

So the third of Foch's tasks during the early months of 1917 had given him yet more experience in dealing with Allies and in the logistical

[16] Nivelle to Ministre de la Guerre, 1 April 1917, *AFGG* 5/1, annex 1108.
[17] Helbronner diary, 1 April 1917, 313/AP/122.
[18] Poincaré, *AS*, 9: 105; Note rédigée par le Général Foch en vue de la réunion du Comité de Guerre, le 5 avril 1917, *AFGG* 5/2, annex 1189.
[19] Letter, Cadorna to his daughter, 12 April 1917, in Cadorna, *Lettere famigliari*, 197.
[20] *AFGG* 5/2, 296–7; *OH Italy*, 28–30.

problems of moving troops and materiel. Weygand too had been given the opportunity to act independently. Any French force to be sent to Italy was designated an army detachment, commanded by an army group commander, thus leaving the way open for Foch to be appointed should the decision to intervene be taken. This did not happen, however, because great changes in the French high command occurred in May.

Foch had not sulked in his tent, although he kept his head well down between January and May. He was keeping away from Paris and the political intrigues that Nivelle was having to endure. 'I shall let politics continue to interfere with military matters without getting mixed up in it, since I don't want to lose in such a bottomless pit the little influence that I may be able to bring to bear on events', he wrote to his wife.[21] This restraint was either due to having had his fingers burned earlier by mixing with politicians hence having learned his lesson, or due to following Clemenceau's advice to be patient, or else he was simply out of contact with Paris. Foch was scornful of the agitation in government circles, and was happy to be out of it all. Because of continuing sabotage by the government, the political direction of the war had slipped from French hands. At least Lloyd George was energetic, unlike his own 'uncertain, hesitant' government.[22] His restraint was noted by General Maurice Pellé, who had been sacked from GQG at the same time as Foch. No other military leader had kept further away from intrigue and politics than Foch, Pellé wrote. His 'dignity' and 'moral worth' at the time of his sacking had been admirable, when he was entirely suitable for the highest command.[23]

While Foch had been in Italy, the Canadian Corps had captured Vimy Ridge, which had been his constant aim in 1915. This operation was part of Haig's preliminary supporting action (the Battle of Arras) for the ill-fated Nivelle offensive, the only Western Front offensive to bear the name of its originator, which began on 16 April, the day after Foch returned to France. In appalling weather conditions of sleet and snow the French armies along the river Aisne attacked uphill towards the crest, the Chemin des Dames, towards the enemy, who knew when and where to expect them. Nivelle's promise to break off the engagement within forty-eight hours if there had been no breakthrough was not kept. Although there had been a measure of success, with over 400 artillery pieces and machineguns and 8000 enemy captured by 20 April,[24] there was general agreement as

---

[21] Letter, Foch to Mme Foch, 3 April 1917, vol. 43.
[22] Foch, Carnets, 13 May 1917, fo. 237.
[23] Letter, Pellé to his family, 17 May 1917, cited in Le Chatelier, Pellé, 2: 41.
[24] Castex, Chemin des Dames, 20.

early as that date that the offensive had failed in its objectives. By 25 April
the offensive had cost 134,000 casualties, of whom some 30,000 had been
killed.[25] When orders to continue attacking were delivered, the men took
their fate into their own hands and went on strike, refusing to undertake
what they considered to be further foolish, because hopeless, attacks.

Foch had judged even sooner what the consequences of the Nivelle
offensive would be. As early as 17 April he told Henry Wilson that Nivelle
was 'done' owing to his failure. Foch also saw that the 'Nivelle' or
'Verdun' method stood condemned, thus justifying his 'Somme' method.
As he told General Fayolle, who had been his Sixth Army commander
there, this was his revenge for the Somme.[26] In a sad note made on 18
April Foch compared the two battles, the Somme in 1916 and now the
Aisne in 1917. On the Somme, he wrote, the French had taken more
prisoners and captured more guns than the inexperienced British, who
suffered great casualties, but the results had been a field marshal's baton
for Haig, a change in the French command, and the German withdrawal
to the Hindenburg Line. In April 1917, on the other hand, the British were
advancing with success but the French had halted. It was a complete turn-
around in the relationship between the British and French armies.[27] What
he called his theory of the 'Somme School' was being justified more each
day, he wrote to his wife: 'all I have to do is to wait'.[28]

President Poincaré had supported Nivelle's offensive, but Painlevé had
been less convinced. Now the War Minister moved quickly to deal with
the military situation. Despite the boost to enemy morale that would be
provided by replacing the French commander-in-chief yet again, after
only a few months in the job, he began that process by appointing
Philippe Pétain to the post of chief of staff of the army within the
Ministry, a decision ratified on 29 April.[29] Foch was pleased to learn of
Pétain's appointment and hoped that Pétain would be able to make his
ideas prevail. He could see that the appointment meant the end of Nivelle,
who now lacked any authority. If the Republic was worried by a victorious
general, he noted, a defeated general was worth nothing.[30]

Pétain had much grander ideas about his new role than Painlevé, and
discussion over the decree defining the powers and responsibilities of the
position was still continuing a fortnight after his appointment.[31] The

[25] Doughty, *PV*, 354.
[26] Wilson diary, 17 April 1917; Fayolle, *CS*, 217 (entry for 21 April 1917).
[27] Foch, Carnets, 18 April 1917, fo. 233.
[28] Foch, Carnets, 8 May 1917, fo. 237; letter, Foch to Mme Foch, 5 May 1917, vol. 43.
[29] Poincaré, *AS*, 9: 120–4, 131.
[30] Letter, Foch to Mme Foch, 30 April 1917, vol. 43; Foch, Carnets, 8 May 1917, fo. 237.
[31] Serrigny, *Trente ans*, 131–2.

position had been more or less in abeyance since the start of the war because the prewar chief of army (Joffre) was CinC designate of the armies in the field. Unlike in Britain, where the CIGS had a completely separate role from that of the CinC in France, Joffre had combined both roles. Painlevé saw the position of chief of the general staff of the French army as 'balancing' that of the commander-in-chief.[32] Pétain himself did not want a job in Paris, but Painlevé had indicated his intention that eventually Pétain should replace, rather than simply balance, Nivelle. Caution was required so as not to give the enemy a good subject for propaganda, and equally so as not to worry the British ally.

On 13 May, Painlevé was able to impose what he had wanted all along and offered the post of CinC to Pétain, thus removing Nivelle. After some 'stormy and violent' Cabinet meetings, opposition from the President of the Republic (who had not forgiven Pétain his comment that 'we are neither governed nor commanded'),[33] and a slight difficulty when Nivelle refused to go quietly, agreement was reached that Pétain would succeed but that there would be no official announcement until 15 May.[34] The careful, methodical school appeared to be the only alternative to Nivelle's so-called 'Verdun school'.

This left the question of who should succeed Pétain as chief of the army general staff. Ribot believed Foch to be suitable because he was known to the Allies. He and Painlevé agreed to propose Foch at the same time as they decided to replace Nivelle.[35] Pétain believed that, while Foch would not do as CinC because he did not know the infantry and the 'soul of the soldier', he had three qualities that fitted him for the role of chief of staff of the army: he would know how to sort things out [il saura se débrouiller] with the Allies; he was a 'reservoir of energy'; and he was 'an honourable [honnête] man'.[36]

After some second thoughts about whether Fayolle might not be a better choice, Painlevé summoned Foch on 11 May. He got to Paris at 9.30pm and the meeting with Painlevé went on until after midnight. On being offered the job, Foch asked for time to think it over since he was a doer ['un exécuteur'] and not 'prepared' for the task on offer. (This is an extraordinary statement from the former student, teacher and comman- dant of the Ecole Supérieure de Guerre, but no doubt reflects his prefer- ence for a field command over a job in the Ministry.) Painlevé gave him

---

[32] Painlevé, *Foch et Pétain*, 121; Renouvin, *Formes du gouvernement*, 83–4.
[33] Pétain had said this to Poincaré at Verdun in 1916; the President had been enraged: see Ferry, *Carnets secrets*, 227, 230.
[34] Ribot, *Journal*, 101 (entry for 15 May 1917); Painlevé, *Foch et Pétain*, 112–20.
[35] Poincaré, *AS*, 9: 135 (entry for 10 May 1917).   [36] Serrigny, *Trente ans*, 137–8.

until 10am, next morning. Foch then asked to see the job specification. This, as noted above, was still under discussion, but Painlevé read to him the proposed decree. Pétain then arrived and professed himself happy to be returning to the armies, seeing no difficulties in the hat-swapping that was proposed. Foch talked it over with Weygand and his son-in-law (Captain Alex Fournier), who both advised 'great caution'. Having composed a note with a provisional acceptance: 'I accept without reservation if I know the full story [si je sais de quoi il s'agit], with reservations if I do not', Foch returned to the Ministry next morning, handed his note over and received Painlevé's agreement to his terms.[37]

After some more havering over Fayolle or Foch in the Conseil des ministres on 15 May, the decision came down for Foch and immediately Poincaré signed the decree naming him.[38] The tasks of the new chief of staff were to provide technical advice to the Minister in several areas: the general conduct of the war and cooperation with the Allies; the operational planning in general terms (although the commander-in-chief had sole responsibility for carrying out those plans); provision of materiel (railways, artillery, aviation and so on); transport of men and materiel within the country; and any other question that the Minister wished to have examined.[39]

The dual appointment of Foch and Pétain met with favour among the British. This is not surprising as Foch at least was a known quantity, and Lloyd George's subterfuge in placing Haig and the BEF under French command for the Nivelle offensive had been resented bitterly.[40] Haig noted that Foch's appointment meant that 'his wide experience of active operations' gave 'the advantage of greater continuity in the French command ... He has always shown that he is prepared to run risks and act on the offensive.'[41] Wilson was, of course, very pleased. He had been acting as Nivelle's liaison officer during the April offensive, and judged the two appointments as '[p]robably the best arrangements under the circumstances', because Robertson and Foch knew each other very well. Wilson was amused 'a good deal to see both French and English people acclaiming him as the man for the post when I remember how these same gentlemen used to say he was too old, and too tired, and too anti-English, & too loquacious & too etc. etc.!'[42] Clive, the head of the British mission at

---

[37] Foch's note in Painlevé papers: 313/AP/134; Mme Foch diary, 13 May 1917.

[38] Poincaré, AS, 9: 138–9 (entry for 15 May 1917). Painlevé's account omits any mention of hesitations.

[39] Guinard, Devos and Nicot, Inventaire: Introduction, 73; AFGG 5/1, annex 1910.

[40] On Haig's subordination to Nivelle, see Greenhalgh, VTC, 138–53.

[41] Haig diary, 15 May 1917.

[42] Wilson letters to Robertson, 16 and 18 May 1917, Robertson mss, 7/5/67 and 7/5/68.

GQG, hence closer to the armies, thought that the dual appointments 'should be a good arrangement, in that Foch has big views, would get on better with politicians than with Pétain, and Pétain is trusted by the army'.[43]

Opinions among the French were more varied. Those whom Foch had offended were not pleased. General Brugère claimed that Foch would make a 'poor CinC' and a 'bad' chief of the army general staff.[44] At General Castelnau's headquarters they were astounded by the news. A character such as Foch's – 'impulsive and brusque' – could not possibly succeed in the post to which he had been appointed. Castelnau himself thought that Foch would be the same as he always had been at all times and in all places: 'impulsive, brutal, spouting pseudo-philosophical formulae'.[45] One of Foch's corps commanders on the Somme, General Guillaumat, hoped that Pétain would be able to overcome the 'disorganisation genius' that was Foch.[46] On the other hand, General Fayolle approved, and General Pellé thought Foch the best prepared 'militarily' for the post.[47]

Some could see the difficult path that lay ahead because of the lack of a clearly defined distinction between the roles of CinC and chief of the army general staff, especially given the very different characters of the two men. The late Professor Pedroncini concluded from his study of the relations between the government and high command during 1917 that the whole year passed in a search for new equilibrium between the two sets of responsibilities, a search that failed.[48] Haig was unsure whether he should deal with Foch or with Pétain (Robertson advised the latter), and Bertie informed London of the 'great antagonism' between the two generals. Among the French, Clemenceau commented in his newspaper that Pétain would not be content as CinC when so much power was held by Foch in the Ministry.[49] Other French press comments were, however, generally positive. Pellé wondered how long, in such a 'delicate situation' the two generals might be able to collaborate.[50] Foch's latest biographer writes of the risk of 'paralysis or explosion' that Painlevé was running in attempting to marry the 'ice' of Pétain to Foch's 'fire'.[51]

---

[43] Clive diary, 15 May 1915, CAB 45/201.   [44] Brugère diary, 12 May 1917, 1K/160.
[45] De Bary memoirs, 17 May 1917, fo. 37; Castelnau letter to his son Louis, cited in Gras, *Castelnau*, 360.
[46] Guillaumat, *Correspondance*, 209.
[47] Fayolle, *CS*, 224 (entry for 12 May 19017); Pellé to Albert Thomas, 25 May 1917, Albert Thomas mss, 94/AP/237.
[48] Pedroncini, 'Rapports', 122.
[49] Bertie to Foreign Office, despatch # 230, 16 May 1917, FO 371/2937.
[50] Pellé to Albert Thomas, 25 May 1917, Albert Thomas mss, 94/AP/237.
[51] Notin, *Foch*, 270.

Foch's new job was not only new in itself, but the context in which he had to operate was also new. The French army had been driven beyond the point of exhaustion and serious acts of indiscipline were the result. It would require time and careful handling by the new commander-in-chief, Pétain, who would need the support of the new chief of staff of the army. If Foch intended to stick to his 1916 ideas about not undertaking large new offensives until the armies were properly equipped for the task, then he would have to support Pétain with programmes for tanks, for aviation and so on. Furthermore, the perilous state of the French army meant that on the Western Front the BEF would be undertaking the main combat role, so Foch would have to reassure the British and to deal with the aftermath of Haig's subordination to the French by cooperating as much as possible. In addition he had to deal with Italy's requests for guns to enable it to carry out the agreed offensive on the Italian front. There were two further factors that created an entirely new situation for Foch. First, the position of Russia worsened as 1917 progressed until it became clear that little more in the way of offensive operations in the east could be expected. The initial optimism after the February revolution was extinguished by the failure in July of the offensive ordered by the new (Socialist) War Minister, Alexandr Kerensky. Second, the USA had declared war on Germany on 6 April, just as Foch left for Italy. Although no one expected immediate American assistance, the administrative arrangements to insert American troops would occupy much time and energy. In short, Foch's new job was a challenge both as regarded his own army and also as regarded the other Entente powers. He was, however, prepared to accept the challenge so long as he knew where he stood.

Despite Foch's feeling that he had been disgraced by his removal from command of the Northern Army Group, the period between January and May 1917 had not been a wasted five months. Nivelle had shown his confidence immediately by using Foch as temporary army group commander and by entrusting him with taking precautionary measures in areas which it was feared were liable to attack. The establishment of plans for transporting Allied troops to Italy would prove to have been a wise decision and useful practice for Foch. Nivelle's successor Pétain had also expressed his confidence in Foch for his experience in dealing with Allies, even though Pétain also feared the political repercussions of passing him over in favour of Fayolle. So Foch had not been long on the sidelines.

There were other benefits from his enforced removal from active command in the field. It gave Foch a break from the campaigning in which he had been involved since the opening weeks of the war – a luxury which few commanding generals enjoyed. Moreover, he had domestic support as his wife and his home were now close by. Madame Foch had moved into their new Paris home on 4 May (on the Avenue de Saxe, close to the Boulevard des Invalides, where Foch had his new office). The three tasks that Foch carried out, in preparing offensive plans for his army group, preparing Plan H against an invasion of Switzerland, and going to Italy to arrange support in case of an attack there, gave him a wider viewpoint, a better understanding of the inter-connectedness of the various fronts. They also gave him greater insights into the logistical problems involved in moving troops and munitions. His chief of staff, Weygand, had also played an important role in accompanying Robertson to Italy and in dealing with the Swiss authorities. This revealed Foch's confidence in him and gave Foch the benefit of a chief of staff with wide, personal experience.

Finally, Foch had been lucky not to be involved in the unfortunate machinations that placed Haig under Nivelle's authority for the spring offensive. Lloyd George's attempt to restrain Haig from undertaking another Somme offensive by subordinating him to the French commander-in-chief left a huge legacy of mistrust between British generals and their political masters. Foch, however, had had nothing to do with the scheming and this made his initial relationship with Haig and Robertson (both of whom he had known, of course, since 1914) much easier at the start of this new stage of his career. Nor had he been involved in the planning and execution of Nivelle's offensive, and so he was not tainted by its failure. Indeed, one of the tasks assigned to him in his new role was to sit on a board of enquiry to look into the conditions under which the offensive had taken place.

Foch's new position as chief of staff of the French army meant that he had to move up a gear and deal directly with the men who had the task of setting the Entente's military policy. He had to shift from the purely military sphere into a world of international conferences and strategic decision-making, but without losing sight of domestic questions. The immediate problem for France's two new commanders, Foch and Pétain, was the state of the army. During May the armies that had taken part in Nivelle's offensive on the Aisne refused to continue to make war the same way, and the troubles persisted into June on the Soissons front, where offensive action was continuing. While Pétain healed the French army by changing methods, improving conditions and restoring the confidence that had been lost through Nivelle's excessive promises, the British army would have to carry more of the burden of the Western Front. The Battle of Arras and the capture of Vimy Ridge had been the British contribution to the northern flank of Nivelle's joint campaign. It would be Foch's job to support Pétain, and to work with the

British, especially his opposite number in London General Sir William Robertson, dealing with the broader strategic questions of the war: the Italian problem, Salonika and Greece generally, the Middle East, the new ally (the United States) and the failing ally (Russia).

Foch was thrown into his new role at the deep end. When his former liaison officer Dillon asked him how he liked his new job, Foch replied: 'I feel like a dog that has just been thrown into the river Seine – I am swimming, swimming!'[52] On 28 and 29 May, barely a fortnight into the job, Foch had a taste of what a large part of it would involve: an Anglo-French conference in London to discuss the perennial, thorny Greek question. Although Foch had had no previous personal experience of the problem – what to do about General Sarrail and the Macedonian front, called by the Germans the largest internment camp in Europe – he impressed the British Cabinet secretary, Sir Maurice Hankey, with his 'remarkable and clear-headed contribution'.[53] Foch argued that withdrawal from Greece was impossible, that the grain harvest of Thessaly should be secured for the Allies, and that the Isthmus of Corinth should be occupied so as to cut off the capital Athens from the pro-German Royalist Army in the Peloponnese and to capture control of the railway through Athens. The conference adopted Foch's views more or less, British objections having centred on the shipping problem that was becoming acute. Therefore Foch emphasised the naval aspects, arguing that Germany's current 'passive policy' on land enabled them to concentrate on offensive action at sea to acquire more bases in the central Mediterranean, thereby intensifying their submarine offensive. So holding the Isthmus and the railway communications would reduce the Allies' dependence on sea transport.[54] It was agreed that a French Senator and former Governor-General in Algeria, Charles Jonnart, be appointed to represent Allied interests as High Commissioner in Greece, and that a conference of naval experts examine the shipping situation.[55] With his usual speed Foch organised Jonnart's mission, allocating Colonel Georges from his Ministry staff to assist him; French troops seized Thessaly and the Isthmus of Corinth on 12 June and Constantine abdicated in favour of his second son, Prince Alexander, two days later. The pro-Entente Eleutherios Venizelos returned as Prime Minister, and Greece joined the Allies in the war.[56] Thus Foch had more than held his

[52] Dillon diary, *Three Wars*, 87 (entry for 24 May 1917).
[53] Hankey, *Supreme Command*, 2: 636.
[54] 'The Allied Policy to be Pursued in Greece', IC 23, 28 May 1917, p. 5, CAB 28/2.
[55] 'General Conclusion of an Anglo-French Conference held at 10, Downing Street, London, on May 28 and 29, 1917', IC 22, CAB 28/2.
[56] Weygand, *IV*, 396–402; IC 22, CAB 28/2.

own at his first Allied conference. This was no small feat: not only mastering a perennial problem from scratch and impressing the super-organised Hankey, but also translating a policy decision into successful action.

The next problem concerned Robertson and the British offensive in Flanders. Foch commented of Robertson that he 'builds small, but he builds solid'.[57] Robertson was somewhat less complimentary, writing in September 1915 that Foch was 'rather a flat-catcher, a mere professor, and very talkative'. (A 'flat-catcher' is a swindler, someone who takes in simpletons.) Yet he was pleased at Foch's appointment ('so long as he doesn't try to command the armies', he told Dillon), and he had written a kind letter of sympathy after Foch's sacking, recalling the latter's 'kindness and cordiality' and his efforts 'to ensure close and cordial relations between the two armies'.[58] To facilitate their working together, Painlevé established a new liaison service between the two War Ministries, bypassing the obvious choice to run it, Henry Wilson. Neither he nor Pétain wished to retain Wilson's services (he had been acting as liaison officer with Nivelle), probably because of his view that Pétain would be a disaster because Pétain represented 'squatting' instead of attacking.[59] Strangely, Foch did not want Wilson either, which rather hurt the latter's feelings – 'he does not want me – and he really is my friend'.[60] The reason may be that Foch believed that Wilson ought to take a field command, as rotation between field and staff jobs was standard practice in the French army, or else, more selfishly, Foch may have thought that Wilson would be more use to him in London. Both men had talked about Wilson's ideas for a 'central organization of the Allies' and Foch had stated enthusiastically that he 'would love to be the French representative'.[61]

Instead of Wilson Painlevé proposed Major (later General) E. L. Spears, who had been liaison officer on the Somme in 1916 with Sixth, then Tenth Armies, whom he knew possibly through his military secretary, Commandant Helbronner, a friend of Spears.[62] Being highly qualified, experienced and a fluent French speaker, Spears was a natural choice, and Robertson (a 'father-figure' for him) was also in favour of the scheme. Despite some misgivings, Spears set off for Paris on 4 May for his new office in the War Ministry on the Boulevard des Invalides, near Foch.[63] The relationship with Foch would deteriorate in 1918, but for the

[57] Spears, *Prelude*, 35.
[58] Dillon diary, *Three Wars*, 87 (entry for 13 May 1917); Robertson letter to George V, 28 September 1915, cited in Holmes, *Little Field-Marshal*, 243; ms letter, Robertson to Foch, 20 December 1916, 414/AP/4.
[59] Haig diary, 1 June 1917.   [60] Wilson diary, 2 June 1917.
[61] Ibid., 17 April 1917; Jeffery, *Wilson*, 192–3.
[62] Spears, *Liaison 1914*, 71; Egremont, *Under Two Flags*, 52.
[63] Spears diary, 4 May 1917; Egremont, *Under Two Flags*, 69.

moment Foch had the benefit of a fluent French speaker to ensure that he and Robertson could act in concert.

As for Haig, the decision to undertake what became the Third Ypres campaign had been taken before Foch was appointed. The British and French governments had agreed in Paris on 4–5 May to 'press Germany' with all their strength (Lloyd George's words). The CinCs and military advisers had agreed unanimously that they had to attack 'relentlessly', but 'with limited objectives, while making the fullest use of our artillery. By this means we hope to gain our ends with the minimum loss possible.' After the reading of their joint statement, Lloyd George proposed the following wording of a resolution: 'The British and French Governments undertake to continue the offensive on the Western Front in accordance with the principles agreed to by Generals Pétain, Nivelle, Robertson and Field-Marshal Haig . . . and to devote the whole of their forces to this purpose.'[64] So Foch had had no input into the decision to continue the offensive. Nevertheless, he knew what he thought about Haig's plans: 'futile, fantastic & dangerous'. He asked Wilson who the 'fool' was who had wanted Haig to carry them out.[65]

If Robertson and Foch were to work together profitably, then the point of discord that Haig's Flanders campaign represented would require resolution. They met privately for the first time in Abbeville on 7 June as the British began their offensive at Messines, the opening action of Third Ypres. Although Robertson stated that agreement on 'general military policy for the future' was vital and that they needed to be frank with each other, nevertheless 'central control' was impossible. So Robertson put Foch on notice that there was to be no repetition of the experiment putting Haig under Nivelle's command. Foch accepted the prior agreement to continue pressing the enemy, but 'no great battle aiming at distant objectives'. He admitted that the effect of such a policy would be to postpone until 1918 any definitive action.[66] Foch claimed later that in the course of the meeting he had put the Ypres campaign 'on trial'; but that Robertson had told him that it was none of his business and put Foch's note with its accusations 'in the waste-paper basket'.[67] This dissension finds no

---

[64] 'Summary of the Proceedings of the Anglo-French Conference held at Paris on May 4 and 5', IC 21, CAB 28/2; Greenhalgh, *VTC*, 150–1.

[65] Wilson diary, 2 June 1917. Callwell, *Wilson* (1: 359), omits the word 'fool'.

[66] 'Conference held at ABBEVILLE on the 7th June, 1917, between General Foch and General Sir William Robertson', 8 June 1917, WO 106/1513; see also the French account in Clemenceau papers, Archives de la Guerre, 6N 68, and in Weygand, Carnets, 6 June 1917, 1K/130/4, partie déposée.

[67] Foch, Journées, 8 June 1917, 414/AP/10, [d] 3. Since there is no date for the compilation of the 'Journées', it is not possible to judge how much truth to ascribe to this, but it accords with the brutal question put to Wilson about who the 'fool' was who wanted Haig to carry out the campaign.

reflection in either the French or the British official accounts of their meeting. Indeed, both accounts emphasise the large degree of agreement between the two men.

When next they met in Senlis three weeks later, the British had a clearer idea of the extent of the troubles in the French army, and so Robertson sought reassurance about its morale. He reported Haig's unshakeable optimism and belief that enemy morale was weakening, so that French support remained a significant factor in the battle. Foch replied that improvements were satisfactory but it could not be hidden that after carrying the heaviest burden of the war for three years the French army was tired.[68] This, however, seems to have been a vigorous enough response for Robertson. He wrote to Haig on 30 June that he was sure that Foch would impress on the French government the 'necessity to give all the help that can be given'. However, it may be that the subsequent talk with Pétain, who had drawn 'sad pictures' and 'talked like a man without a jot of confidence in the future', made Foch's comments seem to Robertson more upbeat by contrast.[69]

Events in Italy had the potential to affect Haig's Flanders offensive. Lloyd George's new War Policy Committee, a small group of Cabinet ministers dedicated to settling the strategy for the rest of 1917 and into 1918, had its first meeting on 11 June. Such a committee might approve the Prime Minister's preferred option of knocking out Austria by an Italian offensive, thereby depriving Haig of guns and men for Flanders. Next Foch met Cadorna at St-Jean-de-Maurienne, near the frontier, on 25 June; Cadorna informed him that the Austrians had already moved five divisions from the Russian to the Italian front. As a consequence, he needed more artillery both to equip his existing divisions with ten instead of eight batteries and to supply a possible further twenty divisions that Italy's infantry resources could create. Foch reminded Cadorna that the transport plans were in place for sending help to Italy in the event of a heavy Austrian attack following a Russian defection, and he asked for Italian labour to be sent to France in return for some of the French production of guns destined for the American army.[70] Cadorna reported the outcome of this meeting to the Italian Foreign Minister, Baron Sidney Sonnino, and recommended that Foch's request for labour be granted. It seemed to Cadorna to be a fair quid pro quo – guns and munitions for

---

[68] Weygand, Entretien du 28 juin 1917, à Senlis, avec le général Robertson, *AFGG* 5/2, annex 596.

[69] Robertson to Haig, 30 June 1917, in Woodward (ed.), *Robertson Correspondence*, # 148.

[70] Echange de vues fait, à Saint-Jean-de-Maurienne, le 25 juin, entre son Excellence le général Cadorna et le général Foch, *AFGG* 5/2, annex 576.

labour – and there was the further advantage that, since the need was to build barracks and so on for the Americans, the presence of Italian labour might be advantageous in Italy's relations with the USA.[71]

Robertson and Foch agreed that there was little point in sending to Italy troops who knew nothing of the terrain, but Foch judged that Cadorna's request for artillery should be conceded. He argued that the Italians had sufficient infantry to attack on a seventy-kilometre front, and if reinforced with British and French artillery they might even reach Trieste, which could have serious consequences for the Austrians.[72] Therefore Haig's demands for every possible man, airplane and gun to be sent to France would create difficulties for Robertson, who would have to fight French pressure as well as pressure from his political masters to divert artillery resources to Italy. At least Foch did not favour sending troops.

Foch's request for Italian labour reflected the domestic problems that he faced. President Woodrow Wilson's signature on the USA's declaration of war on 6 April meant that American troops would cross the Atlantic, train in France, be equipped with French guns, and eventually fight on the French front. Therefore the French War Ministry faced a huge task in building all the facilities that an American army would require – training camps, hospitals, port facilities, and so on, in addition to providing guns and other equipment.

Foch was on the platform to welcome the new American commander, General J. J. Pershing, when he arrived in Paris on 13 June. He had already sent out a 'Note' on 27 May, stating where the American troops were to land, where the training camps were to be sited (Gondrecourt in Lorraine) and where the artillery camp was to be established (Valdahon, near the Swiss frontier). Foch wanted a response within five days from the heads of all the services involved in the establishment of lines of communication, of hospitals and of food rations. He emphasised that it was vital to have all arrangements in place for the efficient disembarkation of the first American troops, as any hitches would produce a negative effect on the US government.[73] Thus the impression that Pershing gives in his memoirs, that he himself gave a lot of thought to the selection of ports for disembarkation and the area of France for training, is false. Both were chosen before he arrived in France. Moreover, there was little choice since northern ports were fully employed servicing the BEF, and railway

---

[71] Cadorna to Sonnino, 27 June 1917, *Documenti diplomatici italiani*, vol. 8, doc. 474.

[72] Weygand, Entretien du 28 juin 1917, à Senlis, avec le général Robertson, *AFGG* 5/2, annex 596.

[73] Foch, Note au sujet des mesures à prendre pour l'arrivée de la première division américaine, 27 May 1917, *AFGG* 5/2, annex 333.

communications in the north were over-stretched. An Atlantic port and new lines of communication to eastern France were the only feasible option, with the added attraction (for the French) that it kept the Americans out of the sphere of British influence.[74]

The first American division arrived in France in time to take part in the 4 and 14 July celebrations, but landed with rifles and service pistols only, no artillery. This caused problems for Foch with both Joffre and Pétain. Joffre had returned from a triumphal mission to the States, having pledged (without authority) that the American army should be autonomous and that France would arm its first division. Joffre wished to 'mother' the young American army and to play a role in negotiations, but Foch insisted that it was the War Ministry's responsibility to provide transport, training camps and so on and that Joffre had no 'proprietorial' interest.[75] As for Pétain, fully occupied with nursing the French army back to offensive health, Pershing's request for more shells for the guns that the French supplied caused him to raise objections. His primary responsibility was to the French army and, before arming the American Expeditionary Forces (AEF), he aimed to replace his own old, slow guns with rapid-firing heavier ones.[76]

So the arrival of the Americans promised some conflict before they could intervene directly in the fighting. However, Foch had the advantage of knowing the new French High Commissioner appointed (to Joffre's displeasure) to Washington to coordinate the various missions. André Tardieu had been on Foch's staff in 1914, and spoke English fluently. Given the Foch–Tardieu collaboration over munitions supply in 1916, the appointment promised to be fruitful. Also, Joffre's *chef de cabinet*, Lieutenant-Colonel Jean Fabry, acted as liaison officer between Foch and Joffre, although the meagre evidence shows that Fabry spoke to Foch's staff officers, Weygand and Debeney, rather than to Foch himself.[77]

The need to equip the Americans pointed up the main domestic task that Foch faced in 1917, namely overseeing the production and supply of armaments. True to his beliefs, expressed many times in 1916, that a plentiful supply of heavy guns was crucial for successful offensive operations, Foch worked closely with Pétain to ensure that the heavy guns programme that Joffre had established was carried out. Both men, despite

[74] Serrigny, 'Armée américaine – son emploi – son entretien', 25 May 1917, 16N 3095, [d] 13, # 35.
[75] Pedroncini (ed.), *Joffre, JM*, 'Note établie à la date du 28 mai (au retour d'Amérique)', 213, 217, 218 (entries for 1 and 3 June 1917); Mme Foch diary, 4 June 1917; Repington, *First World War*, 1: 585–6.
[76] Pedroncini, *Pétain, Général*, 49–50.   [77] Fabry, *Joffre*, 304.

their totally different temperaments, were united in their aims, which the War Minister also shared. Their 'war plan' was to leave nothing to chance, and so a big programme was begun for aviation, tanks, and gas shells. Painlevé claimed that he had never had to settle any difference of opinion during the six months from May to November 1917 when the three men worked to renew the French armies.[78] Direct control over munitions and aviation programmes had been taken from the War Ministry, so it is difficult to know how much credit should go to Foch for France's amazing munitions effort in 1917. However, Louis Loucheur, Under-Secretary of State and eventually (in September) Armaments Minister, knew Foch, had supported his appointment, and was involved as an industrialist in the production of the short 155mm gun that Foch saw as the foundation of the heavy artillery. The two men worked closely together.[79]

With Foch, Pétain and Loucheur working to the same ends – increased munitions production – the provision of shells and guns in 1917 was impressive. The light Renault FT17 tank was developed, and by the end of May 1917 1000 of them had already left the factory. The results in aviation were less impressive. In an often quoted remark of 1912, Foch is reported to have judged the value of aviation for the army to be 'zero' – yet another example of the way in which his prewar writings and sayings have been used against him. During the Battle of the Somme, however, he had been convinced of its value. He wrote to Joffre on 23 November 1916, pointing out the 'striking' proof of the necessity for air superiority that the current battle had shown, and requesting more and better types of aircraft for the future. He ended his letter with the (repetitious) comment: 'Superiority in *aviation* alone allows the necessary superiority in *artillery* to give superiority in the present-day *battle*.'[80] There was no dispute with Pétain over the priority to be given to aviation. Pétain too wanted new models for artillery spotting, collection of intelligence and for bombing raids so as to disrupt enemy defences. Once again, the need to equip the Americans, when it had been assumed (falsely) that the USA constituted an enormous reservoir of raw materials and of trained pilots, affected the French army. For example, Foch sent Weygand to a meeting that agreed on 30 August to supply 5000 French aircraft to create an American air force. Bureaucratic muddles, lack of coordination and division of responsibilities, not to mention doctrinal disputes over the role of aviation as an

[78] Untitled typescript, [late 1929], fos. 13–15, 313/AP/129 [d] 1; Painlevé, *Foch et Pétain*, 128.
[79] Carls, *Loucheur*, 3; Loucheur, *Carnets secrets*, 52.
[80] Letter, Foch to Joffre, 23 November 1916, reprinted as appendix to Pujo, 'La pensée de Foch' [original emphasis].

independent arm or merely as support for the artillery, meant that the agreement was rescinded in May 1918, and Pétain never received satisfaction of his demands.

In a report of 21 November 1917 the head of Pétain's aviation service at GQG, General Duval, warned that France's position was 'very serious'. Without an improvement in the organisation in the interior, the French risked being unable to overcome the enemy in the 1918 battles. Aircraft were being delivered without their guns, and motors without carburettors. Duval forecast that only one-third of the aircraft allocated to the army corps would be fit for service if nothing was done to improve matters.[81] Foch could do little to affect factors outside his direct control, but his notebooks reveal no sense that he was prepared to give precedence to aviation matters. He did act, however, in two further respects, to make improvements. He gave Pétain greater anti-aircraft resources by taking guns from the interior and from four anti-aircraft sections destined for Russia. Also Foch reinforced the liaison between the British and French headquarters, the maritime centre at Dunkirk and the Eiffel Tower radio transmitter to ensure that intelligence about incoming enemy aircraft was shared rapidly.[82]

One other task concerning an internal French matter involved Foch. This was a Commission of Enquiry to 'study the conditions in which the offensive of 16–23 April took place in the valley of the Aisne and to determine the role of the general officers who exercised command'.[83] It was not a tribunal, hence would not impose sanctions. The President of the Commission was General Brugère (with whom Foch had already clashed) and his two colleagues were Foch and General Gouraud (of Gallipoli fame). The law stated that any commission should consist of three generals who had commanded at least an army corps, and in this case it was obviously preferable that they should not have served under Nivelle. Thus, despite their dislike of the task, the three chosen generals were eminently suitable.[84] However, Foch's mind was already made up: the results of Nivelle's offensive were deplorable; the war would now last a year longer than it would have done if the Allies had continued the Somme offensive into 1917; French casualties were over two million, of whom half had been killed; and the Americans would be ready only in 1918.[85] He recognised that Nivelle was responsible for the methods used, that indeed

[81] Duval's report and Pétain's comments cited in Pedroncini, *Pétain, Général*, 60.
[82] Foch, Note pour le ministre de la guerre, and Note pour le cabinet du ministre, both 17 June 1917, *AFGG* 5/1, annexes 517, 516.
[83] 'Commission d'enquête réunie en exécution de la Note Ministérielle No. 18194 du 14 juillet 1917', 5N 255.
[84] Painlevé, *Foch et Pétain*, 181.   [85] Mme Foch diary, 16 August 1917.

he had been chosen precisely for those methods in preference to the slower 'Somme' procedure. However, since Nivelle had maintained his views in the face of criticism from the government, and the government had re-stated its confidence in him, then for what could he be reproached, Foch asked.[86]

The three generals sat for the first time on 22 August. Foch remarked that, although the plan was Nivelle's, the government had set the aims of the attack and had refused his resignation when it became clear that his subordinates did not have any faith in the plan. Foch criticised Nivelle for trying to 'command' Haig, and focused his almost legalistic questioning on munitions supply. He defended his Somme methods against Nivelle's concept of a rapid and brutal offensive. On the Somme, Foch claimed, the aim had never been to break through, but to carry successive objectives in the enemy lines after a violent artillery preparation. The series of attacks had finally caused the German withdrawal to the Hindenburg Line. If the Somme battle had been continued in 1917 but on a wider front, namely about 100 kilometres from Vimy to the Oise river, a further German withdrawal might have been achieved. Foch dismissed Nivelle's claim that the Somme battlefield was 'worn out', too destroyed to permit con-tinuing the battle. The conquest of an enemy position required its destruction by the artillery beforehand, and the area of the Chemin des Dames did not lend itself to such artillery action. Unfortunately, Foch concluded, 'the [Somme] method had been found to be too slow'.[87]

The Commission met on 30 September and 4 October to conclude their report. Its thirty pages of typescript plus folders of annexed docu-ments stated that Nivelle 'had not been up to the crushing task that he had assumed'. Although Painlevé was dissatisfied with a report he described as too much like 'rose water', the Commission was unable to reconvene to reconsider before events in Italy at the end of October supervened.[88]

Foch was absent from some of the Commission hearings because he was obliged to go to London and then GQG about the continuing ques-tion of sending guns to Italy. International and diplomatic matters occu-pied more of Foch's time than domestic concerns, and by the latter half of 1917 the position for the Entente was looking grim. In Russia the provi-sional government that had taken over from the Tsar seemed unable to halt the revolutionary fervour, and the promised Russian offensive – the Kerensky offensive in July which had succeeded initially – had been routed by a powerful German attack. Cadorna's tenth Isonzo battle in May/June – it should have been launched at the same time as Nivelle's, on

---

[86] Foch, Carnets, 14 August 1917, fo. 253.   [87] Séance du 14 septembre, fo. 68, 5N 255.
[88] Rapport, Dossier A, ibid.; Painlevé, *Foch et Pétain*, 182–3.

16 April – had made few gains for huge casualties. Even more worrying, the German submarine offensive was still inflicting huge losses, despite the institution of convoy. By mid-1917 the net loss of world shipping was over two million tons, of which more than half was British.[89]

The Allies met in conference in Paris on 25 and 26 July and then in London on 7 and 8 August in order to discuss this grim situation. Foch was becoming impatient over the strategic drift, and before the Paris conference he wrote a note setting out his thoughts about what the Allies needed to do.[90] The coalition needed to 'discipline' and to 'direct' its actions, he wrote. If the war was not to drag on they had to seize the occasion and take advantage of Austria's weakened state by coordinating a Russian–Italian operation whilst the British and French kept the Germans from reinforcing its ally by their action on the Western Front. The conference required an agreed programme to bring the war to a victorious conclusion as quickly as possible or, were that not possible, one that would permit the Allies to endure as long as needed. From Foch's point of view this meant that a French military programme should be prepared to put to the others. The French high command had to hold on to its 'directing role' and not take a back seat that risked the others' forgetting the significant services that France had provided to the coalition in the first two years of the war. In practical terms, this meant the creation of an Allied general staff in Paris to deal with the multitude of problems that faced the Allies.

The most pressing of these was Russia, and the military met apart from the politicians to produce a memorandum dealing with the worst possible contingency: Russia was forced out of the war but the Central Powers remained intact. They concluded that in that contingency victory might be 'more remote or less decisive' than had been hoped; and recommended a purely defensive posture in secondary theatres, acceleration of the arrival of American troops, and the achievement of 'unity of action' on the Western Front via a 'permanent Inter-Allied military organisation'.[91] When Foch read out their memorandum to the Allied leaders, Lloyd George condemned it as too pessimistic, as containing no more imagination than he had in his thumb (so Weygand reported). Foch gave as good as he got, however, by conceding that, while action in Italy was worth consideration, Franco-British troops could not participate because they were tied up in Haig's Flanders campaign.

---

[89] Hankey, *Supreme Command*, 2: 640.

[90] Note sur le plan d'action de la Coalition à examiner à la prochaine conférence des Alliés, 18 July 1917, *AFGG* 5/2, annex 746.

[91] 'Policy to adopt should Russia be forced out of the war', 26 July 1917, GT 1533, reproduced as annex to Notes of an Allied Conference, 26 July 1917, IC 24(a), CAB 28/2.

Although the conference made no decision as to practical action, Foch was optimistic that Russia would recover, that the Russian tide that was now going out quickly would return. Moreover the country was in such a state of disorganisation that no competent authority existed to sign a peace with the Central Powers.[92] Immediately following the conference (on 28 July) he drew up an outline of the composition and functions of a military mission to be sent to St Petersburg, and the Comité de guerre approved it two days later.[93] As usual, he made a good choice when he selected General Niessel to head it. Niessel was a Russian speaker, and had been under his command on the Somme in 1916, as commander of IX Corps. He had got on well with the British XIV Corps alongside. Niessel tried to get out of the mission, but Foch was inflexible.[94] Although Niessel's mission had been welcomed in Russia, Foch acknowledged in early October that very little more could be expected from the Russian army.[95]

When the Allies met in the second conference in London, the question of guns for Italy arose again. Foch and Robertson had agreed beforehand that it was too late to halt the Flanders offensive, but that consideration should be given to committing resources to Italy because of Austria's weakened state. Lloyd George succeeded in getting the conference to direct the general staffs to prepare plans to strike at Austria, with the Italians supported by French and British heavy artillery.

In addition, Lloyd George grilled Foch in the full session over Russia: would the country 'revive'? and, if not, could the Allies drive their enemies out of France, Belgium, Romania and Serbia? Foch stood up well to the questioning. He rehearsed all the pros and cons to operations elsewhere than the Western Front, but conceded that a 'heavy', although not 'fatal', blow might be struck at Turkey by a landing on the Syrian coast at Alexandretta, in order to cut at Aleppo the main railway line that supplied the Turks in Mesopotamia and Palestine. The Syrian proposal was a master stroke. It had been on Britain's agenda since the days of Kitchener, it satisfied Lloyd George's desire for an outside theatre, but it could not involve any French responsibility because France had no ships.

The Syrian expedition came up for discussion again at an Anglo-French meeting in Boulogne on 25 September, when Foch warned that the biggest difficulty was shipping. Nonetheless he agreed to prepare a plan, despite not seeming 'very ready to play to Lloyd George's desire for a

[92] Colonel Menschaert [Belgian mission to GQG], Report on Foch's views of Eastern Front, 3 August 1917, de Broqueville mss 530, reel 1510/88.
[93] Foch, 'Note sur l'action militaire de la France en Russie', 28 July 1917, 16N 3019.
[94] Niessel, Le Triomphe des Bolchéviks, ii–iii.
[95] Mission belge, 'Situations extérieures', 3 October 1918, de Broqueville mss 530, reel 1510/88.

French expedition to Alexandretta'.[96] Foch's notebooks reveal that a Syrian expedition went against the grain of his thinking. It was only because there seemed to be little chance of a decision in France that he was prepared to work up such a plan, although he did note that the Macedonian sector of the Baghdad to Monastir front was practicable only in winter, when the front from Nieuport to Trieste was not.[97] Furthermore, colonial pressure groups and the French Foreign Ministry were keen to ensure that Syria remained within the French sphere of influence. The Comité de guerre approved Foch's plan on 1 October and sent it to London with the crucial question: could Britain supply the sea transport? The Admiralty's response was entirely negative. The First Sea Lord did not doubt that the French general staff 'fully appreciated' the difficulties of such a landing, but he concluded his evaluation with the comment that the force's composition would indicate that 'no really serious operation [was] contemplated'.[98]

Meanwhile the Italian question remained on the agenda. In Flanders Haig was not achieving any spectacular gains and the rain poured down throughout August. The Italians' eleventh Isonzo attack, on the other hand, had made significant progress. On 18 August they captured four to five kilometres on the Bainsizza plateau, east of the river, but lack of roads prevented Cadorna from bringing up more artillery to exploit the success.[99] To a certain extent, Foch now came round to Lloyd George's views. This represents a great shift in Foch's thinking. The theoretical principle of conducting war – concentrating forces on the main front for the decisive battle against the main enemy – was beginning to look as though it was beyond France's means to achieve. Foch wondered whether, instead of seeking the overthrow of the main enemy, it might be better to isolate him. A further Italian offensive might take the Italian army swiftly to the gates of Trieste and force Austria to the peace table. The necessary condition for such a success was, in Foch's view, a large reinforcement of British and French heavy artillery, and even some infantry divisions.[100] With Haig demanding Robertson's support for the Flanders campaign, the CIGS was unlikely to agree with Foch's new way of thinking. Indeed, the fairly amicable relationship between the two chiefs of staff that had existed since Foch was appointed in May began to break down over the question of sending guns to Italy.

A further reason to support an Italian offensive against Austria lay in the renewal of secret peace talks. Unlike earlier high-level talks, this new

---

[96] Hankey, *Supreme Command*, 2: 699.   [97] Foch, Carnets, 2 September 1917, fo. 258.
[98] Séances du Comité de guerre, 3N 2; Foch's memorandum (translated) and Jellicoe's response in WP56, CAB 27/8.
[99] *AFGG* 5/2, 278.   [100] Foch, Carnets, 2 September 1917, fos. 256–7.

initiative remained within the French army. All year Foch's 2e Bureau, the bureau that dealt with intelligence, had been pushing the concept of a third way between all-out war and peace at any price, namely the detachment of Germany's weakened ally, Austria-Hungary. When the Austrian Count Revertera initiated contact, via a Swiss intermediary, with Commandant Armand of the 2e Bureau, Foch authorised a meeting between the two men. On 24 July 1917 he issued his instructions: allow the conversation to develop, letting it be known that France favoured maintaining the integrity of the Empire, provided that the different nationalities composing it were respected.[101] Nothing came of these talks, which continued into 1918 under Clemenceau, but Foch's willingness to entertain them indicates an open-minded attitude to the prosecution of the war and a move away from the concept of a decisive battle to defeat the enemy's main forces.

After some bad-tempered haggling over Foch's proposal to send to Italy 100 guns taken from France's First Army operating under Haig's command in Flanders, Haig and Pétain agreed that Haig would release a smaller number of guns which Pétain would replace as circumstances permitted; in his turn, Pétain made available a further 104 guns.[102] However, once the guns arrived in Italy, Cadorna changed his mind about continuing the offensive. He was afraid that further heavy losses would prove fatal to the country's morale, already weakened by news of the Russian revolution. Cadorna knew also that the Russian situation had allowed more Austrian and some German divisions to come to the Italian front. Accordingly he informed the Allies that, while he was grateful for the guns, he would use them for a strong defence rather than an offensive. His allies were so annoyed that they decided in Boulogne on 25 September to withdraw the heavy artillery.[103] So Lloyd George's long-held desire to get the Italians onto the offensive and Foch's plan to facilitate this by going over Haig's head to obtain guns came to naught.

Sending guns and men to Italy raised questions of command responsibility and Allied coordination of such decisions. Foch had recommended back in London during the Allied conference that a 'permanent inter-Allied military organisation' should be set up to realise 'unity of action' on the Western Front (see page 240). Robertson's reaction had been a long moan to Haig about the 'hopeless' Foch and his fears that Lloyd George

---

[101] Bourlet, 'Deuxième Bureau', 43–7; Pedroncini, *Négotiations secrètes*, 73–6.

[102] 'Notes of an Anglo-French conference held at 10, Downing Street, 4 September 1917', IC 26, CAB 28/2; Conférence tenue à Amiens, 7 September 1917, *AFGG* 5/2, annex 1050; A.L. pour l'Italie, 7 September 1917, ibid., annex 1051.

[103] 'Conclusions of an Anglo-French Conference, held in the train at Boulogne, 25 September 1917', IC 37, CAB 28/2.

would pick up the proposal for an Allied general staff sitting in Paris, an idea that he (Robertson) rejected.[104] Spears reported that Painlevé wanted an interallied staff for political 'kudos' to make up for the feeling among French politicians that they were losing the 'predominant voice' in the coalition. The French Cabinet had been 'quite annoyed' to hear of Robertson's unfavourable reaction to the idea.[105] Before the next Allied conference convened in August, Painlevé had a long talk with Lloyd George and Lord Milner about nominating Foch as head of an Allied general staff, but Lloyd George counselled patience. Neither the parliament nor public opinion nor the country was ready for such a move.[106]

As soon as Painlevé took over the Premiership from Ribot on 13 September, he asked to meet Lloyd George to discuss unity of command and a British extension of their front so as to release older French territorials from active duty for mobilisation on the land. They met in Boulogne on 25 September with Foch and Robertson in attendance. Beforehand, however, the two Premiers talked alone. According to Painlevé, they agreed a two-step process that would lead to unity of command. First an Allied war committee would be formed with an Allied general staff presided over by Foch, who would command the British and French reserves behind the hinge where the two armies joined in northern France. Wilson would be the British representative in the new organisation. Then, when opinion in Britain permitted, Foch would become Generalissimo of the two armies. This was as much as Lloyd George could concede for the time being, given the views of both the British army and the parliament. The two Premiers agreed to meet in Britain very soon in order to settle the details with the British Cabinet in order that the Allied general staff might be constituted before the end of October. Painlevé's choice fell on Foch because Pétain was ruled out by the disastrous Haig–Nivelle episode, which made subordination of the British army to a French commander-in-chief impossible. Foch, however, was known to the British military from before the war; he had acted with energy and tact between 1914 and 1916; his achievements in Allied councils since May when he was made chief of the army general staff had impressed both Ribot and Painlevé. Lloyd George had no difficulty in concurring in the choice.[107]

Keeping up the pressure, Painlevé returned 'unheralded' to London on 9 October, supported by Foch, Loucheur and various other officials, and

[104] Robertson to Haig, 8 August 1917, Robertson mss 7/7/42.
[105] Spears to General Maurice [DMO in War Office], 27 July and 28 July 1917, Spears mss 1/13/1, LHCMA.
[106] Painlevé, *Foch et Pétain*, 241.   [107] Ibid., 244–9.

bearing a scheme approved by the Comité de guerre. In a meeting at Chequers on 14 October, to Hankey's horror, Lloyd George put the proposal to his colleagues for an Allied war committee, presided over by Foch, and made up of two members from the governments of the constituent countries and a permanent military adviser. According to Hankey, the French were pushing for a preliminary Franco-British agreement that could be presented as a *fait accompli* to the Americans and Italians.[108] As Lloyd George set about obtaining his colleagues' agreement, the stage was set for momentous decisions to be taken about command on the Western Front. The Central Powers then stepped into the picture, and their intervention in Italy on 24 October increased the momentum.

The complicated events of the period May–October 1917 reveal an evolution in Foch's thinking. The war was much more than the Western Front, and Foch had dealt with a wide range of questions and of geography. His special studies had begun the process, but his experience between May and October opened his eyes still further. He had been involved in Greece and had prepared a paper about an expedition to Syria. Russia and Italy were constant concerns; the arrival of Pershing and the AEF was another. Foch had spent a large part of his time in conferences, mainly with the British. He got on well with Robertson, although this state of affairs was about to change. He admired Lloyd George and was able to stand up to him in meetings. He had indeed succeeded in moving up a gear to deal with political as well as military questions.

Perhaps the most surprising element in the evolution of Foch's thinking during 1917 was his partial agreement with Lloyd George over detaching Germany's allies. He faced the reality that the French army might not be able to fight their way to victory in France, thereby showing his willingness to give up the *Entscheidungsschlacht*, or decisive battle, that theory demanded. This explains his constant advocacy of sending guns to Italy to support an offensive against the Austrians; it explains also his approval of the low-level talks between a member of his staff and the Austrian Count Revertera. His notebooks contain frequent references to counting resources and taking decisions based on those counts. Already on 2 May he had told the military correspondent of *The Times*: 'We must eat the wing, then the leg, and so on; but if one tried to swallow the whole chicken at a gulp, one would be choked.'[109]

---

[108] Hankey diary, 14 October 1917, in *Supreme Command* 2: 713–14; Foch, *Journées*, October 1917, 1K/129/2; 'Secretary's Notes of a Conversation at Chequers Court on Sunday, October 14th, 1917, at 10AM', IC 28, CAB 28/2.

[109] Repington, *First World War*, 1: 556.

His record as an administrator was not impressive, but it would have been amazing if it were. His preference was for action, not sitting at a desk. Indeed, when Clemenceau became Premier and War Minister in succession to Painlevé, the need to reorganise was evident. Clemenceau's *chef du cabinet militaire*, General Mordacq, commented that Foch did not appear to have concerned himself with the section of his staff dealing with the 'interior', despite the fact that the interior constituted four-fifths of his service.[110] His role in the country's industrial mobilisation was that of coordinator, but munitions production was well advanced before he became chief of the army general staff, the new Renault tank was under development, only coming into use in 1918, and he seems to have done little to improve the muddled aviation industry.

Foch had shown no signs of strain despite his dislike of a desk job and all the travelling and talking. He coped well with the stresses of the job, despite having told Painlevé that he was not qualified for it. Pétain and Foch had worked well together at first since there was no disagreement between the two men over the need for more and better artillery before undertaking serious military operations. However, by October, when the question of unified command came to the fore, that relationship had come under pressure. Italy was the catalyst.

Italy has figured largely in these pages and the Italian question provides a perfect example of what was wrong with the workings of the Entente in 1917. Hence it reveals what Foch needed to appreciate in order to be able to change those workings. For the Entente 1917 was a particularly bad year: the French army exhausted itself and had be restored; domestically, political instability was increased by the arrests of a *député* (for dealing with the enemy) and of Paul Bolo (for using German money to bribe French newspaper editors); the Russian army dropped out of the Alliance altogether, although the realisation of this dawned only gradually over the months; the submarine campaign was wreaking havoc on Allied shipping; and various peace proposals, more or (mostly) less viable were being floated. Pershing announced during the July conference in Paris that six or possibly eight American divisions could be in France by the end of the year, but that small number depended entirely on finding the necessary shipping. In answer to all these difficulties, the French had three Premiers in 1917 – Briand, Ribot, Painlevé – before Georges Clemenceau finally took the reins in November; and in London Lloyd George was at odds with his military adviser (Robertson) and with Haig. Lloyd George tried to solve his problems first by subordinating Haig to Nivelle and when that

---

[110] Mordacq, *MC*, 1: 45–6.

failed by trying to get the military to agree to support an offensive in Italy to knock Austria out of the war. The latter attempt ran up against two problems. First, as all agreed, it was foolish to give Haig permission to launch Third Ypres simply to call it off by default a few weeks later, by removing guns and even divisions to Italy. Second, Cadorna proved as unreliable as had Nivelle. In January he did not take up Lloyd George's offer of help made during the Rome conference, and then he persuaded a government minister to go to London to plead the case for support. Next he played the French off against the British by requesting help first from one and then from the other. Finally he got agreement to the loan of guns after a successful eleventh battle along the Isonzo in August, and on 23 September informed his Allies that he did not propose to use them. As Lloyd George himself pointed out, the military and political aspects of the Entente were out of sync. Foch had to deal with Robertson, who gradually lost faith in Haig's methods in Flanders but who felt that he had to maintain a united military front in dealing with Lloyd George. Foch disapproved, as did Pétain, of Haig's offensive in Flanders. He appreciated the shipping losses, hence the declared need to capture the submarine bases on the Flanders coast, but Pétain would much have preferred that the British extend their front and allow the French divisions some relief.

The example of guns for Italy in the midst of all the other major problems made the case for unity of command starkly clear. Foch would have had to be blind not to see the muddled motives and disunity and infirmity of purpose among the Allies that characterised his time as chief of the army general staff. The main players were pulling apart rather than together. Lloyd George was using the question of guns for Italy as a way of stopping Haig's operation in Flanders. Robertson supported Haig out of misplaced loyalty. Foch wrote papers about an expedition to Syria in which he had little faith. Events in Italy would continue to dominate the political and military agenda and they provided the catalyst for the decision made there to take a significant step along the path to unified command.

The two Italian names Caporetto and Rapallo (cause and effect, as will be seen) dominated the last weeks of 1917. Caporetto is a little town on the Isonzo river, today in Slovenia and called Kobarid, but in October 1917 it was part of the Austro-Hungarian empire and named Karfreit. Rapallo is a small Italian seaside town some way from the frontier from France. The twelfth Battle of the Isonzo, the Battle of Caporetto, had far-reaching consequences, both military and political (see Map 12). The political decisions made in Rapallo in early November as a result of Caporetto

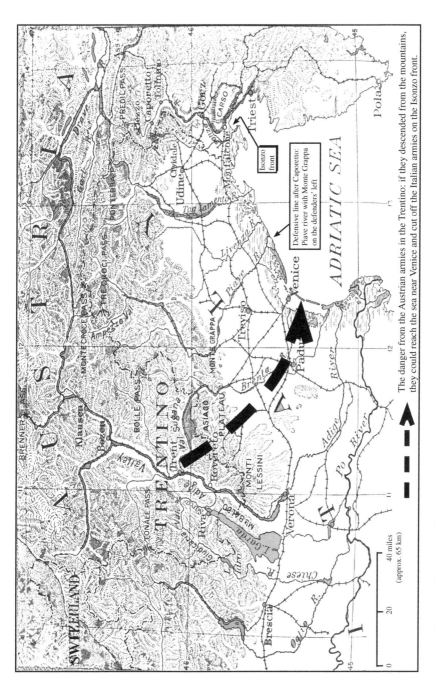

The danger from the Austrian armies in the Trentino: if they descended from the mountains, they could reach the sea near Venice and cut off the Italian armies on the Isonzo front.

Defensive line after Caporetto: Piave river with Monte Grappa on the defenders' left

Isonzo front

Map 12 The Italian Front

began the process, albeit at a very low level, that led in March 1918 to unified command and to Foch's elevation.

Austria's Kaiser Karl knew that his country could not withstand another battle such as Cadorna's eleventh Isonzo had been. Accordingly he asked the German high command for help despite earlier opposition to a joint offensive against Italy.[111] Initially hesitant, OHL's chief of staff Erich Ludendorff agreed because he wished to prop up his ailing ally and prevent any demands for a separate peace. He formed a new German army, the *Fourteenth*, under the command of General Otto von Below, with a Bavarian expert in Alpine warfare, General Krafft von Dellmensingen, as his chief of staff. After inspection of the terrain Krafft advised that an attack down the valley of the Isonzo towards Caporetto, although 'difficult, dangerous and uncertain', was nonetheless possible and ought to be undertaken because the Austro-Hungarians could not be relied upon to withstand another attack there. Accordingly, between 20 September and 22 October Below transferred to Italy his heavy artillery and air units from Riga (where they had just demonstrated their new infantry and artillery tactics with great success against the demoralised Russians), and concentrated his seven German and eight Austro-Hungarian divisions behind the Julian Alps, where the Italian air service could not observe them. The final approaches were made by night, over roundabout routes, with mules (their hoofs muffled) transporting the equipment.

Early in the morning of 24 October *Fourteenth Army* unleashed their attack, using gas and powerful mortar fire. Finally the infantry advanced on the town of Caporetto behind a rolling barrage, whose effectiveness was increased by the morning fog. The Italian Second Army was routed. The attacks continued on 25 and 26 October, and after the loss of the strategic Monte Maggiore, Cadorna ordered a retreat to the line of the Tagliamento river, where he hoped to stand long enough to enable the already prepared defences behind the Piave river to be strengthened. By 10 November the Italians had lost over 10,000 killed, and over 30,000 wounded, with more than a quarter of a million taken prisoner-of-war. They had also lost nearly half their artillery. Deserters and refugees clogged the roads. Cadorna issued a communiqué blaming the disaster on the 'craven' withdrawal without fighting and the 'ignominious' surrender to the enemy of Second Army. He claimed that the government had failed to suppress pacifist and defeatist propaganda, thereby removing any blame from his own shoulders.[112]

---

[111] Cramon, *Quatre ans*, 213.
[112] Procacci, 'Disaster of Caporetto', 143; Thompson, *White War*, 325.

Foch acted immediately. On 26 October he informed Cadorna that, if needed, French troops were 'ready to set off', and copied it to Robertson.[113] Robertson claimed that the Italians had enough men to deal with the enemy offensive; but Foch, who had worked on the relief arrangements earlier in the year, replied that, while he accepted that the Italians did have sufficient men and materiel, 'events' were dominating 'reasoning'. It was in the Allied interest, he stated unequivocally, to support the Italians both morally and materially. To this end he instructed Pétain to put the already arranged relief plan into action by sending to Italy four divisions with heavy artillery and an army headquarters staff, beginning on 28 October using twenty-six (rising to forty) trains per day.[114] He could not have acted more promptly or more effectively. It has to be added, however, that he may have had in mind the subsidiary benefit (for him personally) that some sort of Allied coordination would be needed once all the reinforcements were in place.

However, Foch's rapid action also brought to a head disagreement with Pétain over command of the troops being sent to Italy. At a meeting on 28 October with Painlevé, Pétain insisted that he be in command of the troops that were to be sent, and that he himself would go to Italy. Foch was violently angry, according to a member of Pétain's staff, and claimed the command for himself. Painlevé decided in favour of Foch, no doubt because the choice fitted with the plans that he and Lloyd George had laid to create an allied general staff as a step on the way to unity of command. Moreover, putting the French troops in Italy under Foch was consistent with the situation in Salonika, where troops came under the control of the War Ministry rather than GQG. Foch claimed that he was not pleased to be going, just to 'stick back together again' their allies, but Weygand stated that they ought to have gone to wage war in Italy eight months ago. Although it was likely to be a thankless task, the Italians were experiencing their first taste of German methods and deserved some sympathy.[115] Foch and Weygand left for Italy that evening, Foch having been given full powers to act as he saw fit.[116]

Foch arrived in Treviso by train late on 30 October, but did not meet Cadorna until early the next morning. Foch may have been a little brusque. On being told that Cadorna was in his villa, Foch is said to have responded: 'I haven't come to visit villas'; but Cadorna did not take

[113] Foch to head of military mission, Comando Supremo, and Foch to Fagalde (WO), 26 October 1917, *AFGG* 6/1, annex 22, 23.
[114] Foch to Pétain, and Foch to Robertson, 27 October 1917: both in ibid., annexes 25, 26.
[115] Serrigny, *Pétain*, 170–1; Mme Foch diary, 29 October 1917.
[116] Ordre de mission, 28 October 1917, *AFGG* 6/1, annex 31.

offence. He was impressed by Foch's energy, saying 'he gets on with the job quickly'. A member of Cadorna's staff remembered the pair looking over the maps and Foch saying decisively that various matters should be seen to, whilst Cadorna replied to each that it was already taken care of. So they agreed that they were agreed on what needed to be done.[117] After Robertson arrived the next day, they had another meeting with Cadorna. Foch and Robertson talked privately and composed a note (hand-written by Foch and signed by both men; see Illustration 6) which summarised for Cadorna their joint view. This was Foch's regular way of proceeding: face-to-face discussion, followed by a short written statement so that all knew what had been agreed. The Italian armies were not beaten, the note began; it was simply the Second Army that had been attacked. The other armies were capable of fighting the enemy on the Tagliamento and of resisting on the Piave with the help of the Allied armies that were concentrating in the rear. It was up to the Italian army to defend Italy and up to the Italian high command to set a plan, to hold the important river crossings and to deploy their troops so as to occupy defensive lines behind the rivers.[118]

Foch and Robertson, both sufficiently confident of the Italian capacity to resist, left Cadorna's headquarters, Robertson for Rome and Foch to see King Vittorio Emanuele and the Duca d'Aosta, commanding the Third Army. This was another characteristic of Foch's methods: much travelling and much talking. Foch then travelled to Rome by train with Vittorio Emanuele Orlando, the new Italian Prime Minister. Foch impressed Orlando with his 'serenity', his 'capacity for reasoning and discussion', and his ability to consider other fronts, not simply his own.[119] As a result of his talks with the King and the new Premier, he reported to Painlevé that the Italians were reforming behind the Tagliamento and that he was going to Rome so as not leave to Robertson the 'monopoly' of action.[120] This attempt to prevent Robertson from 'obtaining a preponderating influence' in Rome was reported immediately to London. Spears wrote to the War Office that he did not know whether Foch was acting under instruction or not, but Foch 'seemed to attach a good deal of importance to it'.[121] Thus a contest began to see whether France or Britain would have greater influence over the battered ally. Foch was unwilling to concede to Robertson the ability to claim a

[117] Gatti, *Caporetto*, 277.
[118] Foch/Robertson to Paris (War Ministry), 31 October 1917, *AFGG* 6/1, annex 44.
[119] Orlando, *Memorie*, 234.
[120] Foch to Président du conseil, 1 November 1917, *AFGG* 6/1, annex 46.
[121] Spears to Maurice, 2 November 1917, LSO 157, Spears mss, 1/13/1, LHCMA.

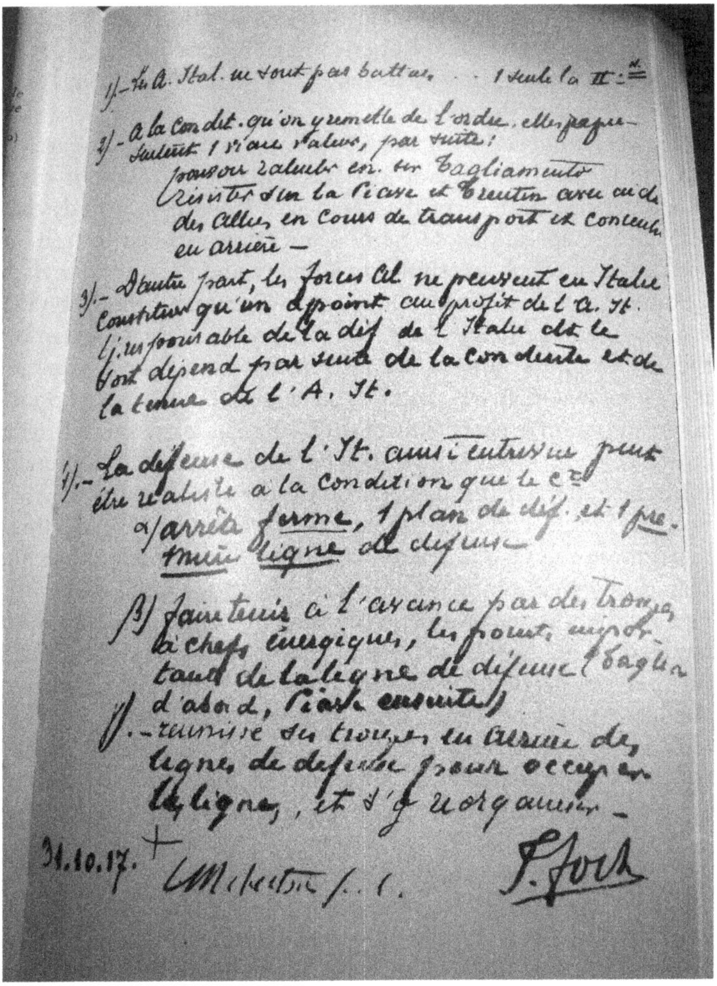
1/- La A. Ital. ne sont pas battues. . . 1 seule la IIe
2/- à la condit. qu'on y remette de l'ordre, elles peuvent seulement 1 si are valeur, par suite;
pouvoir valeur en. sur Tagliamento
résister sur la Piave et continuer avec aide
des Alliés en cours de transport et concentr.
en arrière –
3/- D'autre part, les forces All. ne peuvent en Italie
constituer qu'un appoint au profit de l'A. It.
responsable de la déf de l'Italie dt le
sort dépend par suite de la conduite et de
la tenue de l'A. It.
4/- La défense de l'It. ainsi entendue peut
être réalisée à la condition que le Cdt
a/ arrête ferme, 1 plan de déf. et 1 première ligne de défense
b/ fasse tenir à l'avance par des troupes
à chefs énergiques, les points impor-
tants de la ligne de défense (Taglia
d'abord, Piave ensuite)
c/ - remise des troupes en arrière des
lignes de défense pour occuper
la ligne, et s'y réorganiser –
31.10.17. +
W Robertson
F. Foch

Illustration 6 Foch's hand-written note, countersigned by Robertson, impressing upon Cadorna what needed to be done

greater role.[122] In Rome Foch talked also with Camille Barrère, the French ambassador, and with members of the new Ministry – War Minister General Alfieri, Munitions Minister General Dallolio, Foreign Minister Baron Sidney Sonnino, and again with Orlando. He also talked again

122 Mme Foch, diary 3 November 1917; Dillon, *Three Wars*, 99 (entry for 4 November 1917).

with Robertson in the British embassy, and the two men met once more by chance in the Forum, where they sat on a couple of antique columns and talked about the news that Robertson had just received: Lloyd George and Painlevé were on their way to Italy.[123] The question of an Allied general staff was back on the agenda.

Lloyd George had been furious when news of Caporetto arrived, and he got the Cabinet's approval for talks with Painlevé about the proposed Allied general staff.[124] In the absence of Robertson in Italy the Director of Military Operations, General Maurice, was asked to draw up a draft constitution, which was shown to Painlevé and Pétain and then read to the Cabinet on 1 November. After 'some discussion' the Cabinet accepted the scheme in principle the following day when they were informed that the French government had also accepted it. Lloyd George told his ministers that General Pétain had suggested that the opportunity be taken to obtain greater control of the Italian army by redistributing the entire Western Front to give Haig command from the Channel to a point further south than the line currently occupied by the BEF, whilst he (Pétain) would command thence to the Adriatic. Clearly this proposal owed more to Pétain's desire to keep Foch out of any command in Italy than to any great confidence in Haig's ability to command in France. The fact that he was suggesting placing more of France's defence into Haig's hands is an index of how much he resented Foch's presence in Italy, but no more was heard of Pétain's suggestion.[125] Immediately Hankey and his French counterpart Helbronner drafted some rules for the new committee's secretariat.[126] Hence, within five days of the decision to send troops to Italy a scheme had been fully worked out by the British and French politicians that could be presented to the Italians and other Allies as a *fait accompli*.

Lloyd George and Painlevé arrived in Rapallo, where they had several sessions of talks on 6 and 7 November. Lloyd George argued for Cadorna's removal, but the new Italian government under Orlando had already decided to replace him with General Armando Diaz. Cadorna was appointed alongside Foch and Henry Wilson as the military member on the new proposed organisation. However, this was no longer simply an Allied general staff, but had undergone a name change. Henceforth it was called the Supreme War Council, or, in French, le Conseil supérieur de guerre, and it made its presence felt immediately by constituting itself at

---

[123] Mme Foch diary, 26 November 1917; Weygand, *IV*, 429.
[124] War Cabinet 259A, 30 October 1917, CAB 23/13.
[125] War Cabinets 262 and 263, 1 and 2 November 1917, CAB 23/4.
[126] Hankey diary, 1 November 1917.

the fifth session of the Rapallo conference, which became thereby the first meeting of the SWC.[127]

One problem presented itself immediately. Lloyd George wanted to exclude Robertson, hence his insistence that each 'technical adviser' should act exclusively in that function. Wilson's view was that the military representative should be 'absolutely detached & independent'.[128] Foch, however, made his opinion clear: France was in a different position from the other Allies, since the fighting was taking place on its territory. He intended to keep his present post in addition to the new responsibility and he seems to have believed that he would be able to go his own way in the matter. He told his wife that he would retain his chief of army job and 'shuttle' between Paris and Versailles, where the SWC was to meet.[129]

An interesting sidelight is shone on this episode by Robertson's claim that he had agreed with Foch that both would reject the scheme. He told Spears after he returned to Paris that Foch 'was a silly weak old man'. He continued: 'I told him what to say at Rapallo & he was going to say it & then those damn ministers got round him.' Robertson claimed to have told Foch that he had the whole of England behind him as head of the British amy, and that he would not 'have any nonsense' from Wilson's 'boatload of Generals'. There is no reason to doubt Spears' testimony since it is an unlikely story to invent for a private diary. Moreover Joffre repeated the story, and so it must have had some currency.[130] And we know that Robertson and Foch sat and talked in the Forum, before they went to Rapallo, when Robertson informed his colleague about the scheme that the politicians were bringing with them. It is unlikely, however, that Foch would have agreed to reject the scheme which he had helped draw up, and which offered him a stepping-stone, if nothing more, to greater control.

The politicians and Robertson then returned to their respective capitals, and Foch and Wilson as the SWC's military advisers began their task of studying the Italian front. The enemy had not been inactive during the politicians' meetings in Rapallo. The Germans had crossed the Tagliamento on 3 November, and the Italian retreat to the Piave began the next day. This river was the last major obstacle to the east of the Venetian lagoon, but it was a formidable obstacle. It was very wide in places and subject to flooding, so that a high floodwall had been built on the western side of the river. Cadorna had been preparing the defences for

[127] IC 30, 30a, 30b, CAB 28/2.
[128] IC 30c, 30d, ibid.; Wilson diary, 5 November 1917.
[129] Letter, Foch to Mme Foch, 9 November 1917, vol. 43.
[130] Spears joint diary, 28 November 1917, SPRS 5/17, CCC; 'Note sur l'unité de commandement', 12 December 1917, in Pedroncini (ed.), *Joffre, JM*, 244.

some time and, once the Italians were all across, the remaining bridges were blown. Moreover, now that the Italian front was reduced to less than half its pre-24 October extent, the loss of the Second Army could be absorbed. The left (north) flank of the front was protected by the Monte Grappa and a chain of mountains. So the position did not appear too dangerous to Foch and Wilson, as they began their reporting mission. Moreover, Allied reinforcements were arriving. The French XXXI Corps had disembarked with its infantry and artillery by 6 November, followed by another division on 12 November. The British were somewhat slower because of railway congestion, but the first division had disembarked by 15 November, followed by the second division originally detailed and a further two (much to Haig's disgust) at the end of the month. (Eventually six French and five British divisions were deployed to Italy.)

Foch and Wilson began a regular pattern of daily meetings with Diaz at 9am, followed by trips to various parts of the front, then a talk between Foch and Wilson in the evening.[131] Diaz allowed them to visit wherever and whomever they pleased, and there were daily arguments about where the Allied divisions should be concentrated and daily Fochian exhortations that the Italians should hold on to their present front. Eventually Foch asked for Fayolle to replace him in Italy, and Wilson returned to London on 16 November after he and Foch signed a protocol that assigned the sectors that their respective troops would take over. In a long report to Paris on 16 November Foch wrote that fifteen Allied divisions would be required, unless the Italians retreated still further, and that they would have to remain through the winter to help re-organise and instruct the Italian army.[132]

Meanwhile German and Austrian attacks continued throughout November – what Cyril Falls described as the 'phase of pummelling'.[133] General H. Plumer arrived in Italy on the 13th to take command of the British contingent, unhappy at leaving Flanders just as the British were on the point of capturing Passchendaele village; Fayolle arrived a week later. Foch warned Fayolle that he should not try to take command because the Italians remained responsible for their own defence. Besides, they would not accept French command any more than the British contingent, so Foch advised Fayolle to 'direct matters unobtrusively'. Clemenceau's directions to Fayolle had been to get the Italians in his pocket.[134]

---

[131] Information about Foch's and Wilson's actions is taken from Wilson's diary and from Journal de la première mission du Général Foch en Italie, 1K/129/1.

[132] Rapport, 16 November 1917, *AFGG* 6/1, annex 79.   [133] Falls, *Caporetto*, ch. 9.

[134] Fayolle, *CS*, 245 (entry for 20 November 9117); Mott report # 31 to Intelligence Section, AEF, 6 February 1918, RG 120, E268, folder 737-B.

Foch was not able to leave Italy immediately. On 15 November Poincaré had asked Georges Clemenceau to form a government after Painlevé lost a vote of confidence in the Chamber. Clemenceau took office the next day, retaining the War Ministry, as Painlevé had done. On 18 November he wrote to Foch asking him to remain in Italy after Fayolle's arrival so as to put the new commander fully in the picture, and also to oversee the entry into line of the Allied troops, which took place between 1 and 3 December. On 4 December the Austrians on the Asiago front made further gains, destroying the Italian 29 Division. The Allied troops took part in the see-saw battles over the next three or so weeks that ended on 30 December, when the French *chasseurs alpins* of 47 DI took back the Monte Tomba–Monferena ridge from the enemy (see Illustration 7). Snow put a final halt to operations.

However, Foch did not stay in Italy to oversee the Allied troops in their first operations but returned to France on 23 November. He left an encouraging letter for Diaz, expressing his entire confidence in the Italian army, praising their fine stand on the Piave–Monte Grappa line and promising French aid. He insisted that he had personal experience of stopping a retreat against a victorious enemy, and so knew how difficult the task was.[135] He wrote to his wife that the Italians were gaining in confidence, that the crisis was over, and that Fayolle had arrived. Fayolle was good-humoured, judicious and sensible and would do well, Foch believed, so his 'deliverance' was at hand. Fayolle's comment on seeing Foch off at the station was less warm: 'Good riddance.'[136]

Foch has received much praise for taking prompt, energetic and inspiring action during the Italian crisis. His latest biographer describes him as returning from Italy 'with the prestige of a saviour of a cause that seemed to have been lost'. Having been evicted through the door of the Somme, Foch would return to high command through the 'cisalpine window'.[137] How much of this is deserved, and how much is a result of later hagiography? What was the significance of Caporetto, and did Foch make a difference?

In political and diplomatic terms, Caporetto had important consequences. The USA declared war on Austria-Hungary on 7 December 1917 as a result. Also Caporetto put an end to Lloyd George's grand plan of defeating Austria as a means of attacking Germany. It put an end also to the peace feelers. It provided the Allies with a clear illustration of the need for

---

[135] Foch to Diaz, 23 November 1917, *AFGG* 6/1, annex 108.
[136] Letter, Foch to Mme Foch, 19 November 1917, vol. 43; Fayolle, *CS*, 246 (entry for 23 November 1917).
[137] Notin, *Foch*, 301, 290.

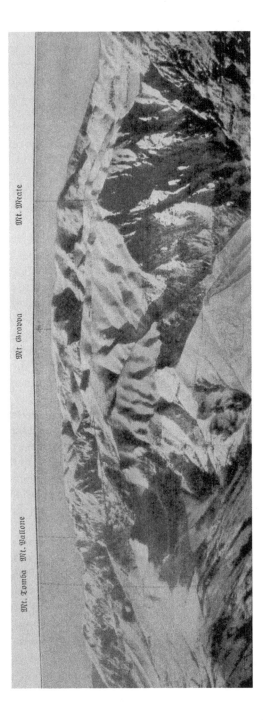

Illustration 7 The Monte Tomba–Monte Grappa massif
The very different terrain of the Italian front gave Foch a wider experience of the war, and of the difficulties of supplying armies fighting there with reinforcements in men and munitions.

supreme command and of the qualities required in the general who would exercise that command. It was a similar crisis, although on a much larger scale, that gave Foch the supreme command five months later. Strange that the man who has the reputation of being the unthinking apostle of the offensive should have achieved his greatest success in *defensive* action at a time of crisis.

In purely military terms, the events between 24 October and the end of the year looked both backwards and forwards. The German army had confirmed the value of the new tactics employed before Riga in a second trial in Italy. A well-coordinated artillery plan, combining gas and explosive shell, a rolling barrage covering the infantry advance, and infiltration tactics to get behind defensive lines thereby dislocating them – all proved that large amounts of terrain could be captured by such methods, without the long preliminary bombardment that eliminated any surprise. Ludendorff would employ these tactics again in March 1918 against the British. On the other hand, Caporetto also revealed the problems that such an approach laid bare. The original German plan had been to stop at the Tagliamento, having achieved the operation's primary aim, namely to bolster the Austro-Hungarian army. However, the stunning successes tempted Below to keep going and the last German divisions did not leave the sector until the end of December, although Ludendorff had always meant them to return to France for the spring offensive and had suggested to the Austrians on 28 November that the Italian offensive should be ended.[138] The temptation to continue with a successful operation that had achieved tactical success, without consideration for the strategic implications, would recur in 1918. Consequently, as the Italian offensive continued longer than planned and the front advanced still further, problems of supplying munitions to the guns when lacking motor vehicles, problems of dealing with thousands of prisoners-of-war, problems of losing control over troops (mainly Austrian) who were ill-clad and ill-fed to the point of starvation when stores of food and clothing were discovered – all these elements would resurface in March and April 1918.

For the Italians Caporetto was an enormous humiliation, and the word is still used today as a metaphor for total disaster. All the ground, or more, that had been captured during the eleven Isonzo battles had been lost in days. Cadorna's humiliation was completed by his removal from command despite his refusal to accept any responsibility for what happened. Coordination between the artillery and infantry was poor to non-existent.

---

[138] *RAW* 13: 301.

Cadorna was a strict disciplinarian, resorting to decimation and using front-line service as a punishment for striking workers from Turin. Certainly morale was low – the war had never been popular in the country at large because there was no sense of national defence such as animated the French – but Cadorna's instant judgement that his Second Army had broken because of cowardice, fanned by pacifist propaganda unchecked by the politicians, was resented deeply. Yet Caporetto united the country as never before. The turnaround in morale was astounding; deserters who had thrown down their weapons and run away straggled back to the armies in large numbers; a new government under Orlando declared a firm intent to continue the war, retreating as far as Sicily if necessary. The chronology shows that while Foch and Robertson, followed by Lloyd George and Painlevé, arrived early in the battle, no Allied troops contributed to the stand on the Piave–Monte Grappa line. They did not move into line until December, although their mere presence must have contributed to the improved Italian morale. Certainly it was a French division that threw the Austrians off the Monte Tomba at the end of the month, but it was Italian troops who held the line and stopped the joint German–Austro-Hungarian assault. Recent research confirms that it was the Italians themselves, rather than Allied troops, who turned around the disaster of Caporetto and recovered to continue resistance to the enemy.[139]

What, then, was Foch's role in all this? Just as the battle looked both forwards and backwards for the Germans, so for Foch the battle reflected 1914 and the stand at Ypres and foreshadowed the crises in March and May 1918. Weygand wrote from Italy to his wife that he was reminded of moments three years earlier, but direct command had been somewhat easier then.[140] Foch himself recalled Ypres during the meetings in Rapallo. Behind the Yser in 1914, he stated, British and French troops had resisted the numerically superior Germans; again at Verdun the French had demonstrated that the defensive had great strength.[141] His former staff officer General Réquin, now with the American mission, wrote to Foch on 23 November: 'Your presence in Italy has restored confidence to even the most pessimistic. It was enough to recall the personal action whereby you galvanised the Allied forces during the Battle of Ypres.'[142]

The particular element that predominated in Italy was the need for tact, as Weygand hinted by his comment that command had been easier at

---

[139] Cassar, *Forgotten Front*, 90; Morselli, *Caporetto*, ch. 7.
[140] Weygand's letter cited in Mme Foch diary, 16 November 1917.
[141] IC 30a, CAB 28/2.
[142] Réquin to Foch, 23 November 1917, Don Lecomte [Réquin], 1K/108/2: pièce 177.

Ypres. Another difference between Ypres and 1917 lay in Foch's refusal to engage the Allied troops in Italy until it became absolutely necessary, and until they were concentrated fully with their artillery and other equipment. Before Ypres Foch had patched the line with troops as they arrived, often lacking their guns, and the result had been a large degree of confusion that took some weeks to sort out after the battle ended. In Italy Foch was under great pressure to engage the Allied reinforcements sooner. The Italians complained bitterly that the Allies had come to Italy only to see how things would turn out.[143] Foch cannot be blamed, however, for such caution. If the Italian front had collapsed entirely, with the Austrians reaching the coast from Asiago and mounting a further attack west of Lake Garda, eleven Allied divisions would not have been sufficient to stop the rout. In such circumstances those eleven divisions would be needed in France. It was only when that danger was over that the Allied troops relieved Italian units in the front line. The Italian complaints foreshadowed those of Haig and his staff in March and April 1918, when Foch would refuse to relieve during a battle. Foch learned from the Italian experience of the inevitable delays involved when troops had to wait for guns and munitions. Thinking about the 1918 campaign, he wrote on 15 November, whilst he was still in Italy, that the coalition needed to establish a defensive plan and to stock-pile munitions on all fronts, so that the infantry would arrive to find their equipment in place.[144]

Foch's achievement in Italy was not the result of military action, but lay rather in the realm of psychology. In his account of the Isonzo battle, General Krafft put the effect on Italian morale as the most significant help that the Allies provided.[145] Foch's speedy recognition of the scale of the crisis and the consequent execution of the prepared contingency plan were perhaps his greatest service to Italy in October 1917. Yet his bustling attitude was not always appreciated. An American liaison officer reporting on events in Italy to General Pershing commented on Fayolle's 'moral authority' over the troops in Italy – Fayolle being fitter than

General Foch in all likelihood, for he is less nervous and less likely by some impatience or loss of temper (and the temptations for these must be numerous) to hurt the Italian pride and make relations difficult. At the same time it is possible that General Foch did much good by telling the Italians some brutal truths when he first arrived.[146]

---

[143] Melograni, *Storia politica*, 490–1.   [144] Foch, Carnets, 15 November 1917, fo. 270.
[145] Krafft von Dellmensingen, *Durchbruch*, 2: 220.
[146] Mott to Chief, Intelligence Section HQ, AEF, 30 November 1917, RG 120, E268, folder 737-B.

General Gathorne-Hardy, Plumer's chief of staff in Italy, was amused by Foch's methods in conference: 'Foch talked all the time', he wrote to his daughter, '& whenever anyone else tried to get in a word, threw up both hands & shouted "Rendez-moi la parole" [let me speak again]'.[147] Angelo Gatti, acting as official historian on Cadorna's staff and a firm supporter of the disgraced Comando Supremo, made a similar comment in his diary about Foch during the Rapallo conference: he kept on talking, and when Cadorna's chief of staff opened his mouth, Foch would say 'be quiet, let me speak'.[148] Cadorna himself, despite his appreciation of Foch's bustle when he first arrived in Italy, was less enthusiastic after his dismissal. He complained to a journalist that Foch and Robertson understood nothing about the Italian front, as proved by the withdrawal of their guns. To another journalist he claimed to have told the two generals: 'if this is all you came to Italy for, it would have been better [to remain in France]. At least we would have saved the coal necessary to transport your troops.'[149] These Anglo-American-Italian comments have a degree of unanimity that suggests they may be trusted.

Less jaundiced observers than Cadorna were, however, full of praise. The French ambassador in Rome reported to Paris that no one could have done better than General Foch, who had gained a beneficial influence at the Italian HQ.[150] Barrère claimed that Foch's optimism and confidence raised everyone's morale. He did not know how things would have turned out without Foch's energy and faith in victory.[151] Orlando told Luigi Albertini, Senator and director of the *Corriere della Sera*, and author of the classic five-volume history of the origins of the war, that Foch

instilled profound respect. He could make mistakes and certainly he erred in judging the situation that confronted him. But optimism was one of the keynotes of his temperament, and he demonstrated it constantly in the even worse crises of the following year, calling on a healthy confidence that he passed on to his subordinates, and he saved his country. As for us as well, undoubtedly he reinforced by his authority the view that we could, we must resist on the Piave, just as he reinforced the view among the Allied governments . . . that victory could not be won without unified command of the coalition forces.[152]

---

[147] Gathorne-Hardy to daughter, 15 November 1917, Gathorne-Hardy mss, 1/2/21.

[148] Gatti, *Caporetto*, 328 (entry for 6 November 1917).

[149] Journalists on *La Tribuna* and *Corriere della Sera* respectively. Malagodi, *Conversazioni*, 1: 207–8 (conversation of 23 November 1917); Morselli, *Caporetto*, 149, note 33 (conversation of 9 November 1917).

[150] Barrère (Rome) to Barthou, 10 November 1917, Paul Cambon mss, PA-AP 42, vol. 68, fos. 59–60.

[151] Charles-Roux mss, PA-AP 037, vol. 3, fo. 269.   [152] Albertini, *Venti anni*, pt 2, 3: 45–6.

Indeed Foch was always optimistic, and in November 1917 optimism was sorely needed. The year that was coming to an end had been a difficult year, with mutinies, pacifist agitation, even treason. French journalists and even a *député* were accused of accepting German money. Russia, France's main ally, had collapsed and Foch's experience over the arrangements for the AEF had shown that much more time was needed before American troops could replace them. The failure of various peace initiatives left the belligerents facing their fourth winter of war with no end in sight. The country's ready acceptance of the combative Clemenceau – 'je fais la guerre' – reflected the same need for positive action and confident optimism.

Foch's optimism and achievement in Italy made a marked contrast with the CinC who had remained in France. When Pétain went over to London with Painlevé before the politicians left for Rapallo, he told the War Cabinet that he 'considered the Italian position to be extremely serious' and (without having been to Italy to see for himself) 'he expressed doubts as to whether the Italian army really existed any longer'. His solution, as noted above, was to divide the command of Allied forces in Belgium, France and Italy by giving the northern portion to Haig and taking the southern, including Italy, to himself.[153] On the other hand, on the day that Cadorna ordered the retreat to the line of the Piave, Wilson noted that Robertson 'wired very pessimistically, Foch not so.'[154]

Pétain was already aware of the risk, as he saw it, that Foch would gain more power, and the acclaim that Foch received for his efforts in Italy increased the fears at GQG. Having failed to obtain command in Italy before Foch left, Pétain allocated Serrigny to Fayolle as his chief of staff as compensation. Serrigny was the former head of Pétain's military cabinet, and it is likely that his appointment was intended to provide Pétain with reliable information about events in Italy. Certainly Foch seems to have believed that this was the case since he warned Fayolle to get rid of Pétain's 'liege man'.[155] The Foch–Pétain competition was highlighted by the fact that the French army was not undertaking operations as Foch returned from Italy. The French victory at La Malmaison on the Chemin des Dames had been eclipsed by Caporetto. Indeed, it was the British tank attack at Cambrai that was filling the newspapers. Herbillon even suspected that Cambrai was a British attempt to prove that they, rather than the French, deserved the supreme command. Criticism began to build that the French army was doing nothing. Former War Minister Millerand, for example, complained that Pétain did not think of attacking.[156]

---

[153] War Cabinet 263, 2 November 1917, CAB 23/4.   [154] Wilson diary, 4 November 1917.
[155] Letter, Serrigny to Pétain, 3 December 1917, cited in Notin, *Foch*, 299.
[156] Herbillon, *Du général*, 2: 169, 173 (entries for 23, 28 November 1917).

Caporetto placed squarely on the table the question of unity of command. A rousing speech by Lloyd George in Paris proclaiming the Rapallo agreement to create the SWC had been followed by disclaimers in both parliaments by both Premiers. Lloyd George stated that unity of command was impossible. As a result the question filled everyone's mind, Herbillon noted, whatever milieu they occupied.[157] Moreover Foch was being criticised for *not* obtaining unity of command whilst in Italy.[158] Fayolle asked specifically for unified command in Italy on 27 November, or at least the creation of an army group of the British and French divisions under his command. Foch consulted Robertson but was told that Plumer had received specific instructions that he was to cooperate fully while remaining completely independent. What was more, Plumer was too highly regarded to be placed in a subordinate position. Consequently Foch replied to Fayolle that 'for the moment' they could not insist.[159] Clearly Foch had a realistic appreciation of the situation.

Clemenceau was equally realistic. The Italian ambassador in Paris reported to Sonnino that he had spoken with the new Premier about the agitation in the press for supreme command in Italy to be given to a French general. Clemenceau had replied that unified command would indeed be an advantage and that Italian acceptance would make persuading the British much easier. After all, the enemy owed their recent successes to their unified command – which is to ignore, of course, the fact that relations between the two Kaisers and their respective high commands were extremely poor. The ambassador concluded that British resistance could not be overcome.[160] General Castelnau attempted to convince Clemenceau that accepting six brains (Haig, Pétain and, eventually, Pershing in France; with Diaz, Fayolle and Plumer in Italy) plus a purely consultative committee was simply asking for trouble. In Clemenceau's opinion, however, 'the situation was not modifiable'.[161] Nevertheless, modifications did occur, as the next chapter will show, which led at last to the imposition of unity of command.

[157] Greenhalgh, *VTC*, 174–7.
[158] Mott report #10, to Intelligence Section, AEF, 10 December 1917, RG 120, E268, folder 737-B.
[159] Foch to Fayolle, 2 December 1917, *AFGG* 6/1, annex 144.
[160] Letter, Bonin Longare to Sonnino, 23 November 1917, in Sonnino, *Carteggio*, 340–3.
[161] Meeting with Clemenceau, 3 December 1917, in Gras, *Castelnau*, 368.

Part II

Supreme command

11 At the Supreme War Council, November 1917–March 1918

Leaving Italy on 23 November, Foch returned to a changed political climate in France. The organisation set up in Rapallo had now been installed in Versailles, and its second session was due to follow the forthcoming Allied conference in Paris. Also, on the 16th Georges Clemenceau had become Premier, replacing Painlevé, thereby realising Foch's long-held desire to see Clemenceau wield political power. Before leaving, he sent the new Premier a telegram of congratulations, to which the latter responded on a very upbeat note. Clemenceau acknowledged that the Italian stand on the Piave was the result of Foch's encouragements, and he approved all that Foch was doing. He wanted Foch to wait a few days until General Fayolle arrived to take over command of the French contingent.[1]

Clemenceau's new role meant a considerable increase in Foch's own chances of gaining greater influence, even of obtaining supreme command. Clemenceau had told Tardieu to tell the Americans that Foch was the man for the job; and he told the head of his military cabinet, General Mordacq, not to trouble about improving the organisation of the general staff in the War Ministry because he (Clemenceau) was determined, whatever the cost, to obtain unity of command with Foch as commander-in-chief.[2] He even told Spears, who passed it on to Hankey, that he was determined to obtain it.[3]

A second source of support came from the Americans. They had sent a delegation under Colonel E. M. House to the Allied conference in Paris and the second session of the Supreme War Council. The Americans were strongly in favour of unified command. Both House and General Tasker H. Bliss, who would become the US military representative on the SWC, wanted to replace '[n]ational jealousies and suspicions and susceptibilities of national temperament' by 'absolute unity of military

---

[1] Letter, Foch to Mme Foch, 18 November 1917, vol. 43; Mme Foch diary, 19 November 1917.
[2] Tardieu, *La Paix*, 43; Mordacq, *MC*, 1: 46.
[3] Hankey diary, 27 November 1917, cited in Roskill, *Hankey*, 1: 465.

control'. Otherwise, Bliss continued, 'our dead and theirs may have died in vain'.[4]

The events that took place between the end of November 1917, when Foch returned to Paris, and March 1918, when the German offensives began, reveal his gradual rise to that supreme command. Although the SWC was the forum in which the arguments over his rise were aired, Foch was not at first part of it. He returned to his old job in the Ministry, since Lloyd George maintained his opposition to the council's permanent military representatives (PMRs) holding any other responsibility. When Lloyd George threatened to leave the conference and return to London if Clemenceau attempted to overturn this provision by dissolving unilaterally an agreement made by his predecessor, Clemenceau called Foch in to see what could be done. Foch suggested appointing Weygand to the SWC; he was given another star and promotion to divisional general so that he would not be too lowly in rank beside his new colleagues.[5] Weygand wrote in his memoirs that Foch did not even have to give him any instructions as each knew the other's thinking so well. Thus Foch had a proxy on the council, and Clemenceau could show his contempt for the whole SWC scheme.

The appointment of Weygand upset both Generals Cadorna and Wilson. The former CinC of the Italian army was 'angry, indignant & contemptuous at Weygand's appointment'; and Wilson was taken down a notch or two by the appointment of one so junior.[6] Wilson was under no illusions as to the source of authority. When he offered Weygand a lift to Versailles for a meeting of PMRs, Foch said there was 'no hurry' for a meeting. Wilson 'pondered' this and concluded that 'Clemenceau intends to direct the whole war by using Foch to work with Robertson & then by sending Weygand here to impose his (Clemenceau's) will on Versailles by Foch through Weygand. This is just the sort of little trick that would appeal to a Frenchman.'[7]

Among French public opinion the SWC was seen as a poor second-best. What was needed was a single commander, not a committee dominated by politicians. The head of the British mission at GQG was told this, and the politicians said the same to Painlevé, both before he went to Rapallo and afterwards.[8] The press also urged the necessity to designate

[4] General T. H. Bliss, Memorandum for the Secretary of War, 18 December 1917, *FRUS, Lansing Papers*, 2: 212.
[5] Weygand, *IV*, 438–41.
[6] Wilson diary, 3, 4 December 1917; Clive diary, 3 December 1917.
[7] Wilson diary, 3 December 1917.
[8] Clive diary, 22, 23, 28 October 1917; Poincaré, *AS*, 9: 349–59 (entries for 3, 4, 10 November 1917).

a single chief. Joseph Reinach (Polybe of *Le Figaro*) scorned what he described as the reconstitution of the Congress of Vienna. Versailles would have a mere three generals amidst a much larger number of politicians. No doubt the representatives would be so numerous that they would have to use the Galerie des Glaces for their meetings.[9] The French ambassador in London called the SWC an aulic (or courtly) council invented by Lloyd George, describing it as simply a 'décor' and not viable.[10]

Lloyd George and Painlevé had invented the council, but Painlevé was now out of office, and Lloyd George had been forced to back down from his position as expressed on his return from Rapallo. Then, at a lunch in the French War Ministry on 12 November, during a speech which even the sober French official history called 'sensational', Lloyd George had qualified the Allied strategy thus far as merely 'stitching' plans together. Certainly, there had been some Allied victories. Yet, when he looked at the casualty lists, he sometimes wished 'that it had not been necessary to win so many'. After his return to London Lloyd George had to face press opposition and parliamentary questions. He stated in the House of Commons that the SWC would have no executive power, and that he personally was 'utterly opposed' to unity of command.[11]

Thus the SWC got off to a very shaky start, yet the task facing the Allies as they assembled in Paris for their conferences was huge: namely, to agree the 1918 campaign. Despite the fact that November was almost over there was no strategic plan yet agreed for the Western Front, and it promised to be a most difficult campaign. The Bolsheviks had taken power in Petrograd and on 27 November had asked Germany for an armistice. On the Eastern Front hostilities would be suspended on 3 December, and Romania would follow suit, signing its own armistice with the Central Powers on 9 December. Signatures on an armistice document merely confirmed a collapse of the Eastern Front that had been obvious for months. German divisions had already begun returning westwards at the beginning of November. On the Western Front the Allies had fewer divisions to counter the increase in enemy numbers, since eleven of them had gone to Italy after Caporetto. The number of trained American divisions in France was still very small.

Consequently, in order to meet the increased threat, it would take *unified* action by (mostly) British and French troops on the Western Front to resist the expected German offensives. The experience of 1917

---

[9] Reinach, 'De l'idée et du projet de Rapallo', *Le Figaro*, 17 November 1917.
[10] Cambon to Xavier Charmes, 21 November 1917, in Cambon, *Correspondance*, 3: 199.
[11] See Greenhalgh, *VTC*, 174–7.

did not bode well for the achievement of such unity. The Nivelle experiment had been a disaster, and for the rest of 1917 the British and French armies had gone their own, completely separate, ways. As General Micheler told Dillon, Haig and Pétain got on very well but they saw very little of each other. Micheler asked Dillon as late as 19 December whether the two commanders-in-chief 'had put their heads together over a common plan for 1918'. Dillon replied that he thought not.[12]

The question that crystallised the twin problems of unified command and of planning for 1918 was that of the establishment of a general Allied reserve, for there was no point having a plan and a supreme commander if he had no troops to command. Thus the thorny problem of how to create a general reserve in the face of resistance from each national commander on the Western Front, despite the SWC's aim to create such a body of troops, came to dominate the winter months. Foch was involved intimately in all the talking and negotiations, which ultimately were fruitless. First of all, however, there was the question of what to do about the ally who did not attend the conferences in Paris and Versailles: Russia.

At exactly the same time that Lloyd George and Painlevé had been stitching up the Western Front in Rapallo, the Eastern Front began unravelling, and unravelling rapidly. There had been little confidence that the Russian army could do anything much to help the Allied cause after the collapse of the Kerensky offensive back in July. Foch and Pétain had ordered contingency plans against the Germans moving divisions from the Eastern Front to France as early as July 1917, despite Lloyd George's scorn at such pessimism.[13] Those contingency plans would now be needed.

The collapse of Russia was of greater significance to the French than to any other ally. Militarily, the return to the Western Front of German divisions freed from the east would mean greater enemy densities in France, where the French were running out of men. Also, the return of Austro-Hungarian troops to Italy would release the German troops who had contributed to the Caporetto success. Economically too, Russia was significant for France. Most of France's overseas investments were in Russia: fully 13bn gold francs' worth, of which 11.5bn was in tsarist bonds. Almost one-third of the total foreign investment in Russia was French (32.6 per cent), with British investment constituting 22.6 per cent. In the Ukraine and Donetz basin, where most of Russia's heavy industry was located, French capital represented between 51 and 97 per cent of total investments in metallurgy and mining.[14] The French government

---

[12] Dillon, *Three Wars*, 104.   [13] Carley, *Revolution and Intervention*, 13.   [14] Ibid., 90.

was spending 125 million francs a month there, mainly in keeping its own people happy by paying out the coupons on the bonds held by French investors.[15] France had been supplying Russia with armaments: 25 million shells, 20,000 machineguns and 1300 field guns.[16] Vast quantities already shipped to Russia were lying about in the northern ports (Murmansk and Arkangel, now ice-bound), and in Vladivostok on Russia's eastern Pacific seaboard, because of bottlenecks on the Russian railways. France desperately needed these armaments because of the commitment to supply the American divisions. Munitions orders for the Americans for the sole month of October, for example, amounted to 620 75 mm guns together with 8 million shells, 260 heavy artillery guns with 1 million shells, plus machineguns and automatic rifles.[17] Already there were murmurings that the Americans would be better equipped than the French unless changes were made.

Finally, France had a great stake in Romania, on Russia's southwestern border. If Russia left the war the Romanians would be unable to continue, surrounded as they were by the Central Powers: Bulgaria and Austria-Hungary. The French had a large military mission there under General Henri Berthelot. The Romanian army had been reinvigorated and rearmed with French expertise and equipment following the disastrous events of 1916, which had caused 400,000 casualties and left two-thirds of the country in the hands of the Austro-Hungarians. Its contribution to the Russian offensives in the summer of 1917 had 'redeemed' the army, but that success was undermined by the Russian collapse when the Central Powers counter-attacked.[18] Consequently a Russian defection would affect all the Allies, especially as the blockade of the Central Powers would be nullified if the grain reserves and raw materials of southern Russian lands fell into their hands (as they did), and above all it would affect the French, both militarily and economically. It is not, therefore, surprising that they should have taken the lead in attempting to keep the Eastern Front alive.

The British too had commitments to the Russians. Over 208,000 tons of shipping had been allocated to various categories of supplies for the period 1 July to mid-September 1917;[19] and this was less than half the amount that had been requested because of the enormous shipping losses

[15] Statement by Pichon, French Foreign Minister, 'Notes of a conversation held at the Ministry of Foreign Affairs, Paris, on December 1, 1917', IC 35(a), CAB 28/3.
[16] Gambiez and Suire, *Première guerre mondiale*, 271.   [17] Kaspi, *Temps des Américains*, 121.
[18] On the 1916 and 1917 Romanian campaigns, see Torrey, *Romania and World War I*, chs. 10–13.
[19] 'British Assistance to Russia – 1917 Programme', 12 July 1017, Cabinet Memo GT 1376, CAB 24/19.

suffered in 1917 after the Germans began their campaign of unrestricted submarine warfare. Britain was also committed to providing credits in the USA for 1.6 million rifles for the Russians, and in Canada for rolling stock to be sent to Vladivostok.[20]

From Romania Berthelot sent a report at the end of November describing anarchy in Russia as 'complete', and the French general staff passed on the report to the British.[21] The effects of such anarchy on public opinion in France, still in a fragile state following the industrial unrest and the military indiscipline of earlier in the year, were potentially severe. Worse still, pacifist and/or revolutionary fever might 'infect' the nation. However, despite the German propaganda effort of firing into French lines projectiles containing Trotskyite manifestoes, the French mood turned to anger at the Russian defection once the second revolution had occurred. Postal control records for the army and prefects' reports for the civilian population kept Foch's office informed about the state of morale.[22]

Thus Foch faced a critical situation caused by the Russian defection as he returned to France. His notebooks reveal his thinking. He had accepted as early as September that the new situation would push back the end of the war until 1919. If the anarchy continued, he wrote on 2 December, it would be necessary to reinforce all the defences in France, Italy and Salonika. Arrangements for moving troops quickly from one threatened point to another (as had happened after Caporetto) would have to be made; and communications would have to be maintained with Moscow if Petrograd fell to the Germans, as seemed increasingly likely when armistice talks broke off on 5 December. An offensive to capture the trans-Siberian railway would have to be prepared.[23] The military mission to the Russian army reported to Foch as chief of the army general staff, and Foch passed on to Pétain on 12 December the frightening figures that he had received from its head, General Niessel. Russian prisoner-of-war camps held 100,000 German and 1.6 million Austro-Hungarian men.[24] If they were released as a result of any peace settlement (and Foch would consider any such release a 'hostile act'), the POWs would swell still further the numbers of troops returning westwards.

As the Allies gathered in Paris, Foch prepared a memorandum on what might be done about Russia. Its collapse meant that communications

---

[20] 'Memorandum for War Cabinet on Supplies to Russia and Roumania', 6 December 1917, GT 2905, CAB 24/35.
[21] 'Summary of report No. 24 of November 30th from General Berthelot', GT 3299, CAB 24/38.
[22] For the evolution in opinion see Nicot, 'Perception des Alliés par les combattants', 46–8.
[23] Foch, Carnets, 29 September and 2 December 1917, fos. 263, 272.
[24] Pedroncini, Pétain Général, 176.

between the western Allies and Romania and southern Russia (where there were still some centres of resistance) were cut. The enemy was now able to advance to crush those centres of resistance and to lay hands on the economic riches and resources of the country. The Ukraine, for example, was one of Russia's main export regions for cereals, mainly wheat and barley. It was vital, therefore, to take 'energetic' measures to support the resistance and to prevent the capture of those economic resources. The way to do this was by taking over the trans-Siberian railway so as to re-establish communications between Vladivostok and Moscow, and to use American and Japanese elements to reinforce the resistance. He proposed direct military intervention in Russia using the railway, whose capture might be represented as a means of safeguarding the arrival of supplies for the capital.[25] Although taking over the railway was an ambitious plan, Foch wished to take pre-emptive action because he feared that Petrograd would be 'boche' by the spring. Before this happened, he wanted Japan and the USA to restore communications between Moscow and the West by capturing the trans-Siberian, using the excuse that its control would permit the Allies to re-supply Moscow.[26]

The Foreign Ministers of France, Britain and Italy met with Colonel House and the Japanese ambassadors to Paris and London in the French Foreign Ministry on 3 December. There Foch read out his memorandum, pointing out that since it had been written the Bolsheviks had captured Vladivostok, thereby threatening American and Japanese interests in the east. As Balfour warned, this might make intervention more desirable, but it also made it an 'operation of great magnitude'. Considerable numbers would be required to capture the 'strongly fortified port' and then to capture and to hold the 'immense length' of the railway. Foch brushed aside the difficulty, asking that a statement of principle be made first. If the situation left Japan and the USA 'indifferent', then there was no need to do anything. Foch had shifted his ground from the support of the considerable French interests tied up in Romania to an appeal to the self-interest of the only two countries that had the means to do anything: the USA and Japan. Eventually they agreed that the Japanese and American representatives should ask their governments without delay to ensure that Russia be supplied via the trans-Siberian railway and to consider what means should be put in place to achieve this, 'even in case of trouble'.[27]

[25] 'Note sur les mesures à prendre à l'égard de la Russie', 30 November 1917, FO 371/3018. This copy of the document, prepared before the meeting, was supplied by the Japanese embassy to the Foreign Office in London.
[26] Foch, Carnets, 15 November 1917, fo. 270.
[27] 'Notes of a Conversation held at the Ministry of Foreign Affairs, Paris, on December 3, 1917, at 11AM', IC 35(b), CAB 28/3.

Next Foch turned to the question of Romania. He proposed an Allied Supply Commission based in the Black Sea port of Odessa to purchase supplies in southern Russia, together with an Allied Railway Commission for the area. The resistance forces should be grouped around the Romanian army, and supported by a propaganda effort. He suggested that credits should be opened to provide the necessary financial support. Once again Balfour demurred. He did not wish to give the impression that the Allies were creating 'a great army, under a French General, for the purposes of the Allies'. Finance was being provided already and House supported Balfour, suggesting that matters should proceed as at present. Foch was clearly pushing policies that went far beyond what the politicians were prepared to accept. On the other hand, he was attempting to act pre-emptively rather than wait upon events, as House and Balfour were recommending.

Foch told his wife[28] that an enormous amount of work had been done that day during the conference, but the fact remains that it was only talk. The representatives had recognised that only the Japanese or the Americans had the resources to intervene in an area (the Pacific) that was in their sphere of interest. Foch had no power to influence, let alone to control, what either country did there. America's armies were forming very slowly, as Foch knew only too well; and the Japanese, despite having been an ally ever since August 1914, had shown no desire to commit troops after their capture of the German naval base of Tsingtau in China back in November 1914.

Maintaining the pressure, the day after the meeting Foch sent a copy of his memorandum to the Japanese ambassador, M. Matsui. It was a slightly longer version and, significantly, more strongly worded. The Russian people were 'gangrened' by the German and Bolshevik propaganda; and Japan and the USA were the only powers who could carry out an Allied intervention policy, given their geographic position and their military resources. He concluded by saying that such were the ideas that had been 'developed' during the meeting.[29] Not surprisingly Matsui protested, very politely, that such ideas had not been accepted, that he and Viscount Chinda, the ambassador in London, had pointed out the inherent dangers, and that all that had been decided was that the representatives should ask their respective governments to obtain detailed information about what was happening in Russia. Matsui passed Foch's

[28] Mme Foch diary, 4 December 1917.
[29] Copy dated 3 December 1917, in Hosoya, *Shiberia*, 19–21; another copy dated 4 December 1917, with a ts addition noting that Vladivostok had been captured, in FO 371/3018.

memorandum on to London, and Lord Bertie was instructed to inform the French Foreign Ministry that the British government could not 'consider themselves as in any way committed to action at Vladivostok or Harbin' – this despite Foch having put forward his ideas 'with great ability'.[30]

Events now moved quickly, and the British reacted by becoming more favourable to intervention.[31] The tsarist army had already started to disintegrate as soon the Russians requested an armistice; and the Romanian armistice was signed on 9 December. After publishing the secret treaties, the Bolsheviks then broke the 1914 Allied agreement by opening unilateral peace negotiations with the Central Powers on 20 December. Although Ukraine did not follow the Bolshevik lead, their resistance would not last long. The Don Cossacks in the area to the east of the Ukraine and north of the Caucasus region, where anti-Bolshevik elements were gathering, seemed to offer the most promising resistance. In the Transcaucasus, Bolshevik influence was at its weakest, and the British wished to support the armies opposing the Turks in order to protect their interests in the Middle East and to prevent pan-Islamic propaganda affecting Persia and India.[32]

Following a suggestion from Cambon, Milner and Lord Robert Cecil of the Foreign Office returned to Paris for further talks on the question of supporting anti-Bolshevik forces in Russia.[33] They hoped that the French might have more reliable information on the position in Ukraine. They met in the French Foreign Ministry on the morning of 23 December with Clemenceau, his Foreign Minister Stephen Pichon, Cambon and Foch. All agreed that it was vital not to let go of the Ukraine, for the area represented the only means of supplying Romania. They agreed also that Russian supplies must be prevented from reaching Germany. The British government accepted Cambon's suggestion of dividing responsibility for the area of southern Russia, with the French looking after Romania and the Ukraine and Britain the rest of southeastern Russia. Here Foch interjected that the Don Cossacks should be counted in with the Ukraine rather than in the British sector. The demarcation line was left to Foch and General Macdonogh to work out between them. This they did before the conference met again in the afternoon.[34]

---

[30] Draft telegram, Foreign Office to Lord Bertie, 13 December 1917, FO 371/3018.
[31] Neilson, *Strategy and Supply*, 294–5.
[32] On these questions, see Kennan, *Russia Leaves the War*, ch. 9.
[33] Cecil, 'Record of interview with French Ambassador', 21 December 1917, FO 371/3018.
[34] 'Conference at the Quai d'Orsay [French Foreign Ministry] held at 10.30AM December 23, 1917', IC 37, CAB 28/3; Milner diary, 23 December 1917, Milner mss, dep. 88.

The final agreement stated that French action was directed north of the Black Sea against the enemy, whereas the British action extended southeast of the Black Sea against the Turks. The French zone covered Bessarabia, Ukraine and the Crimea; the British took the Cossack territories, Armenia, Georgia and Kurdistan. The costs were to be met equally and regulated by an Allied body. Since the French were already funding to the tune of 100 million francs the formation of an army in the Ukraine, this programme was to continue. Thus Foch got his way over maintaining French influence over the most promising (militarily) anti-Bolshevik forces in the Ukraine, but it availed him little, since a peace treaty with the Central Powers was signed on 9 February 1918. This Franco-British convention did not represent an imperialist carve-up of territory, as it was sometimes portrayed later, but an attempt to sustain a front in the east in order to relieve pressure on the west. Foch's agitation had achieved a concrete agreement. The fact that it amounted to little in the end should not detract from the recognition that Foch had argued persuasively enough to unify policy.

The situation in Russia was, he believed, now the dominant question. If the anarchy there continued, it would be vital to consolidate the defences in France, Italy and Salonika, and to supply those armies with increased armaments. The question of transporting troops from one theatre to another to reinforce defensive arrangements at threatened points also needed to be studied, for the experience of Italy had taught its lessons.[35] These musings reveal consideration of all eventualities – not simply unthinking offensives. The principal aim was a wide-front operation; but the defensive had to be settled first, taking into account the Russian situation.

Clemenceau had opened the SWC session on 1 December by calling on the council to 'consider the nature of the military campaigns to be undertaken in 1918' as its first task. The military advisers should take into account conditions in Russia and in Italy, and factor in the new elements: the 'gradually maturing' forces of the new ally, and the shipping situation.[36] Foch himself had already been pondering for some time what the 1918 campaign should be. In September 1917 he wrote that an attack on the principal enemy, the German army, should be undertaken on as wide a front as possible by a combined action of American, Belgian, British and French troops using heavy artillery, with the aim of inflicting a series of defeats that would force the enemy back to a new Hindenburg Line. The French would set the example, but there was no denying that their armies

[35] Foch, Carnets, 15 November 1917, fos. 269–70.
[36] Clemenceau's opening address, 1 December 1917, annex to IC 36, CAB 28/3.

were worn down. The alternative was to isolate Germany by attacking Austria or Bulgaria or Turkey. The first strategy would be more costly but more certain in its effects. The second would be less costly for France and could be carried out when winter weather prevented operations in the north (during what Henry Wilson called the 'mud months'); but it was less certain to produce complete defeat of the enemy, even if that enemy sued for peace as a result. The necessary precondition was to choose between the two.[37]

He had also considered other options. Starving out the enemy (blockade) was no answer because of their interior frontiers with other European sources of food and raw materials, and because the enemy's submarines were working against the Entente's supply lines at the same time. France was exhausted and Britain's army had reached its maximum troop levels. They would have to await the arrival of trained American troops so that all could attack together in 1918; or, if the Russians did defect, they would be obliged to wait until 1919 before they had sufficient superior numbers to undertake a successful operation. If they were forced to wait, the main task would be to enable the country and the army to endure. Manpower would have to be organised to provide men for agriculture so that the country would have enough to eat, men for munitions factories so that the armies would have enough weapons and munitions, and men for the armies so that they could win the war. Then there was the question of the differing needs and interests of the Allies. The British had not been in too much hurry in 1914 and 1915, but now they felt the 'weight of the years', as the French had done from the opening months. The Americans were clearly in less of a hurry to finish the war than the French, who were 'crushed' by the war. The consequence, in Foch's mind, was that a 'general, common direction' was necessary to continue the war.[38]

Pétain too had been thinking about what the 1918 campaign should be. He was in a better position than Foch to put his ideas into practice, and this he had done with a series of 'directives' that modified French army tactics. These had been tested at Verdun and on the ill-fated Chemin des Dames and had been shown to be successful. Unfortunately the latter success, recapturing the fort of La Malmaison, had been overshadowed by the Caporetto disaster, and so there was no great glory gained by what had been planned as a limited operation. Pétain's directives counselled a defensive posture. He set up training schools for the infantry, where his ideas on defence in depth were transmitted, and he developed the other arms, in particular tanks and aviation – all vital matters. No one but Pétain

---

[37] Foch, Carnets, 2 September 1917, fo. 256.   [38] Ibid., 29 September 1917, fo. 265.

could have restored the morale of the French army as he did, yet the fact remains that the Germans were still holding firmly on to French territory and Pétain's achievement in restoring the French army to offensive health was not the sort that could be trumpeted in newspapers.

As for his strategic views, Pétain developed in the latter half of 1917 a proposal for a large offensive into Upper Alsace. Such an attack in a totally new direction would have the benefit of surprise, and if made by a sufficiently large force offered the prospect of seizing significant portions of mineral-rich territory that had been ceded to Germany in the 1871 Treaty of Frankfurt. The possession of such territory would provide bargaining chips in any peace settlement – what Professor Pedroncini called a 'stratégie des gages'. A further advantage accruing from an operation in Alsace would be the forestalling of any German attack through Switzerland (for which eventuality Foch had drawn up 'Plan H' earlier in the year).[39]

A further element of Pétain's thinking about 1918 concerned the question of unified command. Pétain had been lobbying strongly for this, even before the Italian emergency (as we saw in the previous chapter). Clemenceau had refused his request for command over the French troops in Italy. Pétain's chief of staff, Colonel Bernard Serrigny, had put forward a plan as early as April 1917, when Pétain was appointed (briefly) chief of the army general staff, whereby Pétain as the delegate of the French Comité de guerre would assume the 'direction' of troops on the French and Balkan fronts and would 'coordinate' operations with the Allied armies. Pétain's chief of staff in 1917, General Debeney, also had a plan for an Allied chief. In October 1917 he proposed a 'Generalissimo' for the front from Nieuport to Salonika, with an Allied general staff.[40] There was even talk of Joffre returning from retirement in order to do the job.[41] Some believed that he was the only candidate who would be acceptable to the British. Yet Clemenceau realised that political opinion in Britain was too strongly opposed for it to be possible to *impose* unified command. As he told the Deputies' Army Commission, Lloyd George could not concede unity of command because the British parliament would not allow it.[42] In order to accept the necessity, the British themselves would have to request an Allied commander. The only likely way for Haig to bow to the necessity

[39] See Pedroncini, *Pétain Général*, 122–37.
[40] 'Projet de Charte pour le Général Pétain', 30 April 1917, in Serrigny, *Trente ans*, 131–2; General Debeney, 'Organisation du Commandement de la Coalition', 16 October 1917, Fonds Clemenceau, 6N 54.
[41] Mordacq, *MC*, 1: 102.
[42] Audition du Président du conseil, Commission de l'Armée, Chambre des députés, 12 December 1917, C7499.

was through the action of enemy guns – as would prove to be the case a few months later. Haig had made clear that he thought the French army finished, that his ally would do little fighting in the 1918 campaign. This is probably why the two headquarters had done so little joint planning. Plans for the 1916 and 1917 campaigns had been settled well before the end of 1915 and 1916 respectively. Nothing was settled for 1918 by the end of December. Haig and Pétain had not even managed to settle how far the British would extend their line so as to free older Frenchmen to return to the farms to produce enough food so that France would not starve.

At a meeting of the Comité de guerre Pétain had presented his thoughts on what the French might be able to do in 1918. He had prepared some notes in mid-November, but the change in government meant postponement of his presentation. Russia's defection had forced Pétain to delay his proposed offensive in eastern France in favour of a defensive strategy.[43] This meeting must be considered in the light of the considerable dissatisfaction, particularly in parliament, with the military situation. The press was calling for action. The French people were facing their fourth winter at war, and the previous one had been bitterly cold. There was insufficient coal, and rationing had been introduced, even for bread. (Madame Foch noted the start of the distribution of bread ration cards.)[44] Consequently, the Presidents of the two chambers of parliament demanded to be heard in the Comité de guerre.

It met on 13 December, its second meeting since Clemenceau became Premier. The two Presidents wanted to know what the new SWC was and did; and they wanted to discuss also the strategy of limited offensives, of which they disapproved. Pétain responded that, if they knew a better strategy than the one he was proposing, he was prepared to resign, whereupon Clemenceau stated immediately that Pétain was under his orders and that he 'covered' him entirely. Poincaré seconded this, whilst admitting that he was 'temperamentally' in favour of the offensive. Notwithstanding this desire, Pétain's figures on manpower left no room for discussion. Clemenceau was happy that they agreed on this point, but Foch had the last word. The danger must not be exaggerated, Foch said: 'It is easy to stand on the defensive … We can hope to hold easily.' Foch then entertained Pétain to lunch in his home, where Madame Foch noted that Pétain was still 'quite cold', that he had put on weight, and that he talked about the defence of Verdun.[45]

[43] Note pour le Comité de guerre, 18 November 1917, ibid., annex 86, discussed in Pedroncini, *Pétain Général*, 239–44.
[44] Madame Foch diary, 8 October 1917.
[45] Poincaré, *AS*, 9: 411–14 (entry for 13 December 1917); Comité de guerre, 3N2 (which wrongly gives 12 December as date for the meeting); Madame Foch diary, 14 December 1917.

A wide gulf was beginning to open between the strategic ideas of the French CinC and the French head of the army general staff, not to mention the gulf that existed between Pétain and Haig. (Haig told London on 7 January that he favoured a continuation of the Flanders offensive.) Pétain's revised plan proposed four limited offensives in the spring of 1918: two around Reims in the Champagne; one in conjunction with the Americans to capture the Saint-Mihiel salient; and a final, larger action northeast of Reims, supported by a British attack from St Quentin. Only if Russia continued fighting could anything larger be envisaged. In that case, all the actions of the Allies must be coordinated to make a 'joint push aiming to collapse the enemy front'. In addition, the first joint note of the PMRs on 13 December also proposed a defensive strategy.[46]

Foch's staff prepared a response to the Pétain plan, which criticised the four limited offensives, proposing instead a Somme-type wider offensive. Then, on 1 January 1918, Foch prepared a further document embodying his views, which he gave to Weygand to present at the meeting of the PMRs.[47] Thus there was no pretence about who was in the driving seat.

Foch wrote that he expected 'strong' German offensives early in 1918, widely spaced in time and place. They must be met with the defensive arrangements already prepared, and followed by an offensive – 'the only means to obtain victory'. Whether the enemy attacked or not, the Allied armies must prepare to seize the initiative and be ready to undertake limited-objective attacks leading to a combined action aiming at reaching a decision. The enemy might undertake another Verdun-type violent and long-lasting attack intended to break the defenders' morale. The only response, Foch insisted, was a similar action elsewhere, but this must be prepared 'several months in advance'. Foch was thinking of a larger Somme in response to another Verdun, and he referred specifically to those 1916 battles which were the last ones he had dealt with as a field commander. This 'larger Somme' must be a combined effort – combined in the SWC and then prepared in the individual French and British armies. Foch charged Weygand, therefore, with obtaining the plans of the two CinCs and then 'combining' them in the SWC, the only organisation capable of ensuring a common effort. Then the fronts had to be shared out equitably and reserves constituted. This was truly getting back to basics, and Foch was harking back to 1916 ideas in 1918, but he was trying to get a common plan established, which is more than Pétain and Haig had managed to achieve before New Year's Day 1918.

---

[46] Note sur le plan de campagne de 1918, 17 October 1917, *AFGG* 6/1, annex 13; SWC Joint Note 1, 13 December 1917, ibid., annex 179, and CAB 25/120/SWC 15.
[47] Foch to Weygand, 1 January 1918, *AFGG* 6/1, annex 226. See Doughty, *PV*, 408.

This document was followed on 6 January by another 'Note on the current situation', drawn up by Foch's staff, which he handed to the SWC. Taking up the idea of the SWC 'combining' the Allied action, the note stated that three tasks would have to be carried out after the expected enemy attack: husband reserves for the counter-attack; use the bare minimum of reserves to deal with the enemy; and determine the best moment to set the counter-attack in motion. These tasks could not be given to the CinCs because they would know only their own front. Nor could they be given to the SWC, which was a study group not able to take decisive action. Instead a superior command should be created that would cover at least the whole front from the North Sea to Switzerland. The French army chief of staff should fulfil that function.[48] Having delivered that broadside, Foch returned to Italy.

This return was at Clemenceau's insistence. Abel Ferry, prominent *député* and member of the Army Commission, had just returned from an inspection of the French army in Italy and had reported on the Italian army. His report recommended asking Italy for 100,000 labourers. As Clemenceau put it, 'we have 135,000 bayonets there, they can give us 100,000 shovels'.[49] After refusing Pétain's request for the return from Italy of the bayonets of one of the French corps, Clemenceau proposed sending Ferry back to Italy to extract the shovels. He was to take Foch with him to add weight to the arguments.

Ferry's report had criticised Foch over the reorganisation of the Italian army. In the Comité de guerre Foch came in for more criticism from Pétain over the matter and, according to Ferry, put up a 'lamentable' and stumbling defence. Indeed, Foch had written to Weygand, recommending that the SWC encourage the Italian army to regain its cohesion by means of a strong programme of instruction.[50] The SWC was hardly the place, however, for such practical considerations. Clemenceau remarked that he saw that 'General Foch declares on paper that all is well, but that is not the case in reality.' Despite his objections, Foch was ordered to accompany Ferry so as to arrange for an exchange of French and Italian officers. Ferry realised that Foch was annoyed by the criticism ('blessé dans son amour-propre de vieillard, qui ne pisse pas tous les jours') and did not in fact believe that the mission would be successful. Nonetheless Ferry made an effort to win Foch over (using heavy-calibre flattery); but, as he admitted, it was he himself who was won over. Ferry noted in his diary that Foch 'surpassed' all the generals he had known (and as one of

---

[48] Note sur la situation sur le front occidental, 6 January 1918, ibid., annex 237.
[49] Comité de guerre, séance du 3 janvier 1918, 3N 2.
[50] Letter, Foch to Weygand, 27 December 1917, 16N 1773.

the Army Commissioners he must have met a fair number), and Foch's supple and frank attitude when dealing with the Italians won them the 100,000 labourers. The Italians were still grateful for Foch's help after Caporetto. The return to France in the train with Foch was 'most cordial'.[51]

Whilst in Italy Foch agreed to General Fayolle's request to set up an exchange of officers between the French and Italian armies. Fayolle's aim was to attach experienced French staff officers to Italian divisional, corps and army staffs, since the French recognised that it was staff work that had let down the Italian troops. This arrangement was hindered by an insufficient number of qualified French staff officers, and Pétain could not spare any. However, Fayolle and his British counterpart, General Plumer, managed to encourage the Comando Supremo to set up instructional schools such as existed in the British and French armies.[52]

GQG did not wait for Foch's return before composing its response to his broadside. Its 'note' of 8 January, signed by Pétain, admitted that the 'principle' of an Allied offensive was 'unquestionable', yet the principle had to give way before the fact that no American weight would be felt before 1919. He supported his argument by painting a scenario of a double German attack, which the enemy was known to be capable of mounting. Counting the divisions on the hypothetical fronts, and the reserves that would be engaged in the hypothetical actions, Pétain concluded that after maintaining a general reserve of forty divisions a mere two divisions would be left to rotate with the divisions on the attacked front.[53] The 1918 battle would be a defensive one for both British and French, not because their commanders wanted it, but because the lack of resources imposed it.

French manpower resources were indeed diminished. Three divisions were suppressed in November 1917 and nine more suppressions were projected.[54] The critical food situation meant that older territorial troops needed to be freed for agricultural work. Hence the question of the British extension of their front became critical. Lloyd George and Painlevé had agreed that the BEF would take over more front back in September, although neither CinC had been present at the meeting. Haig's Passchendaele operations continued until mid-November, however, with the final gains 'falling short' of what he had wanted to secure before

---

[51] Ferry, *Carnets secrets*, entry for 4 November 1917, and 'Mission à Rome', 15 January 1918, 276–81.
[52] Secret report, Lt Col. T. B. Mott to Chief, Intelligence Section, AEF HQ, 10 February 1918, RG 120, Entry 268, folder 737-B.
[53] Pétain, Note, 8 January 1918, *AFGG* 6/1, annex 242.   [54] Details in Doughty, *PV*, 416.

the winter, and even these might be 'difficult and costly to hold if seriously attacked'.[55] Cambrai followed immediately thereafter, with its initial success on 20 November and subsequent disappointment as the Germans counter-attacked ten days later. As a consequence, the calls for some rest for the BEF were loud and understandable. The French did not see it that way. The British had undertaken Cambrai, some even suggested, to avoid having to take over more front. Haig's relief of the French Third Army (planned to begin on 12 December) was reduced to relief of a single corps, beginning on 10 January, with the British front extending to Barisis by the end of the month.[56]

Clemenceau suggested that the question of the extension of the British front should be put to the SWC to make a decision. Lloyd George agreed, and the PMRs set forth their finding in Joint Note 10 of 10 January 1918. The BEF should take over as far as the Ailette river, with the exact point of juncture to be settled by the two commanders, and arrangements made for intervention by either force in case of enemy attack. This is a classic example of the sort of decision that the PMRs could be expected to discuss and to settle in a non-partisan way. Haig and Pétain, however, showed their lack of respect for the institution by coming to their own private arrangement, which made the extension of the BEF's front less than the SWC had decreed. They showed further disdain by not communicating their scheme for mutual support in case of attack (agreement for which was reached at meetings on 21 and 22 February) until well into March. Finally, they showed what they thought of the SWC's scheme for a general reserve by refusing to cooperate with it. Peter Wright (one of the SWC's secretaries) suggests that the late communication of the mutual assistance scheme was a deliberate attempt to sabotage the general reserve.[57] Foch came back into the picture over this question.

Foch got back from Italy on 15 January and on the 18th had a long talk with Wilson. Wilson was working on a draft resolution about the 1918 campaign to put to the SWC, and had come to the conclusion that a central or general reserve was vital. He suggested that the Germans would make three attacks, beginning the last one only when all the Allied reserves were used up. Keeping a central reserve in hand was, therefore, crucial. Wilson had been promoting this scheme whilst Foch was in Italy, and now explained it to Foch. Not surprisingly Foch agreed, and thought the plan

---

[55] Prior and Wilson, *Passchendaele*, 179.
[56] Pétain to Haig, 14 December 1917, and Haig to Pétain, 18 December 1917, *AFGG* 6/1, annexes 182, 196.
[57] Wright, *At the Supreme War Council*, 86–7.

would 'do very well as a commencement'. He believed that Versailles needed some 'executive power & authority'.[58]

The next day (19th) the PMRs met and discussed Wilson's draft resolution about a general reserve. No size was proposed for it, but the administration of such a body would remain with the CinCs, whilst its 'employment' would be controlled by the SWC. In the face of Weygand's dissent – he said that a reserve without a single CinC was impossible – the PMRs reached no decision.[59] At their next meeting on 21 January, however, the PMRs accepted Wilson's draft plan for the 1918 campaign (it became Joint Note 12) and Weygand withdrew his opposition to a general reserve. He told Wilson that he was sorry he had objected to the plan and was now prepared to agree. Wilson noted that Weygand 'had evidently seen Foch'.[60] At their next meeting the PMRs managed to reach agreement on the text of Joint Note 14, creating a general reserve.[61] The note urged speedy acceptance by the respective governments, who should report the views of their CinCs and chiefs of staff on the 'forces, their placement and the command of this reserve'.

Most commentators see these proceedings as 'intrigues' on the part of Foch to acquire for himself supreme command.[62] Looked at from another point of view, Foch was someone who knew that Pétain would never do the job successfully, and knew that the supreme command had to be in French hands because the French army was the largest and the main front was in France. Most importantly, he knew himself. He had the necessary self-confidence to do what he felt had to be done. He did not hide his wish for supreme command. General Fayolle in Italy, for example, noted Foch's desire to replace Pétain and be the 'director' of the war.[63] This may be arrogant, but a commander who cannot exude confidence can never be a leader whom men will follow.

Foch was fortunate at this stage of his quest for supreme command. Both the British and French PMRs (once Foch had spoken to Weygand) supported the general reserve concept, and now were joined by a very committed American representative. General Tasker H. Bliss had attended the December SWC as the American army chief of staff and

[58] Wilson diary, 9, 10, 11, 18 January 1918.
[59] Minutes of 12th meeting of Military Representatives, 19 January 1918, CAB 25/120/ SWC51.
[60] Minutes of 13th meeting of Military Representatives, 21 January 1918, *AFGG* 6/1, annex 277; Wilson diary, 21 January 1918. Weygand's account of his change of heart is in *IV*, 463.
[61] Procès-verbal, 14th meeting of PMRs, 23 January 1918, *AFGG* 6/1, annex 282.
[62] Especially, of course, Pedroncini: *Pétain Général*, 257 (notes 3 and 4), 267.
[63] Fayolle *CS*, 251 (entry for 12 January 1918).

had returned to the USA with House. After collecting a small staff together he left again on 10 January, passing through London, where he was told about the lack of shipping to ease the manpower shortages, and leaving for Versailles on the 23rd. He became a trusted mediator when the PMRs were unable to reach agreement, and supported strongly the proposal for an Allied reserve.

Foch had a second advantage in that the 'opposition' was not united. Haig and Robertson were scornful, contemptuous even, of the SWC and its military members. Haig commented on Wilson's 'mathematical calculations' from one of his wargames that the BEF should extend his front: 'The whole position would be laughable but for the seriousness of it.'[64] For his part, Wilson was sure that Robertson was doing his best to sabotage the SWC by instigating a press campaign. (Wilson would win that struggle against Robertson, however.) The other focus of opposition was Pétain, but the French CinC had little sympathy or close working relationship with his British counterpart. He and Haig had not cooperated over planning the 1918 campaign despite knowing with certainty that a German attack was inevitable. Their cooperation over extending the British front so as to relieve the French, and over mutual assistance in case of attack, came about purely to avoid having solutions imposed on them by the SWC. Hence Foch could count on strong support from the PMRs and disunity among those who disliked the idea of supreme command that lurked behind the notion of an Allied general reserve.

Robertson arranged a meeting between the French and British chiefs of staff and CinCs, along with Pershing, to establish a measure of agreement *before* the next SWC meeting due at the end of the month. The aim was to 'get at Pershing and ascertain what he is doing' and also to learn what Haig and Pétain were proposing so that he (Robertson) and Foch could help to get done what was needed 'without the interference of the young men at Versailles'. (Foch told Wilson, Britain's 'young man at Versailles', about Robertson's 'little plot to squash the pitch' of the PMRs, about which Foch was 'much amused'.) Robertson explained what he hoped to achieve: to learn from Pershing himself what he intended to do to assist; to consider whether the 'elementary military principle' of a central reserve might be necessary in view of the coming battle; to consider the relative values of each sector of the front to settle what ground might be given up if forced to it and what ground must be kept; finally, to see whether any improvements might be made to railway communications, especially with Italy. The central reserve idea, Robertson hastened to make clear, did not

---

[64] Haig diary, 14 January 1918.

imply removing troops from their commanders, both of whom would continue to command in the west.[65]

At the meeting on 24 January in Compiègne, Pétain's headquarters, Robertson asked what the plans of the CinCs were for mutual support. This led both Pétain and Haig into a discussion of their diminished manpower resources and their respective plans for limited offensives (four French and three British had been earmarked). This caused Foch to lay down the battlelines. The best method of countering a powerful and persistent enemy offensive, Foch asserted, was to carry out a similarly powerful offensive. All available forces, both French and British, must be used for a single plan, not compartmentalised according to the front held by one or the other. Invoking the Somme as the example of a successful counter-attack foiling a powerful enemy onslaught at Verdun, he insisted that a unified plan to be executed when and where the Allies chose with all the means at their disposal had to be prepared well in advance. The Somme could not have been launched without the many months of preparation that had preceded it. He stated that no plans had been made for the '*final battle*' using available British and French troops, as well as American. He wanted no more offensive fronts such as Pétain and Haig had prepared, but a long-term plan.[66]

This is not to say that the Somme had been fought to relieve Verdun. As seen in chapter 7, the Somme had been agreed before the Germans attacked at Verdun. The point here is that the Somme offensive had been decided in principle in December 1915, its date and location had been decided in February 1916, and it began as planned on 1 July. There had been no point 'waiting and seeing' what transpired at Verdun before starting to plan the Somme. It was now already 1918, nearing the end of January, and at the beginning of the month French intelligence had already reported 157 German divisions on the Western Front.[67] By 15 February that number would have increased to 195, the whereabouts of 176 of them being known.[68] Small wonder that Foch's patience was wearing thin.

Certainly Haig and Pétain had been dragging their feet over planning the 1918 campaign. They had only just agreed (contrary to the SWC

[65] Wilson diary, 18 January 1918; Robertson to Haig, 12 and 21 January 1918, in Woodward (ed.), *Robertson Correspondence*, # 205, 206; Haig to Robertson, 20 January 1918, Robertson mss, 7/7/81; Foch to Pétain, 16 January 1918, 16N 1773.

[66] Procès-verbal de la conférence tenue le 24 janvier 1918, au G.Q.G., à Compiègne, *AFGG* 6/1, annex 287.

[67] Rapport du 6 janvier 1918, dated 5 January 1918, ibid., annex 235.

[68] Eventualité d'une offensive allemande sur le front occidental, 15 February 1918, ibid., annex 366.

solution) the extent of the British relief of the French front. They were talking about the mutual support scheme, but the final details were settled only late in February. Longer-term planning was restricted to asking for the return of divisions from Italy and calculations of how many divisions would have to be suppressed for lack of manpower. Foch appears to have been especially aggressive at the meeting. (His wife noted that he had returned from Italy buoyed by his reception there, which may have been a contributing factor.[69]) The several accounts of it all note the acrimony. Haig recorded that Foch 'talked most volubly over the advantages of acting offensively', hence much time was 'wasted'. Spears noted that the two French generals 'were rather short with each other'. Haig concluded that it was evident 'that Pétain thought little of Foch, and that there is considerable friction between them'. There was friction also, according to Haig, between Pétain and Pershing over how little, in the former's view, the Americans were doing 'to fit themselves for battle'.[70]

All in all, not a very productive meeting, and little practical progress was made. Pétain's chief of staff, General Anthoine, said that Foch had made little impression on the two commanders, and liaison officer Herbillon reflected that Foch was predisposed to take a stand against their ideas, which were so different from his own.[71] Foch's former liaison officer for the Somme battle, Colonel Dillon, summed it up neatly: 'The conference was a normal one; no conclusions were reached. It appears that the chief episode was a fight between Pétain and Foch in which the latter lost and made himself rather ridiculous.'[72]

In fact, the dispute was less than it seemed. All agreed that only an offensive could defeat the enemy. Robertson accepted this; and Haig had had to be dissuaded, after all, from continuing the offensive in Flanders. Even Pétain agreed in principle, but he argued that he did not have the means. Moreover, he told Spears afterwards that he had 'painted the situation "particularly black to frighten the Americans", saying "il n'y a rien à faire avec ces gens-là [you can't do anything with these people]"'. So there was no fundamental disagreement with Foch, but rather a divergence of views over how much could be achieved in the coming months.

The benefit from the acrimonious meeting was that there could be no misunderstanding over where each stood. Some practical proposals emerged. Robertson suggested the very next day that he set up direct

[69] Mme Foch diary, 16 January 1918; Wilson diary, 18 January 1918.
[70] Haig diary, 24 January 1918; Spears diary, 24 January 1918.
[71] Herbillon, *Du général*, 2: 198 (entry for 24 January 1918).
[72] Dillon, *Three Wars*, 107. See also Doughty, *PV*, 409–11, and Pedroncini, *Pétain Général*, 248–50.

liaison and 'closer touch' with Foch and Weygand. Once the anticipated battle started, he would move over to live in France with a staff of twelve.[73] Foch agreed to put forward this proposal, but Robertson's removal from office in mid-February finished off this idea. Clemenceau told Herbillon that he envisaged an Allied 'army of manoeuvre' composed of troops from all the Allies, but that the question of who should command it was yet to be considered. Herbillon had already heard this concept bruited widely; and later he heard from Mordacq that Clemenceau favoured Foch for the job.[74] Clemenceau told Wilson in the presence of Lloyd George and Milner that he wanted a large reserve of forty divisions and that he could not accept control of it by France's PMR. Also, Clemenceau told Spears that he accepted the necessity for a general reserve and Spears' suggestion that it be commanded by the chiefs of staff, not by the CinCs, who would each 'look to their front'.[75] Consequently, if Foch had lost the battle in Compiègne on 24 January, he had not lost the war.

The next meeting of the SWC in Versailles between 30 January and 2 February vindicated his views. After much talk about manpower, the SWC accepted thirteen of the fourteen joint notes presented to it. Thus Joint Note 12 on the 1918 campaign, which foresaw little possibility of a decision in favour of the Allies that year even if there was equally little chance of an enemy victory, advised that an offensive against Turkey should be undertaken (after Lloyd George accepted that no troops would be taken from the Western Front for this purpose). However, the fact that the Allies felt confident in their ability to resist an enemy attack on the Western Front did not mean that their defence would be merely passive. An annex to the note spelled out what this meant. Weygand claims that the annex was his addition, but it bears a remarkable resemblance to Foch's letter of 1 January! The acceptance of this annex represented a contradiction: the note prescribes the defensive in the west with an offensive against the Turks, whilst the annex recommends preparing a Western Front operation.

This third session of the SWC also decided to accept the notes concerning the extension of the British front and the creation of a general reserve. Haig had protested that he could not comply with the furthest extension proposed, or even the compromise half-way extension in the note, but he and Pétain agreed privately that the extension carried out so far (up to Barisis on the Oise) was sufficient. This negated the whole purpose of submitting the question to the military representatives, and

[73] Spears diary, 25 January 1918.
[74] Herbillon, Du général, 2: 200, 201 (entries for 25 and 29 January 1918).
[75] Wilson diary, 30 January 1918; Spears diary, 26 January 1918.

may have been done to show them that they were not needed. It would certainly explain why Pétain was content, telling Haig that he would not bother him about the extra front decreed by the joint note.[76]

The general reserve provoked more discussion. After acceptance of the principle, it was agreed to constitute an 'executive committee' to manage the reserve (it became known as the Executive War Board in English, although the French continued to refer to it as executive committee). Lloyd George pointed out that the PMRs' joint note omitted to designate a chairman for the committee. He proposed Foch to preside, claiming that Foch's name inspired total confidence not only because of his military knowledge and experience but also because of his complete loyalty to the Alliance. The Prime Minister recalled Foch's role in Flanders in 1914, and his similar role in Italy in 1917. 'They could be quite sure that as President of the Committee, General Foch would be quite unbiased.' On being asked if America would accept this nomination, General Bliss replied that Foch's name alone justified his designation. According to Hankey, Foch was so overcome by this praise that he was unable to speak.[77]

Foch lost no time in putting the EWB to work. It met for the first time the next day, 3 February. It was, after all, an 'executive' committee and Foch clearly expected that he would be able to 'execute' a policy as a result of the committee's deliberations. The members of the committee were the same as the PMRs except that Foch replaced Weygand. This meant that the PMRs were duplicating themselves to some extent, but with this difference. The French member was now someone of greater authority than Weygand; and Foch was the permanent president, unlike in the PMR meetings when the presidency rotated among the members. The British saw the implication immediately. Haig noted that the decision made 'Foch a "Generalissimo"' to some extent, although he (Haig) believed that he and Pétain got on so well with each other that 'no co-ordinating authority' was necessary as far as they were concerned. General Rawlinson (still in command of Fourth Army but shortly to replace Henry Wilson at Versailles) 'gathered' that Foch had been appointed 'Generalissimo'.[78] The American representative, General Bliss, being more pragmatic and less concerned with prestige, was opposed to the whole idea, arguing that it was a waste of effort and resources to create an organisation to do

---

[76] Haig diary, 2 February 1918.
[77] Minutes of the 5th Meeting, Third Session, IC 43, CAB 28/3; Hankey, *Supreme Command*, 2: 769. Mme Foch records Weygand's account of Lloyd George's praise: diary, 2 February 1918.
[78] Haig diary, 2 February 1918; Rawlinson diary, 6 February 1918, RWLN 1/9.

something which another organisation had already been created to do. The result, he wrote to Secretary for War Newton D. Baker, would be 'unnecessary confusion, friction and delay, at a time when there should exist the utmost clearness of cool and unbiased vision, the utmost harmony, and the utmost rapidity of action'.[79] As events were to demonstrate, Bliss was not wrong.

Although Clemenceau had suggested that the committee create a large reserve of forty divisions, they settled for an initial reserve of thirty French, British and Italian divisions, to include the British and French ones currently in Italy. After some bad-tempered argument over whether the British should contribute nine or ten divisions and the French fourteen or thirteen along with the seven Italian, they agreed the draft of a letter to be sent to the commanders-in-chief informing them of the constitution of the reserve, which it was hoped would be created rapidly. Foch had attempted to railroad the committee, when they split two against two over the number of British divisions to be earmarked, by giving a 'casting vote' in his own favour; but Wilson objected and the committee decided that no voting would take place.[80]

The note describing the EWB's decision was sent to Pétain with a brief covering letter from Foch on 7 February. Naturally Pétain was not pleased, and criticised Foch for his 'crooked' action. Clive reported his views thus: 'he thinks that Gen: Foch has ruined every chance that Versailles had, by forcing the pace since the Conference, and making the peremptory demand for 30 divisions without any attempt to get the C.'s in C. into a mood to agree'.[81] Nonetheless, Pétain agreed to earmark eight divisions, despite allegedly telling Repington that 'if anyone attempted to touch his reserves he would resign'.[82]

As for Haig, Wilson was to give a copy of the note to him personally, but the row that had been simmering between Lloyd George and Robertson now boiled over, and both Wilson and Haig were recalled to London. As a result Wilson replaced Robertson as CIGS, and Rawlinson was chosen to replace Wilson at Versailles. Rawlinson wrote of Foch in his diary: 'I think I can manage him all right, but he will want watching.'[83] In fact Rawlinson remained suspicious of Foch's motives throughout the remainder of his time as Britain's PMR on the council. He warned Wilson, for example, that the cause of Foch's 'present mulish attitude' was that he (Foch)

[79] Cited in Palmer, *Bliss, Peacemaker*, 240.
[80] Minutes of 2nd and 3rd EWB meetings, 5 and 6 February 1918, CAB 25/119.
[81] Letter, Clive to Robertson, 12 February 1918, Robertson mss, 8/5/95.
[82] Clive diary, 8 February 1918, CAB 45/201. This is hearsay evidence, but is plausible.
[83] Rawlinson diary, 23 February 1918, RWLN 1/9. On the supersession of Robertson see Woodward (ed.), *Robertson Correspondence*, ch. 11; and Jeffery, *Wilson*, 210–18.

intended either to claim 'very extended powers' for the EWB, or else to kill it.[84]

Consequent upon this British-caused hiatus, the EWB did not meet again until 2 March. Foch was now even more impatient and bad-tempered. The French and Italian CinCs had responded to the EWB's letter, offering respectively eight divisions and six of the seven requested; but nothing had been received from Haig. Equally the demand that the CinCs communicate their offensive plans to the PMRs for the SWC had been met by the French and Italian commands, but once again the British had not complied. Foch noted formally (according to the British minutes of the meeting which are much fuller than the bare official record of decisions taken) that 'they could not get on with their plans of general co-ordination because the English [sic] Commander-in-Chief had not sent in his schemes'. Rawlinson's excuse for Haig's delay was that his own nomination to replace Wilson 'had introduced further delays and the letter of the 6th February had only formally reached the FIELD MARSHAL the day before yesterday'. Rawlinson's careful choice of words – Foch's '*letter*' of 6 February had only just '*formally*' reached Haig – did not deflect Foch. He interrupted Rawlinson's attempted excuse, saying that Rawlinson 'no doubt meant the official intimation', rather than the fact of the request for divisions for the reserve.[85]

The British official history claims that Haig did not get the EWB letter until 27 February. This may be true literally, but Haig certainly knew what the letter required before he actually set eyes on it.[86] Did Haig wait deliberately until it was too late to supply divisions because the expected German attack was now too close? This is certainly the impression gained from Bliss' attempts to mediate. Bliss noted that Haig had forgotten that the earmarked divisions were *not* to be removed from their own army command until being called upon, when they would come under the commander whose front was being supported. However, Haig told Bliss explicitly during the London SWC meetings that Foch would have 'practical control' and that he (Haig) was 'afraid that his divisions would be taken away from him'.[87] Foch seemed to think that Haig was refusing wilfully to accede to the general reserve. He told Clive that Haig 'had not answered for a month and then refused everything'. It was not his personal

---

[84] Letter, Rawlinson to Wilson, 8 March 1918, enclosing minutes of 6th EWB meeting, Wilson mss, HHW 2/25.

[85] 'Secret and confidential minutes . . . made for the British section alone', 4th EWB meeting, 2 March 1918, CAB 25/119, fo. 48.

[86] Edmonds *et al.*, *OH 1918*, 1: 81; Rawlinson diary, 21 February 1918; Haig diary, 24 and 25 February 1918.

[87] Bliss to General March [Chief of Staff, Washington], 10 April 1918, Bliss mss, cont. 250.

orders that a reserve should be formed, but their governments' orders.[88] Clive, however, was working to bolster Rawlinson's resolve to support the joint arrangements between Haig and Pétain rather than to support Foch's general reserve. Then Clemenceau added his weight to the CinCs rather than to Foch.

Despite attempts by Bliss and Giardino (*vice* Cadorna since 8 February) to suggest compromises, Foch refused to be mollified. 'No bargaining', the British minutes recorded him as saying during the meeting on 4 March: 'Either we are to have it or we are not to have it. I cannot understand it, on the 2nd February everyone agreed to a General Reserve, and on 4th March the FIELD MARSHAL refuses. I have waited a month and I am not going to wait any longer.' Consequently, the EWB sent a joint note to the SWC, dated 7 March, stating that agreement had been reached with the French and Italian CinCs on constituting the general reserve that the council had decreed. The British commander, however, regretted that he could not comply. As a result the EWB was unable to carry out the function which it had been set up to perform, and each representative was 'to so inform his Government and ask for instructions'.[89] These instructions, for Foch, were to wait for the next full SWC session. The EWB itself met twice more: at 3pm on 21 March (by which time the Germans had begun their attacks), and on 23 March, when they agreed to bring back divisions from Italy. The general reserve had shrunk to seven divisions (four Italian, two French and one British), none of them anywhere near northern France.

Bliss claimed in his postwar report on the SWC that, had the reserve been in place, matters might have turned out differently on the days between 21 and 26 March, when the German attacks came near to splitting the French and British armies. Those divisions that had been earmarked for the reserve would have been moved more quickly, but the two CinCs might have had to suffer many more anxious moments as the reserves under their own hand dwindled. Bliss blamed the British government for not enforcing Haig's compliance with the general reserve, and stated: 'Had it been formed early in February as the Executive War Board with its limited powers tried its best to do, the defeat of the British 5th Army on March 21st would most certainly have been promptly checked.'[90] So Foch's bad-tempered handling of the EWB achieved

[88] Clive diary, 11 March 1918.
[89] Joint Note EWB 2, 7 March 1918, CAB 25/120/SWC104.
[90] Bliss, Report of the General Operations of the Supreme War Council, 6 February 1920, in *FRUS, Lansing Papers*, 2: 262.

naught, and the London session of the SWC on 14 and 15 March completed his discomfiture.

The question of the general reserve was the first to be discussed. Clive summed up the proceedings succinctly: 'Foch alone – and beat.' The Allied troops in Italy were all that would constitute the reserve, since Pétain now stated that he could spare no divisions from the front in France.[91] Haig expressed the same point of view with slightly more glee: 'Clemenceau then thoroughly sat on Foch!' In the face of the united stand of the CinCs not to contribute to the reserve, but to rely on their private arrangements, there was little the SWC or Foch could do. A 'masterly' resolution was contrived by Hankey, and despite Foch's vigorous protest was passed. Foch complained that an executive council had been formed but had been deprived of all executive powers. In this he received support from the Americans: Bliss pointed out that the heads of government who formed the SWC had not given any power of veto to the CinCs over the executive board that it had constituted.[92] However, both Lloyd George and Clemenceau contradicted Foch. On the contrary, the EWB had a very important task to carry out, and the nucleus of the general reserve had been decided, which would be extended gradually as American divisions arrived in France.[93] The principle of a general reserve was retained by nominating the divisions in Italy; but those divisions were little use so far away. The French intelligence service had reported on 11 March that the Germans had just changed their codes.[94] Consequently, since they always did this eight to ten days before they launched an attack, little time remained to get the divisions back. Equally, there could be no question of replacing the CinCs at this stage for refusing to obey orders.

Foch returned to the fray the next day. Accepting that the original concept of the general reserve was dead ('we stopped the enemy' on the Marne, on the Yser and on the Piave without such a reserve), he asked for an extension of the SWC's powers by establishing a close liaison with the various armies. He pointed out that he had not received their plans of campaign. The council passed a resolution taking note of Foch's statement, recommending that the Pétain–Haig arrangements for support should be communicated to the PMRs at Versailles.[95] Foch was still 'very sore' about the decision when he saw Wilson that evening.

[91] 'Thursday's meeting', n.d., Clive notebooks, CAB 45/201.
[92] Palmer, *Bliss, Peacemaker*, 249.
[93] 'Procès-verbal of the second meeting of the Fourth Session of the SWC, 14 March 1918', IC 48, CAB 28/3.
[94] Mordacq, *MC*, 1: 217–18.
[95] 'Procès-verbal of the third meeting of the Fourth Session of the SWC, 15 March 1918', IC 50, CAB 28/3.

Weygand had already apologised for his own 'heat' the previous day, and said that, for the first time in the war, Foch was being 'a little difficult'![96]

This raises the question of Clemenceau's attitude to Foch at this juncture. He had already indicated his earlier support for putting Foch into supreme command, and Foch seems to have believed him.[97] Clemenceau told the Senate Army Commission on 20 February that 'insuperable objections' remained to unified command but that the question had been approached much more closely in the SWC than ever before.[98] Yet all the accounts of the London SWC session agree that Clemenceau squashed Foch comprehensively. On the other hand, Clemenceau had also told Haig that the 'surest guarantee of success' was close agreement between the two CinCs. He reassured Haig that he 'would arrange to "écarter" (set aside) Foch gradually'.[99] Yet, three days later, Clemenceau agreed with his military advisor, General Mordacq, that unity of command was essential and that Foch was the man to exercise it ('take the rudder').[100] It would appear that Clemenceau had some idea of taking military control himself. He alarmed Poincaré by stating that he would be able to settle any disputes between Foch and Pétain because, at the moment of any attack, he would be there.[101] Certainly he interfered in purely tactical matters. (For example, he wrote a highly critical letter to Pétain about the construction of the first and second defensive positions.)[102] Either Clemenceau was now regretting Foch's getting so much control, hence was trying to put him down deliberately; or else he was playing a long game, so that when eventually the British had to ask for unified command they could not say that he had been angling to put Foch in all along. There is some support for the latter interpretation. When Wilson told Clemenceau that the problem was that he and Foch were right to insist upon a general reserve, and that Clemenceau, Haig and Pétain were wrong, 'The Tiger agreed absolutely.'[103] Another possibility is that Clemenceau simply did not wish to go against the Haig–Pétain agreement and set up a new arrangement when the expected German offensive was likely to take place soon. He told Spears that he would not interfere, saying that he could not be said 'to be a "Petainite", yet as he is the Commander-in-Chief he must be given a free hand'. Clemenceau had assured Pétain that he would support him

[96] Wilson diary, 16 March 1918.   [97] Ibid., 23 January 1918.
[98] Audition du Président du Conseil, 20 February 1918, fo. 10096, Archives du Sénat.
[99] Haig diary, 24 February 1918.   [100] Mordacq, *MC*, 1: 186 (27 February 1918).
[101] Poincaré, *AS*, 10: 58 (22 February 1918).
[102] Président du Conseil to Pétain, 8 February 1918, *AFGG* 6/1, annex 340.
[103] Wilson diary, 17 March 1918.

and Haig in the London meeting and not permit the reserves to be handled by Versailles in a manner contrary to their wishes.[104]

Foch queried (correctly) Clemenceau's commitment to Versailles. He had been chosen by the British and Italians, but abandoned by Clemenceau in London. Bitterly Foch told Haig after the meeting: 'Only in London can military matters now be regulated.'[105] This situation, Foch wrote in his notebook a few days later, would harm the French interest in the SWC. Clemenceau ought to have supported Foch in London and not 'flirted' with Haig and Pétain. The SWC ought to study the war from the world-wide perspective, and not be restricted to the Franco-British front. Clemenceau was simply being dragged along in the wake of the British, who were thinking solely of domestic politics and of 'the battle with their generals'. So long as it was a question of preparing and organising the war against the Germans, then Foch was your man, he concluded; but the war was 'expiring, languishing'.[106] There could be no clearer expression of his frustration with events just days before the start of the German offensives, and no clearer statement of the reasons for his impatience during the EWB meetings.

Foch's frustration and impatience were entirely understandable. Lloyd George had created the SWC in order to get rid of Robertson. In this he had succeeded, but the march of events in Russia merely proved the SWC's inadequacy when it came to coordinating strategy. Foch had no standing on the SWC until the EWB was established to control an Allied reserve. Haig and Pétain combined to destroy such a reserve before it was created. Foch's relationship with Pétain was difficult. The division of powers between the CinC and the army chief of staff was never clearly delineated. This had mattered less when Pétain was busy with the reforms that put the French army back on its feet. When, however, they met in conference to settle the 1918 campaign, the very real differences in their views and strategic outlook came to the fore. Far from establishing a coordinated programme to counter the increasing German threat, the SWC had simply laid bare the lack of coordination and lack of basic agreement.

The SWC had not even settled the question of Japanese intervention in Siberia. During the two sessions following the silencing of Foch over the general reserve question, the political leaders discussed Siberia and also the possibility of intervention in northern Russia through Arkangel. After much inconclusive talk Balfour was charged with the preparation of a joint

[104] Letter M602, Spears to Wilson, 10 March 1918, Wilson papers, HHW/2/14A/5; Clive diary, 12 March 1918.
[105] Haig diary, 14 March 1918.   [106] Foch, Carnets, 19 March 1918, fo. 297.

document to be submitted to President Wilson. The draft dispatch laid out the arguments for intervention – Japan had the manpower and tonnage to be able resist German domination in Siberia – and accepted that such action would lose half its moral authority unless the USA approved. Thus the President was invited to give consideration to the proposed policy.[107]

Time was running out rapidly. By the time of the London meetings of the SWC – when the Allies also agreed to publish Clemenceau's declaration noting the 'unprecedented outrage perpetrated, under the name of a German peace, on the Russian peoples'[108] – Ludendorff had been freed from the need to consider the Eastern Front. Despite Lenin's and Trotsky's delaying tactics in hopes of inspiring workers in the west to rise up against the war, the Treaty of Brest-Litovsk had been signed between the Bolshevik government and the Central Powers on 3 March. Earlier the Russians had walked out of the negotiations and broken off the armistice, but the Germans simply invaded even more Russian territory. Since there was no longer any Russian army, and since the strikes and mutinies in Germany had been suppressed (although unrest continued in Vienna), Lenin had no cards left to play. So ended Russia's part in the Great War. In George Kennan's elegant words, the treaty represented 'the final stages of that process by which the Russia of World War I was transformed from a failing ally of the Entente into a sullen and disarmed bystander, partially occupied by the enemy, ruled by a group of men who loathed both warring camps with every fiber of their fanatical and profoundly political natures'.[109]

The treaty detached former Russian lands west of the Riga–Brest-Litovsk line (thus some Baltic provinces and Poland came under the Central Powers' jurisdiction), and deprived Russia of much of its coal and heavy industry capability. Also the Russians evacuated the rich lands of the Ukraine, whose delegates had settled a peace treaty with the Central Powers (also at Brest-Litovsk) on 8 February. At least the Western powers now knew what a German peace entailed. Although military action did not stop in the east, finally Ludendorff could concentrate his attention on his strategic gamble for victory in France.

Once again Foch had had impressed upon him the supremacy of the civil power. After sacking him from the Northern Army Group in 1916,

---

[107] 'Despatch to the United States of America', 16 March 1918, IC 52, appendix II, CAB 28/3.

[108] 'Text of the joint declaration published by the Allied governments in conference', ibid., appendix III.

[109] Kennan, *Russia Leaves the War*, 377.

the politicians had squashed his Executive War Board. Thus he had received a second lesson in the limits of power. More positively, he obtained a much wider perspective on the war from his 'special studies' and then from his international contacts. Much of his time as chief of the army staff was spent in conference. The intervention in Italy was a particularly useful dry run for the Western Front in March 1918. Thus his experiences in 1917 were, as it turned out, excellent training for the sorts of problems that supreme command would bring as Ludendorff made his strategic gamble.

12 MICHAEL and GEORGETTE, March–April 1918

Foch returned from London on 18 March. The first of the five German offensives in 1918 on the Western Front, operation MICHAEL (see Map 13), began three days later. The stunning German successes of the opening days supplied, at last, the opportunity for the creation of an Allied unified command.

Operation MICHAEL had been long in the planning. Ludendorff knew that a decision had to be reached as to the war's outcome before the Americans began arriving in great numbers. His general aim was to punch a hole through the front, and to roll up the BEF against the sea. He seems, however, to have wavered over the precise objectives for the three armies devoted to MICHAEL. The offensive covered a 103-kilometre-wide front between the rivers Scarpe (at Arras) and Oise (the junction of British and French armies). Impressive staff work assembled the troops of those three armies with their reserves, positioned 6608 guns, and succeeded in fooling the Allies as to the exact area to be attacked. The artillery expert, Colonel Georg Bruchmüller, had drawn up a bigger version of the fire direction schemes that had proved so successful in Riga; and 125 squadrons of aircraft were hidden well away from enemy reconnaissance. The attack divisions (*Angriffsdivisionen*) had trained and been rested well away from the front, and they were supplemented with specialist units (communications, engineering, medical and so on). The supply question was the most difficult. Difficulties caused by poor roads and railways in terrain which had been fought over for years were exacerbated by lack of motor lorries (as well as rubber for tyres and petrol), and lack of horses for pulling the guns.[1] Troops did not receive the full allocation of food and ammunition. The historian Gerhard Ritter was in the front line near Saint-Quentin, an officer in *Eighteenth Army*. He remembered 'wretchedly equipped supply units, the makeshift vehicles, the dejected nags with their bones sticking out, the largely overage, poorly trained, and thoroughly weary men'.[2] The weather,

---

[1] Zabecki, *German 1918 Offensives*, 86–8.   [2] Ritter, *Sword and Scepter*, 4: 229.

Map 13 Operation MICHAEL, March 1918

however, was on Germany's side. Fine weather had enabled their own necessary reconnaissances of Allied positions, then a couple of wet days prevented the Allies from discovering what was happening, and finally the fine weather returned, creating early-morning fog on the opening day of the attack, 21 March.

Those 6608 guns plus 3535 trench mortars fired 3.2 million rounds on that day, and when the fifty *Angriffsdivisionen* attacked they faced two British armies, General Byng's Third and General Gough's Fifth – a total of twenty-six infantry divisions and 2686 guns (only about one-third of them heavy). Not surprisingly, given the huge disparity, the Germans made large gains. They advanced five kilometres on the 21st, another five the next day, and a further sixteen kilometres on 23 March. Such an advance recalls Caporetto and contrasts with, for example, the British results on 1 July 1916, the first day of the Somme, namely between zero and 1500 *metres*.

Despite being the government's technical adviser, Foch played no role during these days, for Clemenceau did not seek his advice. Instead Clemenceau intervened directly, going to see Pétain at GQG (on 23, 24 and 25 March) and Poincaré in the Elysée on each day of the offensive, with a Conseil des ministres meeting on the 25th. Nor did the SWC convene and request Foch's views. As all had feared, a council was no use in a crisis. In any case, following its decisions in London, the SWC had no reserves for Foch to use.

Given Foch's anger at the preference shown in London for the Haig–Pétain mutual assistance arrangements over the Executive War Board's General Reserve, his impatience at being side-lined may be imagined. Late on 23 March he ordered the commander of the French troops in Italy to return two divisions to France beginning at midday on 25th. The British and French troops in Italy had been earmarked for the reserve, it will be remembered; yet they were not even to hand when needed.

On 23 March Ludendorff's aim changed focus to separating the French and British armies. And not only that: after having separated them the British were to be driven northwestwards into the sea, and the French were to be driven southwestwards. Thus Ludendorff's objectives increased in scope, and on 24 March the *Eighteenth Army* continued across the Somme. Yet it was beginning to falter through fatigue and lack of supplies, despite the human resources in the form of reserve divisions that it had received.[3]

Foch held his peace until 24 March, by which date it was clear that the mutual assistance plan was insufficient. Fifth Army had been destroyed or dispersed, and the Germans had driven an eighty-kilometre wedge between British and French. Pétain was sending reserves, but the British were being forced back northwards and the breach between the British and the French was widening.[4] That morning Pétain sent liaison officer Herbillon to Paris to instruct the government to put pressure on the British to make them do more than they were doing, and to ask Clemenceau to come to GQG in Compiègne that evening. The Premier had already visited Compiègne the previous evening and found army morale to be 'not very brilliant'. Returning to Paris he told Mordacq that, in order to retain any confidence 'after such an interview, you needed

---

[3] Zabecki, *German 1918 Offensives*, 144–6.
[4] For the details of French units sent to the danger zone, see Greenhalgh, 'Myth and Memory'.

a cast-iron constitution'. Nonetheless, he admitted, Pétain was taking action, even if perhaps he did tend to 'see the bad side of events a little too much'.[5]

Foch set down his thoughts in a note for Clemenceau that he handed over personally at 4pm on 24 March, just as the Premier was about to leave for Compiègne to see Pétain again. Thus Foch and his memorandum arrived in between Clemenceau's two visits to Pétain. Foch set out the position as he saw it. The enemy's offensive seemed to have been stopped in the south, but the danger lay in the north, where there were fewer natural obstacles to impede the enemy's progress. Also in the north were two important resources which ought not to be allowed to fall into enemy hands: the railway and road junctions around Amiens, and the coalfields around Béthune and Bruay. In his study of Pétain's command, Professor Pedroncini scorns Foch for not knowing that the danger lay in the enemy action in the south, where most German gains were made, but this is to miss the point.[6] Foch recognised what it was important to defend, and he could not be expected to be as up to date with the military situation as the CinC at headquarters.

He laid out three measures to counter the danger to Allied communications in the north: a step-by-step defence of the vulnerable terrain; action to hold the British to this; and, because however good those British troops were they were outnumbered, a large French reserve concentrated northeast of Amiens to deal with unexpected enemy action or to counter-attack. He suggested that Pétain should be so advised; that Haig should be asked to make known his resources and to hold on; and finally that the 'directing body of the war [presumably the SWC or its EWB] should oversee the execution of these directives once they had been issued'. Otherwise, Foch concluded, the coalition risked having to deal with 'a battle with serious consequences, inadequately prepared, inadequately put in train, and inadequately executed'.[7] These were strong words, and clearly Clemenceau understood the implied criticism. He asked Foch if he was abandoning him. Foch replied that he never abandoned anyone, but 'it was time for everyone to shoulder their responsibilities'.[8]

An hour later, Foch telephoned Henry Wilson, and they agreed that 'someone must catch a hold or we shall be beaten'. Wilson decided to go to France (he left early the next morning). Milner had already left at 12.30, instructed by Lloyd George to report on the situation. (Haig's claims that

[5] Herbillon, *Du général*, 2: 229–31; Mordacq, *Commandement unique*, 59.
[6] Pedroncini, *Pétain Général*, 317–19.
[7] Foch to Clemenceau, 24 March 1918, *AFGG* 6/1, annex 603.   [8] Weygand, *Foch*, 187.

it was his intervention after a late meeting with Pétain on the 24th that brought Milner and Wilson to France are thus disproved easily.)

Clemenceau left for Compiègne after speaking to Foch, taking Mordacq with him. Consequently when he arrived there on the evening of 24 March it was with the memory of the previous evening's conversation with Pétain and that afternoon's conversation with Foch. Returning to Paris after this second meeting, Clemenceau agreed with Mordacq that they, the French, needed to take over the 'strategic direction' of the war, just as earlier in the war it was the French who had stopped German advances, on the Yser, before Ypres and before Verdun. Clemenceau agreed totally when Mordacq urged that they should take advantage of the situation to get the British, Italians and Americans to agree to the designation of Foch as Allied leader.[9] Clearly the direction of the war could not be left to Haig and Pétain, because the latter believed that if they were beaten it would be the fault of the British.[10]

Thus the worsening military situation gave Clemenceau the opportunity to work for Allied unified command. Pétain was still trying to retain contact with Haig and the BEF. He told the Minister for Armaments, Louis Loucheur, that he would not sacrifice Amiens, and that he would go to see Haig personally about restoring the junction of their armies. (This is the famous night meeting after which Haig claimed that he had telegraphed for 'Foch or some other French general who would fight' to take charge – a post hoc and untrue addition to his diary.)

On his return to Paris, Loucheur found that he could not speak to Clemenceau about the serious situation that Pétain had described, because the Premier had just set off for GQG himself. Consequently Loucheur contacted Foch, who came to his office immediately, thereby betraying his (Foch's) impatience and desire to be doing. Loucheur recalled Foch pacing his office like a caged lion. Foch described the situation as 'serious, certainly, but by no means desperate'. He likened the military position to double doors that had been pushed open with each general behind his own door. Whoever pushed back first risked exposing his army. Both generals had resisted the push against the doors 'magnificently', but what was required now was someone to catch hold and to prevent any further retirements. On being asked how he would stop the Germans in Haig's or Pétain's place, Foch replied that he would use his usual method: sticking patches here, there, wherever. Eventually the Germans would come to a halt and the patches of reserves would have covered all the holes.

[9] Mordacq, *Commandement unique*, 63.
[10] Poincaré, *AS*, 10: 86 (entry for 25 March 1918).

Foch also told Loucheur what he had said to Clemenceau about British objections to unified command – that without it they risked a 'catastrophe'. Clemenceau's liaison efforts between Haig and Pétain were not enough. Both generals agreed with Clemenceau when they met in his presence, but afterwards 'each worked separately', albeit 'conscientiously'; and the Germans were taking advantage of this. Loucheur recorded that he was greatly affected by Foch's words and that he hoped to talk to Clemenceau soon.[11]

Thus by 25 March, when both Milner and Wilson were in France, Foch had stated his case for the need for someone to take strategic direction to both Clemenceau and to an influential minister, both of whom had also visited GQG and spoken to Pétain. Foch wrote in his notebook a simple statement of what needed to be done (see Illustration 8):

General P is seeking the liaison with the British right. That's good, [but] not enough. Marshal Haig is pulling back – is going to say his troops are tired ... We must stop him, support him. We must organise so as to have a [mass?] in Amiens so as to counter everything – with this aim put pressure on Pétain.[12]

He was not simply sitting back and waiting for the supreme command to fall into his lap.

The Allied response came together on 25 March. Milner saw Clemenceau in Paris early that morning and found him 'in great form and very full of fight'.[13] He told Milner that important decisions needed to be taken 'at once', and that the junction between the British and French armies must be maintained at all cost. He repeated the argument that Foch had given him in the previous day's memorandum: the danger lay in the north. Clemenceau thought that Pétain would require pressure to make him do more in that respect, and he proposed a meeting of all parties – including Foch – at Compiègne that evening. However, Foch had already arranged to go with Weygand to meet Haig and Wilson at Abbeville, but on hearing just as he was about to get on the train that Clemenceau was calling a conference at Compiègne he ordered Weygand to go alone to meet Haig and Wilson. Clemenceau was the key, and Foch would do better to see Clemenceau rather than Haig.

Nonetheless, the meeting at Abbeville was important, because there Haig revealed his thinking. In a note that he asked Weygand to pass on

---

[11] Loucheur, *Carnets secrets*, 52–3.

[12] Foch, Carnets, n.d. [on or after 24 March 1918], fo. 299.

[13] 'Memorandum by Lord Milner on his visit to France, including the Conference at Doullens, March 26, 1918', 27 March 1918, IC 53, CAB 28/3, p. 1.

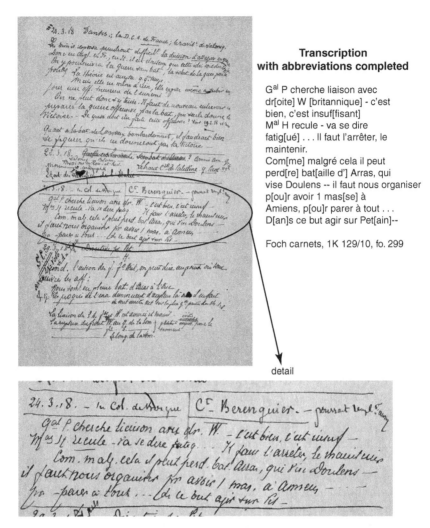

**Transcription
with abbreviations completed**

G^{al} P cherche liaison avec
dr[oite] W [britannique] - c'est
bien, c'est insuf[fisant]
M^{al} H recule - va se dire
fatig[ué] . . . Il faut l'arrêter, le
maintenir.
Com[me] malgré cela il peut
perd[re] bat[aille d'] Arras, qui
vise Doulens -- il faut nous organiser
p[ou]r avoir 1 mas[se] à
Amiens, p[ou]r parer à tout . . .
D[an]s ce but agir sur Pet[ain]--

Foch carnets, 1K 129/10, fo. 299

detail

Illustration 8 Page from Foch's notebook, 24 March 1918

to both Clemenceau and Foch he requested a force of at least twenty
French divisions to come up immediately (Pétain had already dispatched fifteen to cover the breach). Haig wanted those divisions 'to
operate on the flank of the German movement against the English
Army which must fight its way slowly back covering the Channel

ports'.[14] This memorandum corroborates Wilson's view that Haig was 'cowed', because it shows clearly Haig's decision to fall back to the coast. It reveals what Haig's latest biographer calls the 'acute psychological strain' of 23–26 March.[15] Wilson took the opportunity to say 'I told you so', by pointing out that Haig and Pétain had scuppered the general reserve plan and the great breach in the Allied front was the result. Wilson urged, therefore, much greater unity of action, and 'suggested that Foch should coordinate the action'. 'D. H. said that he would prefer Petain but I simply brushed this to one side. Petain is a very inferior person & is now proving all I have said against him. In the end D. H. agreed.'[16] Hence the meeting at Abbeville marked both Haig's admission that he was retiring to the ports, for which he needed the support of twenty French divisions, and also Haig's acceptance of Foch as Allied commander, as Wilson urged.

At the same time as Weygand was talking with Haig, the other leaders were meeting in Compiègne. Clemenceau had included Poincaré (he chaired the meeting), Loucheur and Foch. Milner was the sole British representative. Pétain had the latest intelligence, and he described the state of Gough's Fifth Army (it had ceased to exist) and the steps he was taking to counter the German offensive and stop up the gap. He claimed to be doing all that was possible, given the risk from a German attack to his other fronts. (The Germans put a strong disinformation effort into threatening an attack in the Champagne, on either side of Reims.) Foch 'evidently took a somewhat different view of the situation', as Milner stated in his report to the Cabinet. In what Milner described as a 'long and very energetic statement', Foch argued that the risk to other fronts must be run because the risk to Amiens, if the breach between the two armies grew, outweighed all else. It seemed to Milner that both Poincaré and Clemenceau were in sympathy with Foch's position: they must run that risk and take extreme measures as rapidly as possible. (In private conversation after the meeting Clemenceau told Milner that he sympathised with Foch's attitude.) When Milner stated reasonably that, in the absence of Wilson and the BEF's commander, he could not answer for what the British might be able to contribute, all agreed to meet again the next day 26 March, at Dury, half-way between Haig's and Pétain's headquarters.[17]

In her diary account of this meeting of 25 March – an account which must have originated with her husband – Madame Foch states that it was there decided that Foch would take charge of the 'coordination' of

[14] WO 158/72/4, and *AFGG* 6/1, annex 751.   [15] Harris, *Haig*, 460.
[16] Wilson diary, 25 March 1918.   [17] Milner memorandum, 2–3, CAB 28/3.

304 Part II: Supreme command

the French and British armies in the great battle that was taking place. Clemenceau had tried to run things, she continued, but he did not know what he was doing and had been persuaded (wrongly) by Haig. Now her husband had to 'stick things back together' (a frequent metaphor of his): 'After the Marne, the Yser, Italy, once again it is he who has to put things straight.'[18] This shows Foch's confidence that supreme command would soon be his. Since Wilson had already obtained Haig's acceptance in Abbeville, he was right to be optimistic. He also had the support of a good many at GQG. The head of intelligence wrote that all their hopes were in Foch's designation: 'He seemed to us to be the only man capable of restoring a state of affairs that was becoming more and more dramatic.'[19]

Pétain too was prepared to accept Foch's nomination. Both generals were agreed in their determination to face up energetically to a grave danger. Loucheur recorded that Foch approved Pétain's dispositions while insisting on no hesitation over risks in other sectors of the front.[20] Pétain told Herbillon that same evening that he had explained how the British kept looking to their bases and that he could not impel Haig to maintain contact. The danger was complete separation, with the British forced back to the sea and then forced to surrender. He claimed that Milner was so struck with this picture that he agreed to the designation of Foch as the liaison between the two CinCs.

It's a step towards unified command, Pétain told [Herbillon] in conclusion; it required a crisis to impose it. I hope that it is not too late and that the British, being in the soup [se sentant dans la marmelade], will obey. Foch has all the qualities needed to force them to do so.[21]

Thus Pétain thrust the whole blame for the crisis onto Haig and the British, and he could acquiesce in Foch's elevation because he believed that Foch could make the British do what he himself could not.

Foch and the politicians returned to Paris, where Weygand and Wilson caught up with them after talking with Haig at Abbeville. Weygand delivered Haig's request for twenty divisions; and Wilson suggested that Clemenceau might be made supreme Allied commander with Foch to advise him as his chief of staff. (Was Wilson having second thoughts about giving Foch so much power? or was he counting on

---

[18] Mme Foch diary, 26 March 1917.
[19] Cointet memoirs, Cahier '1918', fo. 21 (24 March 1918).
[20] Loucheur, Carnets secrets, 56.
[21] Herbillon, Du général, 2: 233 (entry for 25 March 1918).

taking advantage of the positive reputation that Clemenceau had among the BEF's leaders?) Foch rejected the idea. He claimed that Clemenceau might be drawn in opposite directions, according to whether he followed Foch's or Pétain's advice. There could be no unity of control if Clemenceau were to agree first with one and then with the other. Foch did not wish to command anything (so Wilson reported him to Milner as saying), he simply wanted 'to have the express authority of the two Governments to bring about the maximum co-operation' between Haig and Pétain. In other words, he wanted 'the same kind of position which he had held once before, at the time of the Battle of Ypres, when Field-Marshal Joffre delegated him to try and get the British and French to work more closely together'. All he wanted this time was a joint designation from the two governments, instead of the solely French designation of 1914. This was a shrewd statement on Foch's part. He and Wilson had worked hand in hand at that time, and Haig too had good memories of First Ypres. The reference to 1914 was the happiest Foch could have chosen. Whether the choice was instinctive or calculated, it worked its effect. Wilson wrote in his diary that he 'arranged that at our meeting at Dury tomorrow I would suggest that he (Foch) be commissioned by both Governments to co-ordinate the military action of the 2 C.inC.s'.[22] Wilson and Milner agreed as they drove to that meeting the next day (26 March) that the 'best solution' under the circumstances was to place Foch in a similar position to the one he occupied in 1914. Milner was convinced that 'whatever might be his other merits or demerits as a soldier, Foch possessed in a quite exceptional degree the promptitude, energy and resource necessary'.[23] Wilson had obtained Haig's agreement to the solution; now Wilson and Milner were also in agreement.

The historic meeting on 26 March – when finally the nettle of unified command was grasped – was held in Doullens, not Dury because Doullens was more convenient for Haig. It has been described by most of the participants and by many historians. There is no need to repeat the details here, except to say that wisely Foch kept his counsel. Pétain gave his 'discouraging' report about the speed with which he could get his divisions to where they were needed, despite his belief that the danger of another German attack on his front in Champagne no longer existed.[24] His words proved unconvincing, and Milner received an impression of 'coldness

[22] Wilson diary, 25 March 1918.   [23] Milner memorandum, 3.
[24] Cointet memoirs, Cahier '1918', fos. 24–5 (26 March 1918). Cointet supports this assertion with Weygand's testimony.

and caution, as of a man playing for safety'. Foch did not speak, but clearly his body language indicated impatience. Milner took the first step, therefore, telling Clemenceau privately that Foch had the 'greatest grasp of the situation', and that he was 'most likely to deal with it with the intensest energy'.[25] And so the deed was done; Loucheur scribbled the agreed form of words; and Foch had his piece of paper. He was commissioned by the British and French governments to *coordinate* the action of the Allied armies on the Western Front. Finally, he could leave his desk in Paris and get back into the field.

The immediate reactions were of relief. Poincaré told Herbillon: 'good work . . . and it was time for it'.[26] Clemenceau admitted, even while writing his explosive *Grandeurs et misères d'une victoire*, how grateful he was that Foch had seized the initiative. If the agreement did not constitute a victory over the Germans, at least it was a victory over the British.[27] According to Milner, Haig looked in much better spirits that evening; according to Wilson, Haig 'looked ten years younger'.[28] As for Foch himself, he was somewhat less categorical about the simplicity of what needed to be done. Before the meeting began he had insisted that his plan was straightforward: he would fight in the north, on the Somme, on the Aisne, in Lorraine, in Alsace. Afterwards, speaking less decisively, he was teased by Loucheur who described him, now that he had his authorisation, as the 'post-paper Foch'. Foch did not find the comment very funny.[29]

Clearly it was Foch's energy, decision and confidence that overcame Pétain's measured but cold approach. Poincaré summed it up neatly: in grave moments Pétain's dark, critical, unquiet spirit did not inspire his listeners because he gave the impression of not believing in himself. (It is noteworthy that his statement that the threat to his front in Champagne no longer existed went virtually unnoticed, probably because it was not stated with conviction.)[30] What was required was Foch's 'cover Amiens at all cost' attitude.[31] Clemenceau thought that Pétain was timid in action and lacking in ideas, although he understood the mentality of his armies. He was an administrator rather than a leader ('un chef'). 'Let others have the imagination and dash, he is in the right place if there are men above him to take decisions if matters are serious.'[32] Certainly Pétain was doing what he could, but the situation was so critical that all the participants

---

[25] Milner memorandum, 4.   [26] Herbillon, *Du général*, 2: 235.

[27] Mordacq, *Commandement unique*, 90.

[28] Milner memorandum, 5; Wilson diary, 26 March 1918.

[29] Mordacq, *Commandement unique*, 80; Poincaré, *AS* 10: 90 (entry for 26 March 1918).

[30] This is why Cointet insists on this point in his memoirs: Cahier '1918', fos. 24–5.

[31] Letter, Poincaré to Clemenceau, 29 March 1918, cited in Duroselle, *Clemenceau*, 689.

[32] Clemenceau to his secretary, Georges Wormser, in Wormser, *Clemenceau*, 215–16.

needed the sense of a single mind taking hold. All mention Foch's energy; and Pétain did himself no favours by comments such as 'the Germans will defeat the British in open battle; after which they will defeat us as well'.[33] Even if Foch did not bring up any more divisions than Petain had already allocated, it is difficult to see how the breach could have been closed if the two commanders-in-chief had been permitted each to pursue his own dispositions.

Clemenceau had been working consistently for unity of command. He knew that it would take German guns to bring the British to accept it and he had enough political nous to wait until conditions forced the British to request it. Hence it seems likely that his silencing of Foch in London less than two weeks earlier over the question of the general reserve was a calculated ploy to show London that he was not forcing the issue. Foch then had the sense to accept (albeit impatiently) his reprimand, and the sense to make his case when the military situation became critical and to wait for its acceptance.

Nonetheless, it was a close-run thing – even though the Reims danger could be ignored by the time the Doullens meeting began. Although Foch commented that he had been given a lost battle and was expected to win it,[34] he had the self-confidence to go out and do just that. He told his wife that the British failure to hold the line of the Somme was shameful, and that Pétain's scattering of divisions between the two armies left a widening breach through which the enemy could pass. Two precious days had been lost, but with God's help it might not be too late. He reported that Haig had said to him that the situation was a repeat of Ypres. Foch's response was a hope that the outcome would be the same as in 1914.[35]

He set to work immediately. As mere coordinator, Foch could not order divisions to move, but he could give pep talks. First of all, at 4pm, he saw General Gough, who did not appreciate the pep talk, but that did not matter since soon he was made the scapegoat and relieved of his command. Then he saw General Fayolle's chief of staff, and next he explained to the GQG liaison officer what he had done. (Pétain had appointed Fayolle to command the Reserve Army Group that he formed to fill the breach caused by the collapse of Fifth Army.) He saw General Debeney commanding First Army in the Reserve Army Group at 7pm, and got back to Paris at 10.15. The next day, 27 March, he saw Generals Humbert, Fayolle, Gough and Byng. Haig authorised him to give 'instructions' to British army commanders and to the reinforcements arriving from the UK. On 28 March, he saw Fayolle again, and Pétain, and had a long meeting

---

[33] Poincaré, *AS* 10: 88 (entry for 26 March 1918).   [34] Liddell Hart, *Foch*, 278.
[35] Mme Foch diary, 27 March 1918.

with Clemenceau and Loucheur in the afternoon. On the 29th a meeting with Haig confirmed 'the increasing concordance of views and mutual confidence' of the two men. The next day his deputy chief of staff reported that the liaison between Debeney's First and Rawlinson's Fourth Army 'seemed to be fixed'. (Rawlinson had taken over from Gough and the remnants of Fifth Army became Fourth Army.) On 30 March Foch issued his first 'Directive générale' after showing it to Pétain, who had no objections.[36]

Also on 30 March Foch entertained Clemenceau, Loucheur and Winston Churchill, who met up with him in Beauvais town hall, his temporary headquarters. Lloyd George had sent Churchill over to France to find out what was happening (much to Wilson's dismay). Clemenceau promised Churchill that they would go to the front and see everything that there was to see. Their party of about a dozen spoke with Foch and Weygand and a couple of other officers. Churchill's account of the meeting is worth citing at length for it rings very true, even allowing for Churchillian embellishment, and it reveals what Foch had grasped but Ludendorff had failed to grasp.[37]

I cannot attempt to reproduce his [Foch's] harangue, but this was his theme: 'Following the fighting of the 21st, the Germans broke through on the 22nd. Oh! oh! oh! How big!' He pointed to a line on the map.

'On the 23rd they advanced again. *Deuxième journée d'invasion. Ah! Ah!* Another enormous stride. On the 24th. *Troisième journée. Aïe! Aïe!*'

But the fourth day there was apparently a change ... '*Oho!*' he said. '*Quatrième journée. Oho! Oho!*'

We all knew that something had happened to the advancing flood. When he came to the fifth day the zone was distinctly smaller. The sixth and seventh zones were progressively smaller still. Foch's voice had dropped almost to a whisper. It was sufficient for him to point to the diminishing zones and with a wave of the hand or a shrug of the shoulder to convey the moral and meaning which he intended.

Until finally, '*Hier, dernière journée d'invasion*' ... And then suddenly in a loud voice, 'Stabilization! Sure, certain, soon. And afterwards. Ah, afterwards. That is my affair.'

He stopped. Everyone was silent.

Then Clemenceau, advancing, '*Alors, Général, il faut que je vous embrasse.*'

Foch had grasped that a breakthrough was always possible, but that it always expired as it ran out of supplies, munitions, energy. Instead of Ludendorff's imprecise aim to break through and then see what could be done, Foch would seek to land a succession of blows, stopping once

---

[36] Timetable and quotations from Allied HQ war diary: GQGA JMO, 26–30 March 1918, 26N 1.

[37] Churchill, *Thoughts and Adventures*, 141–3.

resistance became too strong, in order to attack elsewhere. Before he could adopt this strategy, however, the Germans had to allow him a breathing space to organise the succession of blows, to collect reserves and to replace the lost materiel. At the end of March 1918 he did not have that breathing space.

Foch's only room for manoeuvre, during the last few days of March when the German offensive came to an end apart from a brief flare-up in April, was psychological. The hole that the offensive had created between the two armies left him no strategic choices. Foch knew that the breach had to be closed. In any case, he had no resources, and his role of coordinator did not permit him to issue orders. As historians have recognised, Foch did not dispatch any extra French divisions to the danger zone. All he could do was to exhort. Exhortation was not, however, a negligible tool and the timetable cited above shows how energetically he used it. At times of crisis any sense that someone has taken hold and is doing something is valuable. Haig was visibly shaken (according, at least, to Wilson), and Pétain and his staff had faced the possibility of defeat even if Pétain did not reveal his concerns openly. Under the circumstances, Foch's only possible action was to go personally to the various headquarters and encourage resistance. Foch believed that if a commander was thinking only of the possibility of retirement to a line further back, he was half-way to giving the order. Even if retirement became necessary, at least Foch's exhortations to stand would have delayed the retirement. As Fayolle noted, at least Foch had a plan – cover Amiens, block up the hole: 'Foch conceived the plan, Pétain furnished the means, and I executed it.'[38]

Given these two constraints on his planning – the actions of the enemy, and the lack of troops to command – it is not surprising that when the offensive died away Foch should have started agitating once again for more power.[39] He had been appointed to coordinate, he wrote to Clemenceau, and now that the action had died down there was nothing left to coordinate. Yet planning was needed. Defensive and offensive tasks had to be allocated across all fronts, including Italy. Clemenceau was convinced that Foch was right, and he called Lloyd George over to France to confer. The Americans were present this time as well at the meeting on 3 April in Beauvais. Bliss had always wanted unified command, and the British, including Lloyd George, appeared to have been affected by the tour of the front that they had just made. Consequently Foch's positive statement of the military situation had a great effect on confidence. According to Loucheur, Foch declared that he would stop the enemy where they now stood and, using

[38] Fayolle, *CS*, 264–8 (entries for 27, 30 March, 1 April 1918).
[39] See Greenhalgh, *VTC*, 198–9.

troops collected from other fronts, he would reply to the enemy offensive and go on to counter-attack. 'He knows how to convince people by his personal authority', Loucheur concluded.[40] As a result, Foch's task of coordination was reaffirmed, but this time with the additional clause that 'to this end all the powers necessary for an effective implementation' were conferred upon him by the British, French and American governments. However, the several CinCs were to retain full tactical control of their armies and were given the right of appeal to their respective governments if they believed that an order from Foch placed their army in danger.

Foch told his wife that in the meeting neither Haig nor Pétain had objected, and he anticipated that they would all be able to work together. Betraying a lack of modesty he added that he could have stopped the invasion before the Doullens agreement was made, but he had stopped it afterwards, although what was lost was lost. After Beauvais, they were going to try to recapture it. Pétain came to see him every day and they understood each other very well; as for the British, they were cooperating so long as they were closely watched. He intended to move his headquarters further to the north so as to be closer.[41]

Beauvais town hall was not suitable as a headquarters – the building and the town were too busy. Foch and his staff moved into a quiet château at Sarcus, a little village thirty-six kilometres northwest of Beauvais, which had easy access to main roads and communications. He gathered his small staff from Versailles and his office in the Ministry, thus forming a small coterie of officers whom he knew well. Weygand agreed to leave the SWC and return to the job of chief of staff that he had been carrying out since 1914. General Desticker was his deputy. Commandants Pagezy and Riedinger (the former had been in charge of Northern Army Group's artillery on the Somme), and Capitaines de Mierry and Gerodias joined them, together with Bonnal (in charge of the mess) and Pupier (interpreter). Gradually liaison officers from the Allied armies joined his staff: British General J. P. DuCane on 4 April; American Colonel Bentley T. Mott on 18 April; and Belgian Colonel Menschaert. Two former British officers with Foch, Charles Grant and Eric Dillon, had been liaising with the new Allied CinC since 26 March. Eventually an Italian colonel was attached as well (Colonnello Riccardo Calcagno), and liaison established with Bliss and the American section at the SWC.

Even before moving his headquarters on 7 April Foch issued his second 'directive' on the same day that his powers were increased at Beauvais. He had already stated in his first such directive that he wanted to constitute a

---

[40] As told to Herbillon that evening: *Du général*, 2: 241 (entry for 3 April 1917).
[41] Letters, Foch to Mme Foch, 4 and 5 April 1918, vol. 45.

'masse de manoeuvre'. Hence he wanted strong defensive positions established to defend Amiens and keep the two national armies in contact with each other; but there could be no large-scale reliefs of defenders, because the troops stripped from quiet parts of the line must be kept in reserve for the manoeuvre force.[42] Now his second directive laid out the broad lines of a possible counter-offensive. Basing his ideas on the fact that a fresh German attack was more likely in the north around Arras (because of the strength of their railways) than in south around Montdidier (where their railways were in a worse state and within range of Allied guns), Foch argued for a double offensive. The BEF should attack eastwards astride the Somme, thereby securing Amiens, and the French should attack northwards from Montdidier, thereby freeing the railway line from Amiens. The two attacks would converge, and the southern French operation would provide the best response if the Germans attacked Arras and interfered with the northern British one.[43]

On 5 April Ludendorff discontinued operation MICHAEL 'temporarily' because the 'supply situation' forbade its continuance; by 9 April Foch was sure that the offensive was over. He wondered whether the enemy had been stopped by the Allied resistance, by their difficult communications, or by the bad weather. It was probably a mixture of all three, he concluded.[44] Now he needed to prepare a counter-attack quickly before the enemy could dig in, improve his communications and rest his troops.

David Zabecki's recent study of Ludendorff's 1918 offensives lists several other reasons for the German failure: too much concentration on the tactical level and too little on the strategic; failure to provide the main attack with adequate resources; disunity at the operational level with the two army group commanders involved; friction among the artillery chiefs (despite their proved success, Bruchmüller's ideas did not have universal acceptance); and, most importantly, a series of bad operational decisions as Ludendorff changed objectives during the course of the battle. Zabecki criticises Ludendorff severely for failing to appreciate the vital importance of Amiens and its communications for the maintenance of the BEF in the field.[45] This Foch *did* appreciate. All his efforts were directed during operation MICHAEL to keeping the British and French together in front of Amiens. And his offensive plans were based on the importance of railway communications to both Allies and the enemy.

---

[42] *AFGG* 6/1, annex 1132.
[43] Directive générale no 2, 3 April 1918, *AFGG* 6/1, annex 1374.
[44] Letter, Foch to Mme Foch, 9 April 1918, vol. 45.
[45] Zabecki, *German 1918 Offensives*, 160–72.

However, Ludendorff did not permit Foch the time to form his 'masse de manoeuvre' nor to prepare that counter-attack. Operation GEORGETTE had started life as GEORG, an offensive to clear the British out of Flanders by capturing the line of Flanders hills that overlooked the ports. By the time that Ludendorff brought MICHAEL to a close, GEORG had evolved into KLEIN GEORG and finally GEORGETTE because of a lack of resources. The vast expenditure of men and materiel in March, together with the much longer front that the Germans now had to hold after capturing the old Somme battlefields, meant that the Flanders operation suffered a reduction in scale. *Sixth Army* (in Crown Prince Rupprecht's army group) was to attack along the heights of the Flanders hills, cross the river Lys at Béthune and La Bassée, with Hazebrouck the main objective. Hazebrouck was an important rail junction like Amiens. The offensive was to begin against the weak British and Portuguese forces facing *Sixth Army* on 9 April. Bruchmüller was sent to *Sixth Army* to direct the artillery preparations; men and munitions arrived gradually as MICHAEL wound down.

Allied intelligence got wind of the preparations. In any case, it was obvious that the best thing the Germans could do would be to hit the weakened British further north. Haig had already spoken about the danger after the Beauvais meeting on 3 April, and he wrote to Foch three days later requesting either a strong French offensive to hold down enemy troops, or a French relief of four British divisions south of the Somme, or, third, the placing of four French divisions around Saint-Pol to serve as a reserve for the British. Wilson also wrote to Foch requesting further French help because no French success south of the Somme could compensate for a disaster further north. Foch was open to persuasion. The French intelligence assessments indicated artillery concentrations around Arras, with the 7 April report pointing to the German method for concealing the movements of their attack divisions. These divisions were trained well away from the front, and brought into position by night marches.[46] So Foch was well aware of the danger, and he ordered Pétain (as the Beauvais agreement had now given him the authority to do) to send a force of three cavalry and four infantry divisions to the west of Amiens. He asked Haig to clear areas for these troops and to ensure that road and rail communications were open so that they could move quickly to liberate British reserves, should the need arise.[47] This decision left a mere forty-six French divisions in line with twelve in reserve for the whole front between the river Oise and Switzerland, plus three US divisions.[48]

[46] Intelligence bulletin 1389, 7 April 1918, *AFGG* 6/1, annex 1519.
[47] Note, 7 April 1918, ibid., annex 1516.   [48] *AFGG* 6/1, 427, n. 4.

On 9 April Crown Prince Rupprecht launched his *Sixth Army* against the weakest part of the British front in Flanders, the sector held by First Army's Portuguese troops, who broke. The Germans reached Estaires and the next day forced the evacuation of Armentières (see Map 14). Also on the second day of the offensive, *Fourth Army* began their assault against General Plumer's Second Army in the Ypres salient, and captured Messines. On 11 April the enemy committed a further seven divisions to Flanders – now a total of thirty-one German divisions faced thirteen Allied. The following day found the Germans within six kilometres of Hazebrouck, the vital Allied communications hub; but at this point Ludendorff ordered the armies to concentrate on Bailleul, thus shifting the focus from that important junction to the high ground of the Flanders hills. However, the force of the German assault was now largely spent: *Sixth Army* was exhausted and suffering severe disciplinary problems, and *Fourth Army* did not reach Bailleul until 15 April. The first week of GEORGETTE, or the Battle of the Lys as the British named it, had followed the same trajectory as the MICHAEL operation. Stunning gains in the opening days were followed by a distinct slowing of momentum. Once again operational aims fluctuated. Yet there were also significant differences. Some of those thirty-one German divisions had already been through the MICHAEL mill and so were more easily discouraged; the reason for the day's difference in the start date for the two German armies was an insufficient number of heavy guns for both to begin on the same day; muddy conditions made bringing up food and munitions even more difficult than it had been further south; and German morale was suffering, as 'repulsive scenes of drunkenness' noted by Rupprecht revealed.[49]

When GEORGETTE began on 9 April Foch happened to be at Haig's headquarters because the latter was asking either to shorten his front or to get the support of a further four French divisions. Haig became 'desperately anxious' as this second offensive against the BEF's lines developed. He had already asked Wilson to come to France (he was there 9–10 April), and he spoke to him 'two or three times' of making peace.[50] On 10 April Haig asked again for French help; and on the 11th issued his famous 'backs to the wall' order of the day. Also he sent General Davidson, his head of operations, to Sarcus to press his request. The War Cabinet in London was worried as well by the turn of events, and Milner was sent to France a second time to deal with the crisis. He and Wilson, who joined him in France on the 15th, pressed for flooding to be ordered from St Omer to the coast to halt the German advance, just as the

---

[49] Herwig, *First World War*, 410.   [50] Harris, *Haig*, 469; Wilson diary, 9 April 1918.

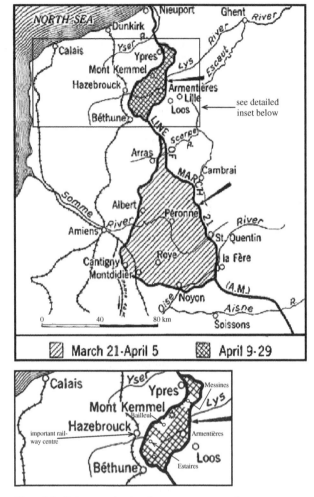

Map 14 Gains made in the MICHAEL and GEORGETTE operations, March–April 1918

flooding of the Yser had stabilised the Belgian front in 1914. The BEF would then retire south of the St Omer line, even though such a move would mean the loss of Dunkirk.

Thus considerable pressure was placed upon Foch. Although he refused Haig's first request on 9 April for more French troops, he had already ordered Pétain, as noted above, to place four infantry and three cavalry divisions in the British sector west of Amiens. This was further south than Haig would have wished, but it gave greater flexibility in that the French units would be able to operate either northwards or southwards as required. He refused Haig's second request on 10 April, but sent a French division to Dunkirk and moved Tenth Army further north, with Fifth Army to follow. When he learned that Plumer had been authorised to abandon the Passchendaele ridge, he sent his deputy chief of staff General Desticker to Plumer's headquarters so that he would have a direct link with the Second Army commander, and he asked the Belgians to come under Plumer's orders. Foch had worked with Plumer in Italy and knew that he could depend on him – indeed, he told Wilson that he thought that Plumer ought to replace Haig.[51] He also asked Pétain for yet another division and ordered Fayolle to support Rawlinson's Fourth Army on the Somme. On 13 April he went in person to see the French Tenth Army and British First Army commanders, and the next day asked the Belgians to extend their front since they had refused to come under Plumer's orders. As a result of his actions the Tenth Army's four divisions in Foch's reserve, with its aviation and artillery, were all in place north of the Somme by 15 April, ready to intervene if necessary.

Meanwhile, Foch had to deal with the politicians, British and French, as well as the military. Haig had enlisted Milner's help in his battle with Foch over reinforcements and, with Wilson, they all met at Abbeville on 14 April. Foch asked Haig to put his demands in writing,[52] and, more helpfully, arranged for the line of defence for Hazebrouck to be placed along the eastern edge of the Nieppe forest, made possible by the Belgian extension of their front. In further meetings on 15 and 17 April, Milner and Wilson continued to press for flooding to be started so as to protect the ports and provide a defendable front for the BEF, but Foch refused to countenance this, merely asking the Military Governor of Dunkirk to prepare for possible flooding and asking Admiral Ronarc'h to make plans for the destruction of the port facilities. Foch also received visits from President Poincaré (who found Foch to be in 'very good form') and Clemenceau. Foch indicated that he believed the German push towards Hazebrouck to be over, and that Arras would be the next target; nevertheless he hoped to be able mount an offensive somewhere else. He informed Poincaré that relations between himself and Pétain were good, but that Pétain recoiled from responsibility. As an 'exécutant' (carrier out of orders), Pétain was 'perfect', Foch said, but he could not be a

[51] Wilson diary, 9 April 1918.
[52] Conference at Abbeville, 14 April 1918, WO 158/72/25, and 15N 10/42.

commander-in-chief.[53] Foch found time in the midst of everything else to press both Poincaré and Clemenceau for a title (Lloyd George agreed to 'Général en Chef des Armées Alliées' on 14 April) and for an official letter of appointment. He received the letter as a brief presidential decree dated 22 April, countersigned by Clemenceau.[54] The letter makes no mention of to whom Foch was responsible, hence by whom he could be sacked. Presumably it was thought that the matter could be left in abeyance whilst the fighting continued.

A week after GEORGETTE began on 9 April, the offensive had run out of steam. Attacks on the Flanders hills and against the new junction between British and Belgian troops both failed on 17 April; true to form, Ludendorff began thinking about another sector, that around Reims. The Allied defence was now in place: Foch spent the nights of 16 and 17 April at Plumer's headquarters so that he could oversee events; and Pétain created an army detachment – the Détachement d'armée du nord (DAN) – to administer the various units that had been sent northwards. By 18 April there were nine French infantry and three cavalry divisions north of the Somme. The DAN came directly under Foch's orders the next day. So, once again, the German onslaught had been stopped. After a pause in offensives they carried out two further operations: an excentric attack on 24 April south of the Somme, at Villers Bretonneux, overlooking Amiens, where initial success was rubbed out when the Australians re-took the town the next day; and on 25 April against one of the Flanders hills, Mt Kemmel, which the French had just taken over from the British. This the Germans captured, much to Haig's disgust. On 1 May Ludendorff closed GEORGETTE down. He had caused the Allies more casualties than his own armies had suffered, but he did not have the reservoir of men that the Americans represented for the Allies, not to mention the results of the harsher conscriptions laws imposed in Britain. German figures for casualties from both MICHAEL and GEORGETTE reveal 325,800 German; figures for the British and the French were 259,779 and 96,467 respectively.[55]

Manpower resources became the urgent question of the hour as a result of those casualty figures. Materiel could be, and was, replaced promptly, but men could not be found so easily. In Flanders the manpower resources were not solely British or French. Foch could call upon the Belgians, and he had already received Pershing's offer to join the battle. Consequently Foch sent a telegram to Bliss at the SWC on 11 April asking if 1 US Division was ready to be sent into the front line. It may be that Foch believed that

[53] Poincaré, *AS*, 10: 123 (entry for 15 April 1918).
[54] Lettre de Commandement, Foch mss, vol. 48, BNF.
[55] *RAW* 14: 255, 300; Edmonds *et al.*, *OH 1918*, 2: 490–3; *AFGG* 6/2, 552.

Bliss had the last word on the deployment of units of the AEF, but it is far more likely that he expected a more helpful answer from Bliss than from Pershing. Whatever the case, Bliss passed the request on to Pershing, who was rather slow to answer. After repeating his request to Bliss the next day, Foch heard in the afternoon that Pershing had agreed, and 1 US Division moved from reserve in General Micheler's Fifth Army into the front line during the night of 24/25 April into First Army's Cantigny sector, northwest of Montdidier.[56] Pershing followed this up with a visit to Foch's head-quarters on 16 April to argue his case for an independent American army. As soon as two, three or four American divisions were able to take part in the war, Pershing intended to take personal command 'in order to sustain the interest of the people of the United States in the war'. This was Wilson's desire as well as that of Secretary of State Baker, Pershing emphasised. He expected two more divisions to be ready quite soon, followed by 2 US Division. Naturally Foch 'agreed to the principle' – 'The understanding on this subject was definite' – but he stated that its execution would depend upon the readiness of the other divisions. Foch could afford to cede the principle while leaving the date, as Pershing recognised, 'indefinite'.[57]

The Belgian refusal to put troops with Plumer stemmed from the constitutional requirement that the King retain command of the Belgian Army. The Belgian decision was looked on critically by GQG, because the French could see that the overriding interest was to prevent any breach between British and French armies. Foch too was unhappy about the decision. When the head of the Belgian mission at GQG argued that the Belgians needed to remain strong around Ypres and the Houthulst forest, Foch replied that the danger there was 'eventual'. The 'immediate and real' danger to Belgium was a German capture of the Flanders hills. This would place the enemy in a position to bombard the rear of the Belgian Army. Foch did not insist, however, telling the officer that he hoped that the situation would not come to pass. He could only pity the Belgians if it did.[58] Obviously Foch realised that there was little point in pressing the matter.

Instead, on 17 April, he went in person to speak to the new Belgian chief of the general staff, General Gillain, and, together with Poincaré, who was on a tour of inspection of the troops in Dunkirk, spoke to the King as well. Foch was worried that the Belgians might abandon the line of the Yser following Plumer's withdrawal from part of the Ypres salient. Foch pointed out to Gillain that the Yser line was very strong: the only two points where it might be crossed were Dixmude and on the coast at

[56] Bliss to Baker, 11, 12 April 1918, Bliss mss, cont. 250; *USAWW: Order of Battle*, 1: 357.
[57] Pershing diary, 16 April 1918.
[58] Rapport # 21, 14 April 1918, Maison Militaire du Roi (Galet), folder 5.

Nieuport. If the Belgian artillery concentrated its fire on those two points, there was little danger. Moreover, Foch pressed, the line of the Yser represented the high point of the Belgian resistance in 1914. It would be a blow to morale to abandon it years later; and it would be an equal blow to let it be known that a line of resistance further back was being contemplated. In an argument that he would repeat in other circumstances, Foch claimed that troops should not be led to believe that another (possibly stronger) line was under consideration. Obviously the high command should prepare for the eventuality of an enemy breakthrough, but general knowledge of the existence of a fall-back position only made the fall-back more likely.[59]

Poincaré attempted to press the advantages of the unified command now that Foch had his title of Generalissimo, but the King refused to be drawn. He could not put any of his troops under the command of a foreign general, although he assured Poincaré that he would be happy to follow Foch's advice as he had known him for a long time and admired him greatly. So the King resisted, politely but firmly, the French attempts to get him to join the unified command, but at least he promised that the Yser would not be abandoned. Furthermore, Gillain assured Poincaré that he and Foch were in complete agreement. It was further agreed that Colonel Menschaert would leave the Belgian mission at GQG to join Foch's headquarters at Sarcus.[60] Nevertheless, the French press continued to publish stories that the Belgian Army was to come under Foch's orders, and the Belgian Premier reported to the King that the same rumours were current in Le Havre. He wondered whether it was a strong French ploy.[61]

In addition to all the travelling and talking Foch also devoted some time to writing a 'note' on defensive doctrine so that all the armies were singing from the same hymnsheet.[62] An energetic, step-by-step defence, based on powerful artillery and a succession of prepared lines, was imperative, whether it involved barring the road to Calais or to the coalmines, or covering the communication hub at Amiens or the Paris–Amiens railway. There must always be at least two defensive positions, just in case the first was destroyed; counter-attacks should be the means of stopping the enemy. Troops used for the counter-attacks should not simply be thrown into battle, but the operation must be well prepared in advance. Foch summed up his thoughts thus: multiply the defensive lines; distribute

[59] General Gillain, Compte-rendu de l'entretien avec le Général Foch, 17 April 1918, ibid.
[60] Poincaré, *AS*, 10: 127–8 (entry for 17 April 1918).
[61] Extracts from Albert's carnets and letter of de Broqueville to the King, cited in Thielemans, 'Le Roi Albert', 93.
[62] Note for Haig, Pétain, French army group and army commanders, 18 April 1918, *AFGG* 6/1, annex 1810.

troops and artillery in depth; prepare counter-attacks and keep fully informed the reserve troops who will carry them out. This note was sent to Pétain, Fayolle and French army commanders, along with five copies to the British. GHQ records show that the five copies were duly forwarded, but Haig makes no reference to Foch's statement of the obvious in his diary.[63] Mordacq claims that Foch was concerned by finding a lack of uniformity in defensive doctrine during his visits to the various armies, but the preparation of such documents (and Foch wrote his own notes) seems unnecessary for a supreme commander.[64]

It is notable how much of all the above was done face to face. Foch 'pursued' his 'two fine fellows', Pétain in the south and Haig in the north, because they needed to be 'held, sustained, maintained' – this was his principal task and he would not fail in it, he told his wife.[65] Foch saw his role as one of encouragement, based on an accurate appreciation of the situation. He stayed overnight with Plumer; he went to see the Belgians; and he saw the politicians as well. Clemenceau's *chef de cabinet*, General Mordacq, noted Foch's bustle and energy and confidence. No doubt, he wrote, such overwhelming activity was necessary, but it also fitted his temperament as CinC. He became even more ardent as the difficulties mounted. This pleased Clemenceau, whom Foch kept informed about events, and the Premier congratulated himself for fighting so hard to obtain the supreme command for Foch. Mordacq compared Foch's command style, favourably, with that of Moltke in 1914. The German commander had remained out of touch in Luxembourg whilst his First and Second Armies fought on the Marne; and it was Colonel Hentsch who acted on the spot.[66] Yet Wilson criticised Foch's hands-on style when he warned Weygand that Foch should not consult British army commanders without asking Haig's permission.[67] (It should be noted, however, that on 26 March Haig had consented to Foch's speaking directly to them.)

Whatever the value of Foch's face-to-face methods during the GEORGETTE offensive, they were, judged solely by results, successful. His parsimony over reserves paid dividends, although at a huge cost to the BEF, whose casualties between 5 and 30 April were 82,000.[68] He had taken huge risks with the remainder of the French front because, despite British fulminations, he had indeed moved French reserves so that they could be used if there was absolutely no alternative. This policy stoked enormous

[63] WO 158/28/66.   [64] Mordacq, *MC*, 1: 306.
[65] Letter, Foch to Mme Foch, 11 April 1918, vol. 45.
[66] Mordacq, *MC*, 1: 304, 307 (16–20 April 1918).   [67] Wilson diary, 16 April 1918.
[68] Edmonds, *et al.*, *OH 1918*, 2: 490.

resentment, both British – they felt that he had not done enough – and French, for doing too much. Yet Foch had the whole front to consider. Haig and GHQ thought that Foch had not done enough because they looked solely to their own armies and their own front. Likewise Pétain: by the end of the battle, he had lost control over the northern sector (the DAN), his front was ninety-seven kilometres longer, and forty-one French divisions had participated in the battle. Reserves behind the remaining front from the river Oise to Switzerland were down to sixteen divisions (of which seven only were fresh) plus three reconstituted cavalry divisions.[69] The balance that Foch maintained between doing the minimum in Flanders so as retain fresh troops in reserve and keeping options open on other fronts was possible only because the power to direct Allied armies was now in one pair of hands.

The battle was over by the end of April, but, true to his nature, Foch was planning to counter-attack. The Allies had managed to double- or even triple-lock the door, he told his wife, and now they had to prepare a response.[70] The great salient that the Germans had created during MICHAEL still threatened Amiens and the routes to Paris. The Paris–Amiens railway could not be used, which left only the single-track line that ran down the coast from Calais. This made communications with Flanders more difficult, although British engineering troops were working hard to increase the capacity of the Somme crossings.[71] Furthermore, in Flanders, German big guns were close enough to the coast to bombard the ports, and close enough to the coalfields to stop the miners working. Hence there were good reasons to take the offensive, and Foch was sure that what he called 'the dimensions of the attack' were fixed by the number of railway lines behind the front. Communications, he wrote, were becoming the determining factors of the war.[72]

We have a clear picture of Foch's basic strategy at this time because his new British liaison officer, General J. P. DuCane, asked Weygand to explain what it was.[73] He wondered what Foch meant by the stock phrases that he kept using. First 'on fait ce qu'on peut' [we do what we can]. This is not as dismissive a phrase as it sounds. Foch meant that, so long as the enemy had the initiative, he had few choices. He had to do what he could to counter the enemy's actions. Second, 'maintain the integrity of the front'. Obviously this was the primordial imperative since, separated, the two armies risked being defeated in detail. United, they had huge areas of France into which to retire should that become necessary. Third, 'never

[69] *AFGG* 6/1, 522, note 6.   [70] Letter, Foch to Mme Foch, 4 May 1918, vol. 45.
[71] Brown, 'Feeding Victory', 136–42.   [72] Foch, Carnets, 21 April 1918, fo. 303.
[73] DuCane report to CIGS, 16 April 1918, in DuCane, *Foch*, 12–15.

withdraw'. In response to Wilson's repeated suggestion that the British withdraw behind St Omer after flooding the front from Dunkirk, Foch replied: 'Why lower the *moral[e]* of your troops by such a retirement and let the enemy advance half-way to Calais without a fight? If you fight, how many weeks, if not months, will it take the enemy to get to St Omer, and how many fresh divisions will he use in the process? Make him a present of nothing.'

The fourth point that DuCane wished to have elucidated was Foch's insistence 'never relieve tired troops during the battle'. The purpose of this was to avoid the dwindling of his reserves. He insisted on maintaining a good supply of fresh troops to meet all contingencies. Obviously, on occasion, it was necessary to feed in troops, but Foch wanted to keep his reserves as fresh as possible, and not feed such troops into the line, taking exhausted troops into reserve in exchange. Fifth, Foch was questioned repeatedly about his priority: the Channel ports or the integrity of the line? Despite the primacy of maintaining a united front, Foch always insisted that he would fight for both. By refusing to contemplate the possibility of being forced to choose, Foch hoped to prevent the British from keeping it at the back of their minds and so being mentally prepared to make that retirement.

Foch's busy advocacy of counter-offensives could not succeed without a resolution of the enormous problem now facing the Allies – that of manpower. However, the Germans were just as exhausted as the hard-pressed British; furthermore, they did not have the fuel or the trucks that the Allies possessed. Consequently, when Ludendorff decided that northern France and Flanders offered little more and he turned to contemplation of the Reims sector, there was an enforced delay before he could mount the next offensive. This gave Foch and the Allies time to deal with the manpower crisis. It demanded a dual focus: Foch had to negotiate with commanders in the field, but it required political action as well. The BEF was worn out; French reserves were dangerously low; and there were too few trained American troops. For all he had a title and strategic direction of the war on the Western Front, it was the Americans who had the manpower and the British who had the ships. It would require diplomacy to make any progress towards building up manpower reserves, and the forum for Allied political action was the SWC.

First of all, the French army. Their casualties were of the order of 92,000 during the two months of March and April. This was nowhere near as great as the British losses, but they were worrying all the same. Pétain asked Clemenceau to release 40,000 workers from French factories and, especially, the miners who were prevented from working the northern coalfields because of the German advances.[74] During the last two weeks of April the class of 1919 was incorporated. Registration had already taken place the previous year, and indeed some of the new recruits had already been taken for reinforcements. Parliament had voted in favour of the incorporation with the highest majority ever reached during the war in such a vote (490 in favour, with seven against).[75] Earlier bills for incorporation had been met with calls for release of the older classes as a quid pro quo. Thus the parliament was firm in supporting a continued war effort.

The French CinC was concerned, however, by the movements of his reserves northwards to support the British. He wrote to Foch on 24 April with a long and strongly worded complaint. The British were suppressing divisions, and their new conscription laws would not produce any effect until later in the year. He had sent forty-seven divisions to relieve or support the British, when the enemy might attack at any moment on the French front and there would be no fresh British divisions to help. The French army asked only to fight – on the British front, the Belgian front, or later on the French front, just as they had fought in 1917 on the Italian front. He concluded that they wanted to be sure that 'the British Army and British Empire were determined, like the French Army and Empire, to make *the maximum effort*'.[76]

The coldness of the tone of Pétain's letter was an index of the worsening relationship between the two men. If Foch had felt after the Beauvais conference that Pétain did not object to his new powers, the German Flanders offensive had changed Pétain's mind. General Brugère heard that Pétain had not liked the Beauvais decision and that his GQG staff had been criticised for poor staff work when they moved from Compiègne. There was 'great tension' between him and Foch, because of his constant talk of the defensive, whereas Foch and Clemenceau were working well together.[77]

As for the BEF, the British had borne the brunt of the two German offensives and had suffered over a third of a million casualties. Consequently Haig informed Foch on 23 April that his losses were so great that five of his divisions had been wiped out totally, and that orders had been issued to reduce another four to cadre. (This process left a skeleton establishment of ten officers and forty-five other ranks, with the rest being re-allocated to other units or to base depots.) Although 268,000 men had been thrown across the Channel within a fortnight of the start of

---

[74] Pétain to War Minister, 20 April 1918, *AFGG* 6/2, annex 40.
[75] Bonnefous, *Histoire politique*, 387.
[76] Pétain to Foch, 24 April 1918, *AFGG* 6/1, annex 1906. Original emphasis.
[77] Brugère diary, 4 and 23 April 1917.

MICHAEL, and new conscription laws had been introduced extending military liability upwards to those aged fifty-five and downwards to eighteen-year-olds, it would take time for the new blood to arrive. Both Haig and Foch knew that they could expect no amelioration before August.

So Foch reacted energetically to Haig's proposal to suppress divisions. A division is the basic building-block of an army, containing all the elements needed (weaponry, engineering, administrative, medical and so on) to engage combat. The numbers of infantry in a division had been decreasing gradually since 1916. Yet, despite this, the firepower of a 1918 division was greater, because each battalion had Lewis guns, trench mortars and rifle grenades. Foch insisted that British divisions should be reconstituted, not suppressed. He wished to maintain the total number of divisions, even if they were depleted in size, so as to maintain operational flexibility and boost his reserves.

The best source of manpower was American. Because of his time as chief of army in Paris in 1917 Foch knew the state of readiness of the American contingents. When the USA declared war there were just over 213,000 officers and men in the regular army and in the National Guard in federal service. The draft had been instituted for men between the ages of twenty-one and thirty; and in July 1917 the AEF and the War Department had developed a thirty-division programme. This aimed to have 1.3 million men in France by the end of 1918, and when MICHAEL began had produced an AEF in France of 318,000 men in eight divisions. By the end of GEORGETTE, a few American engineers and some aviation units had served with the British in Flanders, one more US division had arrived in France, but the three US divisions that had taken over quiet sectors of the French front in Alsace had not been joined by any others.

From the start Joffre had promised autonomy for the AEF, and Pétain had been unable to win the fight over amalgamation of US units in the French army over the winter of 1917/18.[78] When the German offensive began on 21 March, Pershing responded to the crisis by offering to put all the trained US divisions together in I US Corps for Pétain to use as he thought best. Pétain responded that the Americans had neither sufficient staff officers nor artillery to form an entire corps. Three days later, on 28 March, after the Doullens conference, Pershing told Foch in a statement that was splashed over the American press: 'I have come to tell you that the American people would consider it a great honor for our troops to be engaged in the present battle ... the greatest battle of history.' Then the permanent military representatives in Versailles agreed in their Joint Note

---

[78] See Doughty, *PV*, 419–23, and Bruce, *Fraternity*, ch. 5.

18 of 27 March that the US government should permit the 'temporary service of American units in Allied army corps and divisions', and that combat troops only should be sent across the Atlantic during the emergency.[79] Following Wilson's acceptance of this appeal, Pershing crossed to London and reached an agreement with Lord Milner (it was signed on 24 April) that British and American shipping would be used during the month of May to transport combatant troops for training with the British army. The rather vague wording of this (no numbers were specified) was to create dissension during the SWC's May meetings in Abbeville.

For Foch and Pétain, the best use of the AEF units in France was as reinforcements for British and French divisions already in line, and the best use of the manpower still in the USA was to bring infantry and machine gunners in the limited shipping available. The administrative and logistic support for US divisions could wait. The effect was to delay the formation of the autonomous American army that Pershing wanted. The creation of the first US army corps was to have taken place just before 21 March, but events had overtaken the AEF.

Foch spoke to his American liaison officer, Colonel T. Bentley Mott, on 21 April, soon after his arrival at Foch's headquarters. Foch explained his worries and what he hoped from the Americans; and he asked Mott to convey his thoughts to Pershing. Mott accepted Foch's arguments, but Pershing was less than enthusiastic:

P. listened all through then said he had hoped all this thing was settled forever & now it seemed to be dug up; that he was utterly inflexible on the subject & he was going to fight this thing whenever [wherever?] it came up as it had done for now 8 months; that he was going to create American Divs & Corps, that our gen'ls could soon learn – learn by fighting & on my saying that this was expensive in men he said then it could not be helped, that if it cost 20% more in losses for our men to be in American divs. & Corps commanded by American gen'ls, he would coldbloodedly accept this loss rather than put in our rgts singly in the French & Brit Divs.[80]

Pershing dined with Foch on 25 April, and they 'thrashed out' the matter. Pershing remarked that Foch seemed more concerned with the 'transportation of Infantry for service with the French and British than of the formation of an American army. I insisted that we must prepare for the latter.' Then he showed Foch the agreement with Milner. This was the first Foch knew of it, and Clemenceau would broadcast his own displeasure at the French exclusion a few days later during the Supreme War Council meetings. As Grant told the War Office: 'it would have been

---

[79] Joint Note 18, CAB 25/120/SWC148, and *USAWW* 2: 257–8.
[80] Mott diary, 27 April 1918.

very desirable if a summary of the agreement had been telegraphed here as soon as possible afterwards, as General Pershing was the first to inform General Foch of its contents'.[81] Pershing explained that he disagreed with Joint Note 18, and that he had agreed with Milner that infantry would be transported in May on the understanding that the artillery and administrative units would follow in June. Of course, Foch wanted three months' worth solely of infantry and machinegunners. There was little point in the AEF having its artillery if the British were thrown into the sea and the French pushed behind the Loire.[82] However, Pershing was adamant.

General Bliss was present at the meeting at Foch's urgent request. He tried to smooth matters by pointing out that Pershing was unwilling to admit that the emergency measures giving priority to infantry in transportation might last beyond May, whereas Foch wanted those measures to continue beyond May and June.[83] Despite mutual assurances of confidence and cooperation, the meeting did not reach substantive agreement. Foch accepted that if the British really could supply all the shipping that the Milner–Pershing arrangement foresaw, then perhaps entire divisions might be brought across the Atlantic. Yet he insisted on planning for large infantry-only transports in June.

At the end of April, therefore, Foch was faced with Pétain's resentment at having to use up his reserves in supporting the BEF; with Haig's proposal to suppress nine divisions; and with Pershing's continued resistance to any form of amalgamation. In the face of this, French intelligence knew that there were in total 206 enemy divisions on the Western Front, although they knew the whereabouts of only nineteen of the reserve divisions. The whereabouts of the forty-six others were unknown.[84] On the other hand, the Belgians had extended their front and had done very well in resisting German attacks, despite Albert's refusal to put Belgian troops under Foch's command. Further, the Italian II Corps arrived in France between 21 and 27 April. General Diaz had offered their services instead of returning the French units that had been requested. In military terms, then, the manpower position was stable if not good. It was at the political level that important decisions would have to be taken.

Before the main sessions of the SWC on 1 and 2 May, British and French military and political leaders met on 27 April to talk about the American agreement over troops, and also about Wilson's desire that the

[81] Grant to DMO, War Office, 27 April 1918, WO 106/417.
[82] 'Report of Conversation between General Pershing and General Foch at Sarcus, April 25, 1918', in *USAWW* 2: 348–50.
[83] Bliss to Secretary Baker, 27 April 1918, Bliss mss, cont. 250.
[84] Intelligence bulletin 1312, 30 April 1918, *AFGG* 6/1, annex 2097.

BEF withdraw to a line from Béthune, through St Omer to the coast. Clemenceau was angry about the agreement to place American troops with the British in return for shipping transports. He 'did not dispute the desirability of the arrangements made, but he could not understand how such an agreement could have been arrived at without the French being present'.[85] Milner explained the policy as covering 120,000 infantry and machinegunners 'certainly for the first three months', thus revealing a difference of understanding with what Pershing told Foch two days earlier. It was decided, after what Wilson described as 'considerable wrangling & some warmth', to submit the agreement to the full SWC. Then Haig stated that he did not believe that echeloning reserves behind the British front was an adequate solution, because it led to mixing up troops; but Foch maintained his tactic of not taking over sectors whilst a battle was in progress, unless of course it became necessary to do so. In response to Wilson's suggestion about a British withdrawal in the north, Foch rejected the notion. He was fighting to protect the ports and to keep the two armies together. The enemy attacks lost momentum after the first few days, and he saw no reason why succeeding offensives should not suffer the same fate. So the meeting led only to Clemenceau's protest about the Pershing–Milner agreement (beginning a long-drawn-out quarrel about reserves in Britain by asking to send a French expert to look at the War Office's figures) and Haig's and Wilson's complaints of inadequate French support, while Foch maintained his position. He would not give up the ports and he would not relieve troops in the front line while the battle continued.

After the meeting broke up, Wilson pressed Foch again about whether he favoured covering the ports or retiring behind the Somme, but Foch would not be drawn. He 'absolutely refused to consider it even as a problem ... he would not go back a yard ... he would stop the Boches etc. etc.' Despite their friendship, Wilson resolved to pursue the matter. He thought that both Foch and Clemenceau had been difficult during the meeting and that the British needed to assert themselves much more.[86] Tiny cracks were beginning to appear in the façade of Allied unity. Wilson and Haig thought that the BEF was being treated unfairly; Pétain believed that the BEF in France ought to contain a million more men and that Lloyd George was afraid to send them;[87] and Foch and Clemenceau thought that the British and the Americans were making secret agreements that excluded the French.

[85] 'Notes of a Conference held at Abbeville', 27 April 1918, WO 158/72.
[86] Wilson diary, 27 April 1918.
[87] Major Paul H. Clark [Pershing's liaison officer at GQG], Report #57, 28 April 1918, Clark mss.

The three meetings of the fifth session of the SWC took place in Abbeville because it was still too dangerous to have Foch and the three CinCs remove themselves from the battlefield to Versailles. Clemenceau opened proceedings with another complaint about France's exclusion from the US–British agreement on troop transports. Milner and Pershing defended themselves, and Lloyd George attempted to pour oil on troubled waters by pointing out that the interests of the Allies were identical. British losses meant the suppression of ten of their divisions (one more than Haig had signalled earlier), and also meant that French divisions had to be moved to take their place. Consequently both Britain and France required American help, and he appealed to Pershing to permit the extension of the May programme (120,000 infantry and machinegunners only) to June. Pershing was not to be moved. He did not suppose 'that the American army was to be entirely at the disposal of the French and British commands', and he refused to consider the troop transports for June until later in the month.

Foch remained silent at first, but eventually broke in, accepting the principle of a 'homogeneous' American army yet insisting that the situation demanded the extension of the May programme into June. His appointment to supreme command had been sanctioned by the three governments. If he were to be denied a say in such conventions as the Pershing–Milner agreement, then 'his position was stultified' (or, in the French version of the minutes: 'ou bien je n'ai pas de raison d'être'). Foch proposed that he, Pershing and Milner should meet separately and reach an agreement. This proposal was accepted and the meeting adjourned.

When they re-convened the next day, Foch made a long statement to the council. He emphasised the gravity of the present situation, as the Allies' manpower resources dwindled while there was no end in sight. He felt his own responsibilities greatly and asked each government to accept its own responsibility. The losses suffered in the two German offensives had been out of all proportion to previous years. The enemy had available replacements of more than half a million men. It was essential, therefore, in Foch's opinion, that priority should be given to the transport of 120,000 American infantry and machinegunner troops not only during May, but also in June and July. He begged the council to send a statement to the US President pointing out the gravity of the situation. He ended by saying that he spoke as the CinC of the Allied troops in France and that 'his position as such made it imperative for him to submit this request to the Governments of the United States of America, France, and Great Britain. The Heads of these Governments must decide.'[88]

---

[88] 'Procès-verbal of the Third Meeting of the Fifth Session', 2 May 1918, IC 59, CAB 28/3.

This blatant attempt on Foch's part to go over Pershing's head and appeal to President Wilson met with a mixed reception. A member of Pershing's staff, present at the meetings, described Foch as making 'a very long and impassioned harangue', in which he 'practically tried to use his authority as Commander-in-Chief to order General Pershing to agree' – 'in effect, he appealed to this council to force the United States to turn 500,000 or 600,000 infantry and machine guns over to the Allies – that is, to put them at his (Foch's) disposal'.[89] On the other hand, Bliss was more sympathetic. He did not speak during the course of the meetings, as it was his policy to support Pershing in any public forum. As America's PMR, however, he had been involved in drawing up Joint Note 18. He believed that there was 'a great deal in the very earnest remarks of General Foch' – remarks that Pershing qualified in his own diary record as 'dramatic' – and judged that as Generalissimo he deserved the support of each government, which ought to supply what Foch asked.[90]

The final resolution passed by the council was a hybrid. It accepted that an American army should be formed under its own flag as soon as possible; and that in the present emergency priority be given to transporting infantry and machineguns for 'training and service' with French and British armies, on the understanding that they were to be withdrawn and reunited with the AEF at Pershing's 'discretion' after 'consultation' with Foch. It was agreed further that in May priority be given to transporting the infantry and machineguns of six divisions; and that the British would furnish transport for a minimum of 130,000 men in May and 150,000 in June. The first six divisions would go to the British, with the remainder to be allocated at Pershing's discretion. The situation was to be reviewed early in June. This resolution was deemed to constitute the SWC's response to Joint Note 18.[91] Thus Pershing had a written commitment to the formation of an autonomous army, and Foch had slightly more men than the original 120,000 May contingent.

Foch did not get his own way entirely in another matter. The Italian Premier, Orlando, raised the question of the extension of the Beauvais agreement to Italy. His country had not been represented at Beauvais, yet he accepted that if fighting in Italy 'reached the same condition' as the fighting in France then Italy would agree to unity of command in the person of Foch. Otherwise, Foch's role was restricted to the 'coordination' agreed at Doullens. Foch pointed out that the Doullens agreement

---

[89] Colonel L. Eltinge, 'Notes of the Abbeville conference', n.d., RG 120, Entry 268, folder 730.
[90] Letter, Bliss to Secretary Baker, 4 May 1918, Bliss mss, cont. 250.
[91] Resolution no. 6, IC 60, CAB 28/3.

was a dead letter since Beauvais had superseded it, and he 'deprecated the resuscitation of a buried agreement'. Orlando refused to go beyond acceptance of the principle of coordination, and the resolution that was finally adopted reflected his position. Foch was recognised as CinC of Italian troops on the French front; the powers of coordination conferred at Doullens were extended to the Italian front; and Foch would become CinC of all Allied troops on the Italian front if the fighting extended from France into Italy (the Western Front now designated as running from the North Sea to the Adriatic). In one respect this gave Foch even less than the Doullens agreement, because the clause giving the individual national CinCs the right of appeal to their government if they considered that an order given by Foch endangered their army was incorporated. This had not formed part of the Doullens agreement but had been decided at Beauvais.

The SWC decided also to wind up the Executive War Board. Lloyd George explained that the board's powers had been transferred to Foch in his new role. It had done nothing since its proposal for a general reserve had been squashed, and it was now formally dissolved. Foch did not comment on the passing of the organisation that had caused him so much exasperation and had proved inadequate when disaster struck.

The final matter affecting Foch that was settled at Abbeville was the question of the defence of the Channel ports. It was discussed at a separate meeting between the British and French, which included the French Navy Minister and the First Sea Lord, Admiral Wemyss, rather than in a full session of the council.[92] Wilson began by laying out the problem: should the armies north of the Somme retire to the Channel ports, if retreat became unavoidable, or should they fall back along the line of the Somme, thereby keeping in touch with the French armies? He stated that he and Foch had agreed that it was a problem for the two governments to solve. Foch argued that the terrain before the ports meant they were defendable, and Haig agreed. Haig also stated that, however necessary it was to defend the ports, separation was even more dangerous. Lloyd George was not satisfied. He pressed the point that it might become necessary to decide before in fact a retirement became necessary. Foch repeated that it was fundamental to both British and French interests that neither Doullens (where the armies joined) nor the ports should be lost. He went so far as to admit that losing the ports would not mean that all was lost, and that so long as the Allies held together all would not be lost – 'But it would never come to that.' The admirals both agreed that

---

[92] 'Procès-verbal of a Conference held at the Prefect's Private House, at Abbeville, 2 May 1918', IC 56, CAB 28/3.

losing the ports would make the naval war very difficult, and Pétain summed up: 'General Wilson's question was as to whether in the last resort, we should fall back on to the Channel ports or on to the line of the Somme. The answer was: on the line of the Somme.' Thus Pétain cut the verbiage, reasserting the principle of maintaining contact between the armies that he had tried to impose on an unwilling Haig in the days between 21 and 26 March. Foch had not been able to bring himself to say it, because saying it somehow made it more likely. The fact remained that the *only* tactic, if it came to the worst, was to hang together – not separately.

The exchange just described illustrates neatly the reason why Foch was chosen rather than Pétain to lead the Allied armies. A positive 'can do' attitude was needed, rather than cold reality. Foch refused warmly to contemplate losing the ports, even though keeping the armies together was the priority. Pétain faced that possibility coldly. As Clemenceau told the Deputies' Army Commission when he reported to them what had happened at the Abbeville conference, Foch 'inspires everyone with his ardour ... he has everyone's confidence.'[93]

So, between the start of MICHAEL on 21 March and the first week in May, Foch had acceded to supreme command in name, but the limits on that command were also delineated. General Pershing became more obstinate in proportion to the pressure that Foch attempted to apply over the use of his troops. The British, including Wilson, were concerned about the Channel ports, and Foch had no control over naval matters. The Italians accepted Doullens, but not Beauvais. The Belgians did not accept Doullens at all. Pétain was beginning to resent Foch's actions. He had been able to accept Doullens as the only way of controlling Haig, but Beauvais was harder to swallow. The over-arching problem was one of manpower, at a time when Germany still had numerical superiority on the Western Front. The enemy was close enough to the Paris–Amiens railway to interdict its use for troop transports; they were close enough to Calais to be able to bombard it with long-range guns; they were able to shell the coal mines around Béthune and Bruay, dispersing the miners and their families, thereby preventing coal supplies from reaching munitions factories. The emergency was not over.

On the positive side, two great German offensives had been stopped with much exhortation but fewer reserves. The first, MICHAEL, had run its course by the time that Foch took command and it was Pétain who did all

---

[93] Audition de Clemenceau, Commission de l'Armée, Chambre des députés, 7 May 1918, C7500, fo. 58.

and more than he had agreed with Haig. In the second, GEORGETTE, Foch took far greater risks with skewing French reserves northwards than Pétain could have contemplated. Although Foch's insistence on not relieving during the battle was resented and misunderstood, the policy had been vindicated by results. The British and the Americans might not like Foch's operational decisions, but those decisions were accepted and they proved sufficient. He had managed not to lose the military battles, but the political battle over manpower was just as difficult. His opponent Ludendorff did not have to fight on both military and political fronts.

Nevertheless, Foch was thinking of the counter-attack that was needed to deal with the Germans. He had inspired confidence in the government that he would attack when ready, not before.[94] 'When we have patched things up in the north', he wrote in his notebook, 'we must do our accounts and talk about offensives'. He accepted that with 150 Allied divisions against 200 enemy an offensive was impossible for the time being. However, he had a plan for his 150 divisions. Other plans were possible but he intended to carry out his own. This Pétain accepted, but Foch did not trust Haig's acceptance. 'When the moment comes to carry out the plan', he wrote,

there should be no more discussion. If the British high command does not think it possible to carry it out, does not wish to carry it out – if it appeals to the government [. . .] if I am obliged to appeal to my government to discuss the measures opposite the British government, delays and indecision result – which compromise the operation, the effects of the manoeuvre. I am unsure of what I can do. I prefer that another general take responsibility.

Just as in March in London, Foch concluded, when Haig's system – namely his arrangement with Pétain for mutual support – won support over his general reserve, the only thing to do would be to charge Haig with the supreme command.[95] That option does not even bear thinking about.

It is only when considering what might have happened had Pétain and Haig remained in command of their respective halves of the battlefield that the true extent of what Foch's energy and optimism achieved during the MICHAEL and GEORGETTE offensives becomes clear. Haig would have continued to pull back towards the ports, and Pétain would have given up on trying to reach out to him. General Fayolle, commander of the Reserve Army Group, commented of Pétain: 'He says dreadful things [déplorables], showing that he does not believe in the possibility of attack ... This man does not believe in the offensive. Just a little more

[94] Herbillon, Du général, 2: 253 (entry for 4 May 1918).
[95] Foch, Carnets, 30 April 1918, fo. 306.

332 Part II: Supreme command

and he would be a defeatist! He is doing himself harm and it is doubtful whether he will finish the war as commander of the French forces.' These are strong words. Perhaps the most telling comment on Foch's performance during these weeks is the fact that, when Lloyd George, Milner and Clemenceau met alone during the SWC conference to discuss who would replace Foch should he fall ill, 'they were unable to come to a decision'.[96]

---

[96] Fayolle, *CS*, 272 (entry for 30 April 1918); Wilson diary, 2 May 1918.

13 BLÜCHER and GNEISENAU, May–June 1918

MICHAEL and GEORGETTE had failed to defeat the British or to separate them from the French, and left the Germans with a much greater length of front to defend. This meant that they could not devote to a new attack the same resources that they had used in March and April, despite the return of still more divisions from the east. Nor could they mount another attack quickly. Their aim remained the same but now, in order to defeat the British, they needed first to draw away the French reserves that Foch had gathered in the north in support of the BEF by attacking French lines further to the southeast. Once this had been achieved, then another great blow could be struck against the British, an operation code-named HAGEN.

Foch's task was to foil Ludendorff's intentions by regaining the initiative himself. In order to prepare a counter-offensive to achieve this, he had to maintain Allied manpower levels by continuing his campaign against the politicians that he had started in the forum of the SWC, and to employ with the strictest parsimony those reserves that he already had collected. Meanwhile Ludendorff planned a series of operations, the main components of which were operation BLÜCHER along the Chemin des Dames in late May, and its extension, operation GNEISENAU, towards the Montdidier–Noyon line. BLÜCHER constituted a massive surprise attack in the sector where the previous year Nivelle's offensive had foundered. In fact, the battle became known as the 'surprise of 27 May'. It caused chaos in the Sixth French Army, panic in Paris, and brought Foch the closest he had come to being sacked yet again, just as Nivelle had been.

To mount his offensive Ludendorff needed time, and so the Allies benefited from a much-needed breathing space in which to rest and recuperate. GEORGETTE had ended officially on 1 May and it was almost four weeks later, on 27 May, that BLÜCHER began. Foch had already done what he could in the May sessions of the SWC to obtain more American effectives. He did not know where the Germans would attack next, although he assumed that the attack would come at one of several points in the north.[1]

Calm before the storm

The breathing space gave Foch and the Allies time to think about what had happened in March and April, how the supreme command had functioned, and what to do next. Now that he had the liberty to think, Foch began to set down his thoughts about how to proceed. A repetition of the Somme-type artillery battle was useless, he declared. Even a 'brilliant' start, followed by a re-launch, followed by an artillery duel were useless because the Germans had too many divisions, enabling them to block any breach, whilst the Allies had too few to be able to sustain the resultant casualty rate. Instead, what was required was speed to produce a 'penetration' capable of rapidly dislocating the enemy's defensive system. Instead of 'an artillery battle, slow by its nature', the Allies had to fight a 'tank battle', using the tanks either in the initial phase only, or only on part of the front, or else as a means of 'prolonging' the action. The counterpoint was that the Allies had to prevent the enemy from making a speedy break into their own front by stopping him on the front line.[2] If Foch shows no grasp of the *tactical* use of tanks in these jottings, he is clear about their *operational* value and his desire to take advantage of the Allied superiority in tank production.[3] Furthermore, he had seen what German speed achieved between 21 and 26 March, and had noted the meticulous German preparation that enabled that speedy penetration; he had absorbed the lesson that speed of execution was an essential element on the 1918 battlefield.

Meanwhile he drew up for the Allies a vigorous statement of the defensive posture to be adopted north of the Oise, while writing to and talking with them to prepare a counter-offensive stroke by building up a general reserve. Foch insisted that, because the territory that the enemy now occupied was critical, it had become necessary to resist all further attacks. The enemy was simply too close to important Allied positions to permit any other procedure than a step-by-step defence of the ground. The old defensive policy of outpost lines with a line of resistance further back could no longer be justified. In order to be able to carry out this policy, the front now held must be well organised and supported powerfully by increased artillery. Counter-attacks must also be prepared. There must be no voluntary retirements, and any ground lost must be counter-attacked

---

[1] Poincaré, *AS*, 10: 163 (entry for 7 May 1918).
[2] Foch, Carnets, 4 May 1918, fos. 307–8.   [3] Ibid., 7 May 1918, fo. 310.

immediately. In addition Foch recommended steps to be taken to prevent any 'rapid enemy penetration'. Reserve troops holding a series of defensive lines behind the front line must act as a protective barrier for the front-line troops to re-organise and re-form. The enemy must be forced to suspend operations by the high casualties inflicted upon them.[4]

Foch claimed that it was when troops retired that they became disorganised and took most casualties. Hence the most economical method was not to retire. The troops might have disagreed, but Foch was right to insist that in Flanders and Picardy the Allies could not afford to lose any more ground. Moreover, the latter half of Foch's note, in which he described the procedure to follow in case of a 'rapid enemy penetration', reveals that Foch knew that he was preaching an ideal. Despite advice that resisting on the front line was less costly than retiring, he also set out what to do when retirement did occur.

His thinking did not stop there. He wanted to take back the initiative by counter-attacking the Germans, and had asked the Italians to mount an offensive, as well as asking for help from Pershing. The double Franco-British operation that he proposed in Flanders and in Picardy would threaten enemy communications and liberate their own. He wrote to Haig on 3 May suggesting an attack by the Canadian Corps towards Estaires, where he had wanted the Flanders defence to stand during GEORGETTE. If Haig's men could put Estaires under their artillery fire, that would impede any German movement westwards towards the coast or Hazebrouck. The DAN would contribute by ensuring the safety of the Flanders hills that guarded the coast approaches. The other half of the operation in Picardy was to be carried out by Fayolle's Reserve Army Group attacking both flanks of the German salient: from its southern edge northwards towards Montdidier, and with the British eastwards from Amiens, thereby freeing the Paris–Amiens railway. This instruction left Fayolle caught between the offensive Foch and the French CinC who did not believe that the scale of the French casualties permitted such an operation. Fayolle appears to have sided rather with Foch, accepting that it was now Foch in command while blaming Pétain for signing 'absurd' orders.[5] Fayolle was in an impossible position, especially given the different characters of Foch and Pétain.

An offensive required reserves, and Foch was doing all he could to increase the divisions in his general reserve. In Flanders the DAN had three divisions in line, with a further six, plus three cavalry divisions, in

---

[4] Note, 5 May 1918, *AFGG* 6/2, annex105 (sent to Haig, Pétain army group and army commanders, and the Belgian chief of staff).
[5] Fayolle, *CS*, 272 (entry for 7 May 1918).

reserve. In addition, Foch had three divisions in Tenth Army (General Maistre) between Amiens and St Omer, and seven divisions in Fifth Army (General Micheler). The Fifth Army divisions were divided into a Somme group and a larger group in the Oise, with two divisions acting as Pétain's reserve behind the Reserve Army Group, east of that river. As well as gathering reserves Foch wanted a new spirit among the troops. He claimed that the long years spent in the trenches had 'deformed' the infantry, who were 'paralysed' by the machineguns in the new war of movement. The trench war had led to expectations that the artillery should sweep away all machineguns before the infantry advanced, but this was impossible, Foch stated. The answer was more training in small-unit tactics, using the new trench weapons and manoeuvring around obstacles such as machinegun nests instead of attempting to advance in line and stopping when held up.[6] Foch repeated these ideas in a formal letter to Pétain on 11 May, in which he requested that Pétain ensure that subordinate officers apply the doctrine already established so as to correct the errors that trench warfare had introduced. Field commanders had become used to static conditions and, being hesitant, were letting chances escape. The infantry knew only the rigid formations of successive lines supported by the artillery; but the artillery could not provide such support in a war of movement and the infantry had lost the idea of manoeuvre, despite Pétain's already issued note on small-unit tactics. All these imperfections could be correctly rapidly, Foch urged, and he asked Pétain to ensure that junior officers who had no prewar experience apply the doctrine that had already been established.

Clearly Foch was stepping beyond his strategical role in his relationship with Pétain. Foch could not send such letters to foreign generals – they would certainly be ignored as presumptuous and, even worse, would be counter-productive – but the situation was different with his own army. In Foch's defence it should be said that there was no precedent, no job description for him to follow as supreme Allied commander. Equally, neither the British nor French high commands knew what to expect of such a leader. He had been appointed as an emergency measure and it was up to him to create suitable working methods. Certainly he intervened directly with subordinate commanders instead of going through the respective CinCs. For example, he tended to send orders direct to the DAN, instead of through Plumer. DuCane called this 'a weak point in his method of exercising command', and told Wilson in an early account of his impressions of working with Foch that no serious friction had yet

---

[6] Foch, Carnets, 9 May 1918, fos. 309–10.

arisen because of it, but the risk remained. Foch would go personally to sectors under pressure to see conditions for himself, and would issue orders on the spot, using the excuse that such a procedure saved time and that he did not wish to stand on ceremony. However, as DuCane remarked after the war, this habit faded away once the crisis days of April and May were over.[7]

Foch's role was to take strategic direction of the Western Front. For this he needed information and quiet. Although he spent a lot of time travelling, he was able to think and discuss with Weygand along the way, and his regular meals and sleeping habits allowed him the time for reflection that he needed. He spent much time looking at the map on which the positions of Allied and enemy reserves were marked.[8] There were national commanders-in-chief and army commanders with staffs to do the detailed planning. As leader, Foch's role was to inspire and to encourage, just as a school principal imparts an ethos on a school or college and a CEO imparts an ethos to a company. Although Foch maintained only a small staff, there was a constant flow of officers from GQG, from Versailles, from Clemenceau's military cabinet and from the French mission at GQG. 'Old Foch' was 'in and about all day', remarked Grant (one of Foch's British liaison officers), unlike Haig at GHQ, who lived in 'ridiculous ... royal splendour', apart from his staff. Grant was also struck by the 'vast amount of information collected'.[9] It would be impractical for Foch to have a large Allied staff (as Eisenhower had, for example, in the Second World War) because neither Foch nor Weygand spoke English, because of differing systems within the national armies, and also because Foch liked to move near to where operations were taking place. A large staff would make such flexibility difficult. Although a case could be made for the principle that the main staff organisation should be with the Allied CinC, probably at Versailles, this would be entirely contrary to Foch's method of working.[10]

Foch's methods – personal intervention, but no detailed staff work or conferences with the commanders-in-chief all together – caused difficulties with both British and French headquarters. During the fighting there had been no time to ponder the best way to run a supreme headquarters, but the underlying problems surfaced when the fighting ceased. The greatest problems lay between Foch and Pétain, since both were officers in the same national army. The head of the British mission at GQG,

---

[7] DuCane, *Foch*, 6.   [8] Falls, *Foch*, vii.
[9] Grant diary, 14 April 1918; Grant, General Foch's Staff, and method of working, n.d.: both in WO 106/1456.
[10] See Terraine, *Haig*, 426.

General Clive, heard the complaints about Foch's methods and lack of staff directly. Pétain gave Clive to understand that he was 'evidently suppressing himself and practically acting as liaison between Foch and his own staff, for the time being; he would offer to resign, did he not feel that, knowing the French Army as he does, and being constantly with the troops, he is helping the show along.' Clive recorded that Pétain felt his position to be 'very unsatisfactory. He takes it as his duty to stay on and to make no difficulty about doing anything which Foch wants. He says we ought to get back to sectors. Foch [is] in the wrong place, ought to be studying strategy, not tactics. There should be one allied C-in-C for all theatres and one for Western Front.' By 19 May Pétain felt that Foch ought to take over at GQG because he had no 'means of commanding' (in other words, he had no staff), whilst he, Pétain, would become a sort of deputy ('adjoint') 'to see to the execution of Foch's wishes as far as they related to the French Army'. (It was as Joffre's 'adjoint' that Foch had coordinated action in 1914 in the north.) Pétain admitted that there were difficulties with such a scheme: first, Foch's dislike of working with a staff and, second, the probable British objection to be subordinate to GQG. It was one thing to agree to a foreigner as strategic director of operations, but quite another to be under GQG.[11]

Despite Pétain's criticisms of his unsatisfactory position and of Foch's methods, his GQG staff were happy that Foch was in charge. Major Paul H. Clark, Pershing's liaison officer at GQG, was told when Foch was first appointed that he was 'the man for emergencies', and there was 'evident praise and satisfaction' that Foch was in command.[12] Nevertheless, Derby reported as soon as he arrived in Paris to replace the ailing Lord Bertie as British ambassador that he expected friction in the Foch–Pétain and the Haig–Pétain relationships, although the triangular Haig–Foch–Clemenceau one appeared to be working well.[13] Yet Foch praised Pétain highly to the government's liaison officer, Colonel Herbillon. Ever since the unified command had been instituted, Foch said, Pétain had behaved with discipline as a comrade in arms, and Foch appreciated his calm, methodical, disinterested conduct.[14] Foch himself believed that the relationship with Pétain was working well: 'Pétain asks for help and I provide it', he wrote to his wife.[15] Yet Foch recognised Pétain's limitations and the need to play the diplomat with him. They got on well together, Foch

[11] Clive diary, 30 April, 19 May 1918, Clive notebook, 30 April 1918, CAB 45/201.
[12] Clark report # 23, 27 March 1918, fo. 6, Clark mss.
[13] Letter, Derby to Balfour, 22 April 1918, Balfour mss 49,743, fo. 489.
[14] Herbillon, Du général, 2: 253 (entry for 5 May 1918).
[15] Letter, Foch to Mme Foch, 7 May 1918, vol. 45.

claimed, because it was he who decided and who took responsibility for the decision. Although Pétain would always do what Foch asked of him, he would not do it of his own accord for fear of 'disobliging' his subordinates.[16] The acuteness of Foch's perception of Pétain's character is borne out by the events preceding the German attack on the Chemin des Dames described below, when Pétain failed to get the Sixth Army commander to obey his instructions.

Pétain was less happy than Foch's private comments to his wife might suggest. On 12 May he complained to Poincaré that the French troops in Flanders were under Foch's control, not his.[17] When Foch's comments on Fayolle's plan for the offensive out of Montdidier arrived on 13 May, he pointed out their 'contradictions' and 'impossibilities'. He told his sub-chief of staff, General Barescut, that he could not accept Foch's 'tutelage' in an operation involving sending divisions eight to ten kilometres deep into enemy territory. He even refused at first to endorse Foch's plan, because it would become a 'catastrophe', and he threatened to invoke the Beauvais clause by appealing to the government (but did not carry out the threat). Foch was dabbling in politics, Pétain claimed: 'he wants people to say that he is "offensive" and that I am "defensive". So far he has achieved success only in defensive actions, he proved it on the Yser [in 1914] and he is proving it now.'[18] So, for Pétain, the break came over the offensive policy that Foch wished to adopt. The key to that offensive policy was, of course, manpower. The French were happy to see Foch's efforts to persuade the British to enlist more men, but GQG was less happy when Foch insisted on an attack. General Brugère summed up the situation on 22 May: 'Pétain n'est pas bien avec Foch' [is not on good terms with Foch].[19]

Thus far, however, the more important relationship, that between Foch and Clemenceau, was working well. Clemenceau lunched with Foch on 5 May, soon after the end of the May sessions of the SWC, and they spoke of keeping up the pressure on the British and the Americans to increase troop numbers, although they agreed that by-passing Pershing and getting the US government to put pressure on him was probably counter-productive. Clemenceau wanted offensive action and Foch explained the scheme that he had begun to study: a joint attack, with the French aiming northwards from Montdidier and the British eastwards so as to

---

[16] Foch letters to Mme Foch, 25 April, 8 May 1918, ibid.
[17] Poincaré, *AS*, 9: 169 (entry for 12 May 1918).
[18] Extracts from de Barescut diary, entries for 13, 14, 15 May 1918, cited in Notin, *Foch*, 365.
[19] Brugère diary, 22 May 1918, 1K/160.

squeeze out the German salient.[20] Clemenceau sang Foch's praises in the Army Commission hearings in the Senate and in the Chamber of Deputies. He claimed that Foch was 'rejuvenated' and fully in control, although lacking the powers that Napoleon had enjoyed. Foch had to use diplomacy every day with Haig ('not a great soldier') rather than issue orders, yet he had managed to get Haig's agreement 'up to a certain point'.[21] Foch too was content with Clemenceau's handling of the SWC sessions, and praised his energy in suppressing the strikes of munitions workers in St Etienne.[22]

There were not the same complaints from the Americans about Foch's lack of a proper staff. This was because the administrative arrangements for the reception and insertion of the American troops who began arriving in large numbers in May were dealt with by the army general staff in the Ministry in Paris. The administrative burden was huge because the number of US divisions in France doubled in May from the nine present in April. Indeed, Foch was still nominally chief of the army general staff, as General Alby, his second-in-command, always signed his correspondence as acting chief of staff. The proposal to centralise all questions of bringing Allied troops into the line and to create a special section for the Americans came from the general staff of the army, not from Foch himself. On 18 May Foch approved the establishment of the Commissariat général des affaires de guerre franco-américaines, and Tardieu was taken from his Washington High Commission to head it.[23] So administrative matters to do with the AEF were being dealt with and, in any case, Pershing's headquarters were a long way from the action in northern France.

Once those American troops had arrived, however, the question of their deployment continued to be a source of conflict. Although getting more British troops across the Channel was a speedier answer to Germany's numerical superiority in France and Belgium than waiting for American divisions to be trained and equipped, nevertheless it would be American divisions that would tip the scales in the end. So Foch wrote to Pershing on 8 May to accept the latter's offer of three US divisions, and to ask when the next three might be ready to take over a quiet sector of the front, thereby freeing French divisions, as the agreed transport plan brought American infantry and machinegunners across the Atlantic.[24] The 1 US

[20] Mordacq, MC, 2: 9–10.
[21] Audition de Clemenceau, Commission de l'Armée, Chambre des députés, 7 May 1918, C7500, fo. 58; Audition de Clemenceau, Commission de l'Armée du Sénat, 8 May 1918, S-69–7, fo. 10,594.
[22] Foch letters to Mme Foch, 3, 25, 27 May 1918, vol. 46.
[23] GQGA JMO, 10 and 18 May 1918, 26N 1.
[24] Foch to Pershing, 8 May 1918, AFGG 6/2, annex 130.

Division that was already in the front line northwest of Montdidier began planning an operation to capture the village of Cantigny, which became the first American success and a psychological boost. Foch wrote that he had heard much praise of 1 US Division. He also asked for four or five American pilots to be detached to French squadrons, since the French air service had been operating non-stop since 21 March. He ended with flattery: the French had noticed the skill and boldness of these pilots; if four or five completed their training in a French squadron, they would not only render the French a great service but would also follow 'the glorious traditions of the Lafayette squadron [of American volunteers]'.

Foch gave Pershing the impression that he was satisfied with the transport arrangements agreed by the SWC at Abbeville when he saw him in Versailles on 18 May. Madame Foch's diary confirms – she saw her husband the next day for the first time in six weeks – that Foch believed that the council had made an important contribution to solving the problem of getting more American troops to France.[25] Foch seems to have accepted that Pershing would not give up his demand for autonomy, and proposed the creation of an American sector. Pershing indicated that he had ordered his aviation service to supply Pétain with as many pilots as he needed. Also Foch proposed a schedule, in agreement with Pétain, 'prescribing the American troops which shall serve with the French for certain periods of instruction and the duration of those periods'.[26] Foch harked back frequently to getting a definite training timetable settled for the newly arriving Americans during the coming weeks.

In American matters, Foch could count on the support of the American military representative on the SWC, General Tasker H. Bliss. Although Bliss was careful not to disagree openly with Pershing, his views accorded more closely with those of Foch. Bliss had been an advocate of unified command ever since the previous November, when he arrived in France. Immediately following the Abbeville SWC sessions at the beginning of May, he wrote to Secretary of State Baker urging that Foch's wishes be met as far as possible. Since the Allies had agreed unanimously to make him responsible for the Franco-British front, their governments ought to cooperate when he asked for infantry. Bliss ended with a plea not to return to divided responsibility, with three separate and independent nations waging three separate and independent wars against the common enemy. After much thought Bliss informed Clemenceau of the substance of what he had written to Baker, and then wrote to Foch in French with a

---

[25] Mme Foch diary, 19 May 1918.   [26] Pershing diary, 18 May 1918.

translation of what he had said.[27] Thus Foch was assured of support from Versailles in his disputes with Pershing. It is not, therefore, surprising that Foch should have requested as early as 29 March that he and Bliss should meet as frequently as possible and that an American liaison officer be appointed to keep them in touch.[28] This is in contrast to Foch's 'rudely' stated dislike to a British liaison officer of having foreigners at his headquarters.[29]

As far as the British were concerned, Grant at Allied headquarters received frequent complaints from GHQ about Foch's lack of staff. On 29 April, for example, Clive reported to him that not only was 'the French part of the Allied Command ... not working well', but he also

> criticised the working of Foch's staff and talked a good deal about a joint French and British Staff. But as far as G.H.Q. is concerned I don't think he was really making any constructive criticism, or doing more than repeating gossip from the Staff at G.H.Q. No doubt that Foch is too far forward and Pétain too far back but that has nothing to do with minor details of staff work.

Later, Grant heard at GHQ the 'usual abuse of the French and criticism of Foch's Staff' but Davidson backed down when asked to specify: 'The annoying thing is that he talks before the young officers of his staff and allows them to make unfriendly criticisms. They go out to the Armies and repeat this sort of thing to their friends, and so it goes on.'[30] Haig himself told Clive that the whole GQG staff ought to be handed over to Foch.[31]

The British complaints from GHQ reflected in part the experience of subordination to Nivelle in 1917, which had been less than happy. Those senior members of Haig's staff who had not experienced the Nivelle episode were, on the other hand, newly appointed to their jobs and lacked experience of dealing with neighbouring French units. General Herbert Lawrence, for example, became chief of staff only at the end of January, and so had suffered the first German offensive before having to deal with the altered circumstances of the unified command. Other senior members at GHQ were just as lacking in experience: General Sir Travers Clarke replaced the long-serving QMG at the end of December 1917; a month later General Guy Dawnay became Lawrence's deputy and General Edgar Cox became the intelligence chief. Only Davidson remained in

---

[27] Bliss to Baker, 11 May 1918, Bliss mss, cont. 250; Bliss to Foch, 14 May 1918, *AFGG* 6/2, annex 182.
[28] Foch to Bliss and General Giardino [the Italian military representative], 29 March 1918, RG 120, M923, file 201. Colonels Embick, Poillon and Wells were so designated on 16 April 1918, ibid.
[29] Grant diary, 30 March 1918, WO 106/1456.   [30] Ibid., 29 April, 22 May 1918.
[31] Clive notebook, 21 April 1918, fo. 345, CAB 45/201.

post as head of operations under Lawrence. So GHQ either had bad memories of 1917 and the subordination to Nivelle, or else they had little experience of working with the French. Lawrence was a particular problem. Foch noted on 13 May that Lawrence 'rejects everything; proposes nothing; lets no one approach him'. He expanded this in a list: Lawrence '1) does not know; 2) does not want to know when he is informed; 3) digs in his heels against foreigners; and 4) against his government; 5) tries to set one against the other'. Foch was unsure whether Haig simply followed Lawrence in this attitude, or whether he had the same views himself.[32] A British source confirms such lack of cooperation. General DuCane, Foch's liaison officer, found 'very little good to say of the staff at G.H. Q.' when he wrote his postwar memoir. 'In dealing with the French they seemed to me [DuCane] to be petty and to show quite extraordinary hostility ... always suspicious ... Lawrence was exasperating. He could believe no good of the French.'[33]

A further reason for the GHQ staff hostility may have been, as General Pierre Laguiche, the head of the French Military Mission there, reported, a feeling of humiliation that they had needed to call for help at all. On 9 May he suggested that, since the military situation had stabilised and there had been time to reflect, high command perhaps regretted having given away their independence too easily. They blamed both their own government and the French for having imposed an extension of the British front when, as the March events showed, they did not have the means to hold the extra length. Furthermore they blamed the French for prolonging the war when resources needed to be conserved for the economic postwar. The report was not completely negative. Attitudes in subordinate units were noticeably different where staffs attempted to satisfy French wishes, doing so even a little ostentatiously as though to hide a certain scorn.[34]

Haig himself showed no overt signs of hostility. He seems to have been content during May to recuperate from the alarms of the previous weeks; he visited many of his divisions, and his letters home are full of his newborn son. Indeed, he cooperated with Foch over two measures that the Generalissimo proposed as palliatives for the manpower shortages. While the battle was still raging in Flanders, Foch had suggested a scheme of rotating tired British divisions into quiet French sectors (*roulement*) so as to give them time for rest and training and also so as to free French divisions for Foch's general reserve and counter-offensive. Haig had

---

[32] Foch, Carnets, 13 May 1918, fo. 311. '1) Le W. Law ne sait pas; 2) Ne veut pas quand on lui permet de savoir; 3) se braque contre l'étranger et; 4) contre son gouvernement; 5) Tache de les f. bat. l'1 contre l'autre. H. le suit ou participe de la mem natu.'

[33] DuCane, *Foch*, 86.   [34] Report # 7077, 9 May 1918, 15N 11/29.

agreed, and Milner (now Secretary of State for War) had accepted on 19 April that four British divisions would move to the Chemin des Dames, so long as no 'permanent' arrangement was contemplated. Haig could see no reason to object to such a scheme, and he rejected Wilson's immediate and negative reaction.

It was Foch's liaison officers who settled the details of the *roulement* with Weygand, General Davidson from GHQ and General Barescut, sub-chief of staff at GQG. They met at Foch's headquarters on 10 May. Four British divisions constituted as IX Corps under General A. H. Gordon were to occupy a sector currently held by the French with three divisions in line and one in reserve. Davidson insisted that GQG consult with GHQ rather than the corps commander about the state of the divisions, which had been severely mauled in the earlier fighting, before putting them into line. Weygand pointed out that with the possibility of more British divisions being rotated to French sectors, the question of Haig's breaking up nine divisions became acute. The British army would be unable to contribute any divisions at all to a general reserve, which would be needed if the Germans mounted another big attack. Weygand suggested that men engaged in Home Defence in Britain be brought out to France, and the less physically fit category 'B' men also.[35] This procedure – staff meetings to settle administrative matters – had proved successful and Weygand continued with it for the rest of the war. Clive's comment on this procedure – 'I must make this a weekly show' – confirms the utility of the two staffs meeting regularly.[36]

Neither did Haig object any more than he had over the *roulement* to Foch's pressure over getting more men over from England so as to avoid the need to suppress divisions. Haig claimed that the casualties in March and April meant that he had to reduce nine British divisions to a skeleton cadre only. Clemenceau was dissatisfied with the responses of Lloyd George and the War Office to his reiterated demands that the British send more troops across the Channel. There was a deep-rooted French conviction that there were over one million trained men available in Britain.[37] Accordingly Clemenceau called both Foch and Pétain to Fayolle's Reserve Army Group headquarters on 15 May to discuss how to exert pressure through Haig rather than directly on London.[38]

They decided that Foch would call personally on Haig; he went immediately the next day. Haig noted how Foch was 'most pleasant and anxious to be helpful', so clearly he had made his points tactfully. Foch insisted

[35] Conférence tenue à Sarcus le 10 mai 1918, *AFGG* 6/2, annex 142.
[36] Clive diary, 10 May 1918, CAB 45/201.
[37] See Greenhalgh, '1918 Manpower Crisis', 405.   [38] Mordacq, *MC*, 2: 19–20.

that, out of the 1.4 million men in khaki in Britain, '100,000 could be obtained to fill out nine divisions sufficiently to hold a quiet part of the front'.[39] Clemenceau wrote to Lloyd George in similar terms at the same time.[40] The double-pronged attack worked, and Haig agreed to write to the War Office 'asking for men of a lower class than "A" men for this purpose'. It had become received wisdom that the British were hoarding men in accordance with over-generous medical requirements. Foch disapproved of categorising troops into 'A' and 'B' classes, as he told Wilson later, but he used the distinction to win Haig over (successfully) to his way of thinking. The American liaison officer at GQG reported that Foch had been able to convince Haig by his 'earnest presentation'.[41]

The relationship with London ought to have been a little easier now that Wilson was CIGS. Yet, even before the May SWC session, Derby had been worried by what he saw as 'intense bitterness', as Clemenceau became 'very anti-P.M.', and Foch 'anti Henry Wilson'.[42] During the April emergency Wilson had gone to France four times, but he only made one visit in May over and above the SWC conferences of May and June. The easy collaboration of 1914 and 1915 was not repeated. Indeed, it was probably impossible that it should be repeated, not only because of the vastly increased responsibilities of both men, but also because of the omnipresent manpower crisis. Foch's insistence that the British should do more gave rise to much resentment, and when Foch proposed his *roulement* scheme Wilson opposed it strongly. The French meant 'to take us over body & soul', Wilson grumbled, and there were '[n]umberless signs of interference'. He had heard reports from the military attaché and from Clive along similar lines.[43] An American proposal that the Allies should pool their resources raised Wilson's hackles even further.

According to Weygand, it was the manpower question that cast the only 'shadow of a cloud' on the Foch–Wilson relationship.[44] Wilson went to France on 20 May to speak to both Haig and Foch about the numbers of men that the War Office could raise: 2–3000 'A's, 15–16,000 'B's and about 5000 others. According to Wilson, these figures pleased Foch (although fewer than Foch believed possible), but the latter had already told Clemenceau of the difficulties that such a distinction might raise if it became 'definitive'. Foch urged that the formation of 'B' units should be considered purely as a temporary expedient. He did not want a class of

[39] Haig diary, 16 May 1918.
[40] On Clemenceau's 'campaign', see Greenhalgh, '1918 Manpower Crisis', 404–5.
[41] Clark report #75, 18 May 1918, fo. 4.
[42] Derby to Balfour, 28 April 1918, Balfour mss, 49,743, fos. 55–6.
[43] Wilson diary, 12, 14, 15 May 1918. See also Greenhalgh, *VTC*, 213–14.
[44] Weygand, *IV*, 520.

divisions that was good only for holding the line, not for mounting offensive operations.[45] (As will be seen, the German decision to create a dual system of special attack divisions and 'trench' divisions meant that eventually they ran out of trained troops.)

Foch did not neglect the other fronts where he might find support for his proposed offensive. He had already failed in April to get King Albert to accept unified command, and the Flanders coast remained a critical and threatened sector. There had been one bright spot. On the night of 22–23 April a long-planned operation against the Belgian ports of Zeebrugge and Ostend succeeded in partially blocking the former, although an Anglo-French force failed against Ostend. Ostend was attacked again on 9 May, this time successfully. Although the blocking of the two exits from the submarine pens at Bruges had limited effect, the boost to morale was huge. After the two German offensives, at last a naval victory could be cheered. King Albert, however, was afraid for the small stretch of territory over which the Belgian flag still flew. He had resisted French pressure to permit Belgian troops to serve in the army of another nation, but his chief of staff had accepted Foch's note of 5 May, discussed above, in which he urged no retreat. The possibility remained that a retreat (to the sand dunes around Calais if necessary) might have to be ordered. Albert and Lord Curzon were in correspondence about the King's visit to Britain, during which the Cabinet wished to discuss 'certain grave eventualities'. London was discussing evacuating Dunkirk, and Albert's letter to Lord Curzon of 1 May shows clearly his belief that, if it came to a decision between Paris or the ports, his first responsibility was to retain the ports and keep with the BEF. Although he anticipated 'violent' discussion if such an emergency came to pass, nevertheless he was convinced that Anglo-Belgian 'common interest is to defend the coast with the most stubborn energy even if we were reduced to hold on the narrow space of ground along the sea, ground protected by inundations that could be extended from Dunkirk to Calais'.[46]

Of course, Foch would not countenance such action. He went north in person on 22 May, and spoke to the King, to Gillain and several other generals. The Belgian memorandum prepared for the meeting argued the need to hold on to the coast between Nieuport in Belgium and the Somme, because the British might be tempted to withdraw their army to defend Britain if ports such as Dunkirk fell into German hands. Albert himself would be heartbroken if forced to abandon the last remaining

[45] Wilson diary, 20 May 1918; GQGA JMO, 18 May 1918, 26N 1, and doc. # 139.
[46] Letter (in English), King Albert to Lord Curzon, 1 May 1918, in Thielemans (ed.), *Albert Ier*, 469–70; also in 'A' minutes to War Cabinet 405, 6 May 1918, CAB 23/14.

portion of Belgium's territory, and he asked Foch to have all measures ready to flood the land leaving him in the sand dunes protected by the Royal Navy on the sea. The memorandum did make clear, however, that everyone agreed that 'the region must be defended foot by foot and with all possible energy'.[47] Accordingly, Foch departed confident that the Belgians would stand firm, their defensive measures were complete, and preparations had been made to flood, should that become necessary.[48]

There was one other sector of the Western Front, now designated as running from the North Sea to the Adriatic, to consider. Foch wrote to General Diaz on 7 May urging that the Italians take advantage of Austrian inaction and their own numerical superiority (which the Allies lacked in the north) by making as soon as possible a strong offensive on the enemy communications in the Val Sugana, then as now an important route through the Alps. The Italian response was evasive, citing enemy preparations for an offensive in Italy. Foch never managed to overcome Diaz's skill at evasion, despite re-organising the French military mission with the Comando Supremo. General Graziani, commander of the French forces in Italy, reported that the worries of the Italian high command might derive from lack of confidence in the morale of their troops.[49]

So the May days following the end of GEORGETTE were filled with reflections on the German offensives, leading to complaints about the way Foch was directing the Allied armies. His exhortations and attempts to extract more manpower resources led to growing tensions with the British over manpower and with Pétain over strategy. Foch's aim in all his actions was to be able to respond to further enemy action. True to his principle that the only path to victory lay in offensive action, Foch had criticised the limited plan that Fayolle produced for the Montdidier operation. Pétain considered that Foch's criticisms of Fayolle's 'restricted' plans dealt only with tactical matters. In a somewhat abrupt letter written the day after the meeting, Pétain asked Foch to expand those tactical considerations, which 'were not enough to reveal the strategic idea' behind the operation. He ended the letter: 'I should be grateful if you would send a written directive to form a basis for the definitive orders to be given to Fayolle.'[50] In other words, Pétain was attempting to confine Foch to strategy, where the Doullens agreement placed him, so as to leave

---

[47] 'Note rédigée par Galet, au nom du Roi, en vue de la visite du général Foch', 21 May 1918, in Thielemans (ed.), *Albert Ier*, 473–4.
[48] Mordacq, *MC* 2: 37; GQGA JMO, 22 May 1918, 26N 1.
[49] Foch to Diaz, 7 May 1918, Diaz to Foch, 14 May 1918, 15N 43; Graziani to Etat-Major de l'Armée, 23 May 1918, 15N 45.
[50] Pétain to Foch, 16 May 1918, *AFGG* 6/2, annex 197.

himself with the tactics of an operation which would be agreed with the general executing that operation.

The answer came as Directive number 3, dated 20 May.[51] For three weeks the enemy had ceased attacking, Foch stated, but more offensives were to be expected. The Allied armies must be ready to move rapidly onto the offensive whilst they still retained superiority in tanks, aviation and artillery. Foch did not refer to the fact that the Allies were far from having a numerical superiority in infantry. His intelligence report of the same date estimated eighty German divisions in reserve, of which the whereabouts of only thirty-three were known. The estimated figure of 206 German divisions in line had been unchanged since the end of April, but the figure of reserves had increased steadily throughout May, from sixty-four to eighty.[52] Foch listed the two operational aims that he believed their own limited resources permitted and whose importance justified the operations – freeing the Paris–Amiens railway, and freeing the mines in the north. No operation could be contemplated between the Oise and Switzerland because the risk in the north was too great to permit moving troops away from that sensitive sector. The large German salient gave the possibility of mounting convergent attacks in both British and French sectors. Surprise was a vitally important factor, to be achieved by using tanks and the new gas ypérite (a variety of mustard gas); speed was equally important so as to take advantage of any momentary enemy disorganisation. Foch hoped to be ready to attack once he had twenty divisions in reserve, but if the enemy attacked first the Allies might not have enough units for a riposte. So Foch had not changed his thinking about the offensive being the best way to recapture the initiative, nor about the two sectors which promised the most benefit. Yet, in other respects, the directive was pie in the sky. Against eighty German divisions in reserve, he would have a quarter of that number.

Fayolle, who had to carry out the Amiens attack, approved Foch's directive, especially the combined Franco-British nature of the operations, but he could see that Pétain and Foch did not agree. The former exaggerated the enemy's power and so did not want to attack, whereas the latter did not appreciate it fully. Fayolle believed that both were right in their way, and that what was needed was a combination of them both in one man. Fayolle could see that not only should no risks be taken by mounting useless operations but equally that the public needed a significant victory at not too great a cost. He judged, however, that his Montdidier/Amiens operation would achieve that victory. Pétain waited

[51] Directive 3, 20 May 1918, *AFGG* 6/2, annex 214.
[52] Intelligence report, 20 May 1918, 15N 5.

to see the plans that Fayolle drew up rather than producing orders himself.[53] Pétain's final instruction to Fayolle envisaged the employment of twenty-eight to thirty divisions on the southern sector of attack, with a further fourteen to sixteen in the northern, but at the end of the document Pétain laid out a reduced plan in case events interfered with the operation.[54] Pétain's caution could not be suppressed. This instruction was dated 26 May. It was already too late. It was, indeed, enemy offensive action that forestalled Foch's plans (see Map 15).

The 'surprise'

Ludendorff had met the German army group chiefs of staff on 29 and 30 April and they had decided to proceed with BLÜCHER against the Chemin des Dames around 20 May, to be followed by GNEISENAU, a follow-up attack by *Eighteenth Army* from Montdidier to Lassigny about a week later. There were insufficient forces to make the two attacks simultaneous. The aim was simply to 'disrupt the unity of the Allied front opposite Army Group Crown Prince Rupprecht, and create the possibility of renewing the offensive against the British'.[55]

The Germans had been pushed off the Chemin des Dames ridge by the fighting in the latter part of 1917, and the front line now ran north of the Ailette river. Facing the Germans was a succession of rivers, all running more or less east–west, with high ridges separating the river valleys. Between the Ailette and the Aisne was the high Chemin des Dames itself; then there were the rivers Vesle, Ourcq and, finally, the Marne, which the Germans had last seen in 1914. Because of these geographical features the main lines of communication also ran east–west. Since the Germans would be attacking towards the south, they not only had to cross the ridges and the rivers but they would also suffer from the poor north–south communications when supplying their armies. On the other hand, they did have more divisions, returned from the Eastern Front, and were able to allocate twenty-nine attack and ten trench divisions to the operation. The enemy's numerical superiority on the Western Front was great: 206 infantry plus four cavalry divisions to the Allies' 173 infantry plus ten cavalry divisions. Once again, Bruchmüller had the task of drawing up the artillery plan, and Rupprecht's army group in front of the British gave up as much heavy and field artillery and as many engineer, bridging and

---

[53] Fayolle, *CS*, 274 (entries for 19 and 21 May 1918).
[54] Pétain to Fayolle, copied to Foch, 26 May 1918, *AFGG* 6/2, annex 255.
[55] Zabecki, *German 1918 Offensives*, 210.

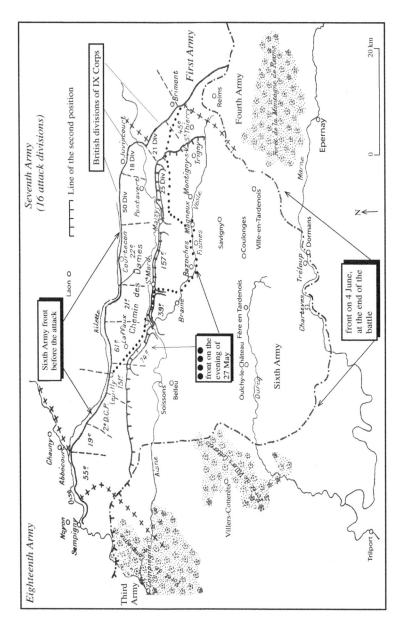

Eighteenth Army

Seventh Army
(16 attack divisions)

Line of the second position

British divisions of IX Corps

Sixth Army front before the attack

front on the evening of 27 May

front on 4 June, at the end of the battle

First Army

Fourth Army

Sixth Army

Third Army

N

0   20 km

Laon

Ailette

Chauny
Abbecourt
Noyon
Sempigny
0.3e
55e
19e
2e D.C.P.
Liguilly
15e
1.74e
61e
La Faux
21e
St-Marle
Courtecon
22e
Chemin   des   Dames
139e
157e
50 Div
Pontavert
Maizy
18 Div
Juvincourt
25 Div
Bazoches
Fismes
Braine
Magneux
Montigny-s-Vesle
Vesle
Trigny
 St-Thierry
45e
21 Div
Brimont
Reims
Savigny
Coulonges
Ville-en-Tardenois
Dormans
Tréloup
Char-teves
Marne
Epernay
Forêt de la Montagne de Reims

Aisne
Soissons
Belleu
Villers-Cotterêts
Fère en Tardenois
Oulchy-le-Château
Ourcq
Forêt de Villers-Cotterêts
Forêt de Compiègne
Triport

Map 15 The 'surprise' of 27 May 1918 on the Chemin des Dames

communication units as it could to Crown Prince Wilhelm's army group for the new operation.

On the Chemin des Dames, the French Sixth Army held the front, under the command of General Duchêne (he had been Foch's chief of staff in XX Corps in 1914). Five tired British divisions, grouped as IX Corps, had joined Sixth Army as a result of the scheme of *roulement* to quiet sectors that Foch and Haig had agreed. This front was outside the Oise to Somme sector, which Foch had designated as too sensitive to permit any retirement, and so Duchêne should have followed the flexible defence-in-depth methods set out by Pétain. His army group commander Franchet d'Espèrey, and Pétain himself, both called his attention to his failure to follow the prescribed doctrine, but Duchêne responded that he was unwilling to abandon the line of the Chemin des Dames after it had cost so many lives to win, a line that was particularly strong. Given Pétain's fight since January 1918 to get his defensive doctrine accepted, his postwar excuse that he had not used the threat of removal from army command to force Duchêne to obey seems feeble. In his report on the 1918 campaign Pétain stated that he was aware of the army commander's disobedience, but the only remedy was to change the commander, and he felt that it would be a 'very serious' matter to do so in the face of an imminent enemy attack.[56] Yet Duchêne's refusal to obey was not recent. After all, Duchêne had been in command of Sixth Army since December 1917, and the army had occupied more or less the same sector since the March 1918 fighting. As Foch was aware, Pétain was known to be unwilling to impose confrontation.[57] Although Pedroncini suggests that Pétain did not want to enter into conflict with Foch because Duchêne's ideas reflected those of Foch more than those of Pétain, it is more likely that Duchêne's abrasive personality was the reason for Pétain's failure to bend him to his way of thinking. Duchêne's brutal ways seem not to have improved since October 1914 when he was chief of staff of Castelnau's Second Army. Abel Ferry's investigation of the 'surprise' offensive on the Chemin des Dames showed that Duchêne's staff did not speak to him during meals. His 'brutality' towards his subordinates and 'rudeness' towards his superiors revealed, in Ferry's view, not strength but 'a spirit of perpetual hesitation'.[58]

Instead of islands of resistance forward of the main defensive position, therefore, Duchêne had eleven French and British divisions in the front line, deployed along the ridge of the Chemin des Dames itself. They had

---

[56] Pétain, *Rapport sur les opérations: Campagne défensive*, pt 4, p. 8.
[57] Even Pedroncini admits as much: *Pétain Général*, 367.
[58] Ibid.; Ferry, *Carnets secrets*, 303–4 (entry for 30 July 1918).

1422 guns and were supported by fourteen squadrons of aircraft. Against them were ranged almost four times as many guns (they included nine of the very heavy long-range 240 mm railway guns), four times as many aircraft, and twenty-nine divisions of infantry.[59] Even if the Germans had not achieved surprise, their overwhelming superiority in guns and men would still have achieved a breakthrough.

The Germans did, indeed, achieve complete surprise. Superb staff work had concentrated the guns, the men and the aircraft in complete secrecy. At 3.40am on 27 May, after Bruchmüller's artillery barrage of only two hours and forty minutes, *Seventh Army* began its infantry assault behind a double creeping barrage. The lead units were on the ridge an hour later and had crossed the Aisne by 10am. They had moved so quickly that Sixth Army was unable to evacuate its artillery. By the end of the day the Germans had expended three million rounds of shell, half of which was gas, and some units were even across the Vesle. The defenders, packed into the front line despite Pétain's instructions, were overwhelmed; Duchêne lost communication with the forward units and did not order the bridges across the Aisne blown in time. He sent his reserves forward and they too were overwhelmed. It was an even worse disaster than 21 March, the first day of the German offensive against the British.

Pétain asked immediately for Fifth Army to be released to him, which left Foch with a mere four divisions in Tenth Army as his general reserve. Foch asked Haig to create a British reserve force in case Tenth Army had to be sent to Pétain also, in addition to a division from the DAN. These measures were not enough. The next day, 28 May, the Germans reached the ridge south of the river Vesle, where they halted because they had reached their objective. Sixth Army was pushed back ten kilometres from the Vesle and German troops entered the outskirts of Soissons. Foch saw Clemenceau and then Pétain that day. Foch told Clemenceau that the Chemin des Dames could very well be a feint and that consequently he did not intend to move all his reserves from Flanders and the Somme. Clemenceau and Mordacq found the atmosphere at Foch's headquarters 'calm', but then they moved on to Pétain's headquarters, where there were 'recriminations' about Foch's insistence on keeping reserves in the north.[60]

On 29 May the German advance continued. Ludendorff had been tempted by the spectacular gains to order his armies to press on. He lost sight of BLÜCHER's original purpose when he ordered two attack divisions to be moved from Rupprecht's army group. His original intention had

---

[59] Zabecki, *German 1918 Offensives*, 215.
[60] Mordacq, *MC*, 2: 42, 45 (entry for 28–29 May 1918).

been to force French units to move, not to move German ones south. The German centre was now nearly at the Marne with very little in the way of defenders in front of them, and Soissons fell. Pétain asked Foch for all the French troops in the north, but, with more than sixty German divisions still in reserve behind Rupprecht's front, Foch did not feel able to accede completely. In any case, it would take time to transport by train all the divisions to the battlefront since his projected offensive to free the Paris–Amiens railway had still not taken place. Instead Foch asked Haig to take over from Tenth Army the task of guarding the junction of the British and French, and he asked the Belgians to extend their front as far as Ypres to help the British. Crisis point was reached on 30 and 31 May. *First Army* attempted, but failed, to encircle Reims in the east; the Marne was crossed at Dormans and a twenty-kilometre stretch of the northern bank occupied; and thousands of prisoners and hundreds of intact guns had fallen into German hands.

By 1 June the Germans were only about sixty kilometres from Paris, but although Ludendorff continued to issue orders to continue the offensive (against Reims in the east and southwestwards on the right flank), BLÜCHER had run its course. As always happened, increasing casualties and difficulties in supplying the forward units halted momentum. The enormous salient that the Germans had created was impossible to feed without adequate railways; Pétain had organised the defence at the bottom of the salient, where two US divisions moved into position around Château Thierry, and he was preparing attacks against its two flanks. More importantly, OHL had informed Rupprecht on 1 June that operation HAGEN against the British – the reason for mounting BLÜCHER – could not now begin before the middle of July. As Rupprecht's chief of staff, General von Kuhl, noted, Ludendorff 'continued to lurch from one tactical success to another, without the slightest idea of "how to end the war or to bring about a decision"'.[61]

Nevertheless the results had been spectacular. The Germans had advanced sixty kilometres in just four days, and had taken some 50,000 prisoners and captured 600 guns. Soissons had been captured, although Reims had resisted. What was less obvious to the shocked Allies, especially to the French, whose capital seemed to be under threat, was the price Ludendorff had paid for these gains: well over 100,000 irreplaceable casualties; five attack divisions, two corps headquarters and large numbers of support and labouring groups removed from Crown Prince Rupprecht.[62] As a result of the 'surprise' of the Chemin des Dames the

---

[61] Kuhl diary, 5 June 1918, cited in Herwig, *First World War*, 415.
[62] Zabecki, *German 1918 Offensives*, 226–7.

consequences for Foch – not only military, but also political and personal – were enormous. His own command, France's future and the fate of the whole Alliance – all were at stake. He had lost command of the Northern Army Group in December 1916, and Nivelle had been sacked for his performance on the exact same Chemin des Dames in 1917. Foch had been a member of the commission of enquiry that had investigated that disaster, so he knew clearly the risk to his own position. Clemenceau recalled in 1929 (on the day after Foch's funeral, hence this memory may not be totally reliable) that Foch's first words to him after the attack was launched were: 'Shall I be court-martialled?'[63]

Despite the risk to his personal position, Foch did not lose his head. His British liaison officer, General DuCane, thought after the war that he had never admired Foch so much as during the May crisis.[64] Clemenceau and Mordacq noted his calm, and his report to Poincaré spoke of the enemy advance being contained.[65] When Herbillon saw him on 3 June, 'solid and confident as always', Foch described a house shaken in a violent wind, the tiles flying off the roof and the walls shaking – 'but the foundations are holding', Foch said, 'and they will continue to hold, that's the important thing'.[66] The gap in the usually daily letters to his wife between 27 May and 4 June betokens the emergency, but after that gap his letters were full of optimism as matters were 'stitched back together' (another favourite simile).[67] A further sign that Foch had not panicked is given by his insistence to Wilson that the forthcoming SWC meetings in Versailles should not be postponed because of the fighting.[68]

Nonetheless, there was considerable criticism of his decisions. Senator and journalist Joseph Reinach claimed that Foch was entirely responsible, because he had refused to believe in an attack in the Aisne department, whereas Pétain had asked for divisions against that possibility.[69] Fayolle blamed Foch for saving British lives at the expense of French ones by keeping the DAN behind the BEF. Later, however, when the situation had calmed down, Fayolle realised that Foch had been correct to some extent, because Ludendorff had clearly not intended to go as far as he had.[70] In the east Castelnau lamented the failure of both Foch and Pétain to foresee events, and the lack of understanding between them, so that there were almost two distinct fronts, the Foch front and the Pétain front,

[63] Suarez, *Soixante années*, 2: 243.   [64] DuCane, *Foch*, 37.
[65] Pedroncini, *Pétain, Général*, 371–2; Weygand, *IV*, 532.
[66] Herbillon, *Du général*, 2: 261 (entry for 3 June 1918).
[67] Letters, Foch to Mme Foch, 4, 5, 6 June 1918, vol. 46.
[68] Wilson diary, 29 May 1918.   [69] Brugère diary, 29 June 1918.
[70] Fayolle, *CS*, 278, 280 (entries for 31 May, 3 June 1918).

with the latter being sacrificed for the benefit of the former.[71] General Micheler (Fifth Army) cannot have been the only commander to wonder why Nivelle was sacked in 1917 but Foch and Pétain remained in position in 1918.[72] The enquiry that Clemenceau instituted on 25 July was less wide ranging and less high powered than the 1917 enquiry upon which Foch had sat. Its terms of reference were limited to the command of Sixth Army and no higher.[73]

The greatest criticism came from parliamentarians. Abel Ferry, now one of the Army Commissioners, thought that the price for getting Foch in supreme command had been too high, because he had covered Calais instead of Paris.[74] His preliminary report for the Chamber of Deputies' Army Commission called for sanctions to be taken. The losses in men and materiel had been severe but, Ferry judged, the moral damage was greater. The French army's prestige had been dented, with the Italians claiming that it had suffered a French Caporetto, and the British claiming that it had suffered a French 21 March.[75] The corridors of the Assemblée nationale ran with rumours and counter-rumours and questions about the rightness of the decision to put Foch in supreme command. Clemenceau appeared before the Deputies' Army Commission on 3 July, but asked the members not to divulge what he had told them. He was less optimistic, he said, than Foch, who was of the opinion that the German offensive would be stopped within a few days.[76] In the Chamber the next day the left put down four interpellations on the military situation. Clemenceau defended both Foch and Pétain vigorously, and he won acceptance for his declaration that it was not the time to discuss such matters while the battle continued, winning the vote to postpone the discussion indefinitely by 377 to 110.[77] Clemenceau's main political opponent, former Premier Briand, declared patriotic support for Clemenceau and told Derby that 'he was a great believer and a strong supporter of Foch'.[78] With such strong backing Foch's position was secure, for the time being at least. Nor was Clemenceau insincere in his support, for he had already told Poincaré

[71] Gras, *Castelnau*, 375.
[72] Micheler, 'Mémoires sur les opérations de rupture du printemps 1917', 1K/113, [d] 6, fos. 152–3.
[73] Rupture du front du Chemin des Dames: Commission d'enquête, 5N 256.
[74] Ferry, *Carnets secrets*, 298 (July 1918).
[75] Rupture du front français le 27 mai 1918 au Chemin des Dames, 17 July 1918, in Ferry, *La Guerre vue d'en bas et d'en haut*, 317–18.
[76] Audition de Clemenceau, 3 June 1918, Commission de l'Armée, Chambre des députés, C7500.
[77] Bonnefous, *Histoire politique*, 390–4.
[78] Dutton (ed.), *Paris 1918*, 27 (entry for 31 May 1918).

that he had complete confidence in the Allied leader and that Foch's decision to weight the reserves in the north was correct.[79]

As for the general mass of Parisians, they seemed to take the threat to Paris less seriously than the politicians. Despite the renewed shelling of the capital by the large railway gun – Madame Foch could hear the booms in Versailles, west of Paris – Sundays in June in the Vincennes and Boulogne woods had never been so busy. When the Germans had last reached the Marne, in 1914, about one million Parisians had fled, but the reduced numbers this time were swelled only by refugees from the fighting who were transiting Paris. The particularly high number of departures from Paris stations on 16 June (82,000) was the result of that date being the first day of the fishing season.[80]

There was no question of the government leaving Paris. Poincaré was adamant that he would not leave as he had in 1914, and the Presidents of the parliament's two chambers stated that they would not authorise the government to leave.[81] Clemenceau was clearly determined to fight on, uttering the words that Winston Churchill heard and echoed a generation later: 'I shall fight in front of Paris; I shall fight in Paris; I shall fight behind Paris.' The capital was placed in the zone of the armies once again, and a defence committee was set up (6 June) to coordinate measures under the Military Governor of Paris. General Guillaumat was brought back from Salonika to take over this command. (There may have been some thought that he ought to be on hand in case anything happened to either Foch or Pétain, or alternatively in case either had to be removed because of public opinion. Guillaumat appears to have believed that he might replace either general.[82]) Foch could be assured, therefore, that he had political support and the Premier's confidence; Poincaré noted how calm and lucid Foch was when he saw him in Paris on 7 June.[83]

The answer to criticisms of Foch's decision to retain French reserves in the north behind the British, thereby running the risk to the defence of Paris, lies in the results obtained. At the price of considerable ill-will – both French because they had to beg for troops to be returned, and British because they were asked to give up those troops – Foch's policy was vindicated when the German offensive ran out of steam. Moreover, the enemy salient that pointed at Paris provided a sound basis for a French counter-attack, since Pétain held both its flanks firmly.

[79] Poincaré, AS, 9: 213 (entry for 2 June 1918).
[80] Mme Foch diary, 28 May 1918; Darmon, Vivre à Paris, 382–7.
[81] Poincaré, AS 10: 205–6, 200–1 (entries for 1 June, 29 May 1918).
[82] Nicol, Uncle George, 166.   [83] Poincaré, AS 10: 222 (entry for 7 June 1918).

It was not simply Foch's handling of the reserves that the 'surprise' of 27 May brought to the fore. More military questions arose from it. Why was it a surprise, and what responsibility must Foch bear for the intelligence failure? What responsibility did other commanders bear, Pétain and army group commander Franchet d'Espèrey, and Sixth Army commander Duchêne? What was the effect on the relationship between Foch and Pétain, and between Foch and Haig?

The intelligence failure was great. Foch received the daily bulletins from both GQG and GHQ, but neither service detected the German buildup of men and guns on the Aisne front. Impeccable staff work enabled Crown Prince Wilhelm's army group to maintain secrecy. Stringent camouflage and concealment measures, strictly enforced discipline over noise and light during the night-time movements, and restriction of knowledge about the forthcoming operation to corps level and above – all contributed to fooling the Allies. The Germans were helped by the heavily wooded terrain where the troops and artillery were concentrated, and also by deception measures such as false wireless traffic. Aerial photography could be carried out only in daylight, in clear weather; observers could not see into wooded areas. Moreover, both the British and French air services had just undergone transformations. The French constituted their Division aérienne on 14 May, under the command of General Duval, head of aviation at GQG; the Royal Air Force had been created on 1 April 1918 by amalgamating the military and naval air services. No night reconnaissance mission was sent over the Aisne sector, but all skirted the area to the west or the east.[84] Briand criticised GQG severely for not sending out aerial observers and claimed to 'know for a fact' that there had been no aerial observation at all in the month before the offensive began. The British too complained about the total lack among the French of aerial observation.[85] These criticisms are unjust. Pétain sent out the Division aérienne in force on 21 May to find out what was happening behind the enemy front, but it failed to find anything.[86] On the evening of 26 May, the aviation of one of Sixth Army's corps reported that there were no signs of an attack: 'absolute calm; no troops, no convoys, no lights, no bivouacs'.[87]

Foch was certainly aware of the poor performance. At the end of April he had called in Commandant Armengaud (he had been in charge of Second Army's aviation in 1914) demanding a better quality of

---

[84] Martel, *French Bombardment Forces*, 349.
[85] Letter, Bliss to Baker, 14 June 1918, cited in Palmer, *Bliss, Peacemaker*, 283.
[86] Laure, *Au 3ème bureau*, 123–4.
[87] Telephone message from 11 CA aviation, 26 May 1918, 20.00, *AFGG* 6/2, annex 291.

intelligence. To Foch's somewhat brutal complaints, Armengaud responded that the Allied armies must be ordered to devote the necessary resources to the task of observation, instead of putting every effort into bombing and fighter missions. He drew up for Foch a 'Note sur l'exploration aérienne' on 7 May, but it had not been approved for putting into effect before the German attack.[88] On the other hand, the Germans too failed later to spot the Allied buildup in the forest of Villers-Cotterêts before the French counter-attack of 18 July. Moreover, as a further mitigating factor in the intelligence failure, at the beginning of May German counter-espionage had destroyed a large network of agents in Belgium and the occupied departments, which interrupted the collection of intelligence at this critical time. Foch urged reconstitution of contact with the enemy lines as a 'vital necessity', but this could not be achieved overnight.[89]

There were, however, some indications of the forthcoming attack, although they appeared very late. British intelligence became aware of the impending attack on 26 May and passed on the information to GQG, but this was less than twenty-four hours before the attack began. The Americans too had reached the conclusion that the Aisne front was to be the target. Captain S. T. Hubbard, in charge of the Order of Battle room at AEF headquarters, deduced to his own satisfaction that the Chemin des Dames was likely to be the next target, between 25 and 30 May. He was sent to GQG with this information and convinced de Cointet, but General Duchêne and his chief of staff did not believe the threat because of the natural strength of the Chemin des Dames position.[90] At Versailles also, where Bliss had a staff officer coordinating all the intelligence reports, the conviction grew that the Aisne was to be focus of the next attack. Bliss was prevailed upon, because of his friendly relations with Foch, to write and warn him. According to the chief of intelligence at AEF headquarters, after the offensive, when Foch was under attack in the parliament, a 'member of Foch's staff' asked Bliss not to make known the existence of his letter because of the 'great pessimism' of those days.[91] Bliss had already mentioned his conviction and the French rejection of his warning to Derby on 31 May in the Paris embassy. However, since the *députés* do not appear to have got hold of the story, presumably Bliss kept quiet thereafter.

[88] Armengaud, *Renseignement aérien*, 170–4.   [89] Lahaie, Renseignement, 665.
[90] Hubbard, *Memoirs of a Staff Officer*, 222–32.
[91] 'Dictated Memoirs of General Nolan, G-2, AEF, concerning his experiences in that headquarters in WW1', 1 March 1936, Nolan mss, box 2, folder 4, fos. 5–6.

At GQG Cointet had believed the two German prisoners who were captured on 26 May, the day before the offensive, when they warned of what was to happen. An officer was sent to Foch's headquarters with the warning, but it was dismissed once again as unreliable. After it became clear that the intelligence had indeed been correct, Foch asked the officer to keep quiet and rewarded him for his discretion by giving him the privilege of acting as orderly on 11 November 1918 when the Germans signed the Armistice.[92]

There were good reasons, of course, to doubt the intelligence. First, it was known that the enemy used disinformation – Pétain had been convinced in March 1918 that his front in Champagne was about to be attacked when it was the British front that was the target. It was wise, therefore, to be cautious. Foch told DuCane on the eve of the Chemin des Dames attack, when finally there were indications that this was indeed the front, that such information 'one gets from all parts of the line every day'. This does not mean that Foch had no use for intelligence reports (as his latest biographer writes), merely that he was rightly cautious about trusting a single piece of intelligence.[93] The British too had dismissed rumours of attack in the Reims area because they believed it was attempt to distract attention from the Arras sector, using bogus wireless traffic as a deception measure.[94] Finally, an enemy attack from north to south with no strategic objective in view made no sense.

So, despite some mitigating circumstances, the 'surprise' was a clear French intelligence failure. Although Foch did not have his own intelligence organisation, it is interesting that Bliss and Cointet both went direct to Foch. Moreover, Foch had tried to improve the aerial observation service. Yet Foch had read the broader strategic situation correctly. As early as 29 May, two days after the assault began, he noted, first, the German success on the Aisne; next the necessity to stop them; then the fact that the safest *strategic* object for the enemy was Abbeville then Calais and the British army. 'But before hitting the British, they want to wear down the French reserves, hence the Aisne battle. It may be followed by other battles on the French front (that will depend on their casualty figures), which is not to say that they were giving up their decisive objective, the British.'[95] Foch concluded that an offensive against the British was still to be expected, and that the British front should be reinforced with divisions brought back from Italy. If, therefore, Foch *had* returned French reserves from the north, he would have played into the enemy's

---

[92] Cointet memoirs, Cahier '1918', fos. 65–6.
[93] DuCane, *Foch*, 36; Notin, *Foch*, 368, speaks of his 'persistent scorn'.
[94] Beach, British Intelligence, 258.   [95] Foch, Carnets, 29 May 1918, fo. 313.

hands. If he had *not* resisted Pétain's and GQG's repeated calls for their return, the losses on the Aisne would have been higher, and Crown Prince Rupprecht's offensive under preparation in the north could have been launched. Foch had enough confidence in his reading of the strategic situation to stick to his policy. The enquiry into the offensive found that the reason for the stunning German success was their overwhelming superiority in men and guns, and bringing back some of the French divisions from the north would not have been enough to even the odds.[96] So Foch was correct too in his policy of pursuing the politicians as energetically as he could over manpower policy.

Other mistakes were made for which Foch could not be held responsible. Duchêne complained that no superior officer came to see him during the first days of the battle, neither his army group commander, Franchet d'Espèrey, nor Pétain.[97] However, Duchêne's failure to blow the Aisne bridges, before the Germans crossed, and his over-confidence generally in the strength of the Aisne positions, cost him his job. On 31 May Foch, Clemenceau and Pétain met and decided that command changes had to be made, despite Pétain's reluctance. Some corps commanders, too, were relieved and replaced by younger, more energetic officers.

Pétain's performance, too, could be criticised. His failure to insist that Duchêne follow his instructions for defence has already been noted. There is anecdotal evidence that he was not even at his command post when the storm broke, but otherwise engaged in Paris.[98] Clemenceau noticed the atmosphere of recrimination at GQG, and recrimination is always a sign of negativity.[99] Commandant Laure of 3e Bureau was working on a radical plan to withdraw Allied troops in the north to below the Somme, and to bring Castelnau's Eastern Army Group forces to support the Marne troops, thereby abandoning Verdun, Nancy and the Vosges. On 30 May Pétain asked Castelnau to prepare in secret the destruction of materiel and installations on his front, and the withdrawal of American and French units of his army group westwards, keeping in contact with the Northern Army Group. Pétain passed Castelnau's plan on to Foch on 4 June, thereby feeding the latter's belief in Castelnau's defeatism. As Foch's memoirs reveal, he had understood that Castelnau had prepared the plan on his own initiative, but Weygand was able to correct this

[96] Rapport de la commission constituée à l'effet d'émettre un avis sur les opérations de la 6e Armée du 26 Mai au 3 Juin 1918, p. 25, 5N 256, dossier A.
[97] Mordacq, *MC*, 2: 44 (entry for 28–29 May 1918).
[98] Wormser, *Clemenceau*, 207, claims Pétain had 'une galante rencontre'. I have found no confirmation of this.
[99] Mordacq, *MC*, 2: 45 (entry for 28–29 May 1918).

mistake in his own memoirs.[100] As for the withdrawal to the Somme, the head of the Belgian mission at GQG reported to the King the reactions of Foch and his staff to the idea. It would be 'folly' to hand over Calais and Boulogne and the mining resources of the north without a fight. Foch claimed that, because the British would take to the boats, the saving of divisions needed to hold the reduced front would be wiped out straight away. He reassured Colonel Menschaert that the front would hold, that Belgium would be secure, and that he should not worry about such a 'mad' scheme.[101]

Although Pétain wrote to Foch on 4 June with his double withdrawal scheme,[102] he had acted more positively over the question of evacuating Reims. Franchet d'Espèrey had ordered this on 31 May, but fortunately subordinate commanders had not obeyed the order. Such a move would have handed the Germans their objective on a plate and allowed them to re-supply their Marne salient. Pétain's order to Franchet d'Espèrey was a forceful command to defend the city although he had no reinforcements to send him.[103] So the failures extended through several levels of command.

As for the British, Haig's lack of generosity in begrudging the release of French troops from his own sector strained relations, although he might be forgiven some *Schadenfreude*. He told Pershing that the French should have foreseen the attack and he criticised their failure to stop the enemy, although he did admit that his words were only a private comment and that he would 'play the game' and do as the French asked 'because he realized the importance of this'. As Pershing remarked to his diary, such criticism was 'rather remarkable in view of the events that took place some two months ago on the British front'.[104] Haig wrote to his wife: 'It seems satisfactory that the blow has fallen on the Aisne front because the French will be obliged to use their reserves, and it gives our tired Div[isi]ons & newly arr[ivin]g American time on which to train ready for the battle.'[105] It was disappointment, therefore, that Haig felt when Foch's repeated calls for more troops arrived. Foch took away his general reserve, Tenth Army, and asked Haig on 3 June to create a replacement British reserve corps of three divisions to be placed astride the Somme, ready to support either the British or the French. Also Foch took a second division from the DAN and finally asked Haig to release some of the US divisions that were

[100] Clark, Report # 86, 31 May 1918; Pétain to Castelnau, 30 May 1918, *AFGG* 6/2, annex 751; Gras, *Castelnau*, 376; Weygand, *IV*, 534.
[101] Menschaert, Report # 31, 8 June 1918, Maison Militaire du Roi (Galet), folder 5.
[102] Pétain to Foch, 4 June 1918, *AFGG* 6/2, annex 1122; Pedroncini, *Pétain Général*, 378.
[103] Pedroncini, *Pétain Général*, 376.   [104] Pershing diary, 30 May 1918.
[105] Haig to Lady Haig, 28 May 1918, acc. 3155, ms. 151.

training with the British. This was a blow. Haig grumbled that sending divisions whose training was almost complete in order to release French divisions in the east for the current battle was a waste. Haig doubted whether the French divisions so relieved would 'ever really fight!', but since Pershing concurred in Foch's decision there was nothing he could do.[106]

The German offensive had given the Americans their first opportunity to make a significant contribution to the fighting. The 1 US Division had already been planning its Cantigny operation, northwest of Montdidier, and it began on 28 May. The original assault went well, but there was a hard battle to retain the captured ground as French men and guns were removed to face the Chemin des Dames threat. The 2 and 3 US Divisions joined the fighting. On 31 May both moved into line near Château Thierry, and helped to stop the Germans crossing the Marne. Then, on 6 June, 2 US Division played a leading role as part of Sixth Army in the Belleau Wood operation. The arrival of significant numbers of fresh, keen American troops on the battlefield gave an important morale boost. Pershing had assured Foch that he would do all in his power to help, despite the latter's refusal ('he would not or could not see') to agree to support troops being transported across the Atlantic. 'He saw no use', Pershing recorded, 'bringing over anything but infantry and machine gun troops'.[107] On the contrary, it was Pershing who would not and could not see that the moment required men in the front line, not men to help create an autonomous American army. Foch continued that battle in the SWC.

The manpower question was even more critical now, following the enormous casualties. The British IX Corps alone suffered 28,703 casualties between 27 May and 19 June.[108] Between 1 May and 5 June French casualties were almost 136,000, of whom more than half (77,163) were killed or missing.[109] Losses were not only high for the Allies. During May the Germans had suffered 138,500 casualties, of whom 16,600 were killed with another 6800 missing, and these were irreplaceable trained troops.[110] Furthermore, since the German attack in the centre had done so much better than on the flanks, they now occupied a deep but narrow salient which could not be supplied adequately. Yet the French army was stretched to breaking point. Pétain informed Foch on 1 June that he had no reserves left; the divisions leaving the front were so worn down that, at best, they could not return before 20 June. The only resource lay among

---

[106] Haig diary, 3 June 1918.   [107] Pershing diary, 30 May 1918.
[108] Edmonds *et al.*, *OH 1918*, 3: 159.   [109] *AFGG* 6/2, appendix I.
[110] *RAW* 14, Beilage 42.

the British and the American divisions in the British sector, or in shortening the front by withdrawal to the line of the Somme and from the east.[111]

Now Foch moved from the battlefront, already well south of the Chemin des Dames, to the battlefront in Versailles, where the SWC held the three meetings of its sixth session on 1–3 June 1918. In dealing with the politicians Foch had to face the grave reports from Pétain about French manpower. He had to deal with Pershing, who was still thinking only of getting his administrative troops across the Atlantic in order to form an independent army. Nor were the British much help. Milner kept saying that he wished the BEF were back in England and he feared that the French would not 'stand a disaster'. Even Foch's old friend Wilson was critical. He wanted Foch to shorten the line in the north, where he had insufficient troops and risked a 'crack'. Repeating the arguments he used before, Wilson wanted flooding and a withdrawal to the St Omer line, despite such a move exposing Dunkirk to capture (hence possibly Calais as well) and leaving the Belgians in great difficulty. 'Dunkirk or no Dunkirk we must shorten our line', Wilson concluded.[112]

At Versailles there were some bad-tempered exchanges about manpower. Pershing recorded Foch as flinging his hands about 'in wild gestures', and repeating 'the only thing that counts is the battle'.[113] During a Franco-British meeting held just before the first session – Clemenceau described the gathering as a committee of the SWC, but it was in fact simply an attempt to get agreement so as to present a united front against Pershing – Foch read out a memorandum that he had prepared. He proposed that President Wilson be asked to increase from 120,000 to 200,000 the number of infantry and machinegunners to be sent to France during each of the months of June and July. Further he proposed that the SWC should ask for an American army of one hundred divisions. Thus far the French and the British agreed. Lloyd George was angered, however, when the discussion turned to the British distinction between 'A' and 'B' men and the alleged British failure to increase effectives before the 21 March offensive. He insisted that Foch remove the figures that he cited in such a 'pernicious paragraph'. Eventually Clemenceau suggested that the memorandum be withdrawn and revised before being submitted to the full SWC. Finally Foch asked that the British divisions in Italy be reduced from twelve battalions to nine, as in France, and appealed 'that the British Government should make every

[111] Pétain to Foch, 1 June 1918, *AFGG* 6/2, annex 968.
[112] Wilson diary, 28 and 31 May 1918.   [113] Pershing diary, 1 June 1918.

effort to maintain their divisions by all the means in their power'. If they did not do so, Foch warned bluntly, they would 'lose the war'.[114]

At the SWC's second meeting, on 2 June, agreement was reached on a telegram to be sent to President Wilson, thanking him for his 'remarkable promptness' during May in sending aid in the crisis. However, the 'utmost gravity' of Foch's memorandum led the assembled Premiers to ask for further help in reducing the enemy's numerical superiority. Otherwise there was 'a great danger of the war being lost'. A copy of the Foch–Pershing–Milner agreement on troop transports was attached: 250,000 men in each of June and July (this being the maximum possible, given British and American shipping facilities), with priority given to providing 170,000 combat troops (140,000 in July) and 25,400 for the railways, with the balance at Pershing's discretion. This was more than Foch had requested, but, although it was recognised that such numbers might mean the dispatch of untrained troops, the present emergency justified the departure from sound training principles.[115]

During the June SWC meetings other matters (command in the Mediterranean; use of Czech troops; intervention in Russia) were discussed, but Foch did not take an active part in these matters. The Allies reached agreement on one topic that would affect Foch and make his supreme command easier. This was pooling of resources. Wilson had been annoyed by the idea, because he saw it as yet another example of a French takeover, but the American suggestion that Clemenceau had accepted was agreed to in the final SWC meeting. Milner had signed for Britain on 29 May, and Clemenceau announced during the meeting that Italy and Belgium also adhered to the scheme for coordinating as far as possible the use of facilities and the distribution of supplies among the Allied armies in France.[116] Thus was created the Military Board of Allied Supply.[117]

As he left Versailles on 3 June, Foch told his wife that the situation was 'good' and that the enemy had been 'stopped'. She noted, however, that the 'stupid' townspeople of Versailles were leaving, tired by nights disturbed by the German railway gun (although the shells did little damage), and fearing the arrival of the enemy in Paris.[118]

---

[114] 'Secretary's notes of a conference', 1 June 1918, with Foch memorandum as appendix, IC 63B, CAB 28/3.

[115] 'Procès-verbal of the second meeting of the sixth session, 2 June 1918', IC 65, CAB 28/4. The American account gives a much better indication of the acrimony: *USAWW* 2: 438–41.

[116] 'Procès-verbal of the third meeting of the sixth session, 3 June 1918', IC 66, annex D, CAB 28/4.

[117] On this board see Greenhalgh, *VTC*, 232–9.   [118] Mme Foch diary, 4 June 1918.

Operation GNEISENAU

On the same day that BLÜCHER ended, 5 June, Foch moved his head-quarters further south to Bombon so as to be nearer French headquarters. He had already moved slightly nearer, to Mouchy-le-Châtel, on 1 June, and he kept Mouchy on as a useful half-way house for meetings with Haig.

Although BLÜCHER was over, the Germans continued preparations for its follow-on exploitation operation, code-named GNEISENAU. It aimed at the Noyon–Montdidier sector, west of the area of the Aisne attack, and would be particularly useful now because success would straighten out the front between the two bulges that Ludendorff had created, the first against the British in March and then against the French on the Aisne. Planning had been continuing since 3 May, and Ludendorff's constant interference in tactical matters meant that the original objectives of the operation were extended to include the line of the Montdidier–Compiègne road, about eight kilometres beyond the little river Matz that gives the French name for the battle.

The Germans were unable to replicate the superb staff work that had characterised the preparation for BLÜCHER. They did not have as much time; the nights were shorter and the cover from wooded terrain less; they lacked ammunition and petrol; and they were suffering badly from the influenza epidemic. Morale was sinking lower and many captured German 'prisoners' were in fact deserters who wished to avoid another offensive operation. Finally luck smiled on the French. On 3 June the French listening station of Mont Valérien, west of Paris, captured a German radio transmission which the cryptologist Capitaine Georges Painvin managed to decipher. It was an order, addressed to a headquarters situated between Montdidier and Noyon, to speed up supplying munitions, even by day if it could be done without being spotted.[119] This confirmed the other indicators which suggested that this area was the next target. Indeed de Cointet had warned GQG as early as 31 May that it would be the Noyon–Montdidier sector in eight to ten days' time.[120] Crucially, the intelligence gave Pétain time to strengthen the front. Moreover, the night-time air reconnaissances were providing useful information about the railway activity behind the German front.[121]

Furthermore, Fayolle kept a close eye on General Humbert command-ing Third Army that would take the brunt of the German offensive. Fayolle insisted on constructing as much of a proper defensive system in

---

[119] Lastours, *Codes secrets*, 46; Cartier, 'Souvenirs', pt 2, 19–20.
[120] Cointet memoirs, Cahier '1918', fo. 76.
[121] Pétain, *Rapport sur les opérations: Campagne défensive*, vol. 5: *La Bataille du Matz*, 6.

depth as time allowed. He supervised Humbert closely to ensure that his instructions were followed. Hence, this time, no divergences such as Duchêne had imposed were tolerated. Nor could commanders complain of having received no visit from superior officers. Clemenceau and Mordacq visited the front on 8 June and spoke with many divisional and corps commanders, as well as with General Humbert. Then they returned to the pessimism of the parliamentary corridors, comforted by the calm confidence they had witnessed.[122] Foch too kept a close eye. He had insisted to Pétain that the national territory had to be defended inch by inch, with a safety-net of troops in the rear to deal with any incursions, and that high command must act with energy and vigilance. In a sentence that must have grated on Pétain, he wrote: '[the high command] must give formal, clear orders, ensure that they are carried out whatever might happen – supervision of orders and subsequent execution must be carried out at all levels'.[123] Foch ended by asking Pétain to send out an order to all troops demanding 'energy and resolution', overseen by 'vigilance and unceasing supervision'. Foch was treading on Pétain's toes here, but obviously he did not want a repetition of the mistakes made on 27 May.

As confidence grew about the date and place of the next German offensive, Foch prepared to move reserve divisions to support Pétain from further north. When he believed at the end of May that the German intention was to get French divisions returned to the Aisne sector, he had resisted and caused Pétain much worry by refusing to meet all his demands. Now, however, Foch knew that the risks in the north were smaller, hence reserves might be moved. This time, he caused much worry to the British whose front was being deprived of troops. On 30 May Foch warned Haig that he might have to move his reserve, Tenth Army, and on 2 June he moved two divisions from the DAN. Next, much to Haig's disgust (as already noted), five of the American divisions that had been training with the BEF were returned to Pershing. He deployed them in Alsace, thereby freeing French divisions for the forthcoming German attack. Finally, on 3 June, Foch asked Haig to position three British divisions as a reserve to replace Tenth Army astride the Somme, ready to intervene either northwards in support of the British or south-wards in support of the French. With British intelligence maintaining that the numbers of German reserves behind Crown Prince Rupprecht's front still posed a considerable threat to the BEF, the stage was set for a serious breach with the British.

[122] Mordacq, *MC*, 2: 67–8.
[123] Foch to Pétain, 6 June 1918, *AFGG* 6/2, annex 1197.

The arguments during the SWC meetings – they were taking place as Foch was making these important decisions about the positioning of reserves – caused even Wilson to be critical. 'I am afraid Foch is going the right way to lose this war', he confided to his diary: 'he will <u>not</u> shorten his line in the north ... & now he wants to pinch all our American Batt[alio]ns & send them to Alsace'. Three days later Wilson was still fuming: 'Foch will lose this war. He spends his time racing about (he has changed his Hd. Qr. again today after 4 days) he can't use his Staff, & he thinks only of blocking holes.'[124] Haig's remarkably ungenerous response to Foch's requests was to declare that it was a 'waste' to send half-trained American troops to the French sector, and that British troops were 'being used up to the last man in order to give the French courage to fight!'[125] He sent copies of his correspondence with Foch over the matter to London, and London took this to be an appeal under the Beauvais agreement, which permitted a commander to refer to his government if he thought that an order of Foch's put his army in danger. How did Foch react to this challenge to his authority?

He did not dispute the risk to the BEF. He knew that the best strategic result for the Germans lay in Abbeville or Calais, namely splitting the British from the French or else capturing a Channel port. A 'British battle' was still to be expected, he noted, but the way to counter the problem of removing French reserves from the British sector was by returning British troops from Italy or by using American troops.[126] When Haig offered to trade the divisions of the DAN for the US divisions that Pershing wished to reclaim, Foch refused.[127] Wilson's complaints about Foch's handling of the war combined with British fears that the French were staring defeat in the face led Lloyd George to send Milner and Wilson to France to settle matters. All met in the War Ministry in Paris on 7 June.[128]

Haig read a prepared memorandum and asked for longer notice of Foch's intentions and the opportunity to appeal against a decision. Foch replied, perfectly reasonably, that enemy action might mean that little notice could be given; if his orders were not to be carried out, he said, then his position became untenable. Haig retorted that, in that case, his right of appeal was worthless. As liaison officer General DuCane summed it up, a 'good deal of steam was blown off on both sides'. Milner and Clemenceau handled matters with great tact. Clemenceau chided Foch for taking

---

[124] Wilson diary, 2, 5 June 1918.   [125] Haig diary, 3, 4 June 1918.
[126] Foch, Carnets, 29 May 1918, fo. 313.
[127] Telegram, GHQ to Foch, 4 June 1918, WO 158/29; Haig diary, 4 and 5 June 1918.
[128] This account is taken from Greenhalgh, *VTC*, 215–20; Milner, 'Record of a visit to Paris – 6–8 June 1918', Milner mss. dep. 670, fos. 343–52; and Wilson diary 7 June 1918.

DAN divisions without advance warning – we saw earlier how Foch tended to give orders to the French troops of the DAN although, nominally, they were under British orders – and Milner supported Foch's need to have his orders obeyed. In Milner's notes, written up immediately after the meeting, he concluded that it was all the result of a 'misunderstanding'. Foch insisted that he would not act 'imprudently', and would not take away reserves from the BEF's front unless and until German intentions were clear. In fact, he had not taken away any reserves, he had simply asked Haig to prepare the move of divisions to the Somme, should they be needed. Better staff work – on Foch's side in issuing orders (Weygand apologised for the muddle), and at GHQ (where Lawrence might have displayed greater confidence instead of telling Milner that the BEF needed to withdraw immediately behind the Somme, or it would be 'too late') – might have avoided the dispute altogether. On the other hand, matters would have come to a head sooner or later, and DuCane for one felt that Haig had simply been testing his government's commitment to the principle of unified command (see Illustration 9).

In the course of the meeting Foch asked Haig for direct confirmation that the guiding strategy remained that the two armies should keep together, doubtless because he had heard reports of the pessimistic talk from Lawrence at GHQ. He appeased Haig after the meeting by agreeing to return at once two of the British divisions in IX Corps on the Aisne, with the remaining three to follow. He flattered Haig by requesting that General Gordon and his corps staff remain with Pétain, as the French army was 'short of corps commanders and staffs': 'It is very satisfactory to find that the French have discovered the value of British staffs & their arrangements', Haig recorded.[129] Wilson was satisfied that the meeting had done 'a vast deal of good'. Foch was not worried by the proceedings. He made no mention of it in his letters to his wife, and took the opportunity to have dinner at home that evening. He was confident about the sector (between Montdidier and Noyon) where the next German attack would take place; he stated that the Americans were arriving 'en masse'; but wished that 'the British would make a bigger effort'.[130] Thus ended the first of the challenges to Foch's authority.

Two days later, on 9 June, the fourth German offensive began, as Foch anticipated. Four divisions were in place in reserve behind Third Army, and three behind General Mangin's Tenth. The French had over 1000 guns and significant air superiority, with all the Division aérienne and the RAF's 9 Brigade. In addition they had 165 tanks. Facing them, *Eighteenth*

[129] Haig diary, 7 June 1918.   [130] Mme Foch diary, 8 June 1918.

Illustration 9 Unified Command
as seen by the German satirical magazine *Simplicissimus*, published in
Munich on 16 April 1918.
French and British dispute the command, but Hindenburg caps them
both with his *Pickelhaube*, claiming 'No, I have it!'

Army had eight attack and sixteen trench divisions available for the first
day, supported by about 500 aircraft and well over 2000 guns. So the
French had double the aircraft but only half the guns deployed by the
Eighteenth Army that had destroyed the British Fifth Army on 21 March.
Bruchmüller's fireplan worked as efficiently as usual, and with double the
number of guns the infantry made significant gains on the left (east) of the
front and in the centre. By the end of the second day (10 June) some units
were across the Matz, but the Germans were hampered in the east by the

American action around Belleau Wood. In order to counter-attack from the west the five divisions of General Mangin's Tenth Army were ordered to take up position on the far left of the French forces.

That same day, however, Foch arrived at Fayolle's headquarters and pressed for acceptance of Mangin's desire to launch his counter-offensive the next day, 11 June. Mangin proposed using four of his five divisions, keeping one in reserve and starting at 11am. Fayolle argued that such a timetable did not leave enough time to get his divisions in place, but Foch supported Mangin. Pétain came to Fayolle's headquarters, but said nothing. As Fayolle remarked, it was clear that one was pushing the counter-attack whilst the other accepted it only unwillingly. In fact Pétain returned next morning and forbade Mangin to use the fifth (reserve) division.[131] Nevertheless Mangin's divisions launched their attack, supported by ground attack aircraft and ten groups of tanks. They recaptured two villages, and took 1000 prisoners and ten guns. They returned to the attack the next day but made few further gains, although they succeeded in disrupting *Eighteenth Army*'s plans. Mangin would have pressed on, but Foch and Pétain agreed on the 13th that the attack should be halted because any further gains would not justify the cost in manpower that might still be required on the Somme. They had benefited from surprise, and that advantage no longer existed. The psychological value of feeling that at last they had hit back rather than simply parrying weighty blows was immense. The Germans too suspended operations on 13 June, although some local attacks continued for two more days.

The cost to both Allies and Germans had been enormous. French casualties in both battles – Chemin des Dames and the Matz – were over 135,000, with 28,600 British and 474 American casualties; and the German figure was 130,370.[132] The French intelligence services had noted the drop in the number of good divisions that the Germans had in reserve. When BLÜCHER began they had eighty-one (sixty-two fresh), but on 8 June before GNEISENAU they had fifty-eight (forty-three fresh) and by 13 June they had only thirty-six fresh divisions out of fifty-one in total.[133] The threat to the north remained as none of Crown Prince Rupprecht's divisions had been moved for GNEISENAU, but the deep German salient as far south as the Marne was untenable without the capture of Reims to free the Reims–Soissons railway; and the fresh American divisions, double the size of British or French ones, were beginning to make their presence felt on the battlefield.

[131] Fayolle, *CS*, 282–3 (entry for 10 June 1918).
[132] Tournès, *Foch et la victoire des Alliés*, 146; Zabecki, *German 1918 Offensives*, 226, 243.
[133] Intelligence reports, 27 May, 8, 13 June 1918, 15N 5.

As for the Italian front, Foch had failed to get Diaz to take action in May. Once BLÜCHER began, Diaz became even more hesitant and the signs that Austria-Hungary was preparing to attack became clearer.[134] Foch had wanted Diaz to forestall the Austrians by attacking first, and he had written on 12 June urging this course of action. However, it was the Austrians who acted.

At a meeting in German headquarters in Spa (Belgium) on 14 May, General Arz von Straussenburg, the Austrian chief of staff, had proposed an offensive in Italy in early June between the rivers Brenta and Piave. Ludendorff and Hindenburg had been happy to approve since such action would support BLÜCHER. Gradually, however, the offensive degenerated into a series of local operations: General Conrad von Hötzendorff wished to attack once again from the Asiago; Boroevic, the commander of the Piave front, wished to launch more than the demonstration called for by the plan approved at Spa. Then the weather turned very wet, which increased the risk of flash floods in the mountains, but the Austrians were so short of food that they had provided the troops with a only few days' worth of rations. Any delay meant that they risked having starving troops for the infantry attack. Next Kaiser Karl insisted on going to the front, where his imperial train interfered with the already inadequate rail facilities and his presence there meant that Arz had to accompany him, thus splitting the high command. The main attack began on the Piave on 15 June and was initially successful. By evening of the same day, however, the Italians had counter-attacked; the Asiago operation had achieved nothing; neither had Boroevic's operation. Next day violent rainstorms transformed the Piave into a raging torrent, so that the Austrian troops who had managed to cross could not be re-supplied. By 24 June the Austrians had been thrown back across the Piave and, despite another two weeks of violent local fighting, they did not mount any further offensives. Indeed Hindenburg suggested that the Austrian offensive be stopped and six Austrian divisions sent to France where the effects of American arrivals were making themselves felt. After an initial refusal, the request was granted. The offensive had cost at least 150,000 casualties and many had deserted before the battle began, warning the Italians of the impending action. The disintegration of the Austro-Hungarian empire continued as the Hungarian parliament demanded that the fate of their divisions should not lie in Austrian hands.[135]

After the Austrian defeat became patent, Diaz still refused to contemplate an Italian offensive. Despite the Austrians' agreement to sending

---

[134] Diaz to Foch, 14 and 28 May 1918, 15N 43, [d] 1.
[135] This account taken from Cramon, *Quatre ans*, 270–83.

divisions to France, and despite the Italians' successful defence, he told Foch that he feared German intervention in Italy.[136] Foch responded that the risk from German intervention was very small, as indeed it was, and he asked Diaz to prepare a jumping-off point in the mountains so as to be ready to go onto the offensive 'on the day when the general offensive on all fronts will be ready'.[137] Foch knew already the broad outline of his strategy. His handling of Diaz, however, was becoming counter-productive. Not only did Foch fail to get him to mount an offensive, but both Diaz and his chief of staff General Badoglio resented the Frenchman's pressure. Wilson visited the British troops in Italy at the end of June. The last time he had been there was with Foch after Caporetto. Wilson thought Diaz was anxious to enrol him on his 'side' against Foch: 'It is quite clear that neither he nor Badoglio like nor admire Foch.'[138]

Reflections on the German offensives and their consequences

So what had Foch learned from these last two German offensives? They confirmed for Foch of the value of surprise, of defence in depth, of intelligence reports, and of coordinated action by tanks, aircraft and infantry. In Zabecki's view Foch 'out-generalled' Ludendorff in these operations.[139] He kept his head and, more importantly, kept his eye on the ball. He never lost sight of the fact that the main threat lay in the British sector in the north, where the enemy could still split apart the Allied armies. His calling a halt to Mangin's counter-offensive illustrates this. The first victory, however minor, that the Allies had seen all year might have tempted a Ludendorff to carry on with the operation. This was what had happened with BLÜCHER. The point had been to draw French reserves from the north, but the result had been to take Rupprecht's troops instead. Once BLÜCHER had stalled, there was no strategic point to GNEISENAU whatsoever. Ludendorff's head of operations had recommended at the planning stage in early May that if BLÜCHER failed in its aim of drawing in French reserves then GNEISENAU should be cancelled.[140] Foch, on the other hand, had put much energy into getting British divisions reconstituted, not suppressed, and in getting the maximum number of American troops to France; he had returned reserves to Pétain drop by drop, at the cost of great anguish at GQG and much

[136] Diaz to Foch, 21 June 1918, 15N 43, [d] 1.
[137] Foch to Diaz, 27 June 1918, 15N 43, [d] 2.   [138] Wilson diary, 27 June 1918.
[139] Zabecki, *German 1918 Offensives*, 231.   [140] Ibid., 245.

political criticism in Paris; he had encouraged the counter-attack as soon as it became possible to launch it. Then he called a halt when continuance would have been too costly. Moreover, he had confirmed Clemenceau in the wisdom of his choice for supreme command. Talking to Poincaré on 2 June Clemenceau declared that Pétain was better in second place than in the first. Fayolle found Pétain's lack of confidence 'despairing'.[141]

If Foch did make a mistake in his handling of BLÜCHER and GNEISE-NAU, it was to grant Ludendorff more strategic sense than he in fact possessed. Foch knew that an attack south from the Aisne led nowhere. As Clemenceau proclaimed, if Paris had to be abandoned he would fight on the Loire, on the Garonne, along the Pyrenees if necessary. So long as the Allied front remained intact, however stretched, and so long as the Allies (the British) retained control of the seas, any increase in ground occupied by the enemy only increased German difficulties. Foch knew this and, assuming that Ludendorff did too, he kept his reserves in the north where lay the only opportunity for a German victory.

The offensives led indirectly to a greater clarity in relations between Foch and Pétain. After smoothing over the dispute with GHQ and Haig's appeal to London according to the Beauvais agreement, Foch had to contend with another appeal against his decisions, from Pétain. Two aspects of Foch's actions troubled him: the deployment of reserves, and Foch's note of 16 June listing the enemy's methods of attack and the best way to counter them. The two German offensives in May and June had wiped out Pétain's reserves, so when he received Foch's order to return the British divisions that Haig had sent (XXII Corps), he was furious. He asked Anthoine to prepare a response, giving the reasons why it was 'imprudent' to continue stripping the French front for the benefit of the British. Pétain declared that he 'persisted in refusing' to give Ypres the same value as Paris; that, rather than sending French artillery to the DAN as Foch had further requested, he wanted the DAN back even if that displeased the British and the Belgians. As for Foch's note, dated the same day, 16 June, Petain declared that he had read it and that he had noted the lack of resources to carry it out. 'It would be interesting to calculate the number of troops', he continued, required by Foch's instructions to hold the front-line positions and man the second positions strongly enough to mount a counter-attack.[142]

Pétain had linked, correctly, the question of obeying Foch's instruction to have enough troops available to contain and then to counter an enemy

---

[141] Poincaré, AS, 9: 213 (entry for 2 June 1918); Fayolle, CS, 283 (entry for 12 June 1918).
[142] Foch note, 16 June 1918, and Pétain note, 16 June 1918, AFGG 6/2, annexes 1580, 1587.

attacking with surprise, violence and speed to the instruction to return troops to Haig. He responded with a double-barrelled refusal. First, he stated that the British had enjoyed two months in which to recover and should be able to hold their shorter front without help from the French, who could not take any more troops away from their own front without grave risk. Accordingly he was sending a copy of his letter with these reasons to Clemenceau. Second, he failed to see the need to add Foch's note about the defensive to the instructions he had already issued, and moreover he did not have the resources to man the lines at the densities that Foch recommended. Accordingly, he had the honour to inform Foch that he did not intend to distribute the note of 16 June to his army commanders, as requested.[143]

Foch reacted immediately. He called Pétain in to his headquarters and lectured him about the right of appeal applying only to the British and the Americans, not to Pétain. According to Foch's latest biographer, this Fochian 'tornado' caused Pétain to consider withdrawing his appeal, conforming to the Generalissimo's instructions. Whatever the effectiveness of Foch's words to Pétain, on 19 June Foch went to see Clemenceau about Pétain's refusal to transmit his note to the French armies.[144]

The Foch–Pétain relationship was becoming distinctly bitter, and Clemenceau made that conflict the subject of the Comité de guerre meeting on 26 June. After describing the earlier disagreement with Haig and the current one with Pétain, Clemenceau told the committee that he would attempt to resolve matters amicably by personal visits to both men. More importantly, the committee 'proclaimed unanimously' the necessity for complete subordination to the orders of the supreme command of the Allied armies. An appeal to the government was permissible in the case of foreign generals, but since Foch and Pétain were in the same army there was no need for such a right of appeal. Henceforth Pétain would have to obey Foch's orders.[145] The testimony of two of the ministers present at the meeting shows why the committee subordinated Pétain to Foch. The Navy Minister, Georges Leygues, described the 'serious conflict' between Foch, whose note was 'completely sensible' and Pétain, whose letter was 'vague, negative'. Louis Loucheur, Munitions Minister, called Foch's note 'remarkable' and Pétain's letter just 'pathos'.[146] The committee's decision is not surprising.

[143] Pétain to Foch, 17 June 1918, *AFGG* 6/2, annex 1605.
[144] GQGA JMO, 18 and 19 June 1918, 26N 1; Notin, *Foch*, 385–6.
[145] Comité de guerre, séance du 26 juin 1918, 3N 2.
[146] Raphaël-Leygues, *Georges Leygues*, 143; Loucheur, *Carnets secrets*, 61.

Foch had proved in Picardy in March and now on the Chemin des Dames in May that he knew how to fight a defensive battle. He had also fostered the first Allied counter-attack from Mangin and encouraged the Americans to attack in their turn, although he had not managed to get the Italians to do likewise. He had survived two appeals against his authority from Haig and from Pétain; and he had survived parliamentary pressure (with Clemenceau's support) for his removal. Pétain recognised Foch's abilities in the defensive battle. He told Barescut on 14 May that Foch was a firefighter, called in to put out the fire but sent away immediately afterwards so that he would not demolish the house.[147] Certainly Foch had extinguished the fire, but Clemenceau would not allow him to be sent away. It remained to be seen how Foch would continue the firefight without demolishing the house.

[147] Barescut diary entry, cited in Notin, *Foch*, 365.

14 MARNESCHUTZ–REIMS and Second Marne, July 1918

After surviving two challenges to his authority, Foch continued to plan his counter-offensive. Haig's appeal to London had resulted in the British government's reaffirmation of unified command, although Foch received a rap over the knuckles about informing the British in advance of moving troops; Pétain's appeal resulted in his subordination to Foch in that now he would have to obey orders. Foch was buoyed further by the Italian successes on the Piave, by the effective contribution of the Americans, and by Mangin's achievement in countering the fourth German offensive on the Matz. There were even more grounds for optimism about the enemy. Foreign Secretary Richard von Kühlmann's speech on 24 June in the Reichstag, which began optimistically, ended with the comment that such a vast coalition war could not be brought to an end by military decisions alone. The speech raised a great scandal on the floor of the Reichstag and led to OHL forcing him from office, but it received immediate coverage in Allied newspapers. A front-page account and editorial comment appeared, for example, in *Le Figaro* of 26 June. Herbillon interpreted the speech as a 'clear' statement that a military victory seemed to Kühlmann to be difficult, not to say impossible.[1]

With these encouraging signs, Foch took two steps to reaffirm his authority: he reinforced his note of 16 June that had provoked Pétain's appeal to the French government, and he issued on 1 July his fourth 'directive' as Allied commander-in-chief. On 27 June Foch's headquarters issued a document about the German method of attack that was distributed to all higher commands, down to divisional level.[2] It was to counter the German methods of brutal, speedy and deep penetration that Foch had issued his note of 16 June on the defensive method to adopt, and now he developed his analysis of the German offensive method by citing extracts from recently captured German documents. Then, in his directive of 1 July, he urged that troops must be well organised and well

---

[1] Herbillon, *Du général*, 2: 280 (entry for 25 June 1918).
[2] 'Mode d'attaque allemande', 27 June 1918, 15N 6, [d] 4.

trained in the necessary defensive methods; commanders must be prepared to act energetically; and transport arrangements must be in place in order to move to any sector which required support reserves collected behind both British and French fronts. Foch still expected that Ludendorff would act with strategic good sense, anticipating that the next German effort would be made either against Abbeville (in order to split apart British and French armies) or against Paris (which would affect only morale, not the military campaign, but which would disorganise government operations).

Also Foch took one further action to reinforce his position vis-à-vis Pétain. General Anthoine, Pétain's chief of staff, had long been a thorn in Foch's side, but Pétain had refused more than once to remove him.[3] The editor of the influential *Echo de Paris* told General Brugère on 10 May that for a long time Anthoine had been telling the press that the only course was to make peace.[4] On 26 June Foch wrote a curt letter to Pétain, informing him that Anthoine had stated that they ought to have made peace in 1916 and now they were beaten.[5] The head of Clemenceau's military cabinet, General Mordacq, was well aware that Anthoine was not the energising influence that Pétain required, quite the opposite, but Pétain threatened to resign if Anthoine were forced out.[6] Foch's response, orchestrated through Clemenceau, was a widely bruited campaign to replace Anthoine by General Buat. In 1915 Buat had worked closely with Alexandre Millerand in the War Ministry, and since the end of 1916 had been in command of the heavy artillery general reserve. He had just been appointed to command Fifth Army, replacing Micheler, in the series of changes made after the Chemin des Dames 'surprise' offensive. Buat himself suspected that he was now about to lose his coveted position as an army commander for the poisoned chalice of GQG.[7]

As soon as Foch had the necessary authority, he moved to override Pétain's objections. In a private meeting with Clemenceau on the same day that the Comité de guerre removed Pétain's right of appeal, Foch and Weygand revealed the two latest instances of Anthoine's overt pessimism: Anthoine had told the Belgian liaison officer at GQG to warn King Albert that his troops were dangerously exposed and that they should pull back behind Dunkirk (an instruction that Foch countermanded immediately); and Anthoine had responded to the news that the extension of railway communications over the Somme would be completed by August by

[3] Weygand, *IV*, 553.   [4] Brugère diary, 10 May 1918.
[5] Copy of letter, Foch to Pétain, 26 June 1918, 1K/129/1, [d] '1914 et ensuite'.
[6] Herbillon, *Du général*, 2: 270–1 (entries for 10, 11 and 12 June 1918).
[7] Ibid., 276–7 (entry for 20 June 1918).

saying that, by then, the Germans would have been victorious 'for several months already'. Clemenceau agreed immediately that Anthoine should be replaced.[8] Pétain accepted the decision sadly, but told Herbillon that he would make no further concessions. Clive thought that Pétain was 'very bitter' about the affair, even indicating that he would prefer to command an army or even an army corps as 'he could not work immediately under F. in any capacity'. In fact, Pétain claimed, the French army 'can't stand the sight of Foch'.[9] This unlikely assessment was probably valid as far as some of GQG were concerned. Pétain's headquarters staff saw Anthoine's removal as the culmination of Foch's long campaign against him, and saw for the fig-leaf that it was the fact that the appointment was actually made by Clemenceau as War Minister, and not by Foch himself. The writer of the press communiqués at GQG called the manoeuvre a 'plot' between the government and Allied headquarters.[10] However, one member at least of the GQG staff, the head of intelligence, did not regret Anthoine's departure. Cointet wrote postwar that Anthoine had long been hateful to his subordinates.[11] As for Anthoine himself, he was bitter enough to go so far as to suggest to Clive that he would be 'delighted' to accept a job at GHQ if Haig had one going![12]

Buat understood that his new role was to facilitate Foch's takeover of the French armies, and that Pétain would be 'suppressed' gradually with himself (Buat) as the 'intermediary' between French and Allied headquarters. When Clemenceau, Foch and Weygand turned up unannounced at Buat's headquarters on the evening of 30 June, Buat was left in no doubt. Foch stated that he was issuing not a request, but an order.[13] Buat was right to be wary. Clearly the relationship between Foch's headquarters and GQG required smoothing. Buat's former boss, Alexandre Millerand, thought that his appointment would be an 'excellent' solution, since Buat had Foch's confidence and would be able to make Pétain conform more strictly to Foch's directions whilst, at the same time, stopping Foch from wounding Pétain's feelings.[14]

So now Foch had every reason to face the coming month of July with confidence. Although intelligence reports made it clear by the end of June that yet another German offensive was to be expected, Foch was very upbeat, as his letters to his wife reveal. Lord Derby, now British

---

[8] Weygand's account in Weygand mss, partie donnée, carton 9, [d] 5. His account in *IV*, 533, omits these details.

[9] Herbillon, *Du général*, 2: 282 (entry for 30 June 1918); Clive diary, 1 July 1918, and notebook, 2 July 1918, CAB 45/201.

[10] Pierrefeu, *G.Q.G.*, 2: 226.   [11] Cointet memoirs, Cahier '1918', fo. 99.

[12] Clive notebook, 30 June 1918, CAB 45/201.   [13] Buat diary, 30 June 1918, ms 5390.

[14] Millerand's words in Herbillon, *Du général*, 2: 277 (entry for 20 June 1918).

ambassador in Paris, visited Foch at Bombon on 21 June and found him 'full of confidence': given another week, Foch declared, 'he would be absolutely prepared' for the next German offensive.[15] Operation GNEI-SENAU (the Battle of the Matz) had ended in the middle of the month, and the longer the renewal of the German offensive was delayed the better equipped the Allies would be to meet it. The crisis was passing, had already passed, Foch wrote; the Austrians were cracking and the Americans arriving. In fact, everything was being put back together.[16]

Even Pétain was upbeat. Foch knew that Pétain had been shaken by the 'surprise' attack on 27 May, but he was keeping a close watch over him, Foch told his wife – 'I won't say like a child, but there is a little of that in it.'[17] However, the sight of truckloads of young, fresh American soldiers inspired Pétain to declare that, if the Allies managed to hold on until the end of June, then they need have no further fears. With their situation now 'excellent', they could get the upper hand in July and so gain victory.[18] It was Foch's obstinate insistence in the SWC that was producing those great numbers of morale-boosting American troops, and it was in the SWC that Foch had to fight another political battle before turning to deal with the enemy. This was the third and final challenge to his authority, and Foch's response to it was probably all the more aggressive because of his success with first Haig then Pétain.

The three meetings of the council's seventh session took place in Versailles on 2, 3 and 4 July. Foch was present at all three, but spoke only briefly during the debate over sending troops to Siberia and northern Russia, the first item to be discussed. President Wilson had agreed to send a small American force to the northern Russian ports, but balked at intervention in Siberia, where Japanese troops would be the only signifi-cant source of military manpower. Wilson had asked Bliss to ascertain Foch's views about the matter. Foch agreed totally with the SWC decision that the Allies should occupy Murmansk and perhaps also Arkangel. The risk of large stocks of Allied materiel falling into German hands was too great to permit inaction. Foch was prepared to accept the diversion of one or two American battalions to Russia, but would object if more troops than this were demanded.[19] It was Foch's agreement to the dispatch of a limited number of Americans to Russia that swung the President's deci-sion for intervention. By the end of June, however, the situation in Russia had changed, for a force of Czechoslovak former prisoners-of-war had

[15] Dutton (ed.), *Paris 1918*, 55 (entry for 21 June 1918).
[16] Mme Foch diary, 26 June 1918.   [17] Letter, Foch to Mme Foch, 25 June 1918, vol. 46.
[18] Pierrefeu, *G.Q.G.*, 2: 191.
[19] Bliss to Baker, 18 June 1918, in Link (ed.), *PWW*, 48: 367–70.

collected along the trans-Siberian railway. They had been taken prisoner by the Russians from the Austro-Hungarian armies, and were liberated following the signing of the peace treaty with the Central Powers. Now they wished to fight against their former Emperor and join the Allies. A second change was more significant. Several German divisions had been moved from Russia to the Western Front, and Foch's view that this action seemed to be 'a decisive military argument in favour of intervention' was relayed to Washington.[20] Foch believed that Allied (including Japanese) intervention in Siberia was 'extremely important' and was required immediately before the winter. He was prepared to allow 8000 US troops to go to Siberia to join the Japanese and Czech volunteers.[21] Bliss's report to Washington of the discussion in the SWC on 2 July gives Foch's view: intervention would shorten the war by reconstituting the Russian front, and the American 100-division programme gave the Allies the necessary numerical superiority.[22] The council decided to commit the agreed forces to northern Russia. It also decided to send rifles and ammunition to Vladivostok to arm the Czechoslovak forces. Foch intervened in the debate on the second day solely over the practical matter of the American artillery resources, concerned that there should not be too great a diminution of the forces in France. As his views about the need to intervene coincided with those of the council, he had no need to do more.

The second item for discussion was more contentious. Foch had prepared for the council meetings with Clemenceau and Pétain, and left it to Tardieu as French High Commissioner for American affairs to press the question of American manpower.[23] This question had evolved since the previous SWC session in June, when the three Premiers had sent a telegram to President Wilson indicating that at least 100 US divisions were needed in France. Then Foch, bolstered by Clemenceau and Tardieu, met Pershing in the latter's headquarters on 23 June, and they had agreed on a programme of 100 divisions by July 1919. President Wilson had not demurred.[24] Because such a huge programme would have an impact on shipping resources, Tardieu had worked on the transport problem. Now, in the first meeting of the July SWC, he claimed that the French could supply machineguns and aircraft (but not horses) to the American troops arriving in such numbers. Tardieu then continued with figures of the

[20] French ambassador to President, 24 June 1918, ibid., 415.
[21] Conversation between Foch and Joffre, 29 June 1918, in Pedroncini (ed.), *Joffre, JM*, 272–3.
[22] Bliss to Secretary of State, Secretary of war and Chief of Staff, 2 July 1918, in Link (ed.), *PWW*, 48: 504.
[23] Letter, Foch to Mme Foch, 30 June 1918, vol. 46.   [24] Beaver, *Baker*, 157–8.

shipping required to transport the troops and large numbers of horses. Lloyd George was outraged. He believed that the shipping question was one that should be settled solely between London and Washington. According to Henry Wilson, the British Premier 'boiled over' and rejected this further attempt to 'take over' the British war effort.[25] Clearly Foch had been wise to leave the presentation of the French view on manpower to Tardieu, and he did not speak during the debate.

It was not, however, in these three formal sessions that Foch's authority was challenged. Rather, behind-the-scenes manoeuvring caused Foch to threaten resignation. Serious cracks were forming in the façade of Allied unity, and Foch was sensitive to what he perceived as further attempts to diminish his authority. The principal problem lay with London. Lloyd George's explosion over Tardieu's mention of shipping for US troops was but one symptom of a growing feeling that unity of command under a French general was leading to French attempts to grab even greater control. Wilson expressed these fears very clearly in his diary: on 11 May he wrote 'the French mean to take us over body & soul'; and on 29 June: 'What is clear is that Clemenceau is trying to grab more and more power, and is trying to brush on one side anybody who gets in the way.' The context for these fears is important. Not only was there an increasingly bitter epistolary war between Lloyd George and Clemenceau over British manpower resources and their use, but the Americans had been pushing for a more efficient use of materiel by pooling resources. London saw this as the distribution of British supplies to the French and Americans; evidently the agreement to constitute the Military Board of Allied Supply, noted in the previous chapter, had not removed British misgivings. All these factors increased British resentment over what they saw as French pretensions.

Two further incidents during the July SWC meetings increased it even more. Clemenceau attacked the Belgian chief of staff over the refusal to join the unified command by placing Belgian troops under Foch's orders. (As constitutional head of the army, King Albert judged that he could not join the Allies in this matter.) Rudely Clemenceau interrupted Gillain when the latter explained that good relations existed between Foch and the Belgian command; then Clemenceau asked that the fact that no Belgian division could become part of any reserve force under Foch's command be noted in the minutes.[26] Henry Wilson thought that this was yet another attempt by both Foch and Clemenceau to get more power, but Gillain's report to the King reveals that Clemenceau prevented Foch from

[25] Wilson diary, 2 July 1918.
[26] 'Second meeting of the seventh session of the SWC', IC 70, CAB 28/4.

speaking during the debate. Furthermore, the following day Weygand spoke privately to Gillain regretting (as did other French generals too) the Premier's behaviour. Foch made the effort to smooth matters by suggesting that domestic political pressures had caused Clemenceau to speak as he did. 'We are in a democracy', Foch told Gillain, 'and, among democrats, action is nothing more than talk. You and I would have settled matters in a few hours.'[27]

The second incident concerned Salonika where, without any consultation with the British, Clemenceau had not only appointed a new commander – Guillaumat had been returned to Paris (as we have seen) and Salonika proved a useful place to park Franchet d'Espèrey, who had been sacked from command of the Northern Army Group following the Chemin des Dames offensive – but he also issued orders to the new French commander to act offensively. These two incidents provoked Hankey to write in his diary: 'Both these cases of Belgium and Salonika are instances of the desperate efforts the French are making to take charge of every phase of the war. As their material resources decrease their ambitions doubly increase.'[28]

So the SWC meetings were taking place in an increasingly acrimonious atmosphere. Although the Allies had beaten off four German attacks, another was expected, despite Foch's optimism. Yet the British were increasingly pessimistic, contemplating a return to a naval strategy with a focus on the Middle East – even contemplating the defeat of France and whether, in that case, the British Empire and America could continue the war.[29] They resented Foch's repeated calls for more men and Clemenceau's criticisms of the British war effort. In an attempt to redress the balance, as they saw it, the British proposed to re-define the responsibilities of the permanent military representatives to the SWC. This would result in a reduction in Foch's autonomy. It represented the third challenge to Foch's authority within a month.

The dispute began with a small private meeting of the French and the British, together with Orlando, following the first day's session. Lloyd George said that he wished to strengthen the SWC, but Clemenceau 'saw no use in the place'. Foch suggested that the council should come under his authority, but Wilson jumped on this idea immediately, saying that the French 'had never made use of Versailles'. They decided that Lloyd George would draft a proposal to put to the council, which Wilson produced: it gave authority in France to Foch, with coordination in

---

[27] Report of General Gillain, 6 July 1918, Maison Militaire du Roi (Galet), folder 5.
[28] Hankey diary, 3 July 1918, HNKY 5/7.
[29] Lloyd George's statement to the Imperial War Cabinet, 11 June 1918, CAB 23/43.

Italy, but 'all other theatres being over the salt water fall to me [Wilson]'. Thus Wilson allocated a larger role to himself (was he tired of being in London whilst all the excitement was in France?) and achieved the imposition of limits on French (and Foch's) pretensions. He knew that any such proposal was likely to be contentious. He ended his diary account of their deliberations thus: 'This will give some fun tomorrow.'[30] Then, before the official sitting on 4 July, there was a another private meeting between Milner and Wilson and, on the other hand, Foch, Weygand and DuCane, when Foch demanded that the British keep up their fifty-nine divisions and create a sixtieth from Category 'B' troops. Wilson and Milner had refused to commit to this, and Lloyd George supported their stance when he joined the meeting. Lloyd George stated categorically that British manpower resources made such a commitment impossible, whilst Wilson intended to take some divisions for service in other theatres once the French front was secure and winter prevented further operations there. According to Wilson, Foch became 'greatly incensed' and warned that Britain would lose the ports and 'would be done' unless divisions were maintained. Wilson claimed to be 'astonished at Foch's angry and almost threatening attitude'.[31] Relations were far from the friendship of 1914, and this was yet another example of excessive (in the British view) French demands.

The official SWC minutes make no mention of any discussion of a proposal to define the responsibilities of the military members of the council. Instead, a resolution (in English only) was slipped into the proceedings right at the end of the last sitting. Its stated aim was to remove any confusion between Foch's role and that of the PMRs. It proposed that, first, the PMRs should study the 'whole field of actual or potential warfare', by taking into account all the broadest factors; second, the PMRs should report their findings to the full council, particularly with regard to the Allied plan of campaign for the autumn and winter, after 'consulting with General Foch as to the prospective situation on the western front'.[32] Clearly Foch's role was to be restricted to the Western Front, and he would simply give his views to the military for incorporation into their recommendations to the full SWC. The SWC would then decide the plan of campaign for the autumn and winter, *not* the 'Général en chef des armées alliées'.

It was the watchful Weygand who noticed the text of the resolution. He had it translated and shown to Foch, who recognised it immediately for the attempt that it was to restrict his influence. Since the British party had

---

[30] Wilson diary, 2 July 1918.   [31] Ibid., 4 July 1918.
[32] Bliss to Lansing and Baker, 4 July 1918, in *USAWW*, 2: 504.

dispersed before the translation was completed, Foch sped off to Paris to confront Clemenceau (whose English was good) and to demand that the wording be changed. When Clemenceau responded that he could not see how a resolution that had been passed officially could be changed, Foch threatened to resign.

What followed was almost farcical, especially given the military situation with a renewed German attack expected shortly. Clemenceau, Foch and Weygand returned to Versailles and confronted Wilson with the resignation threat if the wording were not changed. Then they demanded to see Lloyd George, who was about to go to dinner with the Dominion Prime Ministers who had attended the SWC's final sitting. Instead of his dinner jacket, Lloyd George had thrown on his pyjama jacket[33]– no doubt a deliberate discourtesy, just as the slipping in of the resolution had been a deliberate attempt to limit Foch's powers. Wilson noted that Clemenceau was even angrier with Foch than Lloyd George was. Lloyd George told his counterpart that 'there was a d – sight too much of these Generals threatening to resign & that if they were private soldiers they would be put up against a wall & shot'.[34] Clemenceau replied that, in this case, such action was obviously impossible, but the obstinacy of Foch and Weygand was making him mad: 'when I am *fou* I usually try to kill someone – a general, if possible'. Wilson and Hankey managed to produce an alternative 'horrible hybrid draft' that satisfied everyone.[35] Then this had to be translated and taken to the Italian representative for approval. He objected to a phrase, and the wording went back and forth for several weeks before the matter was finalised. The words 'in consultation with General Foch' were added to the first of the PMRs' tasks; and the second task (to report their views on the autumn and winter campaign) was to be undertaken 'without intruding on the personal studies of General Foch in regard to which he is accountable only to the heads of government'.[36] It is not surprising that Hankey's bureaucratic mind was offended by this 'horrible hybrid' wording.

This petty incident – Wilson thought Foch was 'really childish', and Joffre was highly amused[37]– is revelatory. Foch's over-reaction was probably an indication of the fatigue of the three days spent in official meetings, coupled with angry private meetings with the British. Yet Foch was justified in reacting to this perceived 'lessening of his dignity & power', as Wilson put it. The British intention was indeed to strengthen the PMRs

[33] Weygand, *IV*, 551.   [34] Wilson diary, 4 July 1918.   [35] Hankey diary, 4 July 1918.
[36] 'Resolution 7', 4 July 1918, IC 72, CAB 28/4.
[37] Marginalia ('Et allez donc!' and 'C'est formidable') on the manuscript account by Joffre's military aide, Fonds Fabry, 1K/93/3.

and the SWC at Foch's expense as a response to what they saw as French attempts to take over the whole war effort. Slipping such a resolution into the final minutes was, however, an underhand way of proceeding, although entirely consistent with Lloyd George's methods. (A recent study of Lloyd George as war leader writes of his conspicuous 'deceitful behavior'.[38]) In the 1950s Weygand indicated to an American doctoral student that probably Clemenceau would have rejected the resolution, had it not been introduced when participants were fatigued.[39] The incident reveals further that Foch's threat of resignation was taken seriously. There was simply no one to replace him, and the military position was still tense. Finally, it should be noted that it was the faithful Weygand who noticed the attack on Foch's position, and whose obstinacy was included among the targets of Clemenceau's ire. (By the time that the peace treaty negotiations were concluded in 1919, Clemenceau could barely stand to be in the same room as Weygand.)

Both Clemenceau and Foch were aware that Lloyd George was machinating. The former told Poincaré that Lloyd George's real aim was to get the PMRs to draw up a plan for Palestine, whereas Foch alone would plan for the Western Front. As for Foch, he told his wife that the British always raised difficulties so that he had to stand up to them 'vigorously'.[40] So what appeared from London's perspective to be a French attempt to gather more power was merely, from the French perspective, an attempt to keep the British focused on the Western Front. Foch was not worried by the fuss. With the amended text he believed that he remained his own master, and the PMRs would be confined to the Eastern Front. He knew that Lloyd George might turn his attention to Asia Minor in order to gain some chips [gages] for the peace negotiations. He also knew that Clemenceau had angered the British, not only by his actions at Versailles but also by visiting British troops as though they were controlled by the French government. Clemenceau had not lived for four years with the Allies, Foch told Poincaré, and frequently he offended British sensibilities.[41] Such comments show once again Foch's clear-sightedness and the need to treat allies, Belgian and British, with tact (even while being much more brutal with the French army).

So the July session of the SWC revealed the deterioration in the Franco-British relationship, and also in the Wilson–Foch relationship, whilst at the same time confirming Foch's authority. Wilson wrote to DuCane on 9 July explaining that all that was meant by the resolution was that they

---

[38] Cassar, *Lloyd George*, 12.   [39] Shumate, Allied Supreme War Council, 863, and n. 43.
[40] Poincaré, *AS*, 10: 258 (entry for 8 July 918); Mme Foch diary, 5 July 1918.
[41] Poincaré, *AS*, 10: 261 (entry for 9 July 1918).

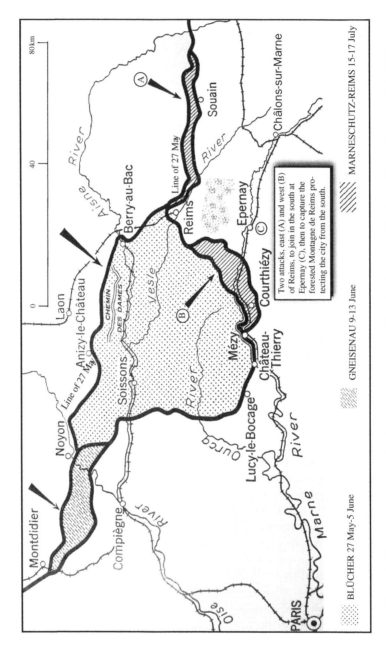

Map 16 The Marne salient, showing the ground gained by the German offensives of May, June and July 1918

The following labels appear on the map:

80km

Aisne River

Line of 27 May

(A)

Souain

Châlons-sur-Marne

MARNESCHUTZ-REIMS 15–17 July

40

0

Laon

Berry-au-Bac

Reims

Vesle River

Epernay

(C)

Courthiézy

Two attacks, east (A) and west (B) of Reims, to join in the south at Epernay (C), then to capture the forested Montagne de Reims protecting the city from the south.

Line of 27 May

Anizy-le-Château

CHEMIN DES DAMES

Vesle

Soissons

(B)

Mezy

Château-Thierry

Noyon

Ourcq River

Lucy-le-Bocage

Compiègne

River

Montdidier

Oise

Marne River

PARIS

GNEISENAU 9–13 June

BLÜCHER 27 May–5 June

should 'look at the picture as a whole', otherwise they would be defeated. There was 'not the slightest idea or intention of interfering with Gen: Foch's command as such'. Nevertheless, he continued, there were other theatres outside France that demanded the British government's attention, and these were 'outside the view & power of the CinC France'.[42] Fortunately the SWC did not provide a forum for yet further deterioration because it did not meet again until October for the discussion of armistice terms. The reason was partly that both Clemenceau and Milner realised that disputes over manpower, over the transport of US troops and over their deployment once transported, risked splitting the Allies and giving comfort to the enemy.[43] A further reason was the enemy action itself. The fifth and final German offensive in the west began eleven days after the vaudeville just described.

Ludendorff's imperative remained the defeat of the British further north, but he had placed himself in a dilemma with his last two offensives. The result of BLÜCHER and GNEISENAU was a deep but narrow salient in the French line, but no means of supplying by railway the troops holding it (see Map 16). There were only two local railway lines running through Soissons at the top of the salient, one of which ran to Reims, which the French still held. Trucks simply could not carry enough food, ammunition and other supplies, even if there were sufficient petrol. Hence Ludendorff faced a choice between abandoning the Marne salient or enlarging it by taking Reims. On 14 June Ludendorff decided to free the Soissons–Reims railway so as to be able to supply his troops in the salient by using lines running through the historic city of Reims. Rather than face the opprobrium that would inevitably follow from shelling the city itself – the cathedral had already been damaged, to international dismay – he decided to make two attacks, one to the east and one to the west of Reims, then to cross the Marne and join up in the south and take Epernay. This would permit the capture of the wooded Montagne de Reims which protected Reims from the south, causing the city to fall and freeing the railway. The two attacks were set for 10 July, with operation HAGEN against the British to follow on the 20th.[44]

True to form, Ludendorff expanded his objectives four days later (on 18 June) by ordering a wider front. Given their past experiences of huge initial success, Ludendorff expected to reach the river Marne on a wide front on the first day of the operation. With thirty-nine divisions Ludendorff now aimed at more than simply capturing Reims to enable railway traffic into the salient; he expected a force-on-force battle to give a

[42] Holograph letter, Wilson to DuCane, 9 July 1918, WO 158/98.
[43] See Greenhalgh, '1918 Manpower Crisis'.   [44] Zabecki, *German 1918 Offensives*, 247–9.

stunning victory that would collapse French morale and force them to sue for peace. As a result, in order to allow all the necessary preparations to be made, operation MARNESCHUTZ–REIMS had to be postponed to 14 July. Then a further day's postponement ensued. So the operation's increased size and objectives meant that it was only on 15 July that MARNESCHUTZ–REIMS was launched, thirty-seven days after the initial warning on 8 June. Such delays only gave the Allies more time to prepare a response.

Ludendorff's changes of plan were not the only German problem. The long hours of daylight made it very difficult to hide their preparations, and the prevailing winds blew the sounds of them south towards the French lines. Although Bruchmüller's successful methods were to be used again, the artillery expert was hampered by reduced numbers of guns. German munitions factories simply could not keep up with the wear and tear since March, and some guns had already been moved north to Crown Prince Rupprecht ready for HAGEN. Furthermore, the poor railway facilities in the salient (the very reason for the offensive) meant that shells had to be moved by road from the railheads. This created traffic jams that could be seen easily from the air, where the Allies had superiority.[45]

Not only were the German preparations more difficult, but Foch and the Allied armies were better prepared. They had experienced Ludendorff's methods during four offensives, and Bruchmüller was providing the artillery plan for the fifth, so the French knew what to expect. Moreover, they had much better intelligence than had been the case before the 'surprise' of 27 May. The head of GQG's 2e Bureau, Colonel de Cointet, recalled that never had the military situation clarified so quickly and so completely as it had before the July offensive. A spy in Crown Prince Wilhelm's staff reported that the Champagne offensive under preparation was the only one under consideration.[46] Although de Cointet was based at GQG, he went frequently to speak with Foch. He enjoyed a better reception from Foch, who accepted his intelligence assessments, than he did from Pétain. At GQG Pétain stated in one of the daily staff meetings that he believed that the Champagne offensive was a feint, as had happened on 21 March, and that he had made plans in consequence. Cointet felt insulted that his judgement had been questioned in an open meeting without his having been consulted beforehand. Clearly de Cointet's optimism and confidence harmonised more with Foch's temperament than with Pétain and his staff.

---

[45] Ibid., 250–5.   [46] Cointet memoirs, Cahier '1918', fo. 101.

One of the several reasons for Foch's better intelligence was his action over aerial reconnaissances. As early as 14 June Foch had ordered his aviation service to make daily sweeps with the same observers over the same terrain in order to increase the chances of catching any enemy buildup.[47] A week later the officer in charge of aviation at Grand Quartier Général Allié (GQGA) was ordered to 'synthesise' all air reconnaissances from the different army groups.[48] The value of strategic reconnaissance was now well recognised as Commandant Paul-Louis Weiller, the son of a prominent Lorraine industrialist and Senator, had convinced Foch's staff to set up a group of two flights of long-range aircraft with the mission of photographing the rear of the whole front every day to a depth of 100 kilometres. (For this purpose, Weiller had developed a camera with an extra-long-focus lens, and methods of revising maps based on aerial photographs. Foch invested Weiller on Armistice Day with the insignia of officer of the Légion d'honneur in recognition of his work.)[49] As for GQG, the 2e Bureau issued strict guidelines for all reconnaissance aircraft that each army group follow a strictly defined programme and submit all information promptly to headquarters.[50] Furthermore, a special study was undertaken of the German railway system and the volumes of men and materiel that could be delivered to a particular front. This report, completed on 22 June, enabled Allied bombers to attack the most vulnerable portions of the German transport system. Cointet felt sufficiently confident in the deductions that he was drawing from such information and from the state of German reserves – deductions that he presented personally to Foch in a note dated 27 June[51] – that he went on leave, secure in his judgement that no fresh German offensive could be mounted before 15 July, even if its precise direction was still unknown.

In order to take advantage of better intelligence about the enemy's plans, Foch needed to be able to ensure that the orders he issued to move Allied units could be carried out. In other words, he needed a larger staff. The shifting about the battlefield of troops of different nationalities caused transport problems. If American troops, for example, were to be moved from the British sector in northern France to the east, railways authorities in the British and French and then American sectors had to be contacted and the movement coordinated. Forty-eight troop trains were required to shift one division in the summer and autumn of 1918, and the

[47] Clive diary, 14 June 1918, CAB 45/201.   [48] Armengaud, *Renseignement aérien*, 181.
[49] Christienne and Lissarague, *French Military Aviation*, 181–4.
[50] Cointet, 'Le Service de renseignements', 30.
[51] Cointet memoirs, Cahier '1918', fos. 92, 94.

greater the mixing of troops, the greater the potential for confusion and delay.[52] Although Foch disliked a large staff, clearly he could not continue to resist, and when he met Wilson at Versailles both men agreed about the necessity for a larger general staff at Allied headquarters.[53] The complaints about Foch's lack of staff, noted in the previous chapter, came to a head on 22 June in a letter from Lloyd George to Clemenceau. This letter must be read in the context of all the resentments in London about France's 'takeover' of the British (and everyone else's) war effort.

Lloyd George had told his Cabinet colleagues that an officer on Pershing's staff had drawn attention to the absence of a proper staff at Foch's headquarters 'which had been responsible for considerable confusion, more particularly in transportation arrangements'.[54] Both Milner and Wilson drafted a letter to Clemenceau that Lloyd George signed, indicating the British worries about Foch's lack of a proper staff. He suggested two solutions: either give Foch an Allied general staff (which Wilson opposed and so Lloyd George did not press this), or else Foch should take over GQG staff and Pétain form a new one to replace it.[55]

Weygand claimed that the transport and supply services at GQG worked so well that the notion of moving them to Allied headquarters was not considered at first. However, GHQ 'took umbrage' at being obliged to ask GQG for transport services when the two headquarters were 'equals in the hierarchy'. It was for this reason, so Weygand judged, that the decision was made to shift more than a hundred general staff from GQG to join the twenty or so at Foch's headquarters.[56] Joffre's testimony provides further evidence of staff resentments. Joffre had heard the complaints, and seems to have interpreted Foch's refusal of Pétain's offer of GQG staff as a power play between GQG, GHQ and GQGA. Pétain suspected a 'trap' (as well he might, considering the decision about removing Anthoine) and decided, according to Joffre, to create a staff 'of the first order' at GQG, while Haig might follow suit at GHQ. Joffre claims that Foch declared himself to be an 'Allied' commander-in-chief and he intended to remain so.[57] It seems likely, however, that Lloyd George's pressure was more decisive than general staff resentment.

In fact, the subject of moving GQG staff to Foch's headquarters was already under consideration. Weygand and DuCane discussed the implications on 24 June, and a week later DuCane informed Wilson that Foch

[52] Henniker, *Transportation*, 423.   [53] Wilson diary, 1 July 1918.
[54] 'X' Committee minutes, X14, 17 June 1918, CAB 23/17.
[55] Lloyd George to Clemenceau, 22 June 1918, Lloyd George mss, F/50/3/2.
[56] Weygand, *IV*, 612.
[57] 'Nécessité de créer auprès le Général Foch un *véritable* E. M. interallié', n.d. [filed between 28 and 29 June 1918], Journal de marche, pièce # 310, Fonds Joffre, 14N 3.

had decided to take the Direction de l'Arrière (DA) from Pétain's staff.[58] Thus Foch did not adopt either of Lloyd George's suggestions, but an intermediate solution. The DA dealt with transport and supply matters in rear areas and formed only one section of GQG's 3e Bureau (operations). The DA carried out the same functions as the QMG and transportation departments at GHQ. Such a move would affect both the French mission at GHQ and the British mission at QGQ.[59] Because these matters would require 'careful working out', Weygand told Grant, it was thought better to delay issuing orders, but Weygand was determined that once Foch and Haig had arranged any transport movement 'the French staff at G.Q.G. should not attempt to make any changes direct with G.H.Q.'[60] Thus the Allied command would have the final say.

Foch drafted a letter explaining that he did not propose to accept Lloyd George's suggestions, but that he did intend to increase his staff in order to deal with administrative matters affecting the Allied armies. He handed it over to Lloyd George, Milner and Wilson in Versailles, and they were completely satisfied with this response.[61] Although Haig seemed content with this decision, his staff at GHQ, in particular QMG Travers Clarke, were outraged.[62] However, because of the myriad complications involved in the change, none of the arrangements were completed before the fighting began again on 15 July with the last German offensive.

The acquisition of a larger staff was not the only change at Allied headquarters. Foch tried also to coordinate the heavy artillery of each national army. This followed logically from the greater control of transport that his new staff would give him, because the resources of all could be gathered together to provide a massive concentration. Furthermore, as currently each army directed its own artillery production programmes without reference to those of an ally, greater coordination in this area would also be productive. Accordingly Foch convened a meeting at his headquarters on 12 July, to be presided over by Weygand, in order to discuss a general Allied production programme and to study how resources of one army might be used in another's sector – in other words, an Allied artillery reserve.[63] So the creation of a more efficient staff organisation at Foch's headquarters was in hand. Foch could leave the detail to Weygand.

[58] DuCane to CIGS, 24 June 1918, WO 158/91.
[59] DuCane to CIGS, 29 June 1918, ibid.
[60] Notes on interview with Generals Foch and Weygand, 9 July 1918, WO 158/88.
[61] DuCane, *Foch*, ch. 8.
[62] Ibid., 67; Haig diary, 3 July 1918; DuCane to CIGS, 5 July 1918, WO 158/91.
[63] Foch to Haig, Pershing, di Robilant [Italian PMR] and Pétain, 10 July 1918, 15N 43.

The largest question for Foch during the pause in the fighting was how to take advantage of the better intelligence by ensuring that his American and British allies were organised to meet the expected renewed offensive. He also had to deal with the effect on the French army of any decisions made in this regard. The Allies had agreed to the 100-division US army for 1919, but the question remained unresolved of how best to use those twelve divisions that were already in France. Seven trained divisions were holding front-line sectors. The remaining five partially trained divisions with both the British and French armies were withdrawn and moved to a quiet sector so as to liberate French divisions. From the French point of view, both Pétain and Foch believed that the best use of the large divisions was to place American regiments with French divisions. In order to press this view on Pershing, Foch and Weygand went to Chaumont on 17 June. Skilfully Foch praised the morale boost that the presence of American soldiers in the front line had provided, and he applied a little blackmail also when he claimed that there had been murmurings amongst some French units about the Americans not taking their share of the fighting. There had also been similar press comment. Foch explained that his tri-fold aim was to build up British manpower, to boost French morale and finally, in August, to create an American army.[64] Pershing was not moved. He did not want to build up other nations' armies but to keep his divisions all together – during July another third of a million US troops arrived in France – and he had already started planning the formation of army corps. Indeed, he thought that poor French and British morale was affecting his men adversely.[65] Consequently, when Foch returned to Chaumont with Clemenceau a few days later and repeated his arguments in favour of some form of amalgamation, Pershing turned down Foch's proposal. Pétain was furious, not only because he would not receive any direct help in the form of US troops, but also because Foch had taken over the negotiations with Pershing.[66] Pershing's liaison officer at GQG reported that the involvement of Foch and Clemenceau was a mistake, because Pétain and Pershing were starting to get on well together. Clemenceau's presence was a mistake, since he thought he understood the Americans, but he did not; Foch's presence was a mistake because his liaison officer, Mott, was 'a fine fellow but had been away too long'.[67] It is unlikely, however, that Pétain would have extracted any greater conces-sions from Pershing.

[64] 'Notes on conversation with General Foch at Chaumont', 17 June 1918, *USAWW* 2: 468–7.
[65] Trask, *AEF*, 77.   [66] Herbillon, *Du général*, 2: 286 (entry for 12 July 1918).
[67] Clark report #128, 6 July 1918.

With his usual realism Foch accepted the inevitable. He discussed with Fifth Army how best to insert the US divisions that still lacked artillery and horses,[68] but at a meeting with Pershing on 10 July he stopped fighting the American CinC. Pershing stated firmly that he wanted to take back those divisions, currently with the British, who had agreed to supply artillery but who lacked horses to pull the guns. He also wanted to collect together the divisions with the French in order to make an American army with its own sector. This sector should be in eastern France so as to avoid congesting still further the lines of communication used by the British and French. Foch responded by saying that he wished to be more American than the Americans, advising Pershing not to leave his divisions with Haig simply because the British could not supply the horses for their artillery units. He accepted that there were now enough American divisions in France to justify the creation of an army, by the end of July. This date is significant because, despite being an advance on 'August', Foch already knew from his intelligence services when and where the next German offensive would fall. He was postponing, therefore, the decision about an American army until the results of that offensive were known. He seemed more concerned about the provision of horses (France was exhausted, and the British were importing them from America), and about using the full available shipping capacity to transport the August contingents from the USA. If some British tonnage remained unused, they might take their ships back, Foch argued. Furthermore he stressed the need to keep up the numbers of British and French divisions, implying that American troops would be required for this purpose.[69] Pershing commented in his postwar memoirs that, although Foch had spoken of an early date for the formation of an American army, he did not seem to believe it possible before September or October.[70]

Decisions about the formation of an independent American army had an impact, of course, on Pétain and the French army. Pershing agreed to leave in Champagne the divisions currently serving with the French, thereby creating his American army in central instead of eastern France. So in mid-July Pétain would have four US divisions on the western flank of the Marne salient (two of which had distinguished themselves at Cantigny and Belleau Wood), two more at the base of the salient, and one supporting General Gouraud's Fourth Army on the eastern flank. Other US divisions held quiet sectors in eastern France, where a further five were

---

[68] Buat diary, 7 July 1918, ms 5390.
[69] 'Conference held on July 10, 1918', *USAWW* 2: 51720; Mott, 'Conversations of July 10, 1918', USMA 1806, box 1.
[70] Pershing, *Experiences*, 2: 146.

in reserve and available if necessary. Foch's efforts in the SWC had paid off handsomely. However, Pétain was furious and he blamed Foch for the loss of GQG's influence over Pershing. He had hoped for some limited amalgamation to pump new blood into French units and to complete the Americans' training with combat experience.[71]

Pétain also had British troops under his command, but on 16 June Foch had asked him to return XXII Corps to Haig, after the previous day's request that Pétain supply more artillery to the DAN.[72] These instructions were among the reasons for Pétain's appeal to Clemenceau described in the previous chapter. The BEF's request for the return of troops reveals the belief, still prevalent in Haig's headquarters, that serious attacks were likely in the Arras and Ypres sectors. This belief was supported by the fact that, as both intelligence services recognised, the numbers of reserves in Crown Prince Rupprecht's army group had not diminished. This was, of course, because Ludendorff intended to attack the BEF once French reserves had been drawn away from the British front. Even when it became clear in July that the French front in Champagne was the next target, GHQ Intelligence still maintained that a major attack was likely against the British front because the Champagne preparations were a feint.[73] This had been the case in March, and may explain the excessive British caution. It is a sad comment, however, on the lack of trust between the two intelligence services, despite the existence since October 1914 of an Allied bureau in Folkestone that centralised intelligence received from secret agents.

Because of this belief at GHQ, Haig was not pleased to learn that Pershing's 'obstinacy' had resulted in the granting of his wish to concentrate his divisions and create an American army. On 18 and 28 June Haig and Foch met at Mouchy-le-Châtel to discuss the return of the French divisions of the DAN to Pétain's command in order to strengthen the Paris defences. Hence Haig was losing both French and American divisions, and it was a similar loss of troops that had provoked Haig's appeal to London. However, Foch seems to have taken to heart the rebuke delivered on that occasion, as the fact of two face-to-face meetings in eleven days reveals.

As Foch's conviction grew that the French front was the target of the next attack – not the British front in Picardy which his directive of 1 July had identified – he decided to shift yet more Allied reserves southwards.

---

[71] Herbillon, *Du général*, 2: 286 (entry for 12 July 1918).
[72] Telephone message, GQGA to GQG, 15 June 1918, and Foch to Pétain, 16 June 1918, *AFGG* 6/2, annexes 1559, 1581.
[73] Beach, British Intelligence, 261–3.

On 7 July he wrote to Haig asking for permission to send an officer to the two British armies next to the French in order to coordinate the reserve force that he (Foch) had ordered Pétain to constitute in a position to move either northwards across the Somme to support the British or else to support Fayolle's Reserve Army Group. For such a reserve force to be effective, Foch argued (correctly, given the initial speed the Germans achieved in the opening phases of their offensives), it had to be able to move speedily. On 12 July Foch wrote again to inform Haig that he had moved the reserve force directly behind the French front, and so wished Haig to move two British reserve divisions (from General Alexander Godley's XXII Corps that had just been returned to Haig's command after taking part in the Matz fighting) to safeguard the junction between British and French armies. Further, Foch warned that he might be obliged to request British help if the German offensive 'absorbed' his reserves. Accordingly he asked Haig to prepare to send three more British divisions to replace them. In the event that the German offensive became so extensive that the likelihood of an attack against the British front was reduced, Foch asked that a counter-offensive be mounted to take advantage of the tired enemy forces. Foch knew that the Germans collected their best troops for any offensive, leaving tired or weak forces as 'trench divisions' [*Stellungsdivisionen*] to hold the trenches.[74] Although addressed to Haig, these two letters were dealt with by GHQ staff as Haig, much to Clemenceau's annoyance, had gone on leave – he was in England from 6 to 14 July, playing golf.[75] Presumably he was not too concerned about the attack against the BEF, which was being used as the excuse for unwillingness to send British forces to Champagne.

Since Haig had been out of touch in England it is not surprising that on his return his response to these repeated requests to shift British reserves southwards should have been so negative. When Haig arrived on the 14th, he was faced with the departure of XXII Corps, authorised in his absence by Lawrence, and a further request for a second group of four divisions. Haig was scornful. 'Apparently without any definite facts to go on', he wrote in his diary, and 'evidently becoming even more anxious', Foch was removing British reserves. Haig's desire to see Foch appointed in March in order to get more French reserves into the British sector had evolved into displeasure at Foch's request for the gesture to be reciprocated. Accordingly he wrote to Foch, asking for an immediate meeting and indicating that he was 'averse' to sending more troops to Champagne, as he still expected the main attack to fall upon his own front. By the time that

[74] Foch to Haig, 7 and 12 July 1918, *AFGG* 6/1, annexes 1822, 1923; WO 158/29/180, 185.
[75] Herbillon, *Du général*, 2: 287 (entry for 13 July 1918).

meeting took place the next day, 15 July, at Mouchy-le-Châtel, the German offensive had begun.

Once again, Foch did his best to be pleasant. He arranged for a 'special lunch' to be provided for his British guests. Haig recorded Foch as 'in the best of spirits', relieved that there had been no attack around Verdun, where he had no reserves. (This was probably padding to impress on Haig how the rest of the French front had been stripped of reserves, as Foch was not expecting any attack at Verdun.) Foch was ready to return the British reserves immediately if an attack occurred on the British front, and so Haig was satisfied, and authorised the sending of the remaining troops that Foch had requested. The British Cabinet, on the other hand, was greatly worried by the move of French troops away from Haig's front. Lloyd George trusted Foch but suspected that Clemenceau was putting undue pressure on him to save Paris and the French army, and so a telegram was sent to Haig reminding him of the right of appeal under the Beauvais agreement if the BEF was endangered.[76] Haig did not rise to the bait.

This new passage of arms with the British CinC demonstrates not only Foch's confidence in his reading of the strategic situation, based on the (accurate) intelligence supplied to him, but also his courage. He was fully aware of the opposition from the British military and politicians. Haig's French ADC, Commandant Gémeau, had reported how badly affected British opinion had been by the Chemin des Dames disaster, to the extent that it was believed in some government circles that the French army was now finished, that France would be forced to make peace, and that the BEF might have to be withdrawn.[77] Gémeau was well informed. The secret 'X' Committee in London (Lloyd George's mini-cabinet) had discussed preventing copies of Hansard being sent abroad because a speech had been made in parliament suggesting that the BEF be withdrawn from France. A week later the 'X' Committee charged Milner with preparing a report on how the war was to be carried on 'if by any chance our European Allies were unable to continue'.[78] A letter from the War Office to Haig, dated 3 July, asked for arrangements to be made to transport two fully equipped divisions from the British reserves back to England 'in case of emergency'. Lawrence's response (in Haig's absence) outlined such a scheme but asked whether Foch had been informed.[79] To

---

[76] Hankey diary, 14 July 1918, in *Supreme Command*, 2: 826.

[77] 'Notes sur le moral britannique', 21 June 1918, 15N 41.

[78] 'Notes of a Conversation', X15, 19 June, and X18, 28 June 1918, CAB 23/17.

[79] 'Scheme "Y": Scheme for transference of forces from France to England in case of emergency', WO 158/65. The latest dated document reads 1 August 1918.

press the point home, Wilson wrote to his 'dear friend' Foch on 12 July, at the request of the War Cabinet, to emphasise British worries at the removal of the French divisions of the DAN and their replacement by half the number of American divisions, who did not have their own artillery. Wilson enclosed a copy of a similar, long letter from Lloyd George to Clemenceau, which spoke of the Imperial War Cabinet's examination of the Western Front and its 'gravest anxiety' caused by evidence (concentrations of enemy artillery) of 'an early and very heavy attack' on the British front. Lloyd George claimed that the unequal distribution of American troops – troops brought across the Atlantic in British ships – was 'indefensible'. He ended his letter with a threat: 'Should the British forces be overwhelmed by superior numbers', Foch would be blamed for the unequal distribution of forces; such feelings 'would undoubtedly be fatal to the continuance' of unity of command (for the securing of which he had 'placed the life of the Government in considerable jeopardy').[80] Neither Foch nor the French government could be in any doubt as to British misgivings.

Yet, despite these threats and urgings, Foch would not be deflected. He had stuck to his guns against Pétain and against the British, although with Pershing he had been forced to concede and to prevaricate. Now he needed to face the enemy. As we have seen, he trusted the French intelligence he was receiving. In addition to the Italian success in June against the Austrians on the Piave and Mangin's success in Champagne, local offensives such as the British attack (by the Australian Corps) on Hamel on 4 July had shown that the Germans could be beaten. At Cantigny 1 US Division had held on and repulsed five German counterattacks. A decision had been made to overcome the transportation problems by moving general staff to his headquarters, although the German offensive would begin before the decision was implemented. In Buat he had a new and more trusted chief of staff at GQG. So Foch was ready. On 14 July he had insisted that the answer to the forthcoming attack was to be the counter-attack planned for Mangin's Tenth Army and Degoutte's Sixth Army against Soissons, with the aim of disrupting the already weak German re-supply facilities in the salient.[81] If Soissons could be re-captured the Germans would be forced to evacuate the salient (see Map 17).

The fifth and what proved to be the last German offensive on the Western Front lacked any element of surprise. On 15 July the artillery

---

[80] Letters, Wilson to Foch, 12 July 1918, Lloyd George to Clemenceau, 13 July 1918, Fonds Clemenceau, 6N 166, [d] 2.
[81] GQGA JMO, 14 July 1918, 26N 1.

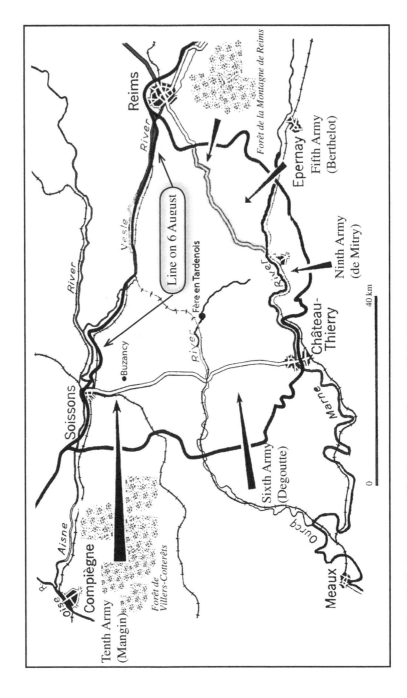

Map 17 Foch's counter-offensive on the Marne, 18 July 1918

preparation started at 01.10 (02.10 French time): 4.5 million rounds were fired but only one-eighth of them were gas, a much reduced proportion from the one-third average of previous attacks. *Seventh Army* required a much longer preparation than in earlier attacks because they needed extra time to build pontoon bridges to cross the Marne, which was wide at this point.[82] On the German left the attack east of Reims failed completely because Gouraud's Fourth Army operated the elastic defence in textbook fashion. The thinly held French outpost line meant that the massive German artillery barrage caused few casualties, and the German infantry attack was held on the main defensive position. Fourth Army inflicted heavy casualties and by the end of the second day (16th) operations were halted in that sector.

On the right the German attack west of Reims made better progress against General Berthelot's Fifth Army, and German infantry crossed the Marne in several places to a depth of five to six kilometres along a fourteen-kilometre front. The varying degrees of successful French resistance did not necessarily mean that Fifth Army was less competent than the Fourth. General Gouraud had commanded Fourth Army since June 1917, and the troops had been holding the same sector since 1914, when they were alongside Foch's Ninth on the Marne. Consequently they were familiar with the terrain and they had had time to make the main defensive position strong enough to resist the German assault. Fifth Army, on the other hand, had been occupying the positions they held on 15 July only since the earlier German offensive on the Chemin des Dames had pushed them there, so they neither knew the terrain so well nor had had time to construct proper defences. Furthermore, General Berthelot had been in command for only ten days, since 5 July, replacing General Buat, who was moved, as noted above, to GQG a mere month after taking over the army command himself. So Fifth Army's comparative lack of success in applying the system of elastic defence did not mean that the system was flawed, nor that Gouraud accepted Pétain's directions while Berthelot, a 'Foch' man, did not. Indeed, Fifth Army artillery played havoc with German bridging operations and the enemy managed to hold only a shallow bridgehead on the south bank of the Marne around the village of Dormans.

Reacting to the German crossing of the Marne, Pétain decided that the situation was too dangerous to permit waiting until 18 July for Foch's planned counter-offensive, and at 10am he ordered Fayolle to suspend preparations so as to free reserves for an immediate riposte to the German

---

[82] Zabecki, *German 1918 Offensives*, 259–60.

advance across the Marne. Fortunately, on his way to meet Haig at Mouchy-le-Châtel, as described above, Foch stopped at Fayolle's head-quarters and so learned of Pétain's order to suspend preparations. Immediately on reaching Mouchy-le-Châtel Foch telephoned GQG and, as he now had the right to do, countermanded the order. There could be no question, Foch said, either of slowing down or, even less, of halting Tenth Army preparations. He did authorise Pétain to take troops, but only if absolutely necessary and only after letting him know immediately if such action were taken.[83] By the afternoon of 15 July, however, the position had stabilised. Fourth Army's stout defence east of Reims meant that its army reserves could be devoted to the badly pressed Fifth Army; although German troops had crossed the Marne on Fifth Army's front, the flanks of the new salient-within-a-salient that the Germans had thus created were holding; finally, following Foch's talk with Haig, agreement had been reached that two more British divisions would be released to support the French, as the enemy was attacking on such a wide front as to make it certain that the Champagne sector was not merely a feint. Foch moved the disembarkation area for the newly arriving British further westwards so as to enable their speedy return to the north should that become necessary. The defence against operation MARNESCHUTZ–REIMS, also named *Friedensturm* or 'peace offensive', was truly international. In addition to the French armies involved, American divisions blocked any German advance towards Château Thierry on the west flank, and II Italian Corps and XXII British Corps were in action on the eastern flank.

The German foothold on the Marne still threatened Reims, but by the end of the second day no further offensive activity took place east of the city. *Seventh Army* was ordered to stop attacks south of Marne next day, but to continue on the north bank of the river towards Reims. On the third day (17 July) Ludendorff left OHL to go to Rupprecht's headquarters to discuss operation HAGEN against the British, but his staff did not believe that he really knew what to do next. By 7.30 that evening the whole German line was 'in a state of chaos', and at midnight OHL authorised a withdrawal from the bridgehead across the Marne.[84]

The tension between the French and Allied headquarters was exacer-bated by the strain. Certainly there was tension between Foch and Pétain, as a curt exchange of letters on 16 July reveals. Foch complained that GQG was not keeping him informed about Pétain's intentions; Pétain replied that the information had already been supplied.[85] Buat remarked that if

---

[83] Telephone message, 12.15pm, GQGA to GQG, *AFGG* 6/2, annex 2012.
[84] Zabecki, *German 1918 Offensives*, 264–5.
[85] Foch to Pétain, and Pétain to Foch, 16 July 1918, *AFGG* 6/2, annexes 2202, 2207.

the correspondence continued with that degree of bitterness the 'inevitable' consequence would be a 'rupture' between the two men, and Buat pledged to do all he could to prevent that. He wondered, however, whether the motive behind Foch's letter – whose complaint was unfounded, Buat claimed, because no instruction left GQG without a copy being sent to Allied headquarters – was to push Pétain to resign, leaving Buat as 'a sort of representative' for Foch at GQG.[86] On the other hand, Foch's complaining letter might simply represent a degree of strain that he hid from his wife. On the same day that he wrote his complaint, he told his wife that the day's 'great battle' had gone very well for the Allies, that the enemy had suffered 'total failure' despite an advance of some four to five kilometres on the Marne, and that in a few days the Allies would have settled matters. He went on to say that he was about to go and see Pétain: 'He always needs to be carried ... followed ... otherwise he would easily weaken.'[87]

Nevertheless, MARNESCHUTZ–REIMS was over and the second Battle of the Marne could begin. Despite Pétain, despite complaints about Foch's staff arrangements, and despite the hurried shifting of troops of four nationalities about and behind the battlefield, Foch's counteroffensive was ready to be launched by the morning of 18 July. Tanks, guns and infantry had been assembled in great secrecy, rivalling German staff work, under cover of the thick forest of Villers-Cotterêts. The German memoir literature refers to this second Marne as Foch's offensive, thereby acknowledging its inspirer, rather than the French CinC or the Allied nature of the forces involved.

Foch's plan was certainly ambitious. The German salient extended like a sack, open at the top and with the bottom below the Marne. Against its western flank, Mangin's Tenth and Degoutte's Sixth Army were to drive eastwards; at the bottom of the sack, Ninth Army (made up of the DAN's units returned from Flanders) was to throw the enemy back across the river; and on the east the badly pressed Fifth Army was to advance northwestwards. With luck east and west could meet across the top of the sack and cut off the enemy troops inside. In all, on a front of 105 kilometres, the four attacking armies contained forty-eight infantry and six cavalry divisions, supported by 540 light Renault tanks, 240 medium tanks, and 1700 aircraft, including a brigade of the RAF.[88] In addition Fourth Army east of Reims was to contribute an artillery barrage that

---

[86] Buat diary, 16 July 1918, ms 5391.
[87] Letter, Foch to Mme Foch, 16 July 1918, vol. 46: 'Il faut toujours le porter à bras tendus, le suivre et le tenir, sans cela il flancherait facilement.'
[88] *AFGG* 7/1, 68, 25.

would keep the enemy guessing as to the main sector of attack. Facing them, French army intelligence reported on 17 July a total of 207 divisions, of which sixty-two (but only thirty of them fresh) were in reserve in the rear.[89]

Of Foch's three national commanders involved in his counter-offensive, Pershing was most fully engaged; Pétain however was still apprehensive, and Haig did not yet accept that it was now impossible for the Germans to mount a Flanders attack. Pershing had agreed at their meeting on 10 July to form his army in the Champagne sector, where most of his front-line divisions were already involved, instead of his preferred Saint-Mihiel. Foch had indicated that he expected both 1 and 2 US Divisions to take part in his counter-offensive, and they were allocated to XX Corps in the middle of Mangin's Tenth Army front. Obviously, if Pershing continued to insist on creating an autonomous American army he would need success in action to prove his ability to handle higher unit formations. Pétain was less positive. The day before the counter-offensive began, he asked Foch to ensure that a second lot of four British divisions would follow those already en route for the French front. Pétain claimed that his reserves were 'insufficient to feed such a strong defensive battle and an offensive that was bound to provoke strong German counter-attacks'. Haig claimed, however, that intelligence suggested an attack against his Second Army in Flanders. Rupprecht's reserves were intact and Crown Prince Wilhelm would not need to take any of them since he had enough reserves of his own. Consequently Haig requested the return of the four British divisions of XXII Corps. Both Haig and Pétain believed themselves to be under-insured.[90]

Neither need have worried. Tenth Army had achieved total surprise on the early morning of 18 July. The infantry debouched from their hiding places in the woods of Villers-Cotterêts, preceded by an intense rolling barrage and swarms of tanks, with aircraft buzzing overhead. By 21 July 1 US Division had crossed both the railway and the only main road running north–south into the salient, the Soissons–Château Thierry road, at Buzancy. Foch's principal aim in mounting the operation, interdicting the enemy's supply lines, had been achieved. This major success was not repeated elsewhere. Fifth Army found it difficult to clear the Marne's south bank of enemy troops, despite the fact that the Germans had already decided to pull back; and the British and Italians on the eastern flank had some very hard fighting in difficult terrain. Sixth Army managed to

---

[89] Compte-rendu de renseignements, 17 July 1918, 15N 5.
[90] Pétain to Foch, 17 July 9118, *AFGG* 7/1, annex 86; Haig to Foch, 17 July 1918, ibid., annex 78, and WO 158/29/91.

liberate Château Thierry on 20 July, but the top of the 'sack' could not be closed, and the Germans succeeded in evacuating both troops and a large proportion of their supplies. By 22 July they had recovered from the surprise and by 3 August were back in the strong defensive positions above the rivers Vesle and Aisne, not much in advance of their position before BLÜCHER.

Although their own casualties were high, Pétain's armies had captured 29,000 German prisoners (a sign of weakening morale), over 800 guns and mortars, and over 3000 machineguns. German casualty figures reached 110,00 for the period 15 July–2 August, and the original forty-eight German divisions in the salient had received a significant blow to their morale.[91] In Crown Prince Wilhelm's *First Army* alone, the total number of wounded who passed through the army's main dressing stations between 15 and 18 July was 7490 – and those killed or taken prisoner must be added to that total.[92] Foch's role was to 'push everyone forward', he told his wife, as the Boche rapidly moved house. Apart from that, he did not know what was happening.[93] This did not stop him from pushing. On 23 July he took a letter personally to GQG pointing out how the enemy was managing to retire in fairly good order, namely by giving strong protection to his flanks and using machinegunners to hold up the pursuers. Foch argued that the best answer was to make a strong flank attack using Tenth Army on a restricted sector of its front, and to avoid distributing effectives and resources piecemeal.[94]

At GQG Foch's advice was seen as interference, and Buat was reduced to asking liaison officer Herbillon to intervene with Mordacq so as to get Clemenceau to insist with Foch that he (Foch) should not interfere in details![95] Further dissatisfaction was generated when the press reports of the fighting heaped all the praise on Foch and Mangin, leaving Pétain and GQG out in the cold. Barescut remarked that no newspaper 'pronounces the name of Pétain'; even Buat thought that there was some 'injustice'.[96]

The fact that MARNESCHUTZ–REIMS had failed and, what was worse, that Foch had been able to mount a successful counter-offensive caused great gloom at OHL. The Kaiser went to see Hindenburg on 18 July and found Ludendorff 'jumpy'; then on 22 July he heard Hindenburg admit 'total

[91] Doughty, *PV*, 473; *RAW*, 14: 502; Zabecki, *German 1918 Offensives*, 271.
[92] Intelligence Report, Army Group German Crown Prince, 17 July 1918 (evening), in *Marne Source Book*, doc. 420.
[93] Letter, Foch to Mme Foch, 21 July 1918, vol. 46.
[94] Foch to Pétain, 23 July 1918, *AFGG* 7/1, annex 256.
[95] Herbillon, *Du général*, 2: 287 (entry for 13 July 1918).
[96] Barescut and Buat diaries cited in Notin, *Foch*, 394.

failure'. This news gave the Kaiser nightmares in which all his English and
Russian relatives marched past, mocking him.[97] Ludendorff was certainly
'jumpy', and became so unhinged as to speak insolently to Hindenburg
and to call on God not to abandon Germany. Crown Prince Rupprecht
saw straight away that HAGEN was henceforth impossible, that the war was
in fact lost, before Ludendorff too accepted that HAGEN should be cancelled. The second Marne battle was a significant turning point, the point
at which the Allies regained the initiative which they never again lost. Fritz
von Lossberg, then *Fourth Army's* chief of staff, recognised this melan-
choly fact. It was not the fighting on 8 August – which Anglophone
historians accept as the beginning of the final Hundred Days to victory –
but rather 18 July that was 'the sharp turning point in the conduct of the
war'.[98] Lieutenant Herbert Sulzbach was ordered back to the Marne front
after a period of rest – 'and it was supposed to be *our* offensive!', he wrote.
As Mme Foch remarked in her diary: 'The Marne doesn't like them, for
them the river is decidedly fatal.'[99]

Foch had been entirely correct to seize the moment. Pedroncini's study
of Pétain's command is not only critical of Foch's methods before MAR-
NESCHUTZ–REIMS but he also downplays Foch's countermanding of the
order to suspend the preparations for the riposte. He concludes that the
appointment of Buat (Pétain's 'friend', who had Foch's 'confidence') and
the removal of Pétain's right of appeal were a quid pro quo for restricting
Foch to strategy, leaving tactical dispositions, especially defensive ones, in
Pétain's hands. Foch's acceptance that the French army could not continue to send French units north to support the BEF and that the next
offensive was likely to fall once again on the French rather than the British
meant, in Pedroncini's view, that 'Pétain's strategic and tactical ideas thus
gained prominence during the waiting period from 15 June to 15 July
1918.'[100] In reality it was Cointet's intelligence assessments that pin-
pointed the forthcoming offensive, rather than Pétain's 'win' in the debate
over strategy. As for the greater success of Gouraud's Fourth Army east of
Reims, it was not simply Pétain's defence tactics but the fact that the
conditions for employing them existed – conditions that were not fulfilled,
as we have seen, in the case of Berthelot's Fifth Army – that counted.

Pedroncini argues further that Pétain did not stop the counter-
offensive, and that the delays caused by the taking away of some of the
troops destined for it had little effect. Moreover, Foch had permitted the

[97] Görlitz, *Kaiser and his Court*, 372–4 (entries for 18, 22, 23 July 1918).
[98] Lossberg, *Meine Tätigkeit*, 351.
[99] Sulzbach, *With the German Guns*, 204; Mme Foch diary, 22 July 1918.
[100] Pedroncini, *Pétain Général*, 386–7.

use of those troops if 'absolutely necessary', so the differences between the two commanders were not all that great.[101] Yet it is the state of mind that is important here: a determination to carry out the planned operation if at all possible versus an acceptance that it might have to be delayed. Once delayed, of course, there would have been no guarantee that the operation would not be delayed yet again and the favourable opportunity lost. On balance, it is more likely that under Pétain the counter-offensive either would not have taken place at all, or would not have had the same force that Foch insisted upon. Indeed, Mangin relates how Pétain and Fayolle came to his observation post on the first evening (18 July), and Pétain said that he had no reinforcements to send to exploit the day's success. Fayolle noted then how 'very restrictive' Pétain was; but Foch ordered a continuation of the offensive and released two more of the British divisions from XXII Corps to join Tenth Army. In what Fayolle described as a 'judicious' instruction, Foch ordered the offensive to continue to 'push hard'.[102] Buat had gone personally to Bombon to argue the need to strengthen Fifth Army, but Foch had forbidden the use of the two British divisions with Fifth Army, instead allocating them to Mangin.[103] It is true that with the failure of MARNESCHUTZ–REIMS the Germans realised that they had lost the war in the west, but an Allied failure to seize and exploit the moment might have meant that the war continued into 1919, with the enemy still occupying French and Belgian territory although on a shorter front. In that scenario there would have been tens, if not hundreds, of thousands more deaths and maimings before peace came.

Foch himself thought that his countermanding Pétain's order to suspend preparations was important. He told Wilson (who had gone to France on 21 July still convinced that Rupprecht would attack the BEF in the north) that when the German offensive began on 15 July Pétain 'at once gave up all idea of counter-attack'. Weygand repeated the same story to DuCane, who passed it on to GHQ.[104] In the glow of the achievement (at last) of a success, Foch and Weygand may have exaggerated the importance of countermanding Pétain's order. However, Cointet tells us how Pétain reacted to the news that Foch had done this. With his 'mine de mauvais jours' (his usual expression on bad news days), Cointet writes, Pétain stated that Foch was biting off more than he could chew. He, Pétain, would wait and see what transpired. Cointet's postwar

---

[101] Ibid., 393–6.
[102] Mangin, *Comment finit la guerre*, 196; Fayolle, *CS*, 290 (entries for 18, 19 July 1918).
[103] Buat diary, 18 July 1918, ms 5391.
[104] Wilson diary, 21 and 22 July 1981; DuCane to CGS, 22 July 1918, WO 158/87.

judgement was that the victory was Foch's – due to his superior military skills and unquenchable energy.[105]

Recent scholarship concurs in this view. Robert Doughty writes: 'Pétain's pessimism colored his assessment of the situation, and had Foch not intervened, he might have delayed, weakened, or canceled Tenth Army's operation.' For Michael Neiberg, Foch turned 'a defensive battle into an offensive battle that changed the entire tenor of the war and made victory in 1918 possible'.[106]

By the end of the second Battle of the Marne, then, Foch had overcome threats to his position, and had gained undisputed authority over his Allies and then over the enemy. Clemenceau and Poincaré responded generously. Mordacq had stated several times that it was time to award a marshal's baton to Foch, and on 22 July Clemenceau agreed: Foch had proved his ability, the honour would prove to the enemy how much confidence they had in the Generalissimo, and obviate any little difficulties resulting from the subordination of Haig, a British field marshal. In the evening of 5 August Clemenceau made one of his frequent visits to Bombon, and pulled out of his pocket what he described as 'a very interesting document' which he meant to read out. He then read the decree naming Foch Maréchal de France. Joffre had been named as the Third Republic's first marshal as a reward for stepping down, but this second award was made in much happier circumstances. Clemenceau's letter to Poincaré requesting the honour spoke of Foch and his soldiers defeating the massive attack to impose a German peace. It went on to list their achievements: Paris freed from danger, Soissons and Château Thierry recaptured, more than 200 villages delivered, 35,000 prisoners and 700 enemy guns captured.

The confidence placed by the Republic and by all its Allies in the victor of the marshes of Saint-Gond, in the illustrious chief of the Yser and of the Somme, has been fully justified. The dignity of marshal of France conferred upon General Foch will not only be a reward for past services, it will preserve even better in the future the authority of the great warrior called to lead the armies of the Entente to the definitive victory.[107]

Both Foch and Clemenceau were overcome with emotion and embraced each other, with Foch agreeing instantly to Clemenceau's suggestion that Pétain should receive the *médaille militaire*.

---

[105] Foch 'veut avoir plus gros yeux que gros ventre': Cointet memoirs, Cahier '1918', fos. 116, 120.

[106] Doughty, *PV*, 470; Neiberg, *Second Battle of the Marne*, 186.

[107] Photograph of Clemenceau's scrawled letter in Weygand, *Foch*, between pp. 226 and 227 (it reads better in French).

15 'Les Boches sont dans la purée': the Hun is really in the soup

Foch did not rest on his laurels. Well before the simple ceremony at his headquarters when he received his marshal's baton (from President Poincaré on 23 August), he was already planning future moves. His plans to free the Amiens–Paris railway and the northern coalmines had long been in the pipeline and he now seized the opportunity to confer with the three commanders-in-chief in France about future operations. Usually, he preferred a less formal, face-to-face approach: this was the sole occasion prior to discussion of armistice terms that Foch called such a conference, its rarity marking its significance. It took place at his headquarters in Bombon on 24 July.

The previous day Foch had asked Weygand to prepare a memorandum to be given to Haig, Pétain and Pershing, together with a questionnaire requesting details of the forces that each Allied army would be able to put into line on 1 January and 1 April 1919.[1] Foch's confidence that his chief of staff would reproduce faithfully his ideas resulted in a more concisely expressed and clearer exposition of his views. Nevertheless, he was capable of concision, as his entry for 24 July in his notebook reveals:

These are the operations to be carried out <u>as soon as possible</u> with the aim of maintaining moral ascendancy over the enemy, maintaining the initiative, maintaining the direction of the war. 2) then a general offensive in the autumn 18; 3) withdrawal [to the] Hindenburg [Line].[2]

Together with their respective chiefs of staff, the Allied and national commanders talked for over two hours before lunch. The memorandum which was read out and translated stated unequivocally that the fifth German offensive had failed; it was time to abandon the defensive attitude that the Allies' numerical inferiority had imposed hitherto and to go onto the offensive. The manpower balance was beginning to move in the Allies' favour: they had greater and fresher reserves; the enemy had been forced to create two 'armies', with the weaker holding the trenches whilst the

---

[1] Weygand, *IV*, 581–2.   [2] Foch, 24 July 1918, fo. 328. Original emphasis.

shock troops received all the resources; the Allies had undoubted superiority in aviation and tanks, and would soon have a greater number of guns; finally, of course, unlike the enemy whose larder was bare, the Americans were continuing to arrive. Consequently, as the enemy had failed when his resources were so much greater than those of the Allies, now the Allies had gained the moral, in addition to the material, ascendancy.

A programme of operations was suggested that would keep the military initiative in Allied hands and improve France's economic life. It involved freeing the railway communications between Paris and eastern France in two sectors: in the Champagne area (where the recent enemy offensive had been defeated and operations were continuing), and around the Saint-Mihiel salient south of Verdun (to be undertaken by the Americans). A third element of the programme was the freeing of the Paris–Amiens railway by combined French and British action. In addition to this concentration on railway communications, Foch proposed action in northern France to liberate the vital coalmining areas and to free the ports, Calais and Dunkirk, from the threat of enemy action. Depending upon how quickly significant results could be obtained in these areas, further action might also be taken before year's end. Finally, the Allied armies must be ready to prevent the enemy from making a strategic withdrawal to shorter lines.[3]

After some initial surprise – Weygand writes, perhaps with exaggeration, of violent surprise and stupor[4] – all expressed general agreement with these strategic principles, although Pétain raised concerns about his reduced resources, not only in men but also in guns, munitions and tanks. He asked for time to think over plans and possibilities.[5] Two days later, he responded that he was in general agreement with the Allied general in chief. He would be able to give General Debeney's First Army the means necessary to join with the British in freeing the Paris–Amiens railway. Equally he would be able to collaborate with the American operation against Saint-Mihiel, in particular by supplying heavy artillery. On the other hand, he did not want French troops involved in the later northern operation against the coalfields and ports because his resources would be exhausted by then, and he wanted to keep the 1919 class (already called up) for operations in the spring.[6] Pétain's cautious response points up the contrast between himself, wishing to limit his army's contribution to any

---

[3] Mémoire, *AFGG* 7/1, annex 276; English translation in *USAWW* 2: 551–2, and Edmonds et al., *OH 1918*, 3: appendix XX.

[4] Weygand, *IV*, 585.

[5] 'Allied Conference at Chateau Bombon', 24 July 1918, *USAWW* 2: 549–50.

[6] Pétain to Foch, 26 July 1981, *AFGG* 7/1, annex 325.

further fighting, and Foch, who had seized the moment on 18 July and now wished to exploit the moral ascendancy that he had gained. Indeed, Foch had already requested (on 20 July) that Clemenceau as War Minister call up the 1920 class so that its training could begin in October ready for 1919, which would be the 'decisive year of the war'. 'The stronger we are', Foch concluded, 'the sooner we shall be victorious, the better we shall be heard'.[7]

As for Haig, he had already been in communication with Foch about the long-delayed Amiens operation. On 17 July Haig had written to ask for the cooperation of the French army on his right (General Debeney's First Army) and for the return of his XXII Corps from the French sector for an operation to advance the Allied lines south and southeast of Amiens to free the railway. The operation should take place as soon as possible, and he had already instructed his First and Third armies to prepare offensive operations in order to mislead the enemy about his true intentions.[8] Consequently, in a Franco-British conversation before the main meeting on 24 July, Haig and Foch agreed to go ahead with the Amiens operation as soon as possible. As a result of this speedy meeting of minds, on 28 July Foch placed Debeney under Haig's command for the operation. This was an astute move. He sent Weygand to deliver the news in person, and Haig was 'pleased that Foch should have entrusted me with the direction of these operations'. The personal attention made a better impression than the 'magnificent lunch' that Foch provided after the commanders' meeting on the 24th (Illustration 10). 'I cannot understand how anyone can work in the afternoon after such a huge meal!', the puritanical Scot wrote in his diary. Nonetheless, he was impressed with the 'great spirits' that all showed during the meeting.[9]

Pershing was delighted at the prospect of the Saint-Mihiel operation because it would help in the creation of the American army, already agreed in principle, and the operation had been under consideration ever since June 1917, when he had first arrived in France. He undertook to enquire about obtaining more American tanks, although he admitted that American production of artillery was far short of what had been planned and promised. Foch pointed out how diminishing numbers of horses meant greater reliance on mechanical transportation for moving guns and munitions across country, and he emphasised that operations would depend to a large extent on the numbers of tanks available. Haig declared that by the end of the summer the BEF would have all the tanks it

[7] Foch to Clemenceau, 20 July 1918, *AFGG* 7/1, annex 178.
[8] Haig to Foch, 17 July 1918, WO 158/29/91, and 15N 10, pièce 114.
[9] Haig diary, 28 July, 24 July 1918; letter, Haig to Lady Haig, 24 July 1918, acc. 3155, ms. 151.

Illustration 10 The supreme and three national commanders on 24 July 1918 in front of Foch's headquarters, after deciding to move onto the offensive

needed; but Pétain stated that the French army was 'very short of tanks' because of earlier losses and breakdown.

So the Allied conference had gone off very well, much more harmoniously than any of the SWC sessions. After the initial surprise at Foch's positive confidence had dissipated, all except Pétain were enthusiastic. In Pétain's case, however, there was the counterweight of a new chief of staff. Weygand recalled Buat's 'wide smile of satisfaction' at the idea of forthcoming operations. Foch could hope that, as Anthoine's replacement, Buat would have a beneficial effect at GQG and on Pétain. Weygand points out that such counter-arguments as were raised during the conference did not reflect opposition to Foch's ideas; rather they were a statement of the difficulties to be overcome.[10]

Now the chances for mounting successfully a coordinated series of Allied attacks were greater because the transport question was on the way to resolution (see earlier pp. 389–91). Because of the onset of the MARNESCHUTZ–REIMS offensive, the complaints about Foch's lack of staff had not been entirely resolved, and the transport question involved control of the railways, which was a matter for civilians as much as for the military. On 20 July General Alby (acting head of the army general staff) and Albert Claveille (engineer, former director of the French state railways, and Minister for Public Works since September 1917) brought a draft decree for the creation of a 'Direction générale de l'arrière', and immediately following the Allied generals' conference they returned with Clemenceau to discuss Foch's objections to the draft. Two days later, on 26 July, the decree was published, placing in Claveille's hands the permanent delegation from the War Minister of authority for the railways. This removed the dual system of military and civilian control which had been much criticised throughout the war; brought together the waterways, ports and other public installations; and, most importantly for military operations and Foch's powers, placed in Foch's headquarters a general officer (whose appointment was agreed by the Minister and Pétain) as the Minister's delegate. This general officer had under his direct orders all the military and civilian personnel working on military transport. Thus Foch had a direct line to the ultimate authority for such transport.

This greater coordination and centralisation in Foch's hands continued apace as the initiative shifted to the Allies. On 31 July, by ministerial decree, all French missions were to report to Foch rather than to GQG 'for all questions to do with the conduct of operations'.[11] Discussions continued with the army general staff in Paris over forming at Bombon the

[10] Weygand, IV, 585.   [11] GQGA JMO, 9 August 1918, 26N 1.

new direction of the rear areas, and Weygand worked with GQG staff on the complicated move of the DA staff from Pétain to Foch's headquarters, despite Buat's reluctance.[12] Arrangements were far enough advanced for a summary of the proposals to be sent to London on 16 August.[13] In addition, Foch took steps to deal with the resources needed for future operations, namely tanks and aviation.

Haig had been impressed by Foch's words during the conference: 'Foch is evidently a great believer in the power of "Tanks".'[14] Moreover, Foch was working on ways to overcome the French army's lack of heavy tanks. On the other hand, production of the light Renault tanks was such that by 27 August the War Ministry had taken delivery of 1960 of them.[15] They were used by the tank crews of the nine new battalions that joined the French army in July and August.[16] Foch wanted much greater coordination in the use of tanks, and already on 14 and 21 June he had sent two projects to General Belin, the French PMR in Versailles, for an Allied tank reserve.[17] He envisaged a reserve on the same lines as the scheme for heavy railway guns that was under consideration. Such a reserve would make heavy tanks interchangeable, to be used where needed; unity of doctrine would also be a good idea. He had asked General Estienne, the head of the French Artillerie d'assaut – although Estienne hated the term 'tanks', the longer French 'assault artillery' was rarely used outside official documents – to preside over an Allied commission of 'particularly competent officers' whose conclusions would be presented for his approval before becoming definitive.

Foch explained his thinking about the use of tanks to Wilson. The CIGS was also thinking about the 1919 campaign, 'based on the employment of tanks on a large scale – both for fighting and for supply', and he asked whether Foch agreed that the Allies should begin immediate planning to place orders for the production of the necessary numbers of tanks. Foch's delay in replying to Wilson's memorandum of 20 July might be another indicator of the growing distance between the two men. Foch criticised Wilson's thoughts about a great offensive with tanks over an eighty-kilometre front, on the grounds that there were few large sectors in France where the terrain was suitable for tanks because of the many rivers.

---

[12] Ibid., 10 and 1 August 1918; Buat diary, 31 July and 1 August 1918, ms 5391.

[13] Grant to DMO, 16 August 1918, WO 106/417.

[14] Haig diary, 24 July 1918; 'Allied conference at Chateau Bombon', 24 July 1981, *USAWW* 2: 550.

[15] 'Situation des chars légers Renault à la date du 27 Août 1918', n.d. [August 1918], Fonds Clemenceau, 6N 54, [d] Divers.

[16] 'Dates d'arrivée des unités d'A.S. aux armées', n.d., 16N 2120, [d] 4.

[17] '1er Projet' and '2e Projet', in Foch to Belin, 14 and 21 June 1918, 15N 94.

He believed also that Wilson's projected figures for tank production were too optimistic, and that any such great tank offensive could begin only late in the year if the Allies had to wait for all the planned production to be delivered before making their move. In other words, Foch appears to be more practical and Wilson the office-bound theorist. Nevertheless, Foch agreed that tanks were 'indispensable to open the way for the infantry and to support its rapid progression', and he foresaw the need to fit trucks with caterpillar tracks so as to carry guns and supplies across devastated terrain now that the armies were on the move. He ended by stating that all the Allies should 'accelerate production' and put their resources in common; that the SWC's tank committee was already working on coordination; and finally that an Allied tank centre was to open soon – 'These are the two organs on which I am counting to use to bring about the best distribution and the best use of our means regarding future operations.'[18]

Foch was indeed using the SWC bureaucracy, as his projects submitted to Belin reveal. The second 'organ' he was developing was a central tactical school for tanks. At its first meeting the Allied tank committee had resolved that such a school should be established because they believed that a successful tank offensive could follow only from combining resources and that 'training must be inter-nationalised'.[19] Accordingly, on 14 July Foch authorised the creation of the 'Centre d'Instruction Interallié d'Artillerie d'Assaut' to function near Fontainebleau from 27 August under the direction of General Estienne, who reported to Foch himself. American, British, French and Italian officers would follow four-day courses, with Britain and France supplying some practice tanks and all four nations supplying the camp's personnel.[20]

Also he worked through the SWC to obtain some British tanks for the French army. The tanks committee's third meeting on 8 July discussed Foch's request for Britain to supply 300 heavy tanks because British production capacity was greater than the BEF's requirements. Foch was convinced, so General Estienne reported, that 'the numbers were superior to the needs' and so he requested delivery of the heavy tanks by September. The reply from the British representative was short. Supplying such a number was 'impossible'. Nothing daunted, next Foch approached General J. E. B. Seely, deputy Minister of Munitions under Churchill, who promised to supply 300 of the latest Mark V (two-star) tanks. Seely

---

[18] Wilson memorandum, 20 July 1918, and Foch to Wilson, 6 August 1918, 15N 94; correspondence between Wilson and DuCane about the delay in WO 158/98.

[19] Procès verbaux of the 3 meetings of the 1st Allied Tank Committee, 6–7 May 1918, CAB 25/121/SWC200; Lt Col. Buzzard, 'Tanks and Mechanical warfare', 14 May 1918, ibid., SWC208.

[20] 'Création d'un centre d'instruction interallié d'artillerie d'assaut', 14 July 1918, 15N 94.

obviously went too far in this promise to Foch, because Wilson wished to keep those later models for the British and to supply 300 of the (now obsolete) Mark Vs instead. Churchill himself saw 'no prospect of meeting the French request' because of munitions workers being withdrawn to be sent to France.[21]

Still Foch did not give up. On 25 July, the day after the generals' conference in Bombon, he spoke with French Munitions Minister Loucheur about getting some tanks from the British.[22] Yet production of all heavy tanks lagged behind Foch's demands. An Allied factory had been built at Châteauroux to produce an Allied tank to the latest design, using French labour, British steel and the new American Liberty motor, but there were constant arguments over allocating the factory's production and no Mark VIII Liberty tank ever left the factory.[23] The Liberty motor was an important element because it was used for aircraft as well as tanks, and American production could not keep up with all the demands from both arms, artillery and aviation. Foch himself was prepared to see a reduction in the numbers of aircraft produced, if there were not enough Liberty motors to go round – he believed that the tank was more important.[24]

All the same, the great value of superiority in the air had been proved, should proof have been needed, by MARNESCHUTZ–REIMS and Second Marne. Not only had air reconnaissance been crucial, but the all-arms battle on 18 July, when infantry, tanks and aircraft combined to strike a massive blow, pointed the way to victory. In aviation matters the SWC was the forum for another threat to Foch's autonomy. The British had created an independent Royal Air Force on 1 April 1918, and then the Air Council in London proposed an independent, strategic bombing force in France, under the command of General Hugh Trenchard. It was based near Nancy in eastern France so that it could bomb German towns and munitions centres. Because of the international character of such long-range bombing, the British Air Minister, Lord Weir, suggested that the SWC should lay down the broad lines for the force, and he sought Clemenceau's support for the scheme because he knew that Foch would prefer to take control himself. Wilson confirmed to the War Cabinet on 24 July the correctness of this view of Foch's intent.[25]

---

[21] Harington, deputy CIGS, to Churchill, 16 July 1918, in Gilbert, *Churchill*, 4, *Companion* 1: 351; and Churchill to Harington, 17 July 1918, ibid., 352.

[22] GQGA JMO, 25 July 1918, 26N 1.

[23] See Greenhalgh, 'First World War Tank', 832, and 'Errors and Omissions', 209.

[24] Foch to Belin, 8 August 1918, 15N 94.

[25] This account of the Independent Bombing Force is taken from Jones, *War in the Air*, 6: 104–17. Wilson had spoken to Foch on 22 July, but there is no mention of the bombing proposal in his diary record of their meeting.

The French representative on the SWC's Allied aviation committee was General Duval, who commanded the Division aérienne as well as heading GQG's aviation service. He had already objected to the British use of the term 'independent' when the aviation committee met on 31 May, arguing that the Allies needed coordination, not independent forces. The committee met again on 21 July after the successful Allied defence and counterattack on the Marne. Duval fought Foch's corner again. Although General F. Sykes gave the British view that strategic bombing was both advantageous and necessary, Duval disputed this. In his view it was certainly advantageous, but it was not necessary (other means could be found) and it was not possible with current resources. Duval believed that bombing forces should be devoted to the battlefield to support the armies. Why, he asked, was it 'more special to bombard Mannheim, inhabited by German civilians, than to bombard Laon, inhabited by German soldiers?' In other words, he brought into question the rationale behind the British proposal for a strategic bombing force independent of Foch. General Trenchard advocated, however, an independent commander for the force, which was already in existence purely as a British force, who would be responsible solely to the SWC.[26] Having failed to reach agreement, the members of the committee passed the ball to the PMRs. They met a week later and accepted the French draft resolution, which proposed that an Allied bombing force be constituted 'as soon as Allied resources in men and materiel' permitted, and that this force 'should be entirely at the disposal of the General Commanding-in-Chief the Allied Armies'. This became Joint Note 35, and the representatives resolved that the 'elaboration of a methodical plan' was expedient, whilst waiting for sufficient Allied resources to permit the force's constitution, which plan 'must be submitted' to Foch and then approved by the SWC.[27] Since the SWC did not meet again to approve the note, Duval's stalling tactic had saved Foch's authority.

The subsequent history of the strategic bombing plan may be told briefly.[28] The British did not give up on their scheme, despite Joint Note 35. Lord Weir roped Derby in to plead the case,[29] and he sent a long note to Clemenceau about the need for a strategic bombing force to destroy German industrial capacity and depress civilian morale – the same arguments would re-surface during the Second World War – and about the need for independent command such as the navy enjoyed. This was passed

---

[26] Procès verbal of the Third Session of the Versailles Inter-allied Aviation Committee, 21 July 1918, CAB 25/122/SWC292, and 4N 10, fos. 3, 8, appendix X.

[27] Draft Resolution: Bombing Air Force, CAB 25/122/SWC296, Annex C; Joint Note 35 and Resolution adopted 3 August 1918, CAB 25/122/SWC299.

[28] See Jones, *War in the Air*, 6: 110–12.

[29] Dutton (ed.), *Paris 1918*, 183, 193 (entry for 6 September 1918).

for comment to Pétain, Foch and Duval on 9 September. As before, Duval rebutted the arguments: there was no reason to separate any bombing force from the military command.[30] Foch's own response was forceful: an independent force meant that resources would be taken from the principal task, that of the army. The existence, let alone the development, of such a force 'exempt' from the 'chief command' was inconceivable.[31] By the time that the War Cabinet in London met to discuss its response, sent on 3 October, the situation on the Western Front had changed radically. The British government was now prepared to accept that General Trenchard's bombing force should be placed under Foch. Clemenceau accepted the British draft proposal on 17 October, and on the 26th Trenchard was notified of his appointment to command the 'Inter-Allied Independent Air Force' with a staff made up of officers from each of the nations supplying aircraft. James Corum has estimated the effects of the strategic bombing carried out: the cost in Allied aircraft destroyed was greater than the damage caused to the German economy. The RAF was losing one expensively trained aircrew for every one or two civilian bystanders.[32] Foch, however, had argued consistently for effective concentration of all aircraft on bombing behind the enemy lines, such bombardment to be under his control.[33]

Tanks and aviation for the French front were not Foch's only worries. No Italian had been present at the Bombon meeting on 24 July, but their continued inaction against the Austrians became an even greater problem for Foch because of Italian demands for greater resources (tanks, lorries, gas shells), more infantry (French and US divisions), and the return of the 60,000 men of the 'Truppe ausiliarie in Francia' (the labour that Foch and Ferry had negotiated with the Italians in January 1918 in return for the French and British divisions serving in Italy since Caporetto). Foch and Clemenceau had discussed the Italian request for tanks and gas shells on 11 July, but so long as the Germans were attacking in France the French could not afford to be generous. The Italians, however, saw only French short-sightedness – if the Germans broke through into Italy they could then threaten southern France – but 'France never looks outside France, and cannot see that the urgent requirements of others can possible [sic] weigh against those of France.' This was the complaint that the British ambassador in Rome passed on to Lloyd George. The Italians complained further that French offers of help came with strings attached, namely the

---

[30] 'Note for M. Clemenceau', in Cabinet du ministre de la guerre to Pétain, Foch and Duval, 9 September 1918, and 'Observations suggérées par la note jointe à ce bordereau', 13 September 1918, both in Clemenceau papers, 6N 54.
[31] Jones, *War in the Air*, appendix VIII.   [32] Corum, *Luftwaffe*, 40.
[33] Dutton (ed.), *Paris 1918*, 153 (entry for 18 August 1918).

extension of Foch's unified command to Italy. This they were not willing to concede.[34] They attempted to enlist British and American help in their quest for greater resources. Finance Minister Francesco Nitti travelled to London and on 24 July (the same day as the commanders-in-chief were meeting in France) attempted to persuade Lloyd George to send the Italians more supplies, and to support their demands for some US divisions.[35] Nitti overplayed his hand by exaggerating the strength of Austrian forces on the Italian front, and gained no concessions from the British. As for the Americans, Italy had been trying to get US divisions ever since the USA joined the war. Pershing had consented to a token force (332 US Infantry Regiment) being dispatched to the Italian Tenth Army, but was unwilling to do more, despite considerable pressure from the American ambassador in Rome.[36] This is not surprising, since Pershing was now fighting to create his independent US army in France. Still Diaz did not give up. On 3 September he called personally on Pershing and asked for twenty divisions to be sent to the Italian front. The interpreter 'had hardly finished translation of this modest request when he [Diaz] made bold to make it 25 divisions'. Pershing did not trouble to explain the reason for turning down the request ('a useless waste of time'), merely stating that it was impossible to satisfy it.[37] One is forced to wonder how Diaz could ever have imagined that Pershing would consent.

The Italian request for the return of their labour battalions from France was more serious, for they were providing an especially important service. They dug trenches, and prepared airfields and barracks; they repaired and built new roads and railways; they established telegraph and telephone lines.[38] These were vital services and they explain Foch's emollient letter to Diaz on 17 July. Foch described how 7000 Italians were constructing new rail communications between the French and British sectors; more than 12,000 were helping to dig defensive positions around Paris; another 30,000 or so were supporting the upkeep of roads and stations behind the front. Finally 4000 were to be used to make up for the casualties that the II Italian Corps had just suffered during the last German offensive. The French had only the highest praise for the Italian workers, Foch wrote, and it would be 'impossible' to interrupt their work now, in the midst of the battle. Taking the Italian workers away would mean that an equivalent number of French soldiers would have to be withdrawn from the French

---

[34] Rennell Rodd to Lloyd George, 12 July 1918, Rennell of Rodd mss, vol. 19.
[35] Cassar, *Forgotten Front*, 170–2.
[36] Sonnino to ambassadors London, Paris, Washington, 19 August 1918, and Washington to Orlando, 1 September 1918, *Documenti diplomatici italiani*, 11: docs. 409, 466.
[37] Pershing diary, 3 September 1918.   [38] For details see Caracciola, *Truppe italiane*, 246.

front to do the work. Foch ended by suggesting that their maintenance in France would not prevent Diaz from taking the offensive: 'the impotence and defeat of the enemy call imperiously for an attack'.[39] Despite this, Mordacq informed Foch on 24 July of the repeated request for the Italians' return. Diaz's lengthy response to Foch's letter was a masterpiece of prevarication, and Foch resorted to going to see Clemenceau to get him to exert some pressure.[40] Once again, Foch refused to return the labour battalions because by now (he wrote on 6 August) the Allies were advancing over a devastated battlefield and Italian labour was needed more than ever. Foch did promise, however, to send some gas shells and three companies of tanks (seventy-five in all) in return for an early date for the start of the Italian offensive.[41] These Italian demands for materiel and for the return of their workers were all distractions from the pressing need to prepare Foch's three offensives to free vital railway communications in France.

Of the three prongs of his planned operations, the northern Franco-British and the eastern American elements required some time for preparation. The central element – carried out by the tri-national armies in Champagne – was the continuation of the Marne battle. Foch's task here was to keep Pétain active. He had already insisted to Pétain that the preparations for its start on 18 July not be delayed. Now he was keeping a close eye on Pétain's conduct of the pursuit of the retreating enemy. On 27 July he sent two letters, urging that Pétain maintain the operations of Sixth and Tenth Armies as vigorously as possible by coordinating them in the general direction of Fère en Tardenois (in the centre of the Marne salient), by supplying fresh units despite Pétain's having very few of them, and by collecting tanks from other parts of the front. Pétain had suggested withdrawing all the tank units because of the losses and damage of the opening days, but Foch vetoed this. Foch's second letter concerned the consumption of shells, which Pétain had warned was becoming worrying. Foch pointed out that consumption was indeed outstripping re-supply by a large factor, but pointed out also that as long ago as 15 June Pétain had warned his armies to be more economical. From the daily figures which GQG supplied (itself an indication of how closely Foch was watching the French army), Foch deduced that Pétain's munitions reserves would last only a few more weeks before being exhausted completely. In other words, once again, Pétain's instructions to his armies were not being observed. Foch advised, therefore, 'rigorous control' of subordinate commands to

[39] Foch to Diaz, 17 July 1918, *AFGG* 7/1, annex 77.
[40] GQGA JMO, 29 and 31 July 1918, 26N 1.
[41] Foch to Diaz, 6 August 1918, *AFGG* 7/1, annex 506.

ensure that orders to be economical were being carried out and that he send a reminder to those subordinates – 'if he had not already done so' – of those instructions.[42]

Although the enemy forces were being pushed back and out of the Marne salient, there was to be no quick victory. It proved impossible to tie the neck of the sack and capture the German forces trapped within; instead the Germans fought a determined and skilful retreat, taking full advantage of the heavily wooded and steep terrain. Consequently Pétain wrote to Foch on 31 July with a situation report on the state of the French armies. He had been short of 112,000 men on 20 July, a deficit that had grown to 120,000 on the 30th despite the reinforcements that he had received. Pétain stated that he had insufficient numbers in the depots to make up such a deficit, and that the French could do no more – 'We are at the very end of our effort.' In addition he had to supply four divisions to General Debeney for the Amiens operation, and the American divisions currently with French units were being removed to constitute the US First Army. Pétain ended his letter with an indirect request that the French should not contribute to the Amiens or the Saint-Mihiel operations: the situation was so serious that he believed Foch should take it into account when evaluating the part the French were to play.[43]

Although Pétain admitted in this 'non possumus' account of his resources that the morale of his 'tired' French divisions leaving the battle was high, he knew that the Germans were suffering just as much. Agents watching trains on the Belgian network reported that between 21 July and 1 August twelve German divisions had left the front north of Cambrai (signifying that operation HAGEN was no more), mostly for the Aisne. An annex to the 2e Bureau's daily intelligence report of 1 August indicated that twenty-one German divisions had moved into the sector between the river Oise and Reims, with another four between Reims and the Aisne.[44] All this information meant that the Germans must be suffering huge casualties. That same day, 1 August, Mangin's Tenth Army captured the heights of Grand-Rozoy (between Soissons and Fère en Tardenois) and entered Soissons the following day. Fayolle noted proudly in his diary that in July his army group had captured over 28,000 German prisoners, over 600 guns, 600 mortars, and well over 4000 machineguns.[45] Although Pétain's armies were indeed fought out (he told Foch on 2 August that

[42] Letters, Foch to Pétain, 27 July 1918, *AFGG* 7/1, annexes 336, 337.
[43] Pétain to Foch, 31 July 1918, ibid., annex 403.
[44] 'Armée allemande à la date du 1er août 1918', 2 August 1918, ibid., annex 429; 'Divisions allemandes dont le déplacement a été constaté', annex to 2e Bureau Compte-rendu de renseignement, 1 August 1918, 15N 5.
[45] Fayolle, *CS*, 293 (entry for 3 August 1918).

he had not one fresh division in reserve),[46] so that the next August days saw them only following up the retreating enemy rather than inflicting any great defeat, the contrast between the positive attitude of the normally careful and methodical Fayolle and the negative attitude of Pétain is marked.

Yet Foch was satisfied. He told his wife that the Germans had engaged a quarter of their entire forces in the Marne salient, and their exhausted divisions were simply trying to evacuate all their materiel. They had not expected such a 'kick' from the French army.[47] When Clemenceau came to see him in Bombon on 30 July, Foch was able to press for the repair of the railway between Château Thierry and Epernay, so as to restore communications between Paris and eastern France.[48] So the aim of freeing the railway along the Marne was accomplished. Although the Allies had not managed to trap the enemy in the Marne salient, the moral victory of enforcing a retreat was enormous. The movement of German troops to the Aisne implied that the preparations for the second element of Foch's strategy, the Amiens operation, had remained a secret.

Haig was much more positive than Pétain. At that same meeting between Clemenceau and Foch, the latter was able to report that Haig was preparing the northern operation with enthusiasm and confidence. In the personal letter that Weygand had delivered asking Haig to take command of a Franco-British force for the action, Foch requested that the date be brought forward from 10 to 8 August. Because the enemy was occupied in withdrawing from the Marne salient, the Germans would be even less prepared for the new attack. So Foch acted to accentuate the element of surprise which he had identified as a factor in the German success of the first half of the year.

His placing of Debeney's First Army under Haig's command was a politically astute move which flattered the British commander. It probably reflected also what Foch had learned from his 1916 experience on the Somme, the sector where this new action was to take place. Then the lack of unified command had made the battle a disjointed affair, with one ally constantly waiting for the other to be ready. With both First Army and Rawlinson's Fourth Army under Haig's command, the problems of 1916 ought not to be repeated. The 1916 experience was probably a factor also in Rawlinson's reaction to the news that he was to fight alongside the French once again. He had already prepared and received approval for his battle plan when he and Debeney met on 26 July with Haig and Foch (who was, Rawlinson noted, 'in the best of form & spirits').[49] Rawlinson had

---

[46] Pétain to Foch, 2 August 1918, *AFGG* 7/1, annex 434.
[47] Mme Foch diary, 30 July 1918.   [48] Mordacq, *MC*, 2: 148.
[49] Rawlinson diary, 26 July 1918.

planned for Debeney to attack south of Montdidier 'in conjunction with' Fourth Army, but Foch stated that he did not have enough troops for a big offensive out of Montdidier and so First Army must attack north of the Avre river, close up to the British. He wanted as strong an attack as possible to exploit the surprise effect. Rawlinson 'strongly deprecated the employment of two armies side by side but Foch insisted & it must therefore be done but it will be very difficult to keep it secret & if we are discovered our chances of a big success will be small'. Having been side-lined after the 1916 Somme battle, Rawlinson was keen for a success and appreciated, as did Foch, the need for secrecy so as to achieve surprise. However, he had to accept a French presence in the battle, even though he believed it reduced his chances of that success, because unified command meant that there was no appeal against Foch's decision.

On 6 August Pétain sent a telegram to Foch saying that the Germans were now solidly installed in their defensive positions on the Vesle river, whose steep northern banks made any French attack very difficult. Consequently he had ordered his two army groups to establish themselves along the southern approaches to the river but at the same time to give the impression to the enemy that they intended to make a strong pursuit. This feint was to safeguard the Amiens operation, which began two days later. So Pétain's armies had forced the enemy to retire and had kept them occupied until the next phase of Foch's plan.

Foch's insistence on speed and secrecy paid dividends. He had kept both the French and British governments in the dark. When Clemenceau arrived at Bombon on the evening of 8 August, the opening day of the offensive, he asked Weygand where Foch had found the divisions to mount such an attack. In order to satisfy Lloyd George's requests to DuCane to find out what was afoot, Foch gave DuCane a couple of scraps of non-committal paper to pass on to London – 'As things are going well, we will continue to act against the enemy' – but threatened that if DuCane ever took advantage of his position to pass on confidential information he would by-pass DuCane altogether.[50] Instead Foch gave Grant instructions on 6 August that he was to go to London, arriving 'very late on the 7th so as to say nothing which could be possibly misused in case events changed'.[51] Even GQG knew nothing about the forthcoming operation, except for Pétain, Buat and Barescut.[52] The secrecy strained relations between Foch and Wilson because Wilson thought that he might be taken into his

[50] Weygand, *IV*, 590; DuCane, *Foch*, 52.
[51] Grant diary, 6 August 1918, WO 106/1456; Grant, 'Some notes made at Marshal Foch's H.Qrs. August to November 1918', fo. 2, ibid.
[52] Clive diary, 8 August 1918, CAB 45/201.

confidence, but Foch said that he was prepared to *talk* to Wilson but not to write to London.[53] Wilson had tried to open a private line to both Haig and Foch. On 3 August he asked both Haig and DuCane to communicate with him privately. Haig rejected such 'an extraordinary proposal': 'It is impossible for a CIGS to exchange opinions on military matters with a C-in-C in the field in *personal* telegrams!'[54] So Wilson was kept out of the loop as well.

The successful maintenance of secrecy increased the surprise in the early morning of 8 August. The British tanks and infantry had been assembled at the last minute, revealing a mastery of staff preparations that equalled that shown by the enemy in the preparation of their attacks. Added to surprise, the weight of the Allied attack increased its effectiveness. Over 800 aircraft of the RAF and the whole of the French Division aérienne (600 aircraft, added to First Army's own aviation resources) vastly outnumbered German airpower, which was mainly engaged in Champagne. Well over 500 British tanks (the whole of the Tank Corps) and ninety French light Renault tanks joined the battle. Finally, over 600 heavy guns in addition to the 700 field guns used for the creeping barrage faced 530 German guns, ninety-five per cent of whose positions were known. The German defences were organised haphazardly, a sign of lowered morale.[55] Ten British divisions with a further one in reserve and ten French divisions (with two more in reserve) faced *Second* and *Eighteenth Armies*, both in Crown Prince Rupprecht's army group and both completely unsuspecting. On 5 August, three days before the attack, Rupprecht's chief of staff reported to OHL that the Entente was 'remarkably inactive'; that both German armies were 'in excellent form'; that most units were 'near full strength' (whereas average battalion strength had fallen from 850 to 600 men since March); and that 'morale was good, defensive positions were satisfactory'.[56]

Fourth Army's infantry attack, spearheaded by the Australian and Canadian corps, began with no prior warning from the artillery at 4.20 am. On their right, First Army began an artillery barrage at the same time, but the infantry did not launch the first of their three staggered assaults until forty minutes later, with the aim of maximising the effect of surprise. The results were stupendous. Fourth Army captured *intact* nearly all the German guns operating south of the Somme. They also took 12,000 prisoners,

[53] DuCane, *Foch*, 52.
[54] Cipher telegram, Wilson to DuCane, 3 August 1918, WO 158/98; Haig's comments on Wilson's telegram in Sheffield and Bourne (eds.), *Douglas Haig*, 437.
[55] Prior and Wilson, *CWF*, 301, 314.
[56] Von Kuhl, cited in Kitchen, *German Offensives*, 222; Herwig, *First World War*, 421.

inflicted three times as many casualties (27,000) as they suffered, and advanced twelve kilometres. First Army did not capture so much ground (seven kilometres), but had forced the passage of the Avre and liberated several villages.

Foch was, of course, delighted and went to congratulate Haig in person. As usual, he wanted to be near the action. He moved his headquarters to an advanced post at Sarcus so as to be nearer to Haig and to Fayolle, from whose Reserve Army Group First Army had been detached and whose Third and Tenth Armies were next in line on the front. Foch wrote to his wife that same day that Amiens was already secure, and he hoped that the whole of the left bank of the Somme might be cleared. Fayolle was primed ready to intervene to extend the battle, if needed. That evening Fayolle went to see the new marshal and found him very excited. He wanted Montdidier captured immediately, but Fayolle counselled patience.[57] The town could be taken only by flank attacks, nipping it off. Further progress was made the next day, 9 August, with the aim of reaching the Roye–Chaulnes–Bray line. Although Fourth Army's attacks were now less well organised because it proved impossible for neighbouring units to know each other's precise position and because some delay occurred in issuing orders for that day (the result of losing time in toasting the successes of the 8th), they captured another 4000 prisoners against stiffening German defences. First Army, however, completed the encirclement of Montdidier so that its fall became simply a matter of time (see Map 18).

Fayolle was right to describe Foch as 'excited' by the gains of 8 August, and Foch intervened directly on the 9th to make sure that Debeney knew that First Army had to reach Roye as quickly as possible. He sent a message to this effect with Colonel Desticker during the morning. The reason for insisting on reaching Roye was that, there, First Army could join with Third Army, thereby extending the front of battle. Next to Third Army was the victor of the Second Battle of the Marne, General Mangin and Tenth Army. The front line ran south from the Somme and then turned east along the Oise and into Champagne. If the battle could be extended as far east as Tenth Army, the German positions along the Vesle and the Aisne, to which they had been driven in July, could be attacked in flank. The enemy would then be forced to relinquish the line of the Vesle. Foch could see enormous possibilities opening up as a result of the Amiens/Montdidier battle and sent yet another message to Debeney ordering him to keep up with the Canadian Corps on his left and push on to Roye 'without losing a minute' and 'with drums beating'.[58]

[57] Fayolle, *CS*, 294 (entry for 8 August 1918). [58] *AFGG* 7/1, annexes, 571, 572.

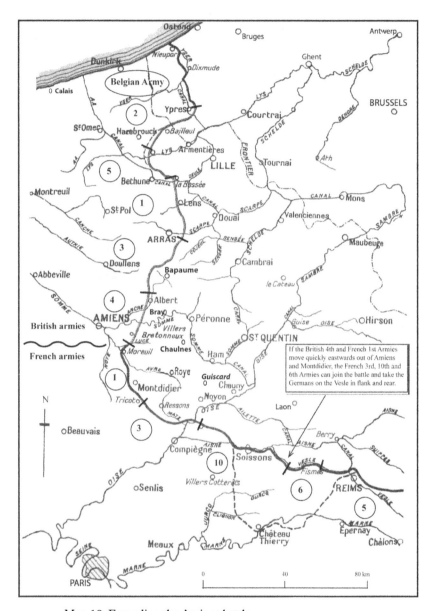

Map 18 Extending the Amiens battle
Position on 7 August 1918, showing the advantage of extending the
battle to the eastern flank after the capture of Montdidier.

Foch's urging was not completely effective, since Haig had to reinforce it. That afternoon he called Debeney in to GHQ, as he had every right to do since First Army was under his orders, to urge exactly the same object, namely an advance on Roye. According to Haig, Debeney demurred, saying that it 'would upset all his plans'.[59]

On 10 August Foch went to see Haig and handed him a 'directive' with instructions that British and French should continue pushing towards Ham on the Somme, with the Fourth Army preparing to cross the river and the French aiming for the Ham–Guiscard road. French Third Army had begun operations to exploit First Army's success and liberate Lassigny and Noyon; Foch asked British Third Army to exploit the enemy's withdrawal as soon as possible by advancing on Bapaume and Péronne. Haig's orders to Rawlinson and Debeney reflected these instructions.[60] When Wilson came over from London to see how matters were progressing and he, Haig and Foch talked on the evening of the 11th, Haig was still in agreement with Foch about 'pushing so far as to get the Boches over the Somme'.[61]

German resistance stiffened considerably on 11 and 12 August, although the French Third Army took more ground, and Mangin was able to issue orders to bring his Tenth Army into the battle. Foch knew that most ground was won on the first day or two of a battle and that further gains lessened gradually. He also knew that he did not want to create a narrow salient such as the one the Germans had created on the Marne. Accordingly on 12 August he wrote to both Haig and Pétain to urge the British to push on to the line of the Somme. In the face of the increased enemy resistance it was pointless to put uniform pressure along the whole front since this would lead only to being weak everywhere. Instead Fourth Army should aim for points that would disorganise the enemy still further, and these attacks should be mounted as soon as possible after the necessary resources in guns, tanks and so on had been collected. As for the French, Mangin's attack east of the river Oise, combined with British Third Army's attack towards Bapaume, would force the enemy to abandon an enormous amount of territory. He ended with the encouraging news from the intelligence service that the Germans had deployed as many as 120 divisions since 15 July, thereby greatly depleting their reserves. Hence the Allies had a splendid opportunity to make further progress.[62]

---

[59] Haig diary, 9 August 1918.
[60] Foch, Directive générale, 10 August 1918, *AFGG* 7/1, annex 593; Prior and Wilson, *CWF*, 333.
[61] Wilson diary, 11 August 1918.
[62] Foch to Haig and Pétain, 12 August 1918, *AFGG* 7/1, annex 631.

Fourth Army's renewed attack was scheduled for 15 August, but a minor revolt by the commander of the Canadian Corps because of the strong German defences facing his men led to a postponement. This in turn led to a disagreeable exchange between Foch and Haig in which Haig claims to have told him 'quite straightly' that he (Haig) was 'responsible for the handling of the British forces'. At this, still according to Haig, Foch was chastened and asked merely that Haig give him early warning of his intentions. However, Foch's responses to the news that Haig had postponed his Fourth Army action tell a different story. Foch accepted that strong enemy resistance required effective artillery preparation before any infantry assault, but he did not want Haig to delay the British Third Army attack towards Bapaume because of Fourth Army's halt. Furthermore, his First Army had already begun its artillery preparation for the agreed 15 August attack, and Fourth Army's halt would seriously affect its operations. First Army was running short of munitions and could not extend its artillery preparation. Foch asked, therefore, that Fourth Army's right support the French and that, should this prove 'absolutely impossible', Haig let him know promptly. Foch did not object to Fourth Army halting to arrange the necessary artillery attack; but he did object to Third Army waiting for Fourth Army before beginning their own operation.

In effect, the Battle of Amiens was over for Fourth Army, but Haig ordered his Third Army to begin the Battle of Albert on 21 August with First Army further north ready to exploit any success. Foch returned Debeney's First Army to French command and, together with Third Army, they made further small advances. This was enough, however, for Mangin to send his Tenth Army northwards from Soissons. Tenth Army captured the enemy's main line of resistance between the Oise and the Aisne and penetrated three to four kilometres beyond, taking more than 8000 prisoners and 100 guns.[63] This was such a significant advance that Pétain ordered his Centre Army Group (Sixth and Fifth Armies) to be ready to seize any opportunity to cross the Vesle on the heels of the enemy. The line of the river Vesle was where the French had halted after Second Marne. So Foch's aim of extending the battle on the flanks was achieved, both in the north by the British and in the east by the French. Both railway lines had been freed; the German withdrawal on the Somme had forced the enemy to leave the Lys salient in Flanders as well, which meant that there was no need to mount the further operation that Foch had included in his 24 July memorandum to safeguard the northern coalfields and the ports. Loucheur reported on 11 August that the output from the Bruay

---

[63] Ibid., 228.

mines was already back to 30,000 tons per month, only 5000 tons down on the pre-April figure.[64] The pursuit continued: the Canadians captured the Drocourt–Quéant switch (it joined the *Wotanstellung*, the Flanders portion of the Hindenburg Line, to the *Siegfriedstellung*); the Australians took Mont St Quentin, north of Péronne, thereby driving the Germans from the Péronne bridgehead; and Mangin reached the Soissons–Chauny road facing the Hindenburg Line. Between 3 and 9 September the enemy's general retreat meant that the Germans were back on their defensive positions; the whole of their gains since 21 March had been wiped out; and they were so short of reserves that Austro-Hungarian troops were brought from Italy to France. Two Austro-Hungarian divisions were included in the intelligence estimate of the enemy reserves on 29 August, following many unconfirmed reports.[65] The August total of German casualties was 228,000, of whom more than half (131,000) were killed or missing.[66] OHL was in total disarray, showering their divisions daily with new regulations about anti-tank warfare.[67] Ludendorff was suffering from nervous exhaustion to the extent that he agreed to accept medical help.

With the greater than anticipated success of the Picardy and Champagne operations, the third prong of Foch's 24 July memorandum, namely the reduction of the Saint-Mihiel salient in order to free the eastern end of the Paris–Nancy railway, became less urgent. From Pershing's point of view, however, he needed to make a success of that operation in order to prove that the AEF was capable of autonomous action. On the same day as the Bombon conference, 24 July, Pershing took command personally of the US First Army, retaining overall command of the AEF. On 9 August Foch and Pershing agreed that fourteen US divisions would be gathered in Lorraine to undertake the proposed operation.[68] Next day the US First Army became effective.

In their meeting on 10 July, when Foch had consented to its formation, most of the US divisions had been in the Champagne area; now, however, the Lorraine sector, where the Americans had built their depots and hospitals, became the focus. At the same meeting Foch had indicated two reasons for not getting too involved in eastern France. First of all, the Allies should keep together in their attacks so as to make the British fight. This was probably a pretext simply to flatter Pershing. Certainly the British had not undertaken offensive operations on their front since MICHAEL and GEORGETTE in March and April, but Foch had no reason

[64] GQGA JMO, 11 August 1918, 26N 1.
[65] Intelligence report 1553, 29 August 1918, 15N 5.   [66] *RAW* 14, Beilage 42.
[67] Sulzbach, *With the German Guns*, 226 (2 September 1918).
[68] Foch to Pershing and Pétain, 9 August 1918, *AFGG* 7/1, annex 569.

(other than London's unwillingness to supply reinforcements in the numbers that Foch believed possible) to suppose that Haig would not mount an offensive at some point. The second reason that Foch adduced was that to follow the reduction of the Saint-Mihiel salient with an advance on Metz was too difficult an undertaking for the 1919 campaign. The argument that the Americans had built their base infrastructure in the area was not valid: infrastructure should follow operations, not dictate them. Foch stated also that freeing the railway communications along the Marne and near Amiens was much more important than the reduction of Saint-Mihiel.[69]

The Germans had held the Saint-Mihiel salient since September 1914; therefore its fortifications were solid. It extended westwards across the Meuse where the eponymous village was situated, and its possession enabled the enemy to interdict the Paris–Nancy railway, which had handicapped the defence of Verdun in 1916. From the apex of the triangular salient on the Meuse, the sector widened so that its eastern base stretched for about forty kilometres. It was about twenty-five kilometres deep. The American plan, long matured, aimed to reduce the large salient by two converging attacks using fourteen divisions, to break through the two lines of the well-fortified *Michelstellung* forming the salient's base; finally to advance towards Metz (in German Lorraine) and capture a main German railway and take control of the approaches to the important Briey iron ore fields. This was a considerably larger operation than Foch's freeing of the Paris–Nancy railway.

Pershing now had an army and a plan, but he needed to collect his scattered divisions and accumulate guns, tanks, munitions and aircraft. Craftily, Foch left Pershing to see Haig alone about the five divisions of US II Corps currently with the BEF. Haig had reacted badly when Foch had taken away the American divisions in June, so his reluctance to get involved again is understandable. Or did he wish to prove to Pershing that commanding an army was rather more difficult than he seemed to think? Whatever the reason, Pershing saw Haig on 12 August and after some unpleasantness it was agreed that Pershing would take back three divisions, leaving the two others with the BEF. Predictably Haig was furious, all the more so since the Battle of Amiens was a mere four days old. It is not clear how much influence Foch had in the compromise that left two American divisions with the BEF (they took part in the breaking of the Hindenburg Line in September). Yet General Harbord's comment is to the point: as Allied CinC Foch could have ordered the US divisions back

---

[69] 'Conversation of July 10, 1918', n.d., Mott papers, USMA 1806, box 1.

and saved Pershing 'a rather uncomfortable visit' to Haig, but 'he left the child on Pershing's lap'.[70]

Another reason for Foch's reluctance to issue the order lies in the delicate state of Franco-British relations over manpower. Wilson was in France between 10 and 12 August, and he had had a 'nice & breezy' argument with Foch, who claimed that the British were prolonging the war by refusing to send men over from Britain and to return the wounded to the front. When Wilson said that the number of British divisions might have to drop to forty to forty-three instead of the fifty-nine to sixty-one that Foch was demanding, Foch became 'rather excited about this & said he would resign'. Wilson became enraged in turn, and told him that 'he would not tolerate that language for a moment'. When Wilson suggested that Foch get the Americans to reduce their battalions from twelve of 1000 men per division to nine of 900 per division, as the British and French had been compelled to do, Foch replied that he did not command the American army. 'Nor do you the British Army', was Wilson's immediate response.[71] Although Wilson claimed that the dispute had done some good and that they were 'as good friends as ever after it', it is likely that Foch still felt some diffidence about removing divisions from Haig's command and was happy to let the American suffer the heat.

Pétain released his US divisions from the Marne and from quiet sectors in the Vosges with less fuss. On 17 August, as theatre commander, he confirmed his general instructions for the attack. Nine US divisions on the southern flank of the salient and five further north in contact with French Second Army were to free the Paris–Avricourt railway and reduce the salient. (Avricourt is the easterly point of the Paris–Nancy line; there is no mention of a further advance on Metz.) Between the two American sectors Pétain was to supply a French force (in the event the three divisions of II Colonial Corps).[72] American historian Robert B. Bruce sees the fact that Pétain gave command of the French forces in the Saint-Mihiel battle to Pershing as providing 'concrete evidence of the vast faith that he had in the military abilities of the AEF and in the leadership capabilities of Pershing and his corps commanders'.[73] One might equally well argue that Pétain wanted to place some tested and reliable French troops into the equation, given that Pershing was insisting on independence – especially since the Americans were using over 3000 French guns (one-third of them manned by French gunners), 267 French tanks (almost half manned by French crews), and the 600 aircraft of the Division aérienne. The French

[70] Yockelson, *Borrowed Soldiers*, 92–7, quotation at p. 96.
[71] Wilson diary, 11 August 1918.   [72] Plan d'attaque en Woëvre, *AFGG* 7/1, annex 711.
[73] Bruce, *Fraternity*, 258.

also supplied the motor transport that moved the US divisions from their previous sectors, and all the shells that were fired in the operation. Haig could not spare the 150 heavy tanks that Pershing had requested, but Trenchard's Independent Bombing Force was added to the aviation resources.

Foch's and Rawlinson's insistence on maintaining secrecy has been noted. The message had not penetrated all the new and inexperienced American headquarters, and Pétain wrote to Pershing on 19 August calling his attention to the talk, in both military and civilian circles, of the forthcoming offensive in eastern France. It was impossible that the enemy remained unaware. Pétain suggested a feint, by sending US officers to Belfort, further south in the Vosges, which would give the impression that something was being prepared in that sector.[74] The 'Belfort ruse', as it became known, appears to have worked to the extent that the French Military Mission in Switzerland reported a state of 'nervousness' in the German command, which requested three German divisions to be sent south to meet any possible threat.[75] Nonetheless, German intelligence had noticed the withdrawal of US divisions from other parts of the front, and had not concentrated their vigilance solely on Belfort. The Saint-Mihiel salient (see Map 19) was, after all, the obvious place for an attack, and the Germans were prepared to receive an assault in either Lorraine, or Alsace, or both.[76]

Next Foch threw the planning into the melting-pot. The Germans along the whole front from Reims to Albert, he boasted to Loucheur, were in 'shreds and tatters'.[77] On 17 August he had approved an operation utilising fourteen US divisions, but, since that date, the British had begun their advance in Flanders, and the Battle of Albert began on 21 August. The French captured Roye on the 27th, Noyon on the 29th; the British took back Bapaume, also on the 29th. Consequently Foch changed his mind about the possibilities for further attacks in 1918 and sent Weygand to check on the progress of the American preparations.[78] He told President Poincaré on 27 August that the enemy was in 'total disarray'. They were making a fighting retreat, but a retreat without order, without planning. Hence, Foch declared, a tight hold must be kept on them: 'light fires everywhere, widen the battle and continue without let-up'.[79] The memorandum of 24 July had forecast that it might be possible

---

[74] Pétain to Pershing, 19 August 1918, *AFGG* 7/1, annex 733.   [75] *USAWW* 8: 62–4.

[76] That German vigilance remained high is confirmed by the translated German operational documents in ibid., 288–301.

[77] Letter, Churchill to his wife, 14 August 1918, in Gilbert, *Churchill*, 4, *Companion* 1: 374.

[78] GQGA JMO, 27 August 1918.

[79] Poincaré, *AS*, 10: 326 (entry for 27 August 1918).

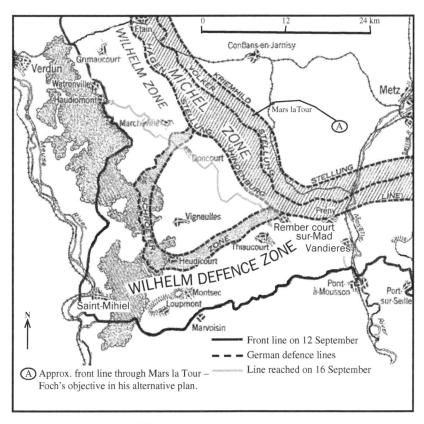

Map 19 Saint-Mihiel, September 1918

to do more, and the first two operations, namely freeing the railways in Champagne and before Amiens, had achieved so much more than had been believed possible. Pershing should not have been surprised, therefore, when Foch turned up at his headquarters on 30 August with a revised plan for the third element of that memorandum, the reduction of the Saint-Mihiel salient.

The revised plan, to take advantage of the enemy's 'disorganisation', proposed a reduced operation against the salient, followed by a Franco-American attack in the direction of Mézières. The Saint-Mihiel action, reduced to eight or nine divisions, was to aim for a line through Vigneulles, cutting the salient and freeing the railway but stopping short of the *Michelstellung* at the salient's base. Then the attack towards Mézières would be made in two parts: on the right, between the Meuse and the Argonne, by French Second Army reinforced by four to six American divisions; on the left, westwards from the Argonne, by French Fourth Army and an American army astride the Aisne. The Saint-Mihiel operation was to be ready by 10 September, to be followed by the Meuse–Argonne attack five to ten days later. General Degoutte would be on hand to help with arrangements for this second proposed, much enlarged, operation.[80] The result was a row with Foch asking Pershing if he intended to do any fighting and Pershing refusing point-blank to fight other than as an American army. 'You may insist all you please', Pershing retorted, 'but I decline absolutely to agree to your plan'. The account of the row on 30 August is always told from the American perspective because the only full account we have is Pershing's, or Pershing's version as told to other Americans.[81] Historians emphasise what a stunning blow Foch's revised plan was, but this is to accept Pershing's virtual obsession with capturing Metz after Saint-Mihiel. Yet, looked at from the French perspective, an interesting question arises. Why did Foch think that he could get Pershing to agree to split up his divisions so soon after receiving authorisation to create the US First Army? That events should have overtaken the 24 July memorandum and imposed a change of emphasis is entirely reasonable. Yet Foch's action in approving an operation on 24 August, cancelling it on 30 August and replacing it with another attempt at amalgamating US divisions into French armies seems uncharacteristically clumsy.

The motive behind Foch's decision was probably political. Haig had been furious when Pershing removed the three US divisions from the BEF. The martyred tone of Haig's letter to him on 27 August is barely veiled: 'I trust that events may justify your decision to withdraw the American troops from the British battle front at the present moment, for I make no doubt but that the arrival in this battle of a few strong and vigorous American Divisions, when the enemy's units are thoroughly worn out, would lead to the most decisive results.'[82] Haig conveyed his feelings to Wilson in London, who felt that removing the divisions was 'a rotten thing to do'. Wilson and Milner expressed their disapproval to Pershing's personal liaison officer in the War Office, Lloyd C. Griscom.[83] This bad feeling fed in to Lloyd George's displeasure at French complaints about British manpower. Pershing's collection of his divisions from Haig had snowballed into Lloyd George's threat that he

---

[80] Foch, Note, 30 August 1918, *AFGG* 7/1, annex 898; English translation in *USAWW* 8: 40–1.
[81] See Smythe, *Pershing*, 174–6.
[82] Cited in Sheffield and Bourne (eds.), *Douglas Haig*, 451.
[83] Griscom, *Diplomatically Speaking*, 358.

would not supply yet more British shipping to transport US troops across the Atlantic. The Prime Minister informed Lord Reading, Britain's ambassador in Washington, that 'until the French and the Americans come to terms with us on the question of the line, I do not propose to give any further assistance in the matter of shipping'.[84]

Clemenceau could not afford to ignore such a threat and its implications. He had gone to Amiens with Lord Derby on 18 August to present Haig with France's highest military honour, the *médaille militaire*. At lunch Haig and Foch voiced their complaints: 'They all have the poorest opinion of Pershing who they say is a most stubborn pig-headed man and who is really the only one of the Americans who thinks that he knows everything and will not recognise that he has much to learn. Haig is particularly bitter.'[85] The next time Clemenceau spoke with Lord Derby, the ambassador reassured him that if it came to a dispute between Pershing and Foch, he believed that President Wilson would support the supreme Allied CinC. Evidently Clemenceau had expressed doubts about whether Foch could command Pershing's obedience, for Balfour informed Derby that Wilson would be 'quite glad of an opportunity of giving Pershing a snub'. Balfour conjectured that if it came to Foch versus Pershing the President would support Foch. Derby passed on to Clemenceau the judgement that Wilson

accepted Foch as being in supreme command and they might rely on him supporting Foch even against Pershing. Clemenceau told me that it was a point on which he had great doubts in his own mind. Things were not going well between Foch and Pershing. Many of Foch's suggestions are ignored by the latter and he had not dared give him an order for the effect it might have on the President. Curiously enough however Clemenceau had told him yesterday the time had come when he must give orders and if they were not obeyed he (Clemenceau) would have to telegraph the President on the subject. He said therefore that the information I gave him was of the greatest value *as it strengthened his hand* [added emphasis].[86]

Now Clemenceau saw Foch every few days. On the evening of 28 August, the day after his second conversation with Derby, Clemenceau had a long private talk with Foch at Bombon. Mordacq had been arguing the case for cancelling Saint-Mihiel completely since the enemy knew that it was coming, and he talked with Weygand about the operations, whilst Foch and Clemenceau conferred privately. It is highly likely that Clemenceau insisted that Foch take the bull by the horns and confront Pershing. As Foch and Haig were in agreement that the most fruitful course was a

---

[84] Lloyd George to Reading, 26 August 1918, Lloyd George mss, F/43/1/15.
[85] Dutton (ed.), *Paris 1918*, 146 (entry for 18 August 1918).
[86] Ibid. 171 (entry for 27 August 1918).

434   Part II: Supreme command

concentric Allied attack, with the Americans aiming for Mézières, Pershing must be made to conform. Clemenceau's talk with Poincaré the next day, 29 August, confirms his intervention. Clemenceau said that Foch was being too soft with Pershing, that he (Clemenceau) wanted the Saint-Mihiel operation postponed, and that it would be better for Pershing to attack in the Argonne, thereby extending the current battlefront.[87]

Clemenceau was also receiving advice from another quarter about the proposed Saint-Mihiel attack. Tardieu, the High Commissioner for American affairs, had been deeply affected by the losses that the AEF had suffered in their earlier operations, and he pointed out to Clemenceau the objections to allowing the Americans to proceed with the Saint-Mihiel operation. Poincaré believed that Clemenceau and Tardieu were bringing pressure to bear on Foch, but that Foch should be free to decide on the operation without interference from the government, especially since Pershing had declared that American losses would not affect American *élan*.[88]

Clemenceau had two further causes for complaint about Pershing. Now that the American CinC had his First Army he wished to be rid of any French (or British) 'tutelage'. Pershing believed that his allies' instruction methods did not suit the American soldier, and he wanted to set up his own officer training schools in France so that the gradual training programme whereby US units were attached to French and British divisions for training could be abolished. Moreover, he recommended taking away from Allied instructors in the USA all officer training, and vetoed the proposed elementary course for staff officers due to start in the War College in Washington on 1 September.[89] Second, the Americans joined the British in refusing to allow the Military Board of Allied Supply to come under Foch's control. They saw that Foch was 'very desirous of effecting' a 'central control in the rear', which would give him much greater control than he already exercised in the zone of the armies. The board believed, however, that armies fought better when segregated, so the national CinCs had to keep control of their lines of communication.[90]

Several pieces of circumstantial evidence strengthen this interpretation of Clemenceau's important role in instructing Foch to make Pershing accept the change of plan. First, the suddenness of the decision to

[87] Poincaré, *AS*, 10: 328 (entry for 29 August 1918).
[88] Ibid., 316 (entry for 21 August 1918).
[89] Colonel Réquin reports, 21 August and 15 September 1918, 15N 78; Kaspi, *Temps des Américains*, 278–82.
[90] Dawes, 'Report of activities for the period August 14 to 31, inclusive', in Dawes, *Journal*, 2: 166; Dawes diary, ibid., 1: 147, 154, 156 (entries for 25, 28, 29 August 1918).

confront Pershing fits with the chronology of Clemenceau's actions, in that Foch acted immediately following Clemenceau's talks with Derby. Then, accounts of the row reveal a real 'dialogue of the deaf', as though Foch were repeating rehearsed arguments. Indeed, Foch's performance was somewhat feeble: by accusing Pershing of not having the necessary services to act independently he was playing straight into Pershing's hands, since it was Foch's own energetic arguments that had prevented administrative troops from crossing the Atlantic in favour of infantry and machinegunners. Pershing mentioned Foch's exhaustion and pale face as he left; this would indicate an unusual degree of strain because the pressure from Clemenceau had forced him to confront rather than to persuade. Further, Foch's notebook contains lists of divisions for the revised operation, but these notes start only on 31 August. Weygand is discreet as always, but he notes the 'underhand' and 'threatening attitude' that Clemenceau was 'pushing'. Even Mme Foch remarked in her diary how the 'impulsive' and 'impressionable' Clemenceau would set off to demolish the Allies, so that her husband was reduced to telling him that they were fighting the Boches, not the Allies.[91] Robert Hanks has analysed Clemenceau's relationship with Pershing. Clemenceau had been enthusiastic about the formation of the US army, Hanks writes, but 'quickly became frustrated with the relative inactivity of the American Army in August and the slow build-up of American forces opposite the St. Mihiel sector'.[92] Finally, of course, Clemenceau would interfere again after his visit to the Meuse–Argonne sector on 28 and 29 September, pressing Foch to demand Pershing's removal; and he was busy pressing his Italian counterpart to get Diaz to launch an offensive as well.

Clemenceau's role here is interesting. If the above interpretation is accepted, then Clemenceau obliged Foch to act to prevent Pershing from pursuing his original plan. The Premier was keeping a close eye on the Generalissimo, and asserting the pre-eminence of the civil over the military power. After the battle Clemenceau claimed that the French had made all the preparations for Saint-Mihiel because the Americans were incapable of acting alone.[93]

On leaving, Foch had left a copy of his new plan with Pershing, but a night's reflection failed to make Pershing any more receptive. He sent a long written response, which Mott translated and handed over late on the 31st. While Pershing accepted Foch's right as Allied CinC to make strategic decisions by which he (Pershing) would abide, yet he refused to

[91] Weygand, *IV*, 602; Mme Foch diary, 16 September 1918.
[92] Hanks, Culture versus Diplomacy, 363.
[93] Poincaré, *AS*, 10: 357 (entry for 24 September 1918).

436 Part II: Supreme command

have four or five of his American divisions used here and six or seven there. He did not believe it possible to do both the Saint-Mihiel operation and another Meuse operation to follow at such a short interval. Given the late arrival of the letter at Bombon, it may be that Pershing waited to send it until after he had seen Pétain that afternoon. It is difficult to tell from the American account of the meeting in Pétain's train whether the French CinC poured oil on troubled waters or fanned the flames. First, Pétain encouraged Pershing to stick to his larger operation against the salient on the grounds that Foch had nothing further to do with it once he had determined the general plan. Also Pétain disapproved of the option of splitting the Americans by placing them on both sides of the Aisne because the terrain was too difficult. On the other hand, Pétain pointed out several times that going against Metz was not possible so long as the Meuse was dominated by German guns. He suggested a compromise: that Pershing take over the whole sector from the Moselle to the Argonne, even though the defence of Verdun ought to remain in French hands. Pétain would leave the French Second Army's commander, General Hirschauer, and 'special services' there until the Americans became familiar with the sector. Finally, Pétain stated that there was insufficient time between the Saint-Mihiel and the Meuse operations for the American staffs to prepare both.[94]

Whatever Pétain's input into Pershing's letter, its sense was plain. Pershing's preference was for an American sector, extending south from Saint-Mihiel; that had been his plan and he expected it to be followed. Nonetheless he would follow Foch's directions as to strategy. Mott thought that Pershing 'evidently took alarm as usual, seeing in it another effort to take part of his army away from him', and that he 'expected to bluff out F, thinking F was merely trying again to use his divs'. Mott continued:

I know P is mad as a hornet. He has no one about him who takes another view of these suspicions of his or who, taking another view, has the courage to announce it. He gets mad & says what he thinks & then all the men in G3 (who are those now most about him) agree & later egg him on, thinking to make themselves agreeable.[95]

It seems that Foch had thought the Americans capable of both operations. Now, however, discussing Pershing's letter with Mott, Foch concluded that Saint-Mihiel should be given up as the concentric operation against

[94] 'Notes on Conversation between General Pershing and General Pétain, August 31, 1918', RG 120, Entry 267, folder 986. Pedroncini makes no mention of this meeting in his study of Pétain's command.
[95] Mott diary, 1 September 1918. G3 is the operations bureau.

Mézières was 'the more fruitful' of the two (see Map 1). Foch explained that when he had presented the 24 July memorandum the Allies had been 'poor', but 'now they were able to take the view of the rich & offer themselves something far bigger'. There should be no let-up. Foch invited both Pershing and Pétain to confer with him in Bombon on 2 September.

That occasion was far less acrimonious, and a compromise was reached. A reduced Saint-Mihiel operation would be undertaken (eight divisions in the main and two in the subsidiary attack), aiming for a line across the salient short of the *Michelstellung* but freeing the Paris–Avricourt railway. It was to begin no later than 10 September followed, no later than 20–25 September, by a strong offensive towards Mézières supported by the Fourth Army on the US First Army's left and resting on the Meuse on its right. This second task was asking a lot of an inexperienced army operating on an approximately 160-kilometre front, in particularly difficult and well-defended terrain (yet another reason for suspecting outside pressure on Foch?). However, if Pershing refused to disperse his divisions as Haig had permitted when the XXII and IX British Corps joined the French, there was no other option. Speed was of the essence and no large-scale movement of French or British divisions in or out of the sector was possible.

In the event, First Army staff managed to produce a revised plan, almost in time. On 12 September the offensive began, two days late but with huge superiority in guns, aircraft and infantry. The Germans had begun pulling out of the salient beforehand, and early on 13 September the American forces attacking from the northern and southern edges of the salient joined hands at Vigneulles. The Americans had captured nearly 16,000 prisoners and over 1000 guns and machineguns at a cost to First Army of 7000 casualties. By forestalling the attack with their withdrawal, the Germans prevented the Americans from gaining an even greater success. At this time Foch was sitting for the painter William Orpen, who recalled that Foch 'was very upset at the Boche getting out of the St. Mihiel pocket in the way they did, without being caught'.[96] Pershing had used his most experienced divisions in the attack, which left the less experienced for the Meuse–Argonne, but he knew that he could not afford to fail at Saint-Mihiel. Captain Michel Clemenceau, serving with the II Colonial Corps, was invited to join the victorious troops who entered the village that had given its name to the whole operation. The operation was closed down on 16 September, amid some regrets that having freed the salient so easily they might have pressed on to Metz after all.

---

[96] Orpen, *Onlooker in France*, 80.

All the objectives set by Foch in July had now been achieved. The Allies were ready to begin a general offensive against the German defensive position of the Hindenburg Line. Yet Lossberg, OHL's defence expert, now chief of staff of General von Boehn's new army group formed between the two crown princes, argued at an army group meeting on 6 September that the Hindenburg Line was no longer strong enough. The German armies should pull back to a much shorter and much safer line between Antwerp and the Meuse, but Ludendorff refused. A staff officer with OHL, Colonel Albrecht von Thaer, wrote on the 15th that they were now fighting for their very existence.[97]

Foch was extremely busy during August and into September, so busy that he could not be with his wife on the fourth anniversary of their son's death. He barely had time to go to church.[98] On the few days that he did not leave his headquarters, he received visits from Clemenceau or foreign generals. His plans outlined in the 24 July memorandum had been even more successful than had seemed possible at the time. He had had to take some hard words from Haig and from Pershing, but their armies had done all that was asked of them and more. In addition, he had three other tasks: firstly, to encourage the Italians, next to bring in the Belgians, and third to work with the SWC. The Italian nut was the hardest to crack and, despite Foch's urging, Diaz had avoided any definite commitment to attack. He saw Diaz in France on 31 August, before the latter's abortive request to Pershing for some US divisions. Diaz asked for four French divisions, but instead had to listen to Foch pressing for an attack. Poincaré had warned Foch to treat Diaz kindly in order to bring the Italians round to the French point of view, but neither kindness nor pressure had any effect.[99]

Nevertheless, there was some cause for optimism about the military situation in Italy. As chief of army in 1917, Foch had authorised the creation of a Czech army made up of prisoners and deserters from the Austro-Hungarian armies captured by the Italians, and, on 21 April 1918, a convention had been signed with the Italian government over their use. Foch appointed Colonel Milan Stefanik to head the Italian Czech Army, which by 20 May numbered 22,000 men formed into a division of two brigades. The presence of these Czech troops had been beneficial during the Austro-Hungarians' June offensive because the enemy withdrew their

---

[97] Lossberg, *Meine Tätigkeit*, 357; Thaer, *Generalstabdienst*, 229.
[98] Letter, Foch to Mme Foch, 22 August 1918, vol. 47.
[99] GQGA JMO, 31 August 1918, 26N 1; Herbillon, *Du général*, 2: 306–7 (entry for 30 August 1918).

Czech and Hungarian troops to the rear to avoid any 'contamination'.[100]
If ever the Italians could be induced to attack, the Czech division should
be able to make a significant contribution. Moreover, Foch was keeping in
close touch with events in Italy. Stefanik sent regular updates, and Foch
received translations of the Austrian daily communiqués and weekly
résumés of the Italian press.[101] On 18 July his new head of the French
mission with Comando Supremo, Colonel Girard, began sending private
reports to Foch on 18 July, by-passing the military attaché in Rome.[102]

King Albert of the Belgians was brought into the battle by an ingenious
compromise. The extension of the battle to Haig's First and Second
Armies in Flanders had brought the active front back to Belgium. The
King had been impressed by Foch's leadership of the Allied forces, and
wrote to his chief of the army staff on 30 August that Foch's command
methods had proved their worth; moreover, the Belgian army should
take inspiration from those methods.[103] Clemenceau had offended the
Belgians, it will be remembered, by his aggressive questioning of Gillain
at the last SWC in July. Now Mordacq attempted to bring about a recon-
ciliation by getting Clemenceau to go and see Albert. They met at the
Franco-Belgian frontier on 7 September and, against all expectations, got
on together very well. Clemenceau judged that the King would not sit idly
by as the British and French advanced, and so he suggested that Foch go to
see him as well.[104] This Foch did on 9 September. He had prepared a plan
for a combined force of the Belgian army, one British army and a small
French one, under the King's nominal command, to expel the invader
from Belgian soil. As the King had no experience of command in the field,
he would be 'assisted' by General Degoutte as chief of staff. Degoutte's
Sixth Army had been relieved from the Aisne as the front line shortened
with the German withdrawal. Since Pershing had declined the offer of
Degoutte's help, the latter was free for this new appointment. On leaving
the King, Foch went immediately to his old headquarters at Cassel, where
he and Gillain met Haig, Wilson (Haig had asked him specially to attend)
and Plumer. It was Plumer's Second Army that would form part of the tri-
national force, and he knew the terrain intimately.

Foch's plan was to exploit the enemy's disarray to cut off his communications with the coast at Bruges and, to cover this move, to occupy the
line of the Lys river thereby preventing any German reinforcements from

[100] Barrère to Ministère des Affaires Etrangères (MAE), 20 May 1915, in Service historique de
la défense, *Stefanik*, doc. 90; Barrère to MAE, copied to Foch, 23 June 1918, 15N 45.
[101] The communiqués are in 15N 45, and the press summaries in 15N 46.
[102] Folder marked 'à part', 15N 47.
[103] King Albert to Gillain, 30 August 1918, cited in Thielemans, 'Le Roi Albert', 106.
[104] Mordacq, *MC*, 2: 231, 215–17 (entries for 5 and 7 September 1918).

the south. This operation would form part of the general offensive of all the Allied armies that was in the planning stage. Foch wanted it to take place at the end of the month, between 20 and 25 September. As always, he insisted that surprise was the main factor in any success, hence speed and secrecy were essential. Haig agreed to place Plumer under the King's command, but refused to allocate the three British cavalry divisions that Foch requested.[105]

Two days later, Albert himself drove to Bombon, and requested a French general as chief of staff and an official 'lettre de service'. Since Degoutte had already been selected, he was called in immediately to meet the King, and Weygand composed the brief (and highly unorthodox) letter of appointment. He got round the difficulty that constitutionally the supreme Allied CinC could not give an order to the King by writing simply: 'H.M. the King of the Belgians takes command of the forces collected together for the Flanders operations ... at his disposition [he] will have General Degoutte and his staff "pour assurer la direction des opérations".' This satisfied both the King and Foch, and copies were sent to Pétain and Haig.[106]

The SWC was the third element. As already seen, Foch was involved in the logistics and supply side of their work, namely in tanks and aviation. In what was probably designed to emphasise the amended decision of 4 July, when Foch had threatened to resign if he was shut out of consultation about future campaigns, he had asked the PMRs to send him their thoughts on operations for the winter and the 1919 campaign. On 26 August, after reading their memoranda, he called in the four PMRs and declared that their views and his were in substantial agreement. Bliss was then 'disquieted' by hearing Foch state that the main point was to defeat the Germans on the Western Front 'thoroughly and crushingly' in 1919. In order to achieve this, Foch insisted that the British and French divisions must be maintained at their current strength at least until next year; that 100 US divisions must be in France by 1 July 1919; and that sufficient tonnage must be found to achieve this. Foch reiterated to Bliss that 'he wanted as much artillery, tanks and aviation as he could get, but that it was "man-power" and again "man-power" that he wanted'. So Foch continued to beat the same drum. However, Bliss's worry was understandable: Washington had already decided that an eighty-division programme was the limit of what was possible; and London was beginning to make difficulties about supplying the tonnage for even that reduced

[105] GQGA JMO, 9, 10 September 1918, 26N 1; Haig diary, 9 September 1918; Wilson diary, 8, 9 September 1918.
[106] Weygand, *IV*, 605–7; *AFGG* 7/1, annex 1074.

programme.[107] Eventually the PMRs put their memoranda together and produced their Joint Note 37, 'Military Policy of the Allies for the Autumn of 1918 and for the Year 1919'. It confirmed the Western Front including Italy as the main theatre of the war, where manpower and materiel resources must be concentrated for the decisive struggle. However, since the full SWC did not meet to discuss and approve the note, it served only to confirm that on 10 September, when it was signed, no one believed that the war would end in 1918.

Yet Foch was optimistic. On 16 August he had told his wife that the Boches were 'dans la purée', up the proverbial creek. A few days later he told her: 'the Boche is letting go everywhere ... we will continue. We will not let go until he gives back what he stole. And if he makes any offers, we will not listen until he is at our mercy.' Finally, in a phrase that echoes faintly Churchillian rhetoric, 'it is the beginning of the end'.[108] Foch did not have any illusions. He told his American liaison officer that the Germans were 'still dangerous, and capable of striking a heavy blow'. Certainly they were in disarray, but they were not 'lying on the ground shouting for help'. Nevertheless, so long as they were giving way, the Allies had to keep pushing 'with everything [they] had'.[109] This push was the planned general Allied offensive to approach and then to break the Hindenburg Line.

[107] Bliss to Baker, 27 August 1918, Bliss mss, cont. 250.
[108] Mme Foch diary, 17 and 25 August 1918.   [109] Mott diary, 1 September 1918.

16   'Tout le monde à la bataille'

Having set the ball rolling, all Foch had to do now was to maintain the momentum with a general offensive. This he did with his customary energy – so much so that to read his directives and instructions for this offensive, planned for the end of September into October, without reference to Germany's approach to President Wilson for an armistice based on the Fourteen Points, is to get no sense that victory was in sight. Pushing everyone into the fight, pushing to maintain maximum pressure on the enemy, was Foch's constant war cry.

When the last Allied effort to win victory began, the Germans were back in the series of defensive positions that Hindenburg and Ludendorff had ordered constructed when they took over the supreme command in 1916, hence called the Hindenburg Line by the Allies. It was not, however, a single line, rather a series of deep positions (some extending as much as ten kilometres), stretching from the Swiss frontier to the North Sea. It consisted of five sections, named after mythical or historical figures. Wotan in the north ran from the coast to Arras. Then the *Siegfriedstellung*, the first to be built and the strongest, extended from Arras to Soissons. Next, Alberich linked Soissons and Laon, and Hagen extended the line to Metz and Strassburg. Behind this first defensive line ran a second, the Hunding Line. It was less deep but took full advantage of the steep wooded terrain, especially in its central section between the Aisne and the Oise rivers. It extended eastwards – the Brunhild and Kriemhild Lines – and northwards to Douai on the river Scarpe – the Herrmann Line. Yet a third line (Freya) had been started behind Hunding, but it was incomplete at the Armistice. Finally, a fall-back position existed: a line from Antwerp on the estuary of the river Scheldt/ Escaut running southeast to the Maas/Meuse north of Verdun. This fall-back position was much shorter, and it was Foch's constant preoccupation that the Germans should not have time to retire there, despite the fact that little had been done to reinforce it because of lack of labour. If the enemy did withdraw that far, certainly most of northern France would have been liberated, but it was a line on which the Germans could rest and re-form through the winter, ready to begin operations again in the spring. Hence Foch's constant urging to hurry and harry the enemy.

So, even if the Allies broke the Hindenburg Line, they would not find themselves in open country, nor would their task be finished. Moreover, just as important as the defensive positions themselves, the railways supplying them were vital (see Map 20). There were two lines, the more northerly from Berlin crossing the Rhine at Köln, thence to Liège; further south the lines passed through Koblenz or Mainz, thence to Metz or Luxembourg. Three rocades linked these two main routes. The first in the east followed the line of the Rhine; the middle one ran through Strassburg, Thionville (north of Metz) and Luxembourg to Namur; and the third in the west, which carried the most traffic, linked Strassburg to Valenciennes in the north, passing through Metz, Longuyon, Mézières and Hirson. At Mézières this third rocade was only forty kilometres distant from the second, and so it could be interdicted by long-range guns if Mézières were captured. The hilly Ardennes left only a narrow gap for railways between Mézières and the Dutch frontier. Although, as 1940 would show, the Ardennes were not impassable, the roads there simply could not carry the volume of traffic required for modern armies. Railways were vital. Foch knew that Mézières was the weak spot in the German supply system.

Although Foch could not know it, Kaiser Karl had been sending his OHL liaison officer to Spa (the German headquarters in Belgium) with urgent statements to the effect that soon Austria-Hungary would be compelled to make a separate peace. Hindenburg's replies stated that the Germans in France had reached the line that they intended to hold [!] and that such an action by the Austrians would give the impression that the alliance was about to break down. Karl was unmoved, and the Austrian peace note was published on 15 September.[1] Clemenceau's response was a ringing speech in the Senate, proclaiming a fight to the finish, of which Pichon sent a copy to Vienna.[2] Foch was aware, therefore, of the state of Austria-Hungary, and French intelligence had reported the presence of two Austrian divisions on the French front, where the estimated number of German divisions declined steadily throughout September. On 25 September, the day before the start of Foch's general offensive, Intelligence reported 129 enemy divisions on the Western Front, with sixty-eight in reserve (of which only twenty were judged to be fresh). A further sign of German difficulties was the confirmation that the class of 1920 was finishing its short period of training and, during

[1] Cramon, *Quatre ans*, 288–93.   [2] Mordacq, *MC*, 2: 229–32.

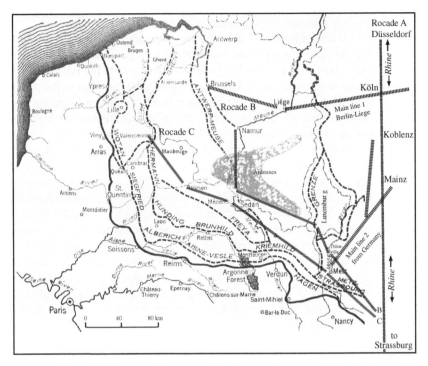

Map 20 Lines of German defensive positions on 1 September with schematic map of main railway communications
Note how Rocade B turns, north of Mézières, to follow the line of the Meuse valley northwards through the hilly and forested Ardennes to Namur.

September, the youngsters were being sent to the depots.[3] At OHL Ludendorff was in a state of nervous collapse, but refused Lossberg's suggestion that an immediate withdrawal be made to the Antwerp–Maas line because the *Siegfriedstellung* was not strong enough.[4] Ludendorff clutched, like a drowning man at a straw (his own words), the news that there was an outbreak of pulmonary plague in France.[5] If Foch did not know of that state of affairs in Spa, at least he knew that in Germany

---

[3] Répartition des divisions allemandes sur le front occidental à la date du 24 septembre 1918, 25 September 1918, *AFGG* 7/1, annex 1287; Compte-rendu de renseignement, 25 September 1918, ibid., annex 1288.
[4] Lossberg, *Meine Tätigkeit*, 357–8 (6 September 1918).
[5] Mertz von Quirnheim, 25 September 1918, in *Ursachen und Folgen*, 2, doc. 363.

morale was suffering. Reports stated that the defeats of July and August had depressed public opinion despite the attempts by the military to play down the reverses and to urge the population to hold on.[6]

French and British morale, on the other hand, was high. Clemenceau and Mordacq toured the liberated areas in the north on 22 September and then went to see Foch in the evening. Clemenceau told him that the desolation caused by the fighting – including the deliberate damage done by the retreating German forces – made both the British and the French, whether general or simple soldier, all the keener to maintain the pressure, sure of success. In response, Foch told the Premier that the Americans were ready, although Pershing still claimed sole direction of his two armies. This was 'most regrettable', Foch said, but there was no point in trying to recriminate or to change the situation because the hour was at hand for the start of the general offensive. All preparations had been made, and 'in four or five days, he would give the signal'.[7]

In reality preparations were still continuing for the new Flanders group and for the Americans. Getting everything ready for the AEF to move their focus from Saint-Mihiel to the Meuse–Argonne took time, and delays were inevitable because of lack of motor transport and the need to move troops only by night to avoid detection. General Degoutte left for Belgian headquarters in La Panne on 12 September, unhappy at his posting, according to Buat. The Belgians lacked equipment of all sorts, and Degoutte asked for labour battalions, guns, munitions, aircraft, cavalry and tanks. Foch overrode Pétain's refusal to supply Degoutte, thereby depriving his own armies. Foch also took a French army corps under his own command, thus lessening Pétain's resources still further.[8] This led to complaints from Buat about the volume of requests and the speed with which they were demanded. 'It's a bit much', he confided to his diary; Foch wants 'to swallow everything before we have even started'.[9]

As a measure to keep the enemy guessing, Foch spent three days between 19 and 22 September in Lorraine, visiting Nancy and Belfort in a disinformation exercise. Cointet had suggested the scheme, which was designed to get German reserves moved south to Alsace to face a non-existent threat of attack from Eighth and Seventh Armies. In 1919 it was discovered that the stratagem had worked, in that the Germans had sent five fresh divisions to the area.[10]

---

[6] 'Situation générale à la date du 30 août 1918', 7N 680.
[7] Mordacq, *MC*, 2: 235 (entry for 22 September 1918).
[8] Buat diary, 11 September 1918, ms 5391; *AFGG* 7/1, 348–50.
[9] Buat diary, 17, 22, 23, 25 September 1918, ms 5391.
[10] Cointet memoirs, Cahier '1918', fo. 151.

The next day, 23 September, Foch called in Haig and Pétain to Mouchy to make the final decisions about the general offensive. The aim was to establish the Allies on a line from Ghent/Gand (the Flanders Army Group of Belgian, British and some French troops, under King Albert) through Valenciennes (the BEF, supported on their right by First Army) to Mézières (the remainder of the French armies, with the Americans on their right). These convergent moves would create a much shorter front, with the possibility of encircling the enemy, who would be forced to evacuate his armies through the inhospitable Ardennes. The rhythm was designed to throw the Germans completely off balance. Beginning with the Franco-American operation to be launched on 26 September, the series was to continue with British First and Third armies the next day, and the Flanders group on the 28th. Then Haig's Fourth and Debeney's First Army were to join in as soon as possible after that. In fact Haig had already decided that the last attack of the series would take place three days after the first, in effect on 29 September.[11] It might have been better to schedule the Americans later in the offensive so as to allow the AEF more time to prepare, since its Saint-Mihiel operation had only closed down on the 16th, but there were good reasons for the order of attacks that was agreed. Because the strongest defences and greatest number of enemy reserves faced the British, Haig wanted reserves drawn away by an attack elsewhere on the first day. Foch wanted the Flanders attack to begin last because there were no Allied reserves to support that front. Consequently the Americans had to start the ball rolling. Foch was 'admirable at making the French generals do what he wants!', Haig noted and everything 'was quickly fixed up'. Foch too was happy with the easy agreement and told his wife that all had been settled 'without any difficulty'.[12]

Things were being settled elsewhere on the front as well. At last, on 19 September, the decree creating the Direction générale des communications et des ravitaillements aux armées (DGCRA) was finalised, although its head did not move from GQG until 9 October – presumably because of the imminent start of the general offensive – and the decree came into effect only a week later. The DGCRA was given responsibility for organising all lines of communication; for coordinating similar services of national armies to avoid duplicating transport; for building new common storage facilities and regulating stations to be shared amongst the Allies; for sharing out facilities in occupation areas and allocating zones between and among the armies; sharing out all the supplies that the Allies agreed to put in common; and coordinating troops and

[11] Foch note, 23 September 1918, *AFGG* 7/1, annex 1257; Haig diary, 21 September 1918.
[12] Haig diary, 23 September 1918; letter, Foch to Mme Foch, 23 September 1918, vol. 47.

supplying transport and evacuation of the wounded.[13] Here was a recipe
for a much more efficient use of the space behind all the armies as, at last,
they began to move forward against the invader. It is a pity that such an
organisation did not begin its work earlier in the war.

At last, events on other fronts were starting to go the Allies' way. In the
Balkans Franchet d'Espèrey's proposed offensive – it had finally obtained the
go-ahead from the British and the Italians – was launched on 15 September.
Although Foch had no authority over the Balkans, he had been pressing
Clemenceau to act, especially given the known poor morale among
Bulgarian troops and the fact that Bulgaria's military pact with Germany
expired on 23 September. The Bulgarian army collapsed and sued for an
armistice. It was signed on 29 September and the German *Eleventh Army*
became disarmed prisoners-of-war. The loss of Bulgaria threatened German
supplies of oil from Romania (its only source) and also threatened its
communications with Turkey. The Ottoman Empire had its own difficulties.
General Allenby's Palestine campaign began on 19 September against an
out-numbered Turkish army and Damascus fell on 1 October.

Foch's final note to Pétain (both American and French forces were
under Pétain's command for the offensive) before the sequenced attacks
of the general offensive began insisted on the need for speed. Foch
declared that US First Army and French Fourth Army together had
numerical superiority over the enemy, hence there should be no hold-
ups, no waiting for further orders to advance. Fourth Army was to keep in
touch with the Americans on their right, but *on no account to slow down their
advance*. He asked Pétain to call on the 'spirit of decision and initiative' of
the commanders under his orders.[14]

On 26 September the AEF set off in fine style, but quickly became
bogged down. Pershing had used in the attack too many of his American
divisions, twice the size of the 1914 British and French ones, against
skilful German defences (mainly machinegunners installed in the prime
defensive territory behind belts of barbed wire). The results were enormous casualties, huge congestion, and an inability either to evacuate the
wounded or to re-supply and feed the front lines. Foch sent one of his staff
to investigate. His report blamed Pershing for not using his staff 'ration-
ally', for not establishing daily transport plans; for failure to transmit
orders securely and speedily, and so on (over eight typed pages).[15]

Next, on the 27th, the British began and advanced towards Cambrai,
making such good progress that they were in the outskirts of the city by the

[13] Buat to all commanding generals, 16 October 1918, 6N 38, [d] 2.
[14] Foch, Note [for Pétain], 25 September 1918, *AFGG* 7/1, annex 1286. Original emphasis.
[15] Commandant Vincent, 'Résumé des observations . . .', 5 October 1918, 15N 11.

third day. Then the Flanders group continued the success by advancing seven kilometres on its first day (28th), reaching Passchendaele on the next. Finally Haig's second attack, that of Fourth Army supported by French First Army, began on 29 September, and ground was gained here too. The *Siegfriedstellung* portion of the Hindenburg Line had been breached by the Canadian Corps near Cambrai, and by the Australian Corps along the Canal du Nord. The French made the least progress during the first four days of the general offensive. First Army had not done much to support the British, and Gouraud's Fourth Army operating on the west of the Argonne slowed as the Americans on their right slowed.

Nonetheless, the shock to the already shaken German armies and its leadership was enormous and decisive. Ludendorff's erratic behaviour could no longer be tolerated and OHL staff forced a decision. On 28 September, as news of the Bulgarian disaster came in and in the midst of the blows to the Western Front that had only just begun, Ludendorff and Hindenburg agreed that the war must be ended and that a broad-based national government must be installed in Berlin to negotiate with the USA on the basis of Wilson's Fourteen Points.

Foch knew of the peace feelers but he did not relax his efforts. On the 26th he moved his command post to be nearer the Franco-American sector, and then moved to Flanders on 29 September. In between times, he saw Secretary of War Baker on 27 September. Baker was visiting the AEF and attempting to sort out the question of transport for the agreed eighty-division AEF as Lloyd George threatened to withdraw British shipping and Pershing still insisted on a 100-division army. When Baker met Foch, it was still the 100-division plan that was on the table, according to the GQGA war diary. They discussed the transport for such an army to be in France by 1 July 1919. Baker's postwar recollection in 1931, however, was that Foch had amazed him by stating that he could win the war with forty US divisions, not the 100 that Pershing was still demanding even though Washington had decided on a lesser programme. It is difficult to judge how much weight to give to Baker's recollection because it reflects neither the contemporary war diary nor Foch's habit of asking for more than he knew to be possible. On the other hand, Baker is unlikely to have dreamed up the exchange, as he gives the detail that he asked the interpreter to repeat his questions, thinking that he had misunderstood Foch's answer. Foch may have had a burst of optimism, but coupled with enough caution that he did not wish it entered in his own official record.[16]

[16] Smythe, *Pershing*, 210–11; Palmer, *Baker*, 2: 348.

Also on 27 September a letter arrived from the Italian Premier. Orlando was well aware that, unless the Italian army made a move, Italy was risking future gains from the peace treaty and Foch's refusal to help if there were another Austrian attack. Orlando summed up the situation as a vicious circle: the Italians were not fighting because they lacked the means, and the Allies refused to provide the means because they were not fighting. Orlando's letter to Foch was an attempt to break out of the circle. In an astute move, he offered battleground authority to Foch, that is, the unity of command that the Italians had refused to accept earlier. In return, Foch should assume full responsibility for the Italian attack and support it with French men and materiel. Foch refused. The SWC's Abbeville agreement stated that Foch's authority would extend to Italy if 'circumstances [brought] about the presence on the Italian front of Allied armies fighting in the same conditions as in France'. Foch replied that the proposed Italian operation affected only a small part of the Italian forces and that Diaz should command it himself. The sole question at the present moment, when the whole front from the river Jordan to the North Sea was being shaken, was whether the Italian high command was prepared to run the risks that were inevitable in war.[17] Clearly Foch's patience had worn thin. He told Mott: 'They are not going to fight & we are not going to send troops to Italy to fight for them. They always want somebody to do their fighting for them.'[18]

Foch also complained about the French army's progress. General Rawlinson was unhappy about the support on his right from First Army, and Foch sent Debeney a personal message urging him to get a move on.[19] Mangin's Tenth Army had advanced four kilometres northeast of Soissons, but only because the enemy had retired. Likewise Fifth Army managed to advance to the river Aisne, behind which the enemy had withdrawn. Fourth Army was keeping pace with the Americans, hence had slowed and eventually stalled, but Gouraud's troops had captured 7000 prisoners. Foch sent a scathing letter to Pétain on 4 October.[20] Fourth Army had made over the past week gains which, although 'no doubt honourable', were less than could have been expected, given the enemy's disorganisation. The battle was neither led nor pushed nor coordinated. Foch saw only 'inert' army corps, corps that did not manoeuvre, that did not exploit success. He urged Pétain to instruct all

---

[17] Orlando to Sonnino, 18 September 1918, in Sonnino, *Carteggio*, 488; Orlando to Foch, 24 September 1918, 15N 43, [d] 3; Foch to Orlando, 28 September 1918, *AFGG* 7/2, annex 38.
[18] Mott diary, 29 September 1918.
[19] Confirmation de message téléphoné, 4 October 1918, *AFGG 7/2*, annex 138.
[20] Foch to Pétain, 4 October 1918, *AFGG* 7/2, annex 137.

army and army group commanders to take personal command and to act with energy. He ended with a rallying cry that reflected his own style of command: 'Animer, entraîner, veiller, surveiller', that is 'inspire, lead, be vigilant, supervise'. Pétain cannot have been pleased to receive such a broadside, especially when GQG was having to cope with demands for tanks from Degoutte in Flanders, and for munitions from the Americans. Buat was exasperated: Foch had 'never been able to take account of what is and what is not possible'.[21]

Foch's biggest disappointment, however, arose from the American attack, which had stalled completely by 29 September. Clemenceau had decided to celebrate his 77th birthday by visiting the fronts in eastern France on the 28th and 29th. His car became stuck in a solid traffic jam. Mordacq claimed that he had never seen anything like it, not even during the retreats four years earlier.[22] On their return to Paris, they learned of the much greater success of the British and Belgians, and on 1 October Clemenceau himself went to Bombon to speak with Foch about the mess behind the American lines.

The appalling confusion that Clemenceau witnessed marked a definite deterioration in Foch–Clemenceau relations. The Premier thought that he had a special rapport with America, having lived there and having married an American wife; also he spoke English. Pershing's French liaison officer thought that this was not entirely a good thing.[23] Clemenceau had already intervened over the Saint-Mihiel operations, and now he was receiving digests of reports from French liaison officers with the AEF, in addition to his own experience of visiting the sector. The liaison reports were uniformly critical.[24] Henceforth Clemenceau badgered Foch constantly about Pershing's performance, suggesting that he ask Wilson to remove the obstinate American CinC. Clemenceau was also less than pleased about Italian inaction, and again blamed Foch (unfairly) for being too soft, for not ordering an offensive in Italy.

Yet Foch had tried to intervene to improve matters in the Meuse–Argonne sector, where the Allies were falling behind the action further west. On 30 September he returned from the north to his headquarters to learn of the crowding and communications difficulties behind the American front, where no progress at all was recorded that day. He wrote a note for Pershing, which he discussed with Pétain the next day.

[21] Buat diary, 8, 9, 17 October 1918, ms 5391.
[22] Mordacq, *MC*, 2: 245 (entry for 28–29 September 1918).
[23] Colonel de Chambrun, as reported by Major Paul H. Clark, Report to Pershing # 128, 6 July 1918, Clark mss.
[24] The report summaries (in Fonds Clemenceau, 6N 53) cited in Hanks, Culture versus Diplomacy, 371.

He proposed widening the American front by using US divisions east of the Meuse and west of the Argonne. These divisions would be placed in the corps of Second French Army, which was already stationed around Verdun. Pershing would take command of the Franco-American forces on both banks of the Meuse, and General Hirschauer would command Second Army on both sides of the Argonne. Foch sent Weygand to Pershing's headquarters with the note that evening. If Foch thought that the stalling of Pershing's offensive might have made him more amenable to combining French and American forces, he was soon disabused.

Weygand returned with Pershing's reply in the evening of 2 October. While Pershing was ready to hand over US divisions currently unemployed in the Saint-Mihiel area to the French, he refused to admit Second Army with its commander and its staffs into his sector. As a compromise, Foch agreed immediately to Pershing's wishes as to command in the Meuse–Argonne sector, but on condition that the Americans re-start operations immediately and that, once begun, those operations should not stop. Pershing's biographer writes that the general detected Clemenceau's hand in the letter, which is possible.[25] Pershing himself reacted badly, claiming that Foch's letter insulted both him and his troops, and he called his liaison officer with Foch, Colonel T. Bentley Mott, to his headquarters on 3 October.

Mott's diary account of what he called 'a nasty mess' is both interesting and enlightening: it shows the positive role that a liaison officer might play, and it elaborates Foch's views of command.[26] (Weygand's own account is discreet to the point of invisibility.) Pershing was furious. The 'insulting' letter was probably the final straw after Clemenceau's inspection of the chaos when Mordacq claimed to have seen in Pershing's eyes the realisation that he had bitten off more than he could chew.[27] Pershing told Mott that Foch's letter implied that he had stopped operations for no good reason, and that he, or his men, or both, lacked energy and courage. Mott admitted that the letter *did* mean that if taken literally, but he denied that such had been Foch's intention. However, 'P said if F does not withdraw that letter & make amends to me I will refuse to have anything to do with him personally hereafter & I will not obey any of his orders that do not fall strictly within his mandate as laid down in the Versailles agreement.' Mott returned to Bombon and had a long talk with Weygand, asking him to get

[25] Foch to Pershing, copied to Pétain, 2 October 1918, *AFGG* 7/2, annex 111, and *USAWW* 2: 617–18; Smythe, *Pershing*, 204.

[26] Mott diary, 7 and 8 October 1918. Pershing's own diary account (8 October 1918), although much briefer, confirms Mott's.

[27] Mordacq, *MC*, 2: 244.

Foch to write again to 'remove the unfortunate impression' produced by his letter. When no letter was forthcoming, Mott spoke again the next day to Weygand, who took him in to see Foch. Foch explained that there could be 'no question of feelings' between himself and Pershing. Each knew the other's views, and his letter referred simply to facts and 'military technique'. Foch rolled out the map, showing the British, French and American armies, whose chiefs had all agreed to the great battle currently under way. 'Everyone must march, and march to the end', Foch stated.

I am the conductor of the orchestra. Here is the American tenor, the French baritone and the British bass. I make them play together. The bass says that he is out of breath, I say no, you are going to play to the end of the piece. I would have preferred General Pershing to place his army west of the Argonne in the Champagne. There the qualities of his troops could be deployed to best advantage; there the difficulties for his inexperienced staffs would have been less. He preferred the sector in the east. I gave way.

Then, Foch continued, when he saw the problems, he offered to insert General Hirschauer, but Pershing refused. 'I could have given the order, but I accepted General Pershing's arguments and I let him do as he wants. But I told him the responsibility is yours. You want to do it your way? Right, but on condition that you begin and do not stop.' When Mott asked whether Pershing would not be the better judge of when to stop, Foch snorted through his moustache: 'Suppose Marshal Haig said my men are exhausted ... I am going to stop', but then it would be too late: 'You should have thought of that beforehand ... you must go on to the end, to your last man.' Foch ended with a threat, saying that he would appeal to Washington to appoint someone who would obey, otherwise he would resign. Since Pershing had threatened that he would have no more 'personal' dealings with Foch, the tension was clearly reaching breaking-point. Yet it fizzled out. Mott returned to Pershing and recounted what Foch had said, adding that Foch had not meant to wound, and Pershing responded: 'He is perfectly right. And there is no misunderstanding. I am going on to the end.' Either Pershing had repented, or perhaps he had heard that Foch had enquired of Bliss whether he would be fit to take over if Pershing fell ill.[28]

Two obstinate men at a critical juncture in the war might have harmed the Allied cause but for the intervention of a liaison officer prepared to act as go-between and smooth the rough edges of any communication. More than this, Pershing's obsession with independence and Foch's impatience as finally he had the enemy on the run might have boiled over if the war

[28] Hanks, Culture versus diplomacy, 376.

had continued into 1919. Any intervention from Clemenceau would have made matters worse. And the unified command was so ill defined – did the 'strategic direction of military operations' mean that Foch could insist on putting Second Army between Gouraud and Pershing? Surely it did, yet Foch preferred to bow to Pershing's refusal. His aim had been to put more experienced French staffs in sector to deal with transport and re-supply of the troops. Short of tying the American tenor to his chair, the French orchestral conductor could only wave his baton to keep everyone singing. Yet, so long as the eastern armies get moving again, Foch noted, 'the matter is without importance'.[29]

Now it was obvious that the whole front of attack needed a breathing space. It was simply impossible to maintain initial progress after a few days. Communications and supply problems were exacerbated by the Germans' 'scorched earth' policy during their fighting retreat. On 4 October an official French announcement was published ordering the enemy to stop such destruction. On 10 October Foch issued another 'directive générale', which recognised that the British in the centre were making the greatest progress. Hence they should press on, and aim to free the Lille region in conjunction with the Flanders group on their left, and on their right First Army should aim to get across the river Serre in conjunction with the Aisne–Meuse attacks. The Allied front line was shortening as their attacks converged. Foch asked for and received two US divisions to be moved to Belgium to exploit the success there, and he dispatched Sixth Army there also. Intelligence estimates of German forces noted the significant reduction in the number of divisions: 188 on 9 October, down from over 200 from April to September.[30]

The Flanders Army Group reached the Lys on 15 October and Ludendorff authorised Crown Prince Rupprecht to abandon the Belgian coast and pull back to the Hermann Line. Albert made a triumphal entry into Bruges on the 20th. Then the British broke the Hermann Line, and between 17 and 21 October liberated the Lille–Roubaix–Tourcoing industrial region. Three French armies broke the same line between the rivers Oise and Aisne and, finally, the Americans cleared the Argonne forest and reached the Meuse at Stenay on 1 November. The Italians had realised that they needed to join in or suffer the consequences during the peace negotiations, and Orlando finally forced Diaz to act. He launched the battle of Vittorio Veneto on 24 October, the anniversary of Caporetto. After an initial setback due to the haste of the final preparations and bad weather, the Italians with the British and French broke through the

[29] Foch, Carnets, 5 October 918, fo. 335.
[30] Compte-rendu de renseignements # 1574, 9 October 1918, 5N 5.

demoralised Austro-Hungarian lines, reaching Udine and Trento and (by sea) Trieste on 3 November.

Success did not breed harmony, however, and none of the above achievements was won without more instances of ill temper. In two further cases the ill temper became a serious threat to the unified command. The first, the row with Haig over the return of Second Army, was, in Haig's biographer's words, 'extraordinarily petty'.[31] Haig had agreed that Plumer's Second Army should form part of the Flanders Army Group under the command of King Albert, and they had achieved considerable success. Foch wanted the King, as a matter of 'galanterie', to enter his capital at the head of an international army, but Haig and, more especially, Lawrence wanted Second Army back. When Haig went to London to discuss armistice terms, he told Lawrence to retrieve his army. On his return to France on 22 October, Haig found that he still had no army and so he and Lawrence went to see Foch on the 24th at French First Army's headquarters. Since both Haig and Foch were equally obstinate, it was agreed that Haig would put in a formal request, which Foch duly refused. The reasons for Haig's insistence are somewhat opaque, based primarily on the fact that the mission for which he had consented to Second Army's becoming part of the Flanders Army Group had been fulfilled, and with great success. The true motives were probably mixed. Haig was already at odds with Foch over armistice terms, and he had asked that some US divisions be allocated to the BEF, even lobbying Clemenceau over the matter, but in vain. Furthermore, he had a low opinion of both the Belgian and the French troops in the Flanders Army Group, and felt that Plumer's Second Army was being used as the battering-ram to 'open the way for the "dud" divisions (of which the rest of the King's army is composed) and ensure that they get to Brussels'.[32] Haig reported the impasse to London, and Wilson and Milner crossed to France to seek a solution.

I have dealt with the implications for the Franco-British command relationship elsewhere, but the quarrel is important for several other reasons.[33] The meeting on 24 October was particularly bad tempered, with DuCane reporting to Henry Wilson that 'it was the most unpleasant meeting he had yet seen'. Grant remarked that Haig and Lawrence 'came with the intention of having a row' and 'seem to have been extremely rude'. As they left Lawrence said to DuCane: 'It is a jolly good thing that there has been a row. Don't you think so?' DuCane did not agree, of course, and told Grant that he had never heard so much nonsense. Lawrence had 'denied that the recent operations of the last three months

---

[31] Harris, *Haig*, 510.   [32] Haig diary, 24 October 1918.   [33] Greenhalgh, *VTC*, 254–61.

were co-ordinated, and apparently without saying so in so many words attacked directly Marshal Foch as Commander-in-Chief of the forces in France'.[34] Haig claimed to be 'disgusted at the almost underhand way in which the French are trying to get hold of a part of the British Army', especially since 'when all is said and done, the British Army has defeated the Germans this year'.[35] Weygand thought that the tone of the conference had been 'deplorable', and he pointed out, correctly, that the role of high staff officers was to prevent such scenes, and that 'this was not the moment to begin a quarrel'.[36] Foch's tact and persuasive skills appear to have failed him at this juncture, but Haig and Lawrence seem to have been determined to make a mountain out of a very small molehill, perhaps because of the sudden access of pessimism that Haig's biographer detects. Whatever the reason for their aggressive pursuit of the matter, the quarrel over Second Army did not augur well for future cooperation. Haig believed that Foch thought himself another Napoleon and had become 'swollen-headed', but his equally strong belief that the BEF had defeated the Germans (forgetting the French help that he had received in March and April) could just as well be thought 'swollen-headed'.[37] Lawrence's role in all has not been examined.

The quarrel highlights also the deterioration in the Wilson–Foch and the Clemenceau–Foch relationships. Wilson discussed matters with Lloyd George and Milner before leaving London and concluded that Haig was in the right: 'Foch wants us to do all the work. The French are not fighting at all & the Americans don't know how so all falls to us.' The supposedly permanently francophile Wilson seems to have changed his tune. After tossing around the idea of getting the British ambassador to talk to Foch after he had already spoken (at Haig's suggestion) to Clemenceau – the involvement of all these personages is an index of how serious the quarrel had become – Wilson decided that he would go to speak to Foch himself. In 1915 he would have gone without ceremony to Foch's headquarters and the pair would have settled matters with a joke. Now, Wilson resolved: 'If I can't persuade Foch to give up his untenable position I shall have to order him but this, of course, is the last thing I want to do. But the 2nd Army <u>must</u> come back to DH.' These words reveal the extent of the changed relationship and the new status of their friendship.[38]

---

[34] DuCane, *Foch*, 74; Grant, 'Some notes made at Marshal Foch's H.Qrs.', fo. 17, WO 106/1456.

[35] Haig diary, 24 October 1918.

[36] Grant, 'Some notes made at Marshal Foch's H.Qrs.', fo. 18, WO 106/1456.

[37] Haig diary, 27 October 1918.   [38] Wilson diary, 24, 27 October 1918.

Derby's account of his intervention reveals how bad the relationship between Foch and Clemenceau had become. Derby had been so impressed by Haig's tale that he thought the matter 'very serious' and he went to see Clemenceau on 27 October, speaking to him 'as a friend to a friend'. Clemenceau confessed 'in the strictest confidence' that he and Foch 'were not on the best of terms'. He told Derby that

> Foch had got a very swollen head, that he would not carry out his orders and altogether made himself extremely unpleasant. He (Clemenceau) had told him 4 times he was to order Pershing to send American Divisions up to the English and each time Foch had refused to carry out his order. He said that always he used to go and see Foch every day but that things were so unpleasant now that he never went.

Three points arise from this litany. First of all, Clemenceau was not the military commander and disposing of US divisions was not his responsibility; second, telling Derby that those divisions were for the BEF was merely telling him what he thought he would like to hear; finally, he had not usually seen Foch 'every day' (every few days would be more accurate), but it was certainly true that the frequency of their meetings had fallen off noticeably. On the other hand, Foch was very busy winning a war. Nevertheless, Clemenceau *did* go to see Foch about the Second Army quarrel, and returned having been converted, so it seemed to Derby, to Foch's point of view.[39]

A compromise was reached very easily, considering the gravity of appeals to London, a threat to resign (by Haig, uttered to Derby), and Clemenceau's involvement. Derby argued that Foch seemed to be seeking a 'loophole' in order to reach a compromise, and he persuaded Haig to write another letter to Foch, stating the reasons why he wanted his Second Army back – Foch had claimed that Haig had never explained them. This is comprehensible as Haig's letter makes no strong case for its return, adding simply that for Foch to retain Second Army, without permission – did Foch really require permission? – 'was to depart from the Beauvais agreement, and in fact strikes at the very foundation of my position as C.-in-C. of the British Expeditionary Forces in France'.[40] Wilson took the letter with him when he went to see Foch the next day, 28 October.

> I had a rather stormy meeting with Foch, but I think I was able to put my case strongly but quickly & to make him understand that he was trying to do a thing which I thought unfair & which he ought not to do. We parted excellent friends. He was very angry with Derby & Clemenceau for mixing themselves up in the business.

[39] Dutton (ed.), *Paris 1918*, 297–8 (entry for 27 October 1918).
[40] Haig to Foch, 27 October 1918, 15N 11/115, reproduced in DuCane, *Foch*, 129–30.

Then back to Embassy for lunch. DH also there & as he had to go & see Foch at 4.O'c. I told him I was sure the old boy would meet him half way now & I suggested asking for the 2nd Army to be given back when it reached the Scheldt. This he did & both he & DuCane telephoned to me tonight to say that everything had gone splendidly at the meeting & flowers & tea & delights! So that corner is turned. What a lot of babies they are.

It seems to have been Foch who made the effort to heal the breach caused by Haig and Lawrence's obstinacy. Haig noted that 'Foch was very pleased to see me, and was evidently anxious to make amends.' Yet DuCane was surely right in his postwar account to write that

it was beyond belief that two men in the position of Foch and Sir Douglas who had taken part together in the making of history, and who had on the whole co-operated loyally throughout the great events of the last three months, should, when their labours were so nearly crowned with complete success, be so little animated by true feelings of comradeship.[41]

Second Army reverted to Haig's command on 4 November, a week before the signing of the Armistice. Foch had not wanted to break up the successful combination in Flanders, and Second Army remained in line between the Flanders Army Group and the BEF. It was fortunate that the end was already in sight when the dispute began. The quarrel signposted, however, another backward step in the relations between Foch and his Premier. This signified an even greater threat to the unified command, and the second case of a dangerous dispute magnified it still further.

This time it was the AEF that was the cause, but the Americans were not the only source of Clemenceau's annoyance with Foch: the Italian inaction and the proposed action against Constantinople were two further bones of contention. Clemenceau complained to both Derby and Poincaré about the (false) Italian press reports that Foch had approved Diaz's waiting tactic. Next, as the Allied leaders were meeting in Versailles and Paris to discuss armistice terms, a dispute arose over whether the British or the French should exploit the Bulgarian and Turkish collapse by making for Constantinople. Although a compromise agreement was reached, Clemenceau was furious with Foch for playing what he called an 'abominable trick' on him over the matter. Clemenceau complained to Poincaré that Foch had 'betrayed' him by promising to support the French position over Constantinople and then taking Lloyd George's side. 'I will never forgive him', Clemenceau declared; 'I'll live with him until war's end, since that is necessary, but I shall never forget it.'[42]

---

[41] Wilson diary, 28 October 1918; Haig diary, 29 October 1918; DuCane, *Foch*, 74–5.
[42] Poincaré, *AS*, 10: 377–8 (entry for 7 October 1918).

Pershing and the AEF were, however, the main sources of complaint, and Haig's speaking to Clemenceau of his request for some US divisions gave the Premier a stick with which to beat Foch. Clemenceau had already seen the chaos behind the American front, and so sending some US divisions to the BEF to exploit the success in the north, instead of merely adding to the confusion in the east, seemed a sensible proceeding. He sent Mordacq to 'negotiate' with Foch about it on several occasions, but Foch always prevaricated.[43] Foch had refused Haig's request for American divisions on the grounds that there were only ten or eleven that were 'worth anything', and that Haig already had two of them. Haig also pressed his case with Pershing himself, who had gone to the BEF head-quarters to ask for some horses to pull his guns. Pershing had replied that he could not spare any divisions. It seems as though amour-propre was getting in the way of the efficient prosecution of the war at this point. Foch's prevarication with Mordacq may have been a reaction to the earlier interference in the Saint-Mihiel affair, or simply an oblique way of telling Clemenceau to mind his own business. Moreover, Foch did send two US divisions to the north, but not to Haig. After correspondence with Pershing on 14 and 15 October, 91 and 37 US Divisions were sent to Sixth Army in the Flanders Army Group, in order 'to exploit the success that had been gained' there.[44] Pershing made a token show of independence in that these two divisions did not figure on the list of possibilities that Foch had suggested. No doubt this deployment added to Haig's frustration over the return of Second Army, and he sent his private secretary to Paris with a letter for Clemenceau: 'He is to ask Clemenceau when I am to get some American divisions! C. had said to me that he was displeased with the way Foch had given in to Pershing's desire for concentrating all his divisions into a "great American Army," and he is to insist on him (Foch) sending as many American divisions as possible.'[45]

On 12 October Pershing had activated the US Second Army, and split his forces, giving up his personal command of First Army in order to constitute himself an army group commander. He went to Foch's head-quarters to explain the command changes and to ask to be placed directly under the orders of the Allied CinC, instead of coming under those of Pétain. Foch agreed, as did Pétain, and this came into effect on 16 October. (Mordacq claims that Pétain showed great generosity in giving up US First Army from his command, but it is far more likely that Pétain was grateful to be rid of the responsibility.[46]) This change gave

[43] On 11, 18, 21, 25 October: Mordacq, *MC*, 2: 267–8.
[44] GQGA JMO, 14, 15 October 1918, 26N 1; *USAWW* 6: 327ff.
[45] Haig diary, 14 October 1918.   [46] Mordacq, *MC*, 2: 277–8 (entry for 15 October 1918).

Clemenceau the opportunity to insist that Pershing must obey Foch's orders, and that, if he did not, Foch should ask President Wilson for a replacement American CinC.[47] Clemenceau had already complained to Poincaré on 4 October about Foch's failure to 'command' Pershing. Although Baker had seen the difficulties during his visit, Clemenceau was scornful of Baker's influence, arguing that Foch should send a report to the 'buddha', the only one with any influence in Washington, namely the President. Now Clemenceau wrote a letter to Foch asking what he had done about the AEF. Mordacq thought the letter was 'dangerous', hence liable to provoke 'a regrettable incident'. So instead Mordacq went to talk to Foch, who explained what Pershing had said about the new command arrangements.[48] It would seem that Foch had spoken very firmly to Pershing about the Americans' lack of progress and failure to supervise the orders of lower commanders. Indeed, Foch had told Pershing that 'results are the only thing to judge by; that if an attack is well planned and well executed, it succeeds with small losses; that if it is not well planned and well executed the losses are heavy and there is no advance'. He did not think Pershing's command changes important, 'so long as he kept things going at the front'.[49] This was enough to reassure Clemenceau and he did not send the 'dangerous' letter.

However, Foch blotted his copybook a few days later when he wrote to Clemenceau about the armistice negotiations under way. These are the subject of the next chapter; their importance here is the effect on relations between the two men. Clemenceau was particularly irritated by what he considered to be military interference in political matters. Foch had requested, as the military adviser to the Allied governments, that he be kept informed of negotiations so that the armistice conditions – a 'military' matter – should be of a nature to ensure that the peace treaty contain the necessary terms for France's security. The question of the Rhineland was important here. To this end, he asked that a representative of the French Foreign Ministry be nominated to liaise with him.[50] Clemenceau responded on 23 October that the role of the military was to offer technical advice that the politicians would accept or reject as they chose, and he appended a copy of a letter from the Foreign Minister. This accepted as legitimate Foch's concerns about the relationship between armistice and

[47] Weygand, *IV*, 628.
[48] Poincaré, *AS*, 10: 373 (entry for 4 October 1918); Mordacq, *MC*, 2: 274–5 (entry for 14 October 1918).
[49] 'Notes on Conversation between General Pershing and Marshal Foch at Bombon, October 13, 1918', *USAWW* 8: 92–4.
[50] Foch to Clemenceau, 16 October 1918, reprinted in Foch, *Mémoires*, 2: 276–8. See also Mordacq, *MC*, 2: 284–5 (entry for 19 October 1918).

peace terms, but rejected any military infringement upon his Ministry's prerogatives. The 'confusion of responsibilities' could only complicate matters.[51]

Despite Mordacq's advocacy of the good sense of Foch's request, Clemenceau refused to concede, and left Mordacq with the realisation that it would be very difficult to re-establish the 'confident and affectionate relations' that had existed between the two men. On the other hand, Weygand was equally suspicious of Clemenceau's motives. He noted that Clemenceau had been to see both Haig and Pétain without consulting with or reporting to Foch. 'It's the game he played in March starting up again', Weygand noted, referring to the way Clemenceau had dealt with Haig and Pétain in the days following the first German offensive of 21 March, when Foch (then chief of staff of the French army) had been left out of the loop (see pages 298–9).[52]

So Clemenceau had built up a fair head of steam by the time he returned to the theme of Foch's refusal to make the AEF and its commander follow orders. On 21 October he sent to Foch what Weygand called a long 'indictment' of the immobility of Pershing's army, and suggested that Foch inform the American President of Pershing's obstinacy.[53] The letter made enough impression on Foch for him to reproduce large extracts in his postwar memoirs, but in its original 'dangerous' version its effect would probably have been even greater. Clemenceau had sent a first draft, written on 11 October, to Poincaré for comment, and Poincaré had strongly advised against sending it on the grounds that it might cause offence. Clemenceau revised it and re-submitted the revision. Once again Poincaré thought it too hard, both on Foch and on the Americans; indeed, it might even drive Foch to resign. Poincaré suggested that, had he been its recipient, the sentence 'The country commands you to command' would have caused his resignation. Then Poincaré made matters very much worse with his next comment. Surely, he chided Clemenceau, Foch was responsible to the US President as commander-in-chief of the American armies, and Clemenceau had no place in that relationship.[54] It was no doubt Poincaré who had put the idea into Foch's head that 'constitutionally' he was not under Clemenceau's orders. When Foch made this comment to Clemenceau early in October, the latter had told him very clearly not to play such games.[55]

[51] See correspondence in Fonds Clemenceau, Armistice, 6N 70.
[52] Mordacq, MC, 2: 285 (entry for 19 October 1918); cahier 6, 19 October 1918, Weygand mss (partie déposée), 1K/130/4.
[53] Weygand, IV, 629.
[54] We have only Clemenceau's own, very angry, account in his 1930 Grandeur and Misery of Victory (pp. 75–88). Poincaré's published diary account is silent.
[55] Martet, Clemenceau, 151.

Yet the constitutional position was not clear. Clemenceau, as War Minister, claimed in his long letter of 21 October to be the constitutional head of the French army – strictly speaking it was the President of the Republic, but he could only act with a minister's counter-signature – yet Foch had been appointed to supreme command by the Allies acting in concert. There is nothing in the agreements signed in Doullens in March or in Beauvais in April to indicate how the unified command might be ended or altered. Clemenceau had the authority to sack Foch as a general officer in the French army, but such an action would probably provoke an immense outcry from France's allies. And who would replace him?

Foch responded gently and briefly to the Premier's letter. He did not refer to Clemenceau's suggestion that he inform President Wilson if Pershing did not 'obey', or refuse the advice of those 'qualified' to give it. Instead he presented a table showing the distribution of the thirty US divisions that he considered 'apt for combat'. (There were many more divisions in France, but the recently arrived were untrained.) Twenty were under Pershing's orders in eastern France; the other ten were allocated to the British front (two divisions), the Flanders front (two divisions) and the French front, including the quiet Vosges sector. Foch pointed out how many casualties the Americans had suffered between 26 September and 20 October (over 54,000) during fighting in particularly difficult terrain against strong enemy resistance. As circumstances changed, Foch wrote, he would alter the ratio of divisions with Pershing to those on other fronts. This was a better method than issuing orders that Pershing's inexperienced divisional and corps commanders could not execute.[56]

Foch's reply is dated 23 October. The Allies were now talking seriously about the armistice terms that each wanted, and between 1 and 4 November US First Army, with massive French artillery support and a seriously weakened enemy, succeeded in making further progress towards Mézières and Sedan in what David Trask has called 'surely the most efficient' operation of the Meuse–Argonne campaign.[57] The dispute between Foch and Clemenceau was not resolved; fortunately for the Allies, it was overtaken by events. Nevertheless, vital questions of balance between the military and civilian powers and responsibilities had been raised. The more successes the Allied armies achieved, the more prestige Foch gained; and the greater his esteem, the greater the suspicions of the old Dreyfusard who headed France's government.

France's head of state, President Poincaré, was also a factor. The antipathy between Clemenceau and Poincaré was long-standing and

---

[56] Reprinted in Foch, *Mémoires*, 2: 250–2.   [57] Trask, *AEF*, 161.

well known. Poincaré had called upon Clemenceau to form a government only when all other candidates had been eliminated. Clemenceau's deteriorating relations with Foch may have been the cause or the result of the growing closeness between the latter and Poincaré. Just as Foch had cultivated Clemenceau between 1914 and 1916, did Foch now cultivate Poincaré? Foch had found the speech that the President gave when he presented his marshal's baton rather uninspired, but he went nonetheless to the Elysée Palace to thank him on 27 August. Poincaré's record of Foch's flattering words on that occasion may reveal excessive politeness or an attempt to strengthen bridges with the man who had been involved in his sacking at the end of 1916.[58] In the matter of the Saint-Mihiel attack, Poincaré had sent his liaison officer to tell Foch that, if any pressure was brought to bear on him over the decision, he (Foch) should let the President know.[59] Furthermore, Poincaré softened a message that Clemenceau wanted delivering to Foch, about placing French divisions with the AEF so as to have a greater influence, by proposing that the message be delivered as a question rather than as a suggestion.[60] In October Poincaré's liaison officer began reporting Foch's views to him directly, and the President appeared at Foch's headquarters in between his visits to liberated towns and villages.

The jealousies and disputes just recounted were an index of the intense pressures of the last weeks of the war, yet often Foch does not receive any credit for the turn-around after the counterstroke of 18 July and his memorandum six days later. David Stevenson, for example, credits Foch only with having 'mellowed and wisened' so that he was able to 'co-ordinate Allied strategy more effectively than would have been possible through bilateral arrangements, eventually delivering the first concerted general offensive for two years'.[61] An uncritical acceptance of Haig's version of events has pushed Foch's contribution into the background. Haig claimed to have imposed on Foch an end to the Battle of Amiens in August and the strategy of concentric attacks converging on Mézières, but neither claim stands up to scrutiny. Foch is accused of missing a great opportunity by not allowing Pershing to capture Metz, imposing instead the costly Meuse–Argonne offensive. Yet no such

---

[58] Letter, Foch to Mme Foch, 24 August 1918, vol. 47; Notin, *Foch*, 404; Poincaré, *AS*, 10: 325–6 (entry for 27 August 1918).

[59] Poincaré, *AS* 10: 316 (entry for 21 August 1918).

[60] Herbillon, *Du général*, 2: 319 (note to entry for 27 September 1918).

[61] Stevenson, *First World War*, 448.

opportunity existed, and Pershing's obstinacy played a large role in events.

As for the final days and the general offensive, once again Foch's role is diminished by referring to the 'Hundred Days'. This is a phrase used in the British histories and, with its Napoleonic overtones, counts the days to victory from the start of the Amiens battle on 8 August. In reality, however, the '112 days' to victory began on 18 July with Foch's counterstroke against Soissons. Mounting the general offensive required more than running from pillar to post, waving his arms, and parroting 'tout le monde à la bataille', all into the fight. Foch did more than simply parrot the cry; he urged, cajoled, persuaded, ordered everyone to join in the battle. The fact that, by the end, everyone *had* joined the battle and driven the enemy to acknowledge defeat is probably the greatest contribution that Foch made to the Allied victory. His 'all-in' battle even drove Ludendorff to physical collapse. Granted, Foch was lucky in that by 1918 the Allies had the technology and the resources that were necessary for that victory; but, without the will and the strategic vision to seize the moment when it appeared, neither technology nor limitless resources could have obtained a victory in 1918 rather than a year later. In 1916 the Somme had shown how little a battle fought side by side could achieve; in 1917 British action at Messines, Passchendaele and Cambrai had no connection to the French offensive on the Chemin des Dames. In 1918 the German offensives revealed the dangers of separate battles. Certainly Foch cried 'tout le monde à la bataille', but he did it sufficiently energetically to get 'everyone' to agree to join in. At the same time, he was thinking about the next battle, the fight over armistice terms.

During October 1918 Foch deployed all his energy in pushing the Allies into their general offensive and in dealing with disputes with the national CinCs and his Premier. At the same time he had to return to the political arena of the SWC to deal with armistice terms. The first German request was sent to President Wilson on 4 October, and five weeks later the Armistice was signed in a railway carriage near Rethondes in the Compiègne forest. The date and the time of that signing have been commemorated annually ever since as marking the end of the war. Yet the armistice agreement was not intended to end the war but to call a truce; it merely caused the weapons to fall silent. That is why the German term – the silencing of weapons – is used for the title of this chapter, rather than the sometimes misinterpreted English/French term.

At OHL headquarters in Spa, the news that on 25 September Bulgaria had requested an armistice, coupled with the start of Foch's general offensive in Belgium and France, caused Ludendorff's physical collapse. His increasing pessimism had already alarmed some OHL staff, who decided on 26 September to call Foreign Minister Paul von Hintze to Spa to discuss the situation. Three days later Hintze and the Kaiser met with Hindenburg and Ludendorff and were told that an immediate *Waffenstillstand* was required to save the army, and that political reform was required to make the country accept it. Ludendorff was convinced that the worsening military situation in both east and west demanded an immediate armistice, but *not* peace negotiations. If the armistice conditions were too hard, he was prepared to fight on. In conference with the OHL section leaders on 1 October Ludendorff informed them that, to avoid the 'catastrophe' of an Allied breakthrough forcing the army back to the Rhine and bringing revolution to Germany, an immediate *Waffenstillstand* was necessary, based on Wilson's Fourteen Points. He told Thaer that 'unfortunately' he saw 'no other way'. However, when Thaer asked Ludendorff whether he believed that the Allies would grant it, and whether, if he were Marshal Foch, he himself would grant such an

armistice, Ludendorff replied: 'No, surely not, rather first grab the opportunity [to gain a breathing-space by requesting an armistice]'. Yet perhaps, he continued, the Allies wanted it: 'in war one can never know'.[1]

Ludendorff pressed Berlin several times during the next few days to
hasten the formation of a new government (he and Hindenburg approved
the appointment of Prince Max von Baden as the new Chancellor on 30
September), but the true military situation took some time to sink into the
new minds in Berlin. OHL had kept both politicians and the German
people in the dark, hence the shock when the Ludendorff–Hindenburg
duo requested that the government negotiate an armistice. Consequently
it was only on the night of 3/4 October that the German government's note
was sent via Switzerland to President Wilson. It asked for the USA to take
steps to restore peace, and also 'in order to prevent further bloodshed' to
arrange a 'general armistice on land, on water and in the air'. The note was
thus not only a request for an armistice, but also for negotiations for a
Wilsonian peace – a peace that they believed would give them more
generous terms than the Entente leaders would offer.

There is no need to go into the Allied negotiations that led to Rethondes,
as they have been well described elsewhere. What is important here is
Foch's attitude and his resultant decisions. They form the background to
the first two stages of the negotiations in which Foch played only a small
formal role. The first stage, following this first German note, consisted of
the ensuing correspondence between Germany and President Wilson, in
which it was agreed finally that Germany would approach Marshal Foch to
ask for terms based on Wilson's Fourteen Points. The second (international) stage lasted from 29 October, when the bilateral USA–Germany
phase ended, to 4 November when the Allies meeting as the SWC agreed
the terms after much discussion. During this second stage Foch talked with
Pétain, Haig and Pershing, but essentially it was his terms that formed the
basis of the agreed military terms that were offered. The third and final stage
covers the days leading up to the signing, when Foch's role was central.

Not until the German note was sent to President Wilson did Foch begin
to think that the war might end in 1918, instead of after another winter at
war. He had told his wife in mid-September that in 1919 the war must
end.[2] Nevertheless, he did not need to begin thinking only in October
about what the armistice conditions should be; he already knew. In his
mind the important question was whether France was to obtain a lasting
peace, not simply territorial and financial reparations that would see the
struggle with Germany begin again in ten or twenty years. Foch wanted a

[1] Thaer, *Generalstabdienst*, 235–6 (entry for 1 October 1918).
[2] Mme Foch diary, 16 September 1918.

'European equilibrium' that would free his children from the threat of an
enemy's 'insatiable ambitions'. The entire 'Prussian' system had developed ideas of conquest and domination in the 65 million inhabitants of the
German Reich, whereas for Foch France's history since the Revolution had
created an entirely different vision of humanity. He concluded that the
Prussian regime and Empire with its capital in Berlin had to be suppressed;
but, since they could be easily reconstituted with, say, Munich as capital,
French security required that Germany's western frontier should be the
Rhine.[3] Foch would never deviate from this belief.

Even though at first Germany was dealing exclusively with the USA,
Foch was sure that it was *his* role to formulate the armistice conditions.[4]
An armistice was a military matter, to be decided in consultation with
Haig, Pétain and Pershing but settled by himself. On 8 October Foch sent
a brief note that Clemenceau had asked for with the terms he considered
essential. These were, first, the occupation of the Rhineland, the German
territory west of the Rhine, with strong bridgeheads on the eastern side;
second, an immediate German withdrawal from all occupied lands,
including Alsace and Lorraine.[5]

The same day the PMRs also formulated their ideas. Their focus
differed from Foch's in that they judged the 'first essential' to be the
'disarmament of the enemy under the control of the Allies', in other
words unconditional surrender. Furthermore, their terms were much
more wide ranging than Foch's, whose thinking was limited to the
Western Front extending from the North Sea to the Adriatic. The
PMRs included evacuation of all the occupied territories in the east,
naval conditions, and a continuation of the blockade. All the measures
were to be executed within three to four weeks, and as a 'material guarantee'– necessary because Germany's 'word cannot be believed'– Metz,
Thionville, Strassburg, Neu-Breisach and Lille, together with the naval
fortifications of Heligoland, were to be surrendered within forty-eight
hours.[6] If the politicians thought Foch's terms harsh, the unconditional
surrender proposed by the PMRs was far harsher.

British, French and Italian leaders happened to be meeting in Paris
when news of Wilson's response was received. It was a stalling reply,
asking for an assurance that the German government in whose name the
note had been sent was indeed able to speak for more than the Imperial

---

[3] Note, n.d. [annotated in Weygand's hand 'before the Armistice'], in Weygand mss, partie
donnée, 1K/130/6, [d] 9.
[4] Herbillon, *Du général*, 2: 326 (entry for 8 October 1918).
[5] Mordacq, *MC*, 2: 266 (entry for 8 October 1918).
[6] Bliss to Lansing *et al.*, 8 October 1918, in Link (ed.), *PWW*, 51: 272–5.

and military authorities who had so far conducted the war. Naturally, the Allied leaders were dismayed by the astute German move to go over their heads across the Atlantic, all the more so because they had just assembled to discuss the further conduct of the war in the Balkans and the Middle East following Bulgaria's defection. Bulgaria had appealed to Wilson to intervene, although the USA had declared war on neither Bulgaria nor Turkey, and Clemenceau was outraged at what he considered American interference in matters which did not concern it. Now American 'interference' in negotiations with Germany based on the Fourteen Points might cause the Allies to forfeit some of their war aims.

It was difficult for the Allied leaders to agree armistice terms with the German notes being sent only to Washington, and without any American political representation in Europe. Moreover, the German action took them by surprise. Nonetheless, meeting on 8 October in the French Foreign Ministry, they discussed both the PMRs' proposals and the note that Foch had given to Clemenceau with what he, as the general in chief of the Allied armies, considered essential.

Foch set out three main conditions and a series of additional ones. First, Germany must evacuate within a fortnight Belgium, France, Alsace-Lorraine and Luxembourg, restoring their populations. Second, Germany must concede two or three bridgeheads, with a thirty-kilometre radius, on the right bank of the Rhine, to enable the Allies to pursue and destroy enemy forces, should peace negotiations fail. Third, Germany must evacuate the left bank of the Rhine within thirty days so that the Allies could occupy and hold those territories as a guarantee that reparations imposed in the peace treaty would be paid. Any war supplies that could not be removed within the time limits must be left behind and not destroyed, and any German troops remaining after the time limit were to be taken prisoner. All German military installations were to be left *in situ* as well as, most importantly, all railway materiel. All the French and Belgian railway materiel that had been taken must be restored. These terms were ferocious, and if accepted would prevent the Germans from re-starting the war in the west because German territory would be occupied and Germany would have no means of sending troops back into France. When they were read out to the assembled ministers, the immediate reaction was that they were too harsh: the Chancellor of the Exchequer, Andrew Bonar Law, said that they amounted to an unconditional surrender, although Orlando conceded that they were confined to military necessities. Lloyd George thought it too early to start discussing terms, which would probably have to be gone over again once President Wilson had finished his correspondence with the new German government. Meanwhile he thought that a simple rejection of the overtures from the Central Powers was sufficient, and preferable to 'the "no" with a swagger' that Foch and the PMRs were proposing.[7] Lloyd George's disapproval of Foch and his proposal was probably sharpened by the previous day's discussion, when Foch had pressed the British Prime Minister to send all category 'A' men in Britain and Ireland over to France, despite Lloyd George's insistence that nothing could enable Britain to put into the field in 1919 an army of the same size as in 1918.[8]

The fact that Foch pressed the British so hard on the manpower question on 7 October, three days after the German request to President Wilson, reveals how little faith he had in the German démarche amounting to anything. He had replied to Bonar Law's questioning at the end of the meeting by saying the Western Front 'was as yet by no means stabilised'. Neither was Sir Henry Wilson impressed. He thought the German action a 'pretty piece of impertinence' – 'let the Boches get behind the Rhine . . . then we can discuss'.[9] Foch's directive of 10 October about operations, discussed in the previous chapter, shows further that he was not disposed to ease the pressure. He directed the British to combine with the Flanders Army Group in freeing the Lille conurbation, and French First Army to combine with the Aisne–Meuse offensive to outflank the line of the river Serre. The next day, 11 October, a German submarine torpedoed and sank the *Leinster*, an Irish mail boat, with 700 passengers on board of whom 176, mainly women and children, drowned. Since naval warfare was continuing, obviously the Germans were not yet admitting defeat. Neither did President Wilson have much faith in Germany's sincerity. Sir William Wiseman, head of British intelligence in the USA, reported to London on 16 October that the President 'does not trust German Government in the least or believe that their overtures are sincere'[10]

An entry in Foch's notebooks dated 12 October gives an unequivocal sense of his opinion. It reads as though he were composing a military address. 'The Boche is on the way out', it begins, and he wants to talk. 'Who', Foch asked rhetorically, 'wants to talk with an adversary who tears up treaties as though they were scraps of paper . . . with no respect for sacred rights, who reduces people to slavery, deports them like cattle . . . Soldiers of liberty, forward, you will avenge your dead, you will deliver humanity' (see Illustration 11).[11]

---

[7] 'Procès-verbal of a conference at the Quai d'Orsay [French Foreign Ministry], 8 October 1918', IC 80, CAB 28/5, with Appendix I: Foch's note.

[8] 'Procès-verbal of a conference at the Villa Romaine, Versailles, 7 October 1918', IC 78, CAB 28/5.

[9] Ibid.; Wilson diary, 5 October 1918.

[10] Wiseman to Foreign Office, sent 16 October 1918, FO 371/3442.

[11] Foch, Carnets, 12 October 1918, fo. 336.

Illustration 11 Foch's Fifteenth Point
'There remains, then, only the fifteenth point'
Although the enemy has torn up the peace treaty and President Wilson's
Fourteen Points, Foch has his sword. But the politicians have blunted
Foch's sword.

After the Germans sent their second note to Wilson, accepting his
Fourteen Points and asking whether all the Allies did also, they received
a somewhat tougher response. Wilson warned that the Germans must
stop their submarine warfare and other 'illegal and inhumane' practices,
wreaking devastation as they retreated. He indicated that the conditions of

any armistice must be left to the 'military advisers' of the Allied and Associated Powers. In his letter to Clemenceau on 16 October asking for liaison with the French Foreign Ministry, Foch wondered what the President meant by 'military advisers', since he considered that the only 'qualified' advisers were the commanders-in-chief, and even then it was *his* role to reach agreement with them and then to advise the government. Having fought off one attempt by Lloyd George in July to restrict his influence on planning the 1919 campaign in favour of the PMRs at Versailles, Foch was not prepared to allow President Wilson to restrict his influence in like manner. As seen in the previous chapter, Foch's attempt in the same letter to give himself greater prominence by requesting direct liaison with the French Foreign Ministry failed utterly when Clemenceau refused. The Premier intended to keep control within his own hands.

Finally, a third German note and third Wilson response signified that talk of an armistice could begin. Wilson communicated all the correspondence to the Allied governments, with the suggestion that they draw up terms that would leave Germany unable to renew hostilities. The German government delayed four days, until 27 October, before responding. Wilson's position – that the armistice should be such as to make it impossible for hostilities to begin again – had concentrated minds in Spa and Berlin. Ludendorff stated that the only possible response was to break off negotiations and resist to the bitter end, with every man going to the armies and every woman to the factories. He went so far as to publish a communiqué to the press declaring that Wilson wanted a military capitulation: this was unacceptable, Ludendorff claimed, and he called on his soldiers to continue to resist with all their force. Ludendorff told the new German War Cabinet that a few more months of war would have the British and French populations clamouring for peace. Self-delusion cannot go much further, and Ludendorff had overstepped the boundary with the Kaiser. On the grounds that Ludendorff had not obtained his permission to publish the press statement, the Kaiser sacked him on 26 October. Hindenburg stayed, however, because the government wanted to take advantage of his almost mythic status as national hero so as to retain some element of stability.[12] The next day the Germans replied to Wilson that they would wait for the Allied proposals for an armistice; thus the first stage of the process came to an end.

The second stage, the international as opposed to bi-lateral discussions, had already begun. On 24 October Clemenceau called both Foch and Pétain to the War Ministry to consider armistice terms. The Premier told

---

[12] Von der Golz, *Hindenburg*, 53–4.

Foch to discuss them with Haig and Pershing, so as to be ready for the SWC meeting that would begin a week later, as soon as the American delegate arrived.[13] He wanted the military to iron out any objections in advance so that at least they would be united when the usual arguments in the SWC began. Although Foch's terms (with additions from Pétain) submitted on 8 October were confirmed there and then, the military position had changed in the meantime. The disaggregation of the Austro-Hungarian Empire had continued apace: Czechoslovakia had already (on 3 October) been recognised as an Entente ally; on 15 October the Poles announced their independence; on 20 October the Hungarians demanded and received control of Hungarian elements in the army. Only two days after Foch's talk with Clemenceau, Kaiser Karl informed Berlin that he was leaving the war and asked President Wilson for an immediate armistice based on Austria's acceptance of his Fourteen Points. Their woes were increased by the long-awaited start of the Italian offensive between mountain and plain. Although it got off to a shaky start, the battle of Vittorio Veneto completed the destruction of the Austro-Hungarian armies. In France and Flanders the Allies were continuing to make progress, although at a slower rate than at the end of September because of the ordered and methodical retreat of the German armies, during which roads and railways were deliberately destroyed so as to slow the pursuit. Nonetheless, Foch was considering a further extension of the battle into Lorraine, an operation that Pétain had been planning for some time. So the Allies were in a better position on 24 October than they had been on the 8th, when Foch drew up his first set of terms. Indeed, their position was so much better that Foch moved the sites of the proposed bridgeheads across the Rhine further north to reflect the Allied advance. Thus Foch was now thinking more about final peace terms than about an armistice. Peace was approaching, he noted on 20 October.[14]

Clemenceau had asked Foch to confer with Haig and Pershing, and he did this immediately, on 25 October. Foch knew that it was important for the Entente to present a single front, hence he was keen to consult with Haig and Pershing even though he reserved unto himself the final decisions about proposed terms.[15] Although Foch received support from Pétain, who was present at the meeting also, Haig and Pershing had different points of view.

Haig had already enquired of the CIGS whether Foch could involve the British army in an armistice and what he should do if he did not agree with any terms that Foch proposed. Wilson's reply avoided the issue. He

[13] Mordacq, *MC*, 2: 292 (entry for 24 October 1918).
[14] Foch, Carnets, 20 October 1918, fo. 338.   [15] Ibid.

pointed out that the correspondence between Washington and Berlin concerned the Fourteen Points, about which the British had reservations. Haig should continue operations, therefore, 'with all the vigour' considered 'safe and possible'; and the press had been warned not to make too much of the German notes.[16] Next Haig was called to London to discuss terms with the inner cabinet. He told Lloyd George, Bonar Law, Milner and the CIGS that the enemy was not so beaten as to accept any terms. On the contrary, they were able to destroy roads and railways and would be able to retire to and hold a much shorter line, especially as they had not yet incorporated their 1920 class. The French were not fighting well, and the Americans were too disorganised to fight well. Consequently Haig's concern was to prevent an undue burden being placed on the under-strength BEF. He recommended 'only' the evacuation of occupied territories in France and Belgium, as well as Alsace and Lorraine, and the return of French and Belgian rolling-stock and repatriation of deported citizens. Yet, as Bonar Law remarked, 'this amounted to complete defeat', and only if Germany were 'in desperate straits' would it consent to such terms. When the First Sea Lord joined the group, he added some naval conditions: the surrender of two out of the three squadrons of German battleships, fifty destroyers, 'a certain number' of light cruisers, and all the German submarines. Wilson read out a letter from General DuCane which gave some details of Foch's thinking: any armistice must ensure that, if it were broken off, the Allies could continue the war under more favourable circumstances than at present; and it must give the Allies 'pledges of value' so as to ensure compliance with the later peace conditions. In other words, Foch insisted on holding some German territory as a guarantee. DuCane stated also that Foch believed that the Armistice terms must be communicated through him to the Germans 'to ensure the interests of the Allied Armies under his command in the event of hostilities being renewed'. Hence Foch had no intention of being side-lined. Wilson tended more to Foch's position than Haig's, because the latter's suggested terms offered no pledge to ensure compliance with peace terms.[17]

Foch knew Haig's views already because the two men had met on 10 October, when Foch had handed over a copy of his proposed terms. Haig's reaction then had been that they amounted to a 'general unconditional surrender' except that the officers would march back with their

---

[16] Haig to Wilson and Wilson to Haig, 13 October 1918, both in Blake (ed.), *Haig Papers*, 331–2.

[17] 'Notes of a conference', X29, 19 October 1918, with appendix, DuCane to Wilson, 17 October 1918, CAB 23/17.

swords and the soldiers with their rifles.[18] When Haig left for London, the French Military Mission at GHQ reported that Haig believed that the Germans were far from defeated but that nevertheless an armistice before the winter might be achieved. (Foch had already received a report that Haig was very conscious that he was commanding the 'last British army' and that he did not have the confidence of his government. An early armistice would meet London's desire to save British manpower.) Because harsh terms would cause a German rejection and more fighting in 1919, Haig's armistice conditions were simply a German withdrawal from occupied territories and Metz and Strassburg, followed, ten days later, by an Allied occupation of Belgium.[19] Foch was sufficiently worried by Haig's reported views to write to Clemenceau on 18 October to warn the Premier that they were 'completely inadequate'.[20] When Foch and Haig met again on 24 October over the Second Army question, Haig argued that it would be safer to have the Germans with their backs to the Rhine, rather than on the right bank facing Allied bridgeheads.[21]

Foch also knew the views of Poincaré and of Pershing, as both men had come to Foch's headquarters on 23 October.[22] It is inconceivable that they would not have talked of armistice terms, especially given Poincaré's well-known view that Germany should be defeated, with no armistice possible so long as any German troops remained on French soil, especially his native Lorraine. The President wished no doubt to ensure that Foch knew his views about any armistice. As for Pershing, although his diary records that he and Foch held similar 'bellicose' views, he told Haig when he saw him later the same day that he was in agreement with the British CinC's opinions.[23]

By their meeting on 25 October, then, Foch had already discussed terms with the national commanders individually. This meeting was, therefore, a formality. General Gillain should have attended also for the Belgians, but was unable to reach Senlis in time. (Foch had moved his headquarters back there, north of Paris, on 18 October.) Haig gave his views first, repeating what he had said in London. Pétain spoke next; his proposals were much tougher than Haig's. Working on the principle that the conditions should provide guarantees and enable the Allies to

---

[18] Haig diary, 10 October 1918.

[19] 'Notes sur l'état d'esprit du Maréchal Haig', 5 October 1918, 'Notes sur les conditions que le Maréchal Haig estime suffisantes pour un Armistice', 18 October 1918, both in 17N 348, [d] 1918.

[20] Foch to Clemenceau, 18 October 1918, 6N 70, [d] 1.   [21] Haig diary, 24 October 1918.

[22] Herbillon, *Du général*, 2: 334 (entry for 22 October 1918).

[23] GQGA JMO, 23 October 1918, 26N 1; Pershing diary, 23 October 1918; Haig diary, 23 October 1918.

re-start hostilities on a more favourable footing, he proposed the occupation of the whole length of the Rhine from the Swiss to the Dutch frontier, since the right bank of the river opposite Alsace-Lorraine was not suitable terrain for a offensive. He suggested holding a twenty-to-thirty-kilometre-wide stretch of the right bank and demanding railway materiel: 5000 locomotives and 100,000 wagons. In addition, he proposed a time limit of three days, which would mean that the Germans would not have time to evacuate all their heavy equipment, especially if they were also forced to hand over 10–15,000 guns. Pershing agreed with Foch and Pétain that terms should not be light. If the Germans were sincere, Pershing claimed, they would accept the Allies' terms. He agreed with the occupation of zones on the Rhine right bank, and added that all U-boats and U-boat bases should be given up so as to keep safe American lines across the sea.[24]

Foch responded to Haig's pessimistic belief in the enemy's capacity to continue resistance by pointing out the damage inflicted on the Germans since July. Certainly the Allies were tired, but so too was the enemy, and 'nothing gives wings to an army like victory'. Foch wanted to keep up the pressure; 'When one hunts a wild beast and finally comes upon him at bay, he then faces greater danger, but it is not the time to stop, it is time to redouble his blows without paying any attention to those he himself receives.' Unlike some of Foch's analogies, this one would prove to be appropriate. Foch would fight on until and wherever the enemy conceded defeat. He also responded to Haig's interjection that naval terms were not their province by agreeing that Pershing's concern for his sea communications was well founded. Having asked whether Haig wished to change his views after hearing Pétain and Pershing speak (Haig did not), Foch closed the meeting by asking the three generals to give him their opinion in writing.

Foch did not spend long digesting his allies' opinions and the day after their meeting, 26 October, sent the final version of his armistice terms to Clemenceau, keeping him fully informed. In essence the terms were the same as those in his 8 October letter, but with a great deal of added detail. General Gillain declared himself in agreement for the Belgian government, and the document was shown to Poincaré the same day. The President expressed no opinion on the proposed terms, but said privately to Weygand, 'My dear general, they will never sign that.'[25]

The seven paragraphs of military terms plus suggested naval conditions were these. First, the immediate evacuation of Belgium, France, Luxembourg and Alsace-Lorraine within a short timetable (fourteen

[24] 'Conference held at Senlis, October 25, 1918', *USAWW* 10: 19–21.
[25] GQGA JMO, 26 October 1918, 26N 1; Weygand, *Foch*, 265.

days) so as to force the Germans to abandon a large part of their materiel to include 5000 guns (approximately one-third of the German army's artillery), 30,000 machineguns (about half the German total), and 3000 *Minenwerfer*. This was not total disarmament, but would seriously hamper any resumption of hostilities. Second, evacuation of the left bank of the Rhine within twenty-two days and evacuation of a neutral zone of forty kilometres on the east bank within a further three days. The Allies would occupy these territories, together with bridgeheads of a thirty-kilometre radius at the main river crossings: Mainz, Koblenz, Köln, Strassburg. Third, no destruction of any kind and no harm to any inhabitant. Fourth, surrender of 5000 locomotives and 150,000 railway wagons. Fifth, communication of the whereabouts of landmines and other explosive devices. Sixth, the naval blockade to be continued until all conditions had been met. Finally, Allied POWs to be returned as quickly as possible. The naval conditions included the surrender of 150 submarines, removal of the surface fleet to the Baltic, disclosure of all mine-fields, and Cuxhaven (on the mouth of the river Elbe) and the island of Heligoland to be occupied by the Allies.[26] These conditions are so severe that Poincaré's reaction – the Germans will never sign them – seems justified.

Did Foch intend that the Germans should refuse to sign? Derby reported that Foch thought that they would so refuse, but that he hoped to have them 'completely beaten by Christmas'.[27] It seems that Foch trod a path between, on the one hand, unconditional surrender, which Foch knew was unacceptable to the Germans and would inspire them to continue their resistance, and, on the other, armistice terms severe enough to ensure that most of France's peace aims would be realised. Foch accepted that the Germans would be unlikely to accept such severe terms immediately, but he believed that continued Allied pressure would force them to accept. He told his wife that, although he did not expect the enemy to sign at first, news of a refused offer of terms would provoke revolution within Germany, whereupon Germany would be forced to concede.[28] In other words, he was taking a calculated risk.

The eighth session of the Supreme War Council convened on 31 October, immediately after Colonel House's arrival in France. The Allies had requested that President Wilson send a representative to join their discussions, and Wilson delegated House, as he had done in 1917, with full authority to execute his wishes.[29] Discussions continued over

[26] Foch to Clemenceau, 26 October 1918, reprinted as appendix to 'Notes of a conversation at the residence of Colonel House', 1 November 1918, IC 87, CAB 28/5.
[27] Dutton (ed.), *Paris 1918*, 321 (entry for 5 November 1918).
[28] Mme Foch diary, 5 November 1918.
[29] Wilson's letter of authorisation in Seymour, *Intimate Papers*, 4: 87–8.

several days, with private meetings in the mornings and full sessions in the afternoons. Foch did not have to mount a very strong defence of his terms, despite the fact that neither Bliss nor Haig was in agreement. Bliss felt strongly that Foch was presenting a political programme for peace terms, whereas Bliss preferred 'the absolute laying down of arms', a true *Waffenstillstand*, as the sole condition. This was unconditional surrender, a position that now Pershing also adopted despite giving suggestions for armistice terms in the conference with Foch, Haig and Pétain.[30] However, Pershing had specified at the start of their discussion that armistice conditions depended upon the various governments accepting that an armistice was possible. Postwar he made no secret of his preference for unconditional surrender. Haig's thinking was completely different. At a meeting of his army commanders he stated that 'the enemy has not yet been sufficiently beaten as to cause him to accept an ignominious peace'.[31] He still sought terms lenient enough to ensure the enemy's acceptance.

The SWC's first meeting began on the last day of October with Foch's summary of the current military situation. Describing the enemy's disorganisation, Foch compared him to a man who has lost his balance, and illustrated his words by rocking back and forth as he spoke.[32] He listed the Allied achievements since 18 July on the Western Front: well over a quarter of a million German casualties; well over 4000 guns captured; and constant forced retreats. In Italy the Austro-Hungarian army had been cut in two by the advance on Vittorio Veneto, and in the east Bulgaria was defeated and the Turks ready to capitulate. So the war was won in the east, but in the west the enemy 'persisted in methodical destruction and accepted battle everywhere'. He was confident, however, that since Germany was now their sole enemy they could continue until its 'complete defeat'.[33] Then the council proceeded to discuss the armistice terms that had been approved that morning at a private meeting in Colonel House's lodgings.

During that morning meeting, House asked Foch whether it was better to continue the war or to grant an armistice. Foch responded with a statement from which he never deviated:

I do not make war [simply] to make war but to obtain results. If the Germans sign an armistice with the conditions necessary to guarantee those results, I am satisfied. No one has the right to prolong the bloodshed any further.

[30] Bliss to Baker, 23 October 1918, in Link (ed.), *PWW*, 51: 434–6.
[31] Haig diary, 31 October 1918.   [32] Aldrovandi, *Guerra diplomatica*, 195.
[33] 'Procès-verbal of the first meeting of the Eighth Session of the Supreme War Council, 31 October 1918', IC 85, CAB 28/5.

House had asked the question in order to deflect from the USA any accusation that Washington had forced an armistice upon the Allies.[34] The statement remained Foch's defence against many accusations that he ought to have carried the war into Germany and forced the enemy's unconditional surrender.

In their private meeting the next day, 1 November, Lloyd George pressed Foch on the question of the Rhine bridgeheads. He wanted to be sure that, if the armistice terms were rejected, there could be no hint that Haig's views on more lenient terms had not been considered. Foch insisted that it was 'essential first to be master of the Rhine', and that Haig's rejection of any occupation of the Rhineland would enable the Germans to get behind the river in a strongly fortified position if they rejected the terms. Lloyd George pressed that the real point was whether the enemy was sufficiently beaten to accept the occupation of German territory. Both Foch and Clemenceau indicated that they felt that, as yet, Germany would not accept. However, as the Allies 'increased [their] advantages', the Germans would concede. At the start of the meeting Clemenceau had read out a report that he had received from Switzerland showing that conditions within Germany were 'extremely bad'. Moreover, Austria's collapse freed Allied troops for the fight against Germany and opened up the possibility of an invasion of southern Germany via Austria. Bullitt Lowry writes of this exchange that 'Foch was admitting that he had drawn up terms the Germans would refuse, and with that refusal in hand, he would continue the war into 1919 . . . Foch and Clemenceau . . . foresaw the offer of those terms, Germany's refusal of them, and then continued Allied and American attacks compelling Germany to accept the terms some time in 1919.'[35] This is a mistaken reading. Foch did not want to risk Germany's acceptance of less harsh terms, leaving France's security in doubt, but he expected that Germany would be forced to accept his terms very shortly. He did not expect to have to fight on into 1919. He told Loucheur about his response to House's question – that he had no right to shed more blood if the Germans accepted the armistice terms – but he went on to say that, if Germany did not accept them, it was better to 'continue the war to victory which was certain'.[36]

After more private and formal discussion of the military terms, they were confirmed on 4 November. The final version was even harsher: 2000 aircraft and 10,000 lorries were to be surrendered in addition to the railway materiel; a financial clause demanded reparation for damage done; naval clauses were stiffened; furthermore, withdrawal of forces in Africa and on the Eastern Front (Foch had drawn up these provisions) was

[34] Weygand, *IV*, 635; Seymour, *Intimate Papers*, 4: 90.   [35] Lowry, *Armistice*, 120.
[36] Poincaré, *AS*, 10: 402 (entry for 1 November 1918).

specified. The armistice was to last for thirty days with the option of renewal, and the Germans had seventy-two hours in which to accept or reject the thirty-five clauses of the armistice offer.[37]

President Wilson was informed immediately of the Allied agreement on terms and he in turn informed Germany that Foch was authorised to communicate them to their representatives. Thus ended the second stage of the armistice talks. Foch had been involved in many of the private and formal meetings, but had not spoken very much. He did not need to, as his military conditions were not only accepted but strengthened. The council never questioned his authority to draw up the military terms, and the document that the PMRs produced seems never to have been discussed. The final stage of the proceedings now began with Foch as master of ceremonies.

Foch spent 5 November dealing with the planning for the Lorraine offensive, and on the next day arranged with General Debeney for the German party to pass through First Army's lines. On the 7th Foch learned their names, and that afternoon left Senlis in his special train for a quiet, secret location in the Compiègne forest. First Sea Lord Admiral Wemyss and three other British naval officers accompanied him. Wemyss recorded: 'The Frenchmen are all naturally very elated but dignified ... calm, the Marshal quiet and confident. He told me he proposed to do as little talking as possible, so that the Germans do it all ... then hand them the terms of Armistice. If they accept the principles, he may discuss details.'[38] By that evening Allied armies had almost reached Sedan, scene of France's humiliation in the Franco-Prussian war.

It is not easy to judge how confident Foch was of Germany's acceptance of the terms during these final days because he said different things to different people. Possibly his own optimism waxed and waned, but it is more likely that he varied his responses according to his interlocutor. He told both House and Lloyd George, for example, that it would take three or four or more months to drive the Germans back to the Rhine if they did not accept the Armistice terms – probably because he did not want to put any brake on the sending of American and British manpower to France. To Loucheur, however, Foch gave the impression that he believed the Germans would sign, but he told Herbillon that he did not believe the Germans to be beaten.[39] In short, Foch did not know what was going to happen. Whatever his degree of optimism or pessimism, on 9 November

[37] Annex L, 'Conditions of an Armistice with Germany, 4 November 1918', IC 95, CAB 28/5.
[38] Wemyss diary, 7 November 1918, WMYS 5/7.
[39] Mantoux [interpreter at the meetings] to House, 6 July 1920, cited in Seymour, *Intimate Papers*, 4: 91; Loucheur, *Carnets secrets*, 65 (entry for 5 November 1918); Poincaré, *AS*, 10: 402 (entry for 1 November 1918).

Foch sent out an order to the Allied CinCs, pressing them to continue and to speed up their action, telling Mordacq and Clemenceau that one never knew with the Boches. On the other hand, he wrote to his wife that the enemy seemed in a hurry to finish with the war: with God's help, he told her, 'our armistice might come out of our talks'.[40] In the afternoon of 10 November, after news of the Kaiser's abdication, Herbillon asked Foch if he had a message for Paris: 'just tell them', Foch said, 'the Germans are beaten, even more beaten than I believed, they are accepting everything'. Despite the departure of their Kaiser, all the German plenipotentiaries were thinking of was finishing with everything and 'capitulation – for it is a capitulation'.[41]

Finally, after a sleepless night on 10/11 November – it was only Foch's second such experience, the first being after the Battle of the Marne in 1914 – the Armistice was signed at 5.15am and came into effect at 11 that morning: see Illustration 12. Admiral Hope, of the British naval delegation, was impressed by Foch's demeanour: 'Foch was splendid, very quiet and dignified and very firm.' The head of the German delegation, Matthias Erzberger, was 'evidently pleased to get it over', whilst the military representative 'seemed to feel it greatly, the sailor did so less, the diplomat didn't say much, but I expect he was thinking a great deal'.[42] That evening DuCane asked Foch whether he was disappointed that the projected Lorraine attack had not taken place. Foch replied that he was not:

I am quite satisfied with the conditions of the armistice. They give us all we want. After all, why does one make war? It is to enforce one's policy. What is our policy? To clear the Germans out of France and Belgium, to make it impossible for them to continue the war, and finally to dictate peace. We shall do all that quicker than if we went on fighting, and, what is more, without any further sacrifice of life. No, I am quite satisfied.[43]

Foch's handling of the armistice negotiations with the Allies and then the presentation of the armistice conditions to the German plenipotentiaries raise three questions. (That asking whether the terms were too harsh is answered by the fact of their acceptance; the military terms were sharpened by the economic conditions that the politicians added; it was the guilt clause and the reparations demands of the peace that were the principal causes of the interwar ill-will, not the armistice conditions

[40] Mordacq, *MC*, 2: 346 (entry for 9 November 1918); letter, Foch to Mme Foch, 7 November 1918, vol. 48.
[41] Foch's words in Herbillon, *Du général*, 2: 346–7 (entry for 10 November 1918).
[42] Admiral Hope, 'Written from a train in Compiègne Forest', in DuCane, *Foch*, 81.
[43] Ibid., 82.

Illustration 12 The final page of the November 1918 Armistice document signed by Foch and Admiral Wemyss for the Allies, and by the German delegation

It illustrated vol. 2 of Foch's *Mémoires*, facing p. 304 (facing p. 559 in the English translation). The armistice documents and the renewals were bound into a single volume, and an image of this signed page is viewable online at www.servicehistorique.sga.defense.gouv.fr/Nouvel-article,194. html

themselves.) First, should an armistice have been agreed at all, rather than continuing the fighting until unconditional surrender? Second, was the Armistice signed too late, in other words, would easier terms offered before Germany descended into revolution have led to greater acceptance of the war's end amid less social turmoil? Finally, the question asked most frequently, was the Armistice premature? Should the Allies have pressed on to Berlin and signed it there, in the capital of the Reich? Could they have done so?

There was never any question of an immediate negative response to the German request to President Wilson to arrange an armistice. Wilson was suspicious of German intentions, as were the Allied leaders, but the negotiations proceeded on the basis that, if the Germans accepted the ground rules laid down, then terms of an armistice would be prepared. As Wilson had said, if the Germans were beaten they would treat; if they were not beaten he did not want to treat with them. Thus Foch did not have to debate whether to accept or reject the idea of an armistice; he simply made sure right from the start that he had a document with prepared terms so that the Germans could not use an armistice as a breathing-space to revive their army. Given his prewar teaching and belief in the 'decisive battle' to end a war, the fact that he did not hesitate to give up that battle in favour of an armistice shows how far he had come mentally since 1914. Nevertheless, he did not ease the military pressure exerted by the Allied armies during November, even though those armies were becoming very tired; nor did he cease preparing for operations should the Germans refuse to sign. It is impossible to predict how the enemy might have reacted to an immediate refusal on 4 October when Germany first contacted President Wilson. The fighting might well have continued into 1919, with considerable bloodshed, if the Allies had fought their way across the Rhine in the face of a *levée en masse*, but with what results it is impossible to say. The variables are too many. As far as Foch was concerned the question did not arise, other than in the form posed by Colonel House on 31 October, when Foch replied that he did not have the right to shed any more blood if the enemy were prepared to give the necessary guarantees.

The second question – would easier terms, offered sooner, have prevented the social turmoil that followed the signing of 11 November? – is equally impossible to answer. The initiative to request an armistice had to come from the Germans; the victorious Allies could not have been expected to halt their advance whilst offering easy terms. Would Haig's proposed terms that excluded the occupation of the Rhineland and any bridgeheads on the right bank have been more acceptable? Yet Foch was certain that the Rhine was the key to France's security, hence essential. The true intention behind Haig's proposed terms was that they should be acceptable to the enemy, because he feared the casualties that would follow a continuation of the fighting. His argument that it would be better to have the enemy on the left bank of the Rhine, should any armistice break down and the fighting be renewed, does not stand scrutiny. As Foch argued when Lloyd George pressed Haig's position in the meeting on 1 November, if the fighting had to be renewed the Allies would be in a better position holding some German territory already and not having to make an opposed crossing of a very wide river. Moreover, the French had neither the capability nor the intention to make such a river crossing. The Allies would be in a better position standing on German territory east of the Rhine if fighting resumed. The last action of the war was an attempt by 163 DI to cross the Meuse near Sedan, which proved that such action was very costly without proper logistic and engineering support, and against a determined enemy.[44]

---

[44] Favreau, 'Le Dernier Combat'.

THE FINAL

TOMMY (ex-footballer): " We was just wipin' them off the face of the earth when Foch blows his whistle and shouts ' Temps! ' "

Illustration 13 The final act
Foch, the referee, blows his whistle and calls time. Whether the ex-footballer British soldier was as keen to continue the fighting as this cartoon implies is moot, but the boasting fits the pub context.

Was the Armistice premature? (See Illustration 13.) This was certainly the postwar claim of Pétain, Pershing and Poincaré, a claim that was given added weight by a second world war. When Foch took the signed armistice to show Poincaré mid-morning on 11 November, he told the President that the Germans had signed, but that 'they did not declare themselves to be defeated and, worse, they do not believe that they are'. Nevertheless, Foch added, he was convinced that if they had not signed the German army would have been forced very shortly to a 'general surrender'. Poincaré wondered whether that outcome might not have been 'safer'.[45] The armistice deprived Pershing of a great victory to obliterate the criticisms made at the start of the Meuse–Argonne offensive. 'What an enormous difference a few more days would have made', he said as the eleventh hour marked the start of the *Waffenstillstand*. Shortly afterwards he remarked that he dreaded Germany's not knowing that 'she was licked'. 'Had they given us another week', he said, 'we'd have *taught* them!'[46] Such comments reveal disappointment rather than disapproval. It was only in the 1930s that he and Pétain 'remembered' how much they opposed the Armistice. Pershing 'manufactured a false diary entry' in his memoirs so as to 'prove' that he favoured unconditional surrender by citing his letter of 30 October sent to the SWC. Indeed, the fuss made over this letter sent after the discussion of proposed terms with Foch, Haig and Pétain is disproportionate. In it Pershing is said to have advocated unconditional surrender, despite having already given his views on armistice conditions without mentioning any opposition to the whole idea. Yet the last paragraph of his letter states that 'complete victory' could be obtained only by forcing an 'unconditional surrender, but if the Allied Governments decided to grant an armistice, the terms should be so rigid that under no circumstances could Germany again take up arms'.[47] This position is little different from Foch's.

Pétain's 'objections' are more significant, if only because of his role in the 1940 armistice. Pedroncini writes that so badly did Pétain want to launch his Lorraine offensive before the Armistice was signed that he wept before Foch, begging him to delay.[48] The evidence that Pedroncini cites for this assertion is not compelling. Admiral Auphan (born 1894) wrote to him in 1971 with the claim that Pétain had told him of this during the Vichy years, when Auphan was a Navy Minister. Thus the claim is tainted both by the age of the two men and by the fact that Pétain had signed the 1940 Armistice under totally different circumstances from those of 1918. Pedroncini cites also, as evidence that Pétain was right and Foch wrong, a letter that the latter wrote to his brother, the Jesuit priest Germain Foch. Foch wrote on 21 November describing the talks with the Germans and claimed that by signing they had escaped the 'complete destruction that was under way and that would be achieved on the 14th'. According to Pedroncini, this shows that in 1918 Foch did not underestimate the

---

[45] Poincaré, *AS*, 10: 413 (entry for 11 November 1918).   [46] Smythe, *Pershing*, 232.

[47] Lowry, 'Pershing and the Armistice', 290, 286.

[48] Pedroncini, *Pétain Général*, 432. See Colonel Guelton's demolition of Pedroncini's assertions in Porte and Cochet (eds.), *Ferdinand Foch*, 177–87.

possible effects of the Lorraine offensive, although he downplayed them in his memoirs where he wrote that the result would be 'a brilliant start, the speedy capture of some tens of kilometres', then a slowing-down as they reached the zone of enemy destructions.[49] Foch's 1918 letter regretted that the Lorraine offensive had not taken place 'from the military point of view', but as the Germans accepted his conditions Foch spared his soldiers further bloodshed, his constantly reiterated reason for his actions. Yet Foch's armistice terms opened the road to the Rhine, not simply to some 'tens of kilometres' in Lorraine. Moreover, Pétain's even tougher armistice terms would also have given the French the Rhine.[50]

Finally, Pedroncini cited the 'deposition' that General Anthoine wrote in 1940 and handed to the Bibliothèque de l'Institut de France in 1943 in a sealed envelope inscribed 'may be opened on 1 January 1972'. In it Pétain's former chief of staff vents all the resentment against Foch that had clearly been building since 1918. Anthoine and Pétain met frequently after the war, and Anthoine never accepted that Foch had made the right decision.[51] Anthoine claimed in his 'deposition' that the Armistice should have been signed on the other side of the Rhine. It was an armistice that killed the Lorraine offensive four days before it was born, an offensive that would have brought about 'that victory which was so much spoken about, as compensation for not having had it'. Anthoine accused Foch of being 'afraid' to continue operations because he (Foch) was under the influence of the British, Henry Wilson in particular, who were no longer interested in the fate of French territory.[52]

Such optimism about the Lorraine offensive (not to mention the idea that Foch was influenced by Wilson) does not ring true when the reason for Anthoine's removal as Pétain's chief of staff is recalled – namely, his persistent pessimistic remarks. Pedroncini does not mention this fact in his discussion of the 1918 armistice. Nor does he mention the single most important fact about Anthoine's 'deposition': its date. He signed it: '11 November 1940, 22 years afterwards'. That is to say, he signed it on the anniversary of Armistice Day, following the 1940 Armistice. These two circumstances render his evidence unreliable.

Indeed, there is no evidence to suggest that Pétain put up any resistance to drawing up an armistice when he, Foch and Clemenceau met privately

---

[49] Foch, *Mémoires*, 2: 264.

[50] Pedroncini. 'L'Armistice du 11 novembre 1918'; letter, Foch to Révérend Père Foch, 21 November 1918, in private hands.

[51] Brugère, *Veni, Vidi, Vichy*, 48–9. The author is the son of the general whose diaries are quoted above.

[52] 'Ma déposition au sujet de ce qu'il m'a été donné de voir directement pendant 14–18', ms. 5394, Bibliothèque de l'Institut, reprinted in *Guerres mondiales et conflits contemporains* 156 (October 1989), 105–7.

on 24 October to discuss terms. Neither Haig's nor Pershing's diary makes mention of any doubts on the part of Pétain. On the contrary, Haig records that Pétain suggested an indemnity so large that Germany would never be able to pay it hence French troops would garrison the Rhineland as a 'pledge' against payment.[53] So all that gives credibility to the judgement that the Armistice was premature is the fact of a second world war and the way the Armistice was twisted in Germany to suit the 'stab-in-the-back' legend. Foch cannot be blamed for lack of foresight. As Lowry put it colourfully: 'If the emperor and the German military chiefs had been stripped naked and loaded with chains while they personally signed an armistice, someone, sometime, would still claim betrayal, and others would believe him.'[54]

Pétain's 'objections' continued postwar. On 26 June 1929, three months after Foch's death, Mott interpreted for Pétain and Pershing when they met in Paris. Both generals claimed that they had no idea why they had been called to Senlis, that Clemenceau and Lloyd George had 'fixed up' the Armistice between them, and that Foch was merely following Clemenceau's instructions. 'We were two innocents who were taken in', Pétain said, complaining that neither he nor Pershing had been asked whether or not to grant an armistice. The German army had been given eight days in which to collect themselves together, instead of being obliged to leave all their equipment behind, with the result that they marched home 'as returning heroes, without any of the stigma of defeat'.[55] Clearly both men felt cheated, although by 1929 Weimar Germany's behaviour had probably sharpened their regrets.

What then was the reasoning behind Foch's decision to accept the possibility of ending the war by an armistice, rather than by a decisive battle? In order to answer that, it is necessary to analyse what Foch knew about the state of the armies, both Allied and enemy. Numerical superiority had swung the Allies' way by the time Foch had to consider his options at the end of October 1918. The number of German divisions calculated by the French intelligence service had dropped from 207 in July to 184 by the Armistice, of which seventeen were in reserve and only two of those were fresh.[56] Yet the number of divisions was only part of the equation. On 9 October Cointet began producing regular maps showing the state of those divisions by marking the fresh and the worn-out in different colours. The Germans had separated their good and bad divisions, Cointet recalled, and the bad ones simply got worse. This was why Foch had argued so energetically against any British ideas to create

[53] Haig diary, 25 October 1918.   [54] Lowry, *Armistice*, 165.
[55] 'The Armistice Terms', Mott mss, a 272–323.   [56] *Why Germany Capitulated*, 27.

second-class divisions with 'B' men.[57] In other respects, too, the number of divisions was misleading because none was at full strength. The earlier influenza epidemic had hit the tired and poorly fed German troops very hard, as deserters and prisoners informed their captors. Out of the 140 divisions engaged between July and November, thirty-five had lost 1–2000 men, captured as prisoners-of-war, and twenty-three had lost 2–3000 men – this in addition to battle casualties and sickness. On 1 October 1918 – when the total establishment of a German division was 11,643 – the *1 Guards Division* was down to about 720 men.[58] The army facing the Allied forces in October was a tenuous 'spider's web', as a member of Crown Prince Rupprecht's staff remarked, and Foch knew this from French and British assessments.[59]

Foch had information not only on numbers, but also on the morale of the German soldier. On 31 October an intelligence report confirmed that indiscipline and revolutionary ideas were making great progress in the German army. A trusted source stated that the poor army morale was the reason why their government requested an armistice. The numbers of German soldiers surrendering, sometimes in groups led by their officers, was an indisputable index of poor morale.[60] Against this, however, those German soldiers who remained in line were still putting up a highly effective resistance.

The state of German domestic morale was another factor in Foch's calculations. German newspapers were read in Switzerland or the Netherlands, and the information they contained was gathered as soon as it appeared and sent to Paris. Ludendorff's departure, for example, was reported on the front page of *Le Figaro* on 27 October, along with the call to continue the fight for an honourable peace for Germany. By war's end the network of Allied agents was large and well established. Intelligence was gathered from the Netherlands and from near the Swiss border, at Annemasse and Belfort, where listening stations to capture German radio transmissions were also set up. The French had intercepted, for example, the first German note to Wilson, sent through Switzerland, before it reached Washington. The French knew that the 'clearly revolutionary nature' of the Kiel insurrection among German sailors that began at the end of October had spread to many north German towns and even to Berlin; the intelligence that on 9 November Berlin was cut off from communications with the outside world and the Stock Exchange closed was reported the very next day.[61]

[57] Cointet memoirs, Cahier '1918', fos. 167–8.
[58] *Why Germany Capitulated*, 29, notes 1 and 2; *German Army Handbook 1918*, 34.
[59] Major Beck, cited in Deist, 'Military Collapse', 204.
[60] Morale report # 606, 31 October 1918, 7N 680; Watson, *Enduring the Great War*, ch. 6.
[61] 'Résumé des renseignements parvenus', # 616, 10 November, 15h., 7N 680.

The army general staff report, dated 30 October, that Foch received from the War Ministry summed up the situation. The signs of enemy weakening had increased during October with 'unprecedented suddenness and intensity' and 'unforeseen speed'. Although the German army remained standing, now without allies, the exhausted nation behind it could no longer offer support.[62] In Freiburg im Breisgau, just across the border from Alsace, where disaffection with the German administration had created an embittered population,[63] the town's morale degenerated markedly. In late August, there was the war's only strike; and soldiers were involved in looting and black marketeering. The garrison's jail could not hold all the military prisoners and there was unrest among soldiers convalescing in the town's hospitals. A virulent form of influenza swept through Freiburg in September, and a morale report of 18 October stated that a large proportion of the garrison had been acting 'oddly for weeks', swearing and agitating 'most repugnantly in public'.[64] Such public events could not have escaped the attention of intelligence gatherers. The *Vossiche Zeitung* was one of the important newspapers monitored regularly, therefore Walther Rathenau's call for 'an insurrection of the people' without delay that the newspaper published on 7 October did not escape attention, especially since Rathenau was a important industrialist with close connections to the German government.[65]

Foch had to balance all these encouraging signs against reports of front-line German troops showing every sign of being able to continue their methodical and destructive retreat. Both GHQ and GQG were aware of this. Haig heard from his XXII Corps commander, General Godley, that the enemy machinegunners were 'most capable' in defending their positions, and were fighting 'a very good rear guard action'. Despite GHQ's general staff comments on the seven days to 24 October – namely, much greater losses among the 'exhausted' enemy than in the BEF; the Belgian army fighting 'with much greater determination' than expected although American losses were heavy 'largely owing to inexperience'; the French, 'though tired', strongly in favour of continuing until 'decisive victory'[66] – Haig had had a sudden attack of 'pessimism'. In London the War Office still judged at the end of October that a German rout was unlikely.[67] At

---

[62] Etat-Major de l'Armée, 2e Bureau A, 'Situation militaire', 30 October 1918, ibid.

[63] Kramer, '*Wackes* at War', 120.   [64] Chickering, *Great War*, 554, 559, 561, 566.

[65] Cited in Geyer, 'Insurrectionary warfare', 459.

[66] Haig diary, 31 October 1918; 'Summary of the military situation in the various theatres of war for the seven days ending 24th October with comments by the General Staff', # 126, WO 106/319.

[67] Harris, *Haig*, 545; Beach, British Intelligence, 280–1; War Office, 'Appreciation of the situation', 30 October 1918, WO 158/85.

GQG Buat told Clark that an armistice was near, not because the enemy was beaten but because of the internal state of Germany. Furthermore Buat complained that Foch did not appreciate the real difficulties still facing the French army, because he did not have anyone on his staff with experience of commanding a large unit.[68] The fighting was fierce in the French First, Fifth and Tenth Armies, and their army group commander, General Fayolle, noted on 2 November that the 'Boche is still holding in front of us'. Herbillon reported to Poincaré that the struggle was not over and that the enemy was still resisting desperately.[69]

Reports of poor discipline, desertions, sickness and poor morale within Germany were at odds, therefore, with the experience of those still in the fight. This distinction between the *Frontkämpfer* and the demoralised rear units would carry over into the postwar revolution and Weimar Republic, creating a 'divided army'.[70] Foch had to juggle these conflicting impressions and judge between allowing the enemy the chance to regenerate its combat power for 1919 behind a shorter, more easily defensible line, and an early armistice in 1918, with the attendant risk that its terms would be rejected. In the event, he chose to offer the harsh terms of an early armistice.

If Foch had a very good idea from his intelligence services what the state of Germany was, both militarily and domestically, he also had to take into account the weapons at his disposal for finishing the war. On the Italian front, General Diaz had achieved a great victory against the disintegrating Austro-Hungarians, yet Foch knew that his urgings had not moved Diaz to attack. It was only the pressure from Orlando and Sonnino, who feared that they would be at a disadvantage in the forthcoming treaty negotiations, that forced Diaz to act. The Belgians were doing very well, but Foch had just had to deal with a recalcitrant Haig, who had demanded the return of his Second Army, the most effective part of the Flanders Army Group. As for the Americans, who now were making good progress, Foch knew how obstinate Pershing was, and Clemenceau had been making matters more difficult. Behind the American armies great logistical problems remained. The British had made it clear that they would not maintain the same number of divisions in 1919, and so the most effective force on the Western Front was a diminishing asset.

The French army itself was 'on its last legs'.[71] It had suffered huge casualties in the early years of the war, when it bore the brunt of the

[68] Clark report, # 233, 1 November 1918, RG 200, Entry 18; Buat diary, 28 October 1918, ms. 5391.
[69] Fayolle, *CS*, 309 (entry for 2 November 1918); Herbillon, *Du général*, 2: 335 (entry for 24 October 1918).
[70] Stephenson, *Final Battle*, ch. 1.   [71] Doughty, *PV*, 504.

fighting on the Western Front, and further huge casualties between March and July 1918 (a fact that Haig seemed unwilling to acknowledge). The total for deaths and prisoners (that is, excluding the wounded) in the French armies had already reached over a million by April 1916; by the beginning of 1918 that figure stood at 1,481,000. By July 1918 it had increased by almost 200,000 more. The total losses for June (81,000) were higher than for any single month of the 1916 battles at Verdun and on the Somme.[72] Although Foch resisted GQG's dissolution of divisions, he could not produce men where none existed, and his disapproval aggravated relations between Allied and French headquarters.[73] Nor was it simply a matter of men. The French had armed the Americans, supplying 75mm guns and heavy artillery as well – over 1800 of the former and about 1000 of the latter, with 10 million shells to fire from them. They supplied 57,000 machineguns, 240 tanks and well over 4000 aircraft.[74] All this was taken from equipment that would otherwise have gone to their own armies. Small wonder that Buat was driven to lament that he sometimes regretted that the Allied CinC was a Frenchman.[75]

Yet, despite being on its last legs, army morale remained high. Morale was rated 'very good' in, for example, General Debeney's First Army, operating on the right of the British. Although Fayolle criticised Debeney for making his attacks on the 'considerable' enemy forces too small and too complicated,[76] nonetheless the president of the postal control commission for First Army concluded, after an examination of almost 30,000 letters during the week 12–18 October, that confidence in victory was 'general' among the troops. They commented in their letters on the easy capture of prisoners, the enemy's depression and his difficulty in removing heavy guns and materiel. The sight of the destruction caused by the retreating enemy caused anger and a desire for vengeance. Most writers mentioned the Armistice, of course, hoping that the end would be reached by Christmas, although a 'good number' were minded to continue operations until the enemy declared himself beaten.[77] Alongside such positive attitudes, however, existed the natural fear of becoming one of the war's last casualties, and Fayolle wondered whether weaker French attacks were the reason for the enemy's steadfastness. After noting the Kaiser's abdication he wrote: 'I fear lest they [the French] leave the field which they

---

[72] 'Pertes des armées françaises', in Guinard, Devos and Nicot, *Inventaire: Introduction*, 213.
[73] Buat diary, 14 October 1918, ms. 5391.
[74] Table in Kaspi, *Temps des Américains*, 243. I have rounded the figures from the four sets there presented.
[75] Buat diary, 19 August 1918, ms. 5391.
[76] Fayolle, *CS*, 305 (entry for 17 October 1918).
[77] First Army, Rapport d'ensemble for week of 12–18 October 1918, 16N 1390.

have fertilised with their blood at the moment of reaping the harvest.'[78] A study of soldiers' letters concluded that the majority of French soldiers accepted the idea of an armistice, but with solid guarantees as to the peace, while a minority wanted an immediate armistice to put an end to the brutality, and another minority wished to keep on fighting until the enemy was crushed totally.[79] Doughty's study of French morale reports indicates that the 'bitter-ender' minority may have been even smaller.[80]

Hence, as weapons against a demoralised enemy who was still fighting hard, Foch had: exhausted but confident French, reluctant British and inexperienced Americans. The Belgians had probably achieved as much as they could after King Albert re-entered Bruges, dismayed to hear as many acclamations for the French troops as for himself.[81] Diaz had already proved a master of evasion and, once the armistice terms that he handed over to the Austro-Hungarians at Villa Giusti were accepted and the Armistice came into force on 4 November, Foch could not expect much more from that front.

One other factor played a part which has sometimes been discounted. Although improvement in the performance of Pershing and the AEF might be expected in 1919, the value of this improvement was an unknown quantity; but the views of the American President were known. Clemenceau and Foch feared that a continuation of the war might increase Woodrow Wilson's influence to the point where France's war aims might be put in jeopardy. In June 1928 Foch admitted to Leo Kennedy, a leader writer for *The Times*, that one of the reasons for ending the war in 1918 was that, if it had continued, leadership of the war would pass to the Americans. Kennedy was interviewing Foch for an article to be published on the tenth anniversary of the 1918 victory, but Foch asked that his words about the Americans not be reproduced. Foch went on to say that he had done the European governments a service by preventing the American take-over, and he knew that Pershing had not been 'pleased that the war came to an end when it did'.[82]

Nonetheless, in the face of all these pros and cons, preparations continued for further operations against the possibility of Germany's refusal of terms. The first concerned the Italians, and was requested by the SWC. It involved an invasion of southern Germany through Austria, after the formation of a group of three armies (thirty to forty divisions), including the British and French divisions currently in Italy (they had played an

[78] Fayolle, *CS*, 309 (entry for 2 November 1918).
[79] Nicot, *Les Poilus ont la parole*, 512–39.
[80] Doughty, 'France and the Armistice of 1918', 5.   [81] Thielemans, 'Le Roi Albert', 110.
[82] Kennedy diaries, 11 June 1928.

important part in the victory of Vittorio Veneto) and also the Czech divisions, whose formation Foch had fostered. The whole was to be commanded by Diaz under Foch's 'strategic direction'. The aim was to defend against any (unlikely) invasion by Germany, to prevent oil or coal reaching Germany, and to establish airfields for long-range bombing of German towns, even Berlin. The railway capacity between Italy and Austria had been calculated, hence the time needed for concentration of the armies. However, given the weather at that time of year and the multi-national nature of the force, it seems unlikely that Foch had much faith in the scheme worked out in conjunction with General Wilson and the Italian and American PMRs, Generals di Robilant and Bliss.[83] Wilson and Foch also discussed privately the use of Franchet d'Espèrey's Salonika army, agreeing that most of it would be required to garrison Serbia, Bulgaria and Turkey. They also agreed that they opposed occupying any Austro-Hungarian territory unless directly concerned with the lines of communication for the operation against Bavaria.[84]

These operations were very much 'just in case' and unlikely to be carried out, but one Western Front operation remained on the cards. This was the Lorraine offensive, whose cancellation reputedly caused Pétain so much pain. It had existed as a project since 7 September, but received Foch's approval only on 20 October. Pétain envisaged employing Castelnau's unused Eastern Army Group, and had been in correspondence with him throughout September and early October over the resources to be devoted to a sixty-kilometre-wide attack with thirty divisions. The aim was to threaten German communications, and capture (with French troops) some German territory as a bargaining chip for the peace negotiations. Cointet had pointed out how the Franco-American advance towards Mézières so threatened the German communications that the enemy would be unable to move troops quickly between the eastern part of the front in Lorraine and the western. Moreover, there were so few enemy troops in the east that the Allies would have a huge numerical superiority. Cointet's argument prevailed and only one day after Foch's directive of 19 October maintained his convergent strategy, Foch gave Pétain the go-ahead. Pétain had already warned Castelnau to be ready, calculating that given the 'transport crisis' it would require three weeks to assemble all the troops for the operation. In addition to twenty-two infantry and three cavalry divisions, Pétain promised 600 tanks, 1200 aircraft and 600 batteries of artillery. Pétain had asked for ten to twelve

[83] 'Operations against Germany through Austria', Annex A to IC 93, 4 November 1918, CAB 28/5.
[84] Wilson diary, 4 November 1918.

US divisions to join Mangin, but Foch replied that that was impossible, and suggested six to eight. Against Duke Albrecht of Württemberg's six tired divisions, three of them *Landwehr* territorials, the Allies had a crushing superiority.[85]

The three weeks' forewarning explains why the operation never took place. Tenth Army and its commander General Mangin had arrived in Lorraine, and Castelnau had ordered him to begin operations on 14 November, but the Armistice was signed before it could take place. Ever since some have argued that an opportunity was lost to inflict a decisive defeat on the German army. Yet it requires a great leap of faith even to assume that the Lorraine operation would have been successful, let alone that it would have had the supposed effect. First, only a few enemy divisions faced the Lorraine force, and they would have pulled back as the Allies advanced, destroying infrastructure as they went. Given the season and the short days, the advance would have petered out in the difficult terrain. Foch knew the terrain because he had been there in 1914, when his XX Corps advanced to Morhange and then was compelled to retreat, and again in 1917 when he was in temporary command of the Eastern Army Group. Second, Foch was not to blame for the inability to get the offensive launched before the Armistice was signed. The DGCRA required twenty-two days after the 27th to complete the transportation, although Foch wanted the attack to start no later than 31 October. The annexes to Pétain's report on the 1918 operations reveal the logistical difficulties (a further reason to discount Pétain's arguments about a 'premature' armistice).[86] At the beginning of November the Allies had to struggle with 2900 kilometres of destroyed or damaged railway tracks, 1383 bridges that had been blown up, and 3180 kilometres of unusable telegraph and telephone lines.[87] The head of the DGCRA had never refused any demand for rail transport during the general offensive, even when it could be avoided, although he always warned that the rope was stretched thin. By the end of October the rope had broken, as Cointet realised when he produced a study of the military railways for Pétain after the war.[88] At the time he had not appreciated the depth of the transport crisis, and this failure explains his 'profound disappointment' and 'grave concern' for the future when he heard that the Germans would sign the armistice.[89]

---

[85] Pedroncini, *Pétain Général*, 426–7; Pétain, *Rapport sur les opérations: Campagne offensive*, pt 6, *Préparation d'une offensive en Lorraine*, annexes 799, 800, 820; Gras, *Castelnau*, 380–1; Cointet memoirs, Cahier '1918', fos. 184–6.

[86] Pétain, *Rapport sur les opérations: Campagne offensive*, pt 6.

[87] *AFGG* 11, 754–5.   [88] Cointet memoirs, Cahier '1918', fos. 186–7.

[89] Ibid., fo. 179 (9 November 1918).

In 1928 Cointet asked Weygand why Foch had delayed authorising the offensive. Weygand replied that Foch did not want 'disconnected' attacks, but only an operation to extend the Meuse/Moselle offensive. Only when this became impossible did he authorise the Lorraine offensive. Weygand confirmed in his memoirs that Foch was determined that no action should take place east of the Meuse until French Fourth and US First Armies were firmly on the way to taking Mézières.[90]

Finally, neither Pershing's cooperation nor Pétain's sense of urgency could be relied upon. Pershing became angry once again at being asked to supply some of his divisions to an essentially French operation. Despite his 1 and 2 US Divisions having done very well under Mangin's command on 18 July, he tried to insist that his six divisions loaned to Mangin operate as an army, and was still arguing the point on 8 November.[91] Nor was Pétain the general to push on rapidly. As noted in the previous chapter, Foch had sent him a scathing letter on 4 October about taking firm control of his subordinates; on 5 November he invited him to begin the attack as soon as possible, without waiting for all the troops to be concentrated, since speed was more important than numbers.[92] Hence it is highly likely that the Allies reached the Rhine more quickly with Foch's armistice than they would have done with Pétain's Lorraine offensive. Even if the Franco-American forces had reached the important Longuyon rail junction, seventy kilometres northwest of Metz, it was a further 200 or so kilometres to the Rhine.

In summary, Foch knew exactly what he wanted from any armistice: the Rhine frontier. On 27 October the notes from the information section of GQG's 2e Bureau stated that Foch had made a 'solemn engagement': 'We are not yet at the Rhine, but we will get there.'[93] Next, the decision that the German request be taken seriously, despite the fears that it was merely a stalling tactic, was taken by the politicians, and Foch's responsibility was to coordinate the settlement of terms. He did not have to decide whether an armistice should be offered, only the terms of that offer. Third, his terms were sufficiently severe to ensure that Germany could not resume hostilities, and they were accepted by all the Allies, including President Wilson. The severity of those terms meant that there was a risk that they might be rejected, but Foch was confident that Germany was beaten. Hence he calculated that the risk that rejection might mean more fighting in 1919 against a somewhat restored enemy was worth taking for the

---

[90] Ibid., fo. 198; Weygand, *IV*, 625–6.   [91] Mott diary, 8 November 1918.
[92] GQGA JMO, 5 November 1918, 26N 1; Gras, *Castelnau*, 381; Mordacq, *MC*, 3: 321.
[93] 'Considérations générales sur la situation actuelle', fo. 7, 16N 1616, [d] Armées allemande et autrichienne.

potential gains from acceptance. He could not lose. Fourth, Foch continued urging his generals to be ready to fight on, should that prove necessary. Finally, the Lorraine offensive was unlikely to have made much difference – the logistical problems were so great that, even if it had proved possible to launch it before the end of November, its effects would have been minor. In any case, once the politicians had decided that an armistice would be offered and once Germany had accepted the offered terms, the idea that the signature could then be delayed in order to allow Pétain to launch his offensive is preposterous. Since the Armistice gave France the Rhine frontier with bridgeheads on the eastern bank more speedily than the Lorraine offensive could have done, the saving in lives was a clinching factor.

Mordacq believed that Foch's Christianity was at the root of his refusal to shed more blood than was necessary. Rather than simple humanity, Liddell Hart suggests that Foch was animated by blind faith: Foch was 'coming to realise ... that the prospects of his offensive were waning and the enemy slipping out of reach', although his 'conviction of what was necessary and his hope of new developments ... combined to reinforce his faith'.[94] This is to make a thoughtless gambler out of Foch, rather than a calculated risk taker. After the risk had paid off, however, regrets were expressed very early that, harsh as it was, the Armistice might have been too lenient. The First Lord of the Admiralty wrote on 12 November, the day after the signing: 'Had we known how bad things were in Germany, we might have got stiffer terms.' Clemenceau expressed the same sentiment to the Senate Army Commission.[95] In January 1919, a pamphlet was produced by the French general staff and translated into English, insisting that Germany had been defeated. The preface (unsigned, but attributed in the German translations to Foch himself) referred to a German press call to the Rhenish provinces to 'give a warm welcome home to the German armies "who, after four years of incessant fighting, were about to return, undefeated and with heads held high, to their native land"'.[96] It may well be that the fierce struggle Foch put up to retain the Rhine frontier during the peace negotiations in 1919 derived from a lurking fear that he might not have done enough in November 1918.

[94] Liddell Hart, *Foch*, 398.   [95] French, 'Had We Known', 86.
[96] *Why Germany Capitulated*, 3.

18   Losing the peace

On 4 December 1918 Foch noted: 'The war is not ended.' He suffered several defeats before the Treaty of Versailles was signed on 28 June, putting an end to the state of war which the Armistice had only suspended. Foch's role in the peace-making was restricted. Clemenceau kept him deliberately at arm's length from the political process by refusing to make him one of the French delegates to the peace conference, on the grounds that he represented the Allies and not France. Nonetheless Foch presided over the Permanent Armistice Commission that the Germans had requested as a means of communicating with the Allies, and the months following the Armistice were hugely important for Foch. He played a significant role in four areas of the peace-making: first, the military conditions involved in renewing the Armistices and in preparing contingency plans to restart hostilities, should the enemy refuse to sign; second, the question of disarmament and the treaty's military terms; third, the problem of Germany's eastern frontier, which involved questions of how to deal with Russia and Bolshevism, and how to create a strong *cordon sanitaire* in a revived Polish state and the successor states to the Austro-Hungarian empire; finally, and most importantly, the question of Germany's western border, which affected not only France's territorial security in the face of any further invasion, but also France's economic security in the face of the possibility of renewed German commercial success whilst French infrastructure (railways, coalmines and so on) remained devastated. It was the last question that haunted Foch and that caused the most friction with Clemenceau and the Allies.

Before negotiations began, however, there was a round of celebrations. Formal entries were made to the cities of the restored provinces: Metz and Strassburg, which became Strasbourg. Foch and Clemenceau were elected unanimously to the Académie Française. There were triumphal visits to Brussels and London. Haig refused to return to London for the latter occasion: 'I have no intention', he wrote in his diary, 'of taking part in any triumphal ride with Foch & a pack of foreigners through the streets of

495

London'.[1] There were other petty remarks during the celebrations. Mordacq had been advancing Pétain's claims to a marshal's baton for some time, and on 17 November Clemenceau told the President that Foch was eager for the honour to be given as soon as possible so that Pétain could enter Metz as a Marshal of France. At the ceremony on 8 December, when Poincaré presented Pétain with his baton, Weygand was overheard to mutter of the recipient: 'And to think we had to drag him here with kicks up the backside.'[2]

By 11 December Foch was in Trèves/Trier, the old Roman town on the Mosel, near to the Luxembourg border, to negotiate the renewal of the Armistice. However, the Germans were already very behindhand with the guns and railway materiel that the armistice terms demanded. Also Foch had had to complain to the German high command about looting and violence against civilians as the German troops retired, especially around Brussels.[3] Because at the next renewal he had to complain again about German slowness, Foch began to fear that within fifteen years or even sooner there would be a war of revenge, despite the German delegation being compliant and seemingly angry with the Kaiser and Berlin. His wife had already realised that the 'Germans do not appear to agree that they have been beaten; we did not take the war to their territory, so they are not defeated, they say'.[4]

Foch's fears were compounded when the peace conference convened on 18 January under Clemenceau's chairmanship. Foch insisted on attending the opening ceremony, despite Clemenceau's refusal to make him one of the French peace delegation. Foch became very impatient with what he perceived as lack of progress, since President Wilson insisted on the League of Nations being settled before proceeding to other matters. Foch feared that the Germans, too, might become impatient and refuse to sign the final peace treaty. In Foch's opinion, Clemenceau was not exercising sufficient control over the proceedings, which led to an angry exchange of words when Foch pointed out how difficult it was to deal with allies. Bitterly Foch wrote: 'I have to go to war to impose peace.'[5] He had thought that obtaining the Rhine frontier at the Armistice facilitated the settlement of peace terms, yet time was slipping away and the Germans were delaying carrying out the requirements of the Armistice. The politicians themselves recognised that the proceedings were too long

[1] Haig diary, 30 November 1918.   [2] Reynaud, *Au cœur de la mêlée*, 910.
[3] Weygand, *Mirages et réalités*, 11; message téléphoné, Foch to German high command, copied to Clemenceau, 14 November 1918, 6N 70, [d] 1.
[4] Foch, Carnets, 15 January 1919, fo. 350; Mme Foch diary, 24 January 1919.
[5] Foch, Carnets, 6 February 1919, fo. 354.

drawn out, and on 24 March they simplified them by acceding to Wilson's suggestion that the heads of government alone (Wilson, with Clemenceau, Lloyd George and Orlando) meet privately, thereby speeding things up. Informally known as the Council of Four, it became known less formally as the Big Four or 'les 4 Bigs'.

Foch suffered defeat after defeat during the peace negotiations. After negotiating the armistice renewals he had to prepare a military occupation in case the Germans refused to sign the peace treaty. On 10 May he presented a confident report to the Big Four: the Allies had at least forty infantry and five cavalry divisions that could be ready to move after a week's warning.[6] The strength of the German forces was nil, Foch claimed, and the Allies could occupy the Ruhr basin easily. Such a move would cut coal supplies immediately to the whole German rail network because the Ruhr was nothing more than 'a great railway interchange'.[7] Yet, six weeks later, when the fear that Germany might not sign had been increased by the German delegation's list of counter-proposals to the proposed treaty, Foch was less confident. On 16 June he told the Big Four that he could certainly march on Berlin with his (now) thirty-nine Allied divisions, but crossing 480 kilometres of hostile territory inhabited by a 65-million-strong population would not be easy. The politicians were angry. Lloyd George accused Foch of mixing policy with strategy because of the latter's proposal to solve the problem by separating the southern German states from the Prussian rump – an eminently sensible proposal given Germany's size – and told him that he should have asked for more resources back in May if he needed them.[8] Nevertheless, the necessary staff work on the logistics of a move into Germany was carried out at Foch's headquarters in Kreuznach, but fortunately the plans were not needed. The message went out to the various Allied headquarters at 20.25 on 28 June that the Germans had signed.[9] Foch had already left for Kreuznach on the 22nd, telling his wife that, unless that Germans were held 'with an iron fist', none of the clauses of the treaty would be executed.[10] His absence from the signing ceremony in the Galerie des Glaces was noted in the press and interpreted as a mark of his disfavour. Foch had no wish to be there. He wrote to his wife: 'Clemenceau understood that my presence in Versailles was pointless, and leaves me here. That's what

---

[6] Mantoux, *Council of Four*, 2: doc. LXXI.
[7] 'Prévisions sur la résistance que pourrait opposer l'Allemagne à une invasion des Alliés', 5 May 1918, 14N 50.
[8] Mantoux, *Council of Four*, 2: doc. CXXVII.
[9] All documents in Fonds Etat-Major Foch, 14N 49, [d] Opérations du printemps 1919.
[10] Mme Foch diary, 22 June 1919.

I wanted.'[11] The Entente's military leader was so out of favour with the politicians that he did not even attend the signing of the peace treaty.

The Big Four did not appear to have taken into consideration the fact that the demobilisation had reduced Foch's scope for manoeuvre in any resumption of hostilities. Although he knew that, temporarily at least, Germany's estimated 450,000 military troops were disorganised and disarmed, he had also lost the battle over the number and nature of the military forces that Germany was to be permitted by the treaty. Foch wanted to limit a future German army to 100,000, based on conscription, whereas the British favoured a 200,000-strong army of volunteers. Bliss was prepared to be even more generous: an army of 450,000 with an officer corps of 15,300. He wanted Germany to be strong enough to defend itself from Bolshevism, but also recommended banning private munitions production and the destruction of 'surplus' weapons.[12] Despite these differences, Foch's report on the proposed military, naval and air terms was handed to Clemenceau on 28 February and put up for discussion the next day. Amid protests that there had been no time to read, let alone digest, the lengthy document, discussion was postponed to 3 March and then again to the 6th. The British Foreign Secretary was dismayed by what he regarded as 'an attempt to induce the Conference to swallow whole the Military proposals for Peace which most of us had seen for the first time that morning'. Balfour thought that Foch was pressuring the meeting when he announced that the rate of demobilisation made the Allied armies 'incapable of effective action in Germany'.[13] Balfour was right, for apparently Foch was attempting to rush through his own proposals. According to the director of the influential *Journal des débats*, Foch had presented them very badly, and answered questions in such an unsatisfactory manner that Balfour refused to accept them. The same source reports that it was at this point that relations between Foch and Clemenceau degenerated markedly, with the Premier tending to the British point of view.[14]

On 7 March Lloyd George intervened with a resolution which would form the basis of the final military terms: voluntary service for German naval, military and air forces, not to exceed 10,000 naval and 200,000 airmen and military, with a minimum period of service of twelve years. This was accepted, but threw Foch's terms back into the melting pot because he wanted a smaller army and conscription, and the air

---

[11] Mme Foch diary, 28 June 1919.   [12] Schwabe, *Wilson and Peacemaking*, 225.

[13] Balfour, 'Notes on the Military Peace Proposals', 5 May [sic, sc. March 1919], FO 800/216.

[14] Correspondence of the Comte de Nalèche, 4 and 7 March 1919, cited in Miquel, *La Paix de Versailles*, 255 n. 1; 257 n. 3.

commission had recommended that Germany be forbidden to have an air force at all. Foch argued that a voluntary army would give Germany a solid core of trained officers and NCOs capable of producing a huge offensive weapon very quickly, especially given the disciplined nature and military inclinations of the general German population and the prevalence of sporting clubs for the young. He insisted that the officer *cadre* was the most important element of an army, since there was more to fear from an army of donkeys led by lions, than from an army of lions led by donkeys.[15]

So, after an altercation with Clemenceau over Lloyd George's resolution, Foch was obliged to re-draft the terms. In the end, they were agreed on 17 March. They retained the voluntary principle and proposed the figure of 140,000 men, but privately Clemenceau, Lloyd George and House agreed to reduce this to 100,000. Hence, as Wilson put it, 'I got my principle but not my numbers, and Foch got his numbers but not his principle. An amazing state of affairs.'[16] The disagreement was kept out of the press, with Clemenceau's (former) newspaper, *L'Homme Libre*, going so far as to report on 17 March that the council had ratified the proposals of the military experts, completely passing over Marshal Foch's role.[17]

As for arming the permitted German army, Foch had rejected its total disarmament as an armistice condition for two reasons. First, it would be impossible to police the surrender of all the weaponry as the German troops returned home; secondly, Germany's natural resources were great, its factories undamaged and its population much larger than France's, so replacements of a better quality could be forged very quickly and, if necessary, in secret. There was little point in imposing a sanction that could not be policed. As he told Henry Wilson, the Allies could 'no more limit the number of men trained to arms in Germany than the Germans could limit the output of coal in England'.[18] More importantly, however, Foch did not want total disarmament because of the Bolshevist threat. For that reason, German troops had remained in the Ukraine at the Armistice until Allied troops could take over.

The Bolshevist threat hung over the settlement of Germany's eastern frontier, a restored Poland and the new successor states to the Austro-Hungarian empire. Once again, Foch suffered a defeat as he was kept out of these discussions. His only role came in the question of returning Polish troops from France to Poland when the Germans refused to allow them passage through the German (for the time being) port of Danzig.

[15] Weygand, *Foch*, 288.   [16] Wilson diary in Callwell, *Wilson*, 2: 173.
[17] Miquel, *La Paix de Versailles*, 262.
[18] Wilson diary, 26 January 1919, in Callwell, *Wilson*, 2: 166.

On 29 March the Big Four asked Foch to negotiate a solution with the leader of the German armistice delegation, Erzberger. President Wilson added that the council 'invite[d] Marshal Foch in a friendly way to be a diplomat rather than a soldier – as far as possible'.[19] Henry Wilson, who was sitting next to Foch in the meeting, recorded Foch's reaction to this invitation: 'The old boy's face was a study, and he put his hand up to his mouth and said in an audible whisper to me ... *Ce n'est pas commode, Henri!*'[20] Foch managed to reach a compromise with Erzberger, probably helped by their prior agreement about the political dangers of Bolshevism. On his return, Foch presented his report and Lloyd George commented (no doubt ironically): 'I believe Marshal Foch has established his qualifications as a great diplomat. We should congratulate him on his skill and success.'[21] Foch himself appears to have been satisfied with what he had learned. 'Germany will not go Bolshevik', he wrote on 4 April, 'it will not go to pieces, despite the revolution, because of the strength of its administration'.[22]

Foch's greatest defeat came over Germany's western frontier and the status of the Rhineland. He had obtained strategic bridgeheads on the east bank of the Rhine as part of the Armistice, and on 25 November 1918 wrote a note for Clemenceau about the Rhine as the 'natural barrier' against France's bellicose and envious neighbour. Foch had considerable support from Poincaré, the French Foreign Ministry, the press and public opinion generally for his stance. Indeed, Clemenceau accepted as an official French war aim Foch's note advocating autonomy for the Rhineland and retention of bridgeheads on the right bank until the provisions of the peace treaty were carried out. Foch argued the case in London, as Clemenceau's proxy. Although Clemenceau was in London at the same time, he left Foch to present the case alone in 10 Downing Street, probably in order to test the waters. The waters proved chilly. To Lloyd George's comment that the Rhinelanders might not like being disposed of by the Allies and might come to constitute another Alsace-Lorraine in reverse, Foch responded that the Allies would conciliate their feelings and woo them with economic advantages. Bonar Law's comment that Germany had said the same thing in 1870 and that the British had been trying for years to conciliate the Irish remained unanswered.[23]

---

[19] Mantoux, *Council of Four*, 1: 73.
[20] 'That's asking a lot!': Wilson diary, 29 March 1919, in Callwell, *Wilson*, 2: 177.
[21] Mantoux, *Council of Four*, 1: doc. XXIII; Hankey, *Supreme Control*, 115.
[22] Foch, Carnets, 4 April 1919, fo. 370.
[23] 'Notes of a conversation at 10 Downing Street, 1 December 1918', IC 97, CAB 28/5.

The French view of the Rhine frontier was solidified in early January. Foch prepared another note, dated 10 January, re-stating his view that France's security demanded that Germany's military frontier in the west be the Rhine. Clemenceau gave André Tardieu, one of the French peace commissioners, the task of preparing the official statement of France's position based on Foch's note. Hence there was no discord between Clemenceau and Foch at this point, and Clemenceau suggested that Tardieu's mémoire might present additional arguments to counter those that he foresaw the Allies raising.[24] It is likely, therefore, that he utilised Foch's testing of the waters in London in order to strengthen the final statement of France's position on the status of the left bank of the Rhine. Indeed, Tardieu's papers in the Foreign Ministry archives reveal that he and Foch worked together on this final statement. The two men knew each other from before the war; Tardieu had been on Foch's staff in 1914, and he had been France's High Commissioner for American affairs, hence in frequent contact with Foch in 1917 and 1918. His papers contain a copy of a Foch draft of his note, dated 5 January, and a copy of Foch's final version, annotated 'Note before modification'.[25] Clearly there was agreement and collaboration between the military and diplomatic elements developing France's Rhineland policy.

When it became clear in March that neither Lloyd George nor Wilson would accept that French policy, the Foch–Clemenceau relationship broke down. Clemenceau accepted the US–British offer of a military guarantee to come to France's aid in case of any German aggression, in return for abandoning the Rhine frontier. It was agreed that there should be a permanently demilitarised zone of fifty kilometres on the right bank, but only an occupation of fifteen years at the Mainz bridgehead, ten years at the Koblenz and five years at the Köln bridgeheads. Clemenceau gave away permanent control of or influence over the left bank in return for a guarantee (which, as it happened, would not be ratified) of military aid if needed against aggression. He had exchanged geographical security for security dependent upon the time taken for any British or American army to reach France. The arrangement had one saving grace: if Germany defaulted on any of the treaty terms such as reparations, then the Rhineland occupation would be continued, or re-started if evacuation had already occurred. Evidently Clemenceau expected such a default. In the Conseil des ministres on 25 April, Clemenceau predicted: 'Germany will go bankrupt and we shall stay where we are, plus the

---

[24] Tardieu, *La Paix*, 164.
[25] Tardieu mss, PA-AP 166, vol. 422, Rive Gauche du Rhin I, folder 'j'.

alliance. Take note, so that you can remind me of that on my tombstone after my death.'[26]

However, Foch could see no saving graces. Clemenceau called Foch in to tell him about the Anglo-American offer on 16 March, before the final agreement was reached. Foch was already angry over Clemenceau's handling of the peace conference, over the lack of progress on the Russian question, and over opposition to his proposed military terms for the peace treaty, and this news was the final straw. It was letting go of the prey for its shadow, he told Clemenceau. Even if the Anglo-American guarantee were honoured, the French would be in the same position that they were in in August 1914, obliged to wait for the military assistance to arrive. When Clemenceau asked whether Foch was breaking with him over the matter, Foch replied that he never broke with anyone: 'You have modified your line of action; I believe that the one we were following is the right one; I'm sticking to it.'[27]

In order to promote the line to which he was sticking, Foch employed several different tactics. He tried to persuade influential people such as Britain's Lord Robert Cecil and Henry Wilson, and Marshal Joffre and even Poincaré to support his point of view; he invoked the help of parliamentarians and the press to publish his views. He tried his own eloquence when he addressed the Conseil des ministres and the Big Four directly. He tried obstruction when he refused to transmit Clemenceau's telegram summoning the German delegates to Versailles. President Wilson was outraged by what he termed Foch's 'rebellion'. He told his Secretary of State that, if he were Clemenceau, he would not allow Foch another opportunity to refuse to have anything to do with the treaty because it did not cede the left bank of the Rhine to France. Lansing recognised, however, that Clemenceau would not break with his military: 'He will undoubtedly make terms with the military crowd and Weygand with his black portfolio and immobile countenance will continue to create situations which require the use of military forces.'[28] Foch's final tactic was a threat to resign, not carried out. All these tactics were in vain, but Foch's tenacity demands admiration!

In his final unannounced appeal to the plenary session of the SWC on 6 May, when Tardieu read out a summary of the treaty's clauses (because there were not enough copies to go round), Foch gave his 'observations' on what he admitted were rumours because he had not yet seen the draft

[26] Private notes made by Jules Jeanneney, Under-Secretary of State for War, supplied to Bariéty and cited in his *Relations franco-allemandes*, 62.
[27] Weygand, *Mirages et réalités*, 39.
[28] Lansing memorandum, 19 April 1919, in Link (ed.), *PWW*, 57: 494.

treaty text. From the military point of view, Foch declared, the five–ten–
fifteen years' occupation was 'worthless', and asked who would be judge
of the 'desirability' of re-occupation if, at the end of the period, the
reparations had not been paid. To illustrate his view of the defensive
barrier, Foch used a metaphor: pointing to the conference room doors,
he said that those present could defend themselves by barricading the
doors, but, if the doors were removed, they had no defence against an
intruder. He ended with this appeal:

> Please to note that I asked that the occupation of the Rhine should be maintained,
> and not that of the Rhineland; that is the point on which our opinions differ . . .
> These are the principal remarks to which I draw your attention; I ask that they
> should be taken into consideration and that account should be taken of my state-
> ment, for I cannot let these provisions pass.[29]

The British delegation agreed that Foch had made his appeal 'clearly
and with dignity'; Hankey thought Foch's criticisms 'devastating'.[30]
Afterwards Foch told Clemenceau that he had spoken so as to be easy in
his conscience. He was satisfied that now an official record existed of his
formal disagreement with the treaty's military terms. (No minutes were
taken at Big Four meetings.) Clemenceau was furious at Foch's behaviour. 'You think the whole world revolves around you', Clemenceau told
him; 'that was the case during the war, but it's all over now'.[31] So finally,
the next day, the peace terms were handed over, without having been read
in their entirety by their authors. 'I don't think in all history this can be
matched', mused Henry Wilson.[32] Foch had received no uncertain lesson
about the primacy of the political over the military, and the relationship
with Clemenceau never mended. On 7 May many newspapers appeared
with large blanks; they had received the formal order that no reference was
to be made to Foch. The direct order from Clemenceau's office was 'no
résumé of the treaty; no reference to Foch'.[33]

American historian J. C. King saw Foch's actions during the seven and
a half months between 11 November 1918 and 28 June 1919 (the Treaty
of Versailles was signed on the fifth anniversary of the assassination in
Sarajevo) almost as insubordination verging on treachery, as a straight
fight between the military and the civilian power. Since there could be no
question that it was the civilian politicians who should forge the peace,

[29] Plenary Session, 6 May 1919, Protocol # 6, *FRUS, PPC*, 3: 333–90, at pp. 387, 386.
[30] Wilson diary, 6 May 1919, in Callwell, *Wilson*, 190; Hankey, *Supreme Control*, 147.
[31] Weygand, *Mirages et réalités*, 53; Mme Foch diary, 7 May 1919.
[32] Wilson diary, 5 May 1919, in Callwell, *Wilson*, 2: 189.
[33] Berger and Allard, *Dessous du traité*, 173, 176.

King could only condemn Foch's 'impeccable patriotism but dubious wisdom'.[34] King believed also that, had Foch prevailed over the Rhineland, France would have been left alone in Europe to face a vengeful Germany; whereas Clemenceau's peace gave France allies, despite the fact that the military guarantee they promised amounted to nothing when the US Senate rejected the peace treaty and Lloyd George rejected the military guarantee. Yet Foch had recognised the military guarantee's fragility and limitations. On the very day of the signing in Versailles, Foch noted that there was no peace – because no frontier, and inadequate reparations lacking guarantees – and no treaty: it solved nothing, did not prevent further Allied demobilisation, and it ruined France, putting the country at the mercy of its allies.[35]

In Foch's defence, his patriotism, courage and energy were undiminished as he fought for France's postwar security just as he had fought in 1918 to defend its territory. His sole wish was that France should not squander the fruits of victory.[36] However, Clemenceau feared a military *coup* and excluded him deliberately from the proceedings. This could only have been hurtful to the man whom he had placed in supreme command a year earlier. Indeed, Clemenceau was deliberately offensive on occasion, telling Foch that he was no longer the centre of attention. Rather more tact and understanding on Clemenceau's part might have avoided some of the unpleasantness. Moreover, less rigidity on Clemenceau's part might have enabled a better use of Foch's eloquence. Hankey (a good judge) remarked how well Foch presented his case to the SWC on 6 May, when it was too late to make any difference; hence Foch's inclusion in the talks at an earlier stage might have obtained 'better' terms (from the French point of view) for France's security in the east against Germany. King concentrates on the Rhineland question, but Foch was excluded from all non-military discussions, and his views in the commission (which he chaired) dealing with the treaty's military terms were overruled. Clemenceau excluded not only Foch, but also the parliament and Poincaré. This was counter-productive, because the resentment created by such exclusion would make any attempt at a military *coup* all the more likely to succeed.

The most effective defence of Foch lies in the fact that there was never any attempt at such a *coup*. Despite much popular support for his stance over the Rhineland, especially among right-wing and nationalist circles, and despite being buttressed by his military prestige, Foch gave no hint that he ever contemplated such a move. It would have been totally out of

[34] King, *Foch versus Clemenceau*, 1.   [35] Foch, Carnets, 28 June 1919, fo. 392.
[36] See Mme Foch diary, 2 and 5 February, 2 April 1919.

character, and the closest he came to it was to discuss a joint resignation with Poincaré.[37] Neither man was prepared, however, to risk a political crisis by taking that dangerous step. King's indignation at Foch's behaviour is misplaced. If Foch had 'cultivated' Clemenceau early in the war as the strongest supporter of his views on how to win the war, the legalistic Poincaré was a weaker ally as he had neither Clemenceau's strength of character nor his political power. Moreover Clemenceau used Foch as a proxy to give an airing to views that Clemenceau knew were unacceptable to the Allies; and he always cited Foch's great service in 1918 as the excuse for his not sacking his troublesome marshal. Besides, Clemenceau might have needed Foch's services once again, if Germany refused to sign the peace treaty and hostilities began again. This was why the Generalissimo was never sacked.

On the other hand, Foch was clearly hitting his head against a brick wall. Clemenceau achieved the best terms that Wilson and Lloyd George were prepared to concede. If Foch had been included, rather than excluded, from the process, he might have managed to accept the inevitable. Neither was holding the Rhine necessarily a guarantee of security. Clemenceau had a study made of the value of rivers as defensive lines; and clearly the growth of military aviation during the war had reduced the value of rivers, even one as wide as the Rhine.[38] The Aisne had not prevented the Germans from breaking through on the Chemin des Dames in May 1918. Yet Foch's concern was to buy time and to prevent the loss of France's valuable metallurgical resources and industries, which were clustered in northeastern France. The Rhine frontier would give the French time in any future war to secure these resources, which they had lost early in 1914 because of their close proximity to the border. His clarity of vision had not deserted him entirely. Britain's security depended on that of France. In an interview with the *Daily Mail* he had warned presciently: 'Next time the Germans will make no mistake. They will break through into Northern France and will seize the Channel ports as a base of operations against England.' In his notebooks, on 18 April, during the agitated days when the Rhine frontier was being settled, Foch wrote: 'Shall we make of France an accursed country, which after losing 1,500,000 men in 1914 will be obliged soon to begin again, so that the women who gave their husbands in 1914 will have to give their sons in the next war?'[39] (See Illustration 14.)

---

[37] Poincaré, *AS*, 11: 390 (entry for 2 May 1919); Mordacq, *MC*, 3: 258 (entry for 4, 5, 6, May 1919); Mme Foch diary, 4 May 1919.

[38] Ministère de la Guerre, 'Valeur Stratégique des rivières', 14 April 1919, 6N 73.

[39] *Daily Mail*, 18 April 1919; Foch, Carnets, 18 April 1919, fo. 376.

THE TIGER: "Curious! I seem to hear a child weeping!"

Illustration 14 Peace and future cannon fodder
Will Dyson's cartoon, published in the *Daily Herald* on 17 May 1919, reflects Foch's fears for the future. As the delegates leave the peace conference, led by Presidents Clemenceau and Wilson, a child who will grow up to become part of the 'Class of 1940' is heard weeping.

Lansing commented on the absence of both Foch and Poincaré on 28 June. He guessed that protocol would have made the President's presence difficult; furthermore, he and Clemenceau detested each other. As for Foch, Lansing judged that his absence signified disapproval of the treaty. Lansing mentioned Foch's 'bitter' address to the SWC on 6 May, and continued: 'Having taken this radical position, to which little or no attention was paid by anybody, he [Foch] would have been in rather an humiliating position if he had sanctioned by his presence the celebration of a treaty to which he had so unequivocally objected. His absence, however, caused general remark, astonishment and regret.'[40] His absence, after more than four years of war, was indeed astonishing and a matter for regret.

---

[40] Memorandum by the Secy of State: 'The signing of the Treaty of Peace with Germany at Versailles on June 28th, 1919', *FRUS, PPC*, 11: 602.

End of Part II

In conclusion: 'Supreme command is less than people think'

The postwar damage to Foch's reputation among the Allies shows how little real understanding there was of Foch's achievements and, more generally, of the role of supreme commander. There was no body of dispatches, no battle plans, no series of orders to Allied commanders to show what Foch had done as Allied commander-in-chief. His 1918 'directives' are merely generalities. His methods – tact and diplomacy – proved ineffective in preserving his achievements for posterity. The damage began with Foch's attempts to enshrine the Rhine frontier in France's security arrangements in the peace treaty; his failure to influence either the treaty or the postwar defence debates reflects the limits on the supreme command.

Foch never ceased his criticisms of the Versailles treaty. On 18 December 1921, returning to France from America, Foch gave an interview to French journalist Stéphane Lauzanne, who cited him as saying: 'The treaty is a bad treaty, bad because it does not give to France its guarantees of security and its guarantees of payment ... I said it, and repeated it, but no one listened.' A few days later, the *New York Times* reported the attempts to hose down reaction to this interview when Foch reached France: 'the Marshal's words and allusions had been incorrectly interpreted and ... what he had said about M. Clemenceau deserving to be hauled before a high court was in the nature of a joke'.[1]

The fight continued even post mortem. Foch had spoken freely, perhaps too freely, to another journalist, Raymond Recouly, in a series of interviews during the decade between the signing of the treaty and Foch's death on 20 March 1929. They met twice monthly on average, and the journalist recorded the salient points of their discussions, which returned frequently to the same themes. His manuscript was prepared for publication and, significantly, Foch made some revisions himself. Then the 1926 financial crisis caused Foch to advise against immediate publication, and so it was not until after his death that the work appeared as a collection of

---

[1] *Le Matin*, 19 December 1921; *New York Times*, 22 December 1921.

the Marshal's views on various topics. The largest section, entitled 'Le Drame du traité de paix', ends with Foch's conclusion that 'not one step' had been taken towards the solution to France's security problem.[2] It was translated into English and the German translation is frequently cited, erroneously, as being Foch's memoirs. To judge by the number of second-hand copies on the bouquinistes' stalls in Paris, *Le Mémorial de Foch* was printed in very large numbers.

The publication galvanised Clemenceau into writing a response. He had not intended to write his memoirs, but he could not help responding to the soldier's Parthian shot. He produced a vigorous first draft, but died in late November 1929 before he could revise it. Nonetheless *Grandeurs et misères d'une victoire* is a highly readable riposte, proof of Clemenceau's unextinguished vigour and of his journalistic skills. It was translated immediately into English (1930). Addressing Foch directly in the work's foreword, Clemenceau said: 'I cannot remain speechless. You challenge me. Here I am.' He accused Foch of unconsciously seeking revenge; he described the Recouly production as an 'impudent farrago of troopers' tales', an 'insult to the days that are gone', a pelting with roadside pebbles that certainly did not redound to Foch's 'glory'.[3]

Clemenceau had recognised that democracies fighting a coalition war had to make a coalition peace, and the elected politicians were the responsible peacemakers. Historian James Headlam-Morley, one of the British delegation at the peace conference, wrote to a friend that 'Foch is an admirable soldier and probably a delightful man, but good soldiers are nearly always bad politicians.'[4] However, Foch was not interested in politics, unlike Hindenburg, and unlike Eisenhower and de Gaulle after the Second World War. Foch declined Poincaré's suggestion that he stand for President of the Republic when the latter's term expired in 1920.[5] He also declined the offer of a Senate seat for Finisterre. He appears not to have expressed strong political opinions. During the Dreyfus re-trials, for example, he was prepared to wait and see the result, contrasting the calm of his barracks with the agitation in Paris.[6] Leo Kennedy of *The Times* noted in 1928 how Foch kept out of politics,[7] unlike Napoleon (who has twenty-two index entries in Liddell Hart's biography of Foch). Clemenceau need not have feared a Napoleonic *putsch* from Foch, who had been removed from command of the Northern Army Group in December 1916 after dabbling in politics.

---

[2] Recouly, *Mémorial de Foch*, 243.   [3] Clemenceau, *Grandeur and Misery of Victory*, 5, 7, 8.
[4] Headlam-Morley, *Memoir of the Peace Conference*, 85.   [5] Weygand, *Mirages et réalités*, 18.
[6] Letter, Foch to Mme Foch, 3 June 1899, 414/AP/11.
[7] Kennedy diary, 1 June 1928, LKEN 1/6.

Politicians, then, comprised the first constraint on Foch's exercise of supreme command. Allies comprised a second. He had learned at Ypres in 1914 that the only method that worked was diplomacy and persuasion, and he continued to apply it in 1918 although then he had greater authority. Yet diplomacy too was limited. Foch did not manage to make Diaz undertake an offensive until the war was almost over and Italian politicians realised that unless the Italian army won a victory they would be at a disadvantage at the peace table. Foch also had limited success against Pershing's obstinacy, but it is likely that Clemenceau's more direct approach, ordering Foch to seek Pershing's replacement, would have been crowned with even less success. President Wilson might have reacted to such pressure by retaining Pershing, whereas there was a good chance that he would have replaced him in 1919 because of his record, if the war had continued.

The lack of any German reaction to Foch's appointment in March 1918 is a further reflection of the limits of supreme command. Crown Prince Rupprecht's published diary, for example, makes no mention of Foch until August. A new configuration in the Allied high command appears to have been no cause for concern to the enemy on the Western Front. On the other hand, by the time the war was lost, it was acknowledged that the supreme command had allowed Foch to accumulate and to use reserves, which surprised Ludendorff and OHL. In his testimony to the parliamentary commission to investigate the causes of Germany's collapse in 1918, General von Kuhl stated that 'it repeatedly proved to be very much to our disadvantage that we never succeeded in attaining such a degree of centralization of the Supreme Command over all the allied armies as was given to General Foch'.[8] Foch's authority had made a difference after all.

His self-imposed tact, persuasion and restraint in his dealings with Allied commanders perhaps made Foch treat his fellow French generals somewhat more harshly. Pétain did not fail to point out the differences in Foch's dealings with Allied and French generals. In his reception speech at the Académie Française after his election to Foch's chair in 1931, Pétain remarked of Foch: 'while he did not hold back from scoring points off the French or the officers of his staff, he employed with the Allied chiefs infinite diplomacy'.[9] Foch's poor relationship with Castelnau, for example, has been mentioned already. Castelnau's biographer cites Foch's advice that Castelnau not be made a marshal at the same time as Pétain, despite the fact that Castelnau was the only army commander of 1914

---

[8] Jan Hoffmann, in Porte and Cochet (eds.), *Ferdinand Foch*, 250; Lutz (ed.), *Causes of the German Collapse*, 133.
[9] Pétain, *Discours de réception*, 62.

then still holding a front-line command: 'One does not give the bâton to the man who was defeated at Morhange.'[10] If true, these words reflect badly on the man who might himself be blamed for the defeat at Morhange in August 1914. However, there was also much parliamentary opposition to Castelnau's elevation. In 1921 there was a flurry of articles in the *Echo de Paris* and the *Revue des Deux Mondes* about Morhange, followed ten years later by disagreement with Foch's account in his memoirs of Castelnau's conduct at the 1914 Battle of Arras. Castelnau even challenged the account of Morhange in the *Guide Michelin*. Obviously he still felt very keenly about his reputation vis-à-vis Foch.[11]

Nor did the tact and diplomacy towards Allied generals prevent postwar disagreements and unpleasantness in Allied countries. Foch had already harmed his reputation during the treaty negotiations by his unremitting struggle to obtain the Rhine frontier for France. Then there were public disputes over wartime events. The Italians, for example, feeling aggrieved by their treatment during those negotiations, resented any suggestion that Foch had saved them after Caporetto. A series of articles argued that Foch had advised a stand on the river Mincio, further back than the Piave, where the stand was in fact made. This inspired French articles denying such an interpretation. Yet, even as late 1974, Foch's supposed desire to stand further back on the Mincio is repeated as a fact.[12]

General Diaz, who took over from Cadorna and commanded the Italian army until war's end, expressed the frequent complaint about Foch, namely that he was too much the professor: 'Foch is no strategist. He's a talker, a man of big phrases.'[13] By the 1930s the tone had become shriller and more critical. Baron Lumbroso, director of the *Rivista di Roma*, recorded the Duke of Aosta saying that Foch explained little, simply repeating the words 'attack', 'manoeuvre' or 'offensive', and sprinkling them with a 'flood' of 'Bon, bon, bon!' Lumbroso's view was that Foch had never won a battle, such as Joffre had done on the Marne, and there was no comparison with Napoleon. General Giardino (the Italian PMR at Versailles) agreed with Lumbroso: there was both a science and an art of war; whoever 'acts' is an artist but whoever 'blathers' may be a scientist/scholar ['chi *blatera*, può essere un scienziato']. For the scientist to be an artist as well, he must state when he will 'act'.[14] It is clear where Giardino placed Foch.

[10] Gras, *Castelnau*, 382. Gras gives no source for his quotation.
[11] See the dossiers 'Polémiques, Opérations de Lorraine', in Castelnau mss, 1K/795/11 and 12.
[12] Fadini, *Caporetto*, 451.
[13] Conversation between Diaz and Malagodi, 29 January 1919, in Malagodi, *Conversazioni*, 2: 507
[14] Lumbroso, *Fame usurpate*, 182, 183, 209–10.

A similar dispute with the Belgians over events in 1914 was even more serious. On the anniversary of the Armistice in 1926 the French newspaper *Le Matin* published an interview with Foch, written by Stéphane Lauzanne, which led to a public exchange of letters between King Albert and Foch. The article implied that it had been Foch's influence and energy that had inspired the Belgians in November 1914 to stand on the Yser. This was not the case (as was seen in the chapter on the Flanders fighting), and the King wrote a personal letter to Foch the very next day, pointing out that the French general arrived at his headquarters three days *after* the order had been given to retreat no further. Thus the impression that the Belgian army would have retreated still further without Foch's intervention was false and he, the King, could not allow such an interpretation to stand.

Foch replied a few days later, distancing himself from the article. He claimed not to have given an interview to Lauzanne (although Clemenceau states that he did 'talk' with him, a nice distinction).[15] Foch stated that he retained 'great esteem' for the Belgian army and 'deep respect for its King'. Both the King's letter and Foch's reply were published in the press. The matter risked blowing up into a diplomatic incident as the Belgian military attaché in Paris became involved, but Lauzanne took the blame. The journalist apologised to Foch, and explained to the King that all armies retreated at one time or another and that no disrespect had been intended; Foch had been 'much less precise' in his words about the Belgians halting the retreat than the account which had already appeared in the *Bulletin belge des sciences militaires*, which showed complete agreement between the Belgian and French commands.

Yet the matter was not settled quite so easily. The military attaché's letter was placed on Foch's personnel file. He claimed that Lauzanne had in fact confirmed the Marshal's words, to the King's irritation. Albert replied to Lauzanne with a very stern letter, since he was tired of the story that had been circulating for six years. Indeed, following several earlier articles, the Belgian army's historical section had decided to investigate the matter and had asked the King for a written account of what happened.[16] The newspaper *Le Matin* had asked permission to publish the two letters (Lauzanne's confirmation and the King's response), but the Royal Palace managed to quash the idea, despite the King being in

[15] Clemenceau, *Grandeur and Misery of Victory*, 132.
[16] See the file 'Bataille de l'Yser en octobre 1914', containing the correspondence and the King's manuscript account, box 1370, files returned from Russia, Army Archives, Brussels.

favour.[17] Thus the row blew over, until Clemenceau reproduced the King's letter in his *Grandeurs et misères*, and reminded his readers of it.

The USA was less of a problem. Although Pershing and Pétain encouraged each other in the view that Foch had signed a premature armistice, Foch enjoyed a triumphal visit there in 1921, when he declared his opinion of the treaty cited at the start of this chapter. The Knights of Columbus presented him with a gaudy baton to add to his French, British and Polish marshal's batons. The American retreat from Europe, however, meant that memories of the war were buried and no resentments over wartime events such as occurred with the Italians and Belgians were aired publicly.

Britain was a different matter, and criticisms soon arose. For example, T. E. Lawrence (of Arabian fame) must have known Foch solely at the time of the peace negotiations, as his description of 'only a pair of frantic moustaches' reflects the tension of those days. J. F. C. Fuller called Foch a 'tactically demented Napoleon'.[18] Henry Wilson might have defended Foch's reputation, but he was assassinated by the IRA in June 1922. It is difficult to judge, however, how warmly the professional friendship would have persisted into the postwar after the events of 1918 had changed Foch's estimation of him. Derby recorded, for example, the 'profound contempt' with which both Foch and Clemenceau regarded Wilson. Clemenceau thought it 'useless' to discuss military matters with him because 'whenever he is asked an opinion all he does ... is to grin from ear to ear, put his left leg over his right shoulder, and to say "Truly I don't know."'[19]

By the time of Foch's own death in 1929, following Haig's the previous year, the battle of the memoirs was in full spate. Foch's own two volumes, published in a single-volume translation in English at the same time as the French, received a very poor reception. An anonymous review in the *Army Quarterly* began by stating that the memoirs were 'disappointing' and 'woefully inaccurate'. The writer went on to blame Foch for exposing Sir John French's right flank during the Battle of the Marne in September 1914, thereby 'slowing' the British advance and allowing the Germans to 'escape': 'The course of the war might perhaps have been different but for Foch's failure to obey orders and inability to grasp a fairly plain situation in the field.' As for events of 1918: 'Now that the various plans of Ludendorff during 1918 are fully known, it is obvious that Haig's

[17] Colonel Blavier, Attaché Militaire, to Ministre de la Guerre, 9 December 1926, in Marshal Foch's personnel file, dossier 'Archives' 1, pièce 2/1.
[18] Lawrence, *T. E. Lawrence to his Biographers*, 47; Fuller, *Conduct of War*, 128.
[19] Dutton (ed.), *Paris 1918*, 237 (entry for 2 October 1918).

deductions as to their nature and scope were more accurate than Foch's.'[20] R. C. K. Ensor in the *New Statesman and Nation* was as disappointed as Renouvin had been – 'what a wonderful body of facts and comments he might have bequeathed to posterity! But the *Memoirs* are not at all like that.' Once again Foch's 'memory' of events is disputed: 'The 1914 narrative is not all satisfactory. Its account of the events is often surprisingly misleading, and it lapses occasionally into even more surprising inaccuracies.'[21] In his anonymous review in the *Times Literary Supplement* Sir James Edmonds complains that the account of 1914 is 'in many places inaccurate and remarkable for what it leaves out', and that the account of 1918 'betrays an old man's vanity, an inclination to attribute too large a share of the final success to the French and a desire to exhibit M. Clemenceau in an unfavourable light'.[22] The most damning review of all was written by General E. L. Spears in the *National Review*. Spears knew Foch well, of course, and clearly had not forgotten the criticisms aimed at him in the last year of the war. According to Spears, Foch's account of the 1914 Battle of the Marne was 'very misleading'; as for First Ypres in October 1914, 'the whole section of the book dealing with this period gives a most exaggerated view of the importance of Foch's interventions, is very unjust to the British, and is an extremely biased and unfair account of what happened'.[23]

Then in 1931 Basil Liddell Hart published the study which has remained the first point of reference for Anglophone historians ever since. Liddell Hart damns with faint praise. In his Epilogue (p. 458) he wrote of Foch: 'In the council of war as in the classroom he was convincing because he was passionately convinced. The more general he was, the better his effect as a general, and the less harm he caused to offset his heartening influence.' These ungenerous comments must be seen in the light of Liddell Hart's conviction that Britain should avoid a Continental commitment and that Foch represented an old-fashioned and out-dated approach to war that had cost Britain dear.[24] Wilson was to blame also since his friendship with Foch had been made possible because he had learned to speak Foch's language from his French nanny. Moreover, Foch was that highly suspicious (to middle-class British) phenomenon, a convinced (although, it must be said, not ostentatious) Catholic. The 'old school' had been discredited, Haig along with Foch, and Liddell Hart

---

[20] *Army Quarterly* (July 1931), 329–36, at pp. 332, 336.

[21] R. C. K. Ensor, 'A Tale Partly Told', *New Statesman and Nation* (4 April 1931), 223–34. Renouvin's comment is cited in the introduction (p. 5).

[22] *Times Literary Supplement*, 19 March 1931.

[23] *National Review*, no. 578 (April 1931), 469–76.   [24] See Reid, 'Young Turks'.

wanted young military thinkers and leaders to come to the fore. Comments such as that just cited – driven by the search for a clever phrase rather than for an insight into Foch's achievements – fill Liddell Hart's pages. Not surprisingly Weygand was outraged. Liddell Hart had thanked him in his Preface for his help but Weygand wrote immediately on the book's publication, denying that he had helped and rejecting the conclusions and tenor of the biography.[25]

Liddell Hart seemed to have been genuinely surprised by the French reaction and the failure to publish a French translation of his book. He believed that it had been 'banned'. In a note about the matter he gave as the reason that 'this first attempt to compile a life of Foch in the light of the historical records now available, German as well as French and British', differed 'too much from the view of the Marshal held in France'. Liddell Hart thought it 'extraordinary' that this book should have proved impossible to publish in France: 'while it demolishes the Foch legend, it gives the real man, great in spite of his proved mistakes'. He concluded that some influence had been brought to bear on the publishing house by the War Ministry.[26] Whether Weygand had any influence over the fate of the book in France is unclear.

The decline in Foch's reputation outside France, where almost every town has its Avenue Foch, reveals a lack of understanding of the limitations on supreme command in a coalition war. The significant difficulties in coordinating the five national armies on the Western Front between the North Sea and the Adriatic and in dealing with the political problems in Allied councils have obscured what Foch achieved in the face of those difficulties and problems. It was an 'illusion', Foch said postwar, to think that a few lines written on a piece of paper could change the course of events within days. Such a decree could not make an impression on commanders of a different nationality; only the man charged with the task of carrying it out could impose his will on his collaborators.[27] Supreme command might indeed be less than ordinary people think it is, as Foch wrote on Recouly's text of their postwar conversations,[28] yet supreme command is considerably more than many remembered.

At the top of the pyramid a commander's role is to make things happen. Foch's strategic vision made things happen in 1918. He made Haig and

[25] Différend Weygand–Liddell Hart, 1K/129/1.
[26] 'Note on the French "banning" of my book on FOCH', n.d., Liddell Hart mss, LH 11/1933/34.
[27] Recouly, *Mémorial de Foch*, 13, 15.
[28] Ibid., frontispiece: 'ne semble pas être ce qu'un vain peuple pense'.

Pétain keep contact in March, and never abandoned the principle that British and French forces should maintain an unbroken front. He made the crucial decision that began the counter-offensives in July. He insisted on always having a strategic reserve, by demanding that Allied governments provide the men, by doling them out parsimoniously when required, and by watching the enemy's reserves very closely. His strategic vision recognised the importance of communications and ensured that the Allies' first task was to free their own before proceeding to converge on the squeeze-point of the German communications around Charleville–Mézières. Domination of the narrow Meuse corridor between Sedan and Mézières ended Ludendorff's control of railway communications and cut off from the Rhine network the German armies and materiel in Belgium and northern France.

Foch secured all these vital achievements with constant energy, with undiminished optimism, and with steadfastness. The Second World War commander, Lord Wavell, identified physical and moral stamina and energy as necessary qualities in a leader. In 1914 Foch displayed greater stamina on the Marne than did Ludendorff at Tannenberg; and in 1918 Foch did not break down during the 27 May emergency, unlike Ludendorff in September. Bethmann Hollweg judged that Ludendorff was 'only great at a time of success'; when 'things go badly he loses his nerve'.[29] Foch always displayed energy, whether on the battlefield or at the conference table. Churchill caught this Fochian quality very well when he described Foch as 'heav[ing] the mighty wave of allied armies' to final victory.[30] A leader must also be optimistic, even during the darkest hours. This quality in Foch marks out the difference with Pétain. His 'can do' attitude contrasted with the latter's more cautious approach. This is not to accuse Pétain of defeatism, as the British official history does in the post-Second World War volumes on 1918. Nor is it to advocate unthinking gung-ho. Rather, Foch's positive attitude proved more inspiring, hence more effective. The energy and the optimism were supported by Foch's steadfastness and courage in maintaining his views. His courage had been evident in 1916 when he insisted on greater resources before mounting the Somme offensive, and is best seen in his fight for the Rhine frontier in 1919. He did not vary in his advice or in his strategy. Henry Wilson tried many times in vain to make Foch withdraw to a shorter line and to flood the Flanders front, but Foch always refused.

After the war Wilson recognised this quality of steadfastness, and that Foch had been right. In April 1920 he declared:

---

[29] Görlitz, *Kaiser and his Court*, 406.   [30] Churchill, *Great Contemporaries*, 194.

Foch possesses qualities which are not possessed by any other soldier I have ever met. Of course he is well versed in the art of war. He has been well trained and has read widely. He has devoted himself exclusively to his profession. He has had no other interests. But beyond that he has an uncanny instinct as to the right thing to be done. He cannot always give you reasons. I think he reasons up to a point and then takes a leap to the conclusion. He jumps over the hills and valleys, but he always lands in the right place. I remember that two years ago this month we all met together, five of us, British and French, including Foch and myself. The position was very serious. Foch wanted to do a certain thing. We all opposed him. His proposals involved the lives of thousands of British troops, so we had a great responsibility. He heard what we had to say, but declined to alter his opinion. He proved right. We were wrong. That is typical of the man. He is the most courageous man I have ever met, and the greatest fighter. He is never done, and you never know when he will spring up at you again.[31]

Thus Wilson noted Foch's clear-sightedness, and another British liaison officer makes a similar judgement. Rex Benson was at GQG in 1918 and remembered Foch's 'intuitive sense and accuracy of foresight which coupled with a wonderful optimism and excellent information services were of inestimable value'. Benson believed at the time that Foch's 'leadership qualifications in 1918 were superb. On the other hand, the French soldiers were far fonder of Petain than they were of Foch!'[32]

A French witness confirms these qualities in Foch. General d'Urbal had commanded Tenth Army in Flanders and Artois in 1914 and 1915. In his memoirs he wrote:

[Foch had] a robust optimism, which allowed him to take a hammering with serenity and to present matters later to himself as having happened as he wished, even when events had knocked his plans. Perhaps this was a front to save his prestige in front of subordinates; perhaps also he did not always fully explain his plans. Whatever the case, if he looked behind through rose-coloured glasses, he saw clearly and correctly when he looked before him. He saw clearly, he saw from on high and he saw from afar. Clarity and common sense were his supreme qualities: clarity of conception, clarity in exposition, clarity in execution. Add to that, logical plans, steadfastness, energy, with exceptional command qualities by which he made his presence felt, upright and inflexibly loyal, and you have the portrait, as he lives in my memory, of this leader who was a great leader and a great character.[33]

D'Urbal's perceptive comments explain how the clear-sighted Foch could have become involved in so many postwar disputes. Evidently Foch's clear-sightedness worked forwards only, and when he looked back in

---

[31] Riddell, *Diary of the Peace Conference*, 190.
[32] Letter, Benson to Lascelles, 10 November 1965, Lascelles mss LASL 5/6/2.
[33] General d'Urbal, *Souvenirs*, 143–4.

later years he saw less clearly and 'remembered' events differently. Yet, as Shakespeare reminds us, old men do forget.

In 1918, however, Foch saw clearly what needed to be done. In this he makes a stark contrast with Ludendorff. Ludendorff could be distracted from his intended aim, as happened in March during Operation MICHAEL, and in July during MARNESCHUTZ–REIMS. In contrast, Foch was not tempted to continue with Mangin's counterstroke in June following Operation GNEISENAU. It was Ludendorff who took risks in 1918, not the man accused postwar of neglecting the 'prudent' option – arranging not to lose – in favour of a 'bold' solution, going all-out and hoping for the best.[34]

Foch's clear sight over the whole battlefront distinguishes him from Haig, Pershing and Pétain as well. Haig could not see beyond the BEF's front, accepting his intelligence advisers' urgings that an offensive on his Flanders front was imminent. Hence Haig was always reluctant to send his own reserves to the French sector. Foch appreciated Haig's loyalty, but believed that the British CinC was not very intelligent.[35] Pershing was obsessed by an independent American operation towards Metz; and Pétain like Haig refused to look beyond his own front. Foch was remarkably prescient about Pétain. As early as February 1916 he wrote to his wife in praise of Pétain's qualities of method and judgement, but added that he feared that success might go to his head, making him the plaything of certain politicians.[36]

Foch's clear-sightedness extended to his views on a future war if France's security was not assured on the Rhine. His comments cited in the previous chapter about French widows having to lose their sons as well were proved prophetic in his own family. His daughter Marie – her grief at losing her husband in 1914 on the same day as Germain Foch had been killed had worried him greatly – lost her only son Jean Bécourt-Foch with the RAF in August 1944. However, the son of Foch's second daughter, Anne Fournier-Foch, made up for the fact that his grandfather had not gone to Berlin for the German Armistice. After escaping from a German prisoner-of-war camp, Henry Fournier-Foch was captured by Red Army troops and, as Tovarich Kapitaine Foch, entered Berlin with them in May 1945. Marshal Zhukov himself awarded him a Red Star.[37]

---

[34] Mayer, *Trois maréchaux*, 179.

[35] 'Comme il est bete [sic]': Dillon's account of Foch's comment soon after the Armistice was relayed to Liddell Hart in May 1937: Liddell Hart mss 11/1937/43.

[36] Letter, Foch to Mme Foch, 8 February 1916, vol. 39: 'c'est que ses succès le grisent et que, la politique aidant, il devienne l'homme de certains politicailleurs'.

[37] Henry Fournier-Foch, *Tovarich Kapitaine Foch: Souvenirs de guerre* (Paris: Editions de la Table Ronde, 2001).

Foch also possessed the quality that Napoleon prized above all others. He was lucky. The obituary published in one of Germany's leading military journals began with the words: 'Foch is dead. With him departs the luckiest general of the world war.'[38] Certainly Foch took the supreme command at a time when American troops were starting to arrive in France, when industrial mobilisation had reached such a pitch in Allied countries that all the enormous losses of materiel in March and April 1918 could be replaced in short order, and when Allied logistics were reaching a level of efficiency that overcame the German submarine war and ensured that civilians were fed, munitions workers had raw materials for their factories, and troops were fed and re-supplied on the battlefield. Yet Foch must take a share of the credit for these achievements. He had urged the need for greater artillery resources in 1916, mounting a political campaign that in part cost him his job. As chief of army in 1917 he had encouraged the provision of munitions. In 1918 he had played a large part in speeding the dispatch of American troops to France. Indeed he was lucky, but he helped to create his own luck.

He was lucky too in his staff. Weygand and Foch worked as one, and the former's loyalty and devotion were exemplary. The fact that the fatherless Weygand (his paternity remains a mystery) joined Foch's staff at the same time as Germain Foch was killed was obviously significant, but they had no disagreements and Weygand proved an ideal interpreter of Foch's often incomprehensible utterances. Yet Weygand was no mere mouthpiece, as his growing stature throughout 1918 reveals (see Illustration 15). He went on to play an important role in the Russo-Polish war, and again in the Second World War after succeeding in 1930 to Foch's former job as head of the French army's general staff. In 1942, after his arrest by the Nazis, he wrote to Mme Foch wondering what the Marshal would now think of him.[39]

Foch's insistence on a small staff and a secluded headquarters contributed to close working relationships. He inspired great loyalty and affection in his liaison officers. DuCane was impressed enough to write an account of the 1918 days which he had privately published; and Mott was generous enough to translate Foch's memoirs for English publication. Cointet, head of intelligence at GQG, went regularly to confer with Foch and wrote in his postwar memoir of the 'indisputable superiority' of Foch's 'military genius, completely inseparable from his unquenchable energy'.[40]

[38] Hermann Stegemann, 'Foch: Versuch einer Deutung', *Wissen und Wehr*, 1929/5.
[39] Weygand to Mme la maréchale Foch, 1 December 1942, 414/AP/12.
[40] Cointet memoirs, Cahier '1918', fo. 120 (latter half of July 1918).

Illustration 15 General Maxime Weygand
General Maxime Weygand (1867–1965), Foch's chief of staff from
August 1914 until after the Treaty of Versailles
Between 1930 and 1935 he occupied Foch's former post as chief of the
army general staff. One of his first tasks (fortunately, after Foch's death)
was to preside over the evacuation of the Rhineland in advance of the
date set down in the treaty.

All these qualities – energy, optimism, steadfastness, clear-sightedness
(and luck) – are necessary in a leader. They enable such a leader to inspire
confidence. As DuCane recognised – and working with both Foch and
Haig, he was uniquely qualified to judge – the ability to inspire

differentiated Foch, who possessed it, from Haig, who did not.[41] Moreover, Foch was able to communicate his confidence to politicians, as Haig was not. Many of Foch's battles were fought with politicians, both French and Allied, over and above those he directed against the enemy. At its most basic, however, leadership consists of being able to act in such a way as to make others follow. As Generalissimo, Foch led the victorious Allied armies to the railway carriage in Rethondes on 11 November 1918, but, to his lasting regret, he was unable to make the peacemakers follow the direction he wished them to take to the Galerie des Glaces in Versailles. He was able to lead because his confidence in himself – a quality that Liddell Hart disparaged – inspired confidence in others. The source of his confidence lay in his intellectual qualities. His note-books reveal a general who gave much thought to the task in hand. He did what he could to apply what he knew. The conflagration of war shaped his thinking, and in turn Ferdinand Foch shaped the Great War.

[41] DuCane, *Foch*, 85.

Bibliography

Since the great majority of books written about the First World War contain of necessity references to Marshal Foch, I have not attempted to suggest any further reading in the notes, nor have I included in this bibliography any work not cited therein. For completeness' sake, I have appended a select list of works dealing solely with Foch. To save space, all works cited in the notes are referred to there by a short title, with the full bibliographical details given below; abbreviated titles are listed at the beginning of the book.

The bibliography is divided into three sections: first a listing of the archival sources used; second, published works cited in the notes, including the American, Bavarian, British, French, German and Italian official histories, and published collections of official documents, which are referred to by title, not corporate author; finally a brief list of the principal biographies and other studies of Foch himself, excluding the multitude of more-or-less hagiographical works published immediately after the war or after his death (for a full bibliography see Porte and Cochet or the earlier Michel).

Note on the three principal collections of Foch papers: these are in the army archives in Vincennes, in the Archives nationales and in the Department of Western Manuscripts of the Bibliothèque nationale de France (Richelieu). To some extent the contents of the first two duplicate each other. I have used the copies of Foch's 'Carnets' in Vincennes (1K/129/10) and the copies of 'Journées' in the Archives nationales (414/AP/10). Both collections contain a large number of photographs, and reveal some arrangement by General Weygand and by the Marshal's grandsons. Madame Foch's original diaries are in 414/AP/13. The BNF has photographic copies of the valuable letters sent almost daily to Madame Foch, and microfilm copies of other correspondence held by the family.

ARCHIVAL COLLECTIONS CITED

A PRIVATE PAPERS

Belgium
King Albert of the Belgians, Maison militaire du roi (Galet), Archives royales, Brussels
Comte de Broqueville, Archives générales du royaume, Brussels
Major Ferdinand de Posch, in private hands [part published, see Vandewoude below]

522

Britain
A. J. Balfour, additional mss, 49,683–49,962, British Library, London
Lord Bertie of Thame, additional mss, 63,011–63,053, British Library, London
General G. S. Clive, LHCMA; and CAB 45/201, The National Archives, Kew
Brigadier The Viscount Dillon, Imperial War Museum, London
General Sir John F. Gathorne-Hardy, LHCMA
Earl Haig, National Library of Scotland, and WO 256, The National Archives, Kew
Lord Hankey of the Chart (Maurice Hankey), CCC
Aubrey Leo Kennedy, CCC
Sir Alan Lascelles, CCC
Captain Sir Basil Liddell Hart, LHCMA
David Lloyd George, Parliamentary Archives, London
Viscount Milner, Bodleian Library, Oxford
General Lord (Henry S.) Rawlinson, CCC, and National Army Museum, London
Lord Rennell of Rodd, Bodleian Library, Oxford
Field Marshal Sir William Robertson, LHCMA
Sir Edward Spears, CCC, and LHCMA
Admiral Sir Rosslyn Wemyss, CCC
Field Marshal Sir Henry Hughes Wilson, Imperial War Museum, London

France
Colonel de Bary memoirs in Castelnau papers, 1K/795/39, SHD/T
Général Henri Berthelot, see USA below
Général Henri Brugère, 1K/160, SHD/T
Général Edmond Buat, Bibliothèque de l'Institut, Paris
Paul Cambon, PA-AP 042, Archives diplomatiques, MAE, Paris
Général Edouard de Curières de Castelnau 1K/795, SHD/T
François Charles-Roux, PA-AP 037, Archives diplomatiques, MAE, Paris
Georges Clemenceau, Département des manuscrits occidentaux, Bibliothèque
    nationale de France, Paris
Général Edmond de Cointet, memoirs, 1K/87, SHD/T
Général Charles Dupont, memoirs, 1KT/526, SHD/T
Colonel Jean Fabry, 1K/93, SHD/T
Maréchal Ferdinand Foch, personnel dossier, 9Y/d 528, and 1K/129, SHD/T;
    414/AP, Archives nationales, Paris; Fonds photographique quarto: vols. 32–54,
    NAF, and Mi 2907, both in Département des manuscrits occidentaux,
    Bibliothèque nationale de France, Paris
Madame la maréchale Foch, 414/AP/13, Archives nationales, Paris
Jacques Helbronner diary in Painlevé mss (see below), vol. 122
Colonel Jacquand in Castelnau mss, 1K/795/36, SHD/T
Marshal Joseph Joffre, 1K/268, and 14N 2–3, SHD/T
Général Octave Charles Lanoix, 1K/106, SHD/T
Charles Meunier[-Surcouf], 1KT/83, SHD/T
Général Alfred Micheler, 1K/113, SHD/T
Paul Painlevé, 313/AP, Archives nationales, Paris
Jean Pierrefeu, 1K/120, SHD/T
Général Maurice Pellé, Bibliothèque de l'Institut, Paris; and correspondence in
    Albert Thomas mss, 94/AP/237, Archives nationales, Paris

Raymond Poincaré, NAF mss 16028–34, Département des manuscrits
    occidentaux, Bibliothèque nationale de France, Paris
Général Edouard Réquin, in Lecomte mss, 1K/108, SHD/T; drawings in
    Bibliothèque de Documentation Internationale et Contemporaine, Hôtel des
    Invalides, Paris
André Tardieu, PA-AP 166, Archives diplomatiques, MAE, Paris
Auguste Terrier, Bibliothèque de l'Institut, Paris
Général Maxime Weygand, 1K/130, SHD/T

United States
Newton D. Baker, Manuscripts Department, Library of Congress,
    Washington, DC
General Henri Berthelot, Hoover Institution, Stanford, CA
General Tasker H. Bliss, Manuscripts Department, Library of Congress
Major Paul H. Clark: Manuscripts Department, Library of Congress; Pershing
    mss, RG 200, National Archives and Records Administration, College Park,
    MD; and Henry J. Reilly mss, box 36, American Army Heritage and Education
    Center, Carlisle, PA
Colonel Edward M. House, diary, Yale University Library [microfilm copy in
    Academy Library, Australian Defence Force Academy]
William Martin, Hoover Institution, Stanford, CA
Colonel T. Bentley Mott, United States Military Academy library, West Point;
    and Virginia Historical Society, Richmond, VA collections A (diary) and B
General Dennis E. Nolan, American Army Heritage and Education Center,
    Carlisle, PA
General J. J. Pershing, Manuscripts Department, Library of Congress

B OFFICIAL RECORDS

Belgium
Archives Générales du Royaume, Brussels; Royal Archives, Brussels; Russian
    Returned Archives, Army Archives, Brussels

Britain: The National Archives, Kew
CAB 23: War Cabinet minutes
CAB 24: Cabinet memoranda
CAB 25: Supreme War Council records
CAB 27: War Cabinet and Cabinet: Miscellaneous committees
CAB 28: War Cabinet: Allied conferences, minutes and papers: IC series
CAB 37: Cabinet Office: Photographic copies of Cabinet papers
CAB 42: War Council: Minutes and papers
CAB 45: Official history correspondence
FO 371: Foreign Office: Political Departments
FO 800: Balfour and Bertie papers
PRO 30/57: Earl Kitchener papers
WO 32: War Office: Registered files

WO 106: Directorate of Military Operations and Military Intelligence
WO 158: Military headquarters correspondence and papers

France
Army Commission proceedings: Chamber of Deputies, series C, Archives
  nationales, Paris; and Senate, Palais du Luxembourg, Paris
Archives de la Guerre, Château de Vincennes, Série N:
  3N Comité de guerre
  4N Conseil Supérieur de guerre (Supreme War Council)
  5N Cabinet du Ministre de Guerre
  6N Fonds Buat; Fonds Clemenceau
  7N Etat major de l'armée (Army General Staff)
  14N Fonds Joffre et Foch
  15N Grand Quartier Général des Armées Alliées (Allied Headquarters)
  16N Grand Quartier Général
  17N Missions militaires françaises
  18N Groupes d'armées
  19N Armées
  22N Corps d'armée
  26N Journaux des marches et des opérations (war diaries): 26N 1: Allied
    headquarters, 1918

**United States: National Archives and Records Administration, College
Park, MD**
Records of the American Expeditionary Forces (World War I), 1917–23, RG 120,
  Entries 267, 268 and M923
Correspondence of the War College Division and Related General Staff Offices,
  1903–1919, RG 165, M1024
Pershing mss, RG 200

PUBLISHED WORKS

Albertini, Luigi, *Venti anni di vita politica*, 5 vols. (Bologna: Nicola Zanichelli,
  1950–3)
Aldrovandi Marescotti, L., *Guerra diplomatica: Ricordi e frammenti di diario
  (1914–1919)* (Milano: Mondadori, 1936)
Allard, Paul, *Les Dessous de la guerre révélés par les comités secrets* (Paris: Les Editions
  de France, 1932)
  L'Oreille fendue: Les Généraux limogés pendant la guerre (Paris: Editions de
  France, 1933)
Anon., 'General Foch at the Battle of the Marne', *Army Quarterly* 21 (October
  1930), 81–6
[Les] Armées françaises dans la Grande Guerre, 103 vols. (Paris: Imprimerie
  Nationale 1922–38)
Armengaud, Général, *Le Renseignement aérien: Sauvegarde des armées* (Paris:
  Librairie Aéronautique, 1934)
Autin, Jean, *Foch ou le triomphe de la volonté* (Paris: Perrin, 1987, 1998)

Baquet, Général L.-H., *Souvenirs d'un directeur d'artillerie* (Limoges/Paris: Charles-Lavauzelle, 1921)

Bariéty, Jacques, *Les Relations franco-allemandes: Après la Première Guerre Mondiale 10 novembre 1918–10 janvier 1925 de l'exécution à la négotiation* (Paris: Editions Pedone, 1977)

Bayerische Kriegsarchiv, *Die Schlacht in Lothringen und in den Vogesen 1914*, 2 vols. (München: M. Schick, 1929)

Beach, James M., British Intelligence and the German Army, 1914–18 (PhD thesis, London University, 2005)

Beaver, Daniel R., *Newton D. Baker and the American War Effort 1917–1919* (Lincoln: University of Nebraska Press, 1966)

Beckett, Ian F. W., *Ypres: The First Battle, 1914* (Harlow/New York: Pearson, 2004)

Berger, Marcel, and Allard, Paul, *Les Dessous du traité de Versailles* (Paris: Editions du Portique, 1933)

Bertie, Francis, *The Diary of Lord Bertie of Thame 1914–1918*, 2 vols. (ed. Lady Algernon Gordon Lennox) (London: Hodder and Stoughton, 1924)

Blake, Robert (ed.), *The Private Papers of Douglas Haig 1914–1919* (London: Eyre & Spottiswoode, 1952)

Bock, Fabienne, *Un parlementarisme de guerre 1914–1919* (Paris: Belin, 2002)

Bonnefous, Georges, *Histoire politique de la Troisième République*, vol. 2: *La Grande Guerre 1914–1918* (Paris: Presses Universitaires de France, 1957)

Bordeaux, Henry, *Histoire d'une vie*, 13 vols. (Paris: Plon, 1951–73)

Bourlet, Michaël, 'Le Deuxième Bureau et la diplomatie secrète: Les négotiations Armand–Revertera de 1917', *Guerres Mondiales et Conflits Contemporains* 221 (2006): 33–49

Brécard, Général, *En Belgique auprès du roi Albert: Souvenirs de 1914* (Paris: Calmann-Lévy, 1934)

Brock, Michael, and Brock, Eleanor (eds.), *H.H. Asquith Letters to Venetia Stanley* (pb. edn, Oxford: Oxford University Press, 1985)

Brown, Ian M., 'Feeding Victory: The Logistic Imperative behind the Hundred Days', in Peter Dennis and Jeffrey Grey (eds.), *1918: Defining Victory* (Canberra: The Army History Unit, 1999), 130–47

Bruce, Robert B., *A Fraternity of Arms: America and France in the Great War* (Lawrence: University Press of Kansas, 2003)

Brugère, Raymond, *Veni, vidi, Vichy* (Paris: Calmann-Lévy, 1944)

Bugnet, Commandant Charles, *En écoutant le Maréchal Foch* (Paris: Grasset, 1929) [translated into English as *Foch Talks* (London: Gollancz, 1929)]

Bülow, General von, *Experience of the German 1st Army in the Somme Battle*, Occasional Paper # 56, Engineer School, US Army (1917) (being a British translation of the German document)

Mein Bericht zur Marne-Schlacht (Berlin: A. Sherl, 1919)

Cadorna, Luigi, *Lettere famigliari* (ed. Raffaele Cadorna) (Milano: Mondadori, 1967)

Callwell, Major-General Sir C. E., *Field Marshal Sir Henry Wilson Bart., G.C.B., D.S.O. His Life and Diaries*, 2 vols. (London: Cassell, 1927)

Cambon, Paul, *Correspondance 1870–1924*, 3 vols. (ed. Henri Cambon) (Paris: Grasset, 1940–6)

Caracciola, Mario, *Le truppe italiane in Francia (Il II Corpo d'Armata – Le T.A.I.F.)* (Milano: Mondadori, 1929)

Carley, Michael Jabara, *Revolution and Intervention: The French Government and the Russian Civil War, 1917–1919* (Kingston: McGill-Queen's University Press, 1983)

Carls, Stephen D., *Louis Loucheur and the Shaping of Modern France* (Baton Rouge/ London: Louisiana State University Press, 1993)

Cartier, François, 'Souvenirs du Général Cartier', *Revue des Transmissions* 85 (July–August 1959): 23–39; 87 (November–December 1959): 13–51

Cassar, George H., *The Forgotten Front: The British Campaign in Italy 1917–1918* (London/Rio Grande: The Hambledon Press, 1998)

  Kitchener's War: British Strategy from 1914 to 1916 (Washington, DC: Brassey's, 2004)

  Lloyd George at War 1916–1918 (London/New York: Anthem Press, 2009)

Castex, Henri, *L'Affaire du Chemin des Dames: Les Comités secrets (1917)* (Paris: Imago, 1998)

Cecil, Hugh P., *Imperial Marriage: An Edwardian War and Peace* (London: John Murray, 2002)

Cendrars, Blaise, *La Main coupée* (Paris: Le Club Français du Livre, 1953)

Chagnon, Louis, '1916 ou l'année de rupture en matière d'utilisation de l'arme aérienne', *Revue Historique des Armées* 242 (2006): 36–47

Chickering, Roger, *The Great War and Urban Life in Germany: Freiburg, 1914–1918* (Cambridge: Cambridge University Press, 2007)

Christienne, Charles, and Lissarague, Pierre, *A History of French Military Aviation* (Washington, DC: Smithsonian Institution Press, 1986)

Christienne, Charles, and Pesquies-Courbier, Simone, 'L'Effort de guerre français dans le domaine aéronautique en 1914–1918', in Gérard Canini (ed.), *Les Fronts invisibles: Nourrir, fournir, soigner* (Nancy: Presses Universitaires de Nancy, 1984), 233–46

Churchill, W. S., *The World Crisis 1916–1918*, pt 1 (London: Thornton Butterworth, 1927)

  Thoughts and Adventures (London: Thornton Butterworth, 1932)

  Great Contemporaries (London: Thornton Butterworth, 1937)

Clemenceau, Georges, *Grandeurs et misères d'une victoire* (Paris: Plon, 1930) [translated into English as *Grandeur and Misery of Victory* (London: Harrap, 1930)]

[Cointet], 'Extraits des souvenirs inédits du Général L. de Cointet: Le Service de renseignements au G.Q.G. français du 15 juin au 15 juillet 1918', *Revue Historique de l'Armée* 24: 4 (1968), 27–40

Colin, Général H., *La Division de fer 1914–1918* (Paris: Payot, 1930)

Cook, Tim, *No Place to Run: The Canadian Corps and Gas Warfare in the First World War* (Vancouver/Toronto: UBC Press, 1999)

Corbett, Julian, *Naval Operations*, 5 vols. (London: Longmans, Green, 1920–31)

Corum, James, *The Luftwaffe: Creating the Operational Air War, 1918–1940* (Lawrence: University Press of Kansas, 1997)

Cramon, General A. von, *Quatre ans au G.Q.G. austro-hongrois pendant la guerre mondiale, comme représentant du G.Q.G. allemand* (Paris: Payot, 1922)

Daille, Général M., *Histoire de la Guerre Mondiale*, vol. 2: *Joffre et la guerre d'usure 1915–1916* (Paris: Payot, 1936)

Darmon, Pierre, *Vivre à Paris pendant la Grande Guerre* (Paris: Fayard, 2002)

David, Edward (ed.), *Inside Asquith's Cabinet: From the Diaries of Charles Hobhouse* (London: John Murray, 1977)

Dawes, Charles G., *A Journal of the Great War*, 2 vols. (Boston, MA: Houghton Mifflin, 1921)

Deist, Wilhelm, 'The Military Collapse of the German Empire: The Reality Behind the Stab-in-the-Back Myth', *War in History* 3: 1 (1996), 186–207

Diesbach, Ghislain de, *La Princesse Bibesco, 1876–1973* (Paris: Perrin, 1986)

Dillon, Brigadier The Viscount, *Memories of Three Wars* (London: Allan Wingate, 1951)

Documenti diplomatici italiani, 5th series, 11 vols. (Rome: Libreria dello Stato, 1954–86)

Doughty, Robert A., 'French Strategy in 1914: Joffre's Own', *Journal of Military History* 67: 2 (2003), 427–54

   Pyrrhic Victory: French Strategy and Operations in the Great War (Cambridge, MA: The Belknap Press of Harvard University Press, 2005)

   'France and the Armistice of 1918', Harmon Memorial Lecture # 51 (2009), http://www.usafa.edu/df/dfh/harmonmemorial.cfm (accessed 26 March 2010)

Dubois, Général, *Deux ans de commandement sur le front de France 1914–1916* (Paris: Lavauzelle, 1921)

DuCane, Lt-Gen. Sir John, *Marshal Foch* (privately printed, 1920), Imperial War Museum, London

Duffour, Général, *Histoire de la Guerre Mondiale*, vol. 1: *Joffre et la guerre de mouvement 1914* (Paris: Payot, 1937)

Duroselle, Jean-Baptiste, *Clemenceau* (Paris: Fayard, 1988)

Dutton, David, 'The Deposition of King Constantine of Greece, June 1917: An Episode in Anglo-French Diplomacy', *Canadian Journal of History* 12: 3 (1978), 325–45

   'The Fall of General Joffre: An Episode in the Politico-Military Struggle in Wartime France', *Journal of Strategic Studies* 1 (1978): 338–51

   The Politics of Diplomacy: Britain and France in the Balkans in the First World War (London/New York: I.B. Tauris, 1998)

Dutton, David (ed.), *Paris 1918: The War Diary of the British Ambassador, the 17th Earl of Derby* (Liverpool: Liverpool University Press, 2001)

Edmonds, Brigadier-General Sir James E., *et al.*, *Military Operations: France and Belgium* (London: Macmillan/HMSO, 1927–47)

Edmonds, Brigadier-General Sir James E., and Davies, Major-General H. R., *Military Operations: Italy, 1914–1918* (London: HMSO, 1949)

Egremont, Max, *Under Two Flags: The Life of Major General Sir Edward Spears* (pb. edn, London: Phoenix Giant, 1998)

[L']Esercito italiano nella Grande Guerra, 1915–1918, 23 vols. in 7 (Rome: Provveditorato Generale dello Stato, 1927–83)

Fabry, Jean, *Joffre et son destin: La Marne, Verdun, La Somme, L'Amérique* (Paris: Lavauzelle, 1931)

Fadini, Francesco, *Caporetto dalla parte del vincitore: La biografia del generale Otto von Below e il suo diario inedito sulla campagna d'Italia del 1917* (Firenze: Vallecchi, 1974)

Falls, Cyril, *Marshal Foch* (London: Blackie & Son, 1939)
   Caporetto 1917 (London: Weidenfeld & Nicolson, 1965)
Farrar-Hockley, Anthony, *Death of an Army* (London: Barker, 1967)
Favreau, Alain, 'Le Dernier Combat: Vrigne-Meuse, 10 et 11 novembre 1918',
   Revue Historique des Armées 251 (2008): 18–34
Fayolle, Maréchal Emile, *Cahiers secrets* (ed. Henry Contamine) (Paris: Plon,
   1964)
Ferry, Abel, *La Guerre vue d'en bas et d'en haut* (Paris: Grasset, 1920)
   Carnets secrets 1914–1918 suivis de lettres et de notes de guerre (Paris: Grasset, 2005,
   revised and expanded edn)
Foch, Ferdinand, *Des principes de la guerre: Conférences faites à l'Ecole Supérieure de
   Guerre* (Paris: Berger-Levrault, 1903)
   [Maréchal Ferdinand Foch], *Mémoires pour servir à l'histoire de la guerre
   1914–1918*, 2 vols. (Paris: Plon, 1931)[translated into English as *The Memoirs
   of Marshal Foch* (London: Heinemann, 1931)]
Foley, Robert T., *German Strategy and the Path to Verdun: Erich von Falkenhayn
   and the Development of Attrition, 1870–1916* (Cambridge: Cambridge
   University Press, 2005)
Foreign Relations of the United States (volumes for 1918, the *Lansing Papers* and the
   Paris Peace Conference)
French, David, '"Had We Known How Bad Things Were in Germany, We Might
   Have Got Stiffer Terms": Great Britain and the German Armistice', in
   Manfred F. Boemeke, Gerald D. Feldman and Elisabeth Glaser (eds.), *The
   Treaty of Versailles: A Reassessment 75 Years on* (Washington DC: German
   Historical Institute/Cambridge: Cambridge University Press, 1998), 69–86
French, Gerald, *The Life of Field-Marshal Sir John French, First Earl of Ypres, K.P.,
   G.C.B., O.M., G.C.V.O., K.C.M.G.* (London: Cassell, 1931)
French of Ypres, Field-Marshal Viscount, *1914* (London: Constable 1919)
Fuller, Major-General J. F. C., *The Conduct of War 1789–1961: A Study of the
   Impact of the French, Industrial, and Russian Revolutions on War and its
   Conduct* (London: Eyre & Spottiswoode, 1962)
Galet, Général, *S.M. le Roi Albert commandant en chef devant l'invasion allemande*
   (Paris: Plon, 1931)
Gambiez, Général F., and Suire, Colonel M., *Histoire de la Première Guerre
   Mondiale*, 2 vols. (Paris: Fayard, 1968)
Gatti, Angelo, *Caporetto: Dal diario di guerra inedito, maggio–dicembre 1917*
   (Bologna: Il Mulino, 1964)
Gazin, F., *La Cavalerie française dans la Guerre Mondiale 1914–1918* (Paris: Payot,
   1930)
[The] German Army Handbook of 1918 (London: Frontline, 2008 [originally pub-
   lished by Great Britain. Army. General Staff, 1918])
Geyer, Michael, 'Insurrectionary Warfare: The German Debate about a *Levée en
   Masse* in October 1918', *Journal of Modern History* 73 (September 2001):
   459–527
Gilbert, Martin, *Winston S. Churchill*, vol. 3: *1914–1916*, and *Companion* volumes,
   and vol. 4: *1917–1922*, and *Companion* volumes (London: Heinemann, 1971,
   1975)

Görlitz, Walter, *The Kaiser and his Court* (London: Macdonald, 1961)

Gough, General Sir Hubert, *The Fifth Army* (London: Hodder and Stoughton, 1931)

Goya, Michel, *La Chair et l'acier: L'Invention de la guerre moderne (1914–1918)* (Paris: Tallandier, 2004)

Gras, Yves, *Castelnau ou l'art de commander* (Paris: Denoël, 1990)

Greenhalgh, Elizabeth, 'Technology Development in Coalition: The Case of the First World War Tank', *International History Review* 22: 4 (2000), 757–1008

'The Experience of Fighting with Allies: The Case of the Capture of Falfemont Farm during the Battle of the Somme, 1916', *War in History* 10: 2 (2003), 157–183

'Myth and Memory: Sir Douglas Haig and the Imposition of Allied Unified Command in March 1918', *Journal of Military History* 68 (July 2004), 771–820

Victory through Coalition: Britain and France during the First World War (Cambridge: Cambridge University Press, 2005)

'David Lloyd George, Georges Clemenceau, and the 1918 Manpower Crisis', *Historical Journal* 50: 2 (2007), 397–421

'Errors and Omissions in Franco-British Cooperation in Munitions Production, 1914–1918', *War in History* 14: 2 (2007), 179–218

Grigg, John, *Lloyd George*, vol. 3: *From Peace to War 1912–1916* (London: Eyre Methuen, 1985); vol. 4: *War Leader 1916–1918* (London: Allen Lane, 2002)

Griscom, Lloyd C., *Diplomatically Speaking* (London: John Murray, 1941)

Guillaumat, Paul (ed.), *Correspondance de guerre du général Guillaumat: 1914–1919* (Paris: Harmattan, 2006)

Guinard, Pierre, Devos, Jean-Claude, and Nicot, Jean, *Inventaire sommaire des archives de la guerre, série N*, vol. 1: *Introduction* (Troyes: Imprimerie la Renaissance, 1975)

Halpern, Paul G., *A Naval History of World War I* (London: UCL Press, 1994)

Hankey, M. P. A., *The Supreme Command, 1914–1918*, 2 vols. (London: George Allen & Unwin, 1961)

The Supreme Command, The Supreme Control at the Paris Peace Conference, 1919: A Commentary (London: George Allen & Unwin, 1963)

Hanks, Robert K., Culture versus Diplomacy: Clemenceau and Anglo-American Relations during the First World War (PhD thesis, University of Toronto, 2002)

Harris, J. P., *Douglas Haig and the First World War* (Cambridge: Cambridge University Press, 2008)

Headlam-Morley, Sir James, *A Memoir of the Paris Peace Conference, 1919* (London: Methuen, 1972)

Henniker, A. M., *Transportation on the Western Front 1914–1918* (London: HMSO, 1937)

Herbillon, Colonel E., *Du général en chef au gouvernement: Souvenirs d'un officier de liaison pendant la guerre mondiale*, 2 vols. (Paris: Tallandier, 1930)

Le Général Alfred Micheler (1914–1918) d'après ses notes, sa correspondance et les souvenirs personnels de l'auteur (Paris: Plon, 1933)

Herr, Général, *L'Artillerie: ce qu'elle a été, ce qu'elle est, ce qu'elle doit être* (Paris: Berger-Levrault, 1923)

Herwig, Holger H., *First World War: Germany and Austria–Hungary 1914–1918* (London: Arnold, 1997)

Hirschfeld, Gerhard, 'Die Somme-Schlacht von 1916', in Gerhard Hirschfeld, Gerd Krumeich and Irina Renz (eds.), *Die Deutschen an der Somme 1914–1918* (Essen: Klartext Verlag, 2006), 79–161

Holmes, Richard, *The Little Field-Marshal: Sir John French* (London: Cape, 1981)

Hosoya, Chihiro, *Shiberia shuppei no shiteki kenkyū [Historical Study of the Siberian Expedition]* (Tōkyō: Yūhikaku, 1955)

Hubbard, Samuel T., *Memoirs of a Staff Officer, 1917–1919* (Tuckahoe, NY: Cardinal Associates, Inc., 1959)

Huguet, Victor J. M., *Britain and the War: A French Indictment* (London: Cassell, 1928)

Humbert, General J., 'Foch et la défense d'Arras 5–6 octobre 1914', *Revue Historique des Armées* 1979/1: 155–76

Jäschke, Gotthard, 'Zum Problem der Marne-Schlacht von 1914', *Historische Zeitschrift* 190 (1960): 311–48

Jauneaud, Marcel, 'Souvenirs de la bataille d'Arras', *Revue des Deux Mondes*, 1 August 1920, 571–98; 15 August 1920, 825–56

Jeffery, Keith, *Field Marshal Sir Henry Wilson: A Political Soldier* (Oxford: Oxford University Press, 2006)

Joffre, Maréchal [Joseph J. C.], *Mémoires du Maréchal Joffre, 1910–1917*, 2 vols. (Paris: Plon, 1932)

Joffre, Maréchal [Joseph J. C.], Ex-Kronprinz Impérial, Foch, Maréchal [Ferdinand], and Ludendorff, Général [Erich], *Les Deux Batailles de la Marne 5–11 septembre 1914, 15–18 juillet 1918* (Paris: Payot, 1928)

Johnson, Douglas W., *Battlefields of the World War: Western and Southern Fronts: A Study in Military Geography* (New York: Oxford University Press, 1921)

Jones, H. A., *The War in the Air: Being the Story of the Part Played in the Great War by the Royal Air Force*, vol. 6 (London: Clarendon Press, 1937)

Kaspi, André, *Le Temps des Américains: Le Concours américain à la France 1917–1918* (Paris: Publications de la Sorbonne, 1976)

Keiger, J. F. V., *Raymond Poincaré* (Cambridge: Cambridge University Press, 1997)

Kennan, George F., *Soviet-American relations, 1917–1920*, vol. 1: *Russia Leaves the War* (Princeton, NJ: Princeton University Press, 1956)

King, J. C., *Generals and Politicians: Conflict between France's High Command, Parliament and Government, 1914–1918* (Berkeley/Los Angeles: University of California Press, 1951)

Foch versus Clemenceau: France and German Dismemberment, 1918–1919 (Cambridge, MA: Harvard University Press, 1960)

Kitchen, Martin, *The German Offensives of 1918* (Stroud: Tempus, 2001)

Kleinhenz, Roland, 'La Percée saxonne sur le front du centre', in François Cochet (ed.), *Les Batailles de la Marne de l'Ourcq à Verdun (1914 et 1918) (Actes du colloque Reims-Verdun 6 et 7 mai 2004)* (Saint-Cloud: 14–18 Editions, 2004), 147–94

Krafft von Dellmensingen, General der Artl., *Der Durchbruch am Isonzo*, 2 vols. (Berlin: Oldenburg, 1923) (= *Schlachten des Weltkrieges*, Bd. 12a, 12b)

Kramer, Alan, '*Wackes* at War: Alsace-Lorraine and the Failure of German National Mobilization, 1914–1918', in John Horne (ed.), *State, Society and*

Mobilization in Europe during the First World War (Cambridge: Cambridge University Press, 1997), 105–24

Krumeich, Gerd, 'Le Soldat allemand sur la Somme', in Jean-Jacques Becker and Stéphane Audoin-Rouzeau (eds.), *Les Sociétés européennes et la guerre de 1914–1918* (Nanterre: Centre d'Histoire de la France Contemporaine, 1990), 367–74

Lahaie, Olivier, Renseignement et services de renseignement en France pendant la guerre de 1914–1918 (PhD thesis, Université de Paris IV, Sorbonne, 2005)

Lastours, Sophie de, *La France gagne la guerre des codes secrets: 1914–1918* (Paris: Le Grand Livre du Mois, 1998)

Laure, Commandant, *Au 3ème bureau du troisième G.Q.G. (1917–1919)* (Paris: Plon, 1921)

Lawrence, T. E., *T.E. Lawrence to his Biographers Robert Graves and Liddell Hart* (London: Cassell, 1963)

Le Chatelier, Jean, *Le Général Maurice Pellé 1863–1924: Lettres et souvenirs*, 2 vols. (privately printed; copy in Bibliothèque de la Guerre, Vincennes, 1984–5)

Lepick, Olivier, *La Grande Guerre Chimique, 1914–1918* (Paris: PUF, 1998)

Liddell Hart, B. H., 'Ferdinand Foch: The Symbol of the Victorious Will', in *Reputations Ten Years After* (London: John Murray, 1928), 157–83

Foch: The Man of Orleans (London: Eyre and Spottiswoode, 1931)

Link, Arthur S. (ed.), *The Papers of Woodrow Wilson*, 69 vols. (Princeton, NJ: Princeton University Press, 1966–94)

Lipp, Anne, 'Les Soldats allemands sur la Somme: Perceptions personnelles et suggestions d'interprétation', in *La Bataille de la Somme dans la Grande Guerre: Colloque du 80e Anniversaire* [Actes du colloque, Péronne, 1–4 July 1996] (Péronne: Historial de la Grande Guerre 1997), 321–35

Lossberg, Fritz von, *Meine Tätigkeit im Weltkriege 1914–1918* (Berlin: E. S. Mittler & Sohn, 1939)

Loucheur, Louis, *Carnets secrets 1908–1932* (ed. Jacques de Launay) (Brussels: Brepols, 1962)

Lowry, Bullitt, 'Pershing and the Armistice', *Journal of American History* 55 (1968): 281–91

Armistice 1918 (Kent OH/London: Kent State University Press, 1996)

Lucas, Colonel Pascal, *L'Evolution des idées tactiques en France et en Allemagne pendant la guerre de 1914–1918*, 4th edn (Paris: Berger-Levrault, 1932)

Lumbroso, Alberto, *Fame usurpate: Il dramma del comando unico interalleato* (Milano: Giacomo Agnelli, 1934-XII)

Lutz, Ralph H. (ed.), *The Causes of the German Collapse in 1918* (Stanford, CA: Stanford University Press, 1934)

Malagodi, Olindo, *Conversazioni della guerra*, 2 vols. (Milano/Napoli: Riccardo Ricciardi, 1959)

Mangin, Général, *Comment finit la guerre* (Paris: Plon, 1920)

Mantoux, Paul, *The Deliberations of the Council of Four (March 24–June 28, 1919)*, 2 vols. (Princeton/Oxford: Princeton University Press, 1992)

Marne Source Book: The German Offensive of July 15, 1918 (Fort Leavenworth, KS: The General Service Schools Press, 1923)

Martel, René, *French Strategic and Tactical Bombardment Forces of World War I* (trans. and ed. A. and S. Suddaby) (Lanham, MD: Scarecrow Press, 2007)

Martet, Jean, *Clemenceau: The Events of his Life as Told by Himself* (London/ New York/Toronto: Longmans, Green and Co., 1930)

Mayer, Lieutenant-Colonel Emile, *Trois maréchaux: Joffre, Galliéni, Foch* (Paris: Gallimard, 1928)

   Nos chefs de 1914: souvenirs personnels et essais de psychologie militaire (Paris: Stock, Delamain et Boutelleau, 1930)

Melograni, Piero, *Storia politica della Grande Guerra, 1915–1918* (Roma: Laterza, 1977)

Messimy, Général, *Mes souvenirs* (Paris: Plon, 1937)

Miquel, Pierre, *La Paix de Versailles et l'opinion publique française* (Paris: Flammarion, 1971)

Missoffe, Michel, *La Vie volontaire d'André Tardieu: Essai de chronologie animée (1876–1929)* (Paris: Flammarion, 1930)

Mombauer, Annika, *Helmuth von Moltke and the Origins of the First World War* (Cambridge: Cambridge University Press, 2001)

   'The Battle of the Marne: Myths and Reality of Germany's "Fateful Battle"', *The Historian* 68: 4 (2006), 747–69

Mordacq, Général, *Le Commandement unique: Comment il fut réalisé* (Paris: Tallandier, 1929)

   Le Ministère Clemenceau: Journal d'un témoin, 4 vols. (Paris: Plon, 1930–1)

Morselli, Mario A., *Caporetto 1917: Victory or Defeat?* (London/Portland, OR: Frank Cass, 2001)

Neiberg, Michael S., *The Second Battle of the Marne* (Bloomington/Indianapolis: Indiana University Press, 2008)

Neilson, Keith, *Strategy and Supply: The Anglo-Russian Alliance, 1914–1917* (London: Allen & Unwin, 1984)

Nicol, Graham, *Uncle George: Field-Marshal Lord Milne of Salonika and Rubislaw* (London: Reedminster Publications, 1976)

Nicot, Jean, 'Perception des Alliés par les combattants en 1918 d'après les archives du contrôle postal', *Revue Historique des Armées* 1988/3, 45–53

   Les Poilus ont la parole. Lettres du front: 1917–1918 (Paris: Editions Complexe, 1998)

Niessel, Général, *Le Triomphe des Bolchéviks et la paix de Brest-Litovsk: Souvenirs 1917–1918* (Paris: Plon, 1940)

Orlando, Vittorio Emanuele, *Memorie (1915–1919)* (ed. Rodolfo Mosca) (Milano: Rizzoli, 1960)

Orpen, William, *An Onlooker in France 1917–1919* (London: Williams & Norgate, 1924)

Painlevé, Paul, *Comment j'ai nommé Foch et Pétain: La Politique de guerre de 1917, le commandement unique interallié* (Paris: Félix Alcan, 1924)

Palazzo, Albert, 'The British Army's Counter-Battery Staff Office and Control of the Enemy in World War I', *Journal of Military History* 63: 1 (1999), 55–74

Palmer, Frederick, *Newton D. Baker: America at War, Based on the Personal Papers of the Secretary of War in the World War*, 2 vols. (New York: Dodd. Mead and Company, 1931)

Bliss, Peacemaker: The Life and Letters of General Tasker H. Bliss (Freeport, NY: Books for Libraries Press, repr. 1970 [1934])

Pédoya, Général, *La Commission de l'armée pendant la Grande Guerre* (Paris: Flammarion, 1921)

Pedroncini, Guy, 'Les Rapports du gouvernement et du haut commandement en France en 1917', *Revue d'Histoire Moderne et Contemporaine* 15 (1968): 122–32

Les Négotiations secrètes pendant la Grande Guerre (Paris: Flammarion, 1969)

Pétain Général en Chef 1917–1918 (Paris: PUF, 1974)

Pétain: Le Soldat et la gloire (Paris: Perrin, 1989)

'L'Armistice du 11 novembre 1918: Prélude à la paix', in Claude Carlier and Guy Pedroncini (eds.), *Les Etats-Unis dans la Grande Guerre 1917–1918* (Paris: Economica, 1992), 205–16

Pedroncini, Guy (ed.), *Journal de Marche de Joffre (1916–1919)* (Vincennes: S.H. A.T./F.E.D.N., 1990)

Pershing, John J., *My Experiences in the World War*, 2 vols. (New York: Frederick A. Stokes Company, 1931)

Pétain, Maréchal, *Rapport du Maréchal Commandant en Chef les Armées Françaises du Nord et du Nord-Est sur les opérations en 1918*, 15 vols. (n.p., n.d.) [copy in Bibliothèque de la Guerre, Vincennes]

Discours de réception de M. le Maréchal Pétain à l'Académie Française (Paris: Nouvelle Revue Française/Plon, 1931)

Philpott, William J., 'Kitchener and the 29th Division: A Study in Anglo-French Strategic Relations, 1914–15', *Journal of Strategic Studies* 16 (1993): 375–407

Pierrefeu, Jean de, *G.Q.G secteur 1: Trois ans au Grand Quartier Général*, 2 vols. (Paris: L'Edition Française Illustrée, 1920)

Poincaré, Raymond, *Au service de la France: Neuf années de souvenirs*, 11 vols. (Paris: Plon, 1928–74)

Porte, Rémy, *La Direction des services automobiles et la motorisation des armées françaises (1914–1919): Vues au travers de l'action du Commandant Doumenc* (Paris: Lavauzelle, 2004)

Porte, Rémy and Cochet, François (eds.), *Ferdinand Foch (1851–1929): Apprenez à penser* (Saint-Cloud: Soteca/Editions 14–18, 2010) [Proceedings of the 2008 Conference, Paris]

Prete, Roy A., The War of Movement on the Western Front, August–November 1914: A Study in Coalition Warfare (PhD thesis, University of Alberta, 1979)

'The Anglo-French Command Crisis of October–November 1914', *Research Studies* 51 (September/December 1983): 112–26

'Le Conflit stratégique franco-britannique sur le front occidental et la conférence de Calais du 6 juillet 1915', *Guerres Mondiales et Conflits Contemporains* 186 (1997): 17–49

Strategy and Command: The Anglo-French Coalition on the Western Front, 1914 (Montréal: McGill-Queen's University Press, 2009)

Prior, Robin, and Wilson, Trevor, *Command on the Western Front: The Military Career of Sir Henry Rawlinson 1914–18* (Oxford: Blackwell, 1992)

Passchendaele: The Untold Story (New Haven/London: Yale University Press, 1996)

The Somme (London: Yale University Press, 2005)

Procacci, Giovanna, 'The Disaster of Caporetto', in John Dickie, John Foot and
    Frank M. Snowden (eds.), *Disastro!: Disasters in Italy since 1860: Culture,
    Politics, Society* (New York/Basingstoke: Palgrave, 2002), 141–64
Pujo, Bernard, 'L'Evolution de la pensée de Foch sur l'emploi de l'arme aérienne
    au cours de son commandement du Groupe d'Armées du Nord en 1915 et
    1916', in Proceedings of the conference 'Adaptation de l'arme aérienne aux
    conflits contemporains', 4–7 September 1984, 211–21
Raphaël-Leygues, Jacques, *Georges Leygues: 'Le Père' de la Marine (ses carnets secrets
    de 1914–1920)* (Paris: Editions France-Empire, 1983)
Recouly, Raymond, *Le Mémorial de Foch: Mes entretiens avec le Maréchal* (Paris:
    Editions de France, 1929) [translated into English as *Marshal Foch: His Own
    Words on Many Subjects* (London: Thornton Butterworth, 1929)]
Reichsarchiv, *Der Weltkrieg 1914 bis 1918*, 14 vols. (Berlin: E. S. Mittler & Sohn,
    1925–56)
Reid, Brian Holden, '"Young Turks, or Not So Young?": The Frustrated Quest of
    Major General J. F. C. Fuller and Captain B. H. Liddell Hart', *Journal of
    Military History* 73: 1 (January 2009), 147–76
Renouvin, Pierre, *Les Formes du gouvernement de guerre* (Paris/New Haven, CT:
    PUF/Yale University Press, 1926)
    Review of Foch, *Mémoires pour servir à l'histoire de la guerre 1914–1918*, in *Revue
    d'Histoire de la Guerre Mondiale* (1931/3), 302–5
    L'Armistice de Rethondes: 11 novembre 1918 (Paris: Gallimard, repr. 2006 [1968])
Repington, Charles à Court, *First World War*, 2 vols. (London: Constable, 1920)
Reynaud, Paul, *Au cœur de la mêlée 1930–1945* (Paris: Flammarion, 1950)
Ribot, Alexandre, *Lettres à un ami: Souvenirs de ma vie politique* (Paris: Editions
    Bossard, 1924)
Ribot, Dr Alexandre (ed.), *Journal d'Alexandre Ribot et correspondances inédites
    1914–1922* (Paris: Plon, 1936)
Riddell, George Allardyce, *Lord Riddell's War Diary, 1914–1918* (London:
    Nicholson and Watson, 1933)
    Intimate Diary of the Peace Conference and After: 1918–1923 (London: Gollancz,
    1933)
Ritter, Gerhard, *The Sword and the Scepter: The Problem of Militarism in Germany*,
    4 vols. (Coral Gables, FL: University of Miami Press, 1969–73)
Rocca, Gianni, *Cadorna* (Milano: Mondadori, 1988)
Rocolle, Pierre, *L'Hécatombe des généraux* (Paris: Lavauzelle, 1980)
Ronarc'h, Vice-Amiral, *Souvenirs de la Guerre* (Paris: Payot, 1921)
Roskill, Stephen, *Hankey: Man of Secrets*, vol. 1: *1877–1918* (London: Collins, 1970)
Roth, François, *Raymond Poincaré* (Paris: Fayard, 2000)
Samuels, Martin, *Command or Control?: Command, Training and Tactics in the British
    and German Armies, 1888–1918* (London/Portland, OR: Frank Cass, 1995)
Scherer, André, and Grunewald, Jacques, *L'Allemagne et les problèmes de la paix
    pendant la Première Guerre Mondiale*, 4 vols. (Paris: Université de Paris,
    Sorbonne, 1962–78)
Schwabe, Klaus, *Woodrow Wilson, Revolutionary Germany, and Peacemaking,
    1918–1919* (Chapel Hill: University of North Carolina Press, 1985)
Seely, J. E. B., *Adventure* (London: Heinemann, 1931)

Serrigny, Général, *Trente ans avec Pétain* (Paris: Plon, 1959)

Service historique de la Défense, *La Mémoire conservée du général Milan Ratislav Stefanik dans les archives du SHD* (Vincennes: Service historique de la Défense, 2008)

Seymour, Charles (ed.), *The Intimate Papers of Colonel House*, 4 vols. (London: Benn, 1926–8)

Sheffield, Gary, and Bourne, John (eds.), *Douglas Haig: War Diaries and Letters, 1914–1918* (London: Weidenfeld & Nicolson, 2005)

Sheldon, Jack, *The German Army on the Somme, 1914–1916* (Barnsley: Pen & Sword Military, 2005)

Shumate, Jr, T. Daniel, The Allied Supreme War Council, 1917–1918 (PhD dissertation, University of Virginia, 1952)

Smythe, Donald, *Pershing: General of the Armies* (Bloomington: Indiana University Press, 1986)

Sonnino, Sidney, *Carteggio 1916–1922* (Roma/Bari: Laterza, 1975)

Spears, E. L., *Prelude to Victory* (London: Jonathan Cape, 1939)

Liaison 1914: A Narrative of the Great Retreat (London: Eyre & Spottiswoode, 1968)

Stephenson, Scott, *The Final Battle: Soldiers of the Western Front and the German Revolution of 1918* (Cambridge: Cambridge University Press, 2009)

Stevenson, David, *1914–1918: The History of the First World War* (London: Allen Lane, 2004)

Stevenson, Frances, *Lloyd George: A Diary* (ed. A. J. P. Taylor) (London: Hutchinson, 1971)

Strachan, Hew, *The First World War*, vol. 1: *To Arms* (Oxford: Oxford University Press, 2001)

Suarez, Georges, *Soixante années d'histoire française: Clemenceau*, 2 vols. (Paris: Tallandier, 1932)

Briand: sa vie, son œuvre, avec son journal et de nombreux documents inédits, 5 vols. (Paris: Plon, 1938–41)

Sulzbach, Herbert, *With the German Guns: Four Years on the Western Front, 1914–1918* (London: Cooper, 1973)

Sweet, Paul R., 'Leaders and Policies: Germany in the Winter of 1914–1915', *Journal of Central European Affairs* 16: 3 (1956), 229–53

Tanenbaum, Jan Karl, *General Maurice Sarrail, 1856–1929: The French Army and Left-wing Politics* (Chapel Hill: University of North Carolina Press, 1974)

Tardieu, André, *La Paix* (Paris: Payot, 1921)

Avec Foch (août–novembre 1914) (Paris: Flammarion 1939)

Terraine, John, *Douglas Haig: The Educated Soldier* (London: Cassell & Co, 2000 [1963])

Thaer, Albrecht von, *Generalstabdienst an der Front und in der O.H.L. aus Briefen und Tagebuchaufzeichnungen 1915–1919* (Göttingen: Vandenhoeck & Ruprecht, 1958)

Thielemans, Marie-Rose, 'Le Roi Albert, le haut commandement et le commandement unique des armées alliées en 1918', in Patrick Lefevre and Piet de Gryse (eds.), *De Brialmont à l'Union de l'Europe Occidentale/Van Brialmont tot de Westeuropese Unie* (Brussels: Musée royal de l'armée/Koninklijk Legermuseum, 1988), 87–127

Thielemans, Marie-Rose (ed.), *Albert Ier: Carnets et correspondance de guerre 1914–1918* (Paris/Louvain: Editions Duclos, 1991)

Thielemans, Marie-Rose, and Vandewoude, Emile (eds.), *Le Roi Albert au travers de ses lettres inédites 1882–1916* (Brussels, Office international de Librairie, 1982)

Thomazi, A., *La Marine française dans la Grande Guerre (1914–1918): La Guerre navale dans la zone des armées du nord* (Paris: Payot, 1925)

Thompson, Mark, *The White War: Life and Death on the Italian Front 1915–1919* (London: Faber and Faber, 2008)

Torrey, Glenn E., *Romania and World War I: A Collection of Studies* (Iasi/Portland, OR: Center for Romanian Studies, 1999)

Tournès, Général, *Histoire de la Guerre Mondiale*, vol. 4: *Foch et la victoire des Alliés* (Paris: Payot, 1936)

Trask, David F., *The AEF and Coalition Warmaking, 1917–1919* (Lawrence: University Press of Kansas, 1993)

Tyng, Sewell T., *The Campaign of the Marne 1914* (London: Oxford University Press, 1935)

United States Army in the World War, 17 vols. (Washington: US Government Printing Office, 1948)

Urbal, General V. d', *Souvenirs et anecdotes de guerre 1914–1916* (Paris: Berger-Levrault, 1939)

Ursachen und Folgen vom deutschen Zusammenbruch 1918 und 1945 bis zur staatlichen Neuordnung Deutschlands in der Gegenwart, vol. 2: *Der militärische Zusammenbruch und der Ende des Kaiserreichs* (Berlin: Dokumentenverlag Wendler, 1957–77)

Vallières, Jean des, *Au soleil de la cavalerie avec le général des Vallières* (Paris: Editions André Bonne, 1965)

Vandewoude, Emile, 'Deux ans près de Foch: Les Carnets de guerre du Major F. Posch, officier de liaison belge, 1915–1916', *Revue Belge d'Histoire Militaire* XXV: 3 (September 1983), 231–66; XXV: 4 (December 1983), 345–68; XXV: 5 (March 1984), 401–20; XXV: 6 (June 1984), 495–518; XXV: 7 (September 1984), 595–626

Varillon, Pierre, *Joffre* (Paris: Fayard, 1956)

Villate, Robert, *Foch à la Marne: La 9e Armée aux marais de Saint-Gond (5–10 septembre 1914)* (Paris: Lavauzelle, 1933) [consulted (unfoliated) online at www.gwpda.org/wwi-www/Foch14/MarneTC.htm, accessed 28 July 2010]

von der Golz, Anna, *Hindenburg: Power, Myth, and the Rise of the Nazis* (Oxford/New York: Oxford University Press, 2009)

Watson, Alexander, *Enduring the Great War: Combat, Morale and Collapse in the German and British Armies, 1914–1918* (Cambridge: Cambridge University Press, 2008)

Weygand, Général Maxime, *Foch* (Paris: Flammarion, 1947)

Mémoires: Idéal vécu (Paris: Flammarion, 1953)

Mémoires: Mirages et réalités (Paris: Flammarion, 1957)

Why Germany Capitulated on November 11, 1918: A Brief Study Based on Documents in the Possession of the French General Staff (London: Hodder & Stoughton, 1919) [translation of *Pourquoi l'Allemagne a capitulé le 11 novembre 1918* (n.p. n.d. (10 January 1918)]

Williamson, Jr, Samuel R., *The Politics of Grand Strategy: Britain and France Prepare for War, 1904–1914* (pb. edn, London/Atlantic Highlands, NJ: The Ashfield Press, 1990 [1969])

Wilson, Keith, *Channel Tunnel Visions: Dreams and Nightmares 1850–1945* (London: Hambledon Press, 1994)

Woodward, David R., *Lloyd George and the Generals* (Newark: University of Delaware Press, 1983)

Woodward, David R. (ed.), *The Military Correspondence of Field-Marshal Sir William Robertson, Chief of the Imperial General Staff, December 1915–February 1918* (London: The Bodley Head for the Army Records Society, 1989)

Wormser, Georges, *Le Septennat de Poincaré* (Paris: Fayard, 1977)
Clemenceau vu de près (Paris: Hachette, 1979)

Wright, Peter E., *At the Supreme War Council* (London: Eveleigh Nash, 1921)

Yockelson, Mitchell A., *Borrowed Soldiers: Americans under British Command, 1918* (Norman: University of Oklahoma Press, 2008)

Zabecki, David T., *Steel Wind: Colonel Georg Bruchmüller and the Birth of Modern Artillery* (Westport, CT: Praeger, 1994)
The German 1918 Offensives: A Case Study in the Operational Level of War (London/New York: Routledge, 2006)
Chief of Staff: The Principal Officers behind History's Great Commanders, 2 vols. (Annapolis, MD: Naval Institute Press, 2008)

PRINCIPAL WORKS DEALING SOLELY WITH FOCH

This select list is given for completeness, and includes works cited in the footnotes.

Aston, Major-General Sir George, *The Biography of the Late Marshal Foch* (London: Hutchinson & Co, 1929)

Atteridge, A. Hilliard, *Marshal Ferdinand Foch: His Life and his Theory of Modern War* (London: Skeffington & Son, 1919)

Autin, Jean, *Foch ou le triomphe de la volonté* (Paris: Perrin, 1987, 1998)

Bugnet, Commandant Charles, *En écoutant le Maréchal Foch* (Paris: Grasset, 1929) [translated into English as *Foch Talks* (London: Gollancz, 1929)]

Falls, Cyril, *Marshal Foch* (London: Blackie & Son, 1939)

Grasset, Col. Alphonse-Louis, *Foch ou la volonté de vaincre* (Paris: Berger-Levrault, 1964)

Haushofer, Karl, *Foch* (Lübeck: Charles Coleman, 1935)

Hunter, Lt Col. T. M., *Marshal Foch: A Study in Leadership* (Ottawa: Directorate of Military Training, Army Headquarters, 1961)

Liddell Hart, B. H., 'Ferdinand Foch: The Symbol of the Victorious Will', in *Reputations Ten Years After* (London: John Murray, 1928), 157–83
Foch: The Man of Orleans (London: Eyre and Spottiswoode, 1931)

Madelin, Louis, *Foch* (Paris: Plon, 1929)

Marshall-Cornwall, James, *Foch as Military Commander* (London: Batsford, 1972)

Martel, André, *Relire Foch au XXIe siècle* (Paris: Economica, 2008)

Michel, Paul-Henri, 'La Vie et l'œuvre du Maréchal Foch: Essai bibliographique', *Revue d'Histoire de la Guerre Mondiale* (April 1929), 143–57

Neiberg, Michael S., *Foch: Supreme Allied Commander in the Great War* (Washington, DC: Brassey's Inc, 2003)

Notin, Jean-Christophe, *Foch* (Paris: Perrin, 2008)

Palat, Général, *La Part de Foch dans la victoire* (Paris: Charles Lavauzelle, 1930)

Philpott, William, 'Marshal Ferdinand Foch and Allied Victory', in Matthew Hughes and Matthew Seligmann (eds.), *Leadership in Conflict 1914–1918* (Barnsley: Leo Cooper, 2000), 38–53

Porte, Rémy and Cochet, François (eds.), *Ferdinand Foch (1851–1929): Apprenez à penser* (Saint-Cloud: Soteca/Editions 14–18, 2010) [Proceedings of the 2008 Conference, Paris]

Recouly, Raymond, *Le Mémorial de Foch: Mes entretiens avec le Maréchal* (Paris: Editions de France, 1929) [translated into English as *Marshal Foch: His Own Words on Many Subjects* (London: Thornton Butterworth, 1929)]

Tardieu, André, *Avec Foch (août–novembre 1914)* (Paris: Flammarion 1939)

Weygand, Général Maxime, *Foch* (Paris: Flammarion, 1947)

  Le Maréchal Foch (Paris: Firmin-Didot et Cie, 1929)

Index

Lightning Source UK Ltd.
Milton Keynes UK
UKOW06f0426131015

260417UK00010B/492/P

9 781107 633858